THE
ANNUAL REGISTER
Vol. 232

ANNUAL REGISTER ADVISORY BOARD

CHAIRMAN

H. V. HODSON

EDITOR

ALAN J. DAY

ASSISTANT EDITOR

VERENA HOFFMAN

JAMES BISHOP
Editor-in-Chief, The Illustrated London News

FRANK E. CLOSE, PhD
Distinguished Professor of Physics, The University of Tennessee
NOMINATED BY
THE BRITISH ASSOCIATION FOR THE ADVANCEMENT OF SCIENCE

M. R. D. FOOT
Formerly Professor of Modern History, University of Manchester
NOMINATED BY
THE ROYAL HISTORICAL SOCIETY

MICHAEL KASER
Fellow of St Antony's College, Oxford
NOMINATED BY
THE ROYAL INSTITUTE OF INTERNATIONAL AFFAIRS

DEREK MORRIS
Fellow of Oriel College, Oxford
NOMINATED BY
THE ROYAL ECONOMIC SOCIETY

ALASTAIR NIVEN
Literature Director of the Arts Council of Great Britain
NOMINATED BY
THE ARTS COUNCIL OF GREAT BRITAIN

Atlantic Alliance

Washington, 21 December 1990: Britain's new Prime Minister, John Major, meets President Bush at the White House, with UK–US military cooperation in the Gulf dominating their discussions.

Associated Press

Saluting the New Germany

Berlin, 3 October 1990: Chancellor Helmut Kohl (*right*), Foreign Minister Hans-Dietrich Genscher (*left*) and Frau Kohl (*centre*) wave to the crowds outside the Berlin Reichstag celebrating the unification of the Federal Republic of Germany and the German Democratic Republic (respectively West and East Germany).

THE
ANNUAL REGISTER

A Record of World Events
1990

Edited by
ALAN J. DAY

assisted by
VERENA HOFFMAN

FIRST EDITED IN 1758
BY EDMUND BURKE

THE ANNUAL REGISTER 1990
Published by Longman Group UK Limited, Longman House.
Burnt Mill, Harlow, Essex, CM20 2JE, United Kingdom

Distributed exclusively in the United States and Canada by Gale Research Company, Book Tower, Detroit, Michigan 48226, USA

ISBN 0-582-07926-8 (Longman)

Library of Congress Catalog Card Number: 4-17979

© Longman Group UK Limited 1991
All rights reserved; no part of this publication may be reproduced, stored in a retrieval system, or transmitted in any form or by any means, electronic, mechanical, photocopying, recording or otherwise without either the prior written permission of the Publishers or a licence permitting restricted copying issued by the Copyright Licensing Agency Ltd.
33–34 Alfred Place, London, WC1E 7DP

British Library Cataloguing in Publication Data
The Annual Register—1990
 1. History—Periodicals
  909.82'8'05   D410

ISBN 0-582-07926-8

Set in Times Roman by
QUORN SELECTIVE REPRO LIMITED, LOUGHBOROUGH
Printed and bound in Great Britain by
WILLIAM CLOWES LIMITED, BECCLES AND LONDON

CONTENTS

	PREFACE TO 232nd VOLUME	xv
	EXTRACTS FROM 1790, 1840, 1890 and 1940 VOLUMES	xvi
	EDITORIAL	1
	CHRONOLOGY OF THE GULF CRISIS	7
I	UNITED KINGDOM	
1	A Stormy Start to the 1990s	10
2	Local Elections and More Poll Tax Controversies	16
3	From Hopes of Peace to the Gulf Crisis	23
4	Seaside Politics	27
5	European Unity and British Divisions	30
6	High Drama and the Fall of a Prime Minister	34
7	A New Government. A New Era?	41
8	Scotland	44
9	Wales	46
10	Northern Ireland	48
II	THE AMERICAS AND CARIBBEAN	
1	United States of America	52
2	Canada	69
3	Latin America: Argentina 74 Bolivia 76 Brazil 77 Chile 78 Colombia 80 Ecuador 81 Paraguay 82 Peru 83 Uruguay 84 Venezuela 85 Cuba 85 Dominican Republic and Haiti 86 Central America and Panama 87 Mexico 91	74
4	The Caribbean: Jamaica 92 Guyana 93 Trinidad & Tobago 95 Barbados 96 Belize 97 Grenada 98 The Bahamas 99 Windward & Leeward Islands 100 Suriname 102 British Dependencies 103 Netherlands Antilles and Aruba 104	92
III	THE USSR AND EASTERN EUROPE	
1	Union of Soviet Socialist Republics	105
2	Poland 114 Czechoslovakia 119 Hungary 124 Romania 127 Bulgaria 130 Yugoslavia 133 Albania 137	114
IV	WESTERN, CENTRAL AND SOUTHERN EUROPE	
1	France 140 Germany 146 Italy 155 Belgium 159 The Netherlands 161 Luxembourg 163 Republic of Ireland 164	140
2	Denmark 167 Iceland 169 Norway 171 Sweden 172 Finland 174 Austria 175 Switzerland 178	167
3	Spain 180 Portugal 183 Gibraltar 185 Malta 187 Greece 188 Cyprus 191 Turkey 192	180
V	MIDDLE EAST AND NORTH AFRICA	
1	Israel	196
2	The Arab World 200 Egypt 204 Jordan 207 Syria 209 Lebanon 212 Iraq 215	200

CONTENTS

3	Saudi Arabia 219 Republic of Yemen 221	
	Arab States of the Gulf 223	219
4	Sudan 228 Libya 231 Tunisia 233 Algeria 237	
	Morocco 241 Western Sahara 244	228
VI	**EQUATORIAL AFRICA**	
1	Ethiopia 246 Somalia 248 Djibouti 250 Kenya 250	
	Tanzania 253 Uganda 255	246
2	Ghana 254 Nigeria 259 Sierra Leone 262 The Gambia 263	
	Liberia 264	257
3	Senegal 265 Guinea 267 Mali 267 Mauritania 268	
	Côte d'Ivoire 269 Burkina Faso 270 Niger 271 Togo and Benin 271	
	Cameroon 273 Chad 274 Gabon and Central African Republic 275	
	Congo 276 Equatorial Guinea 276	265
VII	**CENTRAL AND SOUTHERN AFRICA**	
1	Zaïre 278 Burundi and Rwanda 280 Guinea-Bissau and Cape Verde 282	
	São Tomé & Príncipe 283 Mozambique 283 Angola 286	278
2	Zambia 288 Malawi 290 Zimbabwe 291 Namibia 295	
	Botswana 296 Lesotho 297 Swaziland	298
3	South Africa	299
VIII	**SOUTH ASIA AND INDIAN OCEAN**	
1	Iran 306 Afghanistan 309	306
2	India 311 Pakistan 315 Bangladesh 318 Sri Lanka 321	
	Nepal 324 Bhutan 325	311
3	Mauritius 327 Seychelles, Comoros and Maldives 329	
	Madagascar 332	327
IX	**SOUTH-EAST AND EAST ASIA**	
1	Myanmar (Burma) 333 Thailand 335 Malaysia 337 Brunei 338	
	Singapore 339 Indonesia 341 Philippines 343 Vietnam 345	
	Kampuchea 347 Laos 348	333
2	China 349 Taiwan 357 Hong Kong 359 Japan 360	
	South Korea 365 North Korea 367 Mongolia 368	349
X	**AUSTRALASIA AND SOUTH PACIFIC**	
1	Australia 372 Papua New Guinea 377	372
2	New Zealand	378
3	South Pacific	382
XI	**INTERNATIONAL ORGANIZATIONS**	
1	The United Nations	386
2	The Commonwealth	397
3	The European Community	399
4	Organization for Economic Cooperation and Development 407	
	Comecon (CMEA) 408 Non-Aligned Movement 411	407
5	Council of Europe 414 European Free Trade Association 415	
	Nordic Council 417	414
6	African Conferences and Organizations 419 South Asian Association	
	for Regional Cooperation 422 South-East Asian Organizations 423	
	South Pacific Regional Cooperation 425 Latin American	
	Organizations 425 Caribbean Organizations 427	419

CONTENTS

XII	DEFENCE AND ARMS CONTROL	430
XIII	RELIGION	444
XIV	THE SCIENCES	
1	Medical and Scientific Research	451
2	Technology	459
3	Environment	464
XV	THE LAW	
1	International Law 468 European Community Law 471	468
2	Law in the United Kingdom	474
3	Law in the United States	479
XVI	THE ARTS	
1	Opera 482 Music 484 Dance/Ballet 488 Theatre 491 Cinema 496 Television and Radio 500	482
2	Art 504 Architecture 509 Fashion 511	504
3	Literature	513
XVII	SPORT	525
XVIII	ECONOMIC AND SOCIAL AFFAIRS	
1	Poland and Eastern Europe	536
2	The International Economy	538
3	The Economy of the United States	540
4	The Economy of the United Kingdom	542
5	Economic and Social Data	546
XIX	DOCUMENTS AND REFERENCE	
1	UN Security Council Resolutions on Gulf Crisis	561
2	Treaty on the Final Settlement with respect to Germany	566
3	Charter of Paris for a New Europe	569
4	The UK Conservative Cabinet	576
5	The United States Cabinet	578
	OBITUARY	579
	CHRONICLE OF PRINCIPAL EVENTS IN 1990	595
	INDEX	610
	MAPS AND DIAGRAMS	
	United Germany	150
	Iraq, Kuwait and the Gulf Crisis	201
	Warsaw Pact and NATO Force Reductions under CFE Treaty	435
	Soviet Force Reductions under CFE Treaty	435
	Zonal Force Limits in Europe under CFE Treaty	436

CONTRIBUTORS

EXTRACTS FROM PAST VOLUMES	**M. R. D. Foot,** Former Professor of Modern History, University of Manchester
PART 1	
UNITED KINGDOM, SCOTLAND	**C. J. Bartlett,** FRHistS, FRSE, Professor of International History, University of Dundee
WALES	**Gwyn Jenkins,** MA, Assistant Keeper, Department of Manuscripts and Records, National Library of Wales, Aberystwyth
NORTHERN IRELAND	**Sydney Elliott,** BA, PhD, Senior Lecturer in Politics, The Queen's University, Belfast
PART II	
USA	**Neil A. Wynn,** MA, PhD, Senior Lecturer and Head of History, Polytechnic of Wales
CANADA	**David M. L. Farr,** Professor Emeritus of History, Carleton University, Ottawa
LATIN AMERICA	**Peter Calvert,** AM, MA, PhD, Professor of Comparative and International Politics, University of Southampton
THE CARIBBEAN	**Julian C. J. Saurin,** PhD, Lecturer in International Relations, School of African and Asian Studies, University of Sussex
PART III	
USSR	**Stephen White,** PhD, Department of Politics, University of Glasgow
POLAND	**Z. J. Blazynski,** Author and broadcaster on Polish and communist affairs
CZECHOSLOVAKIA	**Vladimir V. Kusin,** PhD, Chief Analyst, Radio Free Europe-Radio Liberty Research Institute, Munich
HUNGARY	**George Schöpflin,** Joint Lecturer in East European Political Institutions, London School of Economics and School of Slavonic and East European Studies, University of London
ROMANIA	**Gabriel Partos,** Senior Talks Writer, BBC World Service
BULGARIA	**Stephen Ashley,** MA, DPhil, Senior Talks Writer, BBC World Service
YUGOSLAVIA	**J. B. Allcock,** MA, Head of Research Unit in Yugoslav Studies, University of Bradford
ALBANIA	**Richard Crampton,** PhD, Fellow of St Edmund Hall, Oxford, formerly Professor of East European History, University of Kent
PART IV	
FRANCE	**Martin Harrison,** Professor of Politics, University of Keele

CONTRIBUTORS

GERMANY	**Gordon Smith,** BSc(Econ), PhD, Professor of Government, London School of Economics and Political Science
	Adrian G. V. Hyde-Price, BSc(Econ), PhD, Lecturer, Department of Politics, University of Southampton
ITALY	**Muriel Grindrod,** Writer on Italian affairs; formerly Assistant Editor, *The Annual Register*
BELGIUM, NETHERLANDS, LUXEMBOURG	**J. D. McLachlan,** Managing Director, Marketing, Financial Times Business Information
REPUBLIC OF IRELAND	**Louis McRedmond,** MA, BL, Formerly Head of Information in Radio Telefís Eireann, the Irish broadcasting service
NORDIC COUNTRIES	**Hilary Allen,** BSc(Econ), DPhil, Writer on Nordic affairs
AUSTRIA	**Angela Gillon,** Researcher in West European affairs
SWITZERLAND	**Hans Hirter,** Editor, *Année Politique Suisse*, University of Berne
SPAIN, GIBRALTAR	**G. A. M. Hills,** BA, DLit, Writer and broadcaster on Iberian current affairs and history
PORTUGAL	**Manuel Santana,** Portuguese Section, BBC World Service
MALTA	**D. G. Austin,** Emeritus Professor of Government, University of Manchester
GREECE	**Richard Clogg,** MA, St Antony's College, Oxford
TURKEY	**A. J. A. Mango,** BA, PhD, Orientalist and writer on current affairs in Turkey and the Near East

PART V

ISRAEL	**Noah Lucas, PhD,** Fellow in Israeli Studies, The Oxford Centre for Postgraduate Hebrew Studies
ARAB WORLD, EGYPT, JORDAN SYRIA, LEBANON, IRAQ	**Christopher Gandy,** Formerly UK Diplomatic Service; writer on Middle Eastern affairs
SAUDI ARABIA, YEMEN	**R. M. Burrell,** Lecturer in the Contemporary History of the Near and Middle East, School of Oriental & African Studies, University of London
ARAB STATES OF THE GULF	**George Joffe,** Consultant Editor, Economist Intelligence Unit; Director of Research, Geopolitics and International Boundaries Research Centre, School of Oriental and African Studies, University of London
SUDAN	**Ahmed al-Shahi,** DPhil, Lecturer in Social Anthropology, Department of Social Policy, University of Newcastle-upon-Tyne
LIBYA, TUNISIA, ALGERIA MOROCCO, WESTERN SAHARA	**R. I. Lawless,** PhD, Reader in Modern Middle Eastern Studies, Centre for Middle Eastern and Islamic Studies, University of Durham

PART VI

ETHIOPIA, SOMALIA, DJIBOUTI	**Christopher Clapham,** MA, DPhil, Professor of Politics and International Relations, University of Lancaster

CONTRIBUTORS

KENYA, TANZANIA, UGANDA	**William Tordoff,** MA, PhD, Emeritus Professor of Government, University of Manchester
GHANA	**D. G. Austin** (see Pt. IV, Malta)
NIGERIA	**Robin Theobald,** PhD, Principal Lecturer in Sociology, Polytechnic of Central London
SIERRA LEONE, THE GAMBIA LIBERIA	**Arnold Hughes,** BA, Lecturer in Political Science, Centre of West African Studies, University of Birmingham
CHAPTER 3 (SENEGAL to EQUATORIAL GUINEA)	**Kaye Whiteman,** Editor-in-Chief, *West Africa*

PART VII

CHAPTER 1 (ZAIRE to ANGOLA)	**Robin Hallett,** MA, Writer and lecturer on African affairs
ZAMBIA, MALAWI	**Robin Hallett** (see above)
ZIMBABWE	**R. W. Baldock,** BA, PhD, Senior Editor, Yale University Press; writer on African affairs
NAMIBIA, BOTSWANA, LESOTHO, SWAZILAND, SOUTH AFRICA	**Gerald Shaw,** MA, Associate Editor, *The Cape Times,* Cape Town

PART VIII

IRAN	**Keith McLachlan,** BA, PhD, Senior Lecturer in Geography with reference to the Near and Middle East, School of Oriental and African Studies, University of London
AFGHANISTAN, INDIA, BANGLADESH, NEPAL, BHUTAN	**Peter Lyon,** BSc(Econ), PhD, Reader in International Relations and Academic Secretary, Institute of Commonwealth Studies, University of London; Editor, *The Round Table*
PAKISTAN	**David Taylor,** Lecturer in Politics with reference to South Asia, School of Oriental and African Studies, University of London
SRI LANKA	**James Jupp,** MSc(Econ), PhD, FASSA, Director, Centre for Immigration and Multicultural Studies, Australian National University, Canberra
SEYCHELLES, MAURITIUS, MALDIVES	**Jane Davis,** Lecturer, Department of International Politics, The University College of Wales, Aberystwyth
MADAGASCAR AND COMOROS	**Kaye Whiteman** (see Pt. VI, Ch. 3)

PART IX

MYANMAR (BURMA), INDONESIA, PHILIPPINES	**Robert H. Taylor,** PhD, Professor of Politics, School of Oriental and African Studies, University of London
THAILAND, VIETNAM, KAMPUCHEA, LAOS	**Jonathan Rigg,** PhD, Lecturer in South East Asian Geography, School of Oriental and African Studies, University of London
MALAYSIA, BRUNEI, SINGAPORE	**Michael Leifer,** BA, PhD, Professor of International Relations, London School of Economics and Political Science
CHINA, TAIWAN, HONG KONG	**Robert F. Ash,** MSc(Econ), PhD, Chairman, Contemporary China Institute and Senior Lecturer in Economics, School of Oriental and African Studies, University of London

JAPAN	**I. H. Nish,** Professor of International History, London School of Economics and Political Science
SOUTH AND NORTH KOREA	**James H. Grayson,** PhD, Director, Centre for Korean Studies, University of Sheffield
MONGOLIA	**Alan Sanders,** FIL, Lecturer in Mongolian Studies, School of Oriental and African Studies, University of London

PART X

AUSTRALIA	**James Jupp** (see Pt. VIII, Sri Lanka)
PAPUA NEW GUINEA	**Norman MacQueen,** Senior Lecturer in Politics, Sunderland Polytechnic
NEW ZEALAND, SOUTH PACIFIC	**Roderic Alley,** PhD, School of Political Science and Public Administration, Victoria University of Wellington

PART XI

UNITED NATIONS	**Granville Fletcher,** Former Chef de Cabinet, UN European Headquarters, Geneva
COMMONWEALTH	**Derek Ingram,** Editor of *Gemini News Service* and author and writer on the Commonwealth
EUROPEAN COMMUNITY	**Michael Berendt,** Expert on affairs of the European Communities
OECD, EFTA	**Roger East,** Editor of *Keesing's Record of World Events,* founder and director of Cambridge International Reference on Current Affairs (CIRCA)
COMECON	**Michael Kaser,** MA, Reader in Economics, Oxford University and Professorial Fellow of St Antony's College, Oxford
NON-ALIGNED MOVEMENT	**Peter Willetts,** PhD, Senior Lecturer in International Relations, The City University, London
COUNCIL OF EUROPE	**Richard A. Lambert,** Secretary to the UK delegation to the Parliamentary Assembly of the Council of Europe
NORDIC COUNCIL	**Hilary Allen** (see Pt. IV, Nordic Countries)
AFRICAN CONFERENCES AND ORGANIZATIONS	**Kaye Whiteman** (see Pt. VI, Ch. 3)
S. ASIAN ASSOCIATION FOR REGIONAL COOPERATION	**Peter Lyon** (see Pt. VIII, Afghanistan, etc.)
S.E. ASIAN ORGANIZATIONS	**Darren Sagar,** Regional Editor responsible for Asian and Middle Eastern Affairs, *Keesing's Record of World Events*
S. PACIFIC REGIONAL COOPERATION	**Roderic Alley** (see Pt. X, New Zealand, etc.)
LATIN AMERICAN ORGANIZATIONS	**Peter Calvert** (see Pt. II, Latin America)
CARIBBEAN ORGANIZATIONS	**Ciarán Ó Maoláin,** BA, Research Fellow, University of Warwick, writer on Caribbean, Latin American and Pacific affairs

PART XII

DEFENCE AND ARMS CONTROL	**Phil Williams,** PhD, Professor of Security Studies, Graduate School of Public and International Affairs, University of Pittsburgh

CONTRIBUTORS

PART XIII
RELIGION — **Geoffrey Parrinder,** MA, PhD, DD, Emeritus Professor of the Comparative Study of Religions, University of London

PART XIV
MEDICAL AND SCIENTIFIC RESEARCH
TECHNOLOGY

John Newell, Editor, Science, Industry, Medicine and Agriculture, BBC World Services
David Powell, A director of Electronic Publishing Services Ltd; editor, *EP journal.*

ENVIRONMENT — **Lloyd Timberlake,** Director for External Affairs, International Institute for Environment and Development (IIED)

PART XV
INTERNATIONAL LAW — **Christine Gray,** Fellow in Law, St Hilda's College, Oxford
EUROPEAN COMMUNITY LAW — **N. March Hunnings,** LLM, PhD, Editor, *Common Market Law Reports*
LAW IN THE UK — **David Ibbetson,** MA, PhD, Fellow and Tutor in Law, Magdalen College, Oxford
LAW IN THE USA — **Robert J. Spjut,** JD, LLM, Member of the State Bars of California and Florida

PART XVI
OPERA — **Elizabeth Forbes,** Freelance journalist, critic and translator
DANCE/BALLET — **Mary Clarke,** Editor, *The Dancing Times*
THEATRE — **Charles Osborne,** Author; chief theatre critic, *The Daily Telegraph*
MUSIC — **Francis Routh,** Composer and author; founder-director of the Redcliffe Concerts
CINEMA — **Derek Malcolm,** Film critic, *The Guardian*
TV & RADIO — **Raymond Snoddy,** Media correspondent, *The Financial Times*
ART — **Marina Vaizey,** MA, Art critic, *The Sunday Times*
ARCHITECTURE — **Paul Finch,** Editor, *Building Design*
FASHION — **Bonny Spencer,** Fashion editor, *Bella* magazine
LITERATURE — **John Coldstream,** Deputy Literary Editor, *The Daily Telegraph* and *The Sunday Telegraph*

PART XVII
SPORT — **Tony Pawson, OBE,** Sports writer, *The Observer;* cricket, football and fly-fishing international

PART XVIII
CHAPTERS 1 to 4 — **Victor Keegan,** Assistant Editor, *The Guardian*
STATISTICS — **Sue Cockerill,** Former member of the Statistical Department, *Financial Times*
OBITUARY — **H. V. Hodson,** Formerly Editor, *The Annual Register*
MAPS — **MJL Graphics,** N. Yorks, YO14 9BE

ACKNOWLEDGEMENTS

THE Advisory Board again gratefully acknowledges its debt to a number of institutions for their help with sources, references and documents, notably the UK Foreign and Commonwealth Office, the UN Information Centre and the German Embassy in London. Acknowledgement is also due, as the principal sources for the national data sections (showing the situation as at end-1990 unless otherwise stated), to *Keesing's Record of World Events* (Longman), *People in Power* (Longman) and *World Development Report* (OUP for the World Bank). The Board and the bodies which nominate its members disclaim responsibility for any opinions expressed or the accuracy of facts recorded in this volume.

ABBREVIATIONS

ACC	Arab Cooperation Council
ACP	African, Caribbean and Pacific states associated with EEC
AfDB	African Development Bank
AID	Agency for International Development
AIDS	Acquired Immune Deficiency Syndrome
AMU	Arab Maghreb Union
ANC	African National Congress
ANZUS	Australia-New Zealand-US Security Treaty
AR	Annual Register
ASEAN	Association of South-East Asian Nations
CAP	Common Agricultural Policy
CARICOM	Caribbean Common Market
CEEAC	Economic Community of Central African States
CFE	Conventional Force Reductions in Europe
CIA	Central Intelligence Agency
COMECON	Council for Mutual Economic Assistance (CMEA)
CSCE	Conference on Security and Cooperation in Europe
Cwth.	Commonwealth
EBRD	European Bank for Reconstruction and Development
EC	European Communities
ECOSOC	Economic and Social Council (UN)
ECOWAS	Economic Community of West African States
EEC	European Economic Community (Common Market)
EFTA	European Free Trade Association
EMS	European Monetary System
ESCAP	Economic and Social Commission for Asia and the Pacific (UN)
FAO	Food and Agriculture Organization
FBI	Federal Bureau of Investigation
GATT	General Agreement on Tariffs and Trade
GCC	Gulf Cooperation Council
GDP/GNP	Gross Domestic/National Product
IAEA	International Atomic Energy Agency
IBRD	International Bank for Reconstruction and Development
ICBM	Inter-Continental Ballistic Missile
ICO	Islamic Conference Organization
IDA	International Development Association
ILO	International Labour Organization
IMF	International Monetary Fund
INF	Intermediate-range Nuclear Forces
IRA	Irish Republican Army
MBFR	Mutual and Balanced Force Reductions
NAM	Non-Aligned Movement
NATO	North Atlantic Treaty Organization
OAS	Organization of American States
OAU	Organization of African Unity
OECD	Organization for Economic Cooperation and Development
OPEC (OAPEC)	Organization of (Arab) Petroleum Exporting Countries
PLO	Palestine Liberation Organization
SAARC	South Asian Association for Regional Cooperation
SADCC	Southern African Development Coordination Conference
SDI	Strategic Defence Initiative
START	Strategic Arms Reduction Talks
SWAPO	South-West Africa People's Organization
UN	United Nations
UNCTAD	United Nations Conference on Trade and Development
UNDP	United Nations Development Programme
UNESCO	United Nations Educational, Scientific and Cultural Organization
UNHCR	United Nations High Commission for Refugees
UNRWA	United Nations Relief and Works Agency
VAT	Value Added Tax
WHO	World Health Organization

PREFACE

THIS 232nd volume of the *Annual Register* has as its major theme the great international crisis which developed as a result of the Iraqi invasion of Kuwait in early August 1990 and the response of the world community to that aggression. At year's end it was uncertain whether a peaceful solution would be found or whether recourse would be had to war. By the time this preface was written the latter scenario had come to pass. But the record of the year contained in these pages does not 'jump the gun' by taking account of what was to happen in the next. Rather, it describes the various national and international ramifications of the crisis up to the end of 1990, leaving subsequent developments for the 1991 volume. In view of the importance of the Gulf crisis, this 1990 AR contains a special chronology on that theme (see pp. 7–9), in addition to the usual general chronology of the year's major events, appearing towards the end of the book.

But for the Gulf crisis, Europe would again have held centre-stage in the present volume, as the consequences of the historic transformation of 1989 continued to unfold. Democratic elections were held in most East European states, Germany was reunited and an end was officially declared to the Cold War in Europe. This last achievement had a significant impact on the Gulf crisis in terms of unprecedented great-power cooperation within the UN framework, a hopeful departure which is discussed in the editorial (see pp. 1–6). However, as later sections of the volume make clear, the collapse of communism in Eastern Europe and the accelerating disintegration of the Soviet Union itself threw up new political and economic problems.

Other notable events covered in this volume include the dramatic end of the Thatcher era in Britain, the release of Nelson Mandela in South Africa, the admission of independent Namibia to the community of nations, the start of European Community talks on enhanced economic, monetary and political union, the signature of an East-West conventional forces limitation (CFE) treaty, the growth of anarchy and famine in black Africa, the onset of recession in some major industrialized countries, and moves towards international cooperation on environmental problems. Beyond the realms of politics and economics, the customary extensive coverage is given to developments in the spheres of religion, science, the law, the arts and sport (including the World Cup soccer finals held in Italy).

The Advisory Board mourns the death in September 1990 of Anton Logoreci, the AR's valued contributor on Albania for three decades (see OBITUARY). His successor is welcomed to the AR circle, as are a number of other new contributors.

THE ANNUAL REGISTER

200 years ago

1790. *King Louis in confinement.* [Paris, 4 January] The writer [Arthur Young] beheld the extraordinary spectacle of the king of France walking in the gardens with six grenadiers of the bourgeoise militia. That the doors of the gardens were kept shut while he walked in them, in order to exclude all persons but deputies or those who procured admission tickets, from entering. That when he re-entered the palace, the doors of the gardens were thrown open to all persons without distinction, although the queen, with a lady of her court, was still walking in them.

150 years ago

1840. *Steamships in battle.* [4 November] The attack on St Jean d'Acre was, perhaps, the first occasion on which the advantages of steam have been tried in battle. There were four war-steamers engaged in the action, and the shells that were thrown from them did prodigious execution. They were enabled, with rapidity, to take up the most advantageous position, and rendered the greatest assistance during the bombardment. History presents no other instance of the downfall of such a fortress caused by the cannon of ships of war in so short a space of time.

100 years ago

1890. *Speech by Count Moltke in Berlin.* [14 May] 'It has been stated by Radical speakers over and over again that all our military precautions were taken in the interests of the moneyed classes only; that princes alone brought about wars; and that, without them, the nations would dwell side by side in peace and amity. As to the proprietary class—and that is a very large category, embracing in a certain sense almost the whole of the nation—for who has not something to lose?—it certainly has an interest in the maintenance of all those institutions which guarantee undisturbed possession of one's own. But princes and, on the whole, governments do not really bring about wars in our days. The era of cabinet wars is over. We now have only people's wars, and any government that is ordinarily cautious would think twice and thrice before causing a war of that kind, with all its incalculable consequences.'

50 years ago

1940. *Battle of Britain.* The repulse of the great German air attack not only saved England for the time being from the danger of invasion, but also marked a turning-point in the war in that it finally broke down the legend of the invincibility of the German Luftwaffe—a legend which itself contributed not a little to German success. The British people itself had never believed in this invincibility ever since the fight at Dunkirk, and it was now more than ever convinced that it had taken the measure of the enemy and would be able to withstand all his assaults. Speaking in the House of Commons on August 20, Mr Churchill referred with justifiable pride to the manner in which the nation had borne up against the 'cataract of disasters' which had poured out on it in May and June, until now it was 'standing erect, sure of itself, master of its fate, with the conviction of ultimate victory burning unquenchable in its heart'. In the same speech Mr Churchill paid a tribute to the British airmen who, 'undaunted by odds, unwearied by their constant challenge and mortal danger, were turning the tide of world war by their prowess and devotion. Never', he added, in a phrase which at once caught the popular imagination, 'in the field of human conflict was so much owed by so many to so few.'

ANNUAL REGISTER

FOR THE YEAR 1990

EDITORIAL

THE story of 1990 is crowded with events of high and lasting importance to the world: the collapse of the Warsaw Pact, the reunification of Germany, the revolt against communism throughout Eastern Europe, the protest of one Soviet republic after another against subjection to the USSR, East-West agreement to scrap large numbers of prime military hardware in Europe, the fall of a British prime minister of heroic international stature, the rape of Kuwait by Saddam Husain's Iraq, with its dramatic consequences—a unanimous UN Security Council resolution imposing the severest sanctions, followed by the massing of vast forces poised for war in the Arabian desert—moves towards ending apartheid and other developments in southern Africa and Asia which in less hectic times would have made big headlines everywhere. Among all those events, it would be hard at first sight to select that which was the most crucial, judged by its likely impact on global affairs in the last decade of the twentieth century. But, after a little thought, hesitation ends.

The key change was the ending of the Cold War between the communist-authoritarian East and the capitalist-democratic West, formally proclaimed at the summit meeting of the Conference on Security and Cooperation in Europe (CSCE) in Paris on 21 November. Though not yet given that chill name, the great rift yawned in 1947, when Moscow spurned the Marshall Plan, and caused all its satellites to do likewise, as a ploy of 'American imperialism'. Thus the ideological and political motive preceded and inspired the military confrontation. The Soviet Union under Stalin saw itself, falsely, as under mortal threat by a global system—identified with the United States and other Western powers—that was determined to destroy it from without and within. Its reaction was virulently defensive: a massive military build-up, soon to include atomic weapons and give rise to the stance of mutual nuclear deterrence; the political and military subordination of Russia's whole defensive glacis in Eastern Europe; the search in every continent for allies or at least collaborators, who could harass and undermine American 'imperialism'; an immense spy network; negative diplomacy, especially at the United Nations, where the USSR had a Security Council veto; latterly the Brezhnev Doctrine, justifying armed Soviet intervention in neighbouring or allied states.

All this, of course, provoked an equal and opposite reaction in America and the West generally, until there emerged the familiar pattern of two superpowers, each with its allies and associates, each labelled with an ideological epithet opprobrious to its rival—'communist expansionist' or 'capitalist imperialist'. There are many in high office today who in their active careers never knew any other global scene. The young accepted it as part of the natural order. Not only did the confrontation directly govern all Soviet-West relations, all questions of armaments, nuclear proliferation and so on; it coloured almost every issue and area in foreign relations—aid to poor countries, arms supply, economic and diplomatic favours or the opposite, even environmental and health issues, relations with Latin America, with the Middle East, with South-East Asia, India and Pakistan, and many another problem or place.

That such an explosive complex, with its sensors everywhere, never detonated a third world war may be ascribed to the overwhelming deterrence of nuclear armaments, taken with the fact that neither side wanted or intended such an outcome. The Cuban missiles crisis proved that this was the underlying truth. Peace was far from whole, however. In Asia, the Korean and Vietnam wars were immediate products of the global confrontation, and in many a revolutionary or counter-revolutionary struggle in Africa and Latin America the superpowers (with their allies) were active patrons of one side or the other. Though the description was sometimes inexact, the concept of 'proxy wars' was real enough.

Of course there were other forces and motives animating international relations at the same time: national ambition or resistance, racial solidarity, economic interests, religious or cultural affinities, personal aggrandisement, humanitarian sentiment, historic ties and many others. Yet the colour of communist-capitalist conflict was always luminous in the spectrum of external interests of every power, great or small.

It would be hard, therefore, to overstate the supreme importance of the ending of the Cold War in radically changing the whole panorama of world affairs in the 1990s. Things became possible which were almost unthinkable a dozen months previously—like a unanimous Security Council vote on sanctions against a Middle Eastern violator—or became actual instead of being bogged down in viscid negotiations for years on end, like the arms cuts agreed by the CSCE in November.

The lapse of the Cold War could not be written down as a temporary armistice. True, there were clear signs that the revolt of the Baltic and some other republics against Moscow rule, and the Soviet Union's failure to replace an economic command system with a viable competitive economy, were arousing a powerful conservative reaction, especially in the armed forces and the military-industrial complex. But the happenings that provoked reaction could not be undone, nor reversed without a counter-revolution, equally destabilizing. Eastern Europe could not be reconquered. Only in military personnel and hardware, including nuclear armament, did the USSR remain a superpower. A hot war, perhaps fought through proxies, was still a possibility to be guarded against; but a return to the Cold War weapons of ideology, subversion, prestige and propaganda predicated political forces of attraction and repulsion much closer to equality than could be the case between the Western powers and a disorderly and discredited communist rump.

The end of the Cold War could therefore be counted a durable fact. By it, the whole fabric of world affairs was or would soon be altered. The Warsaw Pact having decreed its own dissolution by 1992, its counterpart NATO had to rethink not only its objectives but also the structure of command and disposition of forces designed to secure them. Such defensive alliances assume an actual threat from a known potential enemy; hitherto there was no question about either, but now both were clouded by doubt. Or consider the position of the countries that proclaimed themselves non-aligned: if the world were no longer split into two permanently hostile power groups, with whom were those countries not aligned? Would fresh alignments, based on particular national interests, emerge among lands on the sidelines of a match that was no longer being played, at least according to the old rules?

The concept of a Third World, again, presupposes First and Second Worlds, powerful and self-sufficient, respectively capitalist and collectivist, distinct from the weak and indigent nations who were given that tertiary label. If, now, no sharp line can be drawn between the first and second groups, should we not partition the world, in the context of economic and benevolent relations, in a binary way, between the countries willing and able to give development aid and those anxious and needful to receive it? The latter would certainly include, at this time, countries in Europe striving to escape from command economies. Such reasoning may seem fanciful, but it illustrates how differently we should picture the family of nations in the budding era of the 1990s.

The work of UN subsidiaries like UNESCO, it could be hoped, would no longer be bedevilled by Cold War attitudes. Regional problems would take new shapes. Some would become more complex, as old partisanships revived, and fresh problems would arise—for instance, in Central Europe, where the instabilities and inter-communal conflicts which were once summed up as 'the Balkan problem' had already begun to raise their ugly heads. Such issues, however, would at least have been rinsed of the universal Cold War tinge which disguised their realities.

One region where the end of the Cold War decisively changed the odds and the stakes was the Persian Gulf. It is not hard to guess what, in the era of Brezhnev—to go back no further—would have followed an assault by Iraq upon Kuwait. Iraq, though not a formal ally of the USSR, was its client, largely supplied with Soviet arms and military advice, believed to be developing nuclear and other long-range armaments aimed against Israel, a client, in the same sense, of the USA. Kuwait, an oil-rich monarchy, enjoyed the patronage of the West. The head of the Gulf was a key strategic area on the world map, from the points of view both of the Western powers and of the Soviet Union. So Kuwait's immediate appeal to the Security Council would surely have caused a bitter wrangle and the near-certainty of a Soviet veto. (Witness the fact that the only actual Security Council dissenters were Cuba and Yemen, outlying remnants of the communist league.) The Arab states, leaderless, divided and anxious to avoid taking sides between the superpowers, would have drifted into acquiescence in a *fait accompli*. Independent action by the USA, with Britain doubtless in tow, if confined to economic measures and a maritime blockade, would have been ineffectual, or, if backed by military deployment, would have threatened to trigger a world war.

That is a bleak picture, and a hypothetical one, but it is wholly consistent with the state of international diplomacy and defensive postures in the era of the Cold War. An impotent UN was the inevitable consequence of a global confrontation held rigid at its centre by mutual deterrence but unstable and combustible at its fringes, as in South-East Asia, in Central America and the Caribbean, and in the Persian Gulf.

As for the actual outcome, following vigorous UN reaction, 1990 ended with a dreadful uncertainty. Two vast military complexes faced each other in the Arabian desert, ready for ruthless war. The window of opportunity for its avoidance by Iraqi submission was about to close. If war should come, its outcome was not in serious doubt. However many the human casualties, however great the material destruction, Iraq would be defeated, Kuwait freed and the UN force, with the USA in the van, would be left master of the battlefield. But what then? The long-term security of restored Kuwait would have initial priority. More widely, there was manifest need for an attempt, under the necessary aegis of the UN itself, at a comprehensive settlement in the whole Middle East. The obstacles to achieving it would be little changed. Syria would have replaced Iraq as the major Arab power in the region; the oil-rich monarchies would have been reprieved, and Egypt would also have gained; the basic problem of Israel would be no less in force or difficulty. The more important changes would be external to the region: the demonstration of American might, the enhanced status of the UN, and the participation, as a positive UN member, of the Soviet Union.

All this remained speculative as 1990 ended. Already, however, the UN had been revived as the powerful organ for keeping peace and punishing aggression which its founders—all too well aware of the feeble record of the League of Nations—intended it to be. The veto of the permanent members of the Security Council, combined with the supremacy of the Cold War in diplomatic and military calculations, had emasculated the UN, just as the League had been emasculated by its incompleteness and the timidity of its leading members. In the UN's case, the exception had proved the rule: its effective action in Korea happened when the USSR had absented itself and no veto paralysed the Security Council.

Secondly, the Gulf crisis was the catalyst of an extraordinary change in the relations between Washington and Moscow, the two poles of the Cold War confrontation. There was special significance in the area that turned former political foes into partners in a great international enterprise and in the passage of stern Security Council resolutions. For the Western powers had long striven to deny the Soviet Union any role in the Gulf—an axiom of British policy rooted, indeed, in the century-long rivalry of the British and Russian empires in Central Asia. Now, the West had acknowledged that Soviet Russia must have a role to play in collective action and collaborative diplomacy in the Gulf and its environs; and, if in the Gulf, then surely in other regions where the West had feared its hostile long-term motives. This change in itself solved no problems, but it ended the projection into them of an over-arching external power conflict, and made it much more likely that any attempted solution would endure.

Thirdly, the UN's response to the rape of Kuwait, while concentrating on that cause, inexorably implied that, once Kuwait was liberated and reparation made, the whole UN would have a common and paramount interest in reviewing the whole regional complex on its merits, lest it again threaten major war. That was the reality of 'linkage' between the Kuwait affair and other problems of the Middle East. 'On its merits' meant, among other things, rid of the former impulses of global conflict between two superpowers and their ideologies.

Talk of an 'Arab solution' of the Gulf crisis had been misguided and even dangerous. As an immediate ploy, it smacked of compromise over an issue of violent aggression, pillage and inhumanity as clear-cut as it could be. In that light the idea was mischievous, but as a long-term formula it was even worse. In geographical terms alone, the Arabs are by no means the only peoples of the area, among whom are Jews, Turks, Kurds, Iranians and others, all with their distinct racial and religious interests. If there were any prospect of a Pax Arabica, something could be said for it, but there was not. The Arab world was riven by internal conflict. An 'Arab solution', even if it were to embrace, improbably, a secure Israel, was a propagandist myth.

On its face, the idea of a 'regional solution' made more sense than one based on racial or cultural affections. But if it meant confining the negotiating parties to countries geographically in the Gulf or Middle Eastern region it lacked realism. UN principles of peace and security for all nations were at stake, and the effect of actual UN intervention in the area would not melt away. The region remained a bomb loaded and primed, whose explosion would implicate every continent. And it remained a chief source of that product which fuels the industry, transport and other energy needs of every country, rich or poor, save the most primitive. So a Middle Eastern settlement required not mere ratification by the world community but its constructive participation.

Not that an overall and lasting settlement had much realistic chance of emerging after an Iraq-Kuwait denouement, however attained. The stakes were too high, the conflicts too deep-rooted, the national and cultural emotions too strong. The best that could be hoped for was a *modus vivendi* more stable than the existing powder keg. That its possibility was already seen on a hazy horizon beyond the fog of war was one aspect of the looming of a global comity of nations, no longer split, on every cause, into hostile ideological power groups. The end of the Cold War had raised the long-term hopes of all mankind.

(*London, February 1991*)

CHRONOLOGY OF THE GULF CRISIS IN 1990

National and international aspects of the Gulf crisis feature extensively in the present volume, notably in Pt. V, which includes a map of the region. Readers are also referred to the entry 'Gulf Crisis' in the index for guidance on other relevant coverage.

JULY

24 Iraq reported to have massed 30,000 troops on Kuwait border.
27 Iraqi troops reported to have pulled back following mediation by President Mubarak of Egypt.
31 An estimated 100,000 Iraqi troops reported on Kuwait border.

AUGUST

1   Talks in Jeddah between Iraq and Kuwait broke down.
2   Iraq invaded Kuwait; Emir fled to Saudi Arabia; many countries froze Kuwaiti assets in response; UN Security Council resolution 660 called for immediate and unconditional withdrawal.
3   US and UK announced that naval vessels would be sent to Gulf; Iraqi troops reported to be gathering on Saudi border.
4   EC agreed to impose sanctions against Iraq.
5   Iraq named 'free provisional government of Kuwait' formed of Iraqi nationals.
6   UN Security Council resolution 661 imposed mandatory sanctions, including oil embargo, against Iraq.
7   President Bush ordered US planes and troops to Saudi Arabia; Turkey closed its oil pipeline.
9   Iraq announced annexation of Kuwait; UK announced it would send troops to join multinational force assembling in Gulf. UN Security Council resolution 662 rejected annexation; USSR condemned annexation but warned against military action without UN approval.
10 At emergency Arab League summit in Cairo, 12 nations voted to send pan-Arab force to Saudi Arabia.
    Iraq closed its borders and those of Kuwait.
11 Iraqi troops shot dead Briton fleeing from Kuwait.
12 US Secretary of State Baker announced that deposed Kuwait government had requested enforcement of UN sanctions under article 51 of UN Charter; US and Israel rejected Saddam's peace plan linking withdrawal from Kuwait with resolution of other Middle East problems.
13 US and Britain began naval blockade of Iraq.
14 King Husain of Jordan in Baghdad for talks with Saddam.
15 Iraq announced formal peace settlement of its conflict with Iran, conceding all Iranian demands and release of POWs.
16 King Husain held talks with President Bush at Kennebunkport.
18 UN Security Council resolution 664 urged Iraq to allow departure of all foreign nationals.
19 Iraq began rounding up Western nationals in Kuwait: some were to be detained at military bases in Iraq as a 'human shield' to deter air attacks; UAE agreed to deployment of foreign troops.

CHRONOLOGY OF THE GULF CRISIS

21 Several WEU countries confirmed they were sending troops to Gulf.
22 President Bush ordered call-up of 40,000 US military reservists; Jordan temporarily closed border with Iraq to deal with refugee influx.
23 President Saddam appeared on television with British hostages.
24 Many foreign embassies in Kuwait defied Iraq's order to close and were reported surrounded by tanks and troops.
25 UN Security Council resolution 665 authorized use of 'measures commensurate' to enforce sanctions against Iraq; President Waldheim, visiting Baghdad, secured safe-passage for Austrian nationals.
26 King Husain of Jordan began peace mission among Arab leaders.
27 US ordered expulsion of 36 Iraqi embassy staff.
28 Iraq announced that Kuwait had become its 19th governorate; Saddam declared that all foreign women and children could leave.
29 OPEC members agreed to support Saudi plan for increased oil production.
31 UN Secretary-General in Amman for talks with Iraq's Foreign Minister; Japan offered $1,000 million towards costs of multinational force.

SEPTEMBER

4 British women and children travelled in convoy from Kuwait to Baghdad to await repatriation.
5 Saddam called for overthrow of King Fahd of Saudi Arabia and President Mubarak of Egypt.
6 UK parliament recalled for two-day debate on crisis; Mrs Thatcher announced that British ground forces would go to Gulf.
9 Presidents Bush and Gorbachev held talks in Helsinki; they demanded Iraq's unconditional withdrawal from Kuwait.
10 Iran and Iraq renewed diplomatic links.
13 Britain announced deployment of 7th Armoured Brigade (Desert Rats) in Gulf; UN Security Council resolution 666 approved shipment of food to Iraq and Kuwait in humanitarian circumstances.
16 UN Security Council resolution 667 condemned raids on diplomatic missions in Kuwait.
17 Britain expelled some Iraqi diplomatic personnel.
21 Iraq expelled military attachés of 11 European embassies in Baghdad.
23 Iraq threatened to attack Israel and Middle Eastern oilfields if strangled by sanctions.
24 UN Security Council resolution 669 entrusted sanctions committee to make recommendations regarding countries suffering from effects of trade embargo.
25 UN Security Council resolution 670 called for an air blockade against Iraq.

OCTOBER

8 At least 17 Palestinians died when Israeli troops fired on demonstrators at Temple Mount, Jerusalem; 9 Oct. Saddam threatened retaliatory air strike against Israel.
21 Saudi Defence Minister suggested Kuwait make territorial concessions to Iraq. Former UK Conservative PM Heath on humanitarian mission to Baghdad.
23 33 hostages returned to UK with Mr Heath; Iraqi parliament voted to release all 330 French hostages; petrol-rationing temporarily introduced in Iraq.
28 EC heads of government, meeting in Rome, declared that EC members would not negotiate with Iraq.
29 Soviet envoy Y. Primakov concluded five-day Gulf peace mission with talks in Baghdad with Saddam; UN Security Council resolution 674 condemned Iraq's hostage-taking and pillage of Kuwait.

NOVEMBER

4 US Secretary of State visited troops in Gulf at start of diplomatic mission to European and Arab countries.
6 Saddam ordered release of 106 (mostly Japanese) hostages.
7 Iraq released more hostages in response to visit by former German Chancellor Willy Brandt.
10 US Congress urged President Bush to seek its approval before an attack in Gulf.
11 US Defence Secretary Cheney travelled to Gulf to visit British troops; Chinese Foreign Minister in Baghdad.
15 Egypt, Syria and Kuwait rejected King Hassan of Morocco's call for emergency Arab summit.
18 Saddam said remaining hostages would be released between Christmas and Easter; in talks with President Bush at Oggersheim, Chancellor Kohl urged a peaceful solution of crisis.
19 Iraq announced that it would increase its forces in Kuwait by 250,000 troops.
22 President Bush visited US troops in Saudi desert for Thanksgiving; UK Defence Secretary King announced deployment of further 14,000 British troops in Gulf, bringing total to more than 30,000.
23 President Bush held talks in Geneva with President Asad of Syria, the first such talks for 13 years; Iraq lifted curfew in Kuwait for first time since invasion.
26 British Labour MP Tony Benn on four-day visit to Baghdad.
28 Britain and Syria resumed diplomatic relations; UN Security Council resolution 677 asked Secretary-General to safeguard smuggled copy of Kuwait's population register.
29 UN Security Council by 12–2 vote adopted resolution 678 effectively authorizing use of force against Iraq after 15 Jan. 1991; Cuba and Yemen dissented; China abstained.
30 President Bush offered to send US Secretary of State to Baghdad between 15 Dec. and 15 Jan. for talks with Saddam; he also invited Iraqi Foreign Minister to visit Washington for talks.

DECEMBER

6 President Saddam announced that all Western hostages in Kuwait and Iraq would be freed.
9 Evacuation of Western hostages in Iraq and Kuwait commenced; all were home by Christmas; King Husain called on all Arab leaders to join a dialogue on crisis to run parallel with proposed US-Iraq talks.
12 Saddam sacked Defence Minister Gen. Abdel-Jaber Khalil Shanshal and promoted Maj.-Gen. Saadi Tuma to post.
16 British ambassador left Kuwait; embassy had been besieged for 111 days and was last to close its doors.
17 Royal assent given to UK order for call-up of reservists for Gulf.
24 Saddam declared that Israel would be his first target in event of war.
28 UK Defence Secretary announced biggest call-up of reservists since 1956 Suez crisis.

I THE UNITED KINGDOM

CAPITAL: London   AREA: 244,100 sq km   POPULATION: 57,100,000 ('88)
OFFICIAL LANGUAGE: English, also Welsh (in Wales)
POLITICAL SYSTEM: parliamentary democracy
HEAD OF STATE: Queen Elizabeth II (since Feb '52)
RULING PARTY: Conservative Party (since May '79)
HEAD OF GOVERNMENT: John Major, Prime Minister (since Nov '90)
PRINCIPAL MINISTERS: Douglas Hurd (foreign and Commonwealth affairs), Norman Lamont (Exchequer), Kenneth Baker (home affairs), Lord Mackay of Clashfern (Lord Chancellor), Tom King (defence), Michael Heseltine (environment), Peter Lilley (trade & industry) (*for full list see* DOCUMENTS)
INTERNATIONAL ALIGNMENT: NATO, OECD, EC, Cwth.
CURRENCY: pound sterling (end-'90 £1=US$1.93)   GNP PER CAPITA: US$12,810 ('88)
MAIN EXPORT EARNERS: machinery and transport equipment, mineral fuels and lubricants, manufactured goods, chemicals, financial services, tourism

A STORMY START TO THE 1990s

THE first year of a new decade opened with the Conservative government in deep trouble. It ended with a new tenant in No 10 Downing Street. Not all the protestations of Mrs Thatcher's staunchest supporters that she was still the indispensable leader at home and abroad could silence the mutterings that, however impressive her achievements since 1979, she was not necessarily the best person to lead the Conservatives and Britain in the 1990s. Even so the end, when it came, was sudden. Three turbulent weeks in November sufficed to bring down one of Britain's most remarkable but at the same time one of its most controversial prime ministers.

At the beginning of the year only members of the Labour Party among the politically active had much cause for satisfaction as they savoured their strong and increasing lead in the opinion polls. The weakness of the centre parties and the government's difficulties with the economy, inflation and the new poll tax (officially 'community charge') were doing wonders for Labour's popularity. On the other hand, despite the extensive policy reviews, doubts persisted as to whether Labour's new thinking was sufficiently clear and convincing to translate its current standing into solid and durable support. Although a recent recruitment drive had secured 35,000 new members, total party membership was barely 300,000.

There was, however, evidence to suggest that even 11 years of Thatcherism had failed to win a majority to support most of the basic essentials of the Thatcherite philosophy. Thus Eric Jacobs and Robert Worcester concluded in *We British: Britain under the Moriscope* that a majority still favoured 'a mainly socialist society in which public interest and a more controlled economy are most important' together with 'the social and collective provision of welfare'. Support for trade unions to protect workers' interests was as strong as in 1975. Many Conservatives were among those who wanted to protect the welfare state. Some commentators thought that the most relevant parts of the Thatcherite agenda had already been implemented and much of it accepted, as demonstrated by the efforts of the Labour Party to revise its policies and image.

Conservatives were nervously aware that they had, at best, a little over two years in which to regain public support, and in particular to rebuild confidence in their management of the economy. A heavy responsibility rested on the shoulders of John Major, the new Chancellor of the Exchequer, to rescue the Conservatives from the consequences of the financial miscalculations and improvidence of the late 1980s. He repeatedly emphasized that interest rates would remain high for as long as was necessary to stop the price spiral. In fact his policy could be subjected to a very simple test: if it was not hurting it was not working.

The government was relieved of one embarrassment on 13 March when the six-month old ambulance dispute was finally resolved. The crews had attracted much public sympathy and financial support, helped by their provision of extensive emergency cover during what was often an acrimonious struggle. Though some hardliners were prepared to battle on, a ballot produced a 4 to 1 vote in favour of terms which gave average pay increases of 17.6 per cent over two years, but which did not include a pay bargaining mechanism—a major reason why the affair had developed into the longest public sector dispute since the miners' strike in 1984–85.

The cabinet suffered two surprise resignations early in the year. In January Norman Fowler announced his retirement for personal reasons from the Department of Employment and he was succeeded by Michael Howard. Peter Walker, the longest-serving 'wet' (and described by a Plaid Cymru spokesman as Wales's 'most effective Secretary of State'), handed over his office to David Hunt at the beginning of May.

Government warnings that rising labour costs compared with leading foreign competitors could lead to a rise in unemployment failed to impress wage bargainers. In the first quarter of the year not only were some engineering industries forced to concede a 37-hour working week, but there were fears of a return to a national 'going rate' for wage increases. Unions justified large wage claims by pointing to rising inflation (which stood at 7.7 per cent for the third month running) and to high mortgage rates. Even the director-general of CBI accused the government of scoring 'inflationary own goals' with the poll tax and the uniform business rate, which would hit the retail trade in southern England.

The trade deficit rose again in January—to almost £2,000 million—

while in February most building societies raised their mortgage rate to 15.4 per cent, a sensitive matter for the Conservatives with home ownership now extending to 65 per cent of the population. The numbers of people in arrears with mortgage, credit and rent payments were rapidly rising.

Kenneth Baker, the Conservative Party chairman, conceded on 25 February that the party was facing a 'very serious' time. Over the same weekend Michael Heseltine, who was increasingly seen as the strongest potential challenger to Mrs Thatcher, made the embarrassing suggestion that the controversial community charge should never have been introduced. A week later an opinion poll commissioned by the British Medical Association suggested that 73 per cent of the electorate thought the National Health Service unsafe in Conservative hands.

The poll tax, however, had clearly become the issue of the day, and remained so until the summer. The lengthy passage of the poll tax legislation through parliament finally ended on 18 January, but not without major challenges to the government from many of its own supporters. Both Mrs Thatcher and Chris Patten (Secretary of State for the Environment), as well as the whips, were involved in the talks to contain one of the potentially most serious backbench revolts since 1979. As it was, two divisions found 26 and 31 MPs from both wings of the Tory party voting against the government.

Equally serious was the decision of 18 Conservative local councillors to resign the party whip on 28 February with the result that their party lost control of the West Oxfordshire district council. Their example was followed by nine councillors on Beverley borough council near Hull on 21 March. They complained that the government had consistently failed to listen to grass roots opinion concerning the implications of the tax. There had been no lack of prior warnings.

As the date for implementation neared so the unease among Conservative backbenchers grew in step with the mounting protests from constituents as well as from the opposition parties. Ministers vainly tried to defend themselves with reminders that local government spending had been rising more rapidly than that of central government, that there would have been sharp increases had the rating system been perpetuated, and that the poll tax would make local councillors more accountable.

New calculations showed that many more families would be adversely affected than had originally been projected (Labour claimed that three out of four would be losers), that the average poll tax would be some £85 above the government's estimate of a national average for England of £278 (£175 for Wales), and that many Conservative as well as Labour-held constituencies would see sharp rises in payments by average households. Chris Patten insisted that local councils, and especially Labour ones, were responsible for the national overshoot of some £3,000 million above what the government considered fair and reasonable. A rise of one-third in the old domestic rates would have been needed to meet such extravagance. Councils, not least Conservative ones, retorted that government figures underestimated their inescapable financial commitments and made insufficient allowance for inflation.

Preparations for the introduction of the poll tax in England and Wales in April set off a number of demonstrations, some of them violent. The first of these was in Manchester on 28 February. Among other places to suffer disorder as councils tried to set a figure for the new tax were Swindon, Bristol and Birmingham. There was a particularly serious outbreak outside Hackney Town Hall on the night of 8 March. Some looting occurred, and 33 people were injured. More trouble erupted in Lambeth on the following night.

Conservative attempts to link the Labour Party with anti-poll tax demonstrations were a failure. Labour leaders were quick to dissociate the party from violence and defiance of the law. The Labour leader, Neil Kinnock, speaking in Dunoon on 9 March, branded the extremists as 'toytown revolutionaries' who were playing into the hands of the government. On 28 March the national executive committee (NEC) withdrew its endorsement of three adopted candidates for the forthcoming council elections in Haringey, North London, for their support of a campaign of non-payment and non-setting of the poll tax. Similar action was also taken against candidates in Swansea and Liverpool. On 14 March one Labour MP, Dick Douglas (Dunfermline West), announced that he was resigning the Labour whip as he was determined not to pay the tax. With three other Labour MPs he pledged continuing support for a campaign of civil disobedience—but he opposed violence. He later joined the Scottish Nationalists.

Meanwhile, the Labour leadership continued to wage war on the Militant Tendency, six members being expelled in Glasgow on 24 March. Militant, which had been thrown on to the defensive in 1989, was once again winning attention. It was the leading force in the All-Britain Anti-Poll Tax Federation, and was providing guidance on organization and the tactics that could be employed, for instance, to protect non-payers from seizure of their goods. Such tactics had already been tried and tested in Scotland. Nevertheless, it was evident, as the strength of protest in Conservative Maidenhead demonstrated, and when Tory MPs faced their own constituency supporters, that anti-poll tax campaigners spanned the whole political spectrum.

By 20 March, budget day, morale on the Conservative benches was badly in need of a boost. Even some Tories were beginning to think that there might be some truth in the Labour charge that the government—having blamed everyone since the late 1970s for the country's economic woes—was now left with no-one to blame but itself.

Contrary to the belief of many economists and the City that a tough budget was needed to protect the pound and to prevent a further rise in interest rates, Mr Major chose a 'broadly neutral' policy. He admitted 'the unexpected stubbornness' of inflation, while consumer spending remained surprisingly buoyant. Nevertheless, he decided to raise only £1,000 million (in a full tax year) in additional taxation, mostly from excise duties. The Chancellor feared that a more draconian approach would tip the economy into recession, and he believed that his strategy would cause inflation to begin to fall by the end of the year. He also expected growth in 1991 to return towards a 'sustainable rate of around 2.75 per cent—a figure which some economists noted was disappointingly close to Britain's average growth rate since 1945. Britain, they feared, would remain a low growth economy in search of a miracle.

The main novelty in the budget was the provision of new tax-free inducements for the small saver, notably TESSA, a five-year tax-exempt savings account (maximum £9,000) for all from January 1991. It was important, argued the Chancellor, to revive the 'culture of thrift'. There was also some tax relief for small businesses and further measures were promised to improve labour skills.

The budget gave comfort to the Tory benches, one MP commenting that the Chancellor had put a smile on the faces of his party colleagues 'for the first time for several months'. There was even a welcome from Labour for some measures, such as the reduction in the levy on the football pools on the condition that the money was used to improve the safety of British soccer grounds. But overall Mr Kinnock dismissed it as a 'bits-and-pieces budget; a stop-gap affair', while the shadow Chancellor, John Smith elaborated upon the inflationary own goals which he said the government had scored against itself. The budget would not enable Britain to seize the economic opportunities of the 1990s.

There were serious complaints from the City, notably the charge that Mr Major had left himself with little room for error. More disturbing for those who looked for a pre-election boom in 1991-92 was the rapid decline in the budget surpluses. On the final day of the debate the former Chancellor, Nigel Lawson, argued that until Britain joined the exchange rate mechanism (ERM) of the European Monetary System (EMS) the Government's commitment against inflation would be at risk. He thought the government timetable might prove 'too leisurely'. But Mrs Thatcher, during question time on 27 March, reiterated the conditions she had spelt out at the Madrid summit (see AR 1989, p.37), and merely expressed the hope that entry would occur during her second decade in power.

Nevertheless, demands for ERM entry continued to grow even when the underlying rate of inflation (that is with the exclusion of mortgage rates and the effect of the poll tax) accelerated compared with France and West Germany. The City believed that business confidence would be precarious at best until Britain joined the ERM. Others feared that Britain was jeopardizing its influence over steps to European monetary union. *The Times* of 30 March asked if anyone in places of influence, apart from Mrs Thatcher, opposed early entry.

The government also encountered opposition from its own benches on 26 March when it pushed through its community charge transitional relief scheme. Four Tories voted against, and more than 30 abstained. The dismay over the poll tax extended to sections of the Conservative press. *The Sunday Times* protested on 25 March that the country had been 'lumbered . . . with a tax widely (and rightly) seen as iniquitous'. *The Times* had earlier dismissed it as 'inane'.

The poll tax was the leading issue in the Mid-Staffordshire by-election of 22 March. In a remarkably high turnout (77.5 per cent) Labour spectacularly overturned the Conservative majority of 14,654 at the 1987 general election. For Labour Sylvia Heal polled 27,649 votes against the 18,200 of her Conservative opponent—a majority of 9,449. The Liberal Democrats (with 6,315 votes) alone of the other candidates made any showing. The swing to Labour was more than 21 per cent, the highest in a by-election since 1935. There were equally impressive Labour gains in five local by-elections on the same day. Pollsters estimated that while there had been a sizeable protest vote many people were perhaps beginning to believe that the Labour Party had changed its political character. Tory strategists hoped to gain in the longer run from the apparent return to a two-horse race with the decline of the political centre.

At least the Transport Secretary was able to give pleasure to many when he announced on 27 March that extensive schemes to build new roads in London had been abandoned. Thousands of homes would be saved from demolition. Instead, more limited road improvements were envisaged, and a higher priority given to public transport and cyclists.

The controversy over the community charge, coupled with the general unpopularity of the government, inevitably re-opened the question of Mrs Thatcher's leadership, in part at least because she was seen as the main driving force behind the poll tax. Resignation rumours on 9 March brought firm denials from No 10 and senior Tories. Michael Heseltine was carefully cultivating his image as a staunch Conservative, albeit one who differed from the Prime Minister on the poll tax, the economy and Britain's relations with Europe.

All this political turbulence was paralleled by a succession of violent storms in January and February. Winds of up to 110 miles per hour caused considerable damage, particularly in the south and south-west of England, parts of Wales and Scotland. The death toll for the storm of 28 January finally reached 47, and two more died on 8 February.

The gales of 26–27 February claimed 18 lives. London on the day of the first great storm was described by the police as 'virtually at a standstill'. The Houses of Parliament themselves suffered damage. Seaside towns in the south-west and in North Wales were repeatedly hammered by gales. The sea wall was breached at Towyn (Clwyd), forcing the evacuation of 2,000 people. Serious flooding occurred in the Severn Valley. Preliminary estimates for the total damage reached £5,000 million.

Chapter 2

LOCAL ELECTIONS AND MORE POLL TAX CONTROVERSIES

ON 31 March a huge anti-poll tax rally in the centre of London (variously estimated at between 40,000 and 200,000 people) developed into a major riot. Some 450 people were said to have been injured (including 374 policemen), and there were 339 arrests. Cars and buildings were damaged in Trafalgar Square, Regent Street and Oxford Street, and there were cases of arson and looting. Political activists as well as hooligan elements were involved. Both Conservative and Labour leaders unreservedly condemned the violence and called for stiff penalties against this criminal behaviour. But there were complaints from various quarters that police management of the operation had been flawed, and that there had been over-reaction in the 'second battle of Trafalgar'. This was one of several controversies relating to police conduct in the eyes of the public.

The display of political unity in the Commons was speedily followed by angry exchanges on 2 April when the Home Secretary attacked those Labour MPs who were encouraging people to break the law through the non-payment campaign. 'Do they really expect', he asked, 'those they seek to influence to draw neat distinctions between one sort of law-breaking and another?' A Labour spokesman later described this as an attempt to smear the entire Labour Party by associating it with the violent scenes which people had just seen on television. Labour also warned that if the Prime Minister and some Conservatives persisted in their attempts to smear the opposition they would be doing a disservice to the cause of law and order.

Twenty Labour councils were ordered by Mr Patten on 3 April to cut their community charges. Another London borough was added a week later. Labour accused the government of a 'political fix', and cited examples of high-spending Conservative councils which had been untouched. Council appeals to the High Court, the Court of Appeal and finally the House of Lords were all rejected in the course of June and July. On 19 September, however, the High Court ruled in favour of Lambeth after its revision of its poll tax in response to capping—though at £29 above the government figure. The verdict was upheld by three appeal court judges a week later.

More fuel was added to the flames when many small shopkeepers protested against the introduction of the standard business rate. They were also suffering from the poll tax and high interest rates. Once again the government had provoked its own supporters. Indeed, *The Times* on 2 April thought the tax in its present form was 'beyond coherent redemption'. Others, drawing on Scottish councils' experiences in 1989-90, noted the high collection costs compared with the old rates system, and the large numbers who escaped payment by intent or because of the difficulty of administering the scheme.

On 18 July the Health Secretary, Kenneth Clarke, told the Commons that plans to reform community care for the elderly, disabled and mentally handicapped had been postponed until after the general election to keep down community charge bills and to give local authorities more time in which to prepare for their new responsibilities. The original intention had been to implement the scheme from April 1991, a target criticized by the all-party social services committee as 'unrealistic' within only 18 months of the passage of the legislation. The new system, with its emphasis on domiciliary as well as residential care, was expected to add over £800 million to local authority spending—or an extra £15 on the average poll tax bill. Some government funding was promised to assist the mentally ill in the interval. Conservative as well as Labour councils criticized the postponement.

By July councils were reporting wide differences in the numbers paying the tax. In some areas non-payment was as high as 50 per cent. Mr Patten's own constituency of Bath reported that non-payment was running at 40 per cent. A survey by *The Independent on Sunday* (12 August) suggested that one in four resident in England's cities had paid nothing, and that many councils were having to take out expensive loans to meet the shortfalls. The situation was particularly serious in some London boroughs.

The government's review of the future of the community charge—often described as Mrs Thatcher's 'flagship'—led to an announcement on 19 July that the Treasury would contribute an extra £3,260 million to local government in 1991–92. Transitional relief to those who had previously paid low rate bills would be extended to 11.5 million people (4 million more than were already receiving help) and would run for an additional two years. But 90 per cent of the money was intended to assist local funding in the hope that the average poll tax rise in 1991 would be no more than £22. Organizations representing local councils challenged the government's estimate that local spending need not exceed £39,000 million. They claimed that current services would cost £41,600 million.

The government for its part was planning to improve the mechanism to cap high-spending councils. Among the critics, Simon Hughes for the Liberal Democrats dismissed the latest moves as an unsuccessful attempt to conceal the unfair nature of the charge until after the general election.

One of the worst outbreaks of disorder ever recorded in a British gaol began on 1 April in Strangeways Prison, Manchester. At least 50 persons were injured, one of whom died later. Serious incidents followed in a number of other prisons. These were soon brought under control, but some prisoners held out in the siege of Strangeways until 25 April. Damage was extensive and was estimated at £60 million. A Prison Officers' Association claim that the prison system was 'on the verge of collapse' was described by the Home Office as 'somewhat exaggerated'. But it was accepted that Strangeways was one of the most overcrowded prisons in England and Wales, ten of which were reported to be holding 50 per cent more prisoners than their intended complements. An all-party Commons committee on 19 June described overcrowding and insanitary conditions as the root cause of the Strangeways riot. It also argued that the poverty of life in most prisons did not even have the merit of deterring crime. It called for a government bill to define acceptable minimum standards.

The local elections held on 3 May gave some satisfaction to all the main parties except the Social Democrats (SDP) and the Greens. The recently introduced community charge, with all the controversies it had generated, was the central issue, with the fate of those councils which had set notably high or low charges attracting special attention. Conservatives campaigned forcefully on the issues of efficiency and a sense of financial responsibility in local government. Seats were contested in 152 English metropolitan and non-metropolitan district councils, and in five district councils in Wales. All regional and island council seats were contested in Scotland.

The best measure of party performance was the comparison with the results in the comparable 1986 elections. On this basis, with 5,198 seats at stake, the results were as follows:

	Gains	Losses
Conservatives	165	356
Labour	436	136
Liberal Democrats	144	192
Social Democrats	5	30
Independents	26	57
Others	25	30

In England Labour secured some 40 per cent of the vote against 32 per cent for the Conservatives, a lead of only 8 per cent compared with margins in opinion polls nationally of two or three times that figure. But while the Conservatives were relieved to find that Labour had not done as well as was widely expected, they had still registered their worst-ever result in terms of votes and seats. The Liberal Democrats, with 18 per cent, easily outperformed their recent ratings in the polls, whereas the SDP was almost obliterated. The Green Party had to content itself with a rather disappointing 8 per cent.

The Conservatives made much of their increased majority in Wandsworth, which had set the lowest community charge in England. On the other hand Labour improved on their 1986 election results in some London councils such as Lambeth and Greenwich despite very high community charges. But in general the Conservatives were pleased by their showing in London, the swing to Labour being only of the order of 5 per cent, and they had clearly benefited from the reputation of extremist Labour councils such as Brent. The national average, however, was a more damaging 11 per cent, and resulted in Conservative loss of overall control of councils such as Bath, Kingston upon Thames and Torbay. Opposition to the poll tax was the most obvious cause. In Scotland the only change was in the Borders region where independents narrowly took control.

Labour easily retained the seat in the Bootle parliamentary by-election of 24 May with a swing from the Conservatives of 9.5 per cent. The SDP candidate polled only 155 votes; SDP membership had been halved within a year to around 6,200. On 3 June its national committee agreed by 17 votes to 5 to suspend the party constitution, arguing that the SDP no longer had sufficient support to remain a national party. Dr Owen and his two colleagues in the Commons, with some peers in the Lords, announced that they would continue to sit as independent Social Democrats.

If the SDP ended with a whimper, it could still be argued that in its nine-year existence, in company with the Liberals, it had helped to revise the agenda of British politics. It had been a factor in the notable changes in the Labour Party, just as it had made it easier for the Conservatives to retain power.

The House of Lords on 5 June defeated the second reading of the government's War Crimes Bill by 207 votes to 74. The bill would have given jurisdiction to British courts over a variety of offences committed by alleged World War II war criminals currently resident in Britain. Sir Geoffrey Howe declared on 22 June that the bill would be reintroduced in the next session of Parliament, but added that the Government would be prepared to examine suggested amendments.

In contrast, the Lords gave an unopposed second reading to the government's Broadcasting Bill on 5 June. A number of amendments during earlier stages of the bill's passage had met some of the fears of critics concerning the character and quality of programmes, notably that in exceptional circumstances the Independent Television Commission would give preference to an applicant if the quality of its service was very much higher than that of the highest bidder. Protection from takeovers in the first year of operation (from 1993) by the new Channel 3 and Channel 5 companies was added later. Meanwhile, from 29 April the choice of satellite channels was widened by the launch of British Satellite Broadcasting (see also Pt. XVI, Ch. 1, TELEVISION AND RADIO).

The party battle was increasingly influenced by the approach of a general election—in 1991 or 1992. Labour's revised policy document, *Looking to the Future*, was published on 24 May as the blueprint for the party's election manifesto. It emphasized Labour's determination to control public spending and inflation. The Labour leaders promised a variety of controls—plus entry to the ERM on 'prudent conditions' to give Britain a 'monetary sheet anchor'—to curb rising prices. Bitter exchanges followed with the Conservatives over the extent to which spending would rise under Labour, and the number of people who would find themselves paying higher taxes.

The policy review had been as much an exercise for the re-education of the Labour Party as a weapon in the struggle with the government. It acknowledged that wealth creation had by and large to precede wealth redistribution; that there was much that the market could do better than the state, though it believed that the latter could strengthen the economy with an investment bank to provide long-term capital, and could play a major role in training, retraining, research and development. Labour, too, had to win votes from the prosperous as well as its traditional centres of support among the under-privileged and sections of the professional classes.

Meanwhile, Labour quickly pounced upon Mrs Thatcher's midsummer assertion that 'we will never run out of steam' and her references to further privatization and increased home ownership. The Prime Minister, Labour claimed on 24 June, had 'let slip plans for an extremist fourth-term manifesto born out of the far-right, far-fetched and far-out dogma of fringe research institutes', not to mention her own desire to soldier on as Prime Minister.

The growing numbers of homeless, especially in London, became a significant political issue in the early summer. The government acknowledged that there was a problem, especially with the numerous young people who were sleeping rough in major cities. It was embarrassed by this obvious sign of poverty amid affluence, and the attention it was attracting abroad as well as at home. On 22 June the Housing Minister announced a package of measures, including an advice service for the homeless, backed by a sum of £15 million to try to eradicate the 'cardboard cities'. The government was also trying to accelerate the repair of some 100,000 currently vacant council houses to reduce the homeless total.

Britain's high divorce rates and numerous single-parent families attracted special attention. In July Mrs Thatcher identified the traditional family unit as providing the best start for children. Two Conservative think-tanks were looking for ways to strengthen the family unit. In contrast, Mr Kinnock argued on 20 September that the family was changing, not collapsing. The changes were creating opportunities as well as uncertainties. The government had a moral duty to protect the family, whatever its structure. He promised that a Labour government would introduce subsidized nursery care for all children aged three and four whose parents desired it. Mrs Thatcher preferred employers rather than the state to provide nurseries.

Single-parent families had risen by 140 per cent in the 1980s, and involved 2.4 million children. More than a quarter of those born in 1989 had unmarried mothers. Nearly 800,000 lone parents received income support. The proportion of such parents receiving maintenance payments from their children's fathers had fallen from 50 to 25 per cent, and the government was anxious to devise new ways to compel fathers to meet their obligations.

Criticism of educational standards was intensifying. A number of studies suggested a fall in basic reading and mathematical skills, and worrying comparisons continued to be made with the performance of pupils in the schools of Britain's leading industrial competitors. Many schools were weak in the provision of foreign language and science teaching. Peter Morgan, director-general of the Institute of Directors, argued on 28 July that it was necessary to raise the school-leaving age to 18, to make all schools independent, to increase vocational training among the young, and to end the situation in which much of the educated elite was alienated from business. He complained, too, that 45 per cent of school-leavers had virtually no qualification except 11 years in school.

Earlier in the month the Education Secretary had had to defend himself against charges from right-wing critics that he had 'gone soft' on the reforms of his predecessor. He replied that the commitments to parental influence and freedom of choice were untouched. At the same time he was winning praise in some quarters for his more pragmatic approach to the implementation of recent legislation. In April, for instance, he accepted the advice of the teaching profession that the amount of testing of the National Curriculum in primary schools was unmanageable and could defeat its own purpose. In October it was confirmed that only the 'three Rs' and basic scientific skills would be examined.

The government suffered various embarrassments during the summer. On 27 June it was informed by the EC Competition Commissioner that British Aerospace would have to repay almost £45 million of the 'sweeteners' or 'illegal' financial inducements which it had received from the government to push through the sale of Rover in 1989. Labour was also quickly on the offensive with the conviction on 28 August, after a 112-day trial, of four leading City figures for their part in an illegal share support scheme in the takeover struggle for the Distillers drinks group in 1986. The judge commented that the crime had occurred at a time when takeovers were regarded as battles. Guinness had waged total war against Distillers. The law, letter and spirit of the City's takeover code had all been broken. Labour spokesmen argued that the trial had revealed 'stark flaws' in the regulatory mechanism in the City, and that 'the do-nothing philosophy' of the government had to end. Defenders of the City argued that existing safeguards had been vindicated.

Meanwhile, at the end of June the Commons select committee on energy had produced a highly critical report of the conduct of the Central Electricity Generating Board and of two ministers (Cecil Parkinson, a former Energy Secretary, and Malcolm Rifkind, Secretary of State for Scotland) for their roles in the controversial history of the nuclear power industry. Their ministries had failed until very late in the day to recognize the true cost of running nuclear plant over its whole lifespan, while successive governments had misled parliament and the public into the belief that nuclear power offered the cheapest source of electricity. The committee was critical of the preparations for the abortive bid to privatize nuclear power in 1989—its own warnings to the government in 1988 being among those ignored—and demanded full publicity for all estimated costs before further nuclear construction was authorized.

The government lost the services of Nicholas Ridley as Secretary of State for Trade and Industry on 14 July. He was forced to resign after the publication by *The Spectator* of his outspoken views on Germany (see below p. 32). He was succeeded by Peter Lilley, a strong Thatcherite and described by some Tories as 'bone dry' on economic affairs.

Around this time Mr Kinnock was strengthening his position with a highly successful visit to the United States. He met President Bush in Washington on 17 July, and was well received on Capitol Hill. This and other evidence showed that the US administration, unlike that of President Reagan (especially before the 1987 election), now believed that it could deal with Her Majesty's opposition in the way that had been customary before the early 1980s.

On 25 July the Labour leaders acted against Militant influence in the Liverpool district party (for the second time in five years) when they removed the party whip from 14 councillors who were refusing to support a rents rise. The city faced a projected £3.6 million deficit on the revenue budget, one that was based on the optimistic assumption that most people would pay the poll tax. Mr Kinnock broadened the fight against the Militant Tendency on 1 August by calling on all local Labour parties to back up the efforts of the central leadership to ensure their expulsion.

The IRA stepped up its attacks in mainland Britain. Targets included the Carlton Club and the Stock Exchange. Two soldiers were killed in separate incidents, and on 30 July the Conservative MP, Ian Gow, was assassinated at his home in East Sussex.

On 25 July the Rt Rev Dr George Carey, Bishop of Bath and Wells, was named as the 103rd Archbishop of Canterbury to succeed Dr Runcie in 1991.

Chapter 3

FROM HOPES OF PEACE TO THE GULF CRISIS

THE British government followed the rapid changes in Eastern Europe and the two Germanies with some apprehension. Mrs Thatcher's uneasiness on the subject of German reunification was well known. On 26 March, however, she conceded that 'we shall have to get used to the fact that in future there will be a country in Europe which will be stronger than all the others'. At the same time the British clearly hoped for French reinvolvement in the military side of NATO.

Improvements in Britain's relations with the USSR were highlighted at the end of May by the first royal visit since the fall of the tsars. The Princess Royal toured widely in the Soviet Union. She was soon followed by Mrs Thatcher herself, who unequivocally endorsed President Gorbachev's 'remarkable' reform programme at a dinner in the Kremlin on 8 June. His reforms, she said, represented one of the greatest achievements of the twentieth century.

During the same visit, however, she opposed Soviet suggestions that NATO and the Warsaw Pact should act as parallel linked bodies, and while acknowledging Russian concerns over security declared that a united Germany—assuming it was the wish of the German people—should be part of NATO. The British also argued that economic aid to the USSR should be preceded by economic institutional reforms. Douglas Hurd, the Foreign Secretary, observed that it made sense for holes in pockets to be mended before money was poured into them.

In September Czechoslovakia was the first of the former Soviet satellites to be visited by the Prime Minister. She warned that extensive bureaucratic change and privatization would be necessary to attract large amounts of Western investment and to open the door to Czech entry to the EC. In Hungary she underlined her desire that East European states should ultimately become full members of the Community.

At the NATO summit of 5–6 July the Americans led the way in a revision of the strategy of flexible response so that nuclear arms would now be weapons of 'last resort' (see Pt. XII). Even so, Mrs Thatcher added a gloss of her own to the effect that the 'fundamental NATO strategy of reliance on nuclear weapons and possibility of using them has not changed. The nuclear deterrent, short and long, remains'.

Although the government was patently impressed by developments in Eastern Europe and the great changes in the policies of the USSR, it responded warily to expectations of a 'peace dividend' in the 1990s following official pronouncements that the Cold War was over. The Defence White Paper of 2 April underlined the difficulty of policymaking in a period of rapid change and confusion. The Defence Secretary, Tom King, did announce a cut of 3 per cent in real terms in the estimates for 1990–91. Everyone, he said, had 'great hopes for the future', but hopes were not certainties.

Nevertheless, a £600 million package of savings announced in July included a reduction of 33 aircraft in the Tornado programme. On 25 July Mr King made an interim Commons statement on projected defence savings over the next five years. A cut of nearly one-fifth in overall service personnel was assumed, the main reductions to be in the army. British forces in Germany would be roughly halved. He refused, however, to be drawn on the subject of the 'peace dividend' other than to say that he expected substantial savings towards the end of the five-year period. Even so, some cutbacks in defence employment were being announced before the end of the year.

Mr King also insisted (though he could hardly have expected such early vindication as that provided by the Iraqi invasion of Kuwait in August) that the aim must be the creation of highly efficient, well-equipped, flexible and very mobile forces which could operate both in the NATO theatre and elsewhere. A special strategic reserve based in Britain would have responsibility for 'out-of-area' operations. The Trident programme would continue as planned, and the government intended to purchase tactical air-to-surface nuclear missiles (TASM) to modernize the capability of the Royal Air Force. Mr King warned that there 'were opportunities but also risks in Europe; and elsewhere some worrying trends—not least the proliferation of sophisticated weapon systems'. Given such uncertainties, and the time needed to make major adjustments, a full defence review must of necessity take time.

Agreement was reached on 29 May at a conference in London to phase out the use of chlorofluorocarbons as part of a programme to reduce the depletion of the ozone layer. Four days earlier, at the opening of the centre for climatic prediction and research at the Meteorological Office, Mrs Thatcher pledged the stabilization of British emissions of carbon dioxide at current levels by the year 2005.

A successful meeting took place in July between Mrs Thatcher and Nelson Mandela (the leader of the African National Congress in South Africa) despite the latter's earlier call for British talks with the IRA and Mrs Thatcher's long-standing reservations concerning sanctions against South Africa. In an interview for *The Star* of Johannesburg on 18 July Mrs Thatcher described Mr Mandela as a courageous, sincere and reasonable man who deserved the confidence of white South Africans.

Quiet diplomacy was gradually narrowing the differences between Britain and Iran, a process that was helped by Iran's desire to be readmitted to the world community and, from August, by the Gulf crisis. Diplomatic relations were resumed on 28 October. Statements in Tehran in December, however, suggested that the death sentence pronounced against the author, Salman Rushdie (see AR 1989, pp. 35, 428–9, 493–4, 538), remained in force despite some earlier discreet hints that Iran would not interfere in the internal affairs of other countries.

The Gulf crisis similarly facilitated the restoration of diplomatic relations with Syria on 28 November after a four-year break. Syria stood firmly against Iraq, and rejected international terrorism. There were hopes, too, in Britain that the move might improve the prospects for the release of British hostages in Beirut.

Anglo-Iraqi relations had been in a troubled state before the invasion of Kuwait. The execution took place on 15 March of Farzad Bazoft, an Iranian-born journalist working for *The Observer*, after he had been found guilty of espionage. A British nurse, Daphne Parish, was later released after serving four months of a prison sentence for assisting him. Meanwhile, concern had been mounting at Iraq's efforts to increase the sophistication of its armed forces. On 28 March the discovery was announced of an alleged plot to supply Iraq with nuclear triggers. Equipment bound for Iraq from the United States was seized at Heathrow Airport. Then, on 10 April, customs officials at Teesport impounded a number of large pipes which were alleged to be parts of a 'super-gun' destined for Iraq. The Trade and Industry Secretary assured the Commons on 18 April that the government was satisfied that the pipes were parts of a gun.

The Iraqi invasion of Kuwait on 2 August coincided with a visit to the United States by Mrs Thatcher. She immediately condemned the attack. During the next few days of frantic diplomacy at the United Nations and around the world, Britain—more so than any other nation—showed itself ready to act swiftly and closely in cooperation with the United States. Thus on 8 August Britain was the first to follow the Americans in responding to Saudi Arabia's request for military aid against the large concentrations of Iraqi troops on its border with Kuwait. Two squadrons of fighters were quickly moved to the Middle East, backed by ground-to-air defence units and Nimrod surveillance aircraft. A number of British warships were speedily deployed in the Gulf.

The government's policy received strong backing from the public, although many had reservations concerning the circumstances in which force might actually be used. The only serious dissent came from most, though not all, of the representatives of British Muslim groups, from the extreme left, and from the Green Party and the Campaign for Nuclear Disarmament. Labour left-winger Tony Benn criticized British action in support of the United States and the 'feudal regime' in Saudi Arabia. Others agreed that action was necessary, but speculated uneasily over where it might all end.

Mr Kinnock on 22 August gave the government almost unqualified support. The Labour leader agreed that there could be no bargaining with Saddam Husain over the fate of British subjects in Iraq and Kuwait, one of whom had been shot while trying to escape to Saudi Arabia. Some 150 had been rounded up amid warnings that if Iraqis died in Western attacks so too would the detainees. Mrs Thatcher had declared the day before that no 'civilized country' would try to hide behind 'women and children and use them as human shields'. Douglas Hurd warned that any Iraqi who committed illegal acts should know that he would be 'held personally responsible'. In the first half of September evacuations of British women and children left an estimated 1,400 British subjects trapped in Kuwait.

A two-day Commons emergency debate on the Gulf crisis took place on 6-7 September. The Prime Minister declared that Iraq's actions were a return to the 'law of the jungle'. It was essential to restore the status quo in Kuwait. Both Mrs Thatcher and the Foreign Secretary insisted that Britain could not undertake to 'use no military force without the further authority of the Security Council'. This would run the risk of a veto, and would give encouragement to Saddam Husain. He must be exposed to the certainty of defeat by sanctions and, if necessary, force.

Mr Kinnock agreed that it was 'our unrelenting purpose' to expel Iraq from Kuwait, to restore the legitimate government and to release all hostages. Nevertheless, while promising Labour's broad support, he cautioned against independent military action without a precise UN mandate. Paddy Ashdown for the Liberal Democrats concurred. Former Prime Minister Edward Heath argued that if there were no direct Iraqi attack it was difficult to imagine circumstances in which force could be used without UN authority. He also contended that no permanent solution could be found to the problems of the Middle East without a settlement of the Palestinian question. The Commons voted by 437 to 35 in support of the government.

On 14 September it was announced that the 7th Armoured Brigade (the successor to the World War II Desert Rats) was to be sent to Saudi Arabia in the biggest movement of British troops and heavy armour since the Korean War. At least 8,000 troops were involved. The number of Tornado aircraft was increased to 50, and the anticipated annual costs of the British military deployment in the Gulf doubled to £2,000 million. Mr King again warned that, while Britain sought implementation of UN resolutions by peaceful means, 'other options' remained available.

Twelve days later the Foreign Secretary outlined to the UN General Assembly his ideas for an international effort modelled on the Helsinki security accords to try to resolve Middle Eastern disputes as a whole, including the Palestinian question. He tried to indicate sensitivity to criticisms from Arabs and others that the West was guilty of double standards in its dealings with Iraq and Israel. But the attack on Kuwait, he argued, was unique in its 'simple brutality. . . . Every principle of law was flouted.' British resolve was underlined by the decision in the middle of November to send a further 14,000 troops. Almost half of the British Army of the Rhine was expected to be in the Gulf by the new year, or some 30,000 service personnel in all.

Meanwhile, on 5 November the Gulf crisis had brought an interesting clarification of Labour's thinking on nuclear weapons. Foreign affairs spokesman Gerald Kaufman stated that his party's determination to eliminate these weapons was not bound by any specific timetable, nor did it entail a commitment to scrap the British armoury as long as such arms existed elsewhere in the world.

Chapter 4

SEASIDE POLITICS

THE Gulf crisis added to the uncertainties affecting the British economy. A survey of companies in September found confidence at its lowest level for eight years. The August figures showed a rise in unemployment (to nearly 1.7 million) for the fourth consecutive month. Inflation, at 10.6 per cent, was the highest since February 1982, and the highest of any major developed state even when the effects of the poll tax and mortgage rates had been excluded. The Gulf crisis was held responsible for only about one-third of the rise since July. Britain's current-account deficit for the second quarter reached almost £5,000 million—more than originally estimated—when only a small surplus on invisibles was recorded. Britain's trade deficit remained close to 4 per cent of national income, and thus dangerously dependent on foreign confidence in sterling.

Meanwhile, seaside venues for union and party conferences seemed unusually appropriate after the country had sweltered through the hottest August known since records began in 1659. On 3 August the highest previously recorded temperature in Britain (dating from August 1911) was broken when the mercury reached 98.8°F (37.1°C) in Cheltenham.

One major preparatory step towards the next election was taken by Labour when the TUC conference in Blackpool on 3 September defeated a motion (put forward by the National and Local Government Officers' Association) which demanded the repeal of all Conservative anti-union legislation and the restoration of secondary picketing. In a stormy debate Norman Willis, the TUC general secretary, argued that it was not sensible to ask that unions stand above the law. The movement now had the chance to work within 'a fair system of law. The law is part of our future.' Critics retorted that the general council had become obsessed with public relations and was wrong in its belief that a robust defence of union rights would jeopardize Labour's chances to win power. The motion was defeated by 4,404,000 votes to 3,529,000.

Mr Kinnock, in his conference speech on 4 September, argued that the best hope of the unions for the future lay with a Labour government, one which would be guided not by a policy of favours for one's friends but justice for all. As for those who spoke of betrayals of principles, he stated that his test of principles was how they were put into effect, not how they were paraded for effect. He won a standing ovation from all but about a quarter of the delegates.

The Liberal Democrats opened the party conference season on 15 September. Their best hope was a hung parliament after the next election, while they could draw some comfort from local election support which stood at around 18 per cent—more than double their standing in the opinion polls. But it was evident that they were in need of more than their new emblem (a bird of freedom) to regain public interest. The party had candidates in place in less than one-third of the nation's constituencies.

Mr Ashdown began the Blackpool conference by indicating that if the party were in a position of influence after the election he preferred a deal with Labour, though he did not rule out one with the Tories provided they were not led by Mrs Thatcher. The conference was much preoccupied with electoral and constitutional change, including proportional representation, home rule for Scotland and Wales, and the transformation of the House of Lords into a senate. The party was determined to reduce the powers of parliament and central government. Various measures were proposed to protect the rights of individuals and to bring about a renaissance of local government. The new federal structure would dovetail into 'the new Europe of regions'.

The Liberal Democrats also set out to project themselves as the party which most strongly supported the EC, and included among their objectives a common currency, greater political union and the closer integration of defence policies. Mr Ashdown presented his party as the supporter both of the enterprise culture and social justice. Taxes should be raised if necessary. Liberal Democrat thinking on the environment included the idea of a pollution-added tax (PAT) directed at polluters.

Observers rated the conference a success and detected signs of more public support for the party.

Labour proceeded to Blackpool with less confidence than the government's problems should have warranted. The party had easily held Knowsley South in an unexciting by-election on 27 September, but the low turnout provided no guide to public feeling, while there were hints of weakness in Labour's big lead in the opinion polls. Despite the policy review many people still found Labour's intentions obscure. There was less confidence in Labour's ability to manage the economy and in Mr Kinnock as a potential prime minister than the party would have liked. Fears, too, existed that the Gulf crisis might be helping to restore Mrs Thatcher's image (in March she had been the most unpopular prime minister since the start of opinion polls). The Gulf crisis was apparently causing more concern than prices, the NHS or the poll tax.

Although Mr Baker, the Conservative Party chairman, stated on 24 September that he did not expect his party's Bournemouth conference to be the last before the next general election, Labour delegates met with the question 'Will she, won't she?' very much in mind as they pondered the odds on an election in 1991. Mr Kinnock certainly took no chances, and subordinated party issues and concerns to the need to try to project Labour as ready for government with himself as a prime minister-in-waiting.

Consequently he refused to be bound by an overwhelming vote on 3 October in favour of a reduction in British defence spending to the average of other West European countries, a motion which was supported by six members of the shadow cabinet. He made it clear to the rebels that while such conduct might be tolerated in opposition, in government he would demand absolute loyalty. Contrary to some expectations the party proved overwhelmingly at one with him on the Gulf crisis. An emergency motion opposing British military action without the definite approval of the UN was easily defeated, helped by Mr Kaufman's assurance that UN authorization of the use of force was eminently desirable if at all possible.

John Smith took an austere line on economic policy, warning that wage rises above levels of productivity would cause unemployment. Nor could public expenditure be increased unless people took account of the national interest. The conference, however, called for larger pension increases than he had proposed. It also voted against leadership efforts to revise the automatic reselection process for MPs. But Gordon Brown secured a good reception for his plans for a national investment bank and other schemes to strengthen British industry. His speech coincided with the publication of figures on 1 October showing how far British research and development spending lagged behind that in West Germany and France.

Hard-liners were overwhelmingly defeated when they challenged party policy to retain much of the existing legislation on the conduct of union affairs and industrial relations. Moves to reduce the trade union block vote at future conferences from 90 to 70 per cent, with further cuts as party membership increased, went ahead without difficulty. The revision of party policy-making processes and structure was also approved, the aim being to increase the involvement of individual members very much after the models provided by other West European socialist parties. The conference also aimed to create a balance between the sexes, with the target of an equal number of male and female MPs by the end of the century. Labour underlined its commitments to a united Europe and to the protection of the environment.

The conference did, however, defy the aversion of most of the leaders to proportional representation by voting to look into the various ways by which MPs might be elected. Evidence of growing public interest in the issue helped to swing the vote. The conference also responded in part to the aspirations of black activists by agreeing to the setting up of a black socialist society. It readily approved the institution of a revamped version of the local rating system to replace the poll tax.

Mr Kinnock's conference speech on 2 October outlined Labour's long-term strategy to create a 'capable country' with a productive and competitive economy to meet the challenge of the single European market after 1992. Improvements to the education system were, he argued, the most fundamental requirement. At the end of the conference he warned union leaders that they had a choice between big pay packets and improved public services. They could not have it out of 'both pockets'. An interesting innovation was the singing of Blake's *Jerusalem* as well as *The Red Flag* to end the proceedings. The day, however, was overshadowed by the government's announcement that Britain was to join the ERM (see next chapter).

Chapter 5

EUROPEAN UNITY AND BRITISH DIVISIONS

EUROPE impinged increasingly on British politics and life in 1990. This provoked some vigorous demonstrations of national insularity and even of xenophobia. Nevertheless, work continued apace on the Channel Tunnel, direct physical contact being finally established with the continent on 30 October after three years of digging. But costs continued to rise, while the government—characterized by Labour as the 'Luddites of Europe'—confirmed on 14 June that it was not prepared to put public money into the £3,500 million high-speed Eurorail Joint Venture to link King's Cross to the tunnel. A fast service to Paris would still be possible, but many feared that Network South-East would not be able to meet the demands both of the new service and of existing commuters. The CBI director-general claimed that 'too little investment too late' threatened not only links to the tunnel but Britain's transport infrastructure as a whole.

In June the European Court of Justice ruled that national courts could freeze any law while its compatibility with EC legislation was being tested, thus reinforcing the principle that Community law took precedence over UK acts of parliament. Other controversial decisions led a Conservative MP, Roger Knapman, to complain in the Commons on 16 July: 'I wonder if we are not just sitting here every day, making laws until the European Court decides to overrule them.' He asked: 'What exactly is the state of our sovereignty?' Lord Denning, a former Master of the Rolls, argued on the same day that the European Court's judicial thinking was 'entirely contrary to the English system of justice'.

In an attempt to broaden the debate over a single European currency John Major on 20 June proposed the issue of banknotes denominated in the European currency unit (to be called 'hard ecus') to run alongside national European currencies. Some saw it as primarily a political move to sidestep divisions in the Conservative Party over EC policies. But it could also be regarded as a genuine attempt to offer an alternative to the Delors Plan and the challenges which it presented to national sovereignty. The initial response of most EC members, however, was not encouraging, the scepticism in West Germany being particularly apparent.

At the Dublin summit (25–26 June), although Mrs Thatcher again insisted that the Twelve were sovereign nations, which would yield up parts of their sovereignty only on the basis of joint decisions, she adopted a more cooperative approach than usual. Indeed, until the surprises at the Rome summit in October (see below), it seemed as if British pragmatism and calls for detailed preparation might be making some impact on the proceedings of the Community. Douglas Hurd, the Foreign Secretary, claimed that a 'lot of the political rhetoric had been flushed out'. In keeping with this improved atmosphere, Mrs Thatcher seconded the motion to extend the term of M. Delors as EC Commission President for another two years.

Meanwhile, Anglo-German relations were, not surprisingly, much in the public eye, given the 50th anniversary of the Battle of Britain and the current moves towards German reunification. Until the Gulf crisis the British watched unhappily as West German influence with the United States continued to displace their own. The government did not conceal its unease over the almost indecent haste with which the Germans were pushing towards unity, and was troubled by Bonn's eagerness to give early economic aid to the USSR. The West Germans for their part did not share British interest in the modernization of NATO's short-range nuclear weapons. Criticism by the German media of Britain's economic performance (one expert spoke of British 'casino capitalism' in contrast to his country's longer-term strategies) caused resentment. Late in June, in a radio interview Mrs Thatcher indicated that her admiration for democracy in Germany was tempered by her belief that NATO and the EC were needed to keep a close watch on the reunified giant given the history of that country between 1914 and 1945.

Anglo-German relations hit the headlines once again with the publication on 12 July of Nicholas Ridley's *Spectator* interview. As *The Times* put it, he was 'saying the unsayable'. Mr Ridley, long noted for his frank speaking, bluntly declared with respect to developments in Europe that 'this rushed takeover by the Germans on the worst possible basis, with the French behaving like poodles to the Germans, is absolutely intolerable'. Other unfriendly remarks about German intentions in Europe were recorded in the same interview.

The pound fell temporarily in the midst of the ensuing consternation. Mr Ridley, who was away on a mission to Hungary at the time, expressed his 'very great regret', and unreservedly withdrew his remarks. Initially it seemed that the Prime Minister did not see it as a resignation matter, while the culprit received some backing from those Conservatives noted for their reservations concerning current trends in the EC. But it was estimated that opposition elsewhere in the party was of the order of 7 to 3 against him. The Foreign Office, the Treasury and the governor of the Bank of England were also hostile. Even so, it was not until late on the afternoon of 14 July that Mr Ridley decided to tender his resignation. Mrs Thatcher was criticized for not acting more swiftly and for not doing more to protect Britain's relations with her major EC partners. It was also evident that she deeply regretted the departure of her oldest ideological ally. His going meant that the 'radical' Conservatives had lost one of their two most powerful voices in the cabinet.

There was further excitement when, the very next day, *The Independent on Sunday* revealed that at a seminar at Chequers on 24 March Mrs Thatcher, Mr Hurd and six experts on Germany had discussed not only the problems attendant upon reunification but also the extent to which the German character had changed since the two world wars. The meeting had patronizingly concluded that Britain should be 'nice to the Germans' and that 'there was no longer a sense of historic mission, no ambitions for physical conquest, no more militarism'. But it was the critical references to Germany's past history which inevitably attracted the most attention.

Sir Geoffrey Howe agreed that Germany's strength was causing genuine concern in Britain, but the appropriate response was closer involvement in Europe. He paid tribute to Germany's achievements and 'civilized values'. The premise of British policy was that 'Europe is the most important game in town'. Mr Hurd did his best in Brussels on 16 July to reassure the French and Germans, a necessary move just when Mr Gorbachev was finally conceding that a united Germany could remain in NATO. As for the Ridley and Chequers affairs, the West German Chancellor insisted on 17 July that these had cast no shadow over Anglo-German relations. The good humour displayed by some West Germans suggested that it might be the British who were suffering from angst.

It was widely assumed that the Ridley affair had strengthened the influence of Foreign Office and Treasury thinking on policy towards the EC. Mr Baker, for instance, stated on 18 July that, while stages two and three of the Delors Plan for European economic and monetary union would be deeply divisive and had worrying constitutional implications, the debate in Britain centred on when and how union would take place rather than whether it should occur. The government's concern was with practical matters, not utopian hopes, as demonstrated by Britain's good record in the implementation of EC measures.

The announcement on Friday, 5 October, that Britain would join the ERM in three days' time came as a complete surprise. Interest rates were also cut by one point to 14 per cent. Two leading building societies promptly reduced their mortgage rates. The Treasury chose to peg sterling at DM 2.95, but with the freedom to fluctuate in accordance with the wider ERM 6 per cent margins rather than the normal 2.25 per cent. This choice caused some disappointment among European ministers of finance.

Entry was seen as a momentous step even if the stock market soon lost its initial euphoria. Sir Leon Brittan (an EC commissioner) likened it to crossing the Rubicon in terms of Britain's relations with, and commitment to, Europe. It also marked the end of the floating exchange rate experiment pursued since 1972. As to the government's motivation, Mrs Thatcher denied both that she had abandoned the Madrid conditions for entry (notably that Britain's inflation rate should move closer to the European average), and that the decision was a political one taken especially with an eye to the imminent Conservative Party conference. What mattered was the course of inflation in the future, and here both she and Mr Major claimed that the signs for the next 12 months were encouraging.

But sources in the City asserted on 19 October that the Chancellor and the governor of the Bank of England had both warned Mrs Thatcher that, given her insistence on a cut in interest rates, only simultaneous entry to the ERM would prevent a sharp fall in the value of the pound. There were suggestions, too, that the move was intended to provide more room for manoeuvre on interest rates if fears of a recession were confirmed. In the longer run entry was deemed necessary to give Britain more influence over future EC steps to monetary union.

The Chancellor of the Exchequer denied that he was trying to create a pre-election 'boomlet', and stressed the continuing need to fight inflation. With other ministers he insisted that joining the ERM was not an easy option or a panacea for Britain's economic problems. Wage restraint was vital in the battle against inflation and to prevent a large rise in unemployment. Mr Major warned that he was prepared to raise interest rates again if necessary.

After so many demands across the whole political and business spectrum that the government should take this decision, many were critical over the timing or complained that the motivation was political rather than economic. Even *The Times*, a strong advocate of entry, described the decision as a triumph of politics over economics. Its timing could hardly have been 'less propitious for much of British industry'. Nevertheless speculation concerning a 1991 election revived on the assumption that ERM membership might have beneficial effects on the economy—at least in the short-term. The government might discover a window of opportunity for an early election. One newspaper writer remarked that the Prime Minister had performed a double somersault to grab 'a political lifebelt'.

Labour leaders agreed with the step in principle, but said that a long-term industrial strategy was still necessary if Britain was to take full advantage of entry. Mr Kinnock described it as 'the action of a cornered government' surrounded by the effects of 'its own economic imcompetence'. The reaction among businessmen and economists was mixed. A fall in interest rates coupled with exchange rate stability promised some advantages. But there were many warnings that the ERM would not ease Britain's problems by itself. Unemployment would rise unless there were realistic pay settlements. The CBI believed that the level of pay settlements would have to be halved. Meanwhile, the director-general of the Institute of Economic Affairs compared the action to 'putting a rickety narrow-gauge British train on a wider European track. There is a real fear of derailment.'

The chief regret of some ERM enthusiasts was that Britain had not entered five years earlier (a point made most forcibly by the former Chancellor, Nigel Lawson, in a Commons debate on 23 October) or even under Labour in 1979. The years of painful adjustment might then have been completed, so enabling the British economy to enter the 1990s in a much healthier condition. As it was, Britain had run out of soft economic options.

Chapter 6

HIGH DRAMA AND THE FALL OF A PRIME MINISTER

THE Conservative Party conference met in Bournemouth in the second week in October, but even a fiery and resilient performance by the

Prime Minister did little to boost the morale of those present. Mrs Thatcher promised further radical measures together with another cut in income tax as soon as circumstances permitted. But her dismissal of the new emblem of the Liberal Democrats as a 'dead parrot' seemed less funny a week later when on 18 October that party's candidate, David Bellotti, spectacularly wrested Eastbourne from the Conservatives in a by-election caused by the murder of Ian Gow. The Conservative majority of 16,923 in 1987 was turned into a deficit of 4,550. The Labour candidate almost forfeited her deposit.

There had clearly been a massive protest vote, but both main parties had reason to feel uncomfortable. Labour, for instance, had to make a breakthrough in parts of southern England to be sure of an outright majority in the next election. For the Tories Sir Geoffrey Howe accepted that the result had been a serious disappointment. It was not one which the party could 'take lightly or simply ignore'. Eastbourne was speedily followed by the government's announcement on 24 October of an increase of £1 in child benefit per week (though only for the first-born), the first rise since 1987. In all £5,000 million was added to state pension and welfare payments for young and old.

Meanwhile, inflation had reached 10.9 per cent, and the Chancellor was doing his best to persuade employers and unions that inflationary wage increases would not be offset by a devaluation of sterling. In particular, negotiators must cease to regard inflation as a guide to pay awards—the test should be productivity and competitiveness. But on 31 October the government rejected an offer from the TUC (though not one backed by all the unions) for joint discussion between unions, employers and ministers on the implications of entry to the ERM. The TUC had stated in a recent publication, *Europe 1992 and After*, that it was prepared to play its part in an all-round effort to try to limit job losses over the next five years as the single market made its impact. It was clearly worried by estimates that half a million jobs might be lost by 1995, and was beginning to take some interest in German wage bargaining methods.

All parties were also anxious to demonstrate their interest in the environment, but the publication of a government White Paper, *This Common Inheritance*, on 25 September was critically or coolly received. The bold programme which Chris Patten had outlined a year earlier had been eroded by the growing pressures on government finances. Ministers had no desire to add to the costs of industry and consumers at a time of high inflation, or to the difficulties of privatizing the electricity industry. Any thought of pollution taxes had been rejected. The great majority of the proposals and measures were not new, though plans to stabilize British carbon dioxide emissions from power stations and motor vehicles at 1990 levels by the year 2005 were elaborated. Labour's thinking was outlined in *An Earthly Choice* on 15 October, but environmentalists again found more generalities than substance.

Conservative divisions over Europe were evident at the party conference in mid-October. Mrs Thatcher's emphasis on national independence and her fears that a single currency would mean 'entering a federal Europe by the back-Delors' indicated little movement from her memorable Bruges speech in 1988. Nicholas Ridley dwelt on the golden age of the floating pound between 1980 and 1986, whereas Sir Geoffrey Howe stood out as a leading spokesman for the Europeanists. The Chancellor more guardedly remarked that entry to the ERM did not imply acceptance of the imposition of a single currency, but indicated that his proposals for a 'hard ecu' might evolve to reach the same destination.

The Commons debate on the ERM on 23 October produced a majority of 73 for the government. Eleven Tories voted with the opposition. But there now occurred a sudden and unexpected surge of activity in Europe. The timetable for economic and monetary change was abruptly changed. The British were taken by surprise and found themselves isolated at the Rome summit at the end of October when the other members agreed to begin the second stage of economic and monetary union in 1994 and to aim for a single European currency by the end of the decade. This was too much for Mrs Thatcher. She threatened to veto any attempt to impose a single currency. Nor would she ever agree to submit a bill to Parliament to abolish the pound. 'It would be totally against the feelings of the people. A common currency, yes; a single currency, no.'

The matter was raised in the Commons on 30 October, and again Mrs Thatcher spoke vehemently in defence of British sovereignty and of the role of parliament. At the same time she agreed that the British plan for a 'hard ecu' might eventually lead to a common currency. In the exchanges Labour's position was somewhat weakened by criticism of the EC from some of its left-wing backbenchers. But Labour leaders clarified their position on 28 November when they announced their acceptance in principle of a single European currency. They added, however, that monetary union would be dependent upon a considerable convergence by the economies of member states, a convergence which would include much more than rates of inflation. Nor should monetary union entail uniform economic policies throughout the EC.

The month of November, meanwhile, had been dominated by a crisis of the first order within the Conservative Party, and one which reached its momentous climax with the resignation of the Prime Minister. Margaret Thatcher's statements in Rome and in the Commons at the end of October, given their strident tone as well as their content, had proved too much for Sir Geoffrey Howe. On 1 November—the same day as parliament was prorogued—he tendered his resignation. He insisted that he was '*not* a Euro-idealist or federalist'. But he believed that Britain, after entry to the ERM, had 'a great opportunity at last to shape Europe's monetary arrangements in the years ahead'. Mr Hurd also revealed some disquiet with his comment shortly afterwards that, while the British had to continue to fight their corner in the EC, it could be done without 'frightening ourselves with ogres'.

Mrs Thatcher was now the sole survivor of the cabinet which she had formed in 1979. The rest had retired, resigned or been sacked. Sir Geoffrey's resignation came at a time when the government was far behind Labour in the opinion polls. The pound was already weakening despite entry into the ERM. In yet another cabinet reshuffle John MacGregor took over as Leader of the House, Kenneth Clarke moved to education while William Waldegrave become Health Secretary. Senior ministers did their best to play down the differences in the cabinet and the party, with Mr Hurd and Mr Major in particular working to build a solid consensus on the middle ground (with the 'hard ecu' as its central plank) between the 'Euro-fanatics' and 'Euro-sceptics' on the extremes of the party.

The Queen's Speech on 7 November outlined 15 new bills. The main emphasis was on transport improvements, the fight against crime, and the need to protect the family—not least by ensuring that absent parents contributed to the maintenance of their offspring. The programme was designed to leave ministers free to opt for an election in 1991 or 1992.

Meanwhile, the government was under the sharpest criticism it had encountered for a decade from the CBI. At a conference in Glasgow its director-general bluntly told the cabinet to get its act together— both at home and in Europe—before it was too late. There had been too many self-inflicted injuries during the last three years. Delegates complained of high interest rates and the uniform business rate. They wanted low inflation and a stable currency. They welcomed a promise from the Employment Secretary to raise industrial training standards, but hoped that the City would become less obsessed with quick returns and would give more attention to long-term investment.

The Chancellor's autumn statement on 8 November indicated that estimated public spending in 1991–92 would exceed £200,000 million for the first time, an increase in real terms of 2.2 percent. Large increases in the politically sensitive areas of health, social security and local authority support were mainly responsible. At the same time he was clearly anxious to reassure the financial markets. Mr Major anticipated a year of low growth, but forecast falls in inflation and the trade deficit. John Smith for Labour claimed that the economy was already in recession, and dwelt on the inaccuracy of past Treasury predictions—notably on inflation. Government figures later confirmed that the economy had indeed declined in the second and third quarters of the year—this by official definitions represented a recession. Unemployment topped the 1.7 million mark in October.

Two by-elections on 8 November underlined Tory unpopularity. In Bradford North, where they had run Labour a close second in the general election, the Conservatives were relegated to third place behind the Liberal Democrats. Labour easily retained Bootle for the second time in the year. The Lords committee on economic and monetary union rubbed salt in the government's wounds a day later by supporting the case for a single currency. Herr Pöhl, the president of the German Bundesbank, claimed that an independent European central bank and a single currency offered the only practical route to economic and monetary union.

But Mrs Thatcher, in her speech at the Lord Mayor's Guildhall banquet on 12 November, left no one in any doubt as to her determination to fight off any challenge to her position. She warned Saddam Husain that there would be war unless he evacuated Kuwait in the near future. On Europe, as in her Commons speech of 7 November, she emphasized the need for a practical and evolutionary approach. Yet even her comments in support of the 'hard ecu' failed to dispel the impression she had made with earlier remarks to the effect that few people were likely to use such a currency. This was used by her critics as further proof both of her Euro-scepticism and her tendency to put her own gloss on some aspects of government policy to the discomfort of ministers.

The stage was now set for Sir Geoffrey Howe to explain the reasons for his resignation to the Commons. This he did on 13 November with a vengeance, shedding in the process the label of a 'dead sheep' attached to him some years before by Denis Healey. His speech, though delivered in his customary measured tone, was variously described as 'devastating' or 'vicious'. It was a sweeping indictment of the Prime Minister, and included the charge—cricket analogies being much in favour at the time—that on the subject of the 'hard ecu' Mrs Thatcher had sent her opening batsmen to the crease only for them to find that she had broken their bats before the start of the game.

He further claimed that at the time of the Madrid summit in July 1989 both he and Nigel Lawson (the then Chancellor of the Exchequer) had threatened to resign to extort a pledge from Mrs Thatcher that Britain would enter the ERM when the conditions were right. Sir Geoffrey argued that her 'perceived attitude towards Europe' was creating increasingly serious risks for the future of this country—isolated in Europe once again and thus compelled to struggle to join the club after the rules had been agreed and power distributed to Britain's obvious disadvantage. He similarly disputed the charge that he had resigned because he differed from the Prime Minister simply on questions of style and not substance. Style and substance in any case were often two sides of the same coin. He made it clear that as far as he was concerned the Prime Minister had overstepped the mark too often.

His speech made a leadership contest certain. The party, if it was to have any chance of improving its political standing in the country, had to stop tearing itself apart over Europe and the merits and demerits of Mrs Thatcher. Michael Heseltine as recently as 6 November had denied any thoughts of a leadership challenge. But it was apparent that this time there would be no Sir Anthony Meyer (see AR 1989, p. 32) to act as a 'stalking horse'. Thus Mr Heseltine found his own reputation was at risk if he failed to act, especially when faced by the charge from his critics that he was 'all presentation and no substance'. The time had come to put to the test the four years which he had spent since his resignation in 1986 in cultivating support for a bid for the leadership.

Mr Heseltine duly announced his candidature on 14 November. The essence of his campaign was that after her successes in the 1980s Mrs Thatcher had become too unpopular in the country to lead a Tory recovery. A number of opinion polls could be cited to support his claim that the nation at large saw him as better suited to lead the Conservatives into the next election—and even to victory. His most striking promise was a fundamental review of the poll tax. He differed from Mrs Thatcher on Europe in that he (like Sir Geoffrey Howe) was prepared to proceed pragmatically and more diplomatically on the subject of a single currency. He denied that he was a federalist, but saw a single currency as an ultimate option to be examined, subject to final approval by the parliaments and peoples of Europe. Mrs Thatcher, however, feared that any departure from current policy would begin an unstoppable erosion of national sovereignty.

Speculation mounted that if Mrs Thatcher failed to defeat Mr Heseltine in the first round she might come under pressure from influential Tories to step down. She fought back with the claim that her rival's thinking was 'more akin to some of the Labour party policies: intervention, corporatism, everything that pulled us down'. Mr Heseltine wondered in reply that if this were the case how it was that he had been invited to address so many local Conservative party gatherings in recent years. Mrs Thatcher also raised the possibility of a national referendum on the issue of a single European currency, a suggestion which disturbed some of her leading cabinet colleagues. On the whole it was felt that Mr Heseltine was waging the more effective campaign.

The reactions of some of the serious newspapers were revealing. *The Times* finally declared itself for Mrs Thatcher. *The Financial Times* argued that the post-Thatcher era needed 'to arrive soon', though not in the person of Mr Heseltine. *The Sunday Times* of 18 November, however, pulled no punches despite its past support for the Prime Minister. It bluntly argued that she had become an 'electoral liability'. She was presiding over a new period of 'stagflation', was guilty of 'misplaced chauvinism' over Europe, and bore a special responsibility for the disastrous poll tax. Although the Prime Minister still enjoyed massive support among Conservative activists, in the country at large there was ample evidence of her unpopularity. During the year some MPs (especially those in marginal seats) had become increasingly apprehensive as time began to run out before the next general election, and as they reflected on the disenchantment of their constituents with the government.

In the first ballot Mrs Thatcher (with 204 votes to Mr Heseltine's 152, plus 16 abstentions) was only four tantalizing votes short of the number needed for outright victory. But to the dismay of many Tories the Prime Minister, who was attending the CSCE conference in Paris, immediately announced her intention to continue the fight. In their view the ballot's striking demonstration of the extent of the division in the party called for reflection and consultation before a decision of that order was taken.

Rumours abounded on her return to London on 21 November, but Mrs Thatcher at first resisted any suggestions that she should step down in favour of a candidate—such as Douglas Hurd or John Major—who might have a better chance of uniting the party. The whips and ministers, however, were increasingly persuaded that opinion among Conservative MPs was moving against her. The Prime Minister's staunchest supporters made desperate last-minute efforts to stop the rot. When, late that day, Mrs Thatcher sounded out cabinet ministers individually, she was advised by a clear majority (including even some of her own strongest supporters) that Mr Heseltine might well win the second round and thus capture the premiership. The argument gathered momentum that she should stand down to enable the party to carry out a wider test of opinion. Thatcherism as well as the Conservative Party required a new leader if it was to have any chance of winning the next election.

At a tense and emotional cabinet meeting at 9 am on 22 November Mrs Thatcher told her ministers: 'I have concluded that the unity of the party and the prospects of victory at a general election would be better if I stood down . . . .' In her appeal to ministers to elect one of their number she made plain her desire to thwart Mr Heseltine's ambitions. That afternoon she went to the Commons to face a Labour motion of no confidence in the government. She gave a bravura performance, although she was experiencing one of the most traumatic days of her life.

Tributes abounded, and it was fitting that a Soviet spokesman should have underlined her contribution to the ending of the Cold War, the most noteworthy and unambiguous of her successes as an international figure. Only two days before in Paris she had been a signatory to the Treaty on Conventional Armed Forces in Europe, a fitting climax to her role on the world stage. At home she enjoyed the distinction of having given her name to a political movement, and while she had not rewritten the agenda of British politics unaided since 1979, her personal contribution in terms of drive, energy and exploitation of opportunities was not in question. She was widely acclaimed as the greatest post-war prime minister. Indeed no one politician had made such an impact (controversial or otherwise) on domestic politics since Lloyd George.

There were bitter recriminations among some Conservatives. Those loyal to her to the end spoke of conspiracy and worse. How could so successful and great a prime minister be so shabbily treated? Yet many of those who struck her down did so with reluctance, alarmed by her growing unpopularity in the country and fearful of a Heseltine victory. Opinion polls in November, while serving as no guide to the next election (every new Tory or Labour leader since 1965 had boosted his or her party's poll ratings), gave striking evidence of the widespread desire for a change. In a matter of days Labour's huge lead in the polls had vanished.

Chapter 7

A NEW GOVERNMENT. A NEW ERA?

MRS Thatcher's withdrawal from the contest enabled Douglas Hurd and John Major to throw their caps into the ring. Each could offer himself as a less divisive candidate than Michael Heseltine, and each was strongly backed by cabinet colleagues, with Mr Major also having the support of the Prime Minister.

The polls soon suggested that Mr Major had as much electoral appeal as Mr Heseltine, and furthermore he was strongly favoured by constituency workers. If he was the candidate most closely identified with recent policies, especially those relating to the economy, he was also noted for his interest in social questions. He capitalized on this by putting forward as his main objective the creation of a 'classless society' based on opportunities for all. Indeed, his own career provided the most spectacular example of what he had in mind. His start in life had been less secure than that provided by Mrs Thatcher's grocer father. He had left grammar school at the age of 16, secured a post in the City six years later, and entered parliament in 1979. He had joined the cabinet as Chief Secretary to the Treasury in 1987, and had gone on to serve as Foreign Secretary and Chancellor of the Exchequer.

Mr Heseltine's undoubted appeal in the country at large was balanced by the hostility he had aroused in important sections of the Conservative Party. Mr Hurd's ministerial qualities were acknowledged, but he was still linked in many minds with the Heath government and the Conservative Party of the pre-Thatcherite years.

The ballot on 27 November gave Mr Major 185 votes, only two short of the necessary overall majority. Mr Heseltine (131 votes) and Mr Hurd (56 votes) immediately announced their withdrawal from the contest and gave their backing to Mr Major. He duly took up the reins of office the following day, and (at 47) became the youngest Prime Minister to step into No 10 since Lord Rosebery in 1894. Mr Kinnock called him a 'no majority, no change Prime Minister', and demanded a general election. But for most Conservatives all had turned out far better than had seemed possible after party unity and discipline had begun to unravel at the start of the month. Indeed, a real sense of demoralization and confusion had been spreading long before this.

The changes in the cabinet were highly revealing. Not only did Mr Heseltine return to the government, but his appointment as Secretary of the Environment signalled a readiness to consider radical changes, notably on the poll tax. Mr Major's campaign manager, Norman Lamont, was rewarded with the plum post of Chancellor of the Exchequer. Chris Patten became party chairman, while Mr Baker moved to the Home Office, the previous occupant, David Waddington, becoming Lord Privy Seal and Leader in the Lords. The new Secretary of State for Scotland, Ian Lang, also reflected the 'one nation' Conservative philosophy. Malcolm Rifkind took over Transport in place of Cecil Parkinson, who had resigned from the government.

The choice of ministers was Mr Major's first retort to charges that he was merely a 'mark 2 Mrs Thatcher', and he promptly called upon the party to forget old differences. In a speech on 4 December he promised flexible and common-sense policies. Adjustments would be made where things 'were not quite right'. Later in the month concessions were made on the poll tax to certain needy groups, an extra £42 million was to be paid to haemophiliacs infected with the AIDS virus by contaminated blood, while more urgent action was promised to help those sleeping rough in London.

In the Commons on 5 December Mr Heseltine announced a fundamental review of the structure as well as the financing of local government. Such a review could not produce results before the next general election, although shorter-term changes might be possible. He surprised everyone with his invitation to the opposition parties to join in an investigation of the problems, including the future of the poll tax and its possible alternatives.

The Liberal Democrats responded favourably, but the Labour benches were noisy, critical and wary. Bryan Gould said the offer could be treated seriously only if there were a clear commitment to abolish the poll tax. Nor would Labour participate in any 'cosmetic exercise'. The government should return to a fairer version of a property-based tax. In response to Labour questions Mr Heseltine declared that 'no options are ruled in and no options are ruled out'. Meanwhile, local councils reflected uneasily on the big shortfalls and other problems arising from the poll tax in 1990, and feared new delays and complications in 1991.

There was no softening of the government's policy towards Iraq following Saddam Husain's decision on 6 December to release all the hostages. Mr Hurd told the Commons on 11 December that the 'peace option' meant withdrawal from Kuwait. If the occupation continued Iraq would be forced out. Labour agreed that force might have to be used, but not so long as there was a hope that sanctions would succeed.

On the same day Labour took a highly critical view of the electricity privatization. It claimed that the under-pricing of shares meant a £3,000 million loss for the tax-payer. Ministers stressed that more people had applied for shares than in any other sell-off of public assets. Study of past sales, however, suggested that only about half of the original purchasers had treated them as long-term investments.

The new Chancellor, Mr Lamont, had gloomy economic news on 12 December. He held out no promise of early cuts in interest rates or of an early end to the recession. 'The discipline of the ERM is tough', he added. One of the most obvious signs of a recession came with the unemployment figures for November. These indicated the sharpest rise in nine years. Some comfort was supplied by the fall in inflation to 9.7 per cent.

A big test awaited Mr Major when he met EC leaders in Rome on 14–15 December. He was anxious both to end British isolation and to prevent the formation of a two-tier Community with Britain consigned to the lower level. On the one hand he insisted that he could not put his name to anything which would not be approved by the British parliament and that there was no change of heart on a single currency or a federal Europe. He also privately asked his European colleagues to remember that he had to fight an election in 1991 or 1992. Nevertheless, he gave public assurances that he saw himself as belonging to a generation with a 'very positive' view of the EC. The Community should 'go ahead as twelve. Europe has to march together.' Meanwhile, British delegates were arguing that any future EC changes should leave nation states free to take as many decisions as possible. There should be compelling reasons before the European Commission took control of any issue.

The outcome in Rome could be variously interpreted. No momentous decisions had been made, and therefore it had not been difficult to avoid controversy. M. Delors, having warned of a possible 'political crisis' in the future, appeared to have second thoughts and qualified his remarks. In general, British ministers were able to claim that the atmosphere had been much more relaxed than in recent meetings, and that their European colleagues appeared ready to listen to their plea that practical experience should be given due emphasis in the quest for greater political and economic unity. The 'hard ecu' was still on the agenda with Mr Major still asserting that 'it could evolve into a single currency'.

The EC agreed to lift the ban on new investment in South Africa, a decision for which the British had been pressing for some months. The current deadlock in vital GATT negotiations was also deplored, while Britain closed ranks with its partners on the question of emergency aid to the USSR.

Parliament rounded off the year with majorities against another bid to restore the death penalty. There was also a debate on 18 December on Britain's relations with Europe during which Labour suggested that the Prime Minister was trying to see how long he could sit on the fence with 'pleasantry in place of policy'. Mr Major responded to his critics—including some in his own party—by re-emphasizing the case he had argued in Rome. The future of the 'hard ecu' would be determined by the market. It would depend on the choices of governments, companies and individuals. Experience should precede final commitment to principles. He repeated his belief in closer cooperation between EC members, but not in the creation of a centralized super-state. He fully agreed, however, that difficult discussions lay ahead.

Mr Major took advantage of his first visit as Prime Minister to Washington (21–22 December) to warn that the Americans as well as the EC would have to show more flexibility if the current and very threatening stalemate in the GATT talks was to be eliminated. On the Gulf he stood shoulder to shoulder with President Bush. Both asserted that there was a growing probability of war. The government, as a precaution in case a conflict should last for several months, appealed for extra ammunition from those European allies which had not sent ground forces to the Gulf. It also began to call up reservists.

Chapter 8

SCOTLAND

THE Conservatives continued to face serious problems in Scotland. There was no lessening of the troubles provoked by the community charge, or poll tax. It was estimated that some half a million had failed to pay anything in its first year of operation (1989–90). In December Strathclyde announced that non–payment alone would require an increase of £42 per head (or more than one–sixth) in 1991–92. On 9 July Malcolm Rifkind, the Secretary of State, reported that 150,000 poll tax payers would qualify for transitional relief in 1991 in addition to the 350,000 already receiving help. The scheme would be extended for two years. For Labour, Donald Dewar dismissed the changes as 'a miserable sticking-plaster job'.

On 4 July Mr Rifkind gave up several key provisions in the bill to effect major legal reforms, in the face of opposition from some Tory backbenchers and Scottish lawyers. Agreement was reached with the Scottish Law Society that banks and building societies would not be allowed to carry out conveyancing.

In the regional and island council elections of 3 May the Conservatives secured only 19.5 per cent of the vote against 21.5 per cent by the Scottish Nationalists and 43.5 per cent by Labour. Tories had vainly attacked Labour's proposed tax on property to replace the poll tax. But no party's proposals on local government finance appeared to be winning much favour.

Tory factional in-fighting intensified over party policy, with the Thatcherites supporting the party chairman, Michael Forsyth, and the Scottish Tory Reform Group backing Mr Rifkind. This dissension probably contributed to the resignation on 1 August of Douglas Young, the party's director of campaigns and operations, after only eight months in the post. Mainstream Scottish Conservative opinion opposed Mr Forsyth's undiluted Thatcherism, and his resignation as party chairman followed on 7 September. His successor, Lord Sanderson, promptly reminded Scottish Conservatives that they were members of a broad church. It was important to work with the 'grain of the Scots'. In November John Major, the new UK Prime Minister, chose Ian Lang to succeed Mr Rifkind at the Scottish Office.

At the SNP conference in Perth in September Alex Salmond won the contest for party leader against Margaret Ewing by a surprisingly large margin despite the support given to the latter by the retiring leader, Gordon Wilson. Mr Salmond, more markedly to the left but also reputedly more pragmatic than Mrs Ewing, was anxious to win over disillusioned Labour activitists and supporters. The conference also resolved to continue its campaign of mass non-payment of the poll tax. On 4 October the former Labour MP and non-payer of the poll tax, Dick Douglas (Dunfermline West), joined the SNP.

The Scottish constitutional convention approved draft proposals for a Scottish parliament on 27 September (it was later endorsed at a special ceremony in Glasgow on 30 November, St Andrew's Day). Its writ would extend to all important aspects of domestic policy, including the right to vary income tax within pre-set limits. A form of proportional representation, a charter of rights, and an office to represent Scotland in Brussels were all envisaged. The parliament was perceived as a forerunner of similar assemblies elsewhere in England and Wales. The proposals were dismissed by Mr Rifkind as a 'pious fraud', while the SNP called for a referendum to test the will of the Scottish people.

Labour retained both seats in the by-elections on 29 November in the two Paisley constituencies. The SNP ran strongly in second place, but the Conservatives consoled themselves with a smaller than average fall in their vote, possibly helped by the retirement of Mrs Thatcher.

The steel industry suffered a severe blow when British Steel announced early in the year that it intended to close the Ravenscraig hot strip mill in Motherwell with the loss of 770 jobs in 1991. In November came the news that 1,200 jobs would go with the closure of the Clydesdale tube works in Bellshill, where unemployment was approaching 30 per cent. The demise of the rest of the Scottish steel industry was widely feared. The Scottish Scenic Trust warned at the end of the year that the plight of hill farmers could result in a repeat of the 'clearances' in the Highlands and Islands. Fishermen were again hard hit by EC fish quotas.

But sectors of the economy defied the onset of the recession longer than most parts of the United Kingdom, so that it was not until November that unemployment began to rise. The increase in home ownership continued, with 200,000 public sector houses (or 18 per cent of the total) having been sold to sitting tenants. The North Sea oil industry expanded despite a period of industrial unrest. New American investment promised to strengthen the electronics industry. Ferranti Defence Systems was bought by GEC in January, but its future remained heavily dependent upon the radar contract for the new European fighter aircraft project. Prestwick lost its monopoly of trans-Atlantic flights.

Parts of northern Scotland were severely affected by storms and flooding early in the year. A number of fishing boat incidents apparently involving submarines reached a tragic climax in the Firth of Clyde in November when the *Antares* sank with the loss of four lives. Upon this occasion, and in response to fierce local protests, the Royal Navy on 5 December agreed to keep fishermen informed of future submarine movements.

Chapter 9

WALES

THE resignation, for personal reasons, of Peter Walker as Secretary of State for Wales was the major political event of the early months of the year. His interventionist style had brought him considerable respect in many circles in Wales, though some considered that his reputation was based more on presentation than on substance.

His successor, the MP for Wirral West, David Hunt, was Welsh-born but like Mr Walker had few genuine links with Wales. It was expected that he would take a more Thatcherite line than his predecessor but in the event he pursued similar economic policies to Mr Walker, announcing further developments in the Valleys Initiative programme in December and pressing ahead with plans to attract further foreign investment. However, small businesses were being hit by the recession, failures being 11 per cent up on 1989. Also on the debit side was the closure of the Brymbo Steelworks, near Wrexham, and the rationalization of the Laura Ashley Company. In agriculture it was feared that the 30 per cent cuts in subsidies announced in the autumn would lead to the loss of 24,000 jobs in the industry by the end of the century.

Mr Hunt was the only cabinet minister openly to support Michael Heseltine in the second ballot for the leadership of the Conservative Party. Although he retained his post on John Major's election, his under-secretary, Ian Grist, was dismissed and replaced by the right-wing MP for Pembroke, Nicholas Bennett. This caused much consternation among Welsh Conservative MPs who saw Mr Bennett's elevation as simply a reward for campaigning vigorously on the winning side in the leadership contest. A further complication arose when Mr Grist refused to join the sparse ranks of Welsh Conservative MPs on the Welsh select committee, thereby ensuring that there could not be a Conservative majority on it. By the end of the year the committee's future remained unresolved.

When Mr Hunt was appointed Secretary of State, the Prime Minister once again passed over the loyal minister of state, Wyn Roberts, but he was to be consoled by a knighthood in the Queen's birthday honours list. Sir Wyn was the only government minister to survive the full 11 years of the Thatcher administration in the same post.

Another North Wales Conservative knight, Sir Anthony Meyer, suffered the consequences of his challenge to Mrs Thatcher in November 1989. He was deselected by the Clwyd North West Conservatives, and although he threatened to stand as an independent he changed his mind following revelations of a longstanding relationship with a black jazz songstress.

It was in Sir Anthony's constituency that the major disaster of the year took place. On the night of 26 February a record tidal surge sent a wall of water through the sea defences at Towyn near Abergele, devastating thousands of homes. Although a £10 million project was begun to repair the sea wall there were complaints that the government was unwilling to provide adequate recompense to the town's inhabitants, many of whom had insufficient or no insurance.

A flood of another kind was identified in data supplied by the Office of Population Censuses and Surveys in August. It was reported that 40,000 people had moved into the Welsh heartland of Dyfed, Gwynedd and Powys in the last decade. Ceredigion had the biggest influx of migrants in the United Kingdom, with 9,000 people moving in during the last nine years, while there was a consistent drift of population away from the old industrial areas of South Wales.

One of the consequences of the immigration of English people into rural Wales was to be seen in the teaching of Welsh in schools. When a small group of English parents complained about Dyfed county council's language categorization policy for primary schools, counter-accusations and much bitterness ensued. The parents were supported by the Labour MP for Carmarthen, Dr Alan Williams, whose intemperate criticism of the council led to recriminations among Labour councillors who strongly backed Dyfed's policy. Dr Williams survived an attempt at deselection but the vast majority of parents, both Welsh and non-Welsh, gave overwhelming support for the council's policy in school parent/governor meetings held in the autumn.

The sensational arrest in February of three well-known Welsh actors on suspicion of being involved with the 'Meibion Glyndwr' holiday home arson campaign quickly turned to farce. The actors were soon released without charge and the credibility of the police was damaged, particularly as no adequate explanation was forthcoming on who planted bomb-making equipment near the home of one of the actors. Meanwhile, the true arsonists remained at large, 11 years after the campaign had begun.

Chapter 10

NORTHERN IRELAND

THE saga of the year was Secretary of State Peter Brooke's attempt to develop inter-party dialogue to give the politicians and politics the initiative rather than the paramilitaries and violence. Despite an increase in the level of violence, the economy continued to improve and new developments marked changing shopping and commercial patterns. Older controversies on extradition, collusion, fair employment and integrated education continued. The year also witnessed celebrations on the tercentenary of the Battle of the Boyne and the release of Brian Keenan from captivity in Lebanon. The death was mourned of Cardinal Ó Fiaich (see Pt.XIII & OBITUARY).

Mr Brooke launched a bid for inter-party talks and devolution on 9 January. In a carefully crafted speech in Bangor he professed to detect common ground favourable to devolution. The speech stirred political debate and by 5 February Mr Brooke informed the Unionist leaders, James Molyneaux (UUP) and Rev. Ian Paisley (DUP), that their pre-conditions did not represent 'any insuperable obstacle' to talks. The intervention of the Irish Supreme Court decision in the McGimpsey case, challenging the legality of the Anglo-Irish Agreement, and the renewed extradition crisis in March and April, did not impede progress. Mr Brooke formally stated his willingness to consider an alternative to the Agreement early in May and by 15 June said he was 'astonished at the progress' and envisaged talks after the holidays. However, despite intensive negotiations with Dublin, Mr Brooke told the House of Commons on 5 July that he was unable to report agreement on a schedule for talks; the problem was timing the formal entry of the Irish government into the talks. A conference on 17 July was unable to find a formula and as parliament adjourned on 26 July he undertook to renew his efforts in September amid fears that the process might 'unravel' over the summer.

The Unionist leaders, convinced that Dublin and the Social Democratic and Labour Party (SDLP) were responsible for the failure in July, took a firmer line and insisted that the Republic's constitutional claim be addressed. Mr Brooke's speech at Ballymena on 7 September reflected the changed conditions. In what was read as an ultimatum he warned that he might have to 'set the pace and show the way'; by 26 September he was willing to produce proposals if requested by the parties. However, while a debate opened up in the Republic on articles 2 and 3 of its constitution this was not welcomed by the SDLP, which also seemed reluctant to renew the debate in the terms of July. At the British Labour Party conference in October the SDLP deputy leader, Seamus Mallon, called for the July document to be torn up, a view later supported by the party leader, John Hume. In November a speech by Mr Brooke in his constituency attracted SDLP interest and seemed to re-open the public dialogue of February with Sinn Féin. The Irish presidential election and the Conservative Party leadership election then distracted attention, and by the Christmas recess the gap officially remained 'narrow' but 'substantial'. On 28 December Mr Brooke admitted, in a *Belfast Telegraph* article, that the year had not produced an answer but that there had been 'new thinking about difficult issues, re-analysis of positions and goals, and re-evaluation of the validity of traditional aims in the context of the 1990s'.

At a less esoteric level there were a number of political developments. While the SDLP celebrated its 20th birthday in August, new parties were organizing. The Green Party was launched on 12 February and, like the Conservatives, established a local organization. Both new parties confronted the traditional parties in the Upper Bann by-election in May, when they polled only 1.6 and 2.9 per cent of the vote respectively, with David Trimble (UUP) elected to succeed the late Harold McCusker. The Labour Party annual conference refused to organize in the province and the leader, Neil Kinnock, on a visit in December, confirmed party policy. The Prime Minister, Margaret Thatcher, paid a brief visit on 16 November, a week before her resignation as party leader. Mr Brooke remained the Secretary of State in the government of John Major. The new British-Irish inter-parliamentary body met in February and December in London and Dublin respectively. Unionists refused to take the two seats offered in protest at the Anglo-Irish Agreement. Unionist district councils ended their ban on meetings with ministers.

One opinion poll for the *Belfast Telegraph* and BBC's *Newsnight* at the end of January and the findings of the British Social Attitudes Survey in November questioned the usual assumption that Catholics sought only a united Ireland. British context solutions were as popular as Irish solutions.

During the year 76 people were killed by political violence, 14 more than in 1989; six others were killed elsewhere, three in England and three in Europe. The year seemed even bloodier, as half the deaths occurred in the last four months and 19 died in October alone. However, earlier in the year several incidents resulted in multiple deaths. Of the 76 who were killed 27 were members of the security forces: they comprised seven RUC men and five RUC reservists, seven regular soldiers and eight UDR members. Forty-nine were civilians and the main feature was an increase in the number of tit-for-tat murders. At the end of November a further 500 troops were sent, bringing the total to 11,000, to cope with an anticipated Christmas campaign. Despite four deaths in December, increased alertness may have contributed to a relatively quiet month. The IRA proclaimed a three-day ceasefire over Christmas, their first since 1974.

The general improvement in the economy continued for most of the year. Two new hotels opened in Belfast, two others were planned and another opened a few miles from the international airport. The range of consumer choice in Belfast increased with the opening of the £75 million Castle Court centre and the promise of a new Cooperative shopping complex. Derry attracted the largest US investment to Northern Ireland for ten years when Fruit of the Loom announced £60 million plans for textile and clothing plants. The Derry-Boston venture also promised new commercial developments. In December Eastman/Texmaco investment promised 300 textile jobs on the old Enkalon site in Antrim. In Belfast new office accommodation was commenced by a local property company and the Laganside development continued. The Springvale project also held the promise of much-needed jobs in West Belfast.

There were warnings about economic difficulties ahead. In April the NI Economic Council said that growth in the economy would be less than 2 per cent and that unemployment would increase; the independent NI Economic Research Centre predicted levels of 14 per cent until 1995. The month-by-month reduction in unemployment continued until July; by November it was 96,100 or 13.8 per cent, the first increase in the seasonally adjusted figures since January 1989. Increased public expenditure for 1991–92 was expected to produce 1,800 new jobs. However, the international failure of the GATT talks threatened two sectors of the local economy. Agriculture faced cuts in subsidies of at least 30 per cent despite low farm incomes; the textile industry was experiencing job losses from the existing quotas for imports. One additional cause of uncertainty was the EC decision to cut subsidies to shipbuilding from 20 to 13 per cent.

The expansion and success of air services from Belfast was a factor in the closure of a longstanding ferry service. The Belfast-Liverpool ferry, first established in 1819, ceased to be operated by Belfast Car Ferries when the *St Colum I* sailed from Belfast for the last time on 14 October.

The publication in November of the Family Expenditure Survey figures for 1988–89 quantified the gap in living standards between Northern Ireland and Great Britain. The average weekly disposable income was 22.5 per cent less at £187.83 compared with £242.50; in addition, state benefits accounted for 20.4 per cent of the total. The figures showed NI residents spending more on fuel and power, food, tobacco, clothing and footwear and motoring but less for housing, alcohol, leisure goods and services.

A number of longstanding controversies continued during the year. The issue of extradition from the Republic of Ireland re-emerged in March with the refusal of the Irish Supreme Court to extradite D. Finucane and J.P. Clarke; the refusal was repeated for the former MP, Owen J. Carron, on the basis of the same pre–1987 legislation. After five months' consideration the Anglo-Irish Conference failed to produce an agreed solution.

In May the conclusions of the Stevens inquiry into alleged collusion between the security forces and loyalist paramilitaries were published. Its 83 recommendations aimed to control access to security information and to impose stiff penalties for abuse. It was pessimistic about eradication given the unrepresentative confessional balance in the security personnel. During the inquiry 58 arrests or cases were sent to the DPP at the request of the Stevens team. In addition, the prospect of a new 'supergrass' revealed how extensively loyalist paramilitaries had been penetrated by inquiries.

The new Fair Employment Act became law on 1 January but a section was challenged successfully before the Fair Employment Tribunal in October. The challenge of discrimination by the Roman Catholic bishops against the Education Reform Order's enabling of integrated education was rejected by the High Court in October.

The year witnessed a number of celebrations. The tercentenary of the Battle of the Boyne was celebrated by the Orange Order. However, plans for major demonstrations on the site had to be aborted owing to lack of cooperation by authorities in the Republic. On 24 August Brian Keenan was released in Damascus after 1,574 days held in captivity by pro-Iranian Shia Muslims. Earlier in August the opening of a new church was celebrated at Darkley, south Armagh. In November 1983 the Mountain Lodge Pentecostal mission hall had seen three church elders shot dead and seven worshippers injured in an attack by the Irish National Liberation Army.

II THE AMERICAS AND THE CARIBBEAN

Chapter 1

UNITED STATES OF AMERICA

CAPITAL: Washington DC AREA: 9,372,614 sq km POPULATION: 248,231,030 ('89)
OFFICIAL LANGUAGE: English POLITICAL SYSTEM: democratic federal republic
HEAD OF STATE AND GOVERNMENT: President George Bush (since Jan '89)
RULING PARTY: Republicans hold presidency; Democrats control Congress
PRINCIPAL CABINET MEMBERS: J. Danforth Quayle (Vice-President), James Baker (Secretary of State), Nicholas Brady (treasury), Richard Cheney (defence), Manuel Lujan (interior), Richard Thornburgh (Attorney General) (*for full list see* DOCUMENTS)
INTERNATIONAL ALIGNMENT: NATO, OECD, OAS, ANZUS
CURRENCY: dollar (end–'90 £1=US$1.93) GNP PER CAPITA: US$19,840 ('88)
MAIN EXPORT EARNERS: machinery and transport equipment, agricultural products, chemicals, miscellaneous manufactures, financial services, tourism

THE American people began and ended 1990 preoccupied with foreign affairs. The invasion of Panama, 'Operation Just Cause', which had begun on 20 December 1989 (see AR 1989, pp. 58–9, 79), achieved its main objective when General Manuel Noriega surrendered himself to the US forces on 3 January. The first American troop withdrawals from Panama began that day, and by the end of the year those remaining numbered 10,000. In August American armed forces again faced action, having been quickly sent to Saudi Arabia in order to deter any possible attack by Iraqi forces following their invasion of Kuwait. Although the US troop presence soon vastly exceeded the numbers involved in Panama, and was now part of a multinational force, it was not sufficient to persuade the Iraqi government to withdraw. As the year ended open conflict seemed a real possibility.

These foreign affairs had a considerable impact on President George Bush's popularity. In January he achieved some of the highest-ever ratings in public opinion polls following the invasion of Panama, and the President appeared to have thrown off the indecisive image which had dogged him in 1989. By the end of the year, however, Mr Bush's popularity had fallen to an all-time low as the public voiced doubts about American policy in the Middle East. The President's reputation also suffered as a consequence of his apparent indecisiveness on domestic matters, particularly his so-called 'flip-flops' on the budget and taxation in the face of partisan conflict in Congress. In October the label 'wimp' was being used again, and as the US government seemed unable to act in the face of the Iraqi seizure of foreign nationals as hostages, the President suffered comparison with former President Jimmy Carter. Even more, as Mr Bush continued to build up American military commitments in the Gulf and war seemed imminent, public and congressional opinion appeared to favour a more conciliatory stance.

The President's position was not improved by the mid-term November congressional elections. While the anticipated Democratic landslide did not materialize, the Republicans barely held their own, and the Democratic party appeared to be recovering ground lost during the Reagan years. In the course of the budget dispute the Democrats began to articulate a distinctive policy which appeared to have some appeal to the voters.

Such matters overshadowed almost all other events in the United States in 1990, and there were none of the natural disasters of the preceding year to distract attention from international and political affairs. While California and other western states suffered massive damage due to raging forest fires, the worst disaster, a fire in New York city, was man-made. A total of 87 people, many of Latin American origin, died in a fire which swept through the Happy Land social club in the Bronx, New York city, on 25 March. The fire, apparently started by a 36-year-old Cuban after he had been ejected from the club, was the second worst in the city's history. Mayor David Dinkins promised to tackle the problem of hundreds of similar unlicensed clubs which were violating safety regulations. Equally alarming to most New Yorkers, however, was the mounting level of violence within the city and a feeling that the administration could do little to prevent it. The number of homicides in New York City reached a record level of some 2,200 in 1990.

A more general sense of foreboding came as a consequence of a slow-down in economic growth in the last quarter of the year, and an increase in unemployment. By November unemployment had reached 5.9 per cent, and it was widely acknowledged that the economy was in a down-turn. Thus for many Americans the year ended in a sense of gloom as the country faced the prospect of war abroad and recession at home.

HOME AFFAIRS. Spelling out his agenda for the coming year in the State of the Union address to Congress on 31 January, President Bush began optimistically with a focus on foreign affairs. He looked back to the changes that had occurred in what he called 'the revolution of 1989', and spoke of the start 'of a new era in the world's affairs'. Pointing to the collapse of communism in Eastern Europe, he stated that it was 'time to acclaim a new consensus at home and abroad—a common vision of the peaceful world we want to see'. In furtherance of this aim he proposed that the USA and Soviet Union should 'move forward on a conventional arms control agreement', and that each should reduce their forces in Europe to 195,000. This figure, he said, was 'designed to protect American and European interests and sustain NATO's defence strategy'. Nonetheless, the President argued that America must still continue to modernize its military capabilities and sustain the Strategic Defence Initiative (SDI).

Claiming that America stood at the centre of a 'widening circle of freedom', Mr Bush stated that the challenge was 'to take this democratic system of ours, a system second to none, and make it better'. This 'better America' would be one with full employment, adequate child-care provision, environmental controls, fair treatment for the disabled and provision for the homeless. It would also be a drug-free society. Planning for the future, said the President, included increased savings to expand the 'pool of capital', reduced capital gains taxes to 'encourage risk takers', and improvements in education. The President particularly highlighted education as an investment for the future, and said that by the year 2000 the United States should increase the high school graduation rate to 'no less than 90 per cent' and 'be the first in the world in math and science achievement'. School pupils were probably not pleased to hear this was to be achieved by increasing assessment in critical subjects at various stages in their school careers.

Looking to the future, the President also spoke of 'the safekeeping of America's precious environmental inheritance', and announced the elevation of the Environmental Protection Agency to cabinet rank. A programme called 'America the Beautiful' was to be established to expand national parks and wildlife preserves. Over $2,000 million was budgeted for these activities, including $1,000 million for research in global environmental changes.

The President reiterated the promises made in his election campaign and inaugural address to reduce the budget deficit without introducing any new taxes. In answer to the suggestion that social security taxes be cut, made in December 1989 by Senator Daniel Moynihan of New York, Mr Bush also promised not to 'mess around with social security'. However, he stated that he was 'committed to bring the staggering costs of health care under control', and announced a review of health care costs and provisions.

In the course of his speech the President quoted the example of Private James Markwell, a 20-year-old army medic who had died in the invasion of Panama in 1989. In a letter to his mother, Private Markman had written that he was fighting, and prepared to die, for freedom. President Bush proclaimed that 'freedom is at the very heart of the idea that is America', and ended his message by calling upon all Americans to affirm their allegiance to that idea.

During the State of the Union address President Bush again called for cooperation from Congress. An indication of the likelihood of success in that quarter had already come when some of the President's proposals were given further detail in his budget request for fiscal year 1991 (beginning 1 October 1990) to the joint houses of Congress on 29

January. The request for $1,233,000 million was based upon adherence to the President's promise not to raise taxes, and was designed to ensure that the budget deficit would not exceed $64,000 million. This was to be done by cuts in various programmes and by reforms within the tax system. The budget did, however, mark some move away from 'Reaganomics' in its shift in spending priorities. The defence budget was cut by 2.6 per cent and involved the closure of 35 domestic and 13 overseas bases, and an overall reduction in forces personnel of 38,000. Research spending on the SDI was increased by 22 per cent and provision was also made for the purchase of another five B–2 Stealth bombers. The budget proposed increasing the funding of the National Aeronautics and Space Administration (NASA) by $2,800 million, a rise of 24 per cent. Conscious of some of criticism of high-spending space exploration, the President said that some of the funds would finance a massive study of planet earth, but manned flights to the moon and to Mars were also included.

Domestic budget proposals included increases of only 2 per cent for education, 6 per cent for health and human services, and 29 per cent for housing and urban development. The war against drugs was enhanced by an increase of $1,100 million, bringing its budget to a total of $10,600 million overall. The bulk of the increase was to go to law enforcement rather than treatment or education.

Critics were quick to point out that the proposed budget relied on optimistic forecasts of economic growth, and left the hard decisions with regard to apportioning cuts in spending to Congress. The bulk of cuts were to fall on farm subsidies and on Medicare spending, where the administration hoped to save $8,500 million by reducing payments to hospitals and doctors.

Opposition to the budget led to months of protracted argument and negotiation between the Bush administration and the Democratic-controlled Congress. Following a breakfast meeting with congressional leaders at the White House on 3 July, the President issued a statement which indicated that he was prepared to accept the need for 'increased tax revenues'. It was clear from this that the President had moderated his famous commitment, made in his 1988 election campaign, when he said: 'Read my lips: no new taxes.' After much further discussion, a compromise agreement involving an increase in excise taxes and reduction in benefits, particularly in the Medicare programmes, appeared to have been reached on 30 September, the day before the new budget was due to come into effect. President Bush appealed for support for the agreement in a national television broadcast on 2 October, in which he described the deficit as 'a cancer gnawing away at our nation's health'. However, in the House of Representatives vote on 5 October the measure was defeated by 254 to 179. In the division 105 Republicans opposed to any increase in taxes, and led by the House minority whip, Newt Gingrich (Georgia), joined with 149 Democrats opposed to cuts in benefits to defeat the measure.

When the House of Representatives approved a stop-gap spending bill to enable the government to continue to function in the absence of a budget agreement on 6 October, President Bush vetoed the measure. He said he refused 'to be part of business as usual when we have one deficit after another piling up'. In a subsequent vote to overturn the veto, the House fell six votes short of the necessary two-thirds majority, with 260 votes for and 138 votes against. As a result, non-essential government services were immediately ordered closed, and a number of museums, parks and public places, including the Statue of Liberty and the White House, were closed to the public on 7 and 8 October, the Columbus holiday weekend.

New budget proposals were discussed in the House and Senate on 8 October, and another measure to provide temporary financing for government until 20 October was passed in the House by 305 votes to 105. The President approved the measure, but made it clear that he would not sign further legislation to keep government going unless a satisfactory agreement was reached on the budget. However, Mr Bush created some confusion on 9 October when he indicated in the morning that he might accept increases in income tax in return for cuts in capital gains tax, but in a later meeting with Republican senators declared that 'both were off the table'. Asked to clarify his position while in Florida, Mr Bush replied: 'Let Congress clear it up'; in a flippant comment made while jogging, he said: 'Read these hips.' The President's public changes of mind led to accusations of indecision and weakness, and public opinion polls showed a fall in his popularity from a high of 75 to 80 per cent at the start of the year to 56 per cent in October.

Complex negotiations continued between the White House, Senate and House of Representatives, following which the administration indicated support for a bi-partisan Senate proposal which included a limit on tax-deductible items on incomes over $100,000, increased Medicare charges and higher excise taxes. However, Democrats in the House, led by chairman of the ways and means committee Dan Rostenkowski (Illinois), drew up a plan to raise taxes on the most wealthy from 28 to 33 per cent and to impose a 10 per cent surtax on incomes of more than $1 million. The divided Republicans were unable to produce an alternative measure.

On 18 October the House approved another stop-gap funding measure to enable the government to keep operating for one more week. President Bush signed the measure the following day, but while he indicated a willingness to approve an increase in taxation of the wealthy and to defer a cut in capital gains tax, he said he would not accept the House budget proposals. Lengthy discussions took place to reconcile the House and Senate proposals, and to meet conflicting political demands.

At several points it appeared that the discussions had broken down. However, as Democrats in the House appeared willing to compromise when they abandoned their demands for inclusion of surtax in favour of phasing out personal tax exemptions for those with incomes in excess of $100,000, Mr Bush signed another emergency funding bill on 25 October, the fourth in a month, to enable discussion to continue for two more days.

Not since World War II had Congress remained in session so close to an election day, and with mid-term elections on 6 November rapidly approaching a compromise budget was at last finally agreed. The new proposal was passed by 228 votes to 200 in the House of Representatives on 27 October. The bill was supported by 181 Democrats and 47 Republicans, and opposed by 126 Republicans and 74 Democrats. It was passed in the Senate by 54 votes to 45 on 28 October. Mr Bush said that although 'there are some things in it I had to gag and digest', he would sign it 'because for the first time it makes significant and long-term cuts in federal spending that should have a positive impact on America's economic future'.

The final measure aimed to reduce the budget deficit by $41,400 million. The main differences between the final version and the original agreement in September were an increase in the top rate of tax, a smaller reduction in the Medicare budget and a smaller increase in petrol tax. The agreed bill levelled out the tax 'bubble', an anomaly created by the 1986 Tax Reform Act. This had meant that couples with incomes in excess of $186,000 paid tax at a rate of 28 per cent, while those in the lower income band, $78,000 to $186,000, were taxed at 33 per cent. The new bill provided for a rate of 31 per cent for both groups, and as a result established three income tax rates of 15, 28 and 31 per cent. The $2,050 personal exemptions were to be gradually eliminated for individuals earning more than $100,000, and deductions claimed by individual tax-payers in those brackets, and by couples earning more than $150,000, were to be limited.

Cuts of $42,400 million over five years were made in Medicare through reduced reimbursements to doctors and hospitals. Monthly premiums for beneficiaries were to be gradually increased from $28.60 to $46.50 by 1995. The amount patients were required to pay before receiving benefits was also raised, from $75 to $100. Income levels subject to the 1.45 per cent Medicare payroll tax were increased from $51,300 to $125,000.

The increases in excise tax included an additional 5 cents on the 9 cents a gallon federal gasoline tax and the renewal of the tax on airline tickets which was also increased from 8 to 10 per cent. The tax on a six-pack of beer was doubled, from 16 to 32 cents, taxes on wines and spirits were increased, and those on cigarettes were raised from 16 cents a pack to 20 cents. In addition, a 10 per cent tax was to be charged on purchases of new private planes over $250,000, boats above $100,000, automobiles above $30,000, and furs and jewellery above $10,000.

Additional measures included cuts of $11,900 million over five years in farm commodity programmes, and reductions of $3,700 million over five years in veterans' benefits. Student loan requirements and regulations were tightened to limit defaults on payments. Military spending was cut by $67,200 million. The few benefits came with an increase in the amount of earned income exempt from tax for workers in the lowest income brackets, and a $500 tax credit for tax-payers with children under one year old. Tax concessions were provided for oil and gas developers and for small businesses. With business finally at an end, the 101st Congress adjourned on 28 October, and many congressmen went to meet the voters. A new round of political debate lay ahead for the new Congress, which would begin to consider the 1992 budget in January 1991.

Election campaigning for many American politicians began months before November. Throughout 1990 Democratic and Republican voters selected their respective candidates in a prelude to the final legislative and gubernatorial contests due in autumn. In Texas Ann Richards, the state treasurer, won the Democratic nomination for governor on 10 April after a bitter primary contest with the state district attorney, Jim Mattox. The contest was marked by personal attacks, as Mr Mattox accused Mrs Richards of drug use and the latter accused him of financial impropriety. The Republican nomination was won by Clayton Williams. Voters participated in primary elections in 11 states in June. Among the most important was that of California, where Dianne Feinstein, a former mayor of San Francisco, came from behind to defeat John Van der Kamp, the state's attorney-general, to win the Democratic nomination after an expensive and often unpleasant campaign. Senator Pete Wilson was nominated to oppose her in November for the Republicans. In Iowa the same month an abortion-rights advocate, the state's House speaker, Don Avenson, secured the Democratic gubernatorial nomination in preference to an anti-abortionist. He would face the incumbent Republican, Terry E. Branstad, who opposed abortion.

Race also figured in the primary contests. On 13 June Theo Mitchell became the first black politician to win a major party nomination for state office when he secured the Democratic gubernatorial nomination in South Carolina to face Republican incumbent Carroll Campbell. On the same day a black Republican, Kenneth Harris, defeated the self-proclaimed white supremacist, Ralph Forbes, in a run-off for the nomination for lieutenant-governor. Harvey Gantt, a liberal supporter of abortion and opponent of the death penalty, became the first black Senate nominee in the twentieth century in North Carolina, where he defeated Mike Easley in order to face the right-wing Republican incumbent, Jesse Helms. In Georgia another black candidate was less fortunate. Andrew Young, the former US representative to the UN and twice mayor of Atlanta, was defeated on 7 August in a run-off election against Zell Miller, the state's lieutenant-governor. Although he was the first black candidate to progress beyond the primary stage in Georgia, Mr Young failed to mobilize black voters or to capture white support, and he was considerably outspent by Mr Miller. The Republican candidate, Johnny Isakson, millionaire businessman and minority leader in the state's house of representatives, sought to become the state's first Republican governor since the period of reconstruction after the Civil War.

The last round of primaries was completed in September. Among the most interesting was the Democratic nomination for governor of Florida of a former federal senator, Lawton Chiles, who rejected the negative campaign tactics of personal attack and refused to accept campaign contributions of more than $100; his Republican opponent, incumbent Governor Bob Martinez, was thought to have some $7 million to spend on the campaign in November. While incumbents were renominated in gubernatorial campaigns in New Hampshire, Rhode Island and Wisconsin, newcomers to the political scene were successful for both parties in Massachusetts and Oklahoma. In Massachusetts the disillusionment with the Democratic administration of 1988 presidential candidate Michael Dukakis showed when John Silber, the president of Boston University, came from behind to beat Francis X. Bellotti, a leading Democrat and former state attorney-general. The Republican choice was William Weld, who sought to win the governorship for his party for the first time in 20 years.

It had been anticipated that social issues such as race, abortion and the environment would be significant factors in the actual elections in November. In the event, such matters were pushed into the background by the Gulf crisis and the budget debacle, but even these produced little clear overall effect. There were few pointers towards the 1992 presidential elections, and no clear sense of any prevailing mood or political climate emerged. Despite voter disillusionment expressed in the second lowest turnout of voters since 1942 (36.4 per cent), and some campaigns to 'throw the bums out', most incumbents were re-elected. The system granting office holders greater amounts of public money than their challengers in campaign funds provided a significant built-in advantage, but in a number of states the voters did pass propositions to limit the length of time their legislators could stay in office.

The traditional strong swing against the party controlling the White House did not materialize. The Democrats gained one more Senate seat (to give them 56 to the Republicans' 44), and only seven more places in the House of Representatives, increasing their numbers to 266 compared with 169 Republicans. In the gubernatorial campaigns the Democrats gained eight governorships and lost five, which gave an overall tally of 28 Democrats, 19 Republicans, two independents and one undecided. The Democratic gubernatorial victories were, however, significant in that, coupled with control of state legislatures, the party would have considerable control over reshaping congressional district lines in key states following the 1990 census. This could provide an electoral advantage through to the end of the 1990s.

In one of the most important campaigns in terms of restructuring, Pete Wilson prevented Dianne Feinstein from gaining the Californian state governorship for the Democrats. The two candidates had spent an estimated $40 million, mostly on negative personal attacks. Mudslinging also played a large part in the election in Texas, where Ann Richards came from behind to defeat Clayton Williams and win the state for the Democrats. Mr Williams, a multi-millionaire, spent $8 million on his campaign but alienated voters with his boorishness and his apparent ignorance of legislation. The revelation that he had paid no income tax in 1986, despite his wealth, also cost him support. In another key state, Florida, Lawton Chiles defeated Bob Martinez despite being heavily outspent by his Republican opponent.

Two other women became governors in addition to Mrs Richards. Former state treasurer Joan Finney defeated incumbent Frank Carlson to win Kansas for the Democrats, while Barbara Roberts, a liberal Democrat, became the first female governor of Oregon. In Iowa the Republican incumbent, anti-abortionist Terry E. Branstad, easily defeated Don Avenson. In South Carolina Republican Carroll Campbell easily held off the challenge of Theo Mitchell, while Zell Miller won in Georgia to maintain the Democratic monopoly of control over the governor's mansion.

Independent candidates won the gubernatorial elections in Alaska and Connecticut. A former Republican, Walter Hickel, created the Alaskan Independent Party to win the gubernatorial contest there. Another former Republican and a member of the Watergate commission, Lowell Weicker Jr, formed the Connecticut Party and wrested control of the governorship away from the Democrats, who had held it for 30 years. Elsewhere in New England the Republicans won the elections for governor and treasurer in Massachusetts for the first time since 1968, and Governor John McKernan withstood a strong challenge from Democrat Joseph Brennan in Maine. The largest winning margin for a challenger over an incumbent was achieved by Democrat Bruce Sundlun in Rhode Island when he beat Edward DiPrete by a 4 to 1 ratio.

Democratic Governor Mario Cuomo was elected for a third term in New York state, but his much reduced majority pointed to a fall in support which might undermine any possible future presidential bid. Another likely contender, New Jersey's Senator Bill Bradley, suffered a dent in his aspirations when he only just avoided defeat despite having vastly outspent his Republican opponent. Hopes of higher office were possibly revived for Democratic Senators Paul Simon of Illinois and Al Gore of Tennessee after they both easily secured re-election.

Other significant congressional results saw Senator Nancy Kassebaum (Republican) re-elected in Kansas to remain as one of only two women in the upper house. In Vermont socialist Bernie Sanders became the state's only member of the House of Representatives following a victory over both the Republican incumbent and a Democratic challenger. In North Carolina the conservative Republican, Jesse Helms, defeated the challenge of Democrat Harvey Gantt in a contest in which race had been a major issue. The US Senate thus remained without any black members. On the other hand, Connecticut's Gary Franks became the first black Republican in the House of Representatives since 1935, having defeated a liberal Democrat. Moreover, Sharon Pratt Dixon became the first black woman mayor in a major city when she defeated a member of Mayor Marion Barry's administration in the Washington election (see below for Barry case). Civil rights leader Rev Jesse Jackson was elected as the Washington district's 'shadow senator', a position used to lobby for statehood.

If Mr Bush could take little comfort from the mid-term elections, he could feel some satisfaction over his handling of an appointment to the Supreme Court following the retirement of Justice William Brennan on 20 July. Justice Brennan, aged 84, had been one of the most liberal members of the Court and his retirement reduced the number of remaining liberals to three. While the retirement provided Mr Bush with an opportunity to ensure a solid conservative majority, he also wished to avoid the embarrassment of failing to secure Senate endorsement of his nominee, as had happened when President Reagan nominated Robert Bork in 1987. With decisions pending on cases relating to abortion, the death penalty and civil rights, the President's nomination was a matter of widespread interest and speculation. On 23 July Mr Bush surprised everyone when he named David H. Souter, a relatively unknown federal Appeals Court judge, to fill the post.

Mr Souter, a 51-year-old bachelor educated at Harvard and Oxford, had been a supreme court judge in New Hampshire from 1983 to 1990. The paucity of his public record provided him with an image of anonymity, and most observers waited until the confirmation hearings before passing judgement. The Senate judiciary committee began to hear testimony from Mr Souter on 13 September. Throughout his three-day questioning he proved to be a model of tact and diplomacy, and he refused to be drawn on contentious issues such as abortion on the grounds that he did not want to prejudge any case he might have to consider in the future. After hearing testimony from other interested bodies, the committee voted by 13 to 1 to confirm the appointment on 27 September. Only Senator Edward Kennedy voted to reject the nomination because of Mr Souter's reticence on key issues. The full Senate confirmed the appointment by a vote of 90 to 9 on 2 October.

During the summer the Bush administration suffered particular embarrassment as a consequence of problems arising from the Savings and Loans collapse in 1989 (see AR 1989, pp. 51–2). In August Congress was informed that an additional $100,000 million would be required for the programme to bail out the failed loan companies, and it was estimated that the total amount required would be $500,000 million rather than $166,000 million. These additional costs were expected to make the task of balancing the federal budget even more difficult in coming years.

The President also suffered personal embarrassment because of the involvement of his son, Neil Bush, in the failed Silverado S & L company in Denver. The President's son had become a director of the company in 1985 at the age of 30. He was accused by federal regulators of 'unsafe and unsound practices' in approving loans, and it was suggested in press reports that he might have benefited personally from some business arrangements. He did not, however, face criminal charges, and he maintained that he was not guilty of any wrong-doing.

Congressional ethics were also a matter of public concern, and the Senate voted on 25 July to denounce Republican David Durenberger of Minnesota for 'clearly and unequivocally unethical conduct' with regard to outside income. The Senate ordered Mr Durenberger to pay more than $120,000 in restitution for improper expense claims and receipt of gifts in excess of the approved limits. The following day the House of Representatives reprimanded Barney Frank of Massachusetts (Democrat) for bringing discredit upon Congress through his association with a male prostitute.

Trials arising out of the Iran-Contra affair continued through the year (see AR 1989, pp. 48–9; 1988, pp. 58–9; 1987, pp. 47–51). On 24 January former air force general Richard V. Secord was sentenced to two years' probation, having pleaded guilty to making false statements to congressional investigators. On 5 March the trial of the former National Security Adviser, Rear-Admiral John M. Poindexter, charged with lying to Congress and obstructing investigations into the affair, opened in Washington DC. In the course of the trial the prosecution was successful in eliciting incriminating evidence from Oliver North, the US Marine lieutenant-colonel at the centre of the affair. Originally reluctant to testify against his superior, Colonel North admitted that Admiral Poindexter had supervised the shipment of arms to Iran in November 1985, and that he had also subsequently destroyed documents implicating the then President, Ronald Reagan. In previous testimony Admiral Poindexter had stated that he alone had authorized the Iran-Contra operation, but during his trial he claimed to have acted with the President's approval.

Mr Reagan had invoked executive privilege to deny Admiral Poindexter's lawyers access to diaries and papers and refused to testify in person at the trial. Judge Harold Greene ruled that the former President should testify but allowed videotaped evidence. As a consequence Mr Reagan (79) gave answers to 159 questions in front of videotape cameras in a Los Angeles court on 16 and 17 February, but had repeated difficulty in remembering specific decisions or meetings, and was even uncertain as to the identity of certain members of his administration. He did confirm that he had approved aid to the Contras between 1984 and 1986 when it had been prohibited by Congress. He denied taking part in any illegal activity, or of having any knowledge of profits from the sale of arms to Iran being diverted to Nicaragua. Mr Reagan stated that he believed Admiral Poindexter to be innocent, but after deliberating for six days on 7 April the jury found him guilty. On 11 June Admiral Poindexter was sentenced to six months in prison.

On 20 July a federal Appeals Court in the District of Columbia overturned one of the convictions against Colonel North and ordered a fresh examination of the evidence in relation to the two other convictions. The court ruled that the judge in Colonel North's trial had issued faulty instructions to the jury, and also accepted that witnesses against him might have been 'tainted' by his televised congressional testimony in 1987.

Issues pointing up the existence of continued racial division achieved political and legal prominence during 1990. On 22 October President Bush vetoed an omnibus civil rights bill designed to reinforce federal protection against job discrimination. The bill was intended to overturn Supreme Court rulings which had limited the rights of minorities to challenge discrimination in employment, but according to Mr Bush it would force employers to use quotas based on race or sex. Although his veto was condemned by civil rights leaders, the Senate narrowly failed to achieve the necessary two-thirds majority needed to overturn the veto when it voted on 24 October.

Black politicians experienced mixed fortunes in the course of the year. While Douglas Wilder, the first black governor in US history, was sworn in on 13 January in Richmond, Virginia, another leading black politician and former civil rights leader, Marion Barry, the mayor of Washington DC for 11 years, was arrested on 18 January following an FBI undercover operation. In the course of the FBI's 'sting', Mr Barry was filmed purchasing and smoking the cocaine-based derivative crack in the hotel room of a former girl-friend. Mr Barry was indicted on 15 February on three felony counts of lying to a federal jury and on five counts of cocaine possession. The substitution of the eight-count indictment instead of a single possession charge appeared to be a consequence of Mr Barry's refusal to resign as mayor and insistence on his innocence. Mr Barry pleaded not guilty in a brief court appearance on 28 February and was ordered to stand trial on 4 June. In the lead-up to the trial he continued to protest his innocence and to claim that he was a victim of white harassment. While the jury was still being selected, Mr Barry announced on television that he would serve the remainder of his mayoral term, due to expire on 2 January 1991, but would not stand for re-election in November.

On 10 August the jury of 10 blacks and two whites found Mr Barry guilty of one charge of possessing cocaine, but acquitted him on a second charge of possession and was unable to reach a verdict on the other charges. The prosecution's case had been undermined by poor credibility of key witnesses, and the belief that filmed evidence, which actually showed Mr Barry resisting offers of drugs in the first instance, had only been achieved as a consequence of FBI activities which amounted to entrapment. On 26 October Mr Barry was sentenced to six months in prison and a $5,000 fine. Many observers considered this to be a harsh sentence for a first offence, but the judge cited Mr Barry's 'breach of public trust' as warranting an 'enhanced sentence'. Mr Barry remained at liberty pending an appeal, but failed in his bid to win a council seat in the November elections.

Racial tensions were also high in New York city as a result of court cases. On 17 May Joseph Fama, a 19-year-old Italian-American, was convicted for the murder of Yusuf Hawkins, a black teenager who had entered Bensonhurst, an Italian neighbourhood in Brooklyn, New York, to buy a second-hand car. On 18 May another youth, Keith Mondello, was acquitted of the same charges although he was said to be the ringleader of the gang involved in the attack. A black Baptist minister, Rev Al Sharpton, warned the white community that race violence would result unless both Fama and Mondello were convicted of murder. Several protest demonstrations followed the Mondello verdict and there were reports of revenge attacks by blacks on white youths. A third white youth, John Vento, was sentenced to two to eight years in prison on 14 August in connection with the Bensonhurst attack.

African-Americans were also involved in a boycott of Korean grocery shops in the Flatbush area of Brooklyn following an altercation between a shop worker and a black customer in January. A teacher and 30 black pupils who attempted to defy the boycott were intimidated by pickets on 14 May. Mayor David Dinkins, New York's first black mayor, had been criticized for not actively intervening to lessen racial tensions. On 11 May he condemned any boycott based on race and offered to mediate in the dispute. He also denounced the murder of Yusuf Hawkins, but rejected notions of 'group guilt'. Although his speech was praised in some quarters, several black spokesmen accused him of betraying his black constituents.

Some of the tension was eased when Fama was sentenced to 33 years to life in prison for murder on 11 June, and Mondello was sentenced to five to 16 years for riot and other felony charges. However, the trial of another notorious crime with racial overtones began on 13 June in the case of three black youths accused of the attempted murder and rape of a white female jogger in April 1989 (see AR 1989, p. 53). Throughout the trial the court was picketed by black demonstrators, led by Rev Sharpton, who protested that the youths were being victimized because of their race and that their confessions, later retracted, were the result of police pressure. On 18 August the jury found Raymond Santana (15), Yusuf Salaam (16) and Antron McCray (16) guilty of rape, but acquitted them of attempted murder. The three were each subsequently sentenced to 20 years' imprisonment.

FOREIGN AFFAIRS. President Bush and the Soviet President, Mikhail Gorbachev, each sent televised New Year's messages to the other's country on 1 January. In his, Mr Bush praised Mr Gorbachev as 'a good partner in peace', and assured the Soviet people that he supported the process of reform under way in the USSR. Mr Gorbachev told the Americans that 1990 could be a turning-point in arms limitation and could lead to genuine US-Soviet cooperation.

The changing situation in the Middle East brought some benefits for the USA early in the year. Improved relations with Syria were instrumental in securing the release of two American hostages held in the Lebanon. Robert Polhill, a university lecturer seized by the Islamic Jihad in Beirut in 1987, was handed over to the US ambassador in Damascus on 22 April. On 30 April Frank Reed, the director of the Lebanese International College in Beirut, who had been held hostage by the Islamic Dawn organization since 1986, was released into Syrian custody in west Beirut. In a public statement made after Mr Reed's release President Bush thanked Syria and also Iran for interceding on the hostages' behalf. He made it clear, however, that the US government had made no deals with the kidnappers.

On 31 May–3 June Mr Gorbachev met with Mr Bush in Washington for their second summit, which had been preceded by meetings between Secretary of State James Baker and the Soviet Foreign Minister, Eduard Shevardnadze, in Moscow earlier in May. At that meeting preliminary agreements were reached, and Mr Baker spoke optimistically of moves towards finally signing the Strategic Arms Reduction Treaty (START). When the US and Soviet delegations met in Washington, they held four sessions of formal talks and on 1 June signed several agreements. The two powers agreed to ban the production of chemical weapons and to eliminate all but 5,000 tonnes of existing stockpiles. Both sides undertook to destroy all their stocks once a world-wide ban was agreed. A set of accords normalizing commercial relations between the two countries for the first time in 50 years was also signed, and a long-term grain accord increasing the sale of US grain to the Soviet

Union was agreed. A provisional treaty on nuclear weapons was signed, but comprehensive agreements on reductions in strategic nuclear arms and on conventional weapons in Europe were not achieved.

After informal meetings at Camp David the previous day, the two leaders held a joint concluding press conference on 3 June. Both spoke in terms of the beginning of a new era of Soviet-US relations, and pointed up their successes. However, despite obvious warm personal feelings, both Mr Bush and Mr Gorbachev acknowledged the existence of differences on matters such as the unification of Germany, the independence of Lithuania and the emigration of Soviet Jews. Nonetheless, the informal relations between the two men were warm and they agreed that they would meet on a regular basis in future. Mr Gorbachev invited Mr Bush to the Soviet Union at some future date.

Following the summit, President Bush played host to the other heads of government of the Group of Seven leading industrial powers, (Canada, France, Italy, Japan, West Germany, the United Kingdom and the USA) at Houston, Texas, from 9 to 11 July. The outcome of the meeting was a commitment to assist the Soviet Union with economic aid, although the USA declined to provide direct aid until the Soviet Union reduced military spending. The summit also agreed the continuation of the sanctions imposed upon China following the Tiananmen Square massacre in 1989. Agreement was reached on environmental issues, and the seven promised to undertake 'common efforts to limit emissions of greenhouse gases' and to negotiate 'a global forest convention'.

The issue of agricultural subsidies was included in the Houston discussions, and in the final statement it was asserted that the participants would work to achieve 'progressive reductions in support and protection of agriculture'. It was expected that this agreement would facilitate talks within the General Agreement on Tariffs and Trade (GATT) which followed in Geneva on 23 July. However, disagreement between the USA and European Community (EC) on this particular issue continued. In the course of further discussions in Geneva on 15 October, the USA formally proposed a 75 per cent reduction in internal farm subsidies and a 90 per cent cut in export subsidies by the EC, to begin in 1991–92, but this was not accepted by the EC side.

On 18 July, following meetings of representatives of the five permanent members of the UN Security Council in Paris, Secretary of State Baker announced a dramatic change in US foreign policy towards Kampuchea and Vietnam. He said that the USA would no longer support the seating of the rebel national government of Kampuchea at the United Nations unless the dominant Khmer Rouge group was excluded. The USA was now also prepared to enter into direct discussion with Vietnam on the subject of Kampuchea. Since the 1970s the American government had accepted the Khmers Rouges, despite their appalling record while in power, in order to maintain friendly relations with China. Concern had been growing in America that the Khmers Rouges were growing in strength and could possibly even regain power, and congressional pressure for a change in policy by the Bush administration had been mounting. Mr Baker's announcement marked the first real change in US policy in Indo-China since the US withdrawal from the region in 1975.

In August Mr Baker visited the Soviet Union to take part in informal talks with his Soviet counterpart, Mr Shevardnadze, notably on Afghanistan, Kampuchea, future economic cooperation between the USA and the Soviet Union, and further matters relating to the START treaty which they hoped to finalize by the end of the year. At the end of their talks on 2 August, Mr Baker went to Mongolia, but cut short his visit to meet Mr Shevardnadze in Moscow again to discuss the Iraqi invasion of Kuwait. The two men issued a joint statement condemning the invasion and calling for an international ban on arms sales to Iraq. On 3 October the agreement between the two nations on the Gulf crisis was underlined when they issued a joint statement in New York which called upon the international community to adhere to sanctions against Iraq. This came after Mr Baker and Mr Shevardnadze had announced a comprehensive treaty to limit the size of conventional forces in Europe, as subsequently signed in Paris by the NATO and Warsaw Pact countries on 19 November (see Pt. XII).

The Gulf crisis overshadowed all other international events, and the US government reacted quickly to Iraq's invasion of Kuwait. On 3 August the administration announced the dispatch of naval vessels to the Gulf, and on 7 August the sending of ground troops to Saudi Arabia as part of a multinational force in 'Operation Desert Shield'. The first brigade of the 82nd US Airborne Division was en route for the Gulf within hours of this announcement, and by the end of August 40,000 American troops were in Saudi Arabia. On 22 August President Bush issued an executive order which called up military reservists for the first time since the Vietnam war. By the end of December the American armed forces in the Gulf had risen to 280,000.

In a national television broadcast on 8 August Mr Bush declared that the aims of the US military were 'wholly defensive' and that 'a line had been drawn in the sand'. The American forces would, he said, 'defend themselves, the Kingdom of Saudi Arabia and other friends in the Gulf'. However, the President compared Saddam Husain to Hitler and, declaring that 'appeasement does not work', warned that 'no-one should underestimate our determination to confront aggression'. The overall objective of American policy was therefore to see the Iraqis 'get and go back'. Mr Bush denounced the subsequent detention of foreign nationals in Iraq and Kuwait, and their location near military installations, as contrary to international law and against 'all accepted norms of international conduct'. Nonetheless, Mr Bush did not alter his holiday plans but left Washington on 10 August for his vacation home in Kennebunkport, Maine. The President made clear that he did not want 'to appear held hostage in the White House', a fate suffered by President Carter during the crisis with Iran in 1987–89.

On 9 September the President met Mr Gorbachev in Helsinki for an emergency summit meeting on the Gulf crisis. In a joint statement the two leaders declared that they were 'united in the belief that Iraq's aggression must not be tolerated', and called upon Iraq 'to withdraw unconditionally from Kuwait, to allow the restoration of Kuwait's legitimate government, and to free all hostages now held in Iraq and Kuwait'. Despite this broad agreement, Mr Bush did admit that there were differences, and that Mr Gorbachev had stressed the need for a political solution rather than the possible use of force which the Americans threatened if Iraq refused to accede to UN demands.

In a statement on US policy in the Gulf to a joint session of Congress on 11 September, Mr Bush reiterated American objectives as the unconditional withdrawal of Iraqi forces from Kuwait, the restoration of 'Kuwait's legitimate government', the assurance of stability and security within the Gulf, and the protection of US citizens abroad. He did, however, stress the economic aspects of the crisis and, pointing up the importance of the Kuwaiti oilfields, said: 'We cannot permit a resource so vital to be dominated by one so ruthless'. The President went on to state: 'Iraq will not be permitted to annex Kuwait. That's not a threat, or a boast, that's just the way it's going to be'.

Despite the more aggressive stance of the administration, Defence Secretary Richard Cheney was forced to dismiss the US Air Force Chief of Staff, General Michael Dugan, on 17 September following some intemperate comments to the press. General Dugan had told reporters in the Gulf that the US would bomb Baghdad if war broke out, adding that the bombing would be aimed particularly at Saddam Husain, his family and senior Iraqi military commanders. Mr Cheney said General Dugan had violated standing orders with regard to the public discussion of military affairs, and had shown 'bad judgement at a sensitive time'.

Popular and bi-partisan support for the President's seemingly uncompromising attitude began to wane towards the end of the year. Saddam Husain's announcement at the beginning of December that he would release the hostages was welcomed in America. The change in Iraq's policy was seen by some congressmen as a sign that negotiation was possible, while the administration appeared to insist that force was the only means of enforcing the UN deadline of 15 January for an Iraqi withdrawal from Kuwait. Several former defence secretaries and the Director of the CIA, William Webster, were among witnesses who appeared before the House armed services committee and argued that sanctions should be given time to take effect before a resort to force.

On 20 November a number of congressional Democrats sought to bring an injunction against the President to prevent him from taking offensive action against Iraq without the prior consent of Congress, and Senator Edward Kennedy called for an extension of the 15 January deadline to 2 August 1991.

In the face of such opposition to the use of force, President Bush launched a surprise peace initiative on 30 November, when he called in a television broadcast for direct negotiation with Iraq. To demonstrate that he was prepared 'to go the extra mile for peace', the President suggested that the Iraqi Foreign Minister, Tariq Aziz, should meet him in the White House soon after 10 December and that Secretary of State Baker should go to Baghdad between 15 December and 15 January. Mr Bush indicated his own pessimism when he said: 'I'm not hopeful we're going to get a lot out of this. We're just going the extra mile'. He went on to assure the American and Iraqi peoples that 'should military action be required, this will not be another Vietnam. This will not be a protracted drawn-out war'. Any American life lost, said the President, would be paid for in full by the other side.

Subsequently, the administration called for a US-Iraqi meeting to take place before 3 January. However, it became clear that American aims remained unchanged and that the point of the meeting would be to demonstrate US determination to secure the Iraqi withdrawal from Kuwait. When Iraq proposed that the meeting be held on 12 January, just three days before the UN deadline for the evacuation of Kuwait, the Bush administration reverted to its former less conciliatory language and increased the military build-up in the Gulf. No apparent progress towards a peaceful settlement had been made by the end of the year.

Chapter 2

CANADA

CAPITAL: Ottawa   AREA: 9,970,610 sq km   POPULATION: 26,000,000 ('88)
OFFICIAL LANGUAGES: English and French
POLITICAL SYSTEM: federal parliamentary democracy
HEAD OF STATE: Queen Elizabeth II (since Feb '52)
GOVERNOR-GENERAL: Ramon John Hnatyshyn (since Jan '90)
RULING PARTY: Progressive Conservative Party (since Sept '84)
HEAD OF GOVERNMENT: Brian Mulroney (Prime Minister since Sept '84)
PRINCIPAL MINISTERS: Donald Mazankowski (deputy premier), Joe Clark (external affairs), William McKnight (defence), Michael Wilson (finance), Jake Epp (energy, mines and resources)
INTERNATIONAL ALIGNMENT: NATO, OECD, OAS, Francophonie, Cwth.
CURRENCY: Canadian dollar (end-'90 £1=Can$2.24, US$1=Can$1.16)
GNP PER CAPITA: US$16,960 ('88)
MAIN EXPORT EARNERS: manufactured goods, fabricated and crude materials, agricultural products, tourism

THE terms upon which English- and French-speaking Canadians had lived together in one country were a subject of controversy in 1990. The occasion was the failure of the Meech Lake Accord (see AR 1987, pp. 67–8), a set of amendments to the 1982 constitution designed to make it acceptable to the largely French-speaking province of Quebec. Required to be ratified by the federal and the ten provincial governments by 23 June 1990, the Accord met growing popular opposition in English-speaking Canada as the deadline approached. Some Canadians believed that one of its provisions, describing Quebec as a 'distinct society' with authority to protect and promote French language and culture, placed the province's collective interests over the rights of minorities, women and native peoples. It was also claimed that the Accord weakened the federal government's capacity to institute national social programmes. The lack of public participation in the drafting of the amendments in 1987 was also criticized.

Behind the constitutional debate lay a deeper issue. The Accord had become a symbol, to English-speaking Canada, of a general hostility towards Quebec and to the national government headed by Brian Mulroney. Mr Mulroney was seen as being too eager to placate Quebec's demands. It was charged that federal policies and financial grants were directed to Quebec at the expense of other Canadian provinces. Quebec was viewed as indifferent to the rest of Canada, especially in its passage of a law which banned English in exterior commercial signs (see AR 1988, pp. 70–71).

Nevertheless, as the year began, the Accord had been approved by the federal parliament and the legislatures of eight of the ten provinces. Manitoba and New Brunswick, whose governments had changed since the Accord was drawn up, delayed ratification until public hearings had taken place on the proposed changes. They then suggested amendments to the Accord. In Newfoundland a new government, elected in April 1989, withdrew its predecessor's endorsement of the Accord. In a bid to save the amendments, Mr Mulroney called the ten provincial premiers to a conference in Ottawa beginning on 3 June. In a week of intense bargaining, nine of the premiers approved the Accord, supplemented by additional changes to be considered later. Newfoundland agreed to submit the Accord to a free vote in the legislature. But further obstacles now arose. In Manitoba an aboriginal member of the legislature, hoping to secure concessions for his people, blocked legislative proceedings on the Accord. The federal government offered more time to Manitoba to complete its consideration but not to Newfoundland. Outraged by what he termed unreasonable pressure tactics, the premier of Newfoundland cancelled the vote in the legislature. The 23 June deadline passed and the Accord died.

Quebec premier Robert Bourassa, who had described the Accord as Quebec's 'minimum demands', expressed his profound disappointment at its failure. Quebec, he declared, '*is* a distinct society . . . free and capable of assuming its destiny and its development'. He announced that henceforth he would negotiate directly with Ottawa and not participate in common fronts with the other provinces. He established an all-party commission to explore future constitutional options for Quebec. Support for independence, perhaps accompanied by an economic relationship with the rest of Canada (the plan put forward by the Parti Québécois), rose dramatically in Quebec. The two older national federalist parties, the governing Progressive Conservatives (PC) and the Liberals, were thrown into disarray. Eight federal MPs left their caucuses to sit as *indépendantistes*. They formed a loose grouping, the Bloc Québécois. A senior Quebec lieutenant of Prime Minister Mulroney who was also a close friend, Lucien Bouchard, resigned from the federal cabinet to lead the Bloc. At a by-election in Montreal held on 13 August a Bloc candidate easily defeated representatives of the national parties. The defeat was particularly humiliating to Jean Chrétien, a former Trudeau minister and a strong federalist, who had only recently been chosen as the new leader of the Liberal Party. With the tide of sentiment for independence running strongly in Quebec, Chrétien chose a French-speaking riding in New Brunswick to enter parliament in a by-election on 10 December. Mr Mulroney's credibility was also severely strained by the death of the constitutional amendments. He had made the goal of reconciling Quebec to Canadian federalism a cornerstone of his government's programme ever since it assumed office in 1984. His immediate response was to appoint public and parliamentary inquiries to examine the workings of the Canadian federal system.

A centre-piece of the Mulroney government's economic legislation, a goods and services tax, GST (see AR 1989, pp. 60–1), was approved late in 1990 after unprecedented parliamentary controversy. The measure, although undoubtedly unpopular, was adopted by the PC majority in the House of Commons in April. It then went on to the appointed upper house, the Senate, which conducted public hearings before recommending that the bill should be abandoned. The Mulroney government was furious. It accused the Liberal majority in the Senate, mainly appointments made by former Prime Minister Pierre Trudeau, of obstructing the will of elected members of parliament. It was unreasonable that senators, unaccountable to any constituency, should hold up the government's programme. It was not the first time that the Liberal majority in the upper house had blocked legislation from the Commons. Budget measures had been stalled or amended, as had the 1989 reform of the unemployment insurance system.

Mr Mulroney moved to overcome the Liberal majority. He filled an accumulation of 15 Senate vacancies with loyal supporters of his government. On 27 September he called upon an inherited section of the 1982 Constitution Act to appoint eight additional senators. The provision was intended to be used in the event of a deadlock between the two houses. The new appointments brought PC standing in the Senate to 54 in an expanded 112-seat chamber. (There were 52 Liberal senators, one from the Reform Party, one Liberal independent and four independents.) The Liberal senators vigorously objected to the new appointments. Court challenges were unsuccessful and noisy demonstrations and filibusters disrupted the proceedings of the upper house. On 13 December, after 340 hours of debate and the defeat of more than eight amendments, the GST bill was passed by 55 votes to 49. The government announced that it still intended to begin the collection of the new tax on 1 January 1991.

Unrest among native peoples was a disturbing phenomenon during the summer of 1990. At Oka, a small community on the Ottawa River 60 kilometres west of Montreal, Mohawks blocked a local road to protest against encroachments on land they considered traditional. An attempt on 11 July to clear the roadblock failed, leaving a Quebec provincial police officer dead. A larger group of Mohawks from the Kahnawake reserve across the St Lawrence River from Montreal, in sympathy with the Oka band, blocked a major commuter bridge into the city. There were ugly incidents with the local residents, causing premier Robert Bourassa of Quebec to call in the Canadian army. About 3,300 soldiers moved in to restore order. Negotiations between the Quebec government and the Mohawks, with the federal government (ultimately responsible for Indian affairs) sitting in as an observer, made no progress. On 27 August Bourassa directed the army to dismantle the bridge barricades. This was done peacefully. The Oka Indians held out on a corner of their property until 26 September, when they surrendered. The clashes called attention to the slow process of settling Indian land claims and the deplorable economic and social conditions under which many of Canada's half-million 'treaty Indians' existed. The Mulroney government, joined by some of the provinces, promised to address these problems more vigorously.

With constitutional reform frustrated, combined with Indian unrest and unpopular economic legislation, the fortunes of the Mulroney government plummeted. An October public opinion poll showed the PC with only 15 per cent support among decided voters, compared with over 30 per cent for each of the other national parties, the Liberals and the socialist New Democratic Party (NDP). At the adjournment of the House of Commons for the Christmas recess, party standings were as follows: PC 159; Liberals 80; NDP 44; Reform Party 1; independents 11 (including 9 Bloc Québécois members), for a total membership of 295.

Mulroney left his cabinet virtually unchanged during 1990. The most important appointment was that of a 42-year-old Vancouver lawyer,

Kim Campbell, who became Minister of Justice on 23 February, the first woman to hold this key portfolio. She successfully piloted the government's compromise abortion legislation through the Commons by 29 May, although at the year's end the legislation had still to be approved by the Senate. In May, when Lucien Bouchard left the cabinet to lead the Bloc Québécois in parliament, Robert de Cotret left his economic portfolio to take up Bouchard's post as Minister of the Environment. This new minister's first responsibility was to complete the government's Green Paper on the environment, a statement of principles for environmental legislation begun by M. Bouchard. The paper was published late in the year.

Two provinces went to the polls in 1990. On 6 September a Liberal administration in Canada's largest province, Ontario, was roundly defeated by the NDP opposition. Bob Rae, the 42-year-old leader of the Ontario NDP, became premier on 1 October. The NDP, winning power for the first time in Ontario, benefited from voter disenchantment with the two older middle-of-the-road parties. In addition, the Liberal leader, David Peterson, who had been premier since 1985, suffered from his strong support of the controversial Meech Lake Accord. In Manitoba, on 11 September, a minority PC administration under Gary Filmon improved its standing, winning 30 of the 57 seats in the legislature. Mr Filmon had opposed the constitutional accord and distanced his administration from some of the unpopular policies of the federal PC.

The Canadian economy slid into recession in 1990, the first setback to economic expansion since 1982. The second and third quarters of the year revealed a contracting economy, expected to shrink by 1 per cent over the year. On a seasonally-adjusted annual basis, gross domestic product stood at Can$676,800 million for 1990. Interest rates remained high, as the Bank of Canada sought to control inflation. Higher gasoline prices following the troubles in the Persian Gulf pushed the consumer price index to 5 per cent for the year ending in November. Unemployment, at a seasonally adjusted rate, stood at 9.1 per cent in November, a significantly higher rate than in 1989.

Finance Minister Michael Wilson delivered his sixth budget on 20 February. There were no tax increases for the first time in 22 years, but cuts in government spending and a two-year freeze on federal grants to the provinces for major social programmes. Total federal spending was expected to be Can$147,800 million, leaving a current deficit of Can$28,500 million. Two large projects were cancelled: the construction of a powerful Can$680 million class 8 icebreaker for Arctic waters and a giant oil sands scheme in northern Alberta.

Canada gave full backing to the United Nations' efforts to force Iraq to withdraw from Kuwait. In addition to diplomatic activity, the Canadian government dispatched two destroyers and a supply ship to assist in the economic blockade of Iraq. The ships, stationed in the central Persian Gulf area, carried a complement of 934 sailors and soldiers. In early October a squadron of 18 CF-18 jet fighters was sent to the Gulf to provide air cover for the naval forces.

A modest reduction in Canada's troops stationed in Europe was announced on 21 September. Some 1,400 personnel—airmen, artillerymen and infantry—would be withdrawn in 1991 from a force of 8,000. The two principal Canadian bases, at Lahr and Baden-Soellingen in southern Germany, would remain open.

Chapter 3

LATIN AMERICA

ARGENTINA—BOLIVIA—BRAZIL—CHILE—COLOMBIA—ECUADOR—
PARAGUAY—PERU—URUGUAY—VENEZUELA—CUBA—
DOMINICAN REPUBLIC AND HAITI—CENTRAL AMERICA
AND PANAMA—MEXICO

ARGENTINA

CAPITAL: Buenos Aires   AREA: 2,766,890 sq km   POPULATION: 31,500,000 ('88)
OFFICIAL LANGUAGE: Spanish   POLITICAL SYSTEM: federal presidential democracy
HEAD OF STATE AND GOVERNMENT: President Carlos Saúl Menem (since July '89)
RULING PARTY: Justicialist (Peronist) Party (since Dec '89)
PRINCIPAL MINISTERS: Eduardo Duhalde (Vice-President), Domingo Cavallo (foreign relations), Humberto Romero (defence), Antonio Ermán González (economy), Julio Mera Figueroa (interior), Antonio Francisco Salonia (education & justice)
INTERNATIONAL ALIGNMENT: NAM, OAS
CURRENCY: austral (end-'90 £1=A10,776.25, US$1=A5,583.55)
GNP PER CAPITA: US$2,520 ('88)
MAIN EXPORT EARNERS: wheat, other agricultural produce, manufactures

ON 2 January a 'new year plan' was officially unveiled, centring on the wholesale forcible conversion of the short-term internal debt into long-term external debt denominated in dollars, which Economy Minister Ermán González claimed would put an end to 'the *patria financiera* and the *patria contratista*'. Any illusion that his promises of stable prices would be maintained were soon swept aside, however, and by February looting of supermarkets recurred in Rosario, Córdoba and the province of Buenos Aires. On 25 May, when the IMF resumed payments suspended in February, the austral rose and remained steady for some months.

Following an increase in its size from five to nine members in April, on 14 July the Supreme Court ruled that the privatization of the state airline, Aerolíneas Argentinas, was legal. It was purchased by a consortium of the Argentine domestic airline, Austral, with Iberia of Spain. The sale of ENTel, the state telecommunications monopoly, to a foreign consortium followed, after troops had been called in (6 September) to break a strike.

In late August the Finance Minister was granted extraordinary powers for 60 days and announced a fresh austerity package, which was further extended on 4 September. A further US$8,000 million in government debts to suppliers was converted into bonds, fuel prices and public utility rates were again raised, public sector wages cut and a new threshold imposed on welfare benefits. But on 12 September it was disclosed that the Central Bank had mislaid some US$67,500 million over the previous decade—equivalent to more than a year's revenue at current prices.

On 24 January the Minister of Defence, Italo Lúder, resigned because the President had consulted directly with the Chief of Staff, General Isidro Cáceres; he was replaced by Humberto Romero, who had been his deputy. The government's difficulties were further exacerbated by the very public dispute between the President and his wife, Zulema Yoma de Menem, about his alleged proclivities for other women. The President's personal position seemed strengthened when on 10 August he was elected chairman of the Justicialist (Peronist) Party and his brother, Senator Eduardo Menem, vice-chairman. This followed the resignation of Governor Antonio Cafiero, whose proposed 98 amendments to the constitution of the province of Buenos Aires had been rejected at a referendum five days before.

However, President Menem's choice of Loyalty Day (17 October) to issue a decree curbing the right to strike and obliging public service unions to maintain services precipitated a major split in Peronist ranks, already disturbed by the resignation of the Peronist governors of Jujuy and Chubut, where an unprecedented 'popular revolt' registered public impatience at the drain of funds to Buenos Aires. At the same time, military discontent also grew. Despite warnings by Colonel Mohammed Ali Seneildín, a revolt on 3 December by his supporters, who seized military headquarters with the loss of at least three lives, took the government by surprise. Any question of negotiation was on this occasion speedily rejected and within 48 hours the headquarters was stormed and some 480 lower-ranking personnel who surrendered were charged with insurrection.

The price was President Menem's irreversible decision to issue on 29 December his long-heralded pardon of General Jorge Videla, Admiral Emilio Massera, General Robert Viola, General Ramón Camps and others convicted (or, in the case of General Guillermo Suárez Mason, extradited but not yet tried) for human rights crimes during the 'dirty war'. Predictably, the pardon stunned human rights activists and relatives of the thousands of victims and received only the 'unrepentant ingratitude' of General Videla, who in an open letter to the Army Chief of Staff demanded an apology and 'the restoration of military honour' for having 'defended the nation against subversive aggression'. Mario Eduardo Firmenich, former leader of the Peronist guerrilla movement, the Montoneros, who was also freed, prudently said nothing.

Abroad, at talks held in Madrid on 14–15 February, agreement was reached with the United Kingdom to restore diplomatic relations forthwith. Mario Cámpora, Deputy Foreign Minister and nephew of the former President, was named as the new ambassador to London. On 6–7 July the President of Brazil, Fernando Collor de Mello, visited Buenos Aires and signed a formal statement of intent to establish a joint market by 1995. In September the destroyer *Almirante Brown* and the missile frigate *Spiro* were ordered to the Persian Gulf, and in October President Menem visited Moscow and signed agreements on space research, atomic energy and the drug trade. The visit of President Bush within hours of the end of the military insurrection in December was followed by a declaration in support of the US plan for a pan-American free trade area.

BOLIVIA

CAPITALS: La Paz and Sucre   AREA: 1,099,000 sq km   POPULATION: 6,900,000 ('88)
OFFICIAL LANGUAGE: Spanish, Quechua and Aymará
POLITICAL SYSTEM: presidential democracy
HEAD OF STATE AND GOVERNMENT: President Jaime Paz Zamora (since Aug '89)
RULING PARTIES: Revolutionary Left Movement (MIR) holds presidency, supported by
   Nationalist Democratic Action (ADN)
PRINCIPAL MINISTERS: Luis Ossio (MIR/Vice-President), Carlos Iturralde Ballivián
   (ADN/foreign affairs), Guillermo Capobianco Ribera (MIR/interior and justice),
   Héctor Hormaechea Peñaranda (ADN/defence), David Blanco Zavala
   (ADN/finance)
INTERNATIONAL ALIGNMENT: NAM, OAS
CURRENCY: boliviano (end–'90 £1=Bs6.53, US$1=Bs3.38)
GNP PER CAPITA: US$570 ('88)
MAIN EXPORT EARNERS: natural gas, tin

INFLATION in 1989 had fallen to 16.5 per cent, one of the lowest rates in Latin America, and a modest economic recovery continued. By mutual agreement, in December 1989 Argentina wrote off US$800 million of Bolivia's foreign debt against $300 million owed by Argentina for Bolivian natural gas, after Brazil had permitted Bolivia to renegotiate $41 million of its $380 million debt to Brazil in exchange for a joint energy integration programme. Optimism that at last Chile might agree to restore Bolivia's access to the sea, buoyed by a promise in October 1989 from President Alan García Pérez of Peru that his country would not object, was muted after the suggestion by the Chilean Foreign

Minister on 27 January that the question of access could be divorced from other outstanding issues.

The government announced a crop substitution aid package from the United States which would enable it to eradicate some 6,000 hectares of coca. President Jaime Paz Zamora on 15 January put the value of the illegal trade in coca at US$1,500 million a year, of which over a third, he believed, remained in the country. His Foreign Minister, Carlos Iturralde Ballivián, put the cost of replacement at some $3,500 million over 8 years—well above US estimates.

On 14 February the state of siege imposed following student unrest in November 1989 was formally ended. On 23 September the President reached agreement in talks with Indian leaders and the following day issued decrees securing land rights in Beni and the central Chimanes forest areas.

BRAZIL

CAPITAL: Brasília   AREA: 8,512,000 sq km   POPULATION: 144,400,000 ('88)
OFFICIAL LANGUAGE: Portuguese   POLITICAL SYSTEM: federal presidential democracy
HEAD OF STATE AND GOVERNMENT: President Fernando Collor de Mello (since '90)
RULING PARTY: National Reconstruction Party (PRN)
PRINCIPAL MINISTERS: Itama Franco (Vice-President), Francisco Rezek (foreign affairs), Zélia Cardoso de Mello (economy), Jarbas Passarinho (justice), Ozires Silva (infrastructure)
INTERNATIONAL ALIGNMENT: OAS
CURRENCY: cruzeiro (end–'90 £1=Cz$329.46, US$1=Cz$170.71)
GNP PER CAPITA: US$2,160 ('88)
MAIN EXPORT EARNERS: coffee, iron ore, soyabeans, tourism

ON 15 March Fernando Collor de Mello was sworn in as President, promising a new deal for the poor and war on the elite, tax evaders and the banking community. Practical steps towards these goals included his appointment of Zélia Cardoso de Mello (36) as the world's first woman Minister of the Economy. She promised that inflation would be reduced to 10 per cent a month in six months under the New Brazil (*Brasil Novo*) plan announced by the President. This was backed within days by the establishment of a special unit headed by the head of the federal police, Superintendent Romeu Tuma, to end tax evasion and fraud, although the special powers decreed by the President were subsequently ruled unconstitutional.

Under the plan, the cruzado was abolished and replaced by a new cruzeiro, a 30-day price freeze was imposed, taxes and public utility rates were steeply raised and 24 state agencies closed with a potential loss of 81,000 jobs. Although the President's National Reconstruction Party (PRN) held only 31 of the 570 seats in Congress, as inflation began to fall steeply the plan was approved on 11 April by a majority of 45. As union protests grew against the enforced dismissals, Congress rejected them on 31 May and on 6 June the Supreme Court ruled them unconstitutional. But the government went ahead with its proposals to remove most import tariffs above a common level of 20 per cent, and on 13 September signed a letter of intent with the IMF for a standby credit of US$2,000 million. The government later agreed to resume interest payments to Western government creditors, although talks with creditor banks over the country's US$114,000 million foreign debt broke down at the end of November, when US banks, who had earlier rejected a government proposal to convert their debt into long-term bonds, demanded an immediate year-end payment.

In the meantime, while scandal raged about financial deals involving the President, his advisers and Paulo César ('P.C.') Farias, a self-made millionaire from the President's home state of Alagoas, gubernatorial and municipal elections on 3 October were marked by widespread apathy, with a marked shift to the right and away from the Workers' Party (PT). On 13 October the Justice Minister, Bernardo Cabral, resigned following reports that he had had an affair with the Economy Minister. He was replaced by a former colonel, Jarbas Passarinho, who had held office under military governments.

Previously, on 6 September the President had ordered an inquiry into charges by Amnesty International that death squads (including members of the police) were murdering street children. When some 200 *garimpieros* invaded the tribal lands of the Uru-eu-wau-wau in Rondonia on Christmas Eve, he also ordered a revision of the country's Indian reservations.

CHILE

CAPITAL: Santiago   AREA: 756,600 sq km   POPULATION: 12,800,000 ('88)
OFFICIAL LANGUAGE: Spanish   POLITICAL SYSTEM: presidential democracy
HEAD OF STATE AND GOVERNMENT: Patricio Aylwin Azócar (since March '90)
RULING PARTY: Christian Democratic Party heading 17-party Coalition for Democracy
PRINCIPAL MINISTERS: Enrique Silva Cimma (foreign affairs), Enrique Krauss Rusque
   (interior), Patricio Rojas Saavedra (defence), Alejandro Foxley Rioseco (finance),
   Francisco Cumplido Cereceda (justice), Carlos Ominami Pascual (economy)
INTERNATIONAL ALIGNMENT: OAS
CURRENCY: peso (end–'90 £1=Ch$638.86, US$1=Ch$331.02)
GNP PER CAPITA: US$1,510 ('88)
MAIN EXPORT EARNERS: copper, agricultural products

ON 11 March more than 16 years of military rule came to an end when the former leader of the civilian opposition, Patricio Aylwin Azócar, was sworn in as President in the new Congress building in Valparaiso. Delegations from over 40 countries were present, including the Presidents of Argentina, Brazil and Uruguay, and the Vice-President of the United States, but other foreign dignitaries, including the Prime Minister of Spain and Sir Geoffrey Howe of the United Kingdom, avoided having to meet the outgoing President, General Pinochet, by arriving only after the ceremony was over. Despite tight security precautions, 17 bombs had exploded in the capital the previous day, but in Valparaiso protesters who jeered and threw eggs and tomatoes at Pinochet were kept well back. The new President immediately announced an amnesty for all the 500 political prisoners in custody not accused of violent offences and the creation of a National Commission on Truth and Reconciliation to probe human rights abuses. Moreover, the new Congress, which met on 20 March in Valparaiso, abolished the death penalty, suspended the strict security laws, and agreed tax reforms designed to raise social welfare expenditure by some US$500 million a year. In November, in advance of President Bush's state visit, an outline trade agreement was signed with the United States, which simultaneously lifted its arms embargo and readmitted Chile to the General System of Preferences.

Both left and right claimed responsibility for the shooting on 21 March of General Gustavo Leigh Guzmán, member of the military junta in 1973–78, who had escaped charges of human rights abuses under a later amnesty. However, the discovery of mass graves of former political prisoners at Pisagua (5 June), where the dry conditions of the Atacama desert had preserved them, and subsequently at Chihuio (near Valdivia), led to demands for the resignation of Pinochet from his post as Army Chief of Staff. These were suppressed by force and rebuffed by a military communique justifying the deaths as an 'act of war'. The General boycotted the state funeral on 4 September of the remains of the late President Salvador Allende, which had lain in an anonymous grave in Viña del Mar since his suicide (confirmed by examination of the body) during the 1973 coup (see AR 1973, p. 96). The President, who had supported the coup, was jeered by demonstrators, but said that he had come to give 'testimony to the truth'.

There were right-wing demonstrations on 11 September, as supporters of Pinochet celebrated the anniversary of the coup, but on the same day José Dionisio Suárez y Esquivel, a Cuban exile living in the United States, admitted in Washington that he had participated in the murder of Orlando Letelier on 21 September 1976 (see AR 1976, p. 83), for which he had been indicted together with two senior officers of the Chilean secret police who remained at large in Chile. Meanwhile, in face of corruption allegations, the possibility of General Pinochet's early resignation seemed increasingly likely after a military 'alert' ordered by him on the night of 19 December received only lukewarm support from the army.

COLOMBIA

CAPITAL: Bogotá   AREA: 1,141,750 sq km   POPULATION: 31,700,000 ('88)
OFFICIAL LANGUAGE: Spanish   POLITICAL SYSTEM: presidential democracy
HEAD OF STATE AND GOVERNMENT: President César Gaviria Trujillo (since Aug '90)
RULING PARTY: Liberal Party (PL) heading coalition with Social Conservatives (PSC) and former M–19 guerillas
PRINCIPAL MINISTERS: Luis Fernando Jaramillo (PL/foreign affairs), Julio César Sanchez (PL/interior), Gen.Oscar Botero Restrepo (ind./defence), Rudolf Hommes Rodriguez (PL/finance), Ernesto Samper Pizano (PL/economic development), Jaime Giraldo Angel (PSC/justice)
INTERNATIONAL ALIGNMENT: NAM, OAS
CURRENCY: peso (end–'90 £1=Col$1,026.98, US$1=Col$532.11)
GNP PER CAPITA: US$1,180 ('88)
MAIN EXPORT EARNERS: coffee, oil and oil derivatives

TWO US warships, sent in January by President Bush to Colombian waters without the consent of the Colombian government, were withdrawn two days after their arrival. Meanwhile, despite the kidnapping by agents of the drug syndicates of relatives of key members of government, including the son of the President's chief of staff, military and police action continued. By the end of January the *'Extraditables'* (see AR 1989, p. 71) admitted defeat and released their hostages. Subsequently, President Virgilio Barco, who was hailed with 'profound admiration' by President Bush at a summit meeting on 15 February at Cartagena with the leaders of Peru and Bolivia, laid down his terms. 'It is very clear', he said, 'the drug traffickers have to end their illegal trade, surrender everything and submit themselves to the courts. Colombian law is not negotiable.' On 11 August the acting leader of the Medellín cartel, Gustavo de Jesús Gaviria Rivero (43), cousin of its acknowledged leader, Pablo Escobar Gaviria, was killed by security forces in a gun battle at Medellín.

Meanwhile, on 11 March congressional and municipal elections gave a decisive majority in the new Congress to the Liberals, who won 72 seats in the Senate to 41 for the Conservatives and one to the left-wing Patriotic Union (UP), obtained a substantial majority in the Chamber and regained the control of Bogotá and Medellín which they had lost in 1986. The sole UP senator, Bernardo Jaramillo Ossa, was assassinated at El Dorado airport, Bogotá, on 22 March by a 16-year-old hired assassin. He was the 68th member of the UP to have been killed since 1 January. Despite this, the left-wing April 19 guerrilla movement (M-19) signed a peace treaty with the government on 9 March, formally completing the peace process begun in January 1989, and participated for the first time in the elections. The 39-year-old M-19 leader and presidential candidate of a new left-wing Democratic Convergence alliance, Carlos Pizarro León Gómez, was also shot dead by a contract killer while on board a commercial flight from the capital to Barranquilla on 26 April, and in the two weeks before the presidential election on 27 May some 37 died and 324 were wounded in incidents of violence.

In a low turnout (45.85 per cent), the 43-year-old former Minister of Finance and Interior, César Gaviria Trujillo, who had become the front-runner for the nomination after the assassination of Luis Carlos Galán Sarmineto in August 1989, was the clear winner with 47.4 per cent of the votes cast, to 23.8 per cent for Alvaro Gómez of the National Salvation Movement (a splinter-group of the Conservatives), 12.6 per cent for Antonio Navarro Wolff of Democratic Convergence and only 12.2 per cent for the Social Conservative (PSC) candidate, Rodrigo Lloreda, with a scattering to eight other minor candidates.

Sr Gaviria, who alone among the candidates had stated his implacable opposition to the drug cartels, was sworn in amongst unparalleled security measures on 7 August. He had in effect created a cabinet of national unity, with seven members from his own Liberal Party, four from the PSC and one from M-19, namely its new leader, Antonio Navarro Wolff, who was given the health portfolio. However, a proposition to establish a Constituent Assembly to reform the constitution of 1886 had also achieved overwhelming support, and at elections for the Assembly held on 9 December in a calm atmosphere M-19 members or sympathisers emerged as the largest grouping, though well short of a majority over the 'dinosaurs' of the two traditional parties.

ECUADOR

CAPITAL: Quito AREA: 270,500 sq km POPULATION: 10,100,000 ('88)
OFFICIAL LANGUAGE: Spanish POLITICAL SYSTEM: presidential democracy
HEAD OF STATE AND GOVERNMENT: President Rodrigo Borja Cevallos (since Aug '88)
RULING PARTIES: Democratic Left allied with Christian Democrats
PRINCIPAL MINISTERS: Luis Parodi (Vice-President), Diego Cordovez (foreign affairs), Jorge Gallardo (finance), César Verduga (interior), Jacinto Jouvin (industry & trade), Gen. (rtd.) Jorge Félix (defence), Diego Tamariz (energy and mines)
INTERNATIONAL ALIGNMENT: NAM, OAS
CURRENCY: sucre (end–'90 £1=S/.1,710.15, US$1=S/.891.27)
GNP PER CAPITA: US$1,120 ('88)
MAIN EXPORT EARNERS: oil and oil derivatives, coffee, bananas

ON 20 January the Supreme Court ordered the arrest of former President León Febres Cordero Rivadeneira. Between 1984 and 1988 he had attracted attention as one of the most enthusiastic exponents of free market economics in the region, but his party's defeat in 1988 had been total (see AR 1988, p. 79) and he was now charged with embezzling public funds. Inflation at the end of 1989 had been brought down to an annual rate of just over 54 per cent, and on 18 January President Rodrigo Borja Cevallos announced that in line with the Brady Plan his government would seek to negotiate a 70 per cent reduction on payments of the principal of the country's US$11,100 million foreign debt.

In elections for 60 of the 72 seats in the unicameral National Congress held on 17 June, the main right-wing opposition party made significant gains, winning 17 seats compared with only 11 for the ruling Democratic Left (ID) and 3 for the Christian democratic People's Democracy (DP), which had suspended its alliance with the government in November 1989. The Ecuadorean Roldosista Party (PRE) won 9 seats, the Socialist Party (PSE) 7, the centre-left Concentration of Popular Forces (CFP) and the traditional Liberal Radical Party (PLR) 3 each and the Conservative Party (PCE) 2, four other parties getting one seat each. Bitter struggles with the government followed, and on 18 October an emergency session of Congress removed its president, Averroes Bucaram Ortiz, after the impeachment of two cabinet officers.

PARAGUAY

CAPITAL: Asunción   AREA: 406,752 sq km   POPULATION: 4,000,000 ('88)
OFFICIAL LANGUAGE: Spanish   POLITICAL SYSTEM: republic, under quasi-military rule
HEAD OF STATE AND GOVERNMENT: President (Gen.) Andres Rodríguez (since Feb '89)
RULING PARTY: Colorado Party
PRINCIPAL MINISTERS: Alexis Frutos Vaesken (foreign affairs), Enzo Debernardi (finance), Antonio Zuccolillo Moscarda (industry & trade), Gen. Orlando Machuca Vargas (interior), Hugo Estigarribia Elizache (justice & labour), Gen. Angel Juan Souto Hernandez (defence)
INTERNATIONAL ALIGNMENT: OAS
CURRENCY: guaraní (end–'90 £1=G2,423.40, US$1=G1,255.65)
GNP PER CAPITA: US$1,180 ('88)
MAIN EXPORT EARNERS: cotton, soyabeans, meat

IN March it was reported that the target of 6 per cent growth in 1989 had been achieved and the public sector deficit had been reduced to zero by sharp spending cuts and an increase in tax revenues. Inflation to the end of November 1989 had been 28 per cent. At the inauguration of President Lacalle of Uruguay on 1 March President Andrés Rodríguez of Paraguay joined the Presidents of Argentina, Bolivia, Brazil and Uruguay in signing the Montevideo Declaration reaffirming the right of free passage on the Rivers Paraná and Paraguay. Subsequently, agreement was reached with Colombia on exchange of information concerning drug trafficking. When the Foreign Minister, Luis Maria Argaña, publicly contradicted the stated policy of holding free elections in 1993 by saying that the ruling Colorado Party would never surrender power, he was dismissed in late July and an extensive cabinet reshuffle followed. Gustavo Adolfo Stroessner, son of the former President and once regarded as his political heir, was arrested in Brazil on 9 August and held pending extradition to Asunción to answer charges of corruption already faced by his father.

PERU

CAPITAL: Lima AREA: 1,285,000 sq km POPULATION: 20,700,000 ('88)
OFFICIAL LANGUAGES: Spanish, Quechua and Aymará POLITICAL SYSTEM: presidential democracy
HEAD OF STATE AND GOVERNMENT: President Alberto Keinya Fujimori (since July '90)
RULING PARTY: Change 90 heading national unity coalition
PRINCIPAL MINISTERS: Maximo San Roman Caceres (1st Vice-President), Carlos Garcia Garcia (2nd Vice-President), Juan Carlos Hurtado Miller (Prime minister/economy & finance), Luis Marchand Stens (foreign affairs), Gen. Jorge Torres Aciego (defence), Gen. Adolfo Alvarado Fournier (interior), Guido Pennano (industry), Augusto Antoniolli Vásquez (justice)
INTERNATIONAL ALIGNMENT: NAM, OAS
CURRENCY: inti (end–'90 £1=I/.990,765, US$=I/.513,350)
GNP PER CAPITA: US$1,300 ('88)
MAIN EXPORT EARNERS: copper, petroleum products

THE year began violently when General Enrique López Albújar, former Army Chief of Staff and Defence Minister, was shot dead while alone and unarmed in Lima on 9 January. According to a Senate committee report, 3,198 people had died violently as a result of insurgent and death-squad activity in 1989, compared with 1,986 in 1988, making a total of some 15,800 since 1980. On 7 February a police officer shot and wounded Henry Pease, the United Left (IU) candidate.

In the first round of the presidential elections, held on 8 April despite 'armed strikes' by Sendero Luminoso (SL), the celebrated novelist Mario Vargas Llosa (54), candidate of the right-wing Democratic Front (Fredemo), led eight other candidates with 27.61 per cent of the ballot. He therefore went into a second round with the runner-up (on 24.62 per cent), the 52-year-old former rector of the Agrarian University in Lima, Alberto Keinya Fujimori, whose 'Change 90' movement promised a new face and 'honesty, hard work and technology'. With the President debarred from succeeding himself, the candidate of his ruling Aprista Party came third with 19.17 per cent, and Sr Pease fourth with 6.97 per cent; both the Apristas and the IU lost heavily compared with 1985.

Leaflets circulated on SL's tenth anniversary (17 May) in Ayacucho claimed that the movement had temporarily renounced armed struggle, but 'armed strikes' were resumed in the highlands for the second round, in which voters, apparently alienated by Sr Vargas Llosa's multi-million dollar media campaign and his high-profile middle class and business support, gave Sr Fujimori 56.53 per cent of the votes cast to his rival's 33.92 per cent. Sr Fujimori, who thus became Peru's first President of Japanese origin, was sworn in on 28 July in the presence of the Presidents of Argentina, Bolivia, Chile, Colombia and Venezuela. Lacking as he did a majority in either house of Congress, he formed a government of national unity of non-aligned and independent members, with military figures in the key positions of defence and interior, under a Prime Minister, Juan Carlos Hurtado Miller, from the conservative Popular Action Party (AP), and requested emergency legislative powers for 180 days to tackle the crisis of hyper-inflation compounded by an escalating guerrilla war.

Though the guerrilla attacks continued, shifting their focus from the Andes to the eastern Amazonian provinces, and the former Minister of Labour, Orestes Rodríguez Campos, was assassinated in Lima on 23 September, a shift of government policy was signalled when on 27 September the President rejected US military aid worth $35.9 million, stating that the package did not address the all-round needs of the coca-growing areas and would victimize the peasantry. In December his predecessor's nationalization of the banking system was reversed.

URUGUAY

CAPITAL: Montevideo AREA: 176,200 sq km POPULATION: 3,100,000 ('88)
OFFICIAL LANGUAGE: Spanish POLITICAL SYSTEM: presidential democracy
HEAD OF STATE AND GOVERNMENT: President Luis Alberto Lacalle Herrera (since March '90)
RULING PARTY: National (Blanco) Party heading coalition with Colorados
PRINCIPAL MINISTERS: Gonzala Aguirre Ramirez (Vice-President), Hector Gros Espiell (foreign relations), Juan Andres Ramirez (interior), Enrique Braga (economy & finance), Mariano Brito (defence), Augusto Montesdeoca (industry and energy)
INTERNATIONAL ALIGNMENT: OAS
CURRENCY: new peso (end–'90 £1=NUr$3,028.35, US$1=NUr$1,569.09)
GNP PER CAPITA: US$2,470 ('88)
MAIN EXPORT EARNERS: wool, meat

ON 1 March President-elect Luis Alberto Lacalle was sworn in as successor to Julio Maria Sanguinetti, following meetings with regional Presidents and a six-day official visit to the United States, during which he also met officials of the IMF and creditor banks. By including four members of the opposition Colorado Party in his cabinet he obtained cross-party agreement on a 'social truce' and support for an economic plan to combat inflation. On 2 July Enrique Braga, Economy and Finance Minister, reported that the IMF had agreed a standby credit of US$150 million over 18 months, and on 17 July creditor banks agreed terms for the government to buy-back $1,000 million or some 60 per cent of its medium-term debt.

VENEZUELA

CAPITAL: Caracas AREA: 912,000 sq km POPULATION: 18,800,000 ('88)
OFFICIAL LANGUAGE: Spanish POLITICAL SYSTEM: presidential democracy
HEAD OF STATE AND GOVERNMENT: President Carlos Andres Pérez (since Feb '89)
RULING PARTY: Democratic Action (since Jan '84)
PRINCIPAL MINISTERS: Reinaldo Figueredo Planchart (foreign affairs), Alejandro Izaguirre Angeli (interior), Roberto Pocaterra (finance), Gen. Filmo Lopéz Uzcategui (defence), Vladimir Moreno Guacaran (justice), Enrique Colmenares Finol (energy & mines)
INTERNATIONAL ALIGNMENT: OAS, NAM
CURRENCY: bolívar (end–'89 £1=Bs98.09, US$1=Bs50.82)
GNP PER CAPITA: US$3,250 ('88)
MAIN EXPORT EARNERS: oil, aluminium

THE former Minister of the Interior and Development, José Angel Cliberto, was stripped of parliamentary immunity on 27 January, but when the Supreme Court dismissed charges against several former ministers riots broke out in Caracas and other cities. On 20 March the Planning Minister, Miguel Rodríguez, signed in New York an agreement to restructure debts totalling US$20,500 million with an option for the government to buy in debt at a discount. The agreement, the fourth to be concluded under the Brady plan, was hailed as essential to the anti-inflationary strategy announced by President Carlos Andrés Pérez when he took office on 2 February 1989. Venezuela became a full member of GATT on 8 September.

In February Venezuela and Guyana agreed to the appointment of a special UN representative to mediate in their dispute over the Essequibo region.

CUBA

CAPITAL: Havana AREA: 115,000 sq km POPULATION: 10,500,000 ('88)
OFFICIAL LANGUAGE: Spanish POLITICAL SYSTEM: republic, one-party communist state
HEAD OF STATE AND GOVERNMENT: President Fidel Castro Ruz (since Jan '59)
RULING PARTY Cuban Communist Party
PRINCIPAL MINISTERS: Gen. Raúl Castro Ruz (1st Vice-President, defence), Isidoro Octavio Malmierca Peoli (foreign relations), Gen. Abelardo Colomé Ibarra (interior), Rodrigo García Leon (finance), José López Moreno (planning)
INTERNATIONAL ALIGNMENT: Comecon, NAM
CURRENCY: peso (end–'90 £1=Cub$1.54, US$1=Cub$0.79)
MAIN EXPORT EARNERS: sugar and sugar products

DEVELOPMENTS in Eastern Europe met with an early and decisive rejection by the Cuban regime of any move towards pluralist democracy—market economics having already been rejected by President Castro in his 'rectification campaign' begun in April 1986. In a public statement on 17 February the central committee of the Cuban Communist Party reaffirmed its commitment to marxism-leninism and to a one-party state, and called on its members, through the committees for the defence of the revolution (CDRs), of whom General Sixto Batista was named head, to 'perfect and vitalize' its organization. On 12 March eight human rights activists were detained, accused of creating conditions for a possible US invasion. Test transmissions were jammed of a new Florida-based TV station, 'TV-Martí', aimed at Cuba, while protests were lodged with a range of international bodies. In April the Soviet Deputy Prime Minister, Leonid Abalkin, visited the island to discuss a new trade and aid agreement. Despite growing irritation in Moscow at Cuba's wayward course, the agreement itself, signed on 29 December, guaranteed Cuba's oil supplies for 1991 but ended the oil surplus whose re-export had for many years been the country's main source of foreign exchange.

HAITI AND THE DOMINICAN REPUBLIC

Haiti
CAPITAL: Port-au-Prince   AREA: 27,750 sq km   POPULATION: 6,300,000 ('88)
OFFICIAL LANGUAGE: French   POLITICAL SYSTEM: presidential
HEAD OF STATE AND GOVERNMENT: President Jean-Bertrand Aristide (elected Dec '90)
CURRENCY: gourde (end–'90 £1=G9.66, US$1=G5.00)
GNP PER CAPITA: US$380 ('88)
MAIN EXPORT EARNERS: light manufactures, coffee, tourism

Dominican Republic
CAPITAL: Santo Domingo   AREA: 48,400 sq km   POPULATION: 6,900,000 ('88)
OFFICIAL LANGUAGE: Spanish   POLITICAL SYSTEM: presidential democracy
HEAD OF STATE AND GOVERNMENT: President Joaquín Balaguer (since Aug '86)
CURRENCY: peso (end–'90 £1=RD$21.63, US$1=RD$11.21)
GNP PER CAPITA: US$270 ('88)
MAIN EXPORT EARNERS: sugar, metals, tourism

AFTER the Nicaraguan elections US pressure mounted on General Prosper Avril of HAITI to resign and give way to a civilian government. On 11 April, after five days of demonstrations following the accidental shooting of a schoolgirl in Petit Goave, he handed over power to the 50-year-old Army Chief of Staff, General Herard Abraham, and was escorted to safety. While both rejoicing and violent protests against continued military rule took place, a provisional committee chaired by the radical Catholic priest, Fr Antoine Adrien, proclaimed a general strike. After General Avril had left the country on 12 April Congress accepted the nomination as provisional President of a member of the Supreme Court, 43-year-old Ertha Pascal-Trouillot, after the president of the Court had been disqualified and the vice-president had refused to serve. Mme Pascal-Trouillot soon found herself at odds with the Council of State and on 27 August installed a new cabinet without consulting it. In elections on 16 December violence was surprisingly muted and to general surprise another liberationist priest, 37-year-old

Fr Jean-Bertrand Aristide, took some 67 per cent of the poll against only 15 per cent for the former Finance Minister and World Bank official, Marc Bazin.

In the DOMINICAN REPUBLIC President Joaquín Balaguer, of the ruling Social Christian Party (PRSC), won re-election on 16 May with 35.7 per cent of the votes, against 34.4 per cent for his rival, Professor Juan Bosch of the opposition Dominican Liberation Party (PLD). Government-imposed price rises in August sparked off a two-day general strike which was put down by military force, while work continued on the construction of a massive lighthouse to commemorate Columbus's first voyage to the New World.

CENTRAL AMERICA AND PANAMA

Nicaragua
CAPITAL: Managua   AREA: 120,000 sq km   POPULATION: 3,600,000 ('88)
OFFICIAL LANGUAGE: Spanish   POLITICAL SYSTEM: presidential democracy
HEAD OF STATE AND GOVERNMENT: President Violeta Chamorro (since April '90)
RULING PARTY: National Opposition Union (UNO)
CURRENCY: córdoba (end–'90 £1=C$4,828,750, US$1=C$2,501,943)
GNP PER CAPITA: US$830 ('87)
MAIN EXPORT EARNERS: coffee, cotton, sugar, bananas

El Salvador
CAPITAL: San Salvador   AREA: 21,400 sq km   POPULATION: 5,000,000 ('88)
OFFICIAL LANGUAGE: Spanish   POLITICAL SYSTEM: presidential democracy
HEAD OF STATE AND GOVERNMENT: President Alfredo Cristiani (since June '89)
RULING PARTY: National Republican Alliance (Arena)
CURRENCY: colón (end–'90 £1=C12.26, US$1=C6.35)
GNP PER CAPITA: US$940 ('88)
MAIN EXPORT EARNERS: coffee, cotton, sugar

Guatemala
CAPITAL: Guatemala City   AREA: 109,000 sq km   POPULATION: 8,700,000 ('88)
OFFICIAL LANGUAGE: Spanish   POLITICAL SYSTEM: presidential democracy
HEAD OF STATE AND GOVERNMENT: President Vinicio Cerezo Arévalo (since Jan '86)
RULING PARTY: Christian Democratic Party
CURRENCY: quetzal (end–'90 £1=Q10.03, US$1=Q5.19)
GNP PER CAPITA: US$900 ('88)
MAIN EXPORT EARNERS: coffee, sugar, cotton, petroleum, cardamom, bananas

Honduras
CAPITAL: Tegucigalpa   AREA: 112,000 sq km   POPULATION: 4,800,000 ('88)
OFFICIAL LANGUAGE: Spanish   POLITICAL SYSTEM: presidential democracy
HEAD OF STATE AND GOVERNMENT: President Rafael Leonardo Callejas (since Jan '90)
RULING PARTY: National Party (PN)
CURRENCY: lempira (end–'90 £1=L10.14, US$1=L5.25)
GNP PER CAPITA: US$860 ('88)
MAIN EXPORT EARNERS: bananas, coffee, tourism

Costa Rica
CAPITAL: San José   AREA: 51,000 sq km   POPULATION: 2,700,000 ('88)
OFFICIAL LANGUAGE: Spanish   POLITICAL SYSTEM: presidential democracy
HEAD OF STATE AND GOVERNMENT: President Rafael Angel Calderón Fournier (since May '90)
RULING PARTY: Social Christian Unity Party (PUSC)
CURRENCY: colón (end–'90 £1=C200.01, US$1=C103.63)
GNP PER CAPITA: US$1,690 ('88)
MAIN EXPORT EARNERS: coffee, bananas, tourism

Panama
CAPITAL: Panama City   AREA: 77,000 sq km   POPULATION: 2,300,000 ('88)
OFFICIAL LANGUAGE: Spanish   POLITICAL SYSTEM: presidential
HEAD OF STATE AND GOVERNMENT: President Guillermo Endara (since Dec '89)
RULING PARTY: Authentic Liberal Party (within Democratic Alliance)
CURRENCY: balboa (end–'90 £1=B1.93, US$1=B1.00)
GNP PER CAPITA: US$2,120 ('88)
MAIN EXPORT EARNERS: bananas, prawns, sugar, canal dues

A summit meeting of the Presidents of the five Central American republics, with President Guillermo Endara of Panama observing, took place at Antigua, Guatemala, from 15 to 17 June. At its close the Antigua Declaration was signed, reaffirming the commitment of the signatories to the 1987 Esquipulas II agreement initiated by President Oscar Arias Sánchez of Costa Rica, and affirming the need to achieve regional stability through an economic action plan looking to the 'efficient and dynamic insertion of the region into the world market'.

After a long campaign, marked by large rallies in favour of both sides, on 25 February the voters of NICARAGUA rejected President Daniel Ortega Saavedra and the ruling left-wing Sandinista National Liberation Front (FSLN). Instead, they elected Violeta Barrios de Chamorro, presidential candidate of the National Opposition Union (UNO), a loose coalition of 14 small parties (including Communists), which had received a substantial cash donation from the United States. Sra Chamorro (60), widow of the newspaper publisher Pedro Joaquín Chamorro, whose murder in 1978 had touched off the Sandinista revolution (see AR 1978, p. 82), and member of the first post-revolutionary provisional government (from which she had resigned in 1980—see AR 1980, p. 87), polled some 52 per cent of the vote to 42 per cent for Sr Ortega, while UNO secured 52 seats in the 90-member National Assembly. Her victory, virtually the reverse of the result predicted by public opinion polls, was attributed to war weariness and the endemic economic crisis compounded by the effects of ten years of terrorism and economic sanctions by the government of the United States.

Doubts remained, however, over the future of the estimated 10,000 US-sponsored 'Contra' guerrillas which had fought against the Sandinistas since 1981, given the strong resistance among the 60,000-strong Sandinista Popular Army (EPS) to any deal that included them. Although on 9 March the government freed under amnesty 1,151 Contras and 39 of Somoza's former National Guards, a definitive ceasefire was only reached (on 19 April) through the mediation of Cardinal Miguel Obando y Bravo, Archbishop of Managua. When Sra Chamorro was sworn in on 25 April, she retained Commandante Humberto Ortega Saavedra as interim chief of the armed forces on condition that he renounced political activity. On 25 May the US Congress finally approved US$300 million in aid to Nicaragua, a small fraction of the cost of the civil war over the previous ten years. The final act in the demobilization of the Contras took place at San Pedro de Lóbago on 27 June, when 19,197 had already surrendered under UN-supervised procedures.

Meanwhile, steps were taken to revoke the land reforms of the Sandinista period, although an attempt on 10 May to revoke the rights of public service workers backfired: failure to honour the terms of the settlement led to a massive strike by the National Workers' Front (FNT). While the Sandinista army and police remained loyal and many former Sandinistas were already competing in the private sector, the concession by the government of most of the workers' key demands on 12 July led to a split in the ruling coalition following strenuous objections from the right led by the Vice-President, Virgilio Godoy. However, despite his tacit support for protests, which turned violent, Sandinista support for an agreed economic policy and for the President's son-in-law, Raúl Lacayo, as governor of the Central Bank, defused the confrontation. The army was able to clear the barricades without incident, and by October inflation had fallen from its peak of 115 per cent in May to 30 per cent.

In a broadcast on 7 January President Alfredo Cristiani of EL SALVADOR confirmed that members of the armed forces had been involved in the murders of the six Jesuits on 16 November 1989. On 19 January Colonel Guillermo Benavides, three other officers and five soldiers were formally charged, though key evidence against them was later found to be 'missing'. On 12 January the deputy secretary of the National Revolutionary Movement (MNR), Héctor Oqueli Colindres, spokesperson in Mexico for the Farabundo Martí National Liberation Front (FMLN), was kidnapped in Guatemala and later found murdered. Following preliminary sessions at Geneva on 4 April, however, agreement was at last reached in principle between the government and representatives of the FMLN at Caracas on the future constitutional structure of the country and the role of the army in it, despite a FMLN offensive that left some 48 dead or wounded. However, further talks on 21–6 July, 17–22 August, 13–18 September and the end of October were unsuccessful, and in mid-November, in their biggest military operation for a year, FMLN guerrillas attacked military installations across half the country. In a week of fighting, which left 90 dead and some 300 wounded, they also shot down an air force jet with a Soviet-made SAM-7 ground-to-air missile.

In GUATEMALA the US ambassador, Thomas Stroock, was recalled for consultation on 5 March in protest at the upsurge in political assassinations attributed to right-wing elements in the army. Not until September did President Vinicio Cerezo Arévalo admit that there was a 'possibility' that security forces had been involved in the murder of a US citizen, Michael Devine, on 8 June; despite the murder of Mirna Mack, a well-known anthropologist, a further $50 million in US aid was approved. Meanwhile, with UN mediation, an agreement had been signed on 1 June at San Lorenzo del Escorial between the Guatemalan National Revolutionary Unity (URNG), the government-sponsored National Reconciliation Commission, and representatives of opposition parties, though further talks in September failed to establish any greater agreement. Inevitably, violence continued in the run-up to the elections on 11 November in which there were 12 presidential candidates. With the candidate of the ruling Christian Democrats, Alfonso Cabrera, hospitalized with a ruptured pancreas, Jorge Carpio of the National Centre Union won the first round. A base commander, whose troops fired into a crowd of about 1,500 people in Santiago de Atitlán on 2 December, killing 11 and wounding 19, was relieved of his duties.

On 27 January Rafael Leonardo Callejas was sworn in at the National Stadium as President of HONDURAS in the country's first peaceful transfer of power to an opposition party since 1933. The new government's plans, announced in March, to slash state expenditure by 42 per cent soon ran into waves of protest. Strikes paralysed state services from May onwards and spread to banana growers and oil workers in June.

On 4 February in presidential elections in COSTA RICA, Carlos Manuel Castillo, candidate of the ruling National Liberation Party (PLN), obtained only 47.3 per cent of the votes cast and was defeated by Rafael Angel Calderón Fournier of the opposition Social Christian Unity Party (PUSC), who got 51.4 per cent. In the Legislative Assembly the PUSC won 29 of the 57 seats against 25 for the PLN and 3 for minor parties. A lawyer and former Foreign Minister, the 40-year-old Sr Calderón took office on 8 May for four years, two days after his predecessor's government, under the Brady Plan, had signed an agreement to reduce US$1,500 million of the country's commercial debt by up to 64 per cent. The new government introduced an austerity plan and signed a fresh letter of intent with the IMF on 7 June, though strikes continued.

On 3 January the former military leader of PANAMA, General Noriega, left his refuge in the papal nunciature and surrendered to US occupation forces (see AR 1989, pp. 58–9, 79). He was immediately sent to the United States to face trial on drugs charges. As order returned to the streets, on 13 February the White House announced that the last intervention forces had left Panama. However, by the beginning of March only a tiny fraction of the promised $1,000 million of US aid to rebuild the shattered country and its economy had materialized and President Endara, who on 23 January confirmed that his government intended to abolish the defence forces, held a 13-day hunger-strike in March to dramatize his country's needs. A possible coup was easily suppressed on 16 August and its alleged leader, Eduardo Herrera Hassan, was arrested. The government's national strategy of 'development and economic modernization' received the backing of a $244 million aid package from the US, but the plan, which called for extensive privatization, was opposed by the opposition Christian Democrats (PDC), who held a majority in the Legislative Assembly, and aid was both slow and inadequate. At the year's end more than 2,000 homeless refugees were still living in aircraft hangars.

MEXICO

CAPITAL: Mexico City AREA: 1,958,000 sq km POPULATION: 83,700,000 ('88)
OFFICIAL LANGUAGE: Spanish POLITICAL SYSTEM: federal presidential democracy
HEAD OF STATE AND GOVERNMENT: President Carlos Salinas de Gortari (since Dec '88)
RULING PARTY: Party of the Institutionalized Revolution (since 1929)
PRINCIPAL MINISTERS: Fernando Solana Morales (foreign affairs), Pedro Aspe Armella (finance), Fernando Gutiérrez Barrios (government/interior), Gen. Antonio Riviello Bazán (defence), Ernesto Cedillo Ponce de Leon (planning & federal budget), Fernando Hiriart Balderrama (energy & mines)
INTERNATIONAL ALIGNMENT: OAS
CURRENCY: peso (end–'90 £1=Mex$5,697.82, US$1=Mex$2,952.24)
GNP PER CAPITA: US$1,760 ('88)
MAIN EXPORT EARNERS: oil, motor machinery, coffee, tourism

THE announcement in February that President Carlos Salinas de Gortari was to send a personal envoy to the Vatican to end more than a century of governmental hostility towards the Catholic Church caused strong anti-clerical reaction within the ruling Party of the Institutionalized Revolution (PRI) after papal authorities demanded changes to the 1917 constitution and restoration of full diplomatic relations (broken off in 1865) in advance of the papal visit in May. A debt reduction agreement signed by the government and representatives of creditor banks on 4 February was estimated by the Finance Minister, Pedro Aspe Armella, to save the country some $4,710 million in debt service over four years. On 26 March the President paid an official visit to the United Kingdom on the first leg of a five-nation tour designed to strengthen ties between Mexico and the European Community. On 2 May he announced the sale of the government's majority shareholding in the 19 banks taken over by President Gustavo López Portillo in 1982 (see AR 1982, pp. 95–6). Following the Iraqi invasion of Kuwait on 2 August, he committed Mexico to 'do everything possible . . . to produce all the oil it can' to help keep prices down. The centre-piece of his economic strategy, a free trade agreement with the United States, featured prominently on the agenda of a summit meeting with President Bush at Monterrey on 26–27 November. Questions in the US Congress about Mexico's human rights record and its democratic credentials, which had held up consideration of the free trade agreement, had been raised when protests continued from the newly-founded opposition Party of the Democratic Revolution (PRD) at alleged electoral fraud. Militant supporters occupied town halls in Guerrero in March and were dispersed by force. Three police and four civilians were killed and hundreds wounded, although in April the town halls of Michoacán were cleared without casualties. To safeguard the domination of the PRI, Congress on 15 June enacted a new electoral law guaranteeing a winning party an overall majority of seats if it secured more than 35 per cent of the votes cast and banning the electoral alliances which had aided the PRD in 1988. But there were some signs of change. The 14th national assembly of the PRI enacted substantial reforms to its statutes (3 September), which, though mostly cosmetic, included a formal process of nomination for presidential candidates, who had for many years been nominated by their predecessors (*tapadismo*). In October the President transferred Javier Coello Trejo, head of the anti-narcotics programme, to another post after accusations of corruption and torture.

Chapter 4

THE CARIBBEAN

JAMAICA—GUYANA—TRINIDAD & TOBAGO—BARBADOS—BELIZE—
GRENADA—THE BAHAMAS—WINDWARD & LEEWARD ISLANDS—
SURINAME—BRITISH DEPENDENCIES—NETHERLANDS ANTILLES
AND ARUBA

JAMAICA

CAPITAL: Kingston   AREA: 11,000 sq km   POPULATION: 2,400,000 ('88)
OFFICIAL LANGUAGE: English   POLITICAL SYSTEM: parliamentary democracy
HEAD OF STATE: Queen Elizabeth II
GOVERNOR-GENERAL: Sir Florizel Glasspole
RULING PARTY: People's National Party (PNP)
HEAD OF GOVERNMENT: Michael Manley, Prime Minister (since Feb '89)
PRINCIPAL MINISTERS: Percival Patterson (deputy premier, finance and planning), David Coore (foreign affairs), Carl Rattray (justice), K.D. Knight (national security)
INTERNATIONAL ALIGNMENT: NAM, ACP/EEC, OAS, Caricom, Cwth.
CURRENCY: Jamaica dollar (end-'90 £1=J$14.86, US$1=J$7.70)
GNP PER CAPITA: US$1,070 ('88)
MAIN EXPORT EARNERS: bauxite/alumina, bananas, sugar, tourism

Both the ruling People's National Party (PNP) and the opposition Jamaica Labour Party (JLP) were confronted with leadership problems In 1990. Prime Minister Michael Manley was deputized for by Percival Patterson between May and September as a result of his ill-health. Edward Seaga faced serious challenges to his leadership of the JLP amid accusations from a 'gang of five' senior party members that he was intolerant of dissent to his own personal visions. This tension surfaced most clearly at the annual JLP conference in June, and at year's end Mr Seaga's leadership remained in question.

The PNP government successfully negotiated a new 15-month standby agreement with the International Monetary Fund (IMF), announced on 30 January. Its principal terms were to cut the public-sector deficit from 7.7 to 4.4 per cent of GDP, the reduction of the current-account deficit on the balance of payments from 8.3 to 3.5 per cent of GDP, and an increase in foreign exchange reserves of US$230 million. The municipal elections of 6 March, in which the PNP promised to restore local powers and functions removed under the Seaga administrations, appeared to vindicate PNP policies in the mind of the electorate. The results showed that 12 of the 13 districts remained in PNP hands.

Meanwhile the IMF agreement had opened the way for the rescheduling of external debt through the Paris Club, such that the $140 million due between December 1989 and May 1991 was to be repaid over the next five years. The debt-service ratio stood at 39 per cent of the value of exports, and despite an envisaged annual GDP growth of 3 per cent and the relative buoyancy of the bauxite industry (alumina accounting for 63 per cent of the value of exports), sugar and banana exports, demands on the economy to fulfil government obligations were expected to become severe. Indeed, in March and again in June, Jamaica had already failed to meet the IMF's conditionality tests, which stalled further drawdowns. In the longer term, the government's five-year plan was contingent upon external funding constituting some 42 per cent of the total new investment required.

GUYANA

CAPITAL: Georgetown   AREA: 215,000 sq km   POPULATION: 799,000 ('88)
OFFICIAL LANGUAGE: English   POLITICAL SYSTEM: cooperative presidential democracy
HEAD OF STATE AND GOVERNMENT: President Desmond Hoyte (since Aug '85)
RULING PARTY: People's National Congress (PNC)
PRINCIPAL MINISTERS: Hamilton Green (First Vice-President and prime minister),
   Viola Burnham (Vice-President, deputy premier, culture and social development),
   Carl Greenidge (finance), Keith Massiah (justice)
INTERNATIONAL ALIGNMENT: NAM, ACP/EEC, Caricom, Cwth.
CURRENCY: Guyana dollar (end-'90 £1=G$44.19, US$1=29.56)
GNP PER CAPITA: US$420 ('88)
MAIN EXPORT EARNERS: bauxite, sugar, rice

A Commonwealth advisory group reported at the beginning of the year that Guyana was now ranked below Haiti as the poorest country in the Western hemisphere. During 1989 the first year of the government's economic recovery programme (ERP) had failed to achieve any substantial upturn in the economy, and failures in meeting production targets in bauxite, sugar, diamonds and gold were repeated in 1990. A real fall in GNP of 4 per cent in 1989 continued through 1990, in part provoking an emigration rate of 1,000 people per month. Nevertheless, there were several qualitative changes which held some promise for future substantive economic growth.

Principal amongst these changes was the conclusion of a standby agreement and an enhanced structural adjustment programme with the IMF on 15 June. The two years of frustrated negotiations were successfully concluded only as a result of a prior multilateral facility being provided (via the Bank for International Settlements and a 'support group of countries') to settle arrears of US$229 million owed to the IMF, the World Bank and the Caribbean Development Bank. Arrears on debt repayment had stood at $1,038 million in 1988 out of a total debt of $1,764 million and US support for the ERP for arrears coverage at the beginning of the year did not augur well; unless arrears were cleared, the IMF would not authorize the disbursement of new funds. The terms of the IMF agreement included an immediate currency devaluation of 26.7 per cent from G$33 to G$45 per US dollar (the parallel rate at the officially licenced *cambios* varied between G$54.50 in March to G$100 in October); cuts in public expenditure; elimination of the sugar subsidy; and the removal of selected tax exemptions.

Easing liquidity bottle-necks through new money complemented new initiatives with foreign capital in the modernization and expansion of a variety of economic sectors, including sugar (with Booker Tate), bauxite (with Alcan and Reynolds), telecommunications (with Atlantic Tele-Network, which took an 80 per cent stake in the Guyana Telecommunication Corporation), and, perhaps of lasting significance, the signing of a protocol to link Guyana to the Venezuelan national grid. Notwithstanding such developments, the infrastructural decay (see AR 1989, p. 84) continued with many power cuts, telephone failures and collapsing sea defences. For example, inadequate flood control and the breaching of sea defences resulted in the destruction of some 30,000 of 80,000 acres of mature rice in 1990.

Economic developments were paralleled by the launch of a new political movement on 18 January dedicated to electoral and constitutional reform and greater political pluralism. The Guyanese Action for Reform and Democracy (GUARD) held large rallies throughout the year, adding to considerable pressure from existing opposition formations for the government to create an independent electoral commission and an accurate and updated electoral register in preparation for the general elections constitutionally due by 31 March 1991. Indications of a readiness by the ruling People's National Congress (PNC) to accept a more plural and open political process came with President Desmond Hoyte's first official meeting with the opposition Working People's Alliance (WPA) and with Cheddi Jagan's People's Progressive Party (PPP). However, such initial steps had yet to be translated into concrete political changes by year's end.

TRINIDAD & TOBAGO

CAPITAL: Port of Spain   AREA: 5,128 sq km   POPULATION: 1,200,000 ('88)
OFFICIAL LANGUAGE: English   POLITICAL SYSTEM: parliamentary republic
HEAD OF STATE: President Noor Mohammed Hassanali (since March '87)
RULING PARTY: National Alliance for Reconstruction (NAR)
HEAD OF GOVERNMENT: Arthur Napoleon Raymond Robinson, Prime Minister (since Dec '86)
PRINCIPAL MINISTERS: Sahadeo Basdeo (external affairs and international trade), Selby Wilson (finance), Selwyn Richardson (justice and national security), Bhoe Tewarie (industry, enterprise and tourism), Herbert Atwell (energy)
INTERNATIONAL ALIGNMENT: NAM, ACP/EEC, OAS, Caricom, Cwth.
CURRENCY: Trinidad and Tobago dollar (end-'90 £1=TT$8.21, US$1=TT$4.25)
GNP PER CAPITA: US$3,350 ('88)
MAIN EXPORT EARNERS: oil, chemicals, tourism

BETWEEN 27 July and 1 August members of the Islamic fundamentalist Jamaat al Muslimeen took hostage Prime Minister A.N.R. Robinson and eight of his ministers, and occupied both the parliament building and the television station. After skilful and careful negotiation all hostages were released and the insurrectionists surrendered to the armed forces. During the siege, in which a curfew was imposed across Trinidad, 23 people were killed and 500 injured (mainly in incidents relating to civil disorder and looting).

Despite the violent nature of the attempted coup the government was able to retain its authority and even benefit in the opinion polls from its survival. This was against a background of continuing pressures on the economy arising from government policy. Unemployment remained high at 22.5 per cent (41.4 per cent in the 15–19 age range) and inflation was at least 11 per cent. Despite moving from a negative GDP growth rate in 1988 and 1989 to a predicted positive 1 per cent increase in 1990, this was achieved through strict controls on public spending (including public sector pay) and the redundancies of large numbers of workers in state enterprises.

The introduction in the 1990 budget of a 15 per cent value added tax, basic rate tax cuts from 20 to 15 per cent and the reduction of company tax from 45 to 40 per cent continued the liberalization of the economy as encouraged by the IMF. A new agreement reached with the

IMF in April (to supersede one which ended in February) provided for a new standby facility of US$111 million for 11 months, $55 million in a compensatory finance facility, a World Bank loan of $44 million, and an Inter-American Development Bank loan of $850 million to develop new oil production and improve infrastructure. In addition, the government succeeded in rescheduling debt of $558 million over the next 11 years, while its financial and balance-of-payments position was improved as a result of a rise in oil prices caused by the Gulf crisis.

Nevertheless, the political opposition was growing stronger, with the United National Congress under Basdeo Panday formally taking over the role of official opposition from the People's National Movement in September. The year also saw the creation of a popular and broad-based Summit of People's Organizations, which protested against government policy, particularly in its management of the public sector and the liberalization of the economy. Elections were due at the latest by December 1991.

BARBADOS

CAPITAL: Bridgetown   AREA: 430 sq km   POPULATION: 254,000 ('88)
OFFICIAL LANGUAGE: English   POLITICAL SYSTEM: parliamentary democracy
HEAD OF STATE: Queen Elizabeth II
GOVERNOR-GENERAL: Dame Nita Barrow
RULING PARTY: Democratic Labour Party (DLP)
HEAD OF GOVERNMENT: Erskine Sandiford, Prime Minister (since June '87)
PRINCIPAL MINISTERS: Philip Greaves (deputy premier), Maurice King (foreign affairs, Attorney-General), Evelyn Greaves (trade, industry and commerce)
INTERNATIONAL ALIGNMENT: NAM, ACP/EEC, OAS, Cwth.
CURRENCY: dollar (end-'90 £1=BDS$3.88, US$1=BDS$2.01)
GNP PER CAPITA: US$6,010 ('88)
MAIN EXPORT EARNERS: sugar, tourism, light manufactures, chemicals

AMID accusations of 'government-inflicted economic crisis' from the opposition Barbados Labour Party (BLP) and National Democratic Party (NDP) and growing internal criticism from his own ruling Democratic Labour Party (DLP), Prime Minister Erskine Sandiford was unable to achieve further growth in the economy: annual GDP growth remained at 3.5 per cent both in 1988 and in 1989. Moreover, there were signs of serious shortcomings in important economic sectors. Thus, although the sugar industry was able to fulfil its domestic and European Community quotas, it failed to supply more than 59 per cent of the US quota, and in so doing lost some BD$9.7 million in revenue. (The 1989 sugar crop had been the lowest by volume since 1931.) In addition, tourist stopovers and resultant revenue declined by just short of 7 per cent on the previous year.

In view of declining revenues Mr Sandiford proposed a budget on 2 May designed to encourage agricultural diversification and the regeneration of the sugar industry. Current and capital expenditure was up over 1989 to BD$1,000 million and BD$243 million respectively, whilst revenue was projected to increase by slightly less than BD$100 million to BD$1,000 million. With inflation at 6.2 per cent, the government felt justified in easing credit restrictions in mid-June. On 6 June Dame Nita Barrow was appointed as the new Governor-General of Barbados.

BELIZE

CAPITAL: Belmopan   AREA: 23,000 sq km   POPULATION: 180,000 ('88)
OFFICIAL LANGUAGE: English   POLITICAL SYSTEM: parliamentary democracy
HEAD OF STATE: Queen Elizabeth II
GOVERNOR-GENERAL: Dame Elvira Gordon
RULING PARTY: People's United Party (PUP)
HEAD OF GOVERNMENT: George Price, Prime Minister (since Sept '89)
PRINCIPAL MINISTERS: Florencio Marin (deputy premier, industry and natural
   resources), Said Musa (foreign affairs, economic development and education),
   Glenn Godfrey (tourism, environment, Attorney-General)
INTERNATIONAL ALIGNMENT: NAM, ACP/EEC, Caricom, Cwth.
CURRENCY: dollar (end-'90 £1=BZ$3.86, US$1=BZ$2.00)
GNP PER CAPITA: US$1,500 ('88)
MAIN EXPORT EARNERS: sugar, citrus products, fish, tourism

THE governing People's United Party (PUP) under Prime Minister George Price ran into substantial difficulties and criticism over the introduction of the International Business Companies Act designed to ease the siting of offshore institutions in Belize. Because of the deficiencies exposed in similar projects in the Eastern Caribbean, it was manifest that Belize did not currently possess the supervisory and monitoring capacity to manage such a sector, particularly in view of the growth of the 'laundering' of drugs-related money. Thus the government had to face disapproval from domestic and international sources similar to that engendered by its 1989 Registration of Shipping Act, which sought to exploit the transfer of registration from Panama.

Such attempts to diversify the economic base of the country were reflected in the intentions of the March budget to achieve even greater GDP growth (currently at 8.3 per cent) by public investment in infrastructure, agricultural diversification, and the encouragement of domestic accumulation. As a result of the Gulf crisis and rising oil prices, greater effort was invested in the feasibility project for a hydroelectric generating scheme on the Mucal river which, it was estimated, could provide the country with 70 per cent of its electricity requirements.

GRENADA

CAPITAL: St. George's AREA: 344 sq km POPULATION: 94,000 ('88)
OFFICIAL LANGUAGE: English POLITICAL SYSTEM: parliamentary democracy
HEAD OF STATE: Queen Elizabeth II
GOVERNOR-GENERAL: Sir Paul Scoon
RULING PARTY: National Democratic Congress (NDC)
HEAD OF GOVERNMENT: Nicholas Braithwaite, Prime Minister (since March '90)
PRINCIPAL MINISTERS: George Brizan (finance, trade and industry), Francis Alexis (Attorney-General)
INTERNATIONAL ALIGNMENT: NAM, ACP/EEC, OAS, Caricom, Cwth.
CURRENCY: East Caribbean dollar (end-'90 £1=EC$5.22, US$1=EC$2.70)
GNP PER CAPITA: US$1,720 ('88)
MAIN EXPORT EARNERS: agricultural products, tourism

FOLLOWING the death of the Prime Minister Herbert Blaize on 19 December 1989 (see AR 1989, pp. 88, 555), his deputy, Ben Jones, became Prime Minister until the general election of 13 March, which was won by Nicholas Braithwaite's National Democratic Congress (NDC). Of the five parties which contested the election, only one presented distinctive policies, namely the Maurice Bishop Patriotic Movement (MBPM), but it failed to secure any seats. The distribution of seats after the election was NDC 7, Grenada United Labour Party (GULP) 4, New National Party (NNP) 2 and National Party (TNP) 2. However, the GULP leader, Sir Eric Gairey, failed to be elected, and following disagreements with him two GULP members of parliament went over to the NDC, thereby obviating the need for coalition government.

In view of the NDC's recent assumption of power, Mr Braithwaite's budget of 19 April was intended to provide a planning space for a more radical review of the economy. Such a review was made all the more necessary following a fire on 27 April which destroyed the Finance Ministry, the Treasury, the central post office and the inland revenue headquarters, amounting to the core of the government's administrative apparatus.

Appeal hearings in the Maurice Bishop murder case were finally completed on 19 September after more than two years. It thereby became the longest such case in Commonwealth history and certainly one of the most controversial. Verdicts had not been delivered by year's end.

THE BAHAMAS

CAPITAL: Nassau   AREA: 14,000 sq km   POPULATION: 244,000 ('88)
OFFICIAL LANGUAGE: English   POLITICAL SYSTEM: parliamentary democracy
HEAD OF STATE: Queen Elizabeth II
GOVERNOR-GENERAL: Sir Henry Taylor
RULING PARTY: Progressive Liberal Party (PLP)
HEAD OF GOVERNMENT: Sir Lynden O. Pindling, Prime Minister (since Jan '67)
PRINCIPAL MINISTERS: Sir Clement T. Maynard (deputy premier, foreign affairs), Paul L. Adderley (finance), Darrell Rolle (national security), Sean McWeeney (Attorney-General)
INTERNATIONAL ALIGNMENT: NAM, ACP/EEC, OAS, Cwth.
CURRENCY: dollar (end-'90 £1=B$1.93, US$1=B$1.00)
GNP PER CAPITA: US$10,700 ('88)
MAIN EXPORT EARNERS: tourism, petroleum products

THE year saw a continuation of government policies to deregulate the economy and finance new developments. As a reflection of this, the cabinet was expanded to 15 posts in September and Prime Minister Lynden Pindling assumed the key portfolio of tourism. Total tourist visitors had been up 7.6 per cent in 1989 over 1988, and further investment and marketing campaigns were being planned, particularly in view of the increasingly sharp competition in the Caribbean tourist industry. Furthermore, preparatory legislation was passed for the creation of a stock exchange to consolidate the country's position as a financial centre.

The financial predicament of the islands continued to worsen. By March the national debt had risen to US$799.7 million, an increase of $100 million on the previous year; moreover, the government deficit was $34.9 million over budget for the year 1989/90. In order to stimulate the economy the government borrowed $100 million for 'general development'—borrowing which was criticized by the opposition for the lack of precision in targeting the money. Charges of budgetary laxness were levelled at the government, not least because it had still failed to produce complete national accounts for 1988. However, the weakness of the official opposition meant that there was little threat to the rule of the Progressive Liberal Party, notwithstanding the resignation of the Agriculture Minister in March over allegations of corruption and nepotism.

WINDWARD AND LEEWARD ISLANDS

St Kitts & Nevis
CAPITAL: Basseterre AREA: 260 sq km POPULATION: 42,000 ('88)
OFFICIAL LANGUAGE: English POLITICAL SYSTEM: parliamentary democracy
HEAD OF STATE: Queen Elizabeth II
GOVERNOR-GENERAL: Clement Athelston Arrindell
RULING PARTY: People's Action Movement (PAM)
HEAD OF GOVERNMENT: Kennedy A. Simmonds, Prime Minister (since Feb '80)
CURRENCY: East Caribbean dollar (end-'90 £1=EC$5.22, US$1=EC$2.70)
GNP PER CAPITA: US$2,630 ('88)
MAIN EXPORT EARNERS: sugar, agricultural produce, tourism

Antigua & Barbuda
CAPITAL: St. John's AREA: 440 sq km POPULATION: 78,000 ('88)
OFFICIAL LANGUAGE: English POLITICAL SYSTEM: parliamentary democracy
HEAD OF STATE: Queen Elizabeth II
GOVERNOR-GENERAL: Sir Wilfred Ebenezer Jacobs
RULING PARTY: Antiguan Labour Party (ALP)
HEAD OF GOVERNMENT: C. Vere Bird Sr, Prime Minister (since Feb '76)
CURRENCY: East Caribbean dollar (end-'90 £1=EC$5.22, US$1=EC$2.70)
GNP PER CAPITA: US$3,690 ('88)
MAIN EXPORT EARNERS: tourism, miscellaneous manufactures

Dominica
CAPITAL: Roseau AREA: 750 sq km POPULATION: 82,000 ('88)
OFFICIAL LANGUAGE: English POLITICAL SYSTEM: parliamentary republic
HEAD OF STATE: President Sir Clarence Augustus Seignoret
RULING PARTY: Dominica Freedom Party (DFP)
HEAD OF GOVERNMENT: Mary Eugenia Charles, Prime Minister (since July '80)
CURRENCY: East Caribbean dollar (end-'90 £1=EC$5.22, US$1=EC$2.70)
GNP PER CAPITA: US$1,680 ('88)
MAIN EXPORT EARNERS: bananas, tourism

St Lucia
CAPITAL: Castries AREA: 616 sq km POPULATION: 145,000 ('88)
OFFICIAL LANGUAGE: English POLITICAL SYSTEM: parliamentary democracy
HEAD OF STATE: Queen Elizabeth II
GOVERNOR-GENERAL: Stanislaus A. James (acting)
RULING PARTY: United Workers' Party (UWP)
HEAD OF GOVERNMENT: John Compton, Prime Minister (since '64)
CURRENCY: East Caribbean dollar (end-'90 £1=EC$5.22, US$1=EC$2.70)
GNP PER CAPITA: US$1,540 ('88)
MAIN EXPORT EARNERS: agricultural products, tourism

St Vincent & the Grenadines
CAPITAL: Kingstown AREA: 390 sq km POPULATION: 112,000 ('88)
OFFICIAL LANGUAGE: English POLITICAL SYSTEM: parliamentary democracy
HEAD OF STATE: Queen Elizabeth II
GOVERNOR-GENERAL: David Jack
RULING PARTY: New Democratic Party (NDP)
HEAD OF GOVERNMENT: James F. Mitchell, Prime Minister (since '72)
CURRENCY: East Caribbean dollar (end-'90 £1=EC$5.22, US$1=EC$2.70)
GNP PER CAPITA: US$1,200 ('88)
MAIN EXPORT EARNERS: bananas, tourism, agricultural produce

THE effects of Hurricane Hugo (see AR 1989, p. 90) continued to undermine the Eastern Caribbean economies, including that of ST KITTS & NEVIS, where, for example, the earning of vital foreign exchange from banana exports was expected to decline as production fell from 24,777 tons in 1989 to a projected 18,000 in 1990. New financial support for the banana industry was being negotiated with multilateral agencies.

ANTIGUA & BARBUDA was rocked by an arms scandal beginning with a Colombian government allegation that Israeli-supplied arms had reached the Medellín cartel via the islands with the knowledge of either the Prime Minister, Vere Bird Sr, or his son, the Minister of Communications and Works, Vere Bird Jr. The Deputy Prime Minister, Lester Bird (another son of the Prime Minister), ordered a judicial inquiry into the affair (under the authority of Louis Blom-Cooper QC), whilst Vere Bird Jr was relieved of his duties following the furnishing of incriminating letters that had been allegedly signed by him permitting the arms shipment. The inquiry reported in November and recommended the removal of Vere Bird Jr from office, and noted the widespread corruption in the country. The scandal further undermined confidence in the ruling Antigua Labour Party, and in the Bird family in particular, but the size of its parliamentary majority (15 of 17 seats) meant that the ALP could not be easily dislodged despite growing criticism from opposition groups.

A general election in DOMINICA on 28 May was narrowly won by Eugenia Charles's Dominica Freedom Party (DFP) with the United Workers' Party (UWP), contesting its first election, and the Dominica Labour Party cutting the DFP's majority to one vote. Mrs Charles characteristically dismissed the narrowness of the victory to focus on her project to oversee the construction of a new international airport, for which her government was seeking finance to the value of US$300 million. More immediate concerns following the damage done by Hurricane Hugo were the substantial rise in the trade deficit, the collapse of banana production and revenues, and the rebuilding of tourist facilities. Although post-hurricane aid between during 1989 had been over EC$30 million, this fell short of necessary reconstruction funds.

Like Dominica, ST LUCIA experienced significant drops in banana-related earnings (down 18 per cent). Although winter season tourist bookings were down by as much as 15 per cent, there was an overall increase in visitors in 1989 of 6.4 per cent, which was likely to continue through 1990. Prime Minister John Compton had predicted growth of 6 per cent during 1990, but his claims of 13 per cent unemployment could not deflect opposition charges that unemployment was really as high as 40 per cent and that projected new finance for housing, tourism and agriculture was insufficient to deal with the problem.

Given the monopoly of power held in ST VINCENT by Prime Minister James Mitchell's New Democratic Party (all 15 National Assembly seats), the three main opposition parties (the St Vincent Labour Party, the United People's Party and the Movement for National Unity) began to hold talks on forming an opposition coalition in October. Meanwhile, the government gave the go-ahead for the construction of a new airport on the Grenadine island of Bequia.

SURINAME

CAPITAL: Paramaribo   AREA: 164,000 sq km   POPULATION: 427,000 ('88)
OFFICIAL LANGUAGE: Dutch   POLITICAL SYSTEM: republic, under military tutelage
HEAD OF STATE: John Kraag (acting President since Dec '90)
MILITARY LEADER: Lt.-Col. Désiré (Desi) Bouterse
INTERNATIONAL ALIGNMENT: NAM, ACP/EEC, OAS
CURRENCY: Suriname guilder (end-'90 £1=Sf3.45, US$1=Sf1.79)
GNP PER CAPITA: US$2,460 ('88)
MAIN EXPORT EARNERS: bauxite/alumina, aluminium, rice

TENSIONS between the three key groups in Suriname's political life—the army under Colonel Desi Bouterse, the government and National Assembly under President Ramsewak Shankar, and the rebel Jungle Commando under Ronnie Brunswijk—increased throughout the year as the strength of Colonel Bouterse grew, the authority of the government remained subverted, and the Jungle Commando began to collapse. After a trivial disagreement between Colonel Bouterse and President Shankar, the former resigned his post on 23 December. This was followed on 24 December by a bloodless coup and the unconstitutional installation of an acting President, who accepted the reappointment of Colonel Bouterse as head of the army. During the year there were numerous occasions when Colonel Bouterse publicly challenged government decisions and openly defied government orders.

The promise of an end to the civil strife embodied in the Kourou Agreement (see AR 1989, p. 91) was unfulfilled in 1990 as post-agreement negotiations with the Jungle Commando were alternately conducted by the army and the government. The former had been hostile to the original agreement, whilst the latter was incapable of implementing the terms of the agreement without army cooperation. Thus in January the army replaced the National Assembly negotiators; by March the National Assembly had resumed its role; by September it had ceded it once again to Colonel Bouterse. The lack of negotiating authority and subsequent confusion was compounded by Ronnie Brunswijk's (temporary) decision to abandon the armed struggle and seek asylum in the Netherlands in June. This was indicative of the increasing inter-clan rivalry amongst the rebels and the growing effectiveness of the army.

One important stimulus to Brunswijk's brief removal from Suriname was his arrest by the army following the discovery of over a tonne of cocaine at an army base captured by his Jungle Commando. Although he was released following retaliatory Jungle Commando attacks on power stations and bauxite facilities, which effectively crippled the economy, it was widely believed that sections of the army were involved in extensive cocaine-trafficking operations. (Over one-third of all cocaine imports to the Netherlands arrived via Suriname.) Initiatives by both the French and Dutch governments to facilitate a peace settlement were undermined by the December crisis. The Dutch government announced the immediate suspension of all aid to Suriname following the coup.

BRITISH DEPENDENCIES

Montserrat
CAPITAL: Plymouth   AREA: 102 sq km   POPULATION: 11,900 ('87)
OFFICIAL LANGUAGE: English   POLITICAL SYSTEM: representative democracy
GOVERNOR-GENERAL: David Taylor
RULING PARTY: People's Liberation Movement (PLM)
HEAD OF GOVERNMENT: John Osborne, Chief Minister
CURRENCY: East Caribbean dollar (end-'90 £1=EC$5.22, US$1=EC$2.70)

Anguilla
CAPITAL: The Valley   AREA: 96 sq km   POPULATION: 7,200 ('87)
OFFICIAL LANGUAGE: English   POLITICAL SYSTEM: representative democracy
GOVERNOR: G.O. Whittaker
RULING PARTY: Anguilla National Alliance (ANA)
HEAD OF GOVERNMENT: Emile Gumbs, Chief Minister (since '84)
CURRENCY: East Caribbean dollar (end-'90 £1=EC$5.22, US$1=EC$2.70)
MAIN EXPORT EARNERS: tourism, lobsters

THE battle over the new constitution of MONTSERRAT between Chief Minister John Osborne and the Foreign and Commonwealth Office (FCO) was settled on 19 December 1989 when Mr Osborne conceded the Governor-General's right to control financial services, whilst the FCO dropped claims that the Governor-General could decree certain types of legislation. The constitutional crisis followed the suspension of 75 per cent of licences granted to off-shore financial businesses located in Montserrat since 1978 under the Banking Ordinance of that year. The new Governor-General, David Taylor, had powers to oversee the implementation of new regulatory practices, which had become the model for other off-shore centres in the Caribbean.

Such considerations informed the review carried out by the government of ANGUILLA in its exploration of the possibilities of setting up an off-shore financial service sector. Similar constitutional changes were under negotiation.

NETHERLANDS ANTILLES AND ARUBA

Netherlands Antilles
CAPITAL: Willemstad (Curaçao)   AREA: 800 sq km   POPULATION: 192,000 ('88)
OFFICIAL LANGUAGES: Dutch Papiamento, English   POLITICAL SYSTEM: parliamentary democracy under Dutch crown
GOVERNOR: Jaime Saleh
RULING PARTIES: National People's Party (PNP) heads coalition
HEAD OF GOVERNMENT: Maria Liberia Peters, Prime Minister (since May '88)
CURRENCY: Neth. Antilles guilder (end-'90 £1=NAf3.45, US$1=NAf1.79)
GNP PER CAPITA: US$5,300 ('88)
MAIN EXPORT EARNERS: oil, tourism

Aruba
CAPITAL: Oranjestad   AREA: 193 sq km   POPULATION: 62,365 ('88)
OFFICIAL LANGUAGE: Dutch   POLITICAL SYSTEM: parliamentary democracy under Dutch crown
GOVERNOR: Felipe B. Trompe
RULING PARTIES: People's Electoral Movement (MEP) heads coalition
HEAD OF GOVERNMENT: Nelson Oduber, Prime Minister (since Feb '89)
CURRENCY: Aruba guilder (end-'90 £1=Af3.46, US$1=Af1.79)
GNP PER CAPITA: US$12,000 ('88)
MAIN EXPORT EARNERS: oil, tourism

FOLLOWING a NETHERLANDS ANTILLES general election victory on 16 March for the People's National Party (PNP) led by Maria Liberia Peters, proposals forwarded by the Dutch government for a new constitution, including the separation of the Antilles into two groups (Curaçao and Bonaire on the one hand, and the Windward group on the other), met with stiff resistance. The PNP and its coalition won ten of the 14 seats in Curaçao, thereby ensuring that the pressures for autonomy of Curaçao alone would increase.

In ARUBA the MEP-led government began to have doubts about moving to separate independence from the Netherlands in 1996. With drug-trafficking and concomitant government corruption becoming endemic in the Caribbean, it began to see the advantages of continued Dutch status, possibly as a self-governing commonwealth. Such matters were discussed by Aruban representatives and the responsible Dutch minister in July, although no substantive decisions were taken. Aruba's oil-based economy continued its rapid growth, giving rise to warnings of over-heating.

III THE USSR AND EASTERN EUROPE

Chapter 1

UNION OF SOVIET SOCIALIST REPUBLICS

CAPITAL: Moscow   AREA: 22,403,000 sq km   POPULATION: 286,700,000 ('89)
PRINCIPAL OFFICIAL LANGUAGE: Russian
POLITICAL SYSTEM: federated republic under communist rule
HEAD OF STATE AND PARTY LEADER: President Mikhail Gorbachev (since March '90),
   CPSU general secretary (since March '85)
RULING PARTY: Communist Party of the Soviet Union (CPSU)
PRINCIPAL MINISTERS: Nikolai Ryzhkov (Prime Minister), Yury Maslyukov (first
   deputy premier, chairman of state planning committee), Lev Voronin (first deputy
   premier), Marshal Dmitry Yazov (defence), Boris Pugo (internal affairs), Valentin
   Pavlov (finance), Veniamin Yakovlev (justice)
INTERNATIONAL ALIGNMENT: Warsaw Pact, Comecon
CURRENCY: rouble (end-'90 £1=R1.07, US$1=R0.55)
GNP PER CAPITA: n.a.
MAIN EXPORT EARNERS: oil and oil products, machinery and equipment

THE year 1990 was by general consent the most difficult of the five that had elapsed since Mr Gorbachev launched his programme of *perestroika*. For some, indeed, it was one of the most difficult of the whole Soviet period. The economy, according to official data, actually contracted for the first time since the war, and shortages, inflation and unemployment became established features of Soviet life. The national question, supposedly resolved in principle by the establishment of socialist rule, became increasingly acute. Social tensions worsened, with a rise in reported crime and widening divisions between rich and poor. The Communist Party (CPSU), supposedly the means by which the central leadership ensured its decisions were put into effect, formally abandoned its 'leading role' and suffered a serious loss of members, morale and influence. A series of constitutional reforms saw the establishment of a presidential system of rule, but without any obvious means of implementing its decisions. Even internationally there was less to show than in previous years, with the continuing erosion of communist control in Eastern Europe and slow progress towards the strategic arms agreement that, it had been agreed, would complement the INF accord of December 1987.

In earlier years the central event of the year would undoubtedly have been the party congress, which took place some months ahead of time in July 1990. By the time it convened, however, the CPSU had already lost a substantial part of the authority it once commanded. The most important single development in this connection was the decision taken by the central committee in February 1990 to relinquish the guarantee of its 'leading role' contained in article 6 of the constitution. Mr Gorbachev, who had resisted a challenge to article 6 at the Congress of People's Deputies the previous December, argued that the leading role had in fact already been overtaken by events, in particular the establishment of a wide range of independent political groupings. The party, however, should seek to retain a position of 'political leadership' through the electoral process. The constitution was amended accordingly by the Third Congress of People's Deputies in March; henceforward, the new article 6 suggested, the Communist Party would share the task of forming and administering public policy with other parties and social movements.

The formal loss of its leading position was only one of the ways in which the CPSU saw its formerly unchallengeable position erode over the course of the year. The party, for instance, began to lose members: nearly 1.5 million of them between January and September 1990, of whom 800,000 had simply resigned. The existing membership became increasingly divided, despite the formal prohibition of 'factions' within its ranks. The two groupings that secured the widest attention during the year were the Democratic Platform, whose members called for the CPSU to abandon its leninism in favour of a purely parliamentary role, and the Marxist Platform, whose members called for a party based more closely on the interests and participation of the industrial working class. The party press lost circulation: *Pravda*, for instance, had only 30 per cent of its January subscribers when subscriptions closed for 1991. Members and whole branches began to withhold their dues, and party income as a whole fell by about half. The party's public standing, as measured by opinion polls, declined sharply. Perhaps (for its leaders) most alarming of all, the party began to fragment as an organization. In March and April the Latvian and Estonian party organizations split into independent and pro-Moscow factions; and in December 1990 the Georgian party opted, as the Lithuanians had done the previous year, for full independence.

The 28th party congress, which met in Moscow from 2–13 July 1990, was accordingly a very different gathering from the party congresses that had preceded it. It was the first to meet against a background of demonstrators shouting 'down with the red fascists'. It was the first congress, for many years at least, at which members of the leadership rendered individual account. It was the first congress at any time at which there was a direct contest for the party leadership: Mr Gorbachev originally faced nine challengers and had to be content with three-quarters of the vote in the final choice between himself and a district party secretary. It was the first congress since the late 1920s that adopted no 'guidelines' for the forthcoming five-year plan, reflecting the new view that this was the responsibility of government alone. An entirely new set of party rules was adopted, together with a new 'programmatic declaration', which was meant to guide the party's activities until a new party programme could be adopted. There were calls for the party to drop the word 'Communist' from its title, and the *Internationale* as its anthem. The congress concluded by electing its first-ever deputy leader and a newly-constituted politburo, including the party first secretaries of the 15 republics.

Mr Gorbachev, in his opening address, described the process of *perestroika* as one by which a 'stalinist model of socialism' had been replaced by a 'civil society of free men and women'. The political system, more particularly, had been 'radically transformed' with the establishment of 'genuine democracy' based upon free elections, a multi-party system, human rights and popular self-government. An atmosphere of 'ideological domineering' had been replaced by one of freedom of thought. The crimes of the past had been 'resolutely condemned'. There had been a 'real revolution in people's thinking'; life had become fuller and richer, the 'absurd bans' of the stalinist years had been removed, and scientists and others had been given a much more prominent place in the party's decision-making processes. And new opportunities had opened up for the development of culture, literature and the arts, or what Mr Gorbachev rather grandly called the 'ecology of the soul'.

The congress adopted a formal position on these and other matters with its approval of a declaration entitled 'Towards a humane, democratic socialism'. The declaration made it clear that, for the party, the origins of Soviet difficulties lay in deformations of socialism rather than in the socialist project itself. Party dictatorship had led to popular alienation and lawlessness; nature had been plundered without restraint; and dogmatism had reigned supreme in the sphere of culture. *Perestroika* meant a 'radical turn towards a policy aimed at the country's renovation'; the CPSU itself was presented as a party of the 'socialist choice and communist perspective', seen as a natural stage in the advance of civilization. The declaration incorporated a set of 'urgent anti-crisis measures', including a new union treaty and normalization of the consumer market. Longer-term measures included strengthened civil liberties, a 'stage-by-stage transition to a market system', international cooperation and democratization of the party itself. The declaration was to serve, in effect, as the party's programme until a new text could be adopted at a conference or congress in the first half of 1992.

Mr Gorbachev discussed democratization of the party in his opening address, noting that the party's own organization and role required constant reappraisal. For many years, he argued, the party had served as an extension of the command-administrative system, leading to serious mistakes in its choice of personnel and policies. Millions of party members had been removed from direct control over its affairs, and the result had been a 'climate of indifference, apathy and passivity' in party branches. What would an 'updated CPSU', freed of these defects, look like? It would, Mr Gorbachev suggested, be a party of the 'socialist choice and communist perspective', committed at the same time to the common ideals of humanity. It would be a party 'freed of its ideological blinkers', promoting its policies through dialogue and cooperation with other 'progressive' social and political forces. It would be a tolerant party, based on a recognition of the rights of minorities and 'total freedom of debate'. It would be a 'vanguard' as well as a parliamentary party, organizing in the workplace and in the armed forces as well as on a residential basis. And it would be a self-managing party, based upon the freedom of action of branches and the independence of republican party organizations within a common programme and statute.

The congress took a formal position on these matters with the adoption of an entirely new set of party rules, which introduced some quite significant changes as compared with drafts published earlier in the year and still more so with the rules that had been adopted at the previous congress in 1986. The important principle of democratic centralism was retained, after some discussion, in the final version. There was much more emphasis, however, upon the rights of ordinary members, who were given greater access to information about party committees at all levels and the right to 'evaluate' their work. Branches were to be allowed to express their views on particularly contentious issues before they were considered by the central committee, and had the right to retain up to half of their subscription income. The changes as compared with the rules of 1986 were still more dramatic, including the explicit right to form 'platforms' if not organized factions, greater respect for the rights of the minority and official endorsement of 'horizontal' structures such as political clubs and seminars of a kind that had hitherto been regarded as incompatible with democratic centralism.

The Soviet political system changed still more dramatically with the introduction, in March 1990, of a presidential system of government. The creation of the new presidency had been among the radical proposals announced by Mr Gorbachev at the February central committee plenum at which the constitutionally-guaranteed 'leading role' of the CPSU was relinquished. The introduction of the new system, for which there was no precedent in Soviet or Russian political practice, was justified by Mr Gorbachev as a means of ensuring that swift executive action could take place in circumstances that required it. Despite claims from some deputies that powers of this kind were a step towards dictatorship, Mr Gorbachev insisted that there was an urgent need to 'enhance the mechanism of executive authority in order to ensure the laws work', and he secured the necessary majority at the Third Congress of People's Deputies on 13 March. He was elected to the presidency himself two days later, although by only 59 per cent of the vote in an uncontested ballot.

Any citizen between the ages of 35 and 65 could be elected to the presidency for a maximum of two five-year terms. The President was normally to be elected by universal, equal and direct suffrage, although in the difficult circumstances then obtaining it was agreed that Mr Gorbachev—exceptionally—would be elected by the Congress itself. The President was to report annually to the Congress of People's Deputies and would brief the Supreme Soviet on 'the most important questions of the USSR's domestic and foreign policy'. He would propose candidates for the premiership and other leading state positions; he had a suspensory veto over legislation; and he could dissolve the government and suspend its directives. He could also declare a state of emergency, and introduce direct presidential rule. The President headed a new council of the federation, consisting of the presidents of the 15 union republics, with responsibility for inter-ethnic and inter-republican issues; he also headed a new presidential council, which was responsible for the 'main directions of the USSR's foreign and domestic policy'.

In September 1990 these already impressive powers were extended by parliamentary vote, giving Mr Gorbachev the right to institute emergency measures to 'stabilize the country's socio-political life' for a period of 18 months. Several further changes were made by the Fourth Congress of People's Deputies in December 1990, which completed the move to a fully presidential administration. The council of ministers was replaced by a more limited 'cabinet', headed by a prime minister who (together with his colleagues) would be nominated by the President and accountable to him. The President became head of a new security council with overall responsibility for defence and public order (he himself appointed its other members). He also appointed a new Vice-President responsible for carrying out the functions that were entrusted to him (Gennadi Yanaev, a member of the CPSU secretariat who had formerly worked in the trade union movement and Komsomol, being elected to this position on 27 December). The presidential council, formed the previous March, disappeared, and a reconstituted council of the federation headed by the President became, in effect, the supreme state decision-making body.

The exercise of executive authority, despite these changes, became increasingly problematic during the year as inter-ethnic tension intensified and republican governments insisted on the primacy of their own laws over those of the USSR as a whole. In January 1990 the long-running dispute between Armenia and Azerbaijan over the territorial enclave of Nagorno-Karabakh (see AR 1988, pp. 109–10) erupted into inter-communal violence across the republic and along the Armenian border. The dispute was precipitated by an Armenian decision to extend the provisions of their republican budget and electoral law to Nagorno-Karabakh. Tens of thousands took to the streets in Baku alone, up to 60 people (mostly Armenians) lost their lives in pogroms, and there were further fatalities when a state of emergency was declared by the USSR Supreme Soviet presidium and troops were used to restore order on 19–20 January. The death toll for the month from the conflict was officially put at more than 200; the Azerbaijani first secretary, Abdul Rakhman Vezirov, whose party organization had been powerless to influence events, lost his position as a result.

There was further ethnic conflict throughout the Soviet Union during 1990. Nationalist rioting erupted in the Tadjik capital Dushanbe in February, precipitated by reports that Armenian refugees were to be allocated housing in the city. By the time Interior Ministry troops had restored order party buildings had been attacked and at least 22 people (according to official figures) had lost their lives. There were riots in the Kirghiz capital Frunze, and renewed tensions between Uzbeks and Meskhetian Turks in Samarkand and near Tashkent. In June and July there were further riots and inter-communal clashes in Kirghizia, leaving at least 212 dead (although unofficial sources suggested the loss of life had been at least five times higher). There were inter-ethnic tensions in Moldavia as well, involving Russians and Gagauz Turks as well as the majority Romanian population. Matters reached a critical point when both Russians and Gagauz established their own forms of government and emergency rule was imposed by Mr Gorbachev in December. All told, official Soviet sources reported in August 1990, inter-ethnic conflict since early 1988 had claimed 949 lives; 8,652 had been wounded and about 600,000 had become refugees within their own country.

Inter-republican relations in the USSR entered a new phase when in February 1990 supporters of the Lithuanian nationalist movement, Sajudis, won a majority of seats in the republican parliament, which then, on 11 March, formally declared Lithuania independent. The parliament, hoping to anticipate Mr Gorbachev's acquisition of extensive presidential powers, agreed to reaffirm the republic's declaration of independence of 1918 and declared illegal its incorporation into the USSR in 1940. Mr Gorbachev, addressing the Congress of People's Deputies, described the Lithuanian action as 'illegitimate and invalid' and refused to open negotiations with what remained, in his view, an integral part of the USSR. The central authorities issued an ultimatum demanding the withdrawal of the declaration of independence; when the Lithuanians refused to comply, an economic blockade was imposed on 18 April. These pressures notwithstanding, the neighbouring republics of Estonia and Latvia adopted more cautiously-worded declarations of independence on 30 March and 4 May respectively. The Lithuanian declaration of independence was suspended by parliamentary vote on 29 June, the blockade was ended, and discussions began on an attempt to resolve the dispute; they had not reached an agreed conclusion by the end of the year.

National assertiveness reached by far the largest of the Soviet Union's republics, the Russian, in May 1990, following elections to the republican Congress of People's Deputies at which radical candidates won a third of the votes (and majorities in Moscow and Leningrad). After several ballots the former Moscow party secretary, Boris Yeltsin, was elected chairman of the Russian Supreme Soviet or de facto republican president on 29 May. Mr Yeltsin's political programme combined calls for radical political reform with a strong appeal for Russia's sovereign rights, including separate citizenship, ownership of all the republic's natural resources, an independent foreign policy, and the primacy of republican legislation over that of the USSR as a whole ('reversing the pyramid', as he put it to a press conference shortly after his election). The Russian Congress of People's Deputies resolved to this effect on 12 June. In a separate development, a Russian Federation Communist Party was established on 21 June and Ivan Polozkov, a relatively conservative first secretary from Krasnodar, was elected its first secretary. Other Russian republican institutions, including an Academy of Sciences and a trade union organization, began to be established during the year.

Declarations of sovereignty were adopted by all 15 republics in the course of the year, and by many lower-level bodies as well. In some cases the affirmation to this effect was even more categoric than in the Russian Republic. The Ukrainian and Turkmenian declarations, for instance, proclaimed their republics nuclear-free zones. The Armenian declaration, which followed elections at which nationalists had won a majority of seats, included an assertion of the republic's 'independent statehood', including the right to form its own military units and to control its own natural resources. Nationalists were similarly successful at elections in Georgia in October 1990, when a seven-party Round Table/Free Georgia coalition won 54 per cent of the vote as compared with 29 per cent for the Communists. The veteran dissident Zviad Gamsakhurdia became president and a parliamentary resolution was adopted which, like those in the Baltic and Armenia, committed the republic to a gradual transition to full independence. The fourth Congress of People's Deputies voted, in December 1990, for the basic principles of a new 'union treaty', but some republics refused to take part in the discussion and it appeared unlikely that it would preserve the USSR as Mr Gorbachev had originally intended.

The background to a growing constitutional as well as ethnic crisis was a steadily deteriorating economy. The economic results for 1989, reported in the central press in January 1990, made dismal reading. There had been a 3 per cent increase in GNP and a 2.4 per cent increase in the more familiar Soviet measure, national income produced. The state statistics committee, in its report, nonetheless pointed out that economic development had 'lost momentum', with many of the most important targets not attained. The consumer market was 'tense', with demand continuing to outstrip supply. Inflation was running at a nominal 2 per cent, but unmet demand or 'hidden inflation' increased the figure to about 7.5 per cent. Labour discipline had worsened, with losses of working time up by 30 per cent on the previous year's total. Incomes had risen 12.9 per cent, well over the planned level (and one reason, in itself, for the shortages of consumer goods). Only in the private and cooperative sector was there evidence of advance, with 1,332 industrial enterprises and 4,911 state or collective farms held on a leasehold basis and 4.5 million employed in the cooperative sector alone.

An economic recovery programme had been introduced by the Soviet Prime Minister, Nikolai Ryzhkov, in December 1989, aimed at restoring market equilibrium by 1993. By March 1990 the programme was already judged inadequate in the light of worsening performance indicators, and a deputy prime minister, economist Leonid Abalkin, was asked to prepare a more sweeping package of reform. The government's proposals were finally presented by Mr Ryzhov to the Supreme Soviet on 24 May. They involved a gradual transition to a 'regulated' market in three stages up to 1995, including legal changes, pricing and tax reforms, and a reduction in the scope of central planning. The plan came in for heavy criticism and the Supreme Soviet, on 13 June, called for the government to submit a more developed and coherent programme by 1 September. It did, however, approve the plan in principle, and called upon Mr Gorbachev to take measures towards the same end by presidential decree. The proposed increase in the price of bread was rescinded, but the announcement of proposals for increased prices led to panic buying and the introduction, in several cities, of regulations prohibiting the sale of goods to non-residents.

Discussion of the way forward for economic reform continued over the summer, concentrated within small groups of ministers and their advisers. A more radical plan, put forward by a group under the chairmanship of presidential council member Stanislav Shatalin, advocated a rapid '500-day' transition to a market economy (the Russian Republic itself adopted this programme in September). The government's original proposals remained on the table, Mr Ryzhkov in particular arguing against a package of reforms that would lead to a significant fall in living standards and (probably) political instability. A compromise plan, drafted by Academician Abel Aganbegyan, was also presented to the Supreme Soviet and to republican parliaments. On 24 September the Supreme Soviet voted for a 'unified programme', combining the best elements of all three documents, to be worked out under Mr Gorbachev's supervision. The Supreme Soviet duly approved Mr Gorbachev's proposals on 19 October; they were based upon the principle of 'maximum freedom of economic activity', combined where appropriate with state regulation, and envisaged a transition to a system of this kind in four stages within a 'relatively short time'.

Programmes of this kind, whatever their merits, had begun to appear rather remote from ordinary people as the year concluded. Indeed, opinion surveys suggested that for many people what occasioned most concern was simply surviving the coming winter. Despite a good harvest, there were widespread food shortages and many larger towns and cities—Leningrad on 1 November, for instance—introduced a system of rationing for the first time since the early post-war years. Yet even this did not guarantee supplies. National income fell by 1.5 per cent in the first nine months of the year, on official figures, and inflation was at least 9 per cent. Public finances continued to deteriorate, with the Russian Republic in particular voting to withhold most of its enormous contribution to the all-union budget. In the end the Fourth Congress of People's Deputies, in December, was unable to agree a new budget for 1991 and various emergency measures had to be instituted, including a sales tax and a 'stabilization fund'.

Soviet foreign policy during the year concentrated upon the consequences of the collapse of communist rule in Eastern Europe, particularly for the former German Democratic Republic. At the same time, the dialogue between the superpowers continued, particularly at a summit meeting in the USA in May–June 1990. The summit was the second between Mr Gorbachev and the recently-elected US President, George Bush, following a preliminary meeting off the coast of Malta in December 1989 (see AR 1989, pp. 57–8). The summit was hailed as a new beginning in US-Soviet relations, despite acknowledged and continuing differences on a number of key bilateral and international issues. Formally speaking, the summit resulted in several agreements, including a convention banning the production of chemical weapons and a series of bilateral agreements on arms control, trade, and cooperation in the transport, energy, education and cultural fields. In particular, the Soviet Union secured 'most-favoured-nation' access to the US market for the first time for 50 years. A more far-reaching agreement on reductions in strategic nuclear arms, which at the time of the Malta summit had been thought imminent, was deferred for further discussion. Mr Gorbachev, at the two leaders' concluding press conference, described the summit as an 'event of enormous importance for our bilateral relations and in the context of world politics' and added that one could now speak of a 'new phase of cooperation' between the USA and the Soviet Union.

The US visit followed a two-day visit to Canada. The Soviet President also visited Germany, France and Spain in the autumn, and attended the Paris summit in November for the conclusion of a far-reaching agreement on the reduction of conventional arms within the CSCE framework (see Pt. XII). The Soviet leader's earlier visit to Spain in October led to the conclusion of political and economic agreements; his visit to France resulted in a joint agreement on cooperation (and a doubling of French aid to the USSR). President Gorbachev's visit to Germany in November (where a 20-year friendship and cooperation treaty was signed) followed a meeting between himself and Chancellor Kohl in Stavropol in July at which it was agreed that a newly-unified Germany would be 'sovereign in every way', including its liberty to join the military alliance of its choice (in practice NATO). Soviet troops still in East Germany would be withdrawn over three or four years, in the course of which the West Germans would underwrite their costs; the number of German troops would also be reduced to 370,000 within a comparable period.

The solidity of East-West understanding was tested from August by the outbreak of the Gulf crisis. The Soviet Union had traditionally maintained friendly relations with Iraq, but Foreign Minister Shevardnadze, in a speech at the UN General Assembly on 25 September, characterized Saddam Husain's invasion of Kuwait as an 'act of terrorism against the nascent new world order' and added that the Soviet Union would be prepared to support the use of force against Iraq within a United Nations framework. Mr Shevardnadze's resignation on 20 December, delivered without warning to the Fourth Congress of People's Deputies, occasioned some concern that his policies on these and other matters might be modified. The Congress, however, supported the position that had been taken by Soviet representatives on the matter and insisted in its resolution upon the withdrawal of Iraqi forces from Kuwait.

Meanwhile, Mr Gorbachev's standing, internationally at least, had been further enhanced by the award to him in October of the Nobel Peace Prize, for what were described as his 'many and decisive contributions' to East-West relations.

Chapter 2

POLAND—CZECHOSLOVAKIA—HUNGARY—ROMANIA—BULGARIA—
YUGOSLAVIA—ALBANIA

POLAND

CAPITAL: Warsaw   AREA: 313,000 sq km   POPULATION: 37,900,000 ('88)
OFFICIAL LANGUAGE: Polish   POLITICAL SYSTEM: presidential democracy
HEAD OF STATE: President Lech Walesa (since Dec '90)
HEAD OF GOVERNMENT: Jan Krzyzstof Bielecki (since Dec. '90)
INTERNATIONAL ALIGNMENT: Warsaw Pact, Comecon, but effectively fluid
CURRENCY: zloty (end-'90 £1=Zl.18,382 US$1=Zl.9,524)
GNP PER CAPITA: US$1,860 ('88)
MAIN EXPORT EARNERS: engineering equipment, coal, metals, agricultural produce

THIS was the most trying year of the post-communist transition from a totalitarian command system to a pluralist democracy and free market economy. It ended with Lech Walesa as the democratically-elected President of the Republic but in a climate where domestic politics had become increasingly turbulent and major controversy intensified over the pace and scope of change within the newly-established system.

Guided by the basic principle that all its actions must be based on the rule of law, the Mazowiecki government (see AR 1989, p.113) forced through parliament over ten months a comprehensive package of over 50 acts laying the foundations for a democratic multiparty system and creating conditions for restructuring of the economy.

On 1 January Poland switched to a market economy as envisaged in Mr Balcerowicz's sharp shock treatment (see AR 1989, p.114). Prices rose initially by 38–600 per cent for food and various commodities. Price controls were lifted, wage controls maintained, the centralized distribution system overhauled, a healthy credit system introduced, foreign trade liberalized, and a number of state monopolies broken up. Industrial output declined by 30 per cent, production sales by 37 per cent and real wages by over a third. Nevertheless, a free market had been established: food and other products were readily available, the monthly rate of inflation was reduced from 79 per cent in January to 1.7 per cent in August (rising to 5.7 per cent in October following increased world oil prices), the zloty was stabilized and fully convertible, and the budget balanced. Trade with the convertible currency zone achieved a surplus of $4,100 million and 4,000 million roubles with Comecon.

At the end of the year the value of sold production and wages began to rise, the recession was slowed down to about 15 per cent, but real income still remained about 30 per cent below 1989 level and unemployment stood at 1.3 million, 8 per cent of the workforce.

In July a law on large-scale privatization provided measures for the conversion of 7,600 state enterprises into joint-stock companies and their eventual sale to individuals and companies, including foreign ones, which could be initiated either by the Ministry for Property Transformations or by the workers' council and the enterprise management. In November shares in the first five state enterprises went on sale and were easily subscribed. Minister Kuczynski forecast that 15 per cent of companies would be sold in 1991 and 50 per cent over the next three years. The government would help by distributing free 'privatization coupons' and making loans available for the purchase of up to one-third of the value of privatized firms. On a smaller scale, the privatization of over 200,000 small businesses thrived in December, when 80 per cent of retail trade was in private hands.

In a gesture of approval of the government's economic strategy, nearly all the country's debts of $40,000 million were rescheduled for 14 years. Nevertheless, Poland pressed for an 80 per cent cut in debt-servicing payments which otherwise could jeopardize further economic progress, particularly since direct losses related to the Gulf crisis amounted to $3,000 million. The World Bank approved loans of $900 million to boost exports and natural gas production and to build up market economy.

On the political scene far-reaching changes were initiated by the government in a climate of increasing controversy and confrontational postures. The former ruling Polish United Workers' Party (PUWP) dissolved itself (18 January) and re-emerged as Social Democracy of the Polish Republic (SDRP), a small insignificant grouping. Its assets were taken over by the government Treasury. Parliamentary commissions began drafting a new democratic constitution to be ready for a general election in the spring of 1991. Meanwhile, the Sejm (parliament) removed all vestiges of communism from the 1952 constitution. Censorship and the state mass media monopoly were ended, freedom of association legally guaranteed, and party cells banned from the army. Registering political parties became a strictly technical matter.

The system of justice was reformed, with judges no longer politically appointed but nominated by an independent national judiciary council. The security service and Citizens' Militia were disbanded and replaced by the State Protection Office (OUP), while recruitment to the state police became carefully screened. The new Ministry of Internal Affairs had its staff levels cut by two-thirds and became a strictly civilian department, headed by Krzysztof Kozlowski, a Solidarity journalist who replaced General Kiszczak of the PUWP. In a July reshuffle two other communists left the government, including the Defence Minister, General Siwicki. Vice-Admiral Kolodziejczyk, his successor, and two civilian Solidarity deputies confirmed that Poland's new purely defensive military doctrine envisaged withdrawal from the Warsaw Pact.

The second Solidarity congress in April was a subdued gathering representing just over 2 million members (compared with 10 million in 1981). It re-elected Mr Walesa as chairman and decided to endorse candidates for local elections rather than form a Solidarity political party. As a trade union, it pledged to strive to minimize the social costs of the government's economic policy.

The first post-war free local government elections (on 27 May) were called two years prematurely. As Mr Mazowiecki stressed: 'Until we create genuine self-government we will not be able to overcome the resistance we experience while introducing changes.' Complex new legislation along Western lines decentralized over two thousand municipal councils, making them responsible for drafting and balancing local budgets, for local administration in all fields (including education and the police) and for the management of communal property. In a turnout of 42.72 per cent, Solidarity Citizens' Committees and other Solidarity groupings won 49.65 per cent of seats, independents 38 per cent, the recently-united Polish Peasant Party (PSL) 6.5 per cent, while all other newly-formed political parties, including the SDRP, shared 0.78 per cent.

This was the last time the Citizens' Committees acted as Solidarity's electoral arm. In May Mr Walesa—gradually dissociating himself and Solidarity from the government—called for 'permanent war at the top'. This meant competition between different political forces, speeding up and broadening the changes, increasing public participation in politics and streamlining the government's activities. Mr Walesa accused the government of delays in implementing political and economic reforms, including destruction of old communist structures, and declared his readiness to stand for the presidency.

Mr Mazowiecki in turn emphasized the need for 'consistency and stability' in government, for controlled and deliberate political evolution, and the introduction of changes in the political system following consensus between interested parties. Renouncing revenge and spectacular gestures, he linked implementation to a clear timetable: fully democratic parliamentary elections in early 1991, followed by a new constitution and then the presidential election. Mr Mazowiecki warned against 'demagogy and populism', and against deviation from the tough economic programme and the danger of a 'Polish hell', where Poland's well-being would be threatened in a chaos of conflicting interests.

This controversy of opposing approaches split and politically polarized Solidarity, and the consensus on which the government was based. Political parties, both traditional and newly-formed, remained minor actors on the political stage except for the marginally more successful PSL. Three main political coalition forces emerged from Solidarity, binding a variety of groups and individuals rather than representing any single interest group: a pro-Walesa Centre Alliance formed by Jaroslaw Kaczynski (PC), a pro-Mazowiecki Citizens' Movement Democratic Action (ROAD) and the Democratic Right Forum (FPD). Under its slogan 'Walesa for President', the Centre Alliance demanded General Jaruzelski's resignation and immediate presidential elections. It formed the political centre with the other two groups to its left and right respectively.

Fundamental differences over strategy developed into a political power struggle. At General Jaruzelski's request the Sejm decided to shorten his term of office and passed a law regulating presidential elections, the first in Poland's history, no later than December. The successful candidate had to receive more than 50 per cent of votes cast; otherwise the two highest-placed candidates would compete in a second round for a simple majority.

During an acrimonious presidential campaign, concentrated more on personalities than issues, people became alarmed by the Mazowiecki–Walesa clash and politicians' language and intolerance. Mr Walesa, criss-crossing the country, was the most visible of the six candidates.

Even so, in the first round (25 November), with a turnout of over 60 per cent, he received only 39.96 per cent of the vote. An obscure emigré Polish-Canadian businessman, Stanislaw Tyminski, promising a 'programme of growth to enrich everybody', won 23.1 per cent, pushing Mr Mazowiecki with 18.08 per cent into third place.

This unexpected result shocked people. The Church and all major political organizations except the post-communist SDRP rallied behind Mr Walesa, who was elected in the second round (9 December) by 74.25 per cent to Mr Tyminski's 25.75 per cent, on a turnout of 53.4 per cent. Polish political analysts warned of the existence of a comparatively large 'constituency of disaffection and frustration'. The result was seen as a defeat for both Solidarity wings.

Mr Mazowiecki resigned on 27 November and accepted leadership of the Democratic Union, a hastily-formed Christian-social party of 'constructive opposition' unifying ROAD and FPD. Lech Walesa was sworn in on 22 December and appealed for solidarity among all political forces in the 'extremely difficult task of building the new economic system'. After wide-ranging consultations, which involved Mr Mazowiecki, he asked Jan Krzysztof Bielecki, a successful businessman, radical free marketeer and leader of the Gdansk-based Liberal Democratic Congress, to form a new government.

During 1990 Prime Minister Mazowiecki and Foreign Minister Skubiszewski travelled to Washington, London, Paris, Brussels, Strasbourg and Bonn, stressing Poland's fundamental objective of rejoining Europe. They successfully sought support for Poland's involvement in the 'two-plus-four' talks on German unification when problems of security and borders were discussed, and also secured commitments to economic cooperation. A treaty confirming the existing Polish–German border on the Oder-Neisse line was signed on 14 November in Warsaw by both countries' Foreign Ministers after a dramatic Kohl–Mazowiecki meeting in the frontier town of Frankfurt-Slubice.

In Polish–Soviet relations the principle of equal partnership was fully implemented, while the government maintained contacts on two levels: with central Soviet authorities and separately with governments of constituent Soviet republics, particularly the Russian Federation, Ukraine and Byelorussia. Negotiations began on the withdrawal of Soviet troops by 1991. In April Moscow admitted that the Katyn massacre of Polish officers in 1941 had been perpetrated by the NKVD (see AR 1989, p.116). The fundamental concept of Polish policy was defined by Mr Skubiszewski as one of 'equal proximity' to two powerful neighbours, and as 'a bridge' between Western Europe and the new USSR and perhaps with the emerging independent republics.

CZECHOSLOVAKIA

CAPITAL: Prague AREA: 128,000 sq km POPULATION: 15,600,000 ('90)
OFFICIAL LANGUAGES: Czech, Slovak
POLITICAL SYSTEM: federal parliamentary democracy
HEAD OF STATE: President Václav Havel (since Dec '89)
RULING PARTIES: coalition of Civic Forum (CF), Public Against Violence (PAV) and Christian and Democratic Union/Christian Democratic Movement (CDU/CDM)
PRINCIPAL MINISTERS: Marián Čalfa (PAV/Prime Minister), Václav Vales (unaffiliated/deputy premier, economic reform), Jiří Dienstbier (CF/foreign affairs), Lubos Dobrovsky (CF/defence), Václav Klaus (CF/finance), Petr Pithart (Czech republic premier), Vladimir Meciar (Slovak republic premier)
INTERNATIONAL ALIGNMENT: Warsaw Pact, Comecon, but seeking West European alignment
CURRENCY: koruna (end–'90 £1=K52.72, US$1=K27.32) GNP PER CAPITA: n.a.
MAIN EXPORT EARNERS: machinery, chemicals and fuels, manufactured goods

PROGRESS in democratization was marked along five lines: the rule of communist ideology came to an end; the coercive organs of the old regime were rendered ineffective; the contours of a pluralistic political system began to take shape; foundations were laid for a market-based economy; and important foreign political gains were made. If the popular mood at the end of the year did not reflect full satisfaction with the attainments of the 'velvet revolution', this was mainly due to fear of the consequences of economic freedom and concern about the continued coexistence of the Czechs and the Slovaks in a viable joint state.

Freedom of speech, including cultural liberalization and uncensored media, became complete. Hundreds of new periodicals began publication. The educational system was democratized at all levels. Foreign travel both into and out of the country, as well as international cultural exchanges, grew exponentially. Visa requirements were abolished through agreements with most Western countries. Blank spots in modern history were being filled and communist clichés about the past were being revised. All religions were given free hand. Repertoires of theatres and cinemas reflected the newly-won freedom. These developments gave the public an overwhelming sense of liberty, against which, however, people became aware of problems unknown under the previous command system, such as the difference between freedom and licence or the conflict between cultural desire and economic feasibility.

The Communist Party's bureaucracy was deprived of its authority and influence. Its numbers diminished drastically (from some 10,000 to barely 2,000) as it became clear that it would have to be paid from the party's withering funds rather than subsidized by the state. A law was passed in November forcing the party to transfer to the government all assets it had held on 31 December 1989 and henceforth live off its members' fees alone. The new regime grappled with the reorganization of the dreaded Interior Ministry for the whole year, in particular the political police. While all the nooks and crannies of an extremely complex and secretive apparatus were perhaps not penetrated yet, the large-scale dismissals and disbandments rendered its erstwhile powers largely ineffectual. A number of people seeking or holding office in the new structures had to resign when their past cooperation with the secret police became known. The armed forces went through several waves of reorganization as well. The military budget was cut; civilian service for conscientious objectors was introduced; and the aim gradually to increase the percentage of career soldiers in relation to conscripts was formulated. The army would be made even smaller over the next years, down to some 140,000 instead of the earlier 210,000. Public police felt the effect of an upsurge in popular dislike for excessive regimentation as well, perhaps unduly so, as the crime rate soared.

Multi-party elections to the federal as well as the Czech and the Slovak parliaments took place in June. The Czech Civic Forum and its Slovak counterpart, Public Against Violence (PAV), came out as clear winners, with a joint majority of 170 seats in the 300-strong federal assembly. As umbrella movements associating an array of diverse groups, they were seen by the electorate as the best guarantee against the revival of communist practices. The Communist Party, which underwent a number of personnel and organizational changes during the year (but did not change its name as the fraternal parties did elsewhere in Eastern Europe), retained a relatively strong following of almost 14 per cent, which made it the second largest party in the federal parliament with 47 seats. At the end of the year, the Communist Party claimed 650,000 members or some 38 per cent of the 1,700,000 it had had before the democratic process began.

The Slovak Christian Democratic Movement, with 40 seats for the coalition it headed, as well as virtually all other political groups in Slovakia, campaigned on a national platform in search of more powers for the Slovak legislature and executive. The Slovak National Party, which gained 15 seats at the federal level and 22 in the Slovak National Council, developed into an assertive champion of full independence for Slovakia. A Moravian-Silesian regional grouping and the Hungarian minority party in Slovakia also did well. On the other hand, the traditional parties, including the Social Democrats, polled badly and failed to clear the 5 per cent hurdle needed to gain access to the federal parliament. The Greens did not make it either. On balance, broad-church liberal politics and regional interests fared best and determined the character of the political landscape throughout the year.

The local government election in November produced some decline in support for Civic Forum and the PAV, while the Christian Democrats and independent candidates (who could not compete for parliamentary seats) became stronger. The communists managed to retain a strong presence in local bodies.

Václav Havel was re-elected as President in July for another two years, the same period of office as that of the new parliaments, which were enjoined to draft separate constitutions for the two republics (Czech and Slovak) and for the federation within that time. Mr Havel continued to enjoy esteem and support but critical voices were heard in the latter part of the year about his alleged excessive interference in politics beyond what the presidential statute envisaged. He asked for special powers in December to prevent a possible disintegration of the Czech-Slovak relationship, but parliament itself resolved the threatening impasse and delayed debating the President's request until 1991.

Whereas the PAV stayed more or less united, with increasing accentuation of the Slovak national cause, Civic Forum's political spectrum began to show signs of disintegration in the autumn. Three groups began to organize themselves into more clear-cut political parties: the Democratic Left (with many, but not all, ex-communists of Prague Spring vintage); the Democratic Right; and the Liberal Club, generally considered to represent the political centre. They still existed only as parliamentary factions but it was clear at the end of the year that a division of the over-arching movement into fully fledged parties was only a matter of time. Václav Klaus, the dynamic Finance Minister, became Civic Forum's chairman in October. He was a self-professed rightist and an advocate of ruthless economic privatization.

While it had always been clear that the federal constitution that regulated Czech-Slovak coexistence, and to which the communists paid only lip-service, would have to be overhauled, the depth and fervour of Slovak proposals caught many Czechs by surprise. What the Slovaks regarded as natural in terms of their right to self-determination, many Czechs saw as excessive and in the last instance non-viable. In April the official name of the country was changed to 'Czech and Slovak Federal Republic' (CSFR). The agreement on the distribution of powers that was eventually thrashed out in November and December after long, heated and acrimonious debates transferred a great deal of legislative and executive authority from the centre to the republics.

After intensive debates in the first part of the year, the proponents of radical economic change gained the upper hand over advocates of a more circumspect approach, but some compromises had to be made. In April the first series of laws established conditions for private enterprise, enabled a break-up of the state monopolies and generally liberalized the economic environment. Private, cooperative and state ownership were declared equal before the law. Privatization was to ensue in three phases. The Restitution Law, enacted in October, provided for the return to private owners of some 70,000 properties expropriated by the communists. Adopted in the same month, the Small Privatization Law stipulated the auctioning off to private bidders of over 100,000 small businesses (shops, workshops, restaurants etc.); the auctions were to begin in early 1991. The Large Privatization Law was presented to parliament in the autumn but not debated or approved by the end of the year. It envisaged selling of shares in state enterprises to local and foreign investors as well as distribution of vouchers to all citizens at a nominal price for later conversion into shares.

While the inflation rate reached 14 per cent at the end of 1990, it became clear that it would rise further after most prices had been decontrolled. The government reserved for itself the right of residual price control to mitigate the impact. Concern was expressed over the social cost of rapid privatization and freeing of prices. Unemployment stayed low, at some 40,000 persons by the end of the year (about 0.5 per cent of the labour force), but officials feared it could rise as much as ten times in 1991. Industrial output fell by some 3.5 per cent, mostly on account of discontinued production programmes that had anyway been wasteful or plainly useless.

Foreign trade with the West grew by 4.5 per cent and declined with the Comecon countries by over 14 per cent. The country was badly affected by a 20 per cent reduction of Soviet oil deliveries, the general unreliability of the USSR in complying with earlier contracts, the cancellation of contracts by the German Democratic Republic prior to its accession to West Germany and the loss of an estimated $2,000 million resulting from the international trading embargo on Iraq. On the other hand, Czechoslovakia was admitted to the International Monetary Fund, granted most-favoured-nation status by the USA, and promised loans and credits by several sources in the West. Its gross foreign debt stood at under $8,000 million at the end of the year, a manageable amount fully covered by outstanding Czechoslovak claims against foreign partners. Foreign entrepreneurs invested in about 1,000 joint ventures with Czechoslovak companies, mostly small and medium sized. The most spectacular and important was the agreement between Volkswagen and Skoda, concluded towards the end of the year after a competing offer from Renault and Volvo had been found less advantageous by the Czechs. The German company pledged to invest thousands of millions of Deutschmarks into the modernization and expansion of the car-making plant.

Czechoslovakia projected a favourable international image, as a country where democratization was proceeding apace and prospects for economic rectification were good. President Havel, Foreign Minister Jiří Dienstbier, Federal Assembly chairman Alexander Dubček and many other leading lights of the new regime travelled widely to carry the message to virtually all parts of the globe. A number of foreign statesmen paid visits, including George Bush, Margaret Thatcher, François Mitterrand, Helmut Kohl and Pope John Paul II. In the spring Czechoslovakia joined the Pentagonale initiative to coordinate practical regional interaction with Austria, Italy, Hungary and Yugoslavia. Diplomatic relations were established with Israel, the Vatican and South Korea. Prague supported German unification without reservation from the start. There were untold millions of visiting well-wishers, fact-finders, prospective business partners, volunteers offering all manner of assistance, and plain tourists.

Czechoslovakia negotiated the withdrawal of all the 75,000 Soviet troops stationed on its territory. Some 55,000 men, over 30,000 dependents and most of the equipment had left by the end of the year and the rest were scheduled to follow before July 1991. Czechoslovakia at first believed that a hasty dissolution of the Warsaw Pact would unnecessarily antagonize the USSR and push it into unwelcome 'Asian' isolation, but later it began to campaign for a quick abolition of the Pact's military wing and a reduction of its residual political role to the consultative level. Czechoslovak armed forces were taken out of the Pact's line of command and all but four Soviet military liaison officers were sent home. Prague also said that Comecon was not viable and that it should be replaced by a small agency for economic consultations.

Prague was chosen to house the newly-created permanent secretariat of the Conference on Security and Cooperation in Europe. It was promised membership in the Council of Europe and an association agreement with the European Community next year. Having initially advocated a vision of the future Europe as a congenial fraternity without blocs and military alliances, President Havel and Mr Dienstbier were later ready to accept NATO as the central point of the new international security system.

President Havel symbolically visited both German states (as they then were) in the first days of the year, immediately after his election. He also acknowledged that the Czechoslovaks had used unlawful and immoral force during the expulsion of Germans in the wake of World War II. Some fears were expressed among the public that the new regime was kowtowing to the Germans too much and that German economic might could strangle Czechoslovakia's aspirations to free development. Czechoslovak officials said that the Sudeten German demand for material compensation could only be considered in inter-state talks and in the context of Czechoslovak claims for damages resulting from Nazi occupation.

Among points of friction with neighbouring countries, it was impossible to come to an agreement with Hungary whether the joint hydro-electric system on the Danube ought to be completed (as Czechoslovakia wanted) or scrapped (as Hungary demanded). In fear of too many Polish shoppers buying cheaper Czechoslovak goods, traffic between the two countries remained subject to restrictions. In the latter part of the year, officials and journalists increasingly expressed concern about a possible flood of refugees from an impoverished and disintegrating Soviet Union. A new asylum law was passed, refugee camps were being erected and other precautions were planned.

It was a year of hopeful but somewhat chaotic transition in which some foundations of a democratic future were laid but no solutions could be fully consolidated.

HUNGARY

CAPITAL: Budapest   AREA: 93,000 sq km   POPULATION: 10,600,000 ('88)
OFFICIAL LANGUAGE: Hungarian   POLITICAL SYSTEM: multi-party democracy
HEAD OF STATE: President Arpád Göncz (since Aug '90)
RULING PARTY: coalition led by Hungarian Democratic Forum (HDF)
HEAD OF GOVERNMENT: József Antall, Prime Minister (since May '90)
PRINCIPAL MINISTERS: Géza Jeszenszky (foreign affairs), Lajos Für (defence), Balázs Horváth (interior), Istvan Balsai (justice)
INTERNATIONAL ALIGNMENT: Warsaw Pact, Comecon, but effectively fluid
CURRENCY: forint (end-'90 £1=Ft116.58, US$1=Ft60.40)
GNP PER CAPITA: US$2,460 ('88)
MAIN EXPORT EARNERS: machinery and transport equipment, agricultural products, basic manufactures

THE year began with what can only be described as a political vacuum. The Communist Party had for all practical purposes disintegrated at the end of 1989 and its control over the country through the *nomenklatura* dissolved, with the result that the government and parliament owed no responsibility to anyone except themselves. The general elections in March-April would eventually resolve this, but until then Hungary was governed by a kind of caretaker administration. It was the lack of legitimacy of this government that explained its reluctance to introduce any far-reaching measures to reform the economy. It was felt that only a democratically-elected government should do this.

The elections took place under an unbelievably complicated system that included both an element of proportional representation and direct mandates and resulted in the clear ascendancy of the Hungarian Democratic Forum (HDF). The votes can be seen in the table:

	% of vote	seats
* Hungarian Democratic Forum	42.49	164
Alliance of Free Democrats	23.83	92
* Independent Smallholders	11.40	44
Hungarian Socialist Party	8.55	33
Alliance of Young Democrats	5.70	22
* Christian Democratic Party	5.44	21
Independents	1.55	6
Agrarian Alliance	0.52	2
Joint party candidates	0.52	2

*members of the coalition

Under the leadership of József Antall, a historian, the HDF became the leading element of a three-party coalition including the Smallholders and the Christian Democrats. The HDF was an occasionally uneasy alliance of conservative reformers, a Christian democratic current and the national radical populists. In particular, the populists were generally more radical in their demands than the other currents in the Forum and frequently put pressure on the leadership, but their demands mostly concerned intellectual and cultural matters, rather than economic. The populists were entirely excluded from the government.

The opposition was made up of (i) the Free Democrats, a party led by the Budapest intelligentsia and professing support for both free market and social democratic principles and with considerable support across the country, (ii) the Young Democrats, a professionally-skilled party representing the younger generation; and (iii) the Hungarian Socialist Party, the reform wing of the old Communist Party.

Perhaps the most important event in terms of establishing the constitutional framework for politics was the agreement signed by Mr Antall and the leader of the Free Democrats, János Kis, at the end of April. This document provided that entrenched legislation requiring a two-thirds majority would be restricted to a relatively narrow range of issues and it agreed that the office of president would be held by a Free Democrat, Árpád Göncz, a popular choice. Thereafter, the new government asked parliament for a hundred days' grace, during which time it would formulate a proper social and economic programme.

In the event, the government proved to be surprisingly passive and hesitant in embarking on any serious programme of reconstruction. This was given various explanations. Partly it was attributed to the internal divisions within the coalition, notably the Smallholders' reluctance to make any concessions on their insistence that all land be returned to the 1947 owners, a demand that all other parties found unviable. Second, there was constant criticism from the populists. Third, there was inexperience, both of administering a state machine and formulating strategy. And fourth, there was the personality of Antall himself, who though a strong leader, was most reluctant to take decisions in economic matters. The economic ministers were themselves divided between more and less étatist strategies of reform, so that the indecisiveness of the Prime Minister resulted in near passivity by the end of the year.

Popular discontent rose as a result. This was expressed through the local government election results in early October, in which the opposition parties captured most of the towns, including Budapest, while the coalition parties did uniformly badly. Popular discontent was articulated even more graphically through the so-called taxi-drivers' blockade at the end of October.

When the government announced a 75 per cent increase in the price of petrol, after having denied that any increase was contemplated, taxi drivers in Budapest blockaded the bridges across the Danube and all main intersections, effectively paralysing the city. They called for the rescinding of the prices and negotiations. Eventually a compromise was patched up. What was especially noteworthy about this event was that it spread within hours throughout the country, so that virtually every locality had its blockade, thereby symbolizing solidarity with the drivers and expressing dissatisfaction with the highly-politicized nature of the formal and informal discussions. If the government had not made concessions, the outcome could have been very serious indeed.

In a speech to parliament in December, Mr Antall as good as admitted that his government had not done enough in transforming the economy. He noted that the economic state of affairs was very grave, but his proposed remedies appeared to be rather a programme of pressing on with the existing slow rate of change. A government reshuffle at around the same time held some hope that the new economic ministers would tackle matters with greater urgency, a need that was urgent given an estimated budget deficit of at least 70,000 million forints, as against a projected 20,000 million earlier in the year, and an inflation rate that was at least 30 per cent and rising.

In foreign and defence policy, Hungary found itself somewhat isolated by the end of the year. As the West turned its attention towards the Gulf, few people bothered to pay much attention to the difficulties of a small country like Hungary. In particular, the longstanding problem of the ethnic Hungarian minorities in Romania, Czechoslovakia and Yugoslavia, in different ways, threatened to envenom relations with three of Hungary's neighbours. Equally, Hungary was feeling the chill breeze of being on its own in defence matters, in that it looked as if no international body could be relied on for support in the event that political events abroad threatened to spill over into Hungary. However, on the plus side, Hungary was the first ex-communist country to be admitted to full membership of the Council of Europe and through the Pentagonale (Italy, Austria, Yugoslavia, Czechoslovakia and Hungary), it was participating in an important regional initiative. Moves were also made to achieve closer regional coordination with Czechoslovakia and Poland.

ROMANIA

CAPITAL: Bucharest   AREA: 237,500, sq km   POPULATION: 23,000,000 ('88)
OFFICIAL LANGUAGE: Romanian   POLITICAL SYSTEM: emerging democracy
HEAD OF STATE: President Ion Iliescu (since Dec '89)
RULING PARTY: National Salvation Front (NSF)
HEAD OF GOVERNMENT: Petre Roman, Prime Minister (since Dec '89)
PRINCIPAL MINISTERS: Adrian Nastase (foreign affairs), Col.-Gen. Victor A. Stanculescu (defence), Theodor Stolojan (finance), Doru V. Ursu (interior), Victor Babiuc (justice)
INTERNATIONAL ALIGNMENT: Warsaw Pact, Comecon, but effectively fluid
CURRENCY: leu (end-'90 £1=66.43 lei, US$1=34.42 lei)
GNP PER CAPITA: US$2,540 ('81)
MAIN EXPORT EARNERS: oil, raw materials and metals, machinery and transport equipment, chemicals, tourism

FOR Romanians the year began with high expectations following the overthrow of the Ceauşescu dictatorship in the revolution of December 1989 (see AR 1989, pp. 124–7) but ended in bitter disillusionment for many. Discontent centred on the survival of the communist bureaucracy, which remained entrenched at many levels of power, and on the failure of the ruling National Salvation Front (NSF) to cope with Romania's desperately serious economic problems. The general malaise manifested itself in endemic anti-government protests, demonstrations and strikes.

Controversy surrounded even the revolution itself. The fighting had hardly died down when allegations began to be made that the revolution, sparked off by demonstrations, had been hijacked by communist officials who had earlier been pushed aside by President Ceauşescu. These claims gained greater credibility in August when two leading figures in the revolution, Professor Silviu Brucan and General Nicolae Militaru, lent their authority to the argument that the events of December 1989 were the outcome of a long-standing conspiracy, involving anti-Ceauşescu elements in the Communist Party, the army and the much-feared secret police, the Securitate.

By the time they had made their allegations, both Professor Brucan, initially the NSF's chief ideologist, and General Militaru, for a time Minister of Defence, had been removed from power. They had joined the ranks of those who had either been forced to leave the NSF leadership because of their connections with the Ceauşescu regime (such as Dumitru Mazilu, for a time NSF vice-president) or those who had resigned from it, among them the respected former dissident, Doina Cornea, in protest against the continuing influence of ex-communists.

In spite of the controversy surrounding its origins and membership, the NSF retained its popularity in the immediate aftermath of the revolution and in the period leading up to the presidential and parliamentary elections, postponed from April to 20 May at the opposition's request. The NSF's popularity was boosted by the liberalization that followed the overthrow of the Ceauşescu regime. The authorities re-introduced freedom of travel and emigration. Freedom of religious worship was also guaranteed and the Eastern rite Catholic Church was relegalized in April, leading to the restoration in May of diplomatic relations with the Vatican after a break of 40 years.

The NSF dominated the all-party provisional legislature, the Council of National Unity, formed in February; it could, therefore, claim credit for the above popular measures in the election campaign, during which it also dominated the media. The election results produced a victory for the NSF that was on an even more massive scale than most observers had expected. In the presidential contest Mr Iliescu received 85.07 per cent, against 10.16 per cent for Radu Câmpeanu of the National Liberal Party (NLP) and 4.29 per cent for Ion Raţiu of the Christian Democratic National Peasants' Party (CDNPP). The elections for the new Assembly of Deputies and Senate resulted as follows:

	Assembly %	seats	Senate %	seats
NSF	66.31	263	67.02	92
Hungarian Democratic Union of Romania	7.23	29	7.20	12
NLP	6.41	29	7.06	9
Ecological Movement	2.62	12	2.45	1
CDNPP	2.56	12	2.50	1
Romanian Unity Alliance	2.15	9	2.15	2
Agrarian Democratic Party	1.59	9	1.59	0
Ecological Party	1.38	8	1.38	1
Socialist Democratic Party	1.11	5	1.11	0
Others	8.64	24*	7.54	0

*including 13 allocated seats

Foreign observers reported far more electoral irregularities than in any other East European elections, ranging from multiple voting by the same individuals to the distribution of ballot papers already marked in favour of the NSF. However, the general consensus was that these malpractices did not substantially alter the results. The NSF's landslide victory was attributed to its cautious economic programme, which warned against a speedy transition to a market economy with its consequent high inflation and unemployment. The opposition was disunited and largely out of touch with the electorate, made all the worse by the fact that the revived NLP and the CDNPP were led by elderly emigrés. Among the opposition, only the Hungarian Democratic Union of Romania (HDUR), with its limited ethnic appeal, performed as well as its supporters had hoped.

More alarmingly the NSF's supporters resorted to intimidation as a weapon to frighten off potential backing for the opposition. Physical assaults on the government's opponents continued even after the elections. They culminated in two days of mayhem on 15–16 June, when pro-government miners from the provinces took to the streets of Bucharest, reportedly at President Iliescu's request, to break up anti-NSF demonstrations. Thereafter, the government's reliance on vigilantes and its own authoritarian measures began to undermine its popularity. Discontent also simmered because many people suspected that former Securitate officials remained in positions of power. There were only a few trials of prominent figures in the former leadership, the most celebrated being that of the late President Ceaușescu's son, Nicu, who was sentenced to 20 years' imprisonment for instigating murder during the revolution.

Chronic economic problems had the same negative effect on the government's standing. Early in the year living conditions improved substantially for most Romanians as the authorities allowed more food imports and increased the amount of energy available for domestic use. There was a cut in working hours and the tough labour discipline maintained under Ceaușescu's rule was considerably eased. In the absence of incentives for producers, the effect of these otherwise welcome changes was to reduce output and productivity.

Prime Minister Petre Roman's government had to go back on its pre-election promises. His new administration, formed after the May elections, launched a more determined shift towards a market economy. Huge price increases on a range of goods and services, including clothing and transport, were introduced at the beginning of November, doubling or trebling many prices. However, following widespread protests, the government postponed a planned second round of price rises. Meanwhile, the Roman government had been granted special powers to manage the economy by decree. The coincidence of rising imports (designed to improve the supply of consumer goods) with falling exports brought about by a drop in production resulted in a trade deficit estimated at $1,200 million, which was in stark contrast with the artificially-inflated huge surpluses of the late Ceaușescu years. In an attempt to boost exports the leu was devalued by nearly 70 per cent in November.

The conflict in the Gulf had a major impact on the Romanian economy, which had traditionally been the most dependent of all the Warsaw Pact countries on supplies of oil from the Middle East. The damage caused to Romania in 1990 through loss of export markets in the Gulf and higher oil prices was estimated at around $3,500 million. Romania observed the UN embargo on Iraq and gave its backing to the international coalition against Saddam Husain. However, its relations with the Western world did not improve in line with expectations at the time of the revolution because of the continuation of authoritarian tendencies in the country's leadership. The refusal to allow the exiled ex-King Michael into the country on two occasions, in April and December, created much adverse international publicity. But nothing matched the officially-inspired violent crack-down on opposition supporters by pro-government miners in June in the extent of damage it caused to Romania's reputation abroad. The action was condemned around the world, particularly in the United States. The European Community responded by suspending the signing of a trade and cooperation agreement with Romania.

Relations with Hungary, which improved dramatically during and in the immediate aftermath of the revolution, failed to maintain their momentum. As ethnic Hungarians began to complain about delays in the implementation of promises for the re-opening of Hungarian-language schools, the Hungarian authorities became increasingly critical of their counterparts in Bucharest. Relations between the two countries came under the greatest strain in the aftermath of bloody ethnic clashes in the Transylvanian town of Tîrgu Mureş on 19–20 March, which claimed several lives.

Among the many states alienated by Ceauşescu, the Soviet Union perhaps fared the best in rebuilding relations with Romania, partly because President Iliescu's political outlook in many ways resembled that of Mikhail Gorbachev. The Romanian authorities adopted a cautious attitude to the emergence of Romanian nationalism in the Soviet republic of Moldavia and to demands on both sides of the border that Moldavia be reunited with Romania. But in the overall improvement of ties with the rest of the world, Romania continued to lag behind the rest of Eastern Europe.

BULGARIA

CAPITAL: Sofia   AREA: 111,000 sq km   POPULATION: 8,989,172 ('90)
OFFICIAL LANGUAGE: Bulgarian
POLITICAL SYSTEM: emerging parliamentary democracy
HEAD OF STATE: President Zhelyu Zhelev (since Aug '90)
RULING COALITION: Bulgarian Socialist Party (BSP), Union of Democratic Forces
   (UDF), Bulgarian Agrarian National Union (BANU) and independents
PRINCIPAL MINISTERS: Dimitar Popov (ind./Prime Minister), Viktor Valkov
   (BANU/deputy premier, foreign affairs), Dimitar Ludzhev (UDF/deputy premier),
   Aleksandar Tomov (BSP/deputy premier), Ivan Pushkarov (UDF/trade & industry),
   Ivan Kostov (UDF/finance), Gen.-Col. Yordan Mutafchiev (BSP/defence), Hristo
   Danov (ind./internal affairs)
INTERNATIONAL ALIGNMENT: Warsaw Pact, Comecon, but effectively fluid
CURRENCY: lev (end-'90 £1=L5.37, US$1=L2.78)
GNP PER CAPITA: US$4,150 ('88)
MAIN EXPORT EARNERS: machinery and equipment, agricultural produce, tourism

A year of three prime ministers and four governments saw a drastic economic decline, exacerbated by a lack of progress on market-oriented reform. Despite the optimism generated by mass anti-communist marches at the end of 1989, (see AR 1989, pp. 127–9), Bulgaria's new democrats failed to eradicate the surviving power and influence of the old pro-Soviet nomenklatura. Although there were free elections in June, for the first time in more than 50 years, they resulted in a deadlock between the parties that frustrated the establishment of a stable democratic order. Public opinion became bitterly polarized.

The year began with the Bulgarian Communist Party (BCP) firmly in power, albeit under the leadership of liberals, who had ousted the long-serving dictator, Todor Zhivkov, in November 1989. (Mr Zhivkov spent 1990 either in prison or under house arrest, awaiting trial.) Facing the challenge of a genuine opposition for the first time since the late 1940s, the BCP was obliged to remove guarantees of its leading role from the constitution and embark on a series of organizational and policy changes to give the party an acceptable public image. At a congress between 30 January and 2 February a reformist marxist manifesto was adopted after heated debates. The politburo and the central committee were replaced by a 17-member presidium and a 153-member supreme council, 90 per cent of whose members were newly-elected to party office. State President Petar Mladenov stepped down as leader; chosen as BCP chairman was Aleksandar Lilov, a former top ideologist, who had been purged by Mr Zhivkov in 1983. After a referendum among members, the party altered its name in April, becoming the Bulgarian Socialist Party (BSP) and taking a red rose as its symbol.

The Communists opened round-table talks with the opposition on 16 January. These took more than two months to reach an agreement, partly because of disputes over control of the media. The 16-member Union of Democratic Forces (UDF), formed as recently as December 1989, improved its bargaining position by mounting huge public rallies. The biggest—in Sofia on 25 February—attracted over 200,000 people. Although the UDF failed to win a deferment of parliamentary elections until November, the BCP had to compromise over both the election law and the size and role of the new Grand National Assembly. During February the BCP changed the Prime Minister, replacing Zhivkov acolyte Georgi Atanasov with a more sophisticated politburo veteran, Andrei Lukanov. At the same time, the Bulgarian Agrarian National Union (BANU) withdrew its three cabinet ministers, declaring itself an opposition party. This left the BCP (subsequently the BSP) running a one-party government for the first time since its takeover in 1944.

The elections took place against a background of mounting economic chaos. Because of a collapse in foreign earnings, Bulgaria had suspended both capital and interest payments on its $10,630 million foreign debt. Mr Lukanov adopted a broad rescue package in March, but almost none of its proposals were enforced. In spite of the erosion of living standards, the BSP won the two-stage election on 10 and 17 June, largely because of the support of pensioners and rural voters, who accepted its claim that it could establish a market economy without using shock tactics. The BSP won 211 seats in the 400-member Assembly, as opposed to 144 for the

UDF and 16 for the BANU. The Movement for Rights and Freedoms, representing Bulgaria's ethnic Turks, won 23 seats. The BSP's slender overall majority resulted in six months of chronic political instability and legislative paralysis.

Nationwide protests that the BSP had won by fraud and intimidation erupted as soon as the result was announced. These quickly developed into a movement against President Mladenov, who had been shown on television during the campaign urging that tanks be brought in to disperse a human chain round parliament in December 1989. Although he protested that the videofilm was a montage, Mr Mladenov was eventually obliged to resign on 6 July. After almost a month of inter-party wrangling, the UDF leader, Zhelyu Zhelev, was surprisingly chosen as his successor, following a split in the BSP parliamentary vote. Mr Zhelev handed over the UDF chairmanship to the naturalist Petar Beron, but in December Mr Beron also stepped down amid allegations that he had been a police informer. Filip Dimitrov of the Green Party then took over the UDF leadership.

Mr Zhelev's election as President had fuelled speculation that the UDF would accept Mr Lukanov's invitation to enter a coalition government. This did not happen, however, and it was not until 20 September, three months after the elections, that Mr Lukanov named his new cabinet, consisting of BSP members and two independents. The inexplicable delay had seriously undermined his ability to rule. Even though he produced a credible economic programme, drafted with US expert advice, the UDF and BANU refused to back it, arguing that the Prime Minister would not be able to enact his own policies. The package was, they said, just a trick to defend the interests of the old nomenklatura. Mr Lukanov had been hoping that endorsement of his reforms would unlock funds from the IMF, which Bulgaria had joined in September. Such credits were needed to offset the effects of a major drop in Soviet oil deliveries and the UN embargo against Iraq, which Bulgaria supported.

The deepening recession and the government's inactivity provoked a massive drop in public support for the BSP. On 1 September food rationing, already in force in the provinces, was introduced in Sofia. Bulgaria also endured systematic power cuts and escalating inflation, exceeding 120 per cent by the end of 1990. Feeling himself under threat and weakened by factionalism, Mr Lilov called a second BSP congress in September. It met in an atmosphere of paranoia following a riot on 26 August, when the party headquarters in Sofia was incinerated by an anti-government mob. The congress voted narrowly to retain Mr Lilov as leader, but made no clear resolution of the BSP's policy dilemmas.

In early November Sofia's students resumed their anti-government strikes, appealing for the overthrow of the Lukanov administration. After three weeks the Podkrepa Labour Confederation (which had observer status in the UDF) called a general strike. Once the larger

Confederation of Independent Trade Unions had joined in, Mr Lukanov resigned on 29 November. Complex negotiations followed, which ended in a three-sided coalition government being formed, under Sofia magistrate Dimitar Popov, who had served on the central electoral commission in June. Mr Popov, who had no party affiliations, persuaded both the UDF and the BANU to accept cabinet posts. The year ended with this new government facing up to Bulgaria's economic collapse and political turmoil.

YUGOSLAVIA

CAPITAL: Belgrade   AREA: 255,804 sq km   POPULATION: 23,690,000 ('90 est.)
OFFICIAL LANGUAGES: Serbo-Croat, Macedonian, Slovene
POLITICAL SYSTEM: nominally socialist federal republic, but in transition
HEAD OF STATE: Borisav Jovic, President of federal presidency (from May '90)
PRINCIPAL MINISTERS: Ante Markovic (federal premier), Budimir Loncar (foreign affairs), Veljko Kadijevic (defence), Petar Garacanin (interior), Franc Horvat (foreign economic relations)
INTERNATIONAL ALIGNMENT: NAM, Comecon (associate), OECD (observer)
CURRENCY: dinar (end-'90 £1=Din20.17, US$1=Din10.45)
GNP PER CAPITA: US$2,679 ('89)
MAIN EXPORTS: machinery (esp. transport equipment), metals and metal manufactures, agricultural products and food, tourism

THE new year opened with the launching of one of the principal measures of the Markovic reform programme (see AR 1989, p. 130), the inauguration of a new currency. The new dinar, fully convertible, was pegged until June to the Deutschmark (DM) at 7:1. As wage increases were tied to the exchange rate, this was an important move in the fight against inflation, which fell from 2,700 per cent by the end of 1989 to around zero within three months. The government's inability to capitalize upon this achievement by enforcing other aspects of its reforms resulted in the return of inflation by the end of the year to a rate of 120–130 per cent. The dinar was devalued at the end of December, to 11:1 against the DM.

A major setback in relation to economic reform was experienced in banking. It was discovered in December that the Serbian banks had been conspiring to evade the provisions of recent legislation, by granting massive unsecured credits in order to shore up ailing enterprises in the republic.

The overall economic results for the year were mixed. The attempt to shake out uneconomic enterprises began to work. Most noteworthy was the liquidation of the Slovene ski-equipment company Elan in October. Registered unemployment rose by an estimated 60,000 on the year; industrial productivity fell by around 11 per cent. On the positive side, investment (especially foreign investment) was believed to have shown a substantial rise, and trade (especially with the OECD countries) to have expanded.

In June the Markovic government introduced a second round of reform proposals, including the privatization of socially-owned enterprises, although the economic reforms introduced in 1989 marked time as a consequence of the continuing political uncertainty in Yugoslavia, and especially the unresolved question of the relationship between the republics and the federation.

In January trade talks the Soviet Union addressed the serious imbalance in trade between the two countries. Yugoslav representatives participated in the Paris meeting to discuss a European Bank for Reconstruction and Development. Gerard Collins, the Irish Foreign Minister and current president of the EC Council of Ministers, visited Belgrade for talks on Yugoslavia's relations with EC institutions. In March agreement was reached with the IMF on the granting of an 18-month standby credit agreement, of up to US$600 million. On 17 September Yugoslavia and Italy signed the 'Adriatic initiative' agreement, on environmental protection, transport, tourism and infrastructure.

The League of Communists of Yugoslavia (LCY) finally began its postponed 14th (extraordinary) congress in Belgrade on 20 January. The main items on the agenda were the commitment of the party to political pluralism; Slovene LC proposals for the reform of the LCY into eight independent parties; and renunciation of the constitutional guarantee of the 'leading role of the League of Communists'. Although this last was adopted with only 28 votes against, the Slovene proposals were resoundingly defeated, as were proposals on a clear commitment to civil rights. The Slovene delegation withdrew. After bitter debate the congress was adjourned on 23 January, with no date set for its reconvention. The press announced the LCY 'no longer exists'. Mr Markovic declared that 'Yugoslavia continues to function with or without the LCY'.

On 30 March the LCY failed to secure a quorum for a special plenum called to discuss the situation, after delegates from Croatia and Macedonia as well as Slovenia had failed to appear. The League of Communists of Yugoslavia could be said to have expired at that point.

The creation of political parties continued in the lead-up to the elections for the republican Assemblies. The Movement for All-Macedonian Action held its founding assembly in February—the first of many, which included a revival of the pre-war Democratic Party in Serbia and of the Croatian Peasant Party. By the end of March around 100 'parties' had been identified throughout the federation, with a wide variety of bases. A large number of these appealed to specifically ethnic constituencies, such as Vuk Draskovic's Serbian National Renewal. Several were renamed fragments of the former LCY, such as the Slovene Party of Democratic Renewal. There was a handful of issue-oriented groups, principally farmers' parties in Macedonia and Slovenia, and Greens. Then there were several general formations with broad economic and political platforms, such as social democratic parties and Mr Markovic's own Alliance of Reform Forces.

The cycle of elections to the Assemblies began in April in Slovenia, and was finally completed in December in Serbia. A centre-right alliance of six parties (DEMOS) was returned in Slovenia, and Franjo Tudjman's Croatian National Union in Croatia, ensuring the participation of non-communist representatives in future federal governments. Slobodan Milosevic's Socialist Party of Serbia also secured victory, as did the Communists in Montenegro. But in other republics a process of negotiation was necessary in order to form coalitions, typically of a centre-left orientation, including former Communists.

The progress of federal-republican relations was not made easier by the accession to the federal presidency in May of Borisav Jovic, a staunch supporter of Mr Milosevic. Since his Vice-President was Croatia's Stipe Suvar, the presidency was seriously hampered as an agency for effective and united government. However, following the Knin affair (see below) the Croatian assembly voted to recall Mr Suvar as its representative on the presidency, on the grounds that he was not sufficiently vigorous in pursuit of Croatian interests. He was replaced by Stjepan Mesic, a committed Croat nationalist and associate of Mr Tudjman, who had once been imprisoned for his part in the events of the 'Croat Spring' of 1971–72.

By year's end in every republic except Macedonia a government was installed with a legitimacy undergirded by popular and free elections. Serious and responsible negotiation could take place on the future of the federation, and open the way for economic reform. The constitutional drafts outlined during the year by Slovene, Croatian and Serbian representatives, however, displayed markedly divergent conceptions of a future Yugoslavia.

Constitutional questions, in one way or another, held the centre of the political stage in Yugoslavia throughout the year. The new Slovene constitution (AR 1989, p. 132) was followed in July and September by revised constitutions in Croatia and Serbia. The obvious inconsistencies between each of these documents and the existing federal constitution remained to be negotiated. On 23 December a popular referendum in Slovenia returned a majority of 95 per cent in favour of the republic's withdrawal from the federation if, after a period of six months, a satisfactory accommodation had not been reached on the constitutional issue.

The revision of the Serbian constitution provoked particularly painful conflict. A central issue was the subordination of the former autonomous provinces of Vojvodina and Kosovo to republican authority. The provinces were nominally parts of the republic of Serbia; but their autonomy as republics in all but name occasioned great resentment among some Serbs. While the change passed with little serious opposition in Vojvodina, it occasioned violent resistance in Kosovo, as it spelled the end of all possibility of self-determination for its Albanophone majority (now estimated at around 85 per cent of the population of the area).

The year saw three periods of serious civil disorder in Kosovo. On 24 January the police broke up a large demonstration in Pristina gathered at the provincial headquarters of the LCY to demand extensive political reforms. This began a week of rioting which spread to other towns. At least 26 Albanians and one police officer were shot dead. The riots were the worst seen in the province in the post-war period. The federal state presidency announced 'special measures' in Kosovo on 30 January, although there were clear signs of acute disagreement between the members of the presidency over the appropriate response to the situation. In February units of the Yugoslav National Army were used for the first time to control public order in Kosovo. Slovene (and later Croatian) militia units were withdrawn.

The second period of disturbance came about after 22 March when allegations and rumours of the mass poisoning of Albanian students and children led to more than 100 people being injured in riots in Podujevo alone. The claims about poisoning were officially dismissed. On April 3 Jusuf Zejnulahu, the provincial premier, and other provincial ministers in Kosovo resigned in protest against the excessive brutality of the security forces. The provincial Assembly later refused to accept the resignations, which would have left government in the hands of the ethnic Serb members.

On 18 April the 'special measures' were suspended in Kosovo. The Serbian Ministry of Internal Affairs took direct control of security arrangements in the province from federal authorities. On 24 April Azem Vlasi was released from custody after being acquitted, together with the others formerly charged with him, of counter-revolutionary activity (see AR 1989, p. 132).

The third bout of Kosovo disturbances was in September. They followed the gaoling on 23 August of Hajrullah Gorani, leader of the newly-founded independent trade union movement in Kosovo, for his advocacy of a general strike. On 3 September the union called a general strike in the province, and claimed participation by 200,000 people. The occasion was also intended as a protest against the dismissal of thousands of ethnic Albanians from official posts, their replacement by Serbs drafted in from other parts of the federation, and the institution of compulsory loyalty oaths to the republic for officials and others.

In anticipation of the ratification of proposed changes to the Serbian constitution, the provincial Assembly was dissolved by the Serbian authorities in July. Albanian members of the Assembly thereupon declared an independent republic of Kosovo, within the Serbian republic. Several were later arrested, and many (including Prime Minister Zejnulahu) fled the country.

Ethnic group relations were also strained at the end of July when, at a rally in the village of Srb, a gathering of 100,000 Croatian Serbs declared their own autonomy from Croatia. Two days later leaders of Serb communities in the republic of Croatia formed a Serbian National Council, which rejected the amendments to the republic's constitution and determined to conduct a referendum on questions of cultural autonomy.

In the Croatian towns of Knin, Benkovac and nine other communes with ethnic Serb majorities, disorder broke out in mid-August in connection with the referendum. Serb settlements were blockaded to exclude the republican police force. The Croatian government declared there to be an armed insurrection against the Croatian state.

Following several public disturbances on and after 9 September in Foca (Bosnia), the republican government dissolved the town council and prohibited public gatherings. In the same week in Novi Pazar (Bosnia) police clashed with Muslim supporters of the Democratic Action Party, who tried to disrupt a rally of the Serbian National Renewal.

On the tenth anniversary of the death of former President Tito (4 May) a demonstration in Belgrade of about 2,000 Serbs, organized by three of the new parties, called for the removal of his remains to his native Croatia, and an end to the 'cult of personality'.

An explosion at the Kreka mine in Bosnia on 26 August killed 179 miners, in the worst mine disaster in Yugoslavia's history. Work had resumed only two days before after a strike over pay and poor safety conditions.

ALBANIA

CAPITAL: Tirana   AREA: 29,000 sq km   POPULATION: 3,000,000 ('88)
OFFICIAL LANGUAGE: Albanian   POLITICAL SYSTEM: Communist people's republic
HEAD OF STATE AND PARTY LEADER: Ramiz Alia, President of the People's Assembly
    Presidium (since November '82), PLA first secretary (since April '85)
RULING PARTY: Party of Labour of Albania (PLA)
PRINCIPAL MINISTERS: Adil Carcani (Prime Minister), Hekuran Isai (deputy premier,
    internal affairs), Reis Malile (foreign affairs), Kico Mustaqi (defence), Bujar
    Kolaneci (chairman of state planning commission)
CURRENCY: lek (end-'90 £1=AL10.28, US$1=AL5.33)
GNP PER CAPITA: US$820 ('81)
MAIN EXPORT EARNERS: crude oil, minerals, agricultural products

THROUGHOUT 1990 the regime of Ramiz Alia vainly sought to assuage unrest through concession, each concession serving merely to encourage further demands. Initially the contest was between reformist and hard-line factions within the PLA, but after the upheavals of July it was also openly a struggle against as well as within the ruling party.

The unrest which had broken out in Shkodër in late 1989 continued in the new year with reports of up to 7,000 demonstrators on its streets on 11 and 14 January. Mr Alia told a central committee plenum on 25 January that economic and political reforms would be introduced, but these would not infringe the leading role of the party. In the middle of April industrial unrest appeared with a strike by 2,000 textile workers in Berat, though much of the anger appeared to be directed at the Hoxha clique rather than at the party itself. The 10th central committee plenum which met shortly afterwards acknowledged internal problems such as corruption and the shortage of food and consumer goods; some steps towards relaxing central control of the economy and allowing a small degree of private enterprise were taken.

On 7–8 May parliament approved measures ending the ban on foreign credits and foreign investments. Simultaneous political reforms ended the prohibition of religious propaganda, re-established the Ministry of Justice, reduced the number of capital offences, and allowed defence lawyers. On 6 June it was announced that Albania would sign the Helsinki Final Act and wished to join the CSCE. In the same month an observer delegation was sent to the CSCE human rights conference in Copenhagen.

If these concessions marked the victory of the reformists over the conservatives within the PLA, they by no means put an end to the upheavals. In July came a political earthquake, the shock-waves of which were to be felt for the remainder of the year. In June there had been an official promise that in principle all Albanians would be given passports for foreign travel. On 1 July student demonstrations in Tirana were broken up by the police, after which four protesters, mindful of the June promise and of the actions of East Germans in 1989, fled to the West German embassy. Despite a security cordon around the diplomatic enclosure, over 3,000 more Albanians flooded into the embassy, with 500 also going to the French and 300 to the Italian missions. The regime could not contain such a massive expression of discontent and between 9 and 13 July some 5,000 Albanians were given passports to emigrate.

A shaken leadership made further steps towards economic reform at the end of July, when greater latitude was allowed to enterprises using foreign currency. At the same time, a decree was passed permitting meetings and demonstrations in public places. Any hope that such concessions would purchase prolonged peace were dispelled on 25 October when Ismail Kadare, a distinguished, pro-government author and deputy chairman of the Democratic Front, fled to France declaring there was no prospect of legal opposition in Albania and that the government was not serious in its protestations of reform.

In the next round of concessions, in November, President Alia announced that a commission would study possible changes in the constitution. The expectation was for further economic and administrative decentralization and multi-candidate, though not multi-party, elections. In Shkodër in the same month, for the first time since 1967, a public celebration of the Catholic mass was held, the celebrant being a former international footballer who had spent 25 years in prison. The mass became a regular event, and soon a mosque was also functioning in the city.

Such concessions were not enough to keep the lid on the cauldron of unrest. In the first half of December pressure again approached explosion-point, with students and workers demanding that more than one party should be allowed to contest the elections scheduled for 10 February 1991. There were large demonstrations in Tirana and other cities, with some violence occurring in Shkodër and Elbasan. On 11 December Mr Alia once more opened the safety-valve of concession. In addition to removing five hard-liners from the PLA politburo, he agreed that more than one party could contest the forthcoming elections. A Democratic Party under the leadership of an academic, Gramos Pashko, was formed the following day and legalized on 19 December. Tirana intellectuals also established the Forum for the Defence of Human Rights to seek the release of all political prisoners in the country. The confederation of trade unions announced that it would become an independent organization.

Whilst internal change proceeded at an unprecedented pace, President Alia also sought to open the country to wider foreign contacts. In May UN Secretary-General Pérez de Cuellar visited the country. On 30 July it was announced that relations with the Soviet Union were to be restored, and on Independence Day (28 November) Mr Alia made friendly references to China. There were tentative moves towards the normalization of relations with the United States, Mr Alia visiting that country in September-October, officially to speak at the United Nations. By the end of the year contacts with Britain had begun in Geneva, but prospects of a restoration of diplomatic relations were clouded by the severe sentences handed out in trials held in December.

The removal of statues of Stalin in the week before Christmas symbolized these momentous changes, domestic and foreign, but the break with the past was by no means total. There had been no talk of the party relinquishing its leading role, the secret police were untouched, and by 20 December over 150 people had been sentenced, some of them to as much as 20 years imprisonment, for acts of violence committed during the previous fortnight. Nor was confidence in the future universal. At the close of the year hundreds of ethnic Greeks poured across the southern border despite the winter snows and the continuing danger of fire from Albanian guards.

IV WESTERN, CENTRAL AND SOUTHERN EUROPE

Chapter 1

FRANCE—FEDERAL REPUBLIC OF GERMANY—ITALY—BELGIUM—
THE NETHERLANDS—LUXEMBOURG—REPUBLIC OF IRELAND

FRANCE

CAPITAL: Paris   AREA: 544,000 sq km   POPULATION: 55,900,00 ('88)
OFFICIAL LANGUAGE: French   POLITICAL SYSTEM: presidential parliamentary democracy
HEAD OF STATE AND GOVERNMENT: President François Mitterrand (since May '81)
RULING PARTIES: Socialist Party (PS) holds presidency; government is centre-left coalition of the PS, Left Radicals (MRG), independents and elements of the Union for French Democracy (UDF)
PRINCIPAL MINISTERS: Michel Rocard (PS/Prime Minister), Roland Dumas (PS/foreign affairs), Pierre Bérégovoy (PS/economy, finance and budget), Michel Durafour (UDF/civil service and administrative reforms), George Kiejman (non-party/justice), Jean-Pierre Chevènement (PS/defence), Pierre Joxe (PS/interior)
INTERNATIONAL ALIGNMENT: NATO (outside command structure), OECD, EC, Francophonie
CURRENCY: franc (end-'90 £1=F9.82, US$1=F5.09)
GNP PER CAPITA: US$16,090 ('88)
MAIN EXPORT EARNERS: machinery and transport equipment, manufactures, chemicals, food and beverages, tourism

'FOR over 30 years the world of politics has never seemed so profoundly cut off from the French people.' The terms in which two conservative politicians, Michel Noir and François Léotard, launched their appeal in March for political renovation and a united opposition captured a more general sense of malaise among politicians and the public alike. In many respects it was a wretched, unedifying political year. Lacking a parliamentary majority, the government was obliged by political arithmetic and the injunctions of the President, François Mitterrand, to seek an 'opening to the centre'. It was engaged in a constant balancing act, trying to keep its own supporters happy, occasionally looking for Communist backing for left-wing measures, but more often wooing the 'swing votes' of the centre parties. In Socialist Party (PS) ranks frustration among those who felt that socialism was being sacrificed to mere political survival mingled with the clash of personal ambitions as leading figures scored points with a view eventually to succeeding M. Mitterrand. Months of dogfighting and intrigue culminated in four days of confusion and confrontation at the PS congress in March. None of the five contending factions achieved ascendancy. Although a compromise was finally stitched together, the outcome was public dismay and a party profoundly unsure of its future direction. Uncertainty was sustained by President Mitterrand's failure to back his Prime Minister, Michel Rocard, during the difficult autumn session.

Yet another bid to renovate the failing Communist Party, this time by former minister Charles Fiterman, failed at the 27th congress in December. The general secretary, Georges Marchais, a master at manipulating the party machine, won 99 per cent backing—decidedly unfashionable in 1990. However, he had had to concede something approaching a genuine debate and, exceptionally, critics retained their positions instead of being ejected.

Meanwhile, the orthodox right wrestled with the interplay of personal ambitions and disagreements over how best to meet the challenge from the far-right National Front. Jacques Chirac, the leader of the Rassemblement pour la République (RPR), advocated merging with the centre-right to form a broad-based conservative party. Ex-ministers like Charles Pasqua and Philippe Séguin favoured direct competition with the Front through a more nationalistic stance and a hard line on immigration. In June the RPR and the Union pour la Démocratie Française (UDF) linked in a Union pour la France promising to agree on a single candidate in the next parliamentary and presidential elections. However, friction between M. Chirac and former President Valéry Giscard d'Estaing prevented progress. In December Michel Noir resigned from the RPR in disgust at M. Chirac's leadership, declaring that the party was 'not fit to lead a renewal of our national political life'. With two other deputies he resigned his seat to fight a by-election with a view to founding a new party. The disarray and disrepute of the other parties were all grist to the mill of the National Front. Despite its own internal stresses and adverse reaction to Jean-Marie Le Pen's rejection of the government's stance on the Gulf crisis, the Front continued to hold sufficient support to jeopardize the prospects of the orthodox right.

A number of scandals discredited the political class still further. In the spring parliament approved proposals to end the kickbacks and false invoices that had become an endemic technique of party finance, incorporating an amnesty for earlier offenders. However, the measure was so worded as to remove the threat of prosecution from most of the politicians involved but not the lay figures. This was widely denounced as a self-serving operation by which the politicians looked after their own. It spurred an unprecedented statement by the panel of senior judges considering an impeachment procedure against the former PS minister, Christian Nucci, implicated in the Crossroads of Development scandal (see AR 1987, p. 136). They concluded that prosecution had been rendered impracticable, deploring the decision they felt obliged to reach. Allegations of impropriety led to the resignation of Jacques Médecin, a prominent right-winger and mayor of Cannes, and to the suspension by the Socialists of the mayor of Angoulême.

The morale of parliamentarians was further dented by the frequency with which the government conceded to direct action what it had refused to their arguments. In the spring it was hospital doctors who contested changes in their contracts by demonstrations and strikes. In August farmers' demonstrations against prices for cattle and the effects of the drought extracted the equivalent of £120 million in government aid. In the autumn nationwide demonstrations involving up to 200,000 secondary school pupils, which brought the worst riots in Paris since 1968, forced the government to add 4,100 more posts to the education budget in addition to the 15,000 extra jobs it already provided. The students' success spurred on the legal professions. A series of action days culminated in an unprecedented illegal one-day strike in November over poor working conditions and political interference with the course of justice. This extracted another £500 million for the justice budget.

In contrast, there was no quick-fix remedy for the problems of France's ghetto suburbs, highlighted by rioting at Vaulx-en-Velin, Lyon, in October, after police had killed a pillion passenger in controversial circumstances. M. Rocard appointed a minister for urban affairs after the riots, but there were no ready solutions for the despair that the Vaulx-en-Velin episode laid bare. Earlier, the opposition had condemned the government's 'inaction' over immigration and pressed for a harder line; the consensus M. Rocard sought proved elusive. However, there was unanimous indignation at the profaning of a Jewish cemetery at Carpentras in June and some 200,000 people joined a demonstration in Paris in opposition to racialism and anti-semitism.

Nevertheless, the year brought concrete achievements. The Education Minister, Lionel Jospin, embarked on a reform of primary education aimed at reducing academic failure, and launched a programme of university building to enable the number of students to increase from 1.1 million to 1.15 million over five years. Measures were approved to reform legal aid, restrict publicity for tobacco and alcohol, give temporary workers greater protection, check the laundering of money by drug traffickers and to split the giant posts and telecommunications monopoly. In the autumn parliamentary session the most substantial measure replaced part of the social security contributions paid by employers and employees with a 'general social contribution' on all forms of income. This would be to the advantage of the vast majority of wage-earners but would bear more heavily on the higher paid and some previously exempt pensioners and unemployed people. It was furiously assailed by both the right and the Communists who, for the first time, joined in supporting a censure motion. The government's survival hung in the balance. However, following timely sweeteners to deputies from outside metropolitan France, the 284 votes for the motion were five short of the total required to force M. Rocard's resignation.

Parliament also considered a bill to grant Corsica a semi-autonomous status. There was general agreement that a solution must be found to the problems of the island, but even among government supporters there was considerable resistance to the bill's recognition of the distinct 'Corsican people, a constituent of the French people'. Over the year there were 28 murders and 197 attacks using explosives on the island, compared with 14 and 146 respectively in 1989.

Hurriedly revised in the light of the Gulf crisis, the budget proposed expenditure of the equivalent of £130,000 million, an increase of 4.8 per cent—slightly more than the expected rate of inflation. The deficit would fall from £9,200 million to £8,030 million. Cuts in taxation on companies and some consumption taxes were partly compensated by new taxes and an increase in the wealth tax. The favoured expenditure priorities were education, up by 9 per cent even before the student protests, employment and training, and research and development. Socialist backbenchers were restive at the curbing of public expenditure and at the concessions to industry. Though welcoming the higher wealth tax, they felt the budget further increased inequalities. It was given a particularly rough ride.

In terms of overall economic performance, despite the rise in oil prices, consumer prices were up only 3.3 per cent over the year; although recession was evident in the retail trade figures and industrial production fell slightly, GDP rose 3.0 per cent and earnings 5.2 per cent. Unemployment, at 9.0 per cent, was down slightly. The trade balance showed a small deficit. As almost everywhere, the Bourse had a bad year: shares lost almost a quarter of their value. With a strong franc, the year was notable for a number of major mergers and foreign takeovers. Some £10,000 million was invested outside the country over the year, including at least £3,300 million on buying shares in European industry. In July it was announced that France had completed repayment of its external debt.

OVERSEAS DEPARTMENTS AND TERRITORIES. Guadeloupe continued to count the cost of Hurricane Hugo in September 1989, estimated at £200 million. The government agreed to build 3,500 low-cost houses to replace those destroyed in the storm. In January an official committee chaired by Jean Ripert recommended a programme of 58 measures to be adopted over six years to combat the economic and social disparities between metropolitan France and the overseas departments. It received an unenthusiastic reception from vested interests, and steps to implement it were slow to emerge.

Anxiety continued to grow over the impact of the post-1992 single European market on the cultures and economies of the overseas departments. Nowhere were these more keenly felt than in the Caribbean. In regional elections in October advocates of independence made substantial gains.

The other major area of activity was French Polynesia. Parliament approved a bill increasing the competence of the territorial government, giving greater scope to its president and more autonomy to the territorial assembly.

FOREIGN AFFAIRS AND DEFENCE. Since 1945 relations with Germany had lain at the heart of French foreign policy. Changes in Eastern Europe cast doubt on many longstanding assumptions. President Mitterrand's manifest lack of enthusiasm at the speed of German unification and his emphasis on guarantees for Poland's borders cast a temporary chill over Franco-German relations. There was considerable domestic disagreement on the policy implications. M. Mitterrand advocated a 'confederation' with the East European countries—a formula which appeared to defer full European Community (EC) membership indefinitely. He also pressed for common Community foreign and security policies, not least as a means of containing German power. While advocating reinforcement of EC structures, he was also concerned at the seeping of sovereignty to the Community. He favoured maintaining the European Council's control over policy and increasing the involvement of national parliaments. The right was divided. The UDF tended to favour a federal Europe, while the RPR inclined to a traditional Gaullist preference for a 'Europe of the states'.

The Gulf crisis overshadowed a number of issues which at another time might have assumed greater importance. In January France renounced the sale of frigates to Taiwan after protests from Beijing. In April the last French hostages in Lebanon were freed; the accompanying thanks to Colonel Qadafi of Libya were widely deemed unduly effusive. In May an international tribunal under UN auspices ruled that France had violated the agreement with New Zealand over the *Rainbow Warrior* affair (see AR 1988, p. 145), imposing 'public condemnation' and a 'fine' of £1.2 million. Also in May France sent troops to Gabon to protect French nationals after demonstrations against President Bongo, disavowing any wish to be the 'gendarme of Africa'. After the Franco-African summit in June President Mitterrand's linkage of French aid to progress towards democratization was not well-received by many in his audience. Troops were again dispatched to Rwanda in October. However, in December the refusal of France to intervene in Chad paved the way for the overthrow of President Hissène Habré. In July Anis Naccache, who had been imprisoned for an attempt to assassinate the Shah's last prime minister in 1980, was released, along with four accomplices following a presidential pardon, and returned to Iran. This completed a much-denied deal over the return of French hostages (see AR 1988, p. 145).

In November a meeting between Presidents Mitterrand and Gorbachev at Rambouillet led to a doubling of French aid to the Soviet Union to

£1,000 million. Relations with Algeria were difficult in the wake of the rise of the Islamic parties there and the downgrading of the French language entailed by policies of arabization. Franco-Moroccan relations also deteriorated, following criticism of King Hassan's record on human rights in France. The CSCE meeting in Paris in November to sign the East-West disarmament treaty and other agreements would in normal circumstances have been the high point of the French diplomatic year.

The end of the Cold War in Europe left the Defence Minister, Jean-Pierre Chevènement, struggling to preserve his defence equipment programme against colleagues hoping for a peace dividend. Such demands, he insisted, were 'irresponsible'. Nevertheless, in July he had to announce a reduction of 35,000 in the armed forces by 1995, mainly falling on the army. President Mitterrand promised to cut national service from 12 months to ten and to withdraw French forces from Germany from 1991. Several weapons programmes were cut or pruned, notably the Orchidée battlefield helicopter. Towards the end of the year the Armées 2000 programme foresaw a concentration on mobile armed forces with a long-range intervention capability, using the new Leclerc tank. There would be a continued role for the new Hades missile, a force of Mirage 2000-Ns and the Rafale aircraft in air force and naval service, with a nuclear capability. However, manned bombers and the missiles on the Albion plateau would be phased out, leaving nuclear development mainly with the submarine fleet.

Meanwhile, although France supported the UN response to the invasion of Kuwait, setting aside 20 years of friendly relations with Iraq was not easy. The Defence Minister initially appeared reluctant to accept French military involvement. However, following Iraqi violation of the French embassy in Kuwait, President Mitterrand ordered the expulsion of 29 Iraqis from France and the dispatch of 4,000 more troops. He won the support of all the orthodox parties, with only the Communists and, more surprisingly, the National Front, refusing to join the party consensus. However, his relatively moderate tones and his readiness to accept linkage with the Palestine and Lebanon issues led to France being the first Western country to secure the repatriation of all its hostages in October. In Saudi Arabia the French force was seen as playing something of a lone hand, distancing itself in both space and command from other forces. Nevertheless, with upwards of 10,000 men in the region by the end of the year, the French commitment ranked third only to the Americans and British.

GERMANY

CAPITAL: Berlin AREA: 357,000 sq km POPULATION: 78,300,000
OFFICIAL LANGUAGE: German POLITICAL SYSTEM: federal parliamentary democracy
HEAD OF STATE: President Richard von Weizsäcker (since July '84)
RULING PARTIES: Christian Democratic Union (CDU), Christian Social Union (CSU) and Free Democratic Party (FDP)
HEAD OF GOVERNMENT: Helmut Kohl (CDU), Federal Chancellor (since Oct '82)
PRINCIPAL MINISTERS: Hans-Dietrich Genscher (FDP/Vice-Chancellor, foreign affairs), Gerhard Stoltenberg (CDU/defence), Theo Weigel (CSU/finance), Helmut Haussmann (FDP/economics), Wolfgang Schäuble (CDU/interior), Hans A. Engelhard (FDP/justice)
INTERNATIONAL ALIGNMENT: NATO, OECD, EC
CURRENCY: Deutschmark (end-'90 £1=DM2.88, US$1=DM1.49)
GNP PER CAPITA: US$18,480 ('88)
MAIN EXPORT EARNERS: machinery and transport equipment, manufactures, chemicals

While the above data show the position of unified Germany as at end-1990, the accounts below reflect the fact that unification was not achieved until 3 October. They are divided into two sections, the first covering the former German Democratic Republic (GDR) and the second the Federal Republic of Germany, into which the GDR was merged on the date cited.

GERMAN DEMOCRATIC REPUBLIC

As the new year began, the GDR was suffering from a severe political crisis and escalating social turbulence. The collapse of Erich Honecker's hardline communist regime (see AR 1989, pp. 106–9) had unleashed a rising tide of unrest and resentment. The new government was led by Hans Modrow and a group of reform-minded communists in the restructured Socialist Unity Party of Germany—Party of Democratic Socialism (SED-PDS), and was committed to democratic elections and market-orientated economic reforms. The Round Table (consisting of the SED-PDS, the four 'bloc' parties, the churches and the nine opposition groups) continued to meet twice a week, and provided an important means of consultation between government and opposition. But the government's hopes of stabilizing the country by a programme of reform were shattered by its ill-judged proposal to reconstitute the hated secret police—the Stasi—allegedly to combat the growth in neo-Nazi and anti-Soviet crimes. The Prime Minister formally withdrew these proposals on 12 January. Nevertheless, on 15 January a demonstration against the Stasi led to the first violent incidents in East Germany's peaceful revolution, when the former secret police headquarters was stormed and occupied.

Throughout January the GDR was afflicted by a mounting tide of industrial unrest, as East Germans continued to leave for the West in their thousands. Herr Modrow's political problems were compounded on 20 January, when the popular mayor of Dresden—Wolfgang Berghofer—resigned from the SED-PDS (along with 40 other leading officials), declaring that the party was unreformable. Finally, on 28 January, faced with a rapidly deteriorating economic and political situation, the government proposed the creation of an all-party government of national responsibility, which was to hold office until free elections (the date of which was brought forward from 6 May to 18 March). Thus on 5 February a government was formed in which, for the first time in the history of the GDR, communists were in a minority, although Herr Modrow remained Prime Minister.

By this stage it was becoming apparent that East Germany's days as a separate state were numbered. On 1 February Herr Modrow returned from a visit to Moscow and in an historic speech announced a four-stage proposal for 'overcoming the division of the German nation' by creating a united, but neutral Germany. On 6 February the West German government rejected this proposal, but declared that it was willing to negotiate economic and monetary union (the first stage of Herr Modrow's plan) with the new GDR government. Consequently, on 13-14 February Herr Modrow led a delegation representing all 13 government parties to Bonn to discuss economic and monetary union.

Within the GDR the campaign for the country's first free and democratic elections got under way. From the start the campaign was dominated by the West German parties. They supplied the funds, resources, expertise and even the main speakers for their East German counterparts. This accelerated the realignment of political forces in the east, as electoral groupings corresponding to the parties in the west were formed. The largest such electoral grouping was the Alliance for Germany, comprising the Christian Democratic Union (CDU) and two smaller parties, Democratic Awakening and the German Social Union (DSU). The three liberal parties formed the League of Free Democrats, whilst three left-wing and former dissident groups formed the Alliance '90.

The election campaign itself focused on the issue of the pace and manner of unification. The Alliance for Germany advocated rapid unification on the basis of article 23 of the West German Basic Law, whilst the Social Democrats (SPD) called for a more gradual unification process on the basis of article 146, and stressed the risks of economic hardship that rapid unification involved. The SPD was initially expected to win a sweeping electoral victory. On the day, however, it was the Alliance for Germany which achieved an unexpected triumph, winning 48 per cent of the vote (on a turnout of 93.4 per cent). The PDS (as the former communists now called themselves) achieved a respectable 16 per cent, having campaigned for the preservation of the comprehensive social guarantees currently offered by the GDR. The complete results were as follows:

	% of vote	seats
Alliance for Germany	48.12	
Christian Democrats (CDU)	40.82	163
German Social Union (DSU)	6.31	25
Democratic Awakening	0.99	4
Social Democratic Party of Germany (SPD)	21.88	88
Party of Democratic Socialism (PDS)	16.40	66
League of Free Democrats	5.28	21
Alliance '90	2.91	12
Democratic Peasants Party (DBD)	2.18	9
Greens	1.97	8
Others	1.35	4

The victory of the Alliance for Germany reflected the popularity of Chancellor Kohl's electoral promise, made at a rally on 13 March, for a currency exchange of one-for-one. But above all it indicated the widespread desire for unification, as quickly and smoothly as possible. Henceforth, as the writer Stephen Heym declared, the GDR was destined to be 'nothing but a footnote in world history'.

The CDU candidate for Prime Minister, Lothar de Maizière, immediately began negotiations with the other main parties to form a coalition government. On 12 April, after nearly four weeks of heated wrangling, a 'grand coalition' was formed, consisting of the Alliance, the SPD and the Liberals. The new government's main concern was to negotiate economic and monetary union with the Federal Republic. Negotiations took place against a background of strikes and demonstrations, as East Germans protested against loss of their guaranteed jobs, and against a currency exchange at anything less than one-for-one (as a popular slogan put it, 'without one for one, Germany will not be one'). Despite the protests, however, an agreement on economic and monetary union was reached on 25 April, and on 18 May the State Treaty on 'the creation of a monetary, economic and social union' was formally signed. This treaty was to create a 'social market economy' in the GDR with effect from 1 July. The Deutschmark was to be the common currency, and the Bundesbank the issuing bank. As promised, wages, pensions and savings (up to specified amounts) were to be exchanged on a one-to-one basis.

The first stage of German unification thus took place on 1 July, when the GDR ceded its sovereignty over economic, monetary and social policy to the Bonn government and to the Bundesbank. The overnight transition to a 'social market economy' was not without its costs. Unemployment rose from 272,000 in July to 350,000 at the end of August; by the end of the year it had topped 1 million. Throughout July and August there were strikes by metal and engineering workers, chemical workers, railway men and women, farmers and public transport employees. Their demands included pay rises and 12-month job security guarantees. At the same time, the hoped-for

Western investment proved slow in coming, for a number of reasons: first, uncertainties concerning the legal rights of ownership of land and buildings; second, the chaotic state of the balance sheets of East German firms; and third, the continuing bureaucratic obstacles to Western investment in the GDR. These economic problems were not helped by disagreements within Treuhandanstalt, the trust body created in March to oversee the privatization of East Germany's 8,000 state-owned enterprises. In August disputes over policy at the highest level of Treuhandanstalt led to the resignation of its executive president, Reiner Gohlke.

While the economic situation deteriorated, the coalition government of Herr de Maizière came under increasing strain. The most divisive issues were the timing of unification and the date of the all-German elections. The CDU wanted elections to be held before unification (on the basis of GDR electoral law), whilst the SPD and the Liberals favoured unification first (and elections on the basis of West German law). The political controversy intensified, and on 24 July the Liberals withdrew from the coalition in protest at what they saw as Herr de Maizière's blatant electoral manoeuvering. On 19 August the Social Democrats followed suit.

The break-up of the coalition threatened to disrupt the unification process, because the government no longer possessed the two-thirds parliamentary majority required to amend the constitution. But a political compromise was reached, and on 23 August the Volkskammer (GDR parliament) took the historic decision to join the Federal Republic on 3 October, under article 23 of the Basic Law. The State Treaty on Unification was accepted by the Volkskammer on 20 September, by 299 votes to 80 against (PDS, Alliance '90 and Greens) and one abstention.

At midnight on 2 October, therefore, the German Democratic Republic ceased to exist. Celebrations were held in most East German towns and cities, but the festivities were tinged by a sense of uncertainty about the future. Although the ending of Germany's division was widely welcomed, most East Germans also recognized that economic and social conditions in the five new *Länder* were going to be difficult for many years to come. In his speech at the official unification ceremony, Herr de Maizière declared: 'We are one people, we become one state. It is an hour of great joy. It is the end of some illusions. It is a farewell without tears.' But at the cradle of East Germany's peaceful revolution—the Nikolai Kirche in Leipzig—no service of celebration was held. Instead, a notice was pinned up outside the church saying: 'With 200,000 unemployed we see little cause for celebrating.' These two views epitomized the mixed emotions experienced by many East Germans as they contemplated life in the new, united Germany.

United Germany. Germany became a united country on 3 October 1990 when the five *Länder* (states) of the now-defunct German Democratic Republic (East Germany) became part of the Federal Republic of Germany (hitherto West Germany). With unification Berlin was restored as the official German capital, although the seat of government remained in Bonn.

FEDERAL REPUBLIC OF GERMANY

NOT surprisingly the whole year was dominated by the question of German reunification. The 'peaceful revolution' that had taken place in the GDR the preceding November maintained its momentum in the form of demands for the unification of the two German states. The most dramatic aspect was the speed with which the process was completed. Unity was achieved on 3 October, an event that no-one had thought conceivable less than a year previously.

Much of the credit for this accomplishment was accorded to Chancellor Helmut Kohl and his Foreign Minister, Hans-Dietrich Genscher, since the problems to be resolved—political, constitutional, economic as well as those involving other countries—were formidable. There were two parallel sets of negotiation conducted. One was with the four powers (USA, USSR, Britain and France), which as World War II victors and occupying powers still exercised rights over Germany as a whole, since a peace treaty with Germany had never been concluded. The other set of negotiations solely concerned the two German states and dealt with the constitutional, social and economic aspects of unification.

The decisive breakthrough on the international front occurred on 11 February when, at a meeting in Moscow with Herr Kohl and Herr Genscher, President Gorbachev conceded the principle that Germany should have the right to unify. On 13 February the so-called 'two-plus-four' talks commenced, that is, the Federal Republic and the GDR together with the four 'victor' powers, in order to settle the basis of German sovereignty and to work out the implications for the military alliance commitments of both countries (NATO and Warsaw Pact). Several rounds of meetings followed which ultimately led to the concession on the part of the Soviet Union that a united Germany should continue to be a full member of NATO. In return, the Federal Republic undertook to limit the size of its armed forces to 370,000 men. A treaty was concluded on 12 September which confirmed the unity and sovereignty of Germany within the existing frontiers of the Federal Republic and the GDR (see DOCUMENTS). On the following day the Soviet Union and the Federal Republic initialled a friendship treaty which provided for cooperation in several fields together with a non-aggression commitment. The Federal Republic also promised substantial financial aid and credits to the Soviet Union to help finance the withdrawal of Soviet forces from Germany, the building of homes for them in the Soviet Union, as well as contributing to their support costs in Germany while still in the country. This munificence was in response to the positive attitude taken by the Soviet Union, which could have acted obstructively towards unification.

Related to the two-plus-four talks was the issue of the German-Polish frontier (the Oder-Neisse line). Poland wanted a specific guarantee of its inviolability from the Federal Republic, but Herr Kohl had delayed agreement on the grounds that only a unified Germany could make such a treaty. Eventually (14 November), this treaty was signed and was due to be ratified in 1991 and to include guarantees of the rights of the ethnic Germans still in Poland.

The rapidly worsening economic situation in the GDR, the impatience of the people, the weakening authority of the communist-led government, and the growing numbers of East Germans moving to West Germany—all of these factors made a speedy resolution imperative. GDR elections (18 March) gave the parties favouring unification a large majority, and the government subsequently formed by the Christian Democratic Union (CDU), the sister-party of the ruling party in the Federal Republic, ensured that no insuperable difficulties would arise. The first formal agreement between the two countries was the State Treaty on Economic, Monetary and Social Union, which came into force on 1 July. From that date the Deutschmark became the sole currency, and the exchange rate for East Germans was exceptionally favourable: a one-for-one rate for wages, pensions, rents and most personal savings; and a two-for-one rate for other assets and liabilities.

A major source of dispute was over the constitutional method of unification. Article 146 of the Basic Law originating in 1949 specified that it should come about through the adoption of a new constitution agreed by 'a free decision of the German people'. The West German government did not favour this course for two reasons. One was that the necessity to achieve unification quickly meant that there was insufficient time to draw up a new constitutional document which would find general agreement. The second reason was probably more important: there were no good grounds for scrapping the Basic Law, which had served the Federal Republic so well for 40 years. Instead, article 23 was favoured, providing for 'other parts of Germany' to accede to the Federal Republic, a provision used in the case of the Saarland in 1956. This course was only agreed to by the East German parliament as late as 23 August.

This agreement led to the conclusion of the Second State Treaty (31 August) which, in over 1,000 pages of text, regulated the details of unification relating to specific areas of policy and administration. The treaty laid down that the five newly-reconstituted *Länder* in the GDR (Saxony, Thuringia, Saxony-Anhalt, Brandenburg and Mecklenburg-West Pomerania) should join the Federal Republic on 3 October (see map on p. 150).

The celebrations on this day of unification (henceforth a public holiday) were more muted than was the case on the occasion of the opening of the Berlin Wall in November 1989, since the problems of merging the two societies and economies were becoming apparent. None the less, it was an historic occasion, and much credit went to

Chancellor Kohl, who was widely regarded as the architect of German unity and who had exploited every opportunity to bring it about. Herr Kohl and the CDU were naturally keen to cement the success by holding an early election, but the earliest agreed date was 2 December.

The federal election—the first free all-German election since 1932—favoured the ruling coalition of the CDU, the Christian Social Union (CSU) of Bavaria and the Free Democrats (FDP) with an expected 'unification bonus'. The main opposition party, the Social Democrats (SPD), had been lukewarm in their attitude towards unification. In particular, the SPD's chancellor-candidate, Oskar Lafontaine (who survived an assassination attempt in April), had throughout harped on the problems and costs involved, accusing the government of hiding the facts, especially that taxes would have to rise. Although many believed that Herr Lafontaine would later prove to be right, his negative image harmed the SPD, particularly in the former GDR.

A Federal Constitutional Court ruling on the electoral law required that for this first election the two parts of Germany should be treated as separate entities. The effect of this ruling was that the 5 per cent threshold requirement for parties to win representation in the Bundestag applied separately to the two parts. As a result, the smaller parties in eastern Germany had a better chance of winning seats. The beneficiaries were the Party of Democratic Socialism (PDS), formerly the ruling communist party, and the East German Greens. The results were as follows:

	% of vote	seats
Christian Democrats (CDU/CSU)	43.8	319
Social Democrats (SPD)	33.5	239
Free Democrats (FDP)	11.0	79
Party of Democratic Socialism (PDS)	2.4	17
Greens (East)	1.2	8
Greens (West)	3.9	0
Republicans	2.1	0
Others	2.1	0
		662

The strong performance of the coalition parties, especially the FDP, indicated that the government's complexion would remain unaltered for several years, while the SPD looked set to remain in opposition indefinitely. The party's chief casualty was Herr Lafontaine, who shortly after the election said that he would not take over the posts of party chairman and leader of the parliamentary party. His decision left the SPD in greater disarray, and the party presidium invited Björn Engholm, minister-president of Schleswig-Holstein, to assume the leadership. Other parties were not free from difficulties either. Lothar de Maizière, the former CDU prime minister of the GDR and subsequently a minister in Herr Kohl's cabinet, resigned from his post after allegations that he had worked for the East German state security police (the 'Stasi'). The PDS was continually embarrassed by revelations about the party's finances involving large sums of money in secret accounts held abroad. That the party managed to retain some credibility was due to the new leader, Gregor Gysi, who sought to make the party fit for democratic politics.

Most bruised by the results of the December election were the West German Greens. They had shown a lack of enthusiasm for reunification and still suffered from factional in-fighting. Their decision not to form a single party with their East German counterpart meant that they fell below the 5 per cent hurdle. The Greens were also harmed by the break-up of the coalition with the SPD in West Berlin shortly before the election.

Earlier in the year the SPD had enjoyed a string of successes in *Land* (state) elections. In the Saarland (January) the SPD retained its overall majority, as it did later (May) in North Rhine-Westphalia; also in May the party ousted the CDU/FDP coalition in Lower Saxony, forming a government with the Greens. The SPD for a while had a slight majority in the federal upper house, the Bundesrat, which had significant legislative and budgetary powers. However, the elections in the five East German *Länder* (14 October) gave victory to the CDU in four, with the SPD winning only in Brandenburg. The first all-Berlin election (held on the same day as the federal election) also went to a CDU-led coalition. Berlin was also constituted as a *Land*, so that the federation totalled 16 member-states in all. The increase led to an enlargement of the Bundesrat to 69 member-votes, combined with an alteration in voting entitlement favouring the larger *Länder*.

Towards the end of the year the problems resulting from unification were becoming evident: unemployment in East Germany was running at about 20 per cent, with extensive short-time working in addition. Major re-training schemes were initiated, but there were difficulties in attracting private investment, partly because of uncertainty about property rights but also because of additional burdens in dealing with environmental problems. The Bundesbank was also concerned about the rapid increase in public borrowing. None the less, taking West Germany by itself, economic performance was good, with rises in consumer spending, earnings and GNP, while unemployment fell to 6.7 per cent (from 7.9 per cent in 1989). Consumer prices rose by 3 per cent, with wholesale prices only 1.8 per cent up. One significant trend was the decline on the current-account surplus; it was expected to decline further over the year following.

A continuing cause for concern was the high rate of immigration into West Germany. Despite unification, East Germans in search of better prospects moved westwards at a rate estimated at 20,000 a month, and during the year about 200,000 people applied for political asylum. In addition, the Federal Republic kept to its policy of receiving ethnic Germans from Eastern Europe, totalling about 400,000 in the year. However, the social pressures resulting did not lead to a political backlash: the right-wing Republicans failed to attract significant support in the federal election.

Whatever the outlook for the future, 1990 exceeded all expectations: Germany was once more united, the summer was the best since 1976 (with an excellent vintage), and in August West Germany's soccer team won the World Cup (see Pt. XVII).

ITALY

CAPITAL: Rome   AREA: 301,000 sq km   POPULATION: 57,400,000 ('88)
OFFICIAL LANGUAGE: Italian   POLITICAL SYSTEM: parliamentary democracy
HEAD OF STATE: President Francesco Cossiga (since July '85)
RULING PARTIES: Christian Democratic (DC), Socialist (PSI), Democratic Socialist (PSDI), Republican (PRI) and Liberal (PLI) parties
HEAD OF GOVERNMENT: Giulio Andreotti (DC), Prime Minister (since July '89)
PRINCIPAL MINISTERS: Claudio Martelli (PSI/deputy premier), Gianni De Michelis (PSI/foreign affairs), Virginio Rognoni (DC/defence), Vincenzo Scotti (DC/interior), Giuliano Vassalli (PSI/justice), Salvatore (Rino) Formica (PSI/finance), Cirino Pomicino (DC/treasury)
INTERNATIONAL ALIGNMENT: NATO, OECD, EC
CURRENCY: lira (end-'89 £1=Lit2,177, US$1=Lit1,127)
GNP PER CAPITA: US$13,330 ('88)
MAIN EXPORT EARNERS: machinery and transport equipment, manufactures, chemicals, agricultural products, tourism

WHEN the year opened Giulio Andreotti, now 71 and already five times Prime Minister, had presided over a five-party coalition since July 1989. This coalition—typical of the frequently-changing governments of the past 40 years—included his own Christian Democrats (DC), still the country's largest party, the Socialists (PSI) and three smaller centrist parties, the Social Democrats, Republicans and Liberals. Despite recent changes in the character of the Communist Party (PCI), the country's second-largest party, unwillingness to admit it to government continued.

The early months of the Andreotti regime had passed in, for Italy, unaccustomed political tranquillity. Signor Andreotti was getting on better with the obstreperous PSI leader, Bettino Craxi. Politicians were, in fact, awaiting the outcome of the PCI congress in Bologna on 7–11 March, which was to consider the dramatic proposal made in November 1989 by its leader, Achille Occhetto, to drop the word 'Communist' from its name, abandon the hammer-and-sickle emblem, and seek to join the Socialist International (see AR 1989, p. 154). The 1,000 delegates at the congress were deeply divided: dissidents, including such long-term diehards as Pietro Ingrao, spoke vehemently against any retreat from marxist principles. But on 11 March Signor Occhetto secured 67 per cent of the vote for his reforms; 30 per cent backed the previous 'Eurocommunist' line, while 3 per cent voted for a return to stalinist orthodoxy. After this inconclusive congress no-one quite knew what the party was to be called, and it was popularly referred to as 'la cosa' ('the thing'). At a subsequent party executive, Signor Occhetto secured two-thirds support for a broadening of the party, and in mid-October the decision was finally taken to change the name to 'Democratic Party of the Left' and to make the emblem an oak-tree.

Meanwhile, regional elections held on 6–7 May had provided a warning test for the PCI's new policies. The party sustained its worst losses ever, going down to 23.5 per cent of the total vote, some 6 per cent lower than in the previous regional election in 1985. The DC, slightly up at 35.6 per cent, did not gain from the Communists' decline, and the Socialists, up from 13.3 to 15.3 per cent, did so only marginally. The startling change was in the support for the Lega Lombarda (Lombard League), a northern grouping which campaigned against, as it said, the 'pampered bureaucrats and southern politicians of the government in Rome' and wanted more regional autonomy. It was also accused of racist prejudice against southern Italians.

Whether or not that accusation was justified, there was a good deal of talk about racism in connection with the difficulties that arose over immigrants to Italy from non-EC countries, in particular from North and sub-Saharan Africa. Italy had in the past been a country of extensive emigration of Italian workers. Now the situation had greatly changed: with rising prosperity, fewer Italians needed to seek work abroad, while increasing numbers were arriving to seek work in Italy, a country of relatively easy access. On 3 January an amnesty law came into effect enabling illegal immigrants already in Italy (estimated at perhaps 1 million) to claim a renewable two-year permit on registration by 27 June. From 29 June onwards those who had no guaranteed job or accommodation would be excluded at the frontier. Some thousands did so register, although many visa-less seasonal workers, farm labourers, etc., did not. In mid-March in Florence, to which some 20,000 immigrants had come from Senegal and Côte d'Ivoire in 1989, Africans were attacked by skinheads, and the police ordered the centre of Florence to be placed off-limits to black itinerant traders. The PSI mayor of Florence resigned on 13 March following accusations that he was implementing a racist programme against coloured immigrants; next day the civic authorities agreed to open four areas near the historic centre to African traders.

The President of the Republic, Francesco Cossiga, began taking a more active part in affairs. He was known to be especially interested in institutional reforms. One such reform concerned the use of the referendum, entitling all citizens to register their opinions on controversial questions such as, in the past, divorce and abortion. On 3 June a referendum was held on the use of pesticides and on game shooting, but these subjects met with apathy—only 47 per cent of Italy's 47 million voters registered their votes. As a minimum 50 per cent turnout was needed the laws remained unchanged.

President Cossiga also spurred on parliament to take a more active part against the Mafia. In November he received detailed reports from 60 Sicilian judges asking that more funds should be allocated for combating the spread of the Mafia, and the accompanying drug traffic, to the north. This warning coincided with the news that, in addition to the longstanding Mafia areas of Sicily and Calabria and the Neapolitan Camorra, a 'fourth Mafia' had in recent months established its headquarters in the hitherto Mafia-free south-eastern province of Apulia, which was becoming a centre for drug trafficking and illegal arms shipments. Kidnapping also continued, including threats against children. On 24 June Francesca Porca, the leader of a Sardinian kidnapping gang who had been sought for nearly a decade, was arrested in Rome.

On 20 April 13 suspected Red Brigade members went on trial in Forlì for involvement in the murder of Senator Roberto Ruffilli in 1988 (see AR 1988, p. 158); on 1 June nine were found guilty and sentenced to life imprisonment. This trial marked the virtual end of the Red Brigades, whose leaders were already in long-term custody.

At the other end of the political scale, in the Bologna appeal court on 18 July 13 men, including four neo-fascists who had been sentenced to long terms for alleged involvement in the 1980 bombing in Bologna station, were acquitted for lack of evidence. Among them was Licio Gelli, grand-master of the now-outlawed 'P2' masonic lodge, who, however, was still liable to be held under financial charges. The acquittal produced widespread shock, and Bologna shops closed in protest.

It was Italy's turn to hold the presidency of the European Community (EC) for six months from 1 July, and President Cossiga and Prime Minister Andreotti were keen to make it a success. These hopes were threatened near the beginning, however, when five left-wing ministers from Signor Andreotti's own DC party resigned over a dispute about a bill to regulate broadcasting advertising and media ownership. But the squabble fizzled out and the Prime Minister secured a vote of confidence for his reshuffled cabinet on 29 July. In the early stages Italy's handling of the EC presidency came in for some criticism, especially from Britain, for the spate of dynamic and, as some thought, ill-conceived suggestions put forward by the ebullient Italian Foreign Minister, Gianni De Michelis. But following the Rome summit on 27 October the presidency became better organized. As convinced federalists, the Italians aimed throughout at moves towards European integration.

Faced with the Gulf confrontation, Italy's cabinet on 3 August approved the immediate freezing of Kuwait's assets and suspension of arms exports to Iraq. Among such exports, Italian-made components of the Iraq 'super-gun' project had been seized by the police in mid-May from steel-producing firms in Terni, Naples and Brescia. On 7 August EC ambassadors in Brussels under Italian presidency approved a law to stop Iraq receiving exports worth US$54 million which would have been paid for by oil exports of similar value. Italy itself had been buying 11 per cent of its oil requirement from Kuwait. At a NATO meeting on 9 August Italy put its NATO bases, and specifically Sigonella in Sicily, at the disposal of the USA as staging posts. On that day Italy together with other EC countries refused to close its embassy in Kuwait. Some 450 Italians in Kuwait and Baghdad became hostages; some were later repatriated by the Brandt and other missions and all were released, with other Western hostages, by the year's end. On 11 August the Defence Minister said that the army was technically ready for involvement in an international force, and later in August two frigates (with a support vessel) and a squadron of Tornado aircraft left for the Gulf. On 21 August Italy was one of the WEU countries which agreed to coordinate operations in the Gulf to enforce trade sanctions, and later Italy supported the idea of using the WEU as a defence arm of the EC.

In general, it could be said that the reaction of Italy to the Gulf crisis was of a different magnitude from that of Britain or France. Signor Andreotti's own wait-and-see attitude, influenced by his longstanding sympathies with some Arab countries, contrasted with the dynamism of Foreign Minister De Michelis. Some newspaper editorials in the early stages denounced the government for dithering. Most Italians thought the UN should take the lead, and some 65 per cent were thought to be against military involvement.

A quite different type of international involvement for Italy was tentatively launched in April when leaders from Czechoslovakia, Hungary, Poland, Yugoslavia and Italy (represented by Signor De Michelis) met in Bratislava to debate central European cooperation; this 'Pentagonale' initiative, as it came to be known, met again in Venice on 31 July to discuss the idea of a counterweight to a united Germany.

Early in July Italy, as EC president, became involved in negotiating the passage out of Albania of some 3,000 dissident Albanian refugees who had entered the embassies of Italy and other West European countries in Tirana (see p.138). French and Italian ships on 13 July brought some 4,800 of them to Brindisi, where they were housed in a disused army base before moving on to West Germany and elsewhere. Some were welcomed by longstanding Albanian residents in southern Italy.

On the economic side the great drawback continued to be the huge deficit in public spending. Failure to bring it under control, said the governor of the Bank of Italy on 31 May, would affect Italy's capacity to participate fully in an EC moving closer to economic and monetary union. In January a realignment of the lira within the European Monetary System involved a 3.01 per cent devaluation of the lira against the ecu, putting it into the narrow 2.25 per cent fluctuation band of the EMS. On 27 April a decree was passed discarding the control of capital movement and allowing Italians to open a bank account abroad; this brought Italy into line with the EC directive requiring full liberalization of exchange controls by 1 July. But Italy still remained behind in implementation of a number of EC directives. Petrol prices rose in August as a result of the Gulf crisis, which inevitably had a serious effect on the economy given Italy's heavy dependence on imported oil. Inflation at the year's end was around 6 per cent.

President Cossiga paid an important state visit to Britain from 23–28 October, spending the last two days in Scotland. He addressed parliament, visited Oxford, and inaugurated various exhibitions including that of the Venetian lion on loan (via Fiat) in the British Museum.

President Gorbachev visited Rome on 18 November on his way to the CSCE meeting in Paris. He had an audience with the Pope, met President Cossiga and Prime Minister Andreotti, and signed an agreement concerning Italian economic aid to the USSR.

Italy was host for the 14th World Cup soccer finals for a month from 8 June (see Pt. XVII). Cooperation between Italian carabinieri and visiting police largely averted the feared clashes with spectators. Sandro Pertini, the highly successful President of the Republic from 1978 to 1985, died on 24 February aged 93 (see OBITUARY).

BELGIUM

CAPITAL: Brussels   AREA: 30,500 sq km   POPULATION: 9,900,000 ('88)
OFFICIAL LANGUAGES: French and Flemish   POLITICAL SYSTEM: parliamentary
  democracy, devolved structure based on language communities
HEAD OF STATE: King Baudouin (since July '51)
RULING PARTIES: Christian People's Party (CVP/Flemish), Christian Social Party
  (PSC/Walloon), Socialist Party (SP/Flemish), Socialist Party (PS/Walloon), People's
  Union (VU/Flemish nationalist)
HEAD OF GOVERNMENT: Wilfried Martens (CVP), Prime Minister (since Dec '81)
PRINCIPAL MINISTERS: Philippe Moureaux (PS/deputy premier, Brussels, institutional
  reform, education), Willy Claes (SP/deputy premier, economic affairs and
  planning, education), Jean-Luc Dehaene (CVP/deputy premier, communications,
  institutional reform), Melchior Wathelet (PSC/deputy premier, justice and the
  middle classes), Hugo Schiltz (VU/deputy premier, budget), Robert Urbain
  (PS/finance), Philippe Maystadt (PSC/foreign affairs), Guy Coëme (PS/defence),
  Louis Tobback (SP/interior)
INTERNATIONAL ALIGNMENT: NATO, OECD, EC, Benelux, Francophonie
CURRENCY: franc (end-'90 £1=BF59.75, US$1=30.96)
GNP PER CAPITA: US$14,490 ('88)
MAIN EXPORT EARNERS: machinery and transport equipment, manufactures, chemicals,
  agricultural products

THE strength of the constitution was put to a highly unusual test on 3 April when the King stepped down from the throne for several days because he found it morally impossible to sign a law liberalizing Belgium's abortion laws. During the royal absence, parliament adopted the Abortion Bill under article 82 of the constitution, previously assumed to apply only in cases where the monarch's assent was blocked by physical impossibility such as illness, or material impossibility such as abduction. Though this crisis was surmounted, the consequences included further polarization of the differences between the Flemish and Walloon communities, with the former strongly supporting the monarchy and the latter showing clear republican sentiments.

The continuing importance of the inter-communal problem was also revealed in the performance of the parliamentary working party charged with preparing the way for the third phase of the devolution plan. This body was unable to produce a clear programme for separately electing regional parliaments and for giving the resulting regional governments power to, for example, make their own international agreements. More discussions took place later in the year, but inconclusively.

Wallonia's severe financial problems also took on a clear federal aspect when the Socialists demanded additional income transfers from national government to Wallonia in order to fund the teachers' annual pay increase, which otherwise would have been no more than 2 per cent as against the 6 per cent rise given to teachers in Flanders. Unsurprisingly, this was opposed by the Flemish on the grounds that transfers from national coffers in effect meant a further shift to Wallonia of money raised in Flanders.

A main focus of national attention for much of the year was on the progress of a parliamentary inquiry into police involvement in the case of the Bende van Nijvel terrorist group, active in murders of civilians during the early 1980s. Some evidence suggested that the terrorists may have had links with elements of the gendarmerie and the state intelligence service. The government's response was to announce plans to increase the police and intelligence forces' accountability to government, and to improve cooperation between the separate municipal police, judicial police and the national gendarmerie.

The government joined in supporting UN and EC decisions concerning the Gulf crisis, and offered defensive military assistance. At the same time, special measures were taken to limit the impact of the expected surge in the price of oil. These ranged from energy conservation (including more stringent insulation requirements for new buildings) to, more expediently, reducing the weighting of energy products within the cost-of-living index.

In the economic sphere, the continuing excessively high public deficit was a major preoccupation, causing the government to introduce a 1991 budget allowing no increase in the deficit, in real terms, over the 1990 level. However, tax increases and lower interest payments, achieved by restructuring part of the public debt and also reducing the net borrowing requirement by some one-off expenditure cuts, were the means chosen, rather than the fundamental reductions in public spending widely considered to be necessary in order to achieve a longer-term solution.

The economy performed strongly throughout the year, with industrial output, personal consumption, private-sector investment and employment all on a favourable trend. This was achieved without generating the inflationary pressures that tended to mark most previous phases of economic expansion.

THE NETHERLANDS

CAPITAL: Amsterdam   AREA: 37,000 sq km   POPULATION: 14,800,000 ('88)
OFFICIAL LANGUAGE: Dutch   POLITICAL SYSTEM: parliamentary democracy
HEAD OF STATE: Queen Beatrix (since April '80)
RULING PARTIES: Christian Democratic Appeal (CDA), Labour Party (PvdA)
HEAD OF GOVERNMENT: Ruud Lubbers (CDA), Prime Minister (since Nov '82)
PRINCIPAL MINISTERS: Wim Kok (PvdA/deputy premier, finance), Ien Dales
    (PvdA/home affairs), Hans van den Broek (CDA/foreign affairs), Relus ter Breek
    (PvdA/defence), Koos Andriessen (CDA/economic affairs)
INTERNATIONAL ALIGNMENT: NATO, OECD, EC, Benelux
CURRENCY: guilder (end-'90 £1=f3.25, US$1=f1.69)
GNP PER CAPITA: US$14,520 ('88)
MAIN EXPORT EARNERS: oil and gas, machinery and transport equipment, chemicals,
    agricultural products

THE coalition government of Christian Democrats and Labour, though still very new as 1990 opened, soon proved itself a viable, if uneasy, alliance as both participants compromised on some of their most divergent policies. This was as well since the government's cohesion was tested during the first quarter by pay disputes with the unions representing civil servants and building workers, and by serious protests from farmers over guaranteed prices for cereals. Notwithstanding a succession of public demonstrations, strikes and obstruction of roads, railways and border crossings by the farmers, the government eventually secured agreement without major compromise.

However, these disputes proved to be a measure of popular dissatisfaction, for the municipal elections held on 21 March produced a protest in the shape of a swing against the coalition partners and a very low turnout of voters, particularly Labour supporters. In the cities, Labour lost many seats, while the Christian Democrats also fared worse than in the previous election. The main gainer was D66 (social democratic), though the right-wing Liberals also improved their position. The disappointed Labour Party took the view that it had been too conciliatory towards its coalition partner, thus alienating many of its own voters.

The setback in the local elections was all the more surprising since it followed closely on the unveiling of the Plan for Social Renewal, which was to be the vehicle for the coalition's key policy. Intended to reintegrate the socially disadvantaged into society, the social renewal programme included measures to create jobs, improve the inner cities and help ethnic minorities. However, the absence of any additional funding, beyond that already allocated under existing programmes, meant that the renewal programme was seen more as a re-presentation than a real advance, and hence left voters unimpressed.

In June the delayed revisions to the National Environment Plan were published, focusing on reducing carbon dioxide emissions by cutting energy consumption. However, implementation prospects were undermined by the Senate's further postponing of the debate on abolishing tax deductions on commuters' travelling expenses. At the same time, extra money was allocated for cleaning up ground pollution.

It was hardly surprising when the coalition government showed signs of stress around mid-year. Divergence between Christian Democrats and Labour was clearest over incomes policy, with each party favouring the interests of its own supporters. Ultimately, a compromise agreement was reached for all incomes to be targeted to rise by 0.5 per cent. The 1991 budget presented on 28 September, though showing a reduced deficit overall, embodied substantial funds to support the incomes policy, including continuation of the index-linking of public-sector wages to those in the private sector, and extra resources for public transport and the environment. Partly offsetting these increases, the defence budget was cut (achieved mainly by reducing national military service from 14 months to 12).

The main economic indicators showed varying trends during the year. Consumer spending rose quite strongly in real terms, reflecting the boost given to personal incomes by the tax changes in January, by falling unemployment and by faster wages growth. In response, the rate of inflation quickened. But investment was less buoyant and contributed little to economic expansion, which was unsurprising given that growth in overall industrial production slowed sharply, though manufacturing was relatively unaffected. Unemployment continued to fall.

In September, parliament agreed that the time had come for new investment in South Africa to be permitted again, to be followed by normalization of relations between the two countries. However, this was subsequently watered down to just a renewal of cultural relations until the UN agreed a relaxation of sanctions. The government's response to the Iraqi invasion of Kuwait was to send frigates to the Gulf and to offer a squadron of aircraft to Turkey.

LUXEMBOURG

CAPITAL: Luxembourg　AREA: 3,000 sq km　POPULATION: 375,000 ('88)
OFFICIAL LANGUAGE: Letzeburgish　POLITICAL SYSTEM: parliamentary democracy
HEAD OF STATE: Grand Duke Jean (since Nov '64)
RULING PARTIES: Christian Social People's Party (CSV) and Luxembourg Socialist Workers' Party (LSAP)
HEAD OF GOVERNMENT: Jacques Santer (CSV), Prime Minister (since July '84)
PRINCIPAL MINISTERS: Jacques Poos (LSAP/deputy premier, foreign affairs), Jean Spautz (CSV/interior), Jean-Claude Juncker (CSV/finance, labour and budget), Robert Goebbels (LSAP/economy)
INTERNATIONAL ALIGNMENT: NATO, OECD, EC, Benelux, Francophonie
CURRENCY: franc (end-'90 £1=LF59.75, US$1=LF30.96)
GNP PER CAPITA: US$22,400 ('88)
MAIN EXPORT EARNERS: basic manufactures, machinery and transport equipment, tourism, financial services

ECONOMIC growth slowed during the year: industrial production showed no measurable increase over 1989, investment (other than restructuring by the steel industry) was relatively flat. However, as slack appeared in the economy, inflation remained modest. Unsurprisingly, the government judged that the time was right to supply a stimulus. Accordingly, the new budget introduced a series of important tax cuts. The top rate of personal income tax was lowered from 53 to 50 per cent, with matching cuts in lower tax bands. A bigger cut, from 36 to 30 per cent, was made in the corporate tax rate, aimed at boosting industrial investment. Partly offsetting these incentives, however, there was an increase in VAT rates. Government spending on health and pensions was also planned to rise under the budget's provisions.

In the private sector Luxembourg's largest company, Arbed, which dominated the steel industry, opened discussions with a leading Belgian company about combining their flat steel-making into a single operation that would have nearly a 10 per cent share of the EC market. Discussions were held with the European Commission, whose approval would be required.

The international reputation of the banking industry, which was subject to remarkably few official controls, was harmed by the involvement of a major bank in laundering money originating from the Colombian drugs trade. The resulting $15,000 fine by a US court in February embarrassed the Luxembourg authorities, who came under pressure to modify the Grand Duchy's large degree of banking secrecy.

The Luxembourg franc, at parity with its Belgian counterpart, followed the latter in having its international value linked to the Deutschmark—a move intended to stabilize exchange rate fluctuations.

REPUBLIC OF IRELAND

CAPITAL: Dublin   AREA: 70,280 sq km   POPULATION: 3,500,000 ('88)
OFFICIAL LANGUAGES: Irish and English   POLITICAL SYSTEM: parliamentary democracy
HEAD OF STATE: President Mary Robinson (since Dec '90)
RULING PARTIES: Fianna Fáil (FF), Progressive Democrats (PD)
HEAD OF GOVERNMENT: Charles Haughey (FF), Prime Minister/Taoiseach (since March '87)
PRINCIPAL MINISTERS: John P. Wilson (FF/deputy premier/Tánaiste, marine), Albert Reynolds (FF/finance), Gerard Collins (FF/foreign affairs), Desmond O'Malley (PD/industry & commerce), Ray Burke (FF/justice & communications)
INTERNATIONAL ALIGNMENT: neutral, OECD, EC
CURRENCY: punt (end-'90 £1=IR£1.09, US$1=IR£0.56)
GNP PER CAPITA: US$7,750 ('88)
MAIN EXPORT EARNERS: tourism, machinery and electronic equipment, agriculture

THE government's attention was largely concentrated on European Community (EC) affairs during the first six months of the year, when the Republic held the Community presidency. The Taoiseach (Prime Minister), Charles Haughey, and the Foreign Minister, Gerard Collins, led the EC successfully in the direction it wanted to take after the dramatic events of the previous year in the former Eastern bloc. At the meetings in Ireland of the European Council and the Council of Ministers the Irish presidency encouraged the rapid processing of German reunification, new relationships with the Soviet Union and its one-time satellites, and further development towards monetary, economic and political union within the Community itself.

Only on defence was the Republic tardy in swimming with the mainstream European current. While Mr Haughey reiterated the longstanding Irish commitment to join in the defence of the Community, he held back from any more specific statement of position which might have seemed to undermine the Irish policy of neutrality by moving the country too close to involvement with NATO or the Western European Union. By the end of the year it was clear that the major opposition party, Fine Gael, and the Progressive Democrats (partners in government with Mr Haughey's Fianna Fáil) both favoured a more positive policy on EC defence and it was clear that Mr Haughey would find it difficult much longer to avoid a precise commitment.

Another question which arose after the Irish presidency had ended concerned the GATT negotiations for a new world trade agreement. The proposal by the EC Agricultural Commissioner, Ray MacSharry, for a phased 30 per cent cut in farm supports drew strong criticism from the United States as grossly inadequate but met equally virulent condemnation from Ireland and several other EC countries, which said that so large a reduction would destroy their rural economies. The Irish Farmers' Association demanded that the government maintain its resistance to the cuts when the GATT talks resumed the following February. Ironically, Mr MacSharry was the Irish member of the EC Commission and a former Fianna Fail Minister for Agriculture.

The Gulf crisis had already placed in jeopardy the immediate prospects for Irish farming. UN sanctions, which the Republic was committed to enforcing, prevented payment of a debt of nearly IR£200 million owed by Iraq to the Goodman Group, a consortium of companies which controlled a large part of the Irish meat processing and dairy industries. This shortfall led to the revelation of deep-seated financial difficulties in the group and parliament had to be recalled during the summer recess to enact special legislation, effectively providing shelter for Goodman against precipitate action by its creditors which could have seriously disrupted the important Irish agricultural export trade.

Some 50 Irish citizens were in Kuwait at the onset of the Gulf crisis in August and 300 in Baghdad, the latter mainly medical and paramedical staff at a hospital administered by a subsidiary of the Irish national airline, Aer Lingus. Patient diplomacy, official and unofficial, ensured that a number of the Irish were enabled to return home before the general exit of hostages permitted in December. The Foreign Minister, Mr Collins, earned much credit in August for securing the release of Brian Keenan, a schoolteacher from Belfast who was an Irish citizen and had been held hostage in Beirut for four years. Mr Collins began the process of restoring relations between Iran and the EC during the Irish presidency of the Community; by using the contacts then established he got Iranian backing for the ongoing efforts of Irish diplomats in the Middle East and at the UN to bring about Mr Keenan's release. Mr Keenan provided much information about the conditions under which he and other Westerners had been held in captivity. He had shared much of his ordeal with the British hostage, John McCarthy.

Anglo-Irish relations suffered several setbacks during the year. While the British Northern Ireland Secretary, Peter Brooke, made a good impression in the Republic by his efforts to bring the political parties in the North to the negotiating table, the point at which the Dublin government would become involved in such discussions remained unresolved throughout 1990 (see pp. 48–9). In early July it became apparent that Mr Brooke saw no role for Dublin until 'substantial progress' had been made in the internal discussions. This was unacceptable to the Republic and the nationalist Social Democratic and Labour Party in Northern Ireland. It was clear that a prerequisite to any talks would be a suspension at Northern Unionist behest of the Anglo-Irish Conference. Dublin was reluctantly willing to facilitate this through a formula which would avoid explicit suspension, but could not see its way to opt out in addition from the new negotiations until the point was passed at which the Republic might be able to exert an influence of any weight.

Decisions of the Irish Supreme Court in March and April reawakened tension over extradition for alleged terrorist offences. The closely-reasoned judgments refusing extradition and reversing precedent were based on legislation about to be superseded in part by a law prohibiting the plea in many cases that terrorist activities were 'political offences' for which the accused could not be extradited. Unease, however, was not confined to British commentators: the Progressive Democrats in particular expressed anxiety over the tendency of the Court rulings. On the other hand, no dissenting voices were heard when the British judicial system was criticized in the Republic on various grounds. These included the refusal by the House of Lords to make policemen compellable witnesses at Northern Ireland inquests and the failure to release the 'Birmingham Six' (see AR 1987, pp. 156–7) in light of new evidence, or to expedite a new appeal in the case ordered by the Home Secretary.

Much debate also followed Supreme Court findings that the description of the national territory in article 2 of the Republic's constitution as 'the whole island of Ireland' amounted to 'a claim of legal right' rather than a political aspiration, as had been previously supposed, and that the 're-integration of the national territory' referred to in article 3 was 'a constitutional imperative'. An opposition attempt in parliament to initiate a referendum on re-phrasing the two articles as a statement of aspiration failed but it was clear that a groundswell of opinion favoured altering the constitution lest a tincture of legality might appear to be conferred on the declared objectives of the IRA in Northern Ireland.

The most dramatic event of 1990 was the unexpected election of Mary Robinson as President of the Republic in November. Mrs Robinson was a leading constitutional lawyer and advocate of civil liberties. Although she had no political affiliation herself, she was nominated by the Labour Party and campaigned vigorously throughout the country for a full six months, stressing pluralist values, the equality of citizens and women's rights. She was aided by a sensational upheaval in which Mr Haughey was obliged to dismiss the Fianna Fáil candidate, Deputy Prime Minister Brian Lenihan, from the cabinet over allegations of misleading the public. Nevertheless, Mrs Robinson was seen to have won primarily through her own determination and the attraction of what she represented, especially to women voters. At the age of 46, she was not only the first woman to become head of state but also the youngest President and the first to be chosen by the people without the backing of Fianna Fáil.

Political consequences followed fast upon her success. Fine Gael chose a new leader—John Bruton—to replace Alan Dukes, who was blamed for the party's slump in the opinion polls and the poor showing of Austin Currie, its candidate in the presidential contest. Mr Haughey faced an upsurge of resentment in Fianna Fáil over his treatment of Mr Lenihan. Marital law reform and the alteration of articles 2 and 3 of the constitution came into political discussion, reflecting a concern to be active in areas of interest to President Robinson and therefore, it was presumed, to the citizens who elected her.

In the course of the year the government pressed ahead with plans for the whole or partial privatization of state companies in the fields of insurance, food, oil refining and hotels. A storm of protest followed the provisions for broadcasting made by the Minister for Communications, Ray Burke, which diverted a proportion of the revenue of the national service, Radio Telefis Eireann (RTE), to the independent sector. RTE itself was strongly criticized by cultural bodies when it sought to mitigate its consequent financial problems by restricting the development of its symphony orchestra (the only major professional orchestra in the Republic) and by ending its sponsorship of a leading choir. Despite the agricultural crisis and setbacks in industries from banking to crystal manufacture, the economy performed strongly and recorded a growth rate of some 4 per cent while inflation was contained at under 3 per cent, the lowest level in any EC country with the exception of Denmark.

At Hollywood in March the Irish film *My Left Foot*, about the triumphs and tribulations of the handicapped Dublin writer Christy Brown, won the Oscars for best actor (Daniel Day-Lewis) and the best supporting actress (Brenda Fricker) (see also Pt. XVI, CINEMA). A happy event at mid-summer was the achievement of the Republic of Ireland football team in reaching the quarter-finals of the World Cup under the inspired management of Jackie Charlton (see also Pt. XVII). Thousands of supporters made their way to Italy for the individual matches as Ireland unexpectedly survived several rounds of the competition. The Irish fans won many plaudits for their good humour and exemplary behaviour.

Chapter 2

DENMARK—ICELAND—NORWAY—SWEDEN—FINLAND—
AUSTRIA—SWITZERLAND

DENMARK

CAPITAL: Copenhagen   AREA: 43,000 sq km   POPULATION: 5,100,000 ('88)
OFFICIAL LANGUAGE: Danish   POLITICAL SYSTEM: parliamentary democracy
HEAD OF STATE: Queen Margrethe II (since Jan '72)
RULING PARTIES: Conservative People's Party (KF) and Venstre Liberals (V)
HEAD OF GOVERNMENT: Poul Schlüter (KF), Prime Minister (since Sept '82)
PRINCIPAL MINISTERS: Uffe Ellemann-Jensen (V/foreign affairs), Henning Dyremose (KF/finance), Anders Fogh Rasmussen (V/economic affairs), Hans Engell (KF/justice), Knud Enggard (V/defence), Thor Pedersen (V/interior, Nordic affairs)
INTERNATIONAL ALIGNMENT: NATO, OECD, EC, Nordic Council
CURRENCY: krone (end-'90 £1=DKr11.15, US$1=DKr5.77)
GNP PER CAPITA: US$18,450 ('88)
MAIN EXPORT EARNERS: agricultural produce, machinery and transport equipment, manufactures

THE changes in Europe during 1990 accelerated the positive development of Danish attitudes to NATO and the EC. In January the all-party Defence Commission set up in 1988 delivered its report. All except the Socialist People's Party (SF) accepted NATO membership as the basis of Denmark's future security policy. In September all the parties except the SF voted to send a naval contribution to support the UN embargo in the Gulf.

Support for European integration, including economic and monetary union, was increased by the prospect of German reunification. Danish politicians regarded Germany's closer integration into Western Europe as the best means of lessening any threat to its smaller neighbours and maximizing their influence on European affairs. The greater support for European integration was most marked among previously sceptical Social Democratic politicians and voters. On 18 April the Social Democrats joined with the coalition parties (Conservatives, Liberals and Radical Liberals) and the Centre Democrats in proposing a resolution calling for further EC integration, support for German self-determination, its reunification within an integrated Europe, and a continued US commitment to European security.

Danish ministers, especially the Foreign Minister, urged the Nordic EFTA countries to join Denmark in the EC. They argued that neutrality was no longer an argument against membership for Sweden and Finland, and warned that their influence on EC decision-making would not be increased within the proposed European Economic Area of the EC and EFTA. At the Nordic Council meeting in February Poul Schlüter, the Prime Minister, also argued that solutions to the economic problems facing their countries could be found only within a wider context than the Nordic region.

Mr Schlüter's government made some progress towards correcting the structural imbalances in Denmark's economy. Inflation fell below 3 per cent and a current-account surplus was forecast for the first time since 1963. But growth was low, unemployment high and the budget deficit widening due to lower revenues and higher transfer payments. The government could not implement its plans for tax and labour market reforms due to its lack of a majority and continued disagreements with the Social Democrats. The 1991 budget proposal, published in August, continued its strategy of a tight fiscal policy, public sector and social security cuts, and modest personal tax cuts on higher incomes.

A budget majority including the Progress Party, as in December 1989, was impossible after mid-November when the parliamentary party split after expelling former leader Mogens Glistrup. On 13 November budget negotiations with the Social Democrats also broke down over tax cuts on higher incomes. On 22 November Mr Schlüter called an election for 12 December. The outcome was as follows (1988 result in brackets):

	seats	% of votes
Social Democrats	69 (55)	37.4 (29.8)
Socialist People's Party	15 (24)	8.3 (13.0)
Conservatives	30 (35)	16.0 (19.3)
Liberals	29 (22)	15.8 (11.8)
Radical Liberals	7 (10)	3.5 (5.6)
Centre Democrats	9 (9)	5.1 (4.7)
Christian People's Party	4 (4)	2.3 (2.0)
Progress Party	12 (16)	6.3 (9.0)
Greenland/Faroes	4 (4)	
Other parties	0 (0)	5.2 (4.8)

Despite the Social Democrats' gains, the six non-socialist parties retained their majority. Mr Schlüter continued as Prime Minister of a Conservative-Liberal coalition, the Radical Liberals having withdrawn from government and the Centre Democrats and Christian People's Party having refused to enter it.

ICELAND

CAPITAL: Reykjavik   AREA: 103,000 sq km   POPULATION: 249,000 ('88)
OFFICIAL LANGUAGE: Icelandic   POLITICAL SYSTEM: parliamentary democracy
HEAD OF STATE: President Vigdis Finnbogadóttir (since Aug '80)
RULING PARTIES: Progressive Party (PP), Social Democrats (SDP), People's Alliance (PA), Citizens' Party (CP)
HEAD OF GOVERNMENT: Steingrímur Hermannsson (PP), Prime Minister (since '88)
PRINCIPAL MINISTERS: Jón Baldvin Hannibalsson (SDP/foreign affairs and trade), Olafur Ragnar Grímsson (PA/finance), Halldór Asgrímsson (PP/fisheries), Jón Sigurthsson (SDP/commerce & industry), Óli Th. Gudbartsson (CP/justice)
INTERNATIONAL ALIGNMENT: NATO, OECD, EFTA, Nordic Council
CURRENCY: króna (end-'90 £1=ISK106.23, US$1=ISK55.04)
GNP PER CAPITA: US$20,190 ('88)
MAIN EXPORT EARNERS: fish and fish products, tourism

ON 1 February a national wage agreement for the period to 15 September 1991 was concluded between the government, employers, private and public sector unions, and farmers. Based on forecast 1990 price rises of 6 per cent if the agreement held, wages would rise in stages by 9.5 per cent. There would be compensating wage rises if price increases exceeded specified percentages at certain key dates. Not included in this national agreement were the public sector university graduates (BMHR). Their 1989 agreement guaranteed them larger rises in order to establish parity with private-sector graduate employees.

On 4 May the Independence Party in the Althing was strengthened when the Liberal Right's two representatives joined it. The Independence Party also performed well in the local elections on 26 May, especially in Reykjavik. The election was a setback for the leaders of the Social Democrats and People's Alliance, respectively Jón Baldvin Hannibalsson and Olafur Ragnar Grímsson, who had encouraged joint left lists. Where such lists were presented they performed poorly. In

Reykjavik, where the People's Alliance put up a separate list and the Social Democrats participated in a joint left list, both lost votes. Mr Grímsson's refusal to support the People's Alliance list brought calls for his resignation as party chairman. In June the party's central committee decided not to join common left lists in the April 1991 general election.

By summer inflation was falling fast, but the government feared that compensating pay awards might still be necessary in September, undermining the anti-inflationary impact of the February national wage agreement. The government therefore on 12 June postponed the 4.5 per cent wage increase due on 1 July to members of the BMHR. Other unions had declared that they would demand a similar increase if it was paid. The BMHR appealed to the Labour Court, which on 23 July found in its favour. On 3 August the government annulled the wage rise by provisional law. The BMHR threatened to appeal to the ILO. On 17 July the government, in a further attempt to hold down price rises, reduced VAT in some sectors and postponed some public-sector price rises.

With the other EFTA states Iceland participated during 1990 in the European Economic Area (EEA) negotiations with the EC. On 1 September, in an important move to bring Iceland's foreign currency regulations into line with those in the EC, far-reaching changes were introduced which lifted restrictions on Icelanders' freedom to invest and raise loans abroad. Iceland's main objective in the EEA negotiations was to secure tariff-free access to EC markets for its fish products without in exchange opening up its 200-mile fishing zone to the EC's fleets. Nor could Iceland accept foreign ownership of Icelandic land or energy sources.

Differences emerged within the coalition over the possibility of eventually seeking EC membership. The Prime Minister, Steingrimur Hermannsson of the agrarian Progressive Party, spoke strongly against it. The Social Democrats, at their congress in October, accepted the possibility of membership provided Iceland received guarantees of permanent exclusive sovereignty over its fishing zone and free access for fish products to EC markets. Outside the government Iceland's largest party, the Independence Party, put up the same conditions for any form of relationship without specifying which it would prefer.

NORWAY

CAPITAL: Oslo   AREA: 324,000 sq km   POPULATION: 4,200,000 ('88)
OFFICIAL LANGUAGE: Norwegian   POLITICAL SYSTEM: parliamentary democracy
HEAD OF STATE: King Olav V (since Sept '57)
RULING PARTY: Labour Party (minority)
HEAD OF GOVERNMENT: Gro Harlem Brundtland, Prime Minister (since Nov '90)
PRINCIPAL MINISTERS: Thorvald Stoltenberg (foreign affairs), Sigbjørm Johnsen (finance), Finn Kristensen (petroleum), Johan J. Holst (defence), Kari Gjesteby (justice), Oddrun Pettersen (fisheries)
INTERNATIONAL ALIGNMENT: NATO, OECD, EFTA, Nordic Council
CURRENCY: krone (end-'90 £1=NKr11.35, US$1=NKr5.88)
GNP PER CAPITA: US$19,900 ('88)
MAIN EXPORT EARNERS: oil and gas, machinery and transport equipment, manufactures, chemicals, fish

BY early 1990 inflation was down to 4 per cent and the balance of payments was again in surplus. In mid-March a moderate voluntary national wage agreement was reached for the private sector; the public sector followed. The main problem was record high unemployment of about 5 per cent. Labour Party and trade union calls for higher public spending were resisted by the centre-right minority coalition headed by the Conservative, Jan P. Syse, although in February it brought forward some major public construction projects and announced measures to encourage greater investment in the economy by financial institutions. The government also announced measures to help the northernmost counties, hard hit by a crisis in the fishing industry.

Government policy was to tackle unemployment by structural reforms to encourage efficiency. In February it published plans for greater competition and mergers between Norway's banks. In May it announced plans for a three-year tax reform to stimulate enterprise and savings. A start was made with privatizing state industries. On 1 July remaining foreign-exchange controls were removed. Restrictions on foreign banks were to be liberalized. On 22 October the krone was linked to the ecu to promote currency stability, control inflation and strengthen links with the EC.

The most difficult issue facing Mr Syse's coalition was Norway's relations with the EC, most immediately the EC-EFTA negotiations to create a European Economic Area (EEA). The three parties had been able to coalesce in September 1989 only by putting aside their deep differences on these questions. At their May congress the Conservatives, who favoured membership, described the EEA as an 'unsatisfactory way station' on the road to this goal. The agrarian Centre Party opposed not only membership but any far-reaching adjustment to the EC. The Christian People's Party was divided. So was Labour, which had postponed a decision until 1992. The Progress Party decided in March in favour of applying for membership. Public opinion also seemed to be moving that way.

The EC and EFTA spent until June preparing their negotiating mandates. Both then and later, when negotiations had begun, the Centre Party insisted on rejecting the EC's requirement that Norway repeal its concession laws limiting foreigners' rights to own Norwegian property and businesses. By the autumn the government's inability to resolve its differences threatened the conclusion of an EEA agreement. Throughout October it tried to resolve the concession issue. Finally on 29 October the Centre Party left the coalition and Mr Syse resigned.

The Centre Party then switched its parliamentary support to Labour and on 3 November Gro Harlem Brundtland again became Prime Minister. Holding only 63 of the Storting's 165 seats, her minority Labour government would normally depend for a majority on the Socialist Left, Centre Party and Christian People's Party. However, for any moves to closer association with the EC she could rely on a solid majority composed of Labour, Conservatives and the Progress Party. She immediately announced her readiness to repeal the concession laws in order to conclude an EEA agreement. However, she reacted cautiously to Sweden's suggestion that Norway and Finland join Sweden in a joint application for EC membership in 1991. She insisted that a Norwegian decision could not be taken until 1992.

SWEDEN

CAPITAL: Stockholm   AREA: 450,000 sq km   POPULATION: 8,400,000 ('88)
OFFICIAL LANGUAGE: Swedish   POLITICAL SYSTEM: parliamentary democracy
HEAD OF STATE: King Carl XVI Gustav (since Sept '73)
RULING PARTY: Social Democratic Party (minority)
HEAD OF GOVERNMENT: Ingvar Carlsson, Prime Minister (since March '86)
PRINCIPAL MINISTERS: Odd Engström (deputy premier), Sten Andersson (foreign affairs), Roine Carlsson (defence), Allan Larsson (finance), Laila Freivalds (justice), Rune Molin (industry)
INTERNATIONAL ALIGNMENT: neutral, OECD, EFTA, Nordic Council
CURRENCY: krona (end-'90 £1=SKr10.87, US$1=SKr5.63)
GNP PER CAPITA: US$19,300 ('88)
MAIN EXPORT EARNERS: machinery and transport equipment, timber and wood products, iron and steel, tourism

PRESENTING the 1990 budget on 10 January, Finance Minister Kjell-Olof Feldt called for the conclusion within a month of a moderate two-year national wage agreement to curb Sweden's serious wage-push inflation. By early February the banking system was crippled by strikes, and key groups of public sector workers were threatening to strike. On 8 February Ingvar Carlsson's minority Social Democratic government proposed a two-year wage, price, rent and dividend freeze combined with a strike ban enforced by heavy fines. On 15 February the government was defeated in parliament and resigned. Mr Feldt announced his departure from politics.

On 23 February, having dropped the strike ban and wage freeze, Mr Carlsson was able, with Communist support, to form a new government with Allan Larsson as Finance Minister. On 26 February he won parliamentary support for a new set of measures, including a price and rent freeze, voluntary wage restraint, and public mediators to help negotiate moderate wage agreements.

The mediators began work with inflation at 11 per cent and a widening current-account deficit. The unions demanded compensating wage rises. On 6 April, with Liberal support, the government introduced further austerity measures to cut demand and public spending. The price freeze was abandoned, VAT raised, and promised social reforms postponed.

Simultaneously, however, the government continued the reforms begun by Mr Feldt to encourage enterprise, deregulate the financial system, and harmonize Sweden's economy with the EC. Again with Liberal Party support, the government in April introduced legislation to reduce the highest marginal income tax rate to 50 per cent, extend the goods and services liable to VAT, and tighten up taxes on business and capital. The turnover tax on bonds and stock market transactions would be abolished. From 1 July foreign banks were permitted to own Swedish banks and other financial institutions, and to open branch offices in Sweden. In April the government also announced its intention to begin in July 1991 a five-year phase-out of the agricultural income support system and price regulation which had led to large agricultural surpluses and high food prices.

At the Social Democratic Party congress in September the leadership won support for significant modifications to party policy. The commitment to begin closing Sweden's nuclear power stations in 1995–96 was dropped to open the way for negotiations to find a solution enjoying broad political support. Mr Carlsson also won acceptance for a more positive view of the compatibility of Swedish neutrality with EC membership in post-Cold War Europe. Opinion polls showed that a majority of Swedes now anticipated EC membership by the late 1990s. The Moderates, Liberals and business leaders also supported an early application for membership.

In the autumn worsening economic indicators and devaluation fears led to large currency outflows, which became very heavy in October. Between 12 and 18 October the Central Bank raised interest rates from 12 to 17 per cent. On 26 October the government presented another emergency austerity programme designed to reduce public spending by SKr 15,000 million, including cuts in welfare spending. The government abandoned its commitment to full employment as the price of defeating wage-push inflation, proposed four-year parliaments to bolster political stability, and announced that it would seek support for a declaration in favour of EC membership. On 12 December parliament voted by a large majority of Social Democrats, Moderates, Liberals and Centre

Party to apply for EC membership following completion of the EC-EFTA European Economic Area negotiations, probably in 1991. The proposal was opposed by the Left Socialists and Greens.

FINLAND

CAPITAL: Helsinki   AREA: 338,000 sq km   POPULATION: 5,000,000 ('88)
OFFICIAL LANGUAGES: Finnish & Swedish   POLITICAL SYSTEM: presidential democracy
HEAD OF STATE: President Mauno Koivisto (since Sept '81)
RULING PARTIES: National Coalition (KK), Social Democratic (SSDP) & Swedish People's (SFP)
HEAD OF GOVERNMENT: Harri Holkeri (KK), Prime Minister (since April '87)
PRINCIPAL MINISTERS: Pertti Paasio (SSDP/foreign affairs), Matti Louekoski (SSDP/finance), Jarmo Rantanen (SSDP/interior), Elisabeth Rehn (SFP/defence), Tarja Halonen (SSDP/justice, Nordic cooperation)
INTERNATIONAL ALIGNMENT: neutral, OECD, EFTA, Nordic Council
CURRENCY: markka (end-'90 £1=Fmk6.99, US$1=Fmk3.63)
GNP PER CAPITA: US$18,590 ('88)
MAIN EXPORT EARNERS: timber and wood products, manufactures, machinery and transport equipment, tourism

BY mid-January most unions had settled for moderate two-year wage agreements. The government implemented its promised tax measures, including higher child allowances and lower income tax rates. The wage agreements, combined with high interest rates and tight public spending, were vital to cool down Finland's economy. After a decade of fast growth inflation was 6 per cent and the forecast current account deficit 5 per cent of GDP.

Moves began to ease the inflow of foreign capital. From 1 February foreigners could invest in markka bonds. A committee was examining the Restricting Act of 1939 which prohibited foreign investment in certain sectors of the economy. In the autumn the government proposed that foreigners be permitted to own restricted shares through mutual funds. As of 1 September foreigners could also buy derivative instruments based on Finnish shares and warrants. From January 1991 most foreign exchange controls would be abolished.

Events in Europe presented Finland's policy makers with major challenges. They reacted cautiously to the Baltic states' declarations of independence. President Koivisto recognized the Soviet Union's legitimate security interests in that region. Moscow's moves to a market economy and weakening central economic control put severe pressure on Finnish-Soviet barter-based trading arrangements. In June the Soviet Union proposed that the barter system be replaced by normal trade in convertible currencies from January 1991. The Finns argued for a transitional period. Trade became erratic, with the barter system breaking down as USSR oil exports declined and its shortage of hard currency led to delays in payments. In 1990 trade with the Soviet Union fell to 10 per cent of Finland's total trade and was expected to fall even further.

Economic relations with Western Europe were thus all the more important. Negotiations for a European Economic Area (EEA) continued throughout the year. Public opinion was coming to favour membership, but the government adopted a very cautious position. The Conservatives were more favourable to membership than the Social Democrats. But both stressed the importance of first successfully concluding the EEA negotiations.

The ending of the Cold War was the background to a formal Finnish re-interpretation of the treaties underpinning its post-war foreign policy. On 21 September the government declared that after consultations with the countries concerned Finland no longer considered itself bound by the restrictions on its armed forces contained in the Paris Peace Treaty of 1947. It also regarded as outdated the reference to Germany in the 1948 Finnish-Soviet Treaty. The treaty texts would not be changed. This was a unilateral re-interpretation which would enhance Finnish sovereignty while leaving its foreign policy unaltered. In August the Rural Party left Harri Holkeri's government during the budget negotiations. But with his own Conservatives, the Social Democrats and the Swedish People's Party, he still retained a majority in parliament. The opposition parties began their preparations for the election in March 1991. On 29 March Paavo Väyrynen resigned as Centre Party chairman although remaining its most likely presidential candidate in 1994. He was replaced by Esko Aho. On 25 February the Communist Party announced the transfer of its political activities to a new organization, the Left League. The League, constituted on 29 April, united the majority Communists, minority Communists (who disbanded their electoral organization, Democratic Alternative) and the People's Democrats.

AUSTRIA

CHAPTER: Vienna AREA: 84,000 sq km POPULATION: 7,600,000 ('88)
OFFICIAL LANGUAGE: German POLITICAL SYSTEM: federal parliamentary democracy
HEAD OF STATE: Federal President Kurt Waldheim (since July '86)
RULING PARTIES: Socialist (SPÖ) and People's (ÖVP) parties
HEAD OF GOVERNMENT: Franz Vranitzky (SPÖ), Federal Chancellor (since June '86)
PRINCIPAL MINISTERS: Josef Riegler (ÖVP/Vice-Chancellor), Alois Mock (ÖVP/foreign affairs) Ferdinand Lacina (SPÖ/finance), Franz Löschnak (SPÖ/interior), Werner Fasslabend (ÖVP/defence), Nikolaus Michalek (non-party/justice)
INTERNATIONAL ALIGNMENT: neutral, OECD, EFTA
CURRENCY: schilling (end-'90 £1=Sch20.28, US$1=Sch10.50)
GNP PER CAPITA: US$15,470 ('88)
MAIN EXPORT EARNERS: basic manufactures, machinery and transport equipment, chemicals, tourism

AN era ended on 29 July with the death of Dr Bruno Kreisky (see OBITUARY), the former Federal Chancellor and Foreign Minister, who helped negotiate the State Treaty which restored Austria's independence, and who established 'active neutrality' as the guiding principle of its foreign policy. Since he had also worked especially for a solution of the Middle East problem, it was ironic that his death should have coincided so nearly with Iraq's invasion of Kuwait on 2 August. Austria at once condemned Iraq's use of military force and called for its withdrawal from Kuwait, imposing sanctions on 13 August in compliance with UN resolutions. This message was confirmed by President Waldheim during his visit to Iraq on 25 August, from which he returned with 95 Austrian detainees. On 6 September the Austrian government approved the overflight of US troops and supplies to the Gulf, in a move seen as a significant departure from traditional Austrian practice on neutrality.

Meanwhile, a rising tide of refugees from Eastern Europe, whose numbers threatened to become a divisive electoral issue, was forcing a reassessment of Austria's traditional role as a country of asylum. In March visa requirements were imposed on Bulgarians, Romanians and Turks, and tougher measures, aimed at discouraging illegal immigration and distinguishing economic from political refugees, were introduced. In September visa requirements were reimposed on Poles, and additional troops deployed along the Hungarian border.

Events in Eastern Europe also frustrated Austrian attempts to accelerate progress on its application for EC membership, with the Commission's final opinion not expected before mid-1991 and, as the Austrians saw it, the projected 'European Economic Area' for greater EC/EFTA cooperation no substitute for full membership. Nonetheless, progress towards German reunification, and the continuing diminution of East-West tensions, were effectively removing obstacles from Austria's path and opening up new opportunities. On 20 May the Foreign Ministers of Austria, Italy, Yugoslavia, Hungary and Czechoslovakia—the former Habsburg lands—met in Vienna to form the so-called Pentagonale group, setting themselves to improve regional cooperation, particularly in the fields of transport, communications, the environment, science and technology, culture and tourism. These objectives were confirmed at a summit of heads of government and foreign ministers in Venice in August.

On 6 November, after the successful conclusion of the negotiations for German reunification, Austria formally informed the four signatories of the 1955 State Treaty—the USSR, USA, Britain and France—that it considered articles 12–16 and point 13 of article 22 of the treaty to be obsolete, though remaining committed to the treaty as a whole and to its commitment not to possess, produce or test nuclear, biological or chemical weapons. Articles 12 and 13 prohibited former Nazis from service in the Austrian armed forces, and the acquisition by Austria of various categories of special weapon, including guided missiles. Articles 14, 15 and 16 concerned disposal of war materiel of allied and German origin, and prohibited Austria from assisting German rearmament as well as from acquiring German or Japanese aircraft. Point 13 of article 22 concerned the disposal of certain German assets in Austria. None of the four signatory powers raised objections.

On 18 November the negotiations being conducted in Vienna by the Conference on Security and Cooperation in Europe (CSCE) were successfully completed with the initialling of a Treaty on Conventional Armed Forces in Europe (CFE), providing for extensive measures of conventional disarmament (see Pt. XII). Agreement was also reached on new confidence and security building measures of information and evaluation (CSBM). Both documents were signed at the CSCE summit meeting in Paris in November.

In economic terms 1990 was generally a successful year, although the unemployment rate rose slightly to an estimated 5.4 per cent. Estimated growth in GDP in real terms for 1990 was 4.5 per cent over 1989, with an expected annual rate of inflation of only 3.3 per cent, both figures comparing favourably with most other Western countries.

Politically, the main event of the year was the general election held on 7 October. The campaign was lacklustre, with Austrian voters uneasy about events abroad and dissatisfied with the performance of the grand coalition between the Socialists (SPÖ) and the conservative People's Party (ÖVP), in office since January 1987 and beset by SPÖ scandals and ÖVP internal dissension. The election results confounded predictions. The SPÖ, having decided to exploit the clean image and popularity of its leader, Federal Chancellor Vranitzky, unexpectedly emerged with its vote (42.8 per cent) only slightly down on the 1986 election, so holding all its 80 seats. The Freedom Party (FPÖ), under its controversial leader, Dr Jörg Haider, who had exploited Austrian anxiety about the influx of immigrants and campaigned against corruption, bureaucracy and mismanagement, did well, almost doubling its vote of 16.6 per cent and winning 15 more seats (33 in all). The Greens won ten seats; although their vote remained static at 4.8 per cent, their additional two seats reflected widespread concern over transit traffic problems and energy resources. The main losers were the ÖVP, whose vote slumped disastrously by almost 10 per cent, to 32.1 per cent, so reducing their seats in the National Assembly to 60, a loss of 17.

Having briefly considered, and rejected, an offer of coalition with the FPÖ, ÖVP leader Josef Riegler accepted Dr Vranitzky's offer of negotiations for a new grand coalition. The new government was sworn in on 17 December, after a last-minute flurry when the ÖVP refused to accept the SPÖ's candidate for the justice portfolio. In spite of an agreed programme of record length, featuring further privatization and renewed action on the budget deficit, this did not augur well for the future cohesion of the coalition. It was widely rumoured that senior ÖVP figures favoured coalition with the FPÖ. The creation of a new post for Dr Peter Jankowitsch (SPÖ), as State Secretary in the Federal Chancellery with responsibility for foreign aid and for internal coordination and presentation of EC policy, alongside ÖVP Foreign Minister Dr Alois Mock, was seen as another likely source of future dissension.

SWITZERLAND

CHAPTER: Berne   AREA: 41,300 sq km   POPULATION: 6,720,000 ('90)
OFFICIAL LANGUAGES: German, French and Italian
POLITICAL SYSTEM: federal canton-based democracy
HEAD OF STATE & GOVERNMENT: Arnold Koller (CVP), 1990 President of Federal Council, Minister of Justice
RULING PARTIES: Christian Democratic People's (CVP), Radical Democratic (FDP), Social Democratic (SPS) and Swiss People's (SVP) parties
OTHER MINISTERS: René Felber (SPS/foreign affairs), Otto Stich (SPS/finance), Adolf Ogi (SVP/communications & energy), Flavio Cotti (CVP/interior), Kaspar Villiger (FDP/defence), Jean-Pascal Delamuraz (FDP/economy)
INTERNATIONAL ALIGNMENT: neutral, OECD, EFTA
CURRENCY: Swiss franc (end-'90 £1=SwF2.46, US$1=SwF1.27)
GNP PER CAPITA: US$27,500 ('88)
MAIN EXPORT EARNERS: financial services, machinery, chemicals, tourism

THE ongoing search for Switzerland's role in Europe dominated discussions about Swiss foreign politics and also had its impact on domestic politics. The current negotiations between EFTA and the European Community (EC), envisaging the creation of a European Economic Area (EEA), took, from a Swiss point of view, a rather disappointing turn. The members of EFTA were forced to abandon many of their desired exemptions from EC rules, moreover the EC representatives also made it clear that they were not ready to grant the EFTA countries any right of co-decision in matters concerning the future development of EEA legislation.

The growing fear of a 'satellization' of Switzerland by the EC stimulated the idea that Switzerland should apply for full Community membership. None of the major political parties supported this request, but a committee of politicians from several parties, of trade unionists and journalists started the collection of signatures for a popular initiative which would urge the government to take steps in that direction. Polls showed that the camps of supporters and opponents of EC membership were about the same strength, but they also indicated that the number of citizens undecided on this question had been growing since 1989.

This growing uncertainty about the future of Switzerland was not confined to foreign politics. The Kopp scandal (see AR 1989, p. 176) resulted in a widespread mistrust of Swiss institutions, the greater part of the mass media and the public being shocked at revelations about the activities of the federal prosecution office. Investigations by a parliamentary committee showed clearly that the police had kept under surveillance not only suspect terrorists and spies but also trade unionists, leftists (including members of the co-ruling Social Democratic Party), environmentalists and others.

In 1990 it became even more obvious that Swiss agricultural policy needed deep reform. The GATT Uruguay Round made it evident that Switzerland, as a nation dependent on its worldwide exports of services and manufactured goods, and therefore genuinely interested in a liberalization of international trade, could not maintain its protectionist policies in the agricultural sector. Taxpayers and consumers also manifested their discontent: on 1 April voters rejected a bill which intended to prolong the protectionist regulation of the wine market. Considering this increasing criticism, the Swiss Farmers' Union took the offensive. It submitted a popular initiative, backed by 262,000 signatures, which proposed some reforms but on the other hand stipulated that financial support of farmers was a constitutional duty of the state.

There was no change in the favourable state of federal finances. First estimates revealed that the budgeted surplus of SwF 500 million should easily be attained in 1990. After years of controversy the four governmental parties agreed in parliament on a new structure for federal tax policy. Among the most important decisions was the replacement of sales tax by a value-added tax (VAT), in line with general EC practice. However, the Gewerbeverband (Union of Craft and Small Businesses), which in the 1970s had twice successfully fought in referendums against the introduction of VAT, announced that it would oppose this tax reform in the popular vote scheduled for 1991.

Apart from the future role of Switzerland in Europe, protection of the environment remained the most important political issue. In a popular vote on 23 September Swiss voters approved, by a majority of 55 per cent, a ten-year halt on the construction of nuclear plants. Another popular initiative, which demanded the complete abandonment of nuclear energy, was rejected only by a narrow margin. On the same day, the electorate accepted a new constitutional article giving the federal government some additional powers in the field of energy policy. In spite of persistent pressure by the EC and its member states, the federal government did not depart from its view that the fast-growing international transport of goods should, for environmental reasons, cross the Alps by railway rather than on motorways. It rejected, therefore, the demand to raise the weight limit for trucks from 28 to 40 tonnes and proposed a SwF 10,000 million project for the construction of two new railway tunnels through the Alps.

The number of persons seeking asylum in Switzerland reached a new record. The accommodation and care of these people, mainly from Turkey and Third World countries, created problems, especially in small villages. Nevertheless, the nationalist parties could not take advantage of this situation and suffered heavy losses in elections at cantonal and communal level. Another social issue that strongly occupied the minds of the population was the drug problem. In some towns in German-speaking Switzerland the mere consumption of drugs ceased to be prosecuted by the police, and therefore took place before the eyes of a horrified public. In contrast, the authorities of French-speaking cantons maintained their policy of repression.

Economic growth continued and the level of unemployment remained at a low level of 0.6 per cent. But an increase of the inflation rate to a yearly average of 5.4 per cent gave some reason for concern.

Italian-speaking Flavio Cotti was elected to the annually-rotating post of President of the Federal Council for 1991.

Chapter 3

SPAIN—PORTUGAL—GIBRALTAR—MALTA—GREECE—CYPRUS—TURKEY

SPAIN

CAPITAL: Madrid   AREA: 505,000 sq km   POPULATION: 39,000,000 ('88)
OFFICIAL LANGUAGE: Spanish   POLITICAL SYSTEM: parliamentary democracy
HEAD OF STATE: King Juan Carlos (since Nov '75)
RULING PARTIES: Spanish Socialist Workers' Party (PSOE)
HEAD OF GOVERNMENT: Felipe González, Prime Minister (since Nov '82)
PRINCIPAL MINISTERS: Alfonso Guerra (deputy premier), Francisco Fernández Ordóñez (foreign affairs), Narcís Serra (defence), José Luis Corcuero (interior), Carlos Solchaga (economy and finance), Enrique Múgica Herzog (justice)
INTERNATIONAL ALIGNMENT: NATO, OECD, EC
CURRENCY: peseta (end-'90 £1=Ptas183.70, US$1=Ptas95.18)
GNP PER CAPITA: US$7,740 ('90)
MAIN EXPORT EARNERS: tourism, transport equipment, agricultural products, minerals and base metals

THE Prime Minister, Felipe González, faced an embarrassing situation for nearly the whole of the year. In January Juan Guerra, a brother of Alfonso Guerra, the Deputy Premier, was discovered to have been using for some time an office in government premises in Seville to amass a considerable private fortune through the purchase and sale of real estate. In his dealings he appeared to have used his brother's name. The press fomented the suspicion, even belief, that Alfonso could not have been ignorant of what brother Juan was doing. Alfonso accused the opposition parties of attempting to discredit the Socialist Workers' Party (PSOE), and offered to resign. Sr González defended his deputy, demanding proof of any business connection between the brothers. The PSOE and opposition Popular Party (PP) accused each other of promising favours to contributors to party funds. Some irregularities came to light in the following months. In May Sr González and the PP leader, José María Aznar, agreed that the rules for the acceptance of party funds should be tightened. Meanwhile, the public prosecutor had begun an investigation into Juan Guerra's business, a task which had not been completed as the year ended.

The final composition of the lower house of the Cortes (see AR 1989, p. 181) was finally settled in March. The PSOE had 175 seats out of 350, and therefore not an overall majority. In June the Constitutional Tribunal ruled that the four (Basque nationalist) Herri Batasuna (HB) deputies who had been elected in 1989 could be allowed to take their seats after promising to accept the constitution with the addendum they demanded, that is 'only because it is a legal requirement'. Three did so; the fourth, who had been convicted of terrorist acts and was now in hiding, did not. The government's majority was therefore never at risk.

The PSOE did well in the election for the parliament of Andalucia on 23 June. In spite of the cloud over Alfonso Guerra it obtained a comfortable majority. On the other hand, at the election for the parliament of Euskadi (the Basque region) on 28 October it lost three of its 19 seats. The Basque Nationalist Party (PNV) recovered much of the vote it had lost in 1986 to its splinter group Eusko Alkartasuna (EA) and gained 22. The EA got 9 and the leftist Euskadiko Ezkerra 3, while HB retained its 13 seats with 17.3 per cent of the vote. It was some comfort to the other Basque parties that the appeal of this political wing of the terrorist ETA had not increased since 1986.

In the five months prior to the Basque election, groups of young boys whose allegiance was to HB had caused upwards of £2 million of damage to bank premises, railway carriages, road construction vehicles and cars with French number plates. These youths did not carry explosives, and if caught and convicted (which they rarely were) received light punishments. It was common knowledge in Bilbao and San Sebastian that ETA was interested in the more daring of them as potential recruits. ETA had carried out fewer acts of terrorism than in previous years and received a blow when four of its more important members were arrested in France. They had lists of some of their colleagues in Spain. The Spanish police found and arrested 24 of them.

A 6 per cent salary and wage increase in the public sector was agreed upon between the government and labour unions after much bargaining. The Employers' Federation instructed its members to take that figure as basic, but to offer higher rises in return for agreements on higher productivity. Most enterprises settled well above the recommended amount and there was little industrial trouble.

The unions and the left of the PSOE continued to harass Carlos Solchaga, the Minister of Economy and Finance, on the grounds that his policies were anti-socialist. He did not see his way to raising pensions or unemployment benefits, and estimated that a reduction in the number of hours in the working week was something the country could not afford at present. The credit restrictions and high interest rates which he had imposed midway through 1989 had the required effect. The final GNP growth that year was no higher than 5 per cent, and it was reduced in 1990 to 3.8 per cent. Inflation in 1990 was kept down to 6.4 per cent. Internal demand fell from 7.7 per cent in 1989 to 4.7 in 1990. Sales of consumer durables, especially cars, dropped. Sr Solchaga expected that, even if he relaxed the credit restrictions a little, GNP growth could be brought down further in the new year to under 3 per cent. The government's chief worry was the persistence of high unemployment, at 16.5 per cent the second highest in the EC. At the beginning of December the government invited the Employers' Federation and labour unions to join it in an Economic and Social Council to advise the government on all matters relating to labour.

On 21 May the Chief of the Spanish Defence General Staff and the Supreme Commander of NATO forces in Europe signed the first two of six projected agreements establishing the mechanisms of coordination between Spanish and other NATO military forces (see AR 1988, pp. 183–4). These referred to air and naval forces in the eastern Atlantic and in Spanish air space. Bearing in mind that many in Spain, especially in the PSOE, had voted in the 1985 referendum that Spain should remain in NATO only on the understanding that it would not join the alliance's command structure, the term 'operational control' was used instead of 'command' in the text of these documents. It was accepted that Spanish units could be placed under the 'control' of a foreigner and similarly a Spaniard could have under him units of another state. In courteous regard to Portuguese sensitivities, Spain entered into what was called 'a gentleman's agreement' not to have control of Portuguese units for the present. The Spanish Defence Minister, Narcís Serra, anticipated great delay in the completion of the other documents, with the exception of that governing the operational control of Spanish units in the Strait of Gibraltar. He expected that one to be difficult.

At the CSCE summit conference in Paris on 21 November Sr González expressed his delight at the new order emerging in Europe (see DOCUMENTS). Then, to the surprise of listeners, he voiced the hope that 'such vestiges of the old as . . . the colonial character of Gibraltar' might disappear, for a 'solid order' had to be based on 'solid foundations'. A few days later, in an interview for a British newspaper, he said that in his opinion the United Kingdom had de facto 'lost sovereignty over Gibraltar'. Britain, he explained, was unable to insist that something should be done in Gibraltar as it could in Glasgow; therefore, Britain was in breach of the Treaty of Utrecht, its sole justification for clinging on to the colony.

In the Spanish government's view events in Eastern Europe had in no way made NATO less necessary than before to Western defence and security; the USSR's forces would still be formidable even after they had been reduced as agreed. Nevertheless, Spain considered that Western Europe should accept greater responsibility for its own defence. This responsibility could be assumed either by the Western European Union (WEU) or the EC. It would be quicker through the WEU, since its meetings were attended by both foreign and defence ministers, and the EC contained one neutral member (Ireland) and another with 'neutralist' tendencies (Denmark). On the other hand, if the Community were to move rapidly, as Spain desired, towards political union, the government reckoned that the EC would have to consider the political and economic aspects of security and evolve its own defence and foreign policy.

Spain also considered that now that the threat from Eastern Europe had diminished, attention should be paid to North Africa and the Near East. In May it put to France and Italy the idea of a Conference on Security and Cooperation in the Mediterranean (CSCM) analogous to the CSCE, which had yielded such good results. Spain had in mind inviting countries as far as the Gulf, but France insisted on limiting the invitations to North Africa. The CSCM met in Rome on 10 October, but ended with no agreement other than to meet again in Algiers in 1991.

PORTUGAL

CHAPTER: Lisbon   AREA: 92,000 sq km   POPULATION: 10,300,000 ('88)
OFFICIAL LANGUAGE: Portuguese
POLITICAL SYSTEM: presidential/parliamentary democracy
HEAD OF STATE: President Mário Soares (since March '86)
RULING PARTY: Social Democratic Party (PSD)
HEAD OF GOVERNMENT: Anibal Cavaco Silva, Prime Minister (since Nov '85)
PRINCIPAL MINISTERS: Fernando Nogueira (deputy premier & justice), João de Deus Pinheiro (foreign affairs) Carlos Brito (defence), Miguel Beleza (finance), Manuel Pereira (home affairs)
INTERNATIONAL ALIGNMENT: NATO, OECD, EC
CURRENCY: escudo (end-'90 £1=Esc255.30, US$1=Esc132.28)
GNP PER CAPITA: US$3,677 ('88)
MAIN EXPORT EARNERS: tourism, basic manufactures, textiles, agricultural products

PRIME Minister Cavaco Silva and his ruling centre-right Social Democratic Party (PSD) fought to regain their lead with the electorate after a bruising defeat at the hands of the Socialist Party (PS) in local elections in December 1989. In an early January reshuffle five ministers were replaced, including Deputy Premier Eurico de Melo and the finance and health ministers, close and loyal associates whose public image had become an electoral liability. The Prime Minister used the opportunity to tighten control over the cabinet and major policy decisions, soon making people forget the PS success in the local elections.

The government sought to strengthen political stability when Mr Cavaco Silva decided not to challenge President Mário Soares in his attempt to be re-elected for a second mandate, and offered him PSD support. In parliament the Social Democrats made good use of their absolute majority and did not face much opposition. Critics accused the government of being high-handed and dismissive of dialogue, or complained that reforms were too timid and slow. Ferro Rodrigues, a PS spokesman on economic matters, said that the government had missed the chance to make real structural changes and that, as a result, Portugal was as vulnerable to negative developments as it had been five years ago.

The Socialists, under their new leader, Dr Jorge Sampaio (mayor of Lisbon), tried to improve their electoral profile through their management of local government in major towns like Lisbon and Oporto. PS policies did not differ much from those of the government, being only more emphatic on matters of health, education and housing.

The Communist Party (PC) went on losing prominent members following acerbic debates and splits over developments in Central and Eastern Europe. A leading Communist intellectual, Zita Seabra, was expelled from the party after repeated public appeals to the leadership of Dr Alvaro Cunhal for change and renewal. Dr Cunhal had given his critics an ultimatum to 'shut up or leave'. Following a PC extraordinary national conference in May, major party figures like Vital Moreira and Veiga de Oliveira decided to leave. In July the central committee put forward Carlos Carvalhas as PC candidate for the 1991 presidential elections. His moderate stance and party discipline record had made him heir apparent to Dr Cunhal.

The government tightened credit through increased interest rates and bank lending ceilings in the hope of restraining consumption and inflation, but its efforts were inhibited by high economic growth (4.1 per cent) and a low rate of unemployment (4.5 per cent). For a small country trying to catch up with its European partners, the threat of further inflationary pressures from higher energy costs were particularly unwelcome (Portugal being obliged to import around 83 per cent of its energy). In early September fuel prices rose by up to 8 per cent, following similar increases less than two months before. The government's original target of bringing inflation down to 10 per cent became unrealistic and had to be adjusted to 13 per cent; by December it had become an actual rate of 14.1 per cent.

While inflation appeared to rule out the escudo's entry into the EC's exchange rate mechanism, Portugal was beginning to bring its currency more into line with its European partners. The importance of inflation in timing the escudo's entry was reflected in statements both by the new Finance Minister, Miguel Beleza, and by the governor of the Central Bank, Tavares Moreira. They said that single-digit inflation would be necessary and that Portugal would probably not be ready until late 1991.

Given the choice between growth and inflation, the Prime Minister came out in favour of the former, saying in early November: 'There is no choice. We cannot afford to bring down growth to 2 per cent for the sake of reducing inflation.' With presidential and parliamentary elections due in 1991, Mr Cavaco Silva clearly did not want growth slowing down too fast. It was a year of remarkably few strikes, but in late November farmers in the central region of Ribatejo held big demonstrations in protest against a perceived lack of government protection from foreign competition. Portuguese agriculture remained chronically inefficient, employing about 18 per cent of the national workforce yet contributing only 7 per cent of GDP. The Prime Minister conceded that bureaucracy and vested interests had hampered his efforts at reform, saying that 'many industrialists, while claiming support for free competition and private enterprise, still hanker for state intervention to safeguard their domestic markets and are happy to benefit from whatever subsidies Brussels makes available'.

Greater efforts were made to contain the budget deficit, though expenditure to co-finance EC programmes was kept at a high level at a time of readjustment to remain competitive in the European market (which absorbed 70 per cent of Portuguese exports). The Central Bank expected a manageable end-of-year current-account trade deficit of up to US$1,300 million, representing less than 2 per cent of GDP; although swollen by imported consumer goods, the deficit would be more than offset by direct foreign investment, which had doubled every year in the previous five years, and was expected to reach US$4,000 million by the end of 1990.

The massive sell-off of nationalized industries went on as planned, but faced problems from shaky stock market confidence due to the Gulf crisis and the prospects of world recession. Partially in response to Portuguese business concerns that Portugal was 'up for sale', the government curbed the stakes available to foreigners in several companies due for privatization. Prices on the Portuguese stock market tumbled by nearly 30 per cent across the board over the year. Some dealers, looking for a more predictable market, pinned their hopes on reforms due to be introduced in the spring of 1991, coinciding with fully computerized trading.

GIBRALTAR

CAPITAL: Gibraltar   AREA: 6.5 sq km   POPULATION: 30,000 ('88)
OFFICIAL LANGUAGE: English   POLITICAL SYSTEM: UK dependency, democracy
HEAD OF STATE: Queen Elizabeth II   GOVERNOR: Adml. Sir Derek Reffell
RULING PARTY: Socialist Labour Party (SLP)
HEAD OF GOVERNMENT: Joe Bossano, Chief Minister (since March '88)

In January, a month ahead of the annual meeting of the British and Spanish Foreign Ministers to review the state of the 'negotiation process' agreed by the two sides in Brussels in November 1964 (see AR 1984, pp. 170, 173), Gibraltar received a visit from Francis Maude, then a UK Foreign and Commonwealth Office minister. The object of the visit was to assure the Gibraltarians that the 1987 UK-Spanish agreement on the joint use of the airport in no way altered the status quo on sovereignty over the territory, and to inquire of the Chief Minister, Joe Bossano, whether he still refused to cooperate in the Brussels process. Mr Bossano stood by his decision not to cooperate. In a subsequent interview to a Madrid newspaper, he expressed the view that the British government should tell Spain that it should 'abandon all hope of recovering Gibraltar through the Brussels process'. The airport agreement, he recalled, could be implemented only when the Gibraltar Assembly approved it; but on the eve of its signature by Britain and Spain '17,000 Gibraltarians' had demonstrated publicly that they were opposed to it, and therefore in his view there was no point in putting it to the Assembly.

Mr Bossano was prepared to have Spanish aircraft using the airport on his own terms, that is with Spain having no say in its administration. His government commissioned from a Japanese construction company plans for its possible development. Some were quite ambitious, and included a substantial reclamation of land into the bay to extend the runway and service areas. All envisaged the construction of a new terminal adjacent to the border, with an entrance from each side, so that passengers would go through Spanish or Gibraltarian police and customs controls but not both. This was as far as Mr Bossano was prepared to go towards the UK-Spanish agreement. Tristan Garel-Jones, who had succeeded Mr Maude at the FCO, visited Gibraltar in September, and found Mr Bossano unyielding on both the Brussels process and airport agreement.

There were a few Gibraltarians who considered Mr Bossano's attitude towards their northern neighbour unrealistic. Gibraltar had grown prodigiously as an off-shore financial centre, and was still growing. By the end of 1990 there were 41,000 companies registered there. On reclaimed land a group of Danish investors was building a £100 million finance and administrative centre. As housing was scarce in Gibraltar, over 2,000 Gibraltarians and expatriate businessmen were already residing north of the border. Without closing the frontier the Spanish authorities could make commuting extremely tiresome.

One of these Gibraltarians was a young lawyer, Peter Montegriffo. In January he broke away from the opposition Labour Party because it was not challenging the government's boycott of the Brussels process, and founded his own Social Democrat Party. Towards the end of the year it had attracted a sufficient number of adherents for the Labour

Party to hold talks with it with a view to reunification. Nothing came of them, but the next election was not due for over a year.

On his election in March 1988 Mr Bossano had stated that the Gibraltarians had 'the moral right to self-determination'. In order to exercise it they had to have 'economic self-sufficiency'. Under his guidance Gibraltar was fast becoming self-sufficient, and there was much talk there of a future as an independent city-state.

MALTA

CAPITAL: Valletta   AREA: 316 sq km   POPULATION: 348,000 ('88)
OFFICIAL LANGUAGE: Maltese, English   POLITICAL SYSTEM: parliamentary democracy
HEAD OF STATE: President Vincent Tabone (since April '89)
RULING PARTY: Nationalist Party
HEAD OF GOVERNMENT: Edward Fenech Adami, Prime Minister (since May '87)
PRINCIPAL MINISTERS: Guido De Marco (deputy premier, foreign affairs, justice),
    George Bonello Du Puis (finance), Ugo Mifsud Bonnici (education, interior)
INTERNATIONAL ALIGNMENT: NAM, Cwth.
CURRENCY: lira (end-'90 £1=Lm0.57, US$1=Lm0.30)
GNP PER CAPITA: US$5,190 ('88)
MAIN EXPORT EARNERS: tourism, manufactured goods, machinery

FOR many Maltese the notable event of the year was the visit by Pope John Paul II on 25–27 May. It was the first papal visit in the islands' history despite their long and devout commitment to Rome. A celebratory mass was held in St John's Co-Cathedral in Valletta attended by such numbers as to suggest that the secular-clerical disputes of the past were greatly reduced if not quite ended. Further distinction for Malta came at the 45th session of the UN General Assembly when, on 18 September, Guido de Marco, formerly Minister for the Interior and Justice, was chosen unanimously as president of the Assembly, succeeding Joseph Garba of Nigeria.

The government continued to look for a secure place in the troubled world of the Mediterranean. On 2 February the Prime Minister, Dr Fenech Adami, and the Libyan Secretary for Foreign Liaison, Jadallah Azouz al-Talhi, renewed the economic and security accord between the two republics for a further five years, though with reduced emphasis on military cooperation. On its opposite flank, the government continued to press the case for full European Community (EC) membership, submitting a formal application on 16 July, the fourth country to do so after Cyprus, Austria and Turkey. None was likely to succeed before the completion of the single market in 1992.

The shadow of the impending Gulf war seemed unlikely to extend directly to Malta—its traditional fortress role was now a tourist attraction—but there were fears of its adverse effect on the islands' main source of revenue, tourism, which during the year contributed over 20 per cent of GNP. The budget gave total expenditure at Lm 332.7 million, against revenue (including EC grants to combat marine pollution) at Lm 330 million. Emphasis was still on infrastructural development, including tourist facilities, for which responsibility was shared by no fewer than three ministries.

GREECE

CAPITAL: Athens   AREA: 132,000 sq km   POPULATION: 10,000,000 ('88)
OFFICIAL LANGUAGE: Greek   POLITICAL SYSTEM: parliamentary democracy
HEAD OF STATE: President Konstantinos Karamanlis (since May '90)
RULING PARTY: New Democracy (ND)
HEAD OF GOVERNMENT: Konstantinos Mitsotakis, Prime Minister (since April '90)
PRINCIPAL MINISTERS: Athanassios Kanellopoulos (deputy premier, justice) Antonis Samaras (foreign affairs), Yannis Varvitsiotis (defence), Souris Kouvelas (interior), Georgios Souflias (economy, tourism), Yannis Palaiokrassas (finance)
INTERNATIONAL ALIGNMENT: NATO, OECD, EC
CURRENCY: drachma (end-'90 £1=Dr301.73, US$1=Dr156.33)
GNP PER CAPITA: US$4,800 ('88)
MAIN EXPORT EARNERS: tourism, merchant marine, textiles, agricultural products

ON 8 April Greece underwent its third general election in less than a year. It was held under the highly proportional electoral system adopted by Andreas Papandreou's PASOK government just before leaving office. This had resulted in hung parliaments in the June and November 1989 elections (see AR 1989, pp. 187–8). Many observers had predicted a similarly inconclusive outcome to the April election but this was averted by the narrowest of margins. Konstantinos Mitsotakis's New Democracy (ND) party marginally increased its share of the vote to 47 per cent, while PASOK's share fell from 41 to 39 per cent. The (communist) Alliance of the Left and Progress vote dropped from 11 to 10 per cent. ND won 150 seats, exactly half of the 300-strong parliament, PASOK 123 and the Left Alliance 19.

The electoral system gave four seats to independents, two to candidates representing the Muslim (predominantly Turkish) minority in Western Thrace (before 1989 candidates from the Turkish minority had contested elections on the tickets of the major parties), one to the Ecologists and one to Democratic Renewal, an ND breakaway group. The latter party's decision to support New Democracy in parliament was enough to ensure that Mr Mitsotakis was called upon to form a government. On 27 April he won a formal vote of confidence by a margin of 152 to 146.

The election was held shortly after the expiry, on 30 March, of the five-year term of the President, Christos Sartzetakis. The relative strength of the parties in parliament under the all-party 'ecumenical' government, headed by the 85-year-old Xenophon Zolotas, which had resulted from the November 1989 election, and the constitutional requirement of a minimum 180 votes in parliament meant that there was no possibility of the election of a candidate against the wishes of Mr Mitsotakis. In May Konstantinos Karamanlis, aged 83, a former conservative Prime Minister and President between 1980 and 1985, was elected to the presidency for a five-year term. He received 153 votes—a simple majority in parliament sufficing under the constitution in the wake of an election.

Mr Mitsotakis made it clear soon after his election victory that he intended to revise the electoral law to prevent a repetition of the political uncertainties of 1989–90. The new law was passed in November. In time-honoured fashion this was crafted so as to favour the incumbent party. The simple proportional system introduced by Mr Papandreou was replaced by a variant of the 'reinforced' proportional system adopted in most post-war elections. By insisting on a 3 per cent threshold for a party to be represented in parliament, the bill ensured that independent Muslim candidates would stand no chance of election. The exclusion of party alliances from the third distribution of seats was clearly directed against the possibility of a future PASOK/communist coalition. The passing of the bill also had the effect of making it less likely that the opposition parties would be tempted to try to overthrow New Democracy's very slim majority in parliament, for its 47 per cent of the vote would now produce a majority of between 15 and 20 seats.

One reason why Mr Mitsotakis had been unable to exploit more effectively the aura of scandal attaching to PASOK was that he had made no attempt to disguise the fact that the seriousness of the country's economic position would demand harsh measures. His opponents, indeed, accused him of being an advocate of 'Balkan Thatcherism'. The IMF, the OECD and the European Commission all made gloomy comments on the severity of the country's economic plight. As soon as he had gained a majority in parliament, Mr Mitsotakis announced an austerity programme aimed at tackling what he described as the country's worst economic crisis in the post-war period. Swingeing increases in the cost of public utilities, in the price of petrol and of alcohol were matched by increases in the differential rates of VAT. A surcharge was introduced on professional incomes and non-reinvested company profits in 1989. The measures, which were estimated to add some 3.5 points to an existing rate of inflation of 18 per cent, were aimed at reducing the public-sector deficit from over 20 per cent of gross domestic product to 10 per cent by the end of 1992. The Prime Minister also announced an end to the index-linking of incomes and a return to free collective bargaining. Plans were established for the privatization of the hugely indebted and overmanned 'problematic' companies that had been taken into state ownership. The measures were bitterly criticized by the opposition, and President Karamanlis was moved to urge that care be taken that the incidence of austerity measures was equitably distributed. These, coupled with proposals to rationalize the arcane system of pension provision, provoked widespread strikes in the public sector and in the banking system.

Another high priority was to mend fences with Greece's European partners and, in particular, with the United States. After visiting every European Community capital Mr Mitsotakis in June became the first Greek premier to visit the White House for 25 years. One outcome of the improved climate in relations with Washington was the renewal in July for a further eight years of the US-Greece defence cooperation agreement. As had been previously announced, the USA intended to close down the Hellenikon air base adjacent to Athens airport and the communications facility at Nea Makri near Marathon. Some of their functions were henceforth to be transferred to the Suda Bay air and naval base near Chania in Crete and to an electronics surveillance station at Gournes. In May Greece for the first time recognized the existence of Israel *de jure* but not its sovereignty over the occupied territories.

There was considerable tension, however, in relations with immediate neighbours. Whatever momentum existed for an improved climate in relations with Turkey deriving from the Davos Agreement of January 1988 was finally dissipated. In February Greece demanded the recall of the Turkish consul-general from Komotini in Western Thrace after he had made reference to the damage suffered by his 'fellow-countrymen' following clashes between Greeks and Turks which had resulted in considerable damage to Muslim-owned property. In retaliation, Turkey had demanded the recall of the Greek consul-general in Istanbul. Tempers flared again at the time of the renewal of the US bases agreement. For short periods in May and June road communications between Greece and Yugoslavia were blocked by Yugoslav Macedonian demonstrators demanding the recognition of the 'Macedonian minority' in Greece and there were fears in Athens that the federal government in Belgrade had taken up the cause of 'Aegean Macedonia'.

Relations with Albania were tense throughout the year as a result of fears for the Greek minority, 400,000-strong in the estimation of the Athens government. In January Sokrat Plaka, an under-secretary in the Albanian Foreign Office, visited Greece at Albania's request to try to allay reports that would-be defectors had been tortured to death. Subsequently, Albania announced that passports would be issued to those that wanted them. The numbers of those crossing the frontier illegally increased gradually throughout the year, while just before the year's end the trickle became a flood, arousing suspicions in Athens that the Albanian government was applying pressure on members of the Greek minority to leave.

The campaign to hold the 1996 Olympics in Athens, on the centenary of the first modern games, had been launched by PASOK and was taken up with equal enthusiasm by the ND government. There was widespread disappointment, therefore, when in September the International Olympic Committee announced that the Greek bid had failed.

A proposal in December to release the three main protagonists in the April 1967 military coup and others imprisoned following the downfall of the dictatorship in 1974 was rescinded after vociferous opposition objections and disquiet on the part of some members of the ruling ND party.

CYPRUS

CAPITAL: Nicosia AREA: 9,250 sq km POPULATION: 687,000 ('88)
POLITICAL SYSTEM: separate presidential democracies in Greek area and in Turkish Republic of Northern Cyprus (recognized only by Turkey)
HEADS OF STATE AND GOVERNMENT: President Georgios Vassiliou (since Feb '88); Rauf Denktash has been President of Turkish area since Feb '75
PRINCIPAL MINISTERS: (Greek Cyprus) Georgios Iacovou (foreign affairs), Georgios Syrimis (finance), Christodoulos Veniamin (interior), Andreas Aloneftis (defence), Nikolaos Papaioannou (justice)
INTERNATIONAL ALIGNMENT: (Greek Cyprus) NAM, Cwth
CURRENCY: Cyprus pound (end–'90 £1=£00.83, US$1=£00.43)
GNP PER CAPITA: US$6,260 ('88)
MAIN EXPORT EARNERS: tourism, textiles, agricultural products

UN-sponsored efforts to resolve the island's communal and de facto political divide met with no more success this year than they had in 1989 (see AR 1989, pp. 189–90). Although talks between the Greek and Turkish Cypriot leaders were resumed in New York in February, by early March they had broken down, with each side blaming the other for the deadlock. The key stumbling-block was Greek Cypriot resistance to the demand of Rauf Denktash, president of the self-styled Turkish Republic of Northern Cyprus (TRNC), that Turkish Cypriots should be recognized as a 'people' with the right to self-determination in UN terms. For President Georgios Vassiliou, the Greek Cypriot leader, this smacked of an aspiration to de jure secession or partition. While accepting that Turkish Cypriots constituted a 'community', he condemned the Denktash 'people' concept as moving the goalposts of the longstanding understanding that the aim of the talks was a bizonal federal republic that would remain one sovereign country.

Back in the TRNC, Mr Denktash called an early presidential election on 22 April and duly obtained a further five-year mandate for his uncompromising stand in the inter-communal talks. He received 67.5 per cent of the vote, soundly defeating presidential aspirants who favoured more concessions to the Greek Cypriots. In subsequent TRNC parliamentary elections on 6 May, the ruling National Unity Party also trounced the opposition, winning 55 per cent of the vote and 34 of the 50 seats. The other 16 seats went to the conservative/socialist Democratic Struggle coalition, which took 44 per cent of the vote on a platform attacking Mr Denktash's 'intransigence' in the negotiations.

The onset of the Gulf crisis from early August effectively placed the Cyprus question on the international backburner for the duration. It remained to be seen whether the eventual outcome of that larger dispute would lead on to a resolution of the Cyprus problem. Optimists thought it might, in that Greece and Turkey, respectively protectors of Greek Cyprus and the TRNC and both members of NATO, would come under serious Western pressure to knock Cypriot heads together and implement the UN plan. Pessimists pointed to the likelihood that Turkey would expect concessions on Cyprus as the price of its support for the US-led anti-Iraq coalition and that agreement with the Greeks would therefore become even more problematical. They also noted that many Greek Cypriots could not resist drawing parallels between the Iraqi invasion of Kuwait and the Turkish military occupation of northern Cyprus dating from 1974.

In the latter part of 1990 Turkish Cyprus was plunged into economic crisis by the collapse of the London-based conglomerate Polly Peck International and the preferment of fraud charges in Britain against its Turkish Cypriot chairman, Asil Nadir. Once described by Mr Denktash as the 'economic commander' of Turkish Cyprus, Mr Nadir had built an international fruit-packaging and tourist empire which was said to account for up to a third of the TRNC's GDP. Efforts by London administrators of the bankrupt concern to locate its allegedly sizeable assets in northern Cyprus had made little progress by year's end.

The Nicosia government submitted a formal application for full membership of the European Community (EC) on 4 July. As with other declared aspirants, however, no substantive progress on the Cyprus application was expected to be made before the completion of the EC's single European market, scheduled for the end of 1992.

TURKEY

CAPITAL: Ankara   AREA: 781,000 sq km   POPULATION: 57,200,000 ('90)
OFFICIAL LANGUAGE: Turkish   POLITICAL SYSTEM: parliamentary democracy
HEAD OF STATE: President Turgut Özal (since Nov '89)
RULING PARTY: Motherland Party (MP)
HEAD OF GOVERNMENT: Yildirim Akbulut, Prime Minister (since Nov '89)
PRINCIPAL MINISTERS: Ahmet K. Alptemocin (foreign affairs), Hüsnü Dogan (defence), Abdülkadir Aksu (interior), Adnan Kahveci (finance and customs), Mahmut Oltan Sungurlu (justice)
INTERNATIONAL ALIGNMENT: NATO, OECD, ICO
CURRENCY: lira (end-'90 £1=LT5,547.91, US$1=LT2,874.56)
GNP PER CAPITA: US$1,280 ('88)
MAIN EXPORT EARNERS: textiles, iron and steel, agricultural products, tourism

THE Gulf crisis made a powerful impact on Turkey. Politically it confirmed Turkey's position as a firm ally of the United States, and demonstrated the limits of its earlier efforts to cultivate its southern

Arab neighbours. The importance of the American alliance had grown as a result of the decision taken on 5 February by the Council of the European Community to accept the recommendation of its Commission that Turkey's application for full membership should not be considered until 1993 at the earliest. Furthermore, while the Commission recommended that Turkey's relations with the Community should in the meantime be strengthened, this approach was hampered by Greece, which tried to force Turkey into concessions on Cyprus by obstructing the Community's aid initiatives. In the event, Turkey continued to back the Turkish Cypriot leader, Rauf Denktash, who was re-elected on 22 April as president of the Turkish Republic of Northern Cyprus (a state recognized only by Turkey). As inter-communal negotiations remained stalled, the Turkish Prime Minister Yildirim Akbulut visited Northern Cyprus in October and reaffirmed his country's support of Turkish Cypriots in their quest for equal status within a freely-negotiated federation (see also p. 191).

The strengthening of the American alliance became a prime objective of President Turgut Özal, who conferred with President George Bush in Washington on 18 January. A major obstacle was removed on 27 February when an attempt to commemorate the deportation of Ottoman Armenians 75 years earlier was defeated in Congress. Turkey thereupon lifted the restrictions which it had placed on American military operations in NATO bases in Turkey.

A deterioration of Turkey's relations with its southern Arab neighbours also preceded the Gulf crisis. In spite of protests by Syria and Iraq, backed by other Arab states, Turkey interrupted the flow of the Euphrates for one month from 13 January, and began to fill the Atatürk dam, forming the core of the vast south-east Anatolia irrigation and hydro-electric project. The dam was topped out on 27 August, and in a series of meetings in Baghdad and Ankara Turkey refused to improve on its promise to release across its southern border an average of 500 cubic metres of water per second, or roughly half of the flow of the Euphrates. However, the outbreak of the Gulf crisis did lead to an improvement of Turkish relations with Syria, which President Özal visited in October in the course of a tour of Arab states within the coalition against Iraq.

Turkey's own firm stance against the Iraqi invasion of Kuwait was demonstrated on 6 August when it decided to comply immediately with the UN sanctions resolution by closing the twin oil pipeline from Kirkuk to the Turkish Mediterranean terminal at Yumurtalik and by ending all commercial exchanges with Iraq and occupied Kuwait. On 12 August parliament in Ankara authorized the government to use armed force, but only if the country were itself attacked. This proviso was lifted by a further vote on 5 September when the government received full authority to send armed forces abroad and allow foreign troops on Turkish soil. Two visits paid to Ankara by US Secretary of State James

Baker, immediately after the outbreak of the crisis in August and then again in November, and a trip by President Turgut Özal to Washington in September served to coordinate policy and to determine measures to meet the losses which sanctions had caused to the Turkish economy. On 10 August the NATO council reaffirmed that it would come to the aid of Turkey, if the latter were attacked. At the end of the year arrangements were made to station a small NATO allied mobile force in Turkey.

By the end of the year, thanks largely to US prompting, Turkey had secured US$1,900 million in crisis aid, with more to come in the new year. The largest single donor was Saudi Arabia, which made a grant of US$1,160 million to cover part of Turkish purchases of crude oil.

Turkey responded to the end of the Cold War by proposing the creation of a Black Sea cooperation area, which was discussed in Ankara in December with representatives from the Soviet Union, Bulgaria and Romania. Turkey extended commercial credits to all three countries, relations with Bulgaria having improved considerably with the ending of discrimination against the ethnic Turkish minority in that country.

In domestic politics the opposition criticized President Özal's unequivocal alignment with the United States and argued that he was exposing the country to the risk of an unnecessary war. In addition, both Professor Erdal İnönü's Social Democratic and Populist Party (SDPP) and the Party of the Right Path (PRP), led by Mr Özal's conservative rival, ex-Prime Minister Süleyman Demirel, claimed that by taking personal charge of policy the President was exceeding his constitutional powers.

There were difficulties inside the government too. The Foreign Minister, Mesut Yilmaz, resigned on 20 February and was succeeded by a former deputy premier, Professor Ali Bozer; the latter resigned in turn on 11 October and was replaced by a former finance minister, Ahmet Kurtçebe Alptemoçin. Finance Minister Ekrem Pakdemirli was succeeded by Adnan Kahveci (a presidential adviser) and the Defence Minister, Safa Giray, was replaced by Hüsnü Dogan (a cousin of the President). Finally, the Chief of the General Staff, Necip Torumtay, resigned on 3 December and was succeeded by General Dogan Güreş, commander of the land forces.

At the end of the year, Mr Özal declared that he would seek a constitutional amendment to provide for the direct popular election of the president and allow him to maintain his links with the political party which supported him. He added that he wanted presidential elections to be synchronized with parliamentary elections (due in November 1992).

In local elections held in some districts in March and August the ruling Motherland Party (MP) obtained 37 and 24 per cent of the poll respectively, but the parliamentary opposition also did badly, disaffected voters switching to minor parties. The secretary-general of the SDPP, Deniz Baykal, thereupon resigned and challenged the party leader, Professor Erdal İnönü. At a special convention on 29 September Professor İnönü was re-elected, while Mr Baykal was replaced by Hikmet Çetin. A group of left-wing dissidents from the SDPP formed a new Toiling People's Party, while the Turkish United Communist Party, which was now tolerated, sought to join other dissidents in a Socialist Unity Party.

There was concern over the resurgence of terrorism, while a decision by parliament to allow freedom of dress in academic premises (and, by implication, the wearing of headscarves by women students) revived controversy over the place of Islam within the secular republic. The campaign by the Kurdish secessionist terrorist organization PKK (Kurdish Workers' Party) continued in the south-east, where, according to official figures, some 1,500 people had been killed overall by year's end. Emergency powers in the area were tightened to allow forcible resettlement and control of information. Elsewhere, both right-wing and left-wing terrorists carried out over 20 murders, the former striking at outspoken defenders of secularism and the latter at persons associated with the repression of revolutionaries after the 1980 military intervention. Two prominent academics (Professors Muammer Aksoy and Bahriye Üçok) and two journalists were killed by Islamic extremists.

The Gulf crisis slowed, but did not stop, a remarkable resurgence of economic activity. Thanks partly to a good harvest after the 1989 drought, the economy was estimated to have grown by a record 9 per cent during the year. However, this was achieved at the cost of high inflation and a deteriorating balance of payments. By the end of December the consumer price index had risen by 60 per cent year-on-year. As growth and a liberalization of tariffs sucked in more imports, the trade gap more than doubled to US$8,600 million by the end of November. However, tourism was little affected by the Gulf crisis, and with the help of tourist receipts and workers' remittances the deficit in the balance of payments amounted to $2,300 million for the year as a whole, after two years of surplus.

The rapid increase in the cost of living strained industrial relations and the year ended with the threat of a general strike. However, organized labour represented less than 10 per cent of the working population, and strikes, which often resulted in high wage settlements, caused little disturbance to daily life.

V THE MIDDLE EAST AND NORTH AFRICA

Chapter 1

ISRAEL

CAPITAL: Jerusalem AREA: 22,000 sq km POPULATION: 4,800,000 ('90)
OFFICIAL LANGUAGE: Hebrew POLITICAL SYSTEM: parliamentary democracy
HEAD OF STATE: President Chaim Herzog (since May '83)
RULING PARTIES: coalition led by Likud with small religious and nationalist parties
HEAD OF GOVERNMENT: Yitzhak Shamir, Prime Minister (since Oct '86)
PRINCIPAL MINISTERS: David Levi (deputy premier/foreign affairs), Moshe Nissim (deputy premier/trade and industry), Moshe Arens (defence), Yitzhak Modai (finance), Dan Meridor (justice), David Magen (economy and planning)
INTERNATIONAL ALIGNMENT: backed by US
CURRENCY: new shekel (end-'90 £1=NIS3.99, US$1=NIS2.07)
GNP PER CAPITA: US$8,650 ('88)
MAIN EXPORT EARNERS: diamonds, machinery, agricultural produce, tourism

A period of instability marked by the resignation of Ariel Sharon from the government on 18 February, in protest at what he considered its soft policies towards the Palestinians, culminated in the collapse of Israel's fragile 'national unity' coalition in mid-March. Labour refused, in effect, to concede to its Likud partner a monopoly over tactical policy-making in dealing with the Palestinians. Likud was determined to stall any talks, while Labour reaffirmed its commitment to negotiating a settlement with the Palestinians.

Shimon Peres gambled that he could bring the government down and form a Labour-led coalition, on the basis of a promise of support from Interior Minister Arie Der'i, then a rising star of the dovish Shas party, on whose votes the government depended. The defection of a Liberal faction within Likud rendered Labour technically the largest party in the Knesset, and thereby eligible to lead a new government. But, before becoming on 15 March the first Prime Minister in Israel's history to lose a parliamentary vote of confidence, Yitzhak Shamir finessed Mr Peres by dismissing him to forestall his resignation. The result was that the Likud ministers, albeit lacking the confidence of a majority of the Knesset, continued in office as a caretaker government without Labour's participation, and Mr Peres was forced to negotiate from the wilderness for the formation of a new coalition.

Upon exhausting his allowance of three weeks for intricate bargaining with the minority religious parties, Liberal splinter-groups and individual mavericks, Mr Peres asked the President to recall a reluctant Knesset from its Passover recess, claiming to have mobilized a majority to support a new Labour-led government. The Labour leader's arithmetic was faulty, however, as he did not make due allowance for individual waywardness nor for the fragility of promises received from the ultra-orthodox, whose commitment to participate in politics at all was at best wavering. The last-minute defection of two representatives of the orthodox Agudah party scuttled Mr Peres's plan, depriving him of the needed marginal vote. Extra time granted by the President to Mr Peres was now used by Shas to change *its* mind about supporting Labour. Once again Mr Peres was foiled, leaving the President no choice but to assign to Mr Shamir the task of forming a new government.

The wheeling and dealing associated with coalition bargaining brought politics into some disrepute among the general public. Movements for reform of the electoral system attracted increasing attention following a rally in April of 150,000 demonstrators in the streets of Tel Aviv, and the presentation of a petition bearing half a million signatures to the President. Amongst the most popular suggestions for reform was the idea of direct election of the Prime Minister. There was little evidence in the Knesset, however, that the members were willing to change the rules under which they themselves had been elected to office.

On 11 June the Prime Minister succeeded in mustering the confidence of the Knesset for an ideologically more narrowly-based coalition than any previous government in Israel's history. In the aftermath of his humiliation, it was a matter for general surprise that Mr Peres's leadership of the Labour Party survived a challenge from his long-time rival, Yitzhak Rabin, in July.

From the moment of its formation the new government, based on Likud together with three ultra-religious parties and three secular parties of the far right, imposed a virtual freeze on the 'peace process'. On 3 July the Israeli ambassador to Egypt, Shimon Shamir (an academic peace activist who had been appointed in 1988 during Mr Peres's tenure as Foreign Minister), announced his resignation. He made it clear to the Egyptians that the Israeli government's policies could not be reconciled with his own concept of peace diplomacy, which he shared with many Egyptian colleagues. The United States in mid-June, to Israel's satisfaction, broke off its 'dialogue' with the PLO. Taking advantage of Washington's global preoccupations, the government rode out US displeasure, and succeeded in sustaining its negative posture on the Palestinian issue to the year's end.

Until late November, when the orthodox Agudah finally joined the government, the Likud coalition had no spare votes in hand to assure its majority in the Knesset. However, opinion surveys showed that the country at large was moving steadily to the right. When the Iraqi invasion of Kuwait plunged the whole region into crisis, a hard-line approach to the Palestinians and to the suppression of their continued uprising had become the prevailing wisdom of the general public. This attitude was merely reinforced by the apparent widespread Palestinian support for Saddam Husain's aggression. Now even in the camp of the doves, foremost among them deputy Yossi Sarid, expressions of doubt were voiced about the wisdom of negotiating with the Palestinians and about the prospects for a settlement with them in the absence of peace with the Arab states.

Violence associated with the Palestinian uprising continued throughout the year at a level averaging about one Arab fatality per day and one Jewish victim per week. The forms of protest became more random, increasingly involving individual Palestinians stabbing Jews, and Jewish vigilantes killing in retaliation. Also, armed incursions from neighbouring states became more frequent. In February a terrorist attack on an Israeli tourist bus in Ismailia in Egypt claimed 11 lives, and in May a demented Israeli fired indiscriminately on a group of Arab workers, killing seven. In November the assassination in New York of Rabbi Meir Kahane, founder of the racist party Kach, was followed by anti-Arab demonstrations and rioting at his funeral in Jerusalem.

A climax of violence and hysteria was reached on 8 October when the police killed at least 17 and injured over a hundred Palestinians involved in a violent riot aimed at Jewish worshippers and at the police garrison on the Temple Mount in Jerusalem. The Israeli government refused to cooperate with a UN mission appointed by the Security Council to investigate the killings. Israel's own Zamir commission of inquiry into the incident found that the police had shown insufficient preparedness in the light of unrest manifest in the area.

In the Gulf crisis Israel had no quarrel with the American preference that it should lie low, to forestall Iraq's hope of exploiting enmity for Israel to undermine the Arab coalition aligned with the UN forces. The Temple Mount shootings for a time raised Israel's profile, but on the whole it managed to stay out of the limelight, while making it abundantly clear that it would massively retaliate in the event of any Iraqi strike upon Israel. The UN Security Council passed three strong censure motions against Israel in the aftermath of the Temple Mount killings, and in December resolved to undertake close monitoring of the Israeli occupation and to provide international protection for the Palestinians. It was by no means clear, how, in the absence of Israeli cooperation, they intended to implement this resolution. Israel merely shrugged off the unwelcome attention and continued to apply its relatively draconian measures, including occasional deportations regarded abroad as illegal.

Distribution of gas masks and other measures of readiness for a Gulf war notwithstanding, the population seemed more nervous about the Palestinian turbulence and indeed about the severe drought and the problems of absorbing mass immigration from the Soviet Union, than about the apocalyptic threat from Iraq.

Some 200,000 immigrants, of whom 185,000 came from the Soviet Union (two-thirds of these in the last six months of the year), comprised a rate of influx not seen since the flood that followed the establishment of the state. There was a good deal of friction and resentment on the part of young Israelis priced out of rental accommodation by the pressure of grants from public funds allowed to Russian immigrants to ease their absorption. But the reception of the newcomers was generally enthusiastic, regardless of the dubious Jewish credentials of many. Housing was the most pressing problem, solved in part by the import of caravans, and the use of hotel space vacant as a result of a drastic reduction in tourism. In spite of the economic burdens generated by the political crisis and the mass immigration, the annual economic statistics, remarkably, showed some improvement. Inflation for the year registered 17.5 per cent compared with 20 per cent in 1989; moreover, after many years of stagnation there was a significant 5 per cent real growth in the economy.

Minister of Interior Arie Der'i (Shas) was subjected to police investigation as soon as the new government was installed in June. Whether coincidentally or as a punishment for his temporary disloyalty to the Likud, Mr Der'i's meteoric career was at the very least stalled by allegations, still under investigation and also *sub judice* at the year's end, that he had systematically channelled government funds to religious institutions to reward his supporters. Further allegations, that he had ordered the tapping of telephone conversations of his accusers, were somewhat overshadowed in December by a swingeing report by the outspoken State Comptroller, Miriam Ben-Porath, confirming a host of financial malpractices in the conduct of the Shas party. It was widely expected that the Attorney-General would press criminal charges against many of Mr Der'i's colleagues.

Reversing an earlier and widely-criticized decision, the Attorney-General in December filed criminal charges against all the senior bankers associated with the bank shares scandal of 1983, in which a large number of people lost their savings and the cost of which was ultimately borne by the taxpayer.

These scandals paled into insignificance in December in comparison with the exposure of General Rami Dotan, head of the equipment branch of the Israeli air force, who was reported to have confessed to taking bribes in excess of US$10 million over an eight-year period in the course of military procurement activities. Amidst a barrage of public criticism, and in the context of a petition submitted by a concerned citizen to the civilian High Court of Justice to cancel any such deal, it was reported that the military investigators would permit a plea-bargain offering General Dotan relative leniency in return for naming his accomplices and disclosing details of how he had managed to pull the wool over the eyes of senior colleagues for so long. Air force morale was undoubtedly undermined by the episode, the first of its kind on such a scale.

On 31 December the Israel Antiquities Authority confirmed the removal on grounds of ill-health of Professor John Strugnell of Harvard University from his post as editor-in-chief of the Dead Sea Scrolls. Widely suspected of anti-semitic prejudice, as expressed most recently in vituperative references to Judaism in an extended interview published in November in Israel's leading daily, *Ha'Aretz*, Professor Strugnell was held responsible by many scholars for undue delay in publication of the fragments. Professor Emanuel Tov of the Hebrew University of Jerusalem was appointed to head the international team of scholars engaged in deciphering the esoteric fragments of parchment.

Chapter 2

ARAB WORLD—EGYPT—JORDAN—SYRIA—LEBANON—IRAQ

Developments in the Arab world, and elsewhere, were dominated by the Gulf crisis in 1990, rendering them so inter-connected that inclusion of the usual cross-references would unacceptably interrupt the text of the remaining chapters of this section, which should be read as a whole. Readers are also referred to the chronology of the Gulf crisis published on pp. 7–9, and to the entry 'Gulf crisis' in the index for guidance on relevant coverage elsewhere in this volume.

THE ARAB WORLD

THE end of the Cold War and the truce between Iraq and Iran suggested that the superpowers would push their clients towards a developing if imperfect peace. Instead, the President of Iraq made 1990 the Middle East's most tragic year since 1967. But already the rising tide of Jewish immigration to Israel, the political changes in Jerusalem and the consequent breakdown of the peace process had raised tensions everywhere. On 2 August this was heightened, and the Arab world divided, by Iraq's invasion of Kuwait.

Even before Shimon Peres had lost his moderating influence, the Israeli government was still stalling on Secretary Baker's proposals of October 1989 (see AR 1989, p. 200). On 17 January Prime Minister Shamir (Likud) said that the Jewish exodus from the USSR required the incorporation into 'Big Israel' of the occupied territories (OT). On 19 January the authorities arrested Faisal al Husaini, the best-known resident Palestinian leader. The US government, already critical of Likud's inflexibility, warned against settling immigrants in the OT including east Jerusalem. A terrorist attack on an Israeli bus inside Egypt on 4 February made Mr Shamir even more inflexible, as did the Labour Party's subsequent departure from government (see p. 196).

THE ARAB WORLD 201

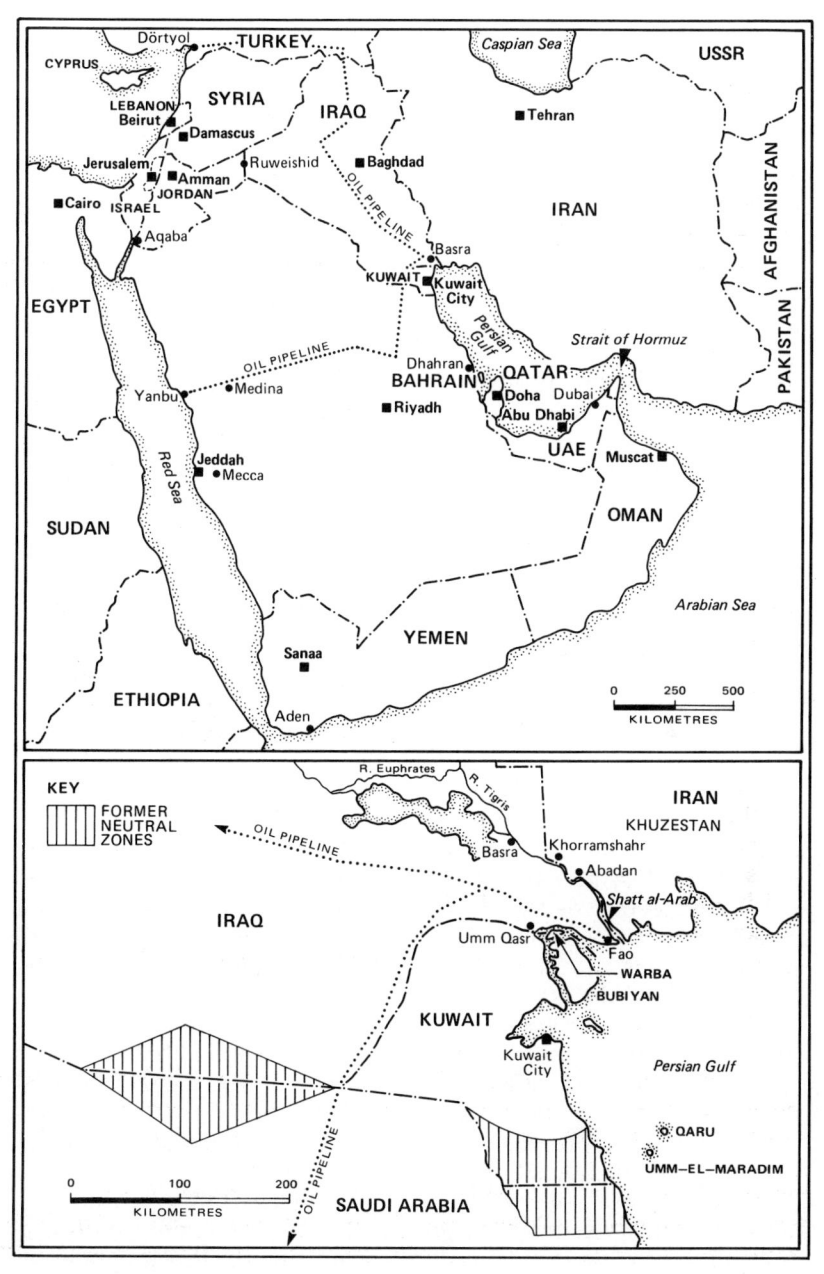

Territorial relationship of Kuwait and Iraq: showing the wider regional context above and the particular situation of Kuwait below.

Peace was further threatened when on 20 May an Israeli gunman shot a group of Palestinians inside Israel and provoked an unsuccessful attack on 30 May on a Tel Aviv beach by a Palestinian splinter group.

On 25 May Yassir Arafat, the PLO chairman, had attended a UN Security Council meeting in Geneva and advanced a five-point plan to re-launch the peace process. On 31 May a resolution, based on one of his points and suggesting a UN mission to the OT, was vetoed by the US in its anger at the previous day's attack; and on 20 June Mr Arafat's prolonged failure to condemn the raid gave the US government a pretext for suspending its long-running dialogue with the PLO. On 13 June Secretary Baker had publicly criticized Mr Shamir's unhelpful attitude to the peace process.

Meanwhile, developments in Baghdad were blowing everything off course. On 28 May, at an emergency summit of the Arab League, called on Iraq's initiative to discuss the mass migration of Soviet Jews, President Saddam Husain threatened to use all Iraq's weapons against Israel if attacked. The Syrian President and four other Arab rulers stayed away, while King Husain of Jordan supported Iraq. Egypt could not prevent the final communique from violently attacking the US. The voices of moderation on both sides were muted; the Israeli ambassador to Egypt resigned and the Israelis closed Faisal al Husaini's offices in Jerusalem.

In July Iraq turned menacingly on its small Gulf neighbours, accusing Kuwait and the UAE of over-production of oil at the behest of the West. Following Iraqi mobilization against Kuwait, Egyptian and Saudi intervention was half-hearted and ineffective, nor did the US and other Western powers react strongly. On 2 August Iraq's invasion of Kuwait split the Arab League. When a majority of its foreign ministers condemned the invasion and demanded an Iraqi withdrawal, Iraq was supported by Jordan, Yemen, Sudan, the PLO and some others. At a later meeting of League heads of state, 12 voted for a motion condemning Iraq and calling on Arab forces to defend Saudi Arabia and other states against aggression; six withheld support; and three (Iraq, Libya and the PLO) voted against.

The UN's economic sanctions at first hurt some of Iraq's neighbours more than the aggressor. Jordan and Egypt found their nationals returning in thousands, unemployed, penniless and no longer producing valuable remittances. Jordan and other Arab states were further hit by the loss of their exports to, and transit trade with, Iraq and Kuwait and some by the cutting of oil supplies.

The Kuwait crisis dislocated the Arab League. Chedli Klibi, the Tunisian secretary-general, resigned in a dispute with the Saudis over his handling of the contentious debates on Kuwait. Then Iraq objected to the agreed move of the League's headquarters back to Cairo which it had previously accepted. Despite these inevitable objections, the secretariat had in fact been reinstated in the Egyptian capital before the year was out (see also p. 236).

Iraq's attack on Kuwait set Arab against Arab. Egyptian, Syrian and Moroccan troops began arriving in Saudi Arabia and might soon be firing on other Arabs. Because of widespread pro-Palestinian and anti-American sentiment, the governments opposing Saddam Husain had little popular support except in Egypt.

Palestinian support for Iraq undermined what standing the PLO still had with the anti-Saddam governments and with the outside, and especially the Western, world. A September meeting in Amman of Palestinians previously opposed to the PLO's dialogue with the US, such as George Habbash of the PFLP and Naif Hawatmeh of the DFLP, was opened by the speaker of the Jordanian parliament representing King Husain. It vehemently attacked America and Saudi Arabia; the latter then took vengeful action against Jordan.

There had been a long lull in the *intifada* in the OT and casualties had fallen. On 8 October a group of Jewish zealots planned to invade the Haram al Sharif (Temple Mount). The police reportedly prevented them, but many Arabs gathered to protest, stones were thrown, the police opened fire and at least 17 Arabs were killed on holy ground, in one of the worst incidents of the Palestinian uprising.

The emotion thus generated threatened the cohesion of the anti-Saddam alliance. This consideration, and Israel's defiance of US advice, induced the US government to alter its line at the UN. Within four days a unanimous resolution condemned the Israeli action and endorsed the Secretary-General's proposal to send an investigative mission to Israel (although the Shamir government declined to receive it).

Violence continued for the rest of 1990, outrage provoking outrage. When the notorious Rabbi Meir Kahane was assassinated by an American Arab in New York, two Arabs in Tel Aviv were immediately murdered in reprisal. On 29 December five Palestinians were killed in Gaza; next day a Jew was found murdered in Haifa. The extreme Muslim group Hamas was gaining ground from the PLO; four of its members were deported from the OT after Hamas had murdered three Jews in Jaffa.

Such deportations violated the Geneva convention, which the UN Secretary-General now invoked. The US hesitated to support a resolution to censure Israel and protect Palestinians because the text also demanded an international conference, which the US thought premature. But when it was redrafted to make the conference non-mandatory, the US agreed to support its description of east Jerusalem as part of the OT, and on 20 December it was unanimously approved. Some Arab representatives in New York, including the PLO's, had cooperated with their Western colleagues to achieve this result.

EGYPT

CAPITAL: Cairo   AREA: 998,000 sq km   POPULATION: 50,200,000 ('88)
OFFICIAL LANGUAGE: Arabic   POLITICAL SYSTEM: presidential democracy
HEAD OF STATE & GOVERNMENT: President Mohammed Husni Mubarak (since '81)
RULING PARTY: National Democratic Party (NDP)
PRINCIPAL MINISTERS: Atif Sidqi (Prime Minister), Youssef Sabri Abu Taleb (deputy premier; defence), Ahmed Esmat Abdul Meguid (deputy premier, foreign affairs), Kamal Ahmet Ganzouri (deputy premier, economy and planning), Yusuf Amin Wali (deputy premier, agriculture), Mohammed Ahmed al Razaz (finance), Farouk Seif al Nasr (justice)
INTERNATIONAL ALIGNMENT: NAM, Arab League, OAPEC, ACC, OAU, ICO, Francophonie
CURRENCY: Egyptian pound (end-'90 £1=LE5.51, US$1=LE2.86)
GNP PER CAPITA: US$660 ('88)
MAIN EXPORT EARNERS: oil and gas, cotton, tourism, agricultural produce

THIS was a bad year for Egyptian diplomacy: the US-PLO dialogue it had sponsored broke down and Iraq invaded Kuwait after persuading President Husni Mubarak of its peaceful intentions. Egypt had to send forces to Saudi Arabia, and the Gulf crisis cost it many thousands of jobs and damaged its balance of payments. However, the Americans became politically more dependent on Egypt and thus more generous to it. Though fundamentalist outbreaks continued, they were unconnected with Egypt's stand against Iraq.

The Palestine peace process remained suspended, despite Shimon Peres's encouraging forecasts during his mid-January visit as Israeli Foreign Minister; on 4 February it was further prejudiced by a murderous attack inside Egypt on an Israeli tourist bus. Two organizations, one Palestinian, the other a hitherto-unknown Egyptian group, claimed responsibility. The Egyptian authorities denounced the attack unreservedly; President Mubarak telephoned condolences to Mr Shamir. But his efforts were brushed aside in Jerusalem, where Mr Shamir and others criticized Egypt's role in the peace process and the alleged bias of its media (which others found distinctly anti-Palestinian). Much later, in November, a deranged Eqyptian policeman crossed the frontier and shot four Israelis.

The threat to the Palestinians posed by Soviet Jewish migration to Israel was strongly felt in Egypt; some Jews arrived, embarrassingly, via Cairo. In a communique of 23 February President Mubarak opposed Jewish settlement in the occupied territories, as he did during his May visit to Moscow, the first by an Egyptian President since 1981. He publicly deplored the breakdown of the US-PLO talks.

Relations improved with most Arab states, especially Syria. Early in May the Egyptian leader made the first presidential visit to Damascus since 1977; and though diplomatic relations with Libya had not been restored, President Mubarak received Colonel Qadafi in Aswan in February and visited Tobruk for a meeting in March. He tried to believe in Iraq's good intentions, despite Saddam Husain's increasing stridency towards Egypt's Western friends, and apparently succeeded.

Relations with Sudan continued uneasy; its Prime Minister, General Bashir, visited Cairo in February.

Everything changed with the Kuwait crisis. On 22 July Iraq's Foreign Minister visited Cairo; President Mubarak publicly forecast that Iraq and Kuwait would resolve their dispute and reportedly advanced a plan to settle it. On 25 July, after visiting Baghdad, Kuwait and Riyadh, he announced that Iraqi and Kuwaiti delegations would meet in Jeddah and that Saddam Husain had promised not to attack Kuwait or move his forces towards it, this despite firm evidence that 30,000 Iraqi troops were already mobilizing on the border.

The invasion was thus a humiliating surprise for President Mubarak. He firmly condemned it but hoped that it could be handled 'inside an Arab framework'. After initial denials that Egypt would send forces, its first detachment reached Saudi Arabia on 12 August after a difficult Arab League conference. President Mubarak raised no objection to the despatch of US troops. On 21 August he appealed to Saddam Husain to leave Kuwait and avoid a destructive war. The Iraqi leader merely called on Egypt to 'side with the Arab poor'; his clandestine radio was already inciting Egyptians to overthrow their government.

By end-September Egypt's expeditionary force had reportedly reached about 35,000 men. President Mubarak's firm stand and support of the US did not, as feared, intensify fundamentalist opposition; too many Egyptian migrants had seen Saddam Husain's fist in front of their noses. Many thousands of them fled from Kuwait and Iraq; even the Muslim Brotherhood supported the Egyptian leader. When popular indignation turned on the Palestinians after Mr Arafat backed Iraq, President Mubarak tried publicly to reassure them in the face of virulent press attacks.

Religious fanatics had since January been making trouble in Upper Egypt and elsewhere. People were killed in Asiut, Copts being a particular target. In April, in another serious incident in the Fayyum (see AR 1989, p. 203), about 15 fundamentalists were shot by the police. In June Nasser's son Khalid (see AR 1988, p. 207) returned voluntarily from Yugoslavia and went on trial with other members of a subversive group calling itself 'Egypt's Revolution', but he was immediately released on bail. By May 400 people had reportedly been arrested; in October there were officially 670 political detainees. In July Egypt, more humane than most Arab governments, freed 14 fundamentalists on appeal after confirmation that they had been tortured. The then Interior Minister, General Zaki Badr (see AR 1989, p. 203), who had been particularly criticized by Egyptian human rights groups for such excesses, had been sacked in January. In October some Palestinians and Iraqis, reportedly sent as saboteurs, were arrested. On 13 October the president of the Egyptian parliament, Rifa'at Mahjub, was shot dead in Cairo; Baghdad denied responsibility.

In April three new political parties were permitted, including a Green party, but a neo-Nasserist one was forbidden. On 19 May the Supreme Constitutional Court ruled the existing parliament void because it had been elected under legislation discriminating against independent candidates. It was dissolved on 12 October after a referendum; fresh elections followed on 29 November. The government's National Democratic Party won 348 of the 444 seats; some opposition parties, though nominally boycotting the elections, gained representation by allowing their members to stand as independents. Twelve women were elected.

Service of Egypt's debts of around US$50,000 million was now costing at least $2,500 million annually and imported food over $12,000 million. Foreign exchange remained short and protracted negotiations with the IMF failed to produce a standby credit, without which other creditors would not reschedule. The government was, as usual, reluctant to do all the Fund wanted, particularly in devaluing the Egyptian pound, unifying its various exchange rates, replacing differential interest rates with a single, higher rate, and above all in cutting the budget deficit by reducing subsidies. The Fund was insisting on a further budget cut of 30 per cent.

In spring the government raised the price of oil products, cigarettes and the *official* prices (largely academic, because the goods concerned were obtainable only on the free market) of certain basic foodstuffs; later, electricity prices also rose. These increases were the most severe since 1977, when they had provoked riots (see AR 1977, p. 182). A modest transfer of industry from the public to the private sector had begun. But all this did not satisfy the IMF and no agreement had been reached by year's end.

The Kuwait crisis made things both worse and better. The mass return of migrants meant losing their remittances and having to provide for them at home; receipts from tourism and Suez Canal dues fell sharply and exports to Iraq and Kuwait stopped. According to the World Bank, Egypt was losing $3,500 million annually. But its oil was fetching much higher prices and production had nearly reached 1 million b/d. Egypt's plight, and its indispensability to the anti-Saddam coalition, brought substantial aid from rich countries and also persuaded them to cancel some of Egypt's debts, particularly the $7,000 million of military debts to the USA. The United States was already supplying free a tenth of Egypt's large imports of wheat. Other debts of about $14,000 million to European and Arab institutions seemed likely to be forgiven. The Kuwait government-in-exile promised to honour pledges of economic aid given before the invasion; and Egypt reportedly signed agreements for the provision of $445 million to resettle returning emigrants.

JORDAN

CAPITAL: Amman AREA: 97,000 sq km POPULATION: 3,900,000 ('88)
OFFICIAL LANGUAGE: Arabic POLITICAL SYSTEM: monarchy
HEAD OF STATE AND GOVERNMENT: King Husain ibn Talal (since Aug '52)
PRINCIPAL MINISTERS: Mudar Badran (Prime Minister, defence), Salem Massadeh (deputy premier, interior), Marwan al-Qasem (deputy premier, foreign affairs), Bas-el Jardaneh (finance), Yousef Mubaideen (justice)
INTERNATIONAL ALIGNMENT: NAM, Arab League, ACC, ICO
CURRENCY: dinar (end-'90 £1=JD1.24, US$1=JD0.64)
GNP PER CAPITA: US$1,500 ('88)
MAIN EXPORT EARNERS: phosphates, chemicals, cement

KING Husain's alliance with Iraq's bankrupt government divided him from rich and powerful friends, Arab and foreign, in a conflict for which he bore no responsibility and from which Jordan could only suffer; but it evoked unthinking enthusiasm among Jordanians. This set their political inclinations dead against their economic interests. How could such an experienced statesman have fallen into this predicament?

With the quickening migration of Soviet Jews came the danger of Israel's settling them in the occupied territories (OT). If persisted in, this would, King Husain feared, force Palestinians to flee to Jordan, turning it, as many Israelis wanted, into a replacement Palestinian state. He voiced these fears in February when the Arab Cooperation Council (ACC) met in Amman. Statistics already showed the *intifada* causing a net movement of Palestinians into Jordan.

President Saddam Husain's denunciations of this new danger, which threatened Jordan above all, strengthened the close links between them and dominated the Arab League's emergency summit in May. King Husain fully supported the Iraqi President against the moderating influence of Egypt and Saudi Arabia.

He was also responding to domestic pressure. The 1989 elections (see AR 1989, p. 206) had encouraged the nationalist and especially fundamentalist agitation which the many Palestinian deaths at Israeli hands had excited. In the Kuwait crisis popular sentiment was overwhelmingly pro-Iraqi; many volunteered to fight with Iraq and trade unions and professional bodies urged a boycott of American goods.

The King could see how potentially disastrous the crisis was for Jordan, and tried, though without much hope, to avert it. After the invasion Jordan remained formally neutral, as its economic interests required, and continued to recognize the Kuwaiti government, but its sympathies remained with Iraq; the King himself 'regretted', but did not expressly condemn, the invasion. Having on 3 August voted against condemning Iraq in the Arab League, Jordan 'expressed reservations' and abstained on 10 August when an anti-Iraq resolution was carried against opposition. Thereafter King Husain constantly advocated an 'Arab' solution and condemned non-Arab intervention. Two days after visiting Saddam Husain, the King flew to America on 14 August to see

President Bush but did not, as forecast, bring a letter from the Iraqi leader. Mr Bush promised help for Jordan's financial predicament: trade with Iraq, the main market for Jordan's exports and the source of its oil and transit trade, was now barred by UN sanctions. At first Jordan would not embargo food and medicine, but by November these too were covered.

Jordanians fleeing Iraq and Kuwait, and other Arabs and Asians whose only way home was through Jordan, flocked in. On 22 August the frontier had to be closed temporarily to ease the resulting congestion. By 31 August 225,000 refugees, many penniless, had reportedly arrived but could not immediately be moved on and had to live under canvas at the height of the desert summer. Those awaiting onward transport fell in October to 700. Altogether, at least 800,000 had passed through. Jordan sought, but did not immediately receive, compensation of $40 million for its expenditure.

The country was already losing migrants' remittances, export proceeds and customs duties on goods in transit, besides having to meet the cost of importing oil at increased prices (though oil from Iraq was reportedly still arriving at 40 per cent of its normal rate, the cost being set against Iraq's large debts to Jordan). In a memorandum of 22 August to the Security Council Jordan put its losses at $4,000 million annually and a UN official estimated that the crisis was costing Jordan 30 per cent of its GNP. Besides President Bush's offer of US help there were others, conditional on observance of the UN sanctions, from the European Community, which would pay Jordan $500 million (from the $2,000 million earmarked for countries hit by the crisis), Japan, Kuwait's government-in-exile and Saudi Arabia, the last proving less than generous.

King Husain's walk on the tightrope required concessions to the feelings of his subjects, to which his constitutional reforms in 1989 had given more voice. In September he allowed a conference of 'anti-imperialist' Arab organizations (including those of his former Palestinian enemies, George Habbash and Naif Hawatmeh, whom he received on this occasion) to be held in Amman. Rhetorical attacks were made on anti-Saddam regimes such as Riyadh, with calls for their overthrow. The Saudis immediately expelled Jordanian diplomats and interrupted their oil supplies, claiming that Jordan had not paid for them.

The King rushed about as usual, visiting Washington, London and Paris in particular, without apparently much to show for it. He was often in the Gulf seeking money, for even before the Kuwait crisis Jordan was in difficulties.

In March the Ministry of Finance put reserves at $380 million, insufficient to meet debt service of $500 million. In May the King told his Arab colleagues that of $350 million expected in Arab aid only $30 million had arrived; just before the Kuwait crisis Jordan's total foreign debts were over $8,000 million. Missions from the IMF came and went, usually complaining of continuing food subsidies and other unorthodoxies. To meet growing unemployment it was proposed to reduce the numbers of foreign (especially Egyptian and Filipino) workers in agriculture, industry and tourism by deporting foreigners lacking work permits and by fixing minimum wages to attract Jordanians.

On 1 January Prime Minister Mudar Badran won a vote of confidence in parliament, after promising to abolish martial law, reform judicial procedures, increase political freedom, and restrict the consumption of alcohol; later he sanctioned cancellation of laws against the Communist Party and allowed freer movement to and from the West Bank. Roughly half the political prisoners still held were released. On 9 April the King appointed a royal commission to draft a charter to regulate political life; some left-wingers and fundamentalists agreed to join it.

There was still much discontent, more freely expressed than before. Emotion was generated by the Kuwait crisis and by Israel's routine repression in the OT. The new left-inclined or fundamentalist deputies forced the government increasingly to follow their wishes, e.g. by purging allegedly corrupt officials. Deputies also criticized failures to curb unemployment and maintain food subsidies. In October over half the deputies formed themselves into a 'National-Islamic' bloc. In November a member of the Muslim Brotherhood was elected speaker of the parliament. The same tendency in elections to professional bodies and trade unions put left-wingers and fundamentalists in control. In April academics from Yarmuk University who had been sacked on political grounds (see AR 1986, p. 189) were reinstated.

SYRIA

CAPITAL: Damascus   AREA: 185,000 sq km   POPULATION: 11,600,000 ('88)
OFFICIAL LANGUAGE: Arabic   POLITICAL SYSTEM: presidential
HEAD OF STATE AND GOVERNMENT: President Hafiz al-Asad (since March '71)
RULING PARTY: Baath Arab Socialist Party
VICE-PRESIDENTS: Abdul Halim Khaddam, Zuheir Masharqa
PRINCIPAL MINISTERS: Mahmud Zuabi (Prime Minister), Gen. Mustafa Tlas (deputy premier, defence), Salim Yassin (deputy premier, economic affairs), Faruq al-Shara (foreign affairs), Khalid Ansari (justice)
INTERNATIONAL ALIGNMENT: NAM, Arab League, OAPEC, ICO
CURRENCY: Syrian pound (end-'90 £1=LS40.56, US$1=LS20.02)
GNP PER CAPITA: US$1,680 ('88)
MAIN EXPORT EARNERS: oil, cotton, textiles

SYRIA, once the Arab world's odd man out, regained a more central position and replaced its dependence on the USSR with a rapprochement with the West and the conservative Arab states. Its anti-Iraq stand alienated it from most Palestinian groups, but things became easier in Lebanon. If the new policy was unpopular in Syria itself, it hardly showed.

The changes in Eastern Europe irked Syria, which pretended that its relations with Russia had not changed. The regime shrugged off reports that Moscow was reducing the numbers of its advisers and denied that *perestroika* would suit Syria. On 8 March President Hafiz al-Asad denounced the migration of Russian Jews to Israel, which he blamed on the US for refusing them visas. The Soviet ambassador said his government would no longer support Syria's aim of strategic parity with Israel. In April President Asad visited Moscow for the first time for three years; both sides protested that their alliance was still strong.

In April Syria met Arab pleas for less hostility to Iraq by declaring that it supported any country being threatened by Israel. But President Asad was affronted by Iraqi claims to lead the Arabs and refused to attend the Baghdad summit abruptly called by President Saddam Husain and Yassir Arafat for 28 May. When in May President Mubarak visited Damascus and begged Syria to join the Middle East peace process and be reconciled with Iraq, President Asad was unforthcoming; Iraq had once again just rejected any collaboration with him. On 27 May Damascus announced that President Asad would not go to Baghdad and soon resumed its usual anti-Iraqi propaganda. President Asad returned his Egyptian counterpart's visit in mid-July and they agreed to meet annually.

Relations with Iran, so long allied with Syria, appeared to cool temporarily when it leaked out that Tehran had not rebuffed Iraqi advances. In January Turkey cut the flow of the Euphrates for a month to fill the new Atatürk dam. The Minister of Foreign Affairs personally complained to Ankara, which counter-complained of Syria's aid to Kurdish guerrillas.

President Asad, Saddam Husain's arch-enemy, was the first Arab leader to condemn Iraq's invasion of Kuwait. Syria voted with the anti-Iraq majority in the Arab League and on 20 August despatched its first troops to Saudi Arabia; by November about 20,000 Syrian troops were there. This improved relations with the West, as had Syrian help in securing the release of its hostages in Lebanon. President Asad was visited in September by US Secretary Baker and in November met President Bush in Geneva; Mr Bush greeted him as a coalition partner. Britain, however, refused to join in by resuming relations, and single-handedly prevented the lifting of EC sanctions until Mr Major had replaced Mrs Thatcher as Prime Minister. The UK Foreign Secretary announced the resumption of relations on 28 November.

In September President Asad, on his first visit to Tehran, agreed with President Rafsanjani in condemning Iraq but would not join in his censures on the US presence in the Gulf. Iran now seemed to accept Syria's attempted pacification of Lebanon, where the Syrians had disarmed Iran's Shia clients as well as their own.

The Syrians helped the Lebanese government re-establish itself against the militias. In his final showdown with Michel Aoun, President Hrawi invoked Syrian help to expel him from the presidential palace; this done, it was Syrian forces who dismantled the barriers between east and west Beirut. Syria's strength in Lebanon was now used to support the Lebanese government against the militias.

It was always easier to follow Syria's foreign policy than its domestic politics, where President Asad was never without his opponents. In early 1990 a group of them, including his predecessor, Amin al-Hafiz, met in Paris, and relatives of political prisoners and 'the disappeared', both Syrian and Palestinian, demonstrated in Damascus. The Kuwait crisis confronted President Asad, not only with his old antagonist, PLO chairman Yassir Arafat, but with the anti-Arafat Palestinian groups, who sided with Iraq and left for Baghdad. August brought denials that pro-Iraqi demonstrations in Damascus and other cities had been forcibly suppressed.

On 26 February President Asad promised more pluralism, political and economic; but only in the framework of the official coalition, the National Progressive Front, and the doctrines of socialism. New courts were instituted to try civil servants for abuse of power and dereliction of duty; old emergency laws were to be re-examined, to confine their scope to threats to state security and public order.

Parliament was dissolved in February and elections held on 22 May. The number of deputies rose from 195 to 250 to admit more independents. In a 60 per cent turn-out, 84 independents were elected, the rest being Baathists (134) or from parties associated with them.

Two new oil finds reportedly brought Syria's total production to 430,000 b/d and oil now composed 25 per cent of Syria's total exports; these figures antedated the price rises after the Kuwait crisis. A large 1989 trade surplus was trumpeted, but became less impressive when examined in detail. Syria now owed the USSR $9,000 million for arms and was still over $200 million in arrears with the IMF. Its foreign debts represented 35 per cent of GNP and service on them 24 per cent of export proceeds. New restrictions limited the use that Syrian migrants could make of their earnings and their ability to import valuable goods.

LEBANON

CAPITAL: Beirut   AREA: 10,500 sq km   POPULATION: 2,670,000 ('85)
OFFICIAL LANGUAGE: Arabic   POLITICAL SYSTEM: presidential, based on power-sharing
HEAD OF STATE AND GOVERNMENT: President Elias Hrawi (since Nov '89)
RULING PARTIES: government of national unity
PRIME MINISTER: Omar Karami (since Dec '90)
INTERNATIONAL ALIGNMENT: NAM, Arab League, ICO, Francophonie
CURRENCY: Lebanese pound (end-'90 £1=LL1597.4, US$1=LL827.67)
GNP PER CAPITA: n.a.
MAIN EXPORT EARNERS: agricultural products, precious metals and jewels

LEBANON emerged from 1990 in better shape. Outside meddling decreased; the Gulf crisis inhibited Iraq, and eventually discouraged France, from supporting General Michel Aoun; Syria cultivated statesmanship and the United States non-intervention; Iran became less disposed to support Shia extremists. Lebanese seemed less cowed by militia leaders; war-weariness grew. Syrian troops forced General Aoun to end his squat in the presidential palace and cleared Tripoli of militias while President Elias Hrawi's government pursued the Taif reforms (see AR 1989, p. 210). The south changed little; Israel retained its security zone and its policy of instant reprisals.

Secondary civil wars continued on either side of the Muslim-Maronite divide, with heavy loss of life. In January, after a week's bloody fighting between the Syrian-backed Amal and the Iranian-backed Hizbullah, inter-Christian battles resumed in east Beirut.

The Hrawi regime in west Beirut was successfully challenging General Aoun's in the east; this involved quarrels between the two, some serious, some ludicrous, such as General Aoun's attempt to prevent Mr Hrawi calling himself President. In Damascus on 21 January Mr Hrawi agreed with President Asad on steps to enhance his government's authority. The Syrian leader offered to help evict General Aoun from east Beirut and to stop Iranian irregulars crossing into Lebanon from Syria, while the Lebanese army in west Beirut would begin disarming the Muslim militias; on 29 January a Syrian military mission reached Beirut to oversee implementation of these decisions.

Already there had been minor incidents between General Aoun's men and the smaller Forces Libanaises (FL) under Samir Geagea, but on 30 January their skirmishes became more serious, with many killed. General Aoun seemed on top and, when Maronite clerics arranged a ceasefire, attacked again.

This internecine fighting in east Beirut strengthened the government in west Beirut, whither many east Beirutis escaped. Rejecting General Aoun's offer of compromise, Mr Hrawi insisted that he leave the palace at Baabda. The Maronite patriarch supported Mr Hrawi, wanted his authority extended over all Lebanon and summoned a Christian peace conference, which General Aoun boycotted and tried to shell. On 3 April Mr Geagea, for the FL, having recognized President Hrawi and the 1989 Taif agreement, invited the west Beirut army commander, General Lahud, to occupy the army barracks in east Beirut.

Meanwhile there were other combats, though less bloody, between the Muslim militias Amal and Hizbullah in west Beirut and further south, until in late May the Syrians attempted to disarm both.

Western attention naturally concentrated on the fate of the hostages remaining in west Beirut. In April two Americans, Robert Polhill and Frank Reed, were released separately, by shadowy Iranian-influenced organizations. The Shia extremist leader, Husain Musavi, protested against such releases, pointing to the US Congress vote to recognize Israel's title to east Jerusalem. President Bush thanked Syria and Iran for their help. Two Swiss Red Cross workers and an Irish schoolteacher were released in August. This left a few American and British hostages, including Terry Waite, unreleased. Forty Shias held by the Israeli-controlled South Lebanese Army (SLA) were released on 1 October.

General Aoun's conflict with Mr Geagea and President Hrawi continued. Maronite clerics began in June to promote a compromise based on modifications to the Taif agreement, which Aoun had rejected; their plan was supported by the papal nuncio and perhaps the French. President Hrawi rejected it on 25 June. In mid-July he invited General Aoun to accept the Taif agreement, a reunited central Beirut cleared of militias and a merger of his troops with those commanded from west Beirut by General Lahud. General Aoun rejected these proposals.

On 28 July President Hrawi embargoed fuel supplies to General Aoun's enclave, which from 10 August was fully blockaded. On 21 August the parliament approved the constitutional reforms, set out in the Taif agreement, to give parliamentary parity to Muslims and Christians by allotting each the same number of seats (instead of the previous ratio of 6 Christians to 5 Muslims) and to enhance the powers of the prime minister while reducing those of the president. President Hrawi signed the bill on 21 September but it was immediately rejected by General Aoun. Thereupon, on 28 September, the blockade of the Aoun enclave round the presidential palace at Baabda was tightened and manned by regular soldiers, replacing FL militiamen.

General Aoun's supporters attempted to rally Christian and anti-Syrian emotions with a mass demonstration on 1 October which was bloodily disrupted, allegedly by Mr Geagea's men. The latter was also suspected of the murder on 21 October of an Aoun supporter, Dany Chamoun, son of the former President, with his wife and children; Mr Geagea had allegedly been behind the similar massacre of the Franjieh family (see AR 1978, p. 184). This roused feeling on the Christian side and support for the blockade weakened.

On 10 October President Hrawi asked the Syrians to expel General Aoun from the palace, which was achieved by 13 October, though with heavy casualties; these reportedly occurred after Aounists had made treacherous use of a white flag. General Aoun himself fled to the French embassy, which had remained in touch with him throughout, though the President had begged diplomatic missions to avoid such contacts. The government, intending to try General Aoun for mutiny and misuse of public funds, refused to allow him out of the country.

Syrian forces immediately began dismantling the barriers dividing the city and on 24 October President Hrawi ordered the militias to hand over to the army and leave Beirut; the Syrians had already in September removed them from the Lebanon's second city, Tripoli. The Beirut militias had apparently not been disarmed; they were now free to move south. The Hizbullah would not agree even to that; and as late as 20 November the FL were reportedly also refusing to leave. Other Muslim militias duly went; Israel reacted to their arrival by attacking PLO and Hizbullah positions. Late in the year a new national unity government was finally installed in Beirut, headed by Omar Karami as Prime Minister and including the leaders of most of the militia factions.

Unlike Beirut, this year in the south differed little from previous years. There was sporadic activity by different guerrilla bands, often fighting each other, with the Iran-oriented Hizbullah being usually opposed to Syria's protegés, Amal, and their allies of the mainstream Palestinian groups. Dissident Palestinian groups like the DFLP of Naif Hawatmeh were also active. Whenever the Israelis decided that things had gone too far, and especially when they thought their own public opinion demanded it, they cracked down from the air or with lightning raids outside their security zone.

Economic activity somehow continued amidst fighting and disorder; its temperature could be read from the rate of the Lebanese pound. This started at 600 to the US dollar, fell at one point in September to 1,200 but had improved to 827 by the end of the year. Reserves still stood at $800 million, comfortably more than the estimated $250 million of debts. The budget presented in April showed a deficit amounting to 60 per cent of total spending, of which internal debt service was the biggest item; revenue was reduced by non-payment of taxes and customs duties, both mainly the result of militia domination.

IRAQ

CAPITAL: Baghdad AREA: 438,000 sq km POPULATION: 17,600,000 ('88)
OFFICIAL LANGUAGE: Arabic POLITICAL SYSTEM: presidential
HEAD OF STATE AND GOVERNMENT: President Saddam Husain (since July '79), also Chairman of Revolutionary Command Council and Prime Minister
RULING PARTY: Baath Arab Socialist Party
PRINCIPAL MINISTERS: Taha Yasin Ramadan (first deputy premier), Tariq Aziz (deputy premier, foreign affairs), Gen. Abdel-Jabbar Khalil Shanshal (defence), Samir Mohammed Abdul Wahhab (interior), Brig.-Gen. Hussein Kamil (oil), Akram Abdel-Qader Ali (justice), Mohammad Mehdi Saleh (trade & finance)
INTERNATIONAL ALIGNMENT: NAM, Arab League, OPEC, OAPEC, ACC, ICO
CURRENCY: dinar (end-'90 £1=ID0.59, US$1=ID0.31)
GNP PER CAPITA: US$3,020 ('80)
MAIN EXPORT EARNERS: oil and gas

PRESIDENT Saddam Husain became increasingly belligerent until, virtually bankrupt and determined to dominate the Arab world, he threatened and then invaded Kuwait. The world awoke too late, but then believed that economic sanctions would force Iraq out. Saddam Husain defied them, impounded foreign nationals and kept them hostage till Christmas. The USA and its European and Arab allies, having accumulated large forces in the peninsula, obtained the Security Council's authorization to use them, unless, by 15 January 1991, Iraq evacuated Kuwait and restored its legitimate government (see DOCUMENTS). Iraq refused to comply.

Iraq's motives were obvious. It owed an estimated $70,000 million, costing $8,000 million to service; post-war reconstruction would need further billions, besides the cost of essential civilian and unceasing military imports. The fading Iranian threat made Iraq's Gulf creditors less generous.

Oil revenues fell with falling prices, which Iraq blamed on overproduction elsewhere. In April a Tehran newspaper correctly forecast Iraq's attempt to frighten Gulf Arabs out of their petrodollars; on 3 May Tariq Aziz, the Iraqi Foreign Minister, duly denounced still unnamed Arab states; on 22 May the Oil Minister named them as Kuwait and the UAE.

All this reinforced the aggressive impression left by Saddam Husain's rhetoric against the West and Israel. In February he demanded the withdrawal of US forces from the Gulf. The West angered him by criticizing his 15 March execution of Farzad Bazoft (see AR 1989, page 214). In early April he threatened Israel with chemical reprisals should it attack Iraq. Clamorous meetings and organized anti-Western demonstrations proclaimed Iraq's leadership of the Arab world.

Iraq continued developing its armaments. British customs intercepted components useable for formidable unconventional weapons. Similar discoveries followed in the USA and elsewhere. Baghdad sought a rapprochement with Iran to cover its eastern flank; in May Saddam exchanged letters with Tehran and on 3 July their Foreign Ministers met in Geneva.

The crisis thus prepared erupted on 17 July when Iraq accused unnamed Arab states of helping America undermine Arab security. Tariq Aziz complained of Kuwait to the Arab League; it had encroached on Iraqi territory, 'stolen' Iraqi oil worth $2,400 million and not cancelled Iraq's debts. These attacks were accompanied by large Iraqi troop movements; on 24 July Iraq had 30,000 men on Kuwait's frontier and, a week later, 100,000.

Arab and Western reactions were incredulous and supine. Egypt's President secured, innocently believed and transmitted to Kuwait Saddam Husain's promise not actually to use the forces deployed. A transcript, later divulged by Iraq, of the US ambassador's last interview with Saddam Husain showed that she and her government had swallowed similar assurances, and given the Iraqi leader the impression that America would not intervene if Iraq pursued its claims against Kuwait.

OPEC agreed to raise its reference price and avoid increasing total OPEC production; Kuwait and the UAE undertook to reduce theirs by around 20 per cent. But at a last-minute Iraqi-Kuwaiti meeting in Jeddah Iraq also demanded Kuwaiti compensation for the 'stolen' oil, blanket cancellation of debts of $10,000 million, the surrender of the Kuwaiti islands of Bubiyan and Warba, and another $10,000 million as a gift. The Kuwaitis reportedly agreed to cancel the debts and cede Warba but refused the rest. Having accepted Iraq's proposal to transfer the talks to Baghdad, they believed that negotiation was continuing.

Iraq's forces invaded and occupied Kuwait on 2 August. Soon abandoning a pretence of responding to popular Kuwaiti appeals, Iraq was by 5 August treating it as Iraqi, formally annexed it on 9 August and on 28 August declared that it had become Iraq's 19th governorate. International reaction to the invasion was swift, unanimous and unambiguous. Iraq was blockaded by US and British ships implementing UN sanctions; its assets in the US and Britain were frozen on the first day of the invasion and its oil exports halted by the closure of pipelines through Turkey and Saudi Arabia.

Thereafter, Iraq manoeuvred ceaselessly to delay the onset of war. One tactic was to demand 'linkage' between Kuwait and Palestine: the 'question of Kuwait' (not that of Iraqi withdrawal) was linked to Israeli withdrawal from the occupied territories. Saddam Husain believed that the arrival of US forces in Saudi Arabia would win him Arab public opinion. To exploit it, on 12 August he proposed a bargain whereby, provided Israel withdrew from the occupied territories and Syria from Lebanon, arrangements could eventually 'be formulated for the situation in Kuwait'. These weasel words were unconvincing, since the Iraqi leader constantly stressed that he would never surrender Kuwait.

He also endeavoured to blackmail actual or potential opponents. There were threats to Israel and to neighbouring oilfields. By mid-August Iraq was using the thousands of non-Arab nationals in Kuwait and Iraq as a brake on allied action against it. Iraqi and Kuwaiti airports were closed and foreigners, especially British and American, progressively seized as 'guests', some being then quartered around possible targets for allied bombing. Baghdad's TV exploitation of child hostages proving counter-productive, it was announced on 28 August that women and children could leave.

On 23 October the Foreign Minister told an American delegation that all hostages would be released if the UN guaranteed a 'move towards peace'; in another variant, all could leave if the major powers promised not to attack Iraq. One ploy followed another till Iraq announced on 7 December that the guests, having served their purpose, would now be released en bloc.

Besides blackmail, there was bribery, mainly directed at other Arab states and peoples. After the 12 August initiative—aimed at seducing the peoples, and embarrassing the rulers, of Jordan, Egypt and Saudi Arabia—came promises to all and sundry of cheap oil. Some reports spoke of Iraq tempting other Arab governments with bits of a defeated Saudi Arabia: King Husain of Jordan would recover his grandfather's domain in the Hejaz and Yemen the Asir, while Egypt would be bribed with money. For though Saddam Husain had initially disclaimed hostility to Saudi Arabia, by early September his propaganda was urging the Saudi, and Egyptian, peoples to overthrow their governments.

One little bribe had had to be paid on the nail—the surrender to Iran of all that Iraqis had been fighting and dying for in eight years of war. On 14 August Saddam wrote to President Rafsanjani agreeing to 'adopt' (i.e. reinstate) the 1975 Algiers agreement, withdraw all Iraqi troops from Iranian territory and repatriate all Iranian prisoners. This followed vain attempts to appease Iran with lesser concessions.

Western governments did not allow concern for the hostages to influence their policy, but a series of self-appointed emissaries flocked in, asking Saddam Husain to release them. Such efforts began with President Waldheim of Austria and continued with, among others, former UK Prime Minister Edward Heath, former West German Chancellor Willy Brandt and British Labour leftwinger Tony Benn; from the US, the boxer Muhammad Ali and the Rev Jesse Jackson also made the trip to Baghdad. The Iraqi government was constantly talking (like many of these personalities) of 'dialogue', 'political solutions' or an 'Arab' solution, without even conditionally promising to restore Kuwait's independence.

Iraq evidently meant to keep Kuwait. It was garrisoning and fortifying

Kuwaiti territory and dismantling the state, politically and physically, by looting its capital equipment, encouraging its inhabitants to leave and replacing them by Iraqis.

On 30 November President Bush offered to receive Iraq's Foreign Minister and send his own to Baghdad. Saddam Husain correctly interpreted this invitation as a matter of US domestic politics: any Iraqi-US talks, he insisted, would have to cover peace in general and Palestine in particular and would exclude the status of Kuwait. For him the US proposals offered just another means of delaying military action against him.

International opposition to Iraq was hardly monolithic. At the Security Council, Yemen and Sudan were reluctant to join it and the Arab public was dominated by pro-Palestinian sympathies. Moscow, for decades Iraq's ally, had never been in a hurry to scrap large investments. It had also to consider the many Soviet nationals in Iraq, whose government quickly turned on its former protector, making difficulties over releasing them and deriding the 'has-been' superpower. By year's end some were still there, despite several visits by a key Soviet official, Yevgeny Primakov, whose influence in Baghdad proved less than supposed. Saddam Husain had never hesitated to discard past friends when, like Moscow, they had lost their utility.

The effect of US sanctions and the departure of thousands of non-Iraqis on Iraq's economy and morale was problematical. Although rationing of food (and, briefly, of petrol) was introduced, there was reportedly little real hardship, despite propaganda claims that, because of sanctions, many, especially children, were dying for lack of food or medicine. The sudden flight of many (not all) foreign workers must have imposed a strain as more and more Iraqis were called up.

Defiance of the UN by this second-rate power, dependent on but now deprived of its oil revenues, showed the mesmeric power of one man over a long-cowed people and was based on much economic and technical preparation.

Chapter 3

SAUDI ARABIA—REPUBLIC OF YEMEN—ARAB STATES OF THE GULF

SAUDI ARABIA

CAPITAL: Riyadh   AREA: 2,150,000 sq km   POPULATION: 13,000,000 ('88 est.)
OFFICIAL LANGUAGE: Arabic   POLITICAL SYSTEM: monarchy
HEAD OF STATE AND GOVERNMENT: King Fahd ibn Abdul Aziz (since June '82), also Prime Minister
PRINCIPAL MINISTERS: Crown Prince Abdallah (first deputy premier), Prince Sultan (second deputy premier, defence), Prince Nayef (interior), Prince Saud al-Faisal (foreign affairs), Muhammad Ali Aba al-Khail (finance & national economy), Hisham Nazer (petroleum), Mohammed ibn Ibrahim ibn Jubair (justice)
INTERNATIONAL ALIGNMENT: NAM, Arab League, OPEC, OAPEC, GCC, ICO
CURRENCY: riyal (end-'90 £1=SRls7.18, US$1=SRls3.72)
GNP PER CAPITA: US$6,200 ('88)
MAIN EXPORT EARNERS: oil and gas

THE year was, without doubt, the most momentous since the foundation of the kingdom in 1932. Iraq's invasion of Kuwait demonstrated the country's vulnerability; and having sought external defence assistance Saudi Arabia was, by late December, playing host to nearly half a million troops from more than 20 countries—the overwhelming majority of whom were non-Muslims. The tradition of quiet and cautious diplomacy had to be abandoned, and as all pretence of Arab unity vanished there was a sharp change in the pattern of regional political and economic relations. The international concern which focused on the Gulf crisis brought new, and in some cases unwelcome, attention by foreign journalists, while the presence of American women soldiers in the kingdom caused consternation among some Saudis. In the final weeks of the year, as the threat of military action to end Iraq's occupation of Kuwait grew, so too did uncertainty about several aspects of the country's future.

Even before the sudden eruption of the crisis in August, the year had not been an easy one. In January Amnesty International published a report alleging that suspected political opponents had been tortured and imprisoned without trial. This was strongly denied by the government. In early February three officials at the Saudi embassy in Bangkok were assassinated, and the government forbade its subjects to travel to that country. The dispute with Australia over the delivery of sheep continued (see AR 1989, p. 216), and the quarrel later involved animals from New Zealand. For the third consecutive year the government issued bonds to help cover the projected budget deficit, and in June it was announced that these would be available for purchase by certain categories of foreign investors. Worries persisted, until August, about the low price of oil, and the government continued to try and negotiate offset agreements for the purchase of arms and military equipment. In

July the prominent Saudi businessman, Adnan Kashoggi, was acquitted of fraud charges in New York.

As the world price of gold fell sharply at the end of March, and again in May and June, the government denied widespread reports that the Saudi Arabian Monetary Agency was selling large quantities of bullion. Talks with Tehran over the number of people permitted to join the pilgrimage collapsed in May, and for the third consecutive year no Iranians took part. The pilgrimage was marred by great tragedy on 2 July, when over 1,400 people were killed during a stampede in a grossly overcrowded tunnel near Mecca. The majority of the victims came from Turkey and Indonesia, and it was 36 hours before the authorities admitted that the accident had occurred.

The Chinese Foreign Minister, Qian Qichen, visited Saudi Arabia in July and diplomatic relations were established with Beijing. Following a visit by Foreign Minister Prince Saud al-Faisal to Moscow in September, diplomatic relations were restored with the USSR after a break of over 50 years. In late November the government announced that it was lending some $4,000 million to the Soviet Union.

The kingdom had taken a leading role in the attempts to resolve the increasingly acrimonious dispute between Iraq and Kuwait, so that the invasion on 2 August clearly came as a great shock. Once again the local media did not report the event for two days, and when the news was released many citizens immediately transferred money abroad. After a visit by the US Secretary of Defence, Richard Cheney, the King invited US forces to help defend the country, and the first units began to arrive on 8 August. These were later followed by troops from a number of states which had supported the Arab League's decision on 10 August to send a pan-Arab force to Saudi Arabia. Later in August several members of the Western European Union announced that they would also be sending troops. The government agreed to make a large financial contribution to the cost of maintaining those forces, and it also cut Iraq's oil export pipeline across the kingdom. From mid-August the country's level of crude oil production rose sharply and by the end of the year it was well over 8 million b/d.

Relations with the neighbouring states of Jordan and Yemen deteriorated rapidly after the invasion. The Saudi ambassador in Washington, Prince Bandar bin Sultan, made an astonishing television attack on King Husain, and he repeated this denunciation in an open letter published in several leading newspapers on 26 September. The Saudi government recalled its ambassador from Amman on 6 October, oil supplies to Jordan were cut, Jordanian-registered lorries were denied entry to the kingdom, and many Jordanian immigrant workers were expelled. Those regional countries which supported Riyadh, notably Egypt, Turkey and Syria, received financial aid on an undisclosed, but significant, scale.

On 21 October the Minister of Defence, Prince Sultan, and later

King Fahd, appeared to suggest that if Iraq withdrew from Kuwait some of Baghdad's territorial claims might be negotiable. But as President Saddam Husain's attacks on the Saudi royal family became increasingly vehement and bloodthirsty, hopes of a peaceful end to the crisis evaporated. In December the government took the unprecedented step of refusing to receive the Algerian President, Bendjedid Chadli, who had been on a peace mission to Baghdad.

President Bush visited US troops in Saudi Arabia on Thanksgiving Day, and Vice-President Quayle did so in December. On 6 November, after seeing American women soldiers driving trucks, a small number of Saudi women staged a demonstration in Riyadh demanding similar rights, but the government insisted on retaining its traditional ban on such activities. On 8 November the King announced his intention to create a Consultative Council, all the members of which would be appointed not elected. On 30 November a serious fire at the massive Ras Tanurah oil refinery cut output of certain products by half. The ban on the holding of non-Islamic religious services within the kingdom was reported to have caused some disquiet at Christmas among some contingents of foreign troops, whose chaplains had to be referred to as 'welfare officers'.

REPUBLIC OF YEMEN

CAPITAL: Sanaa   AREA: 540,000 sq km   POPULATION: 11,000,000 ('90 est.)
OFFICIAL LANGUAGE: Arabic   POLITICAL SYSTEM: presidential
HEAD OF STATE AND GOVERNMENT: President (Gen.) Ali Abdullah Saleh (since May '90)
VICE-PRESIDENT: Ali Salim al-Bid (since May '90)
PRINCIPAL MINISTERS: Haidar Abu Bakr al-Attas (Prime Minister), Hasan Mohammed Makki (first deputy premier), Gen. Mujahid Yahya Abu Shawarib (deputy premier, internal affairs), Gen. Salih Ubayd Ahmed (deputy premier, security & defence), Abdul Karim al-Iryani (foreign affairs), Alwi Salih al-Salami (finance), Abdel Wasi Ahmed Sallam (justice)
INTERNATIONAL ALIGNMENT: NAM, Arab League, ACC
CURRENCIES: rial & dinar, YRls26=YD1 (end-'90 £1=YRls23.27, US$1=YRls12.06)
GNP PER CAPITA: US$580 ('88)
MAIN EXPORT EARNERS: oil, agricultural products

As for all its Arab neighbours, the Iraqi invasion of Kuwait had a major impact on the pattern of Yemen's external relations. These had already been affected by the sudden unification in May of the two former components of the state, the (North) Yemen Arab Republic (YAR) and the People's Democratic Republic of (South) Yemen (PDRY). That deed alone would have made 1990 an important year. The fact that war within the Arabian peninsula, involving large numbers of foreign troops, became increasingly likely made it also a difficult and troublesome one. Little of the euphoria over unification survived the new and uncomfortable circumstances which arose out of the crisis over Kuwait.

Plans for the unification of the two Yemeni states had been announced in November 1989 (see AR 1989, p. 218), but some observers had found it difficult to believe that the envisaged timetable of 12 months was realistic. As elsewhere in the world, however, events moved much faster than had been anticipated. In January the marxist government in Aden began to liberalize the PDRY's very weak economy as it became clear that subsidies from the USSR had come to a sudden end. At the same time official spokesmen admitted that the PDRY government had, in the past, 'taken a wrong stand' over Islam. A number of political prisoners were released in Aden and it was announced in March that the country's secret police would be disbanded. Some of the public statues of Marx and Lenin also began to disappear. In early May Aden restored diplomatic relations with Washington after a break of over 20 years and shortly afterwards it was stated that the armed forces of the two Yemeni states had, in effect, been merged.

The final declaration of unification was made on 22 May, six months in advance of the proposed date. As expected General (formerly Colonel) Ali Abdullah Saleh, the YAR's head of state, became President of the new Republic, and Ali Salim al-Bid, secretary-general of the PDRY's ruling Yemeni Socialist Party, became Vice-President. The two existing parliaments were merged, and new elections for a National Assembly were promised by the end of 1992.

The unification was met with widespread, but not universal, domestic acclaim. It was reported that some of the Islamic fundamentalist members of the YAR's Assembly had abstained on the unification vote, while some PDRY politicians expressed anxiety about the retention of 'progressive' policies on issues such as the rights of women in the new Republic. There were reported to have been a number of small bomb explosions in Sanaa prior to the unification announcement; these were believed to have been the work of Islamic extremists. The new state took over the YAR's membership of the Arab Cooperation Council, and it was soon visited by Presidents Saddam Husain of Iraq and Mubarak of Egypt.

Commentators were divided over the reasons for the advancement in the date of unification. Some suggested that this had been done to forestall growing opposition to the move from Saudi Arabia. The new Republic had a larger population than the kingdom, and it possessed the sole functioning parliament in the Arabian peninsula. While the Saudi government publicly welcomed the unification, it was believed that Riyadh would continue to support northern tribal leaders who were deeply suspicious of the marxist politicians in Aden.

Relations between Sanaa and Riyadh deteriorated rapidly in the aftermath of the Iraqi invasion. It was the new Republic's misfortune to be the Arab member of the UN Security Council for 1990, and as an ally of Iraq it did not immediately condemn Baghdad's action. At the debate on the first relevant Security Council resolution (660) the Republic's ambassador simply absented himself from the voting. Yemen then abstained on resolutions 661, 665, 666 and 674. It voted in favour of resolutions 662, 664, 667, 669, 670 and 677, and it voted against resolution 678 authorizing the possible use of force against Iraq after 15 January 1991 (see DOCUMENTS). This voting record in New York infuriated the Saudi government. The same was true of the Republic's abstention at the Arab League meeting on 10 August in Cairo, which called for the creation of a pan-Arab military force in Saudi Arabia, and its support for a resolution bitterly critical of the USA as well as of Israel at the League summit in Tunis on 18 October. More than 70 of the 80 Yemeni diplomats in Saudi Arabia were expelled in September, as were many of the estimated 1.5 million Yemeni immigrants working there. Amnesty International reported in November that some had been arrested and ill-treated in makeshift detention centres. The Saudi authorities declared that in future Yemeni immigrants would not be eligible for four-year work permits and that, like other foreign workers, they would now require individual Saudi sponsors. As emigré remittances had long been a major source of foreign exchange earnings, the long-term economic effects of those decisions and expulsions were potentially very serious.

In late August the government ordered the expulsion of the British consul-general on the grounds that he had been spying on ships sailing through the Gulf of Aden—some of which were believed to be breaking UN sanctions against Iraq—but this decision was quickly reversed. There were several later reports of anti-US and pro-Iraqi demonstrations in Sanaa.

ARAB STATES OF THE GULF

United Arab Emirates
CONSTITUENTS: Abu Dhabi, Dubai, Sharjah, Ras al-Khaimah, Fujairah, Umm al-Qaiwain, Ajman
FEDERAL CAPITAL: Abu Dhabi AREA: 77,700 sq km POPULATION: 1,600,00 ('88)
OFFICIAL LANGUAGE: Arabic POLITICAL SYSTEM: federation of monarchies
HEAD OF STATE AND GOVERNMENT: Shaikh Zayad bin Sultan al-Nahayyan (Ruler of Abu Dhabi), President of UAE (since '71)
CURRENCY: dirham (end-'90 £1=Dh7.03, US$=Dh3.64)
GNP PER CAPITA: US$15,770 ('88)
MAIN EXPORT EARNERS: oil and gas

Kuwait
CAPITAL: Kuwait AREA: 18,000 sq km POPULATION: 1,900,000 ('87)
OFFICIAL LANGUAGE: Arabic STATUS: under Iraqi occupation
HEAD OF STATE AND GOVERNMENT: Shaikh Jabir al-Ahmad al Jabir as-Sabah (Emir since Dec '77)
CURRENCY: dinar
GNP PER CAPITA: US$13,400 ('88)
MAIN EXPORT EARNERS: oil and gas

Oman
CAPITAL: Muscat AREA: 300,000 sq km POPULATION: 1,400,000 ('88)
OFFICIAL LANGUAGE: Arabic POLITICAL SYSTEM: monarchy
HEAD OF STATE AND GOVERNMENT: Sultan Qaboos bin Said (since July '70)
CURRENCY: rial (end-'90 £1=OR0.38, US$1=OR0.25)
GNP PER CAPITA: US$5,000 ('88)
MAIN EXPORT EARNERS: oil and gas

Qatar
CAPITAL: Doha AREA: 11,400 sq km POPULATION: 411,000 ('88)
OFFICIAL LANGUAGE: Arabic POLITICAL SYSTEM: monarchy
HEAD OF STATE AND GOVERNMENT: Shaikh Khalifah bin Hamad al-Thani (Emir since Feb '72)
CURRENCY: riyal (end-'90 £1=QR6.97, US$1=QR3.61)
GNP PER CAPITA: US$9,930 ('88)
MAIN EXPORT EARNERS: oil and gas

Bahrain
CAPITAL: Manama AREA: 685 sq km POPULATION: 473,000 ('88)
OFFICIAL LANGUAGE: Arabic POLITICAL SYSTEM: monarchy
HEAD OF STATE AND GOVERNMENT: Shaikh Isa bin Sulman al-Khalifah (Emir since Nov '61)
CURRENCY: dinar (end-'90 £1=BD0.72, US$1=BD0.37)
GNP PER CAPITA: US$6,340 ('88)
MAIN EXPORT EARNERS: oil and gas, aluminium

FOR the Arab states of the Gulf 1990 was dominated by Iraq's invasion of Kuwait and by the consequent US-led and UN-backed military confrontation with the Iraqi army there. The invasion, in the early morning of 2 August, was mounted by a 100,000-strong force equipped with 400 tanks, which rapidly overran limited Kuwaiti resistance and fanned through the Emirate. It came in the wake of a growing Iraqi diplomatic campaign against Kuwait as a result of Kuwaiti crude production in excess of its quota during the previous year. Although Kuwait's OPEC quota was 1.5 million b/d during 1990, its production level had ranged between 2.15 million b/d (March) and 1.75 million b/d (July).

Indeed, it was only at the mid-year OPEC meeting on 27 July that both Kuwait and the UAE agreed to observe their quotas and support an official price rise from $18 to $21 per barrel, against Iraqi demands that it should rise to $25. Iraq had, by then, added other items to its complaints, demanding development aid from Kuwait ($10,000 million), insisting that Kuwait forgive Iraqi war debts from the Gulf War against Iran ($20,000 million) and requiring compensation for oil allegedly 'stolen' by Kuwait from the jointly-owned Rumailah oil field ($2,400 million). Kuwait had held out against these demands and an additional demand for Iraqi control of the islands of Warba and Bubiyan (controlling access to the Iraqi ports of Khor al-Zubair and Umm Qasr), only conceding to some just before the invasion itself. Kuwait apparently agreed to abandon its claim for the repayment of war debts, as well as paying $1,000 million compensation for Iraq's Rumailah oil claim and a further $500 million towards development expenditure for the Iraqi economy.

It was not enough, however, to avoid the invasion and the Kuwaiti government was forced to flee to Saudi Arabia. Despite early Iraqi hints that it would withdraw, and Baghdad's attempts to create a 'patriotic' Kuwaiti government, within one week of the invasion Iraq annexed Kuwait and ten days later Kuwait became Iraq's 19th province. At the same time, the former Kuwait-Iraqi border—now the provincial boundary between Basra and Kuwait provinces—was redrawn to include disputed areas (Warba and Bubiyan islands, the border area around Abdali and the southern part of the Rumailah oil field) within Basra province.

The Iraqi army in Kuwait was also reinforced and, by the end of the year, its strength had grown to 290,000 men, with 2,000 main battle tanks, 1,600 armoured personnel carriers and 1,600 artillery pieces. It was drawn up in three fixed defensive lines: along the Saudi-Kuwaiti border, through the centre of Kuwait and along the new provincial boundary to the north. It was backed up by a reserve in Basra province consisting of Iraq's best troops (the Republican Guards and the Special Forces)—totalling 240,000 men with a further 2,000 tanks. Despite the massing of awesome US-led allied forces in Saudi Arabia and US insistence on a complete Iraqi withdrawal and the restoration of the Kuwaiti government, Baghdad obdurately continued to insist up to the end of the year that Kuwait's absorption into Iraq was irreversible and that 'sacrifices' could only be made by Iraq in return for a generalized peace settlement throughout the Middle East, including the Palestinian issue.

Inside Kuwait itself the new authorities embarked on a policy of systematic repression and pillage, at the same time opening the borders with Saudi Arabia to allow Kuwaitis trapped by the invasion to flee. Some 200,000 Kuwaiti citizens had been abroad when the invasion happened and a further 400,000 had fled the Emirate by the end of the year, leaving between 200,000 and 350,000 citizens in Kuwait, together with a large foreign community. This consisted of 250,000 Palestinians (50,000 had also fled), 50,000 Iraqis and around 150,000 Asians. The Kuwaiti government, under the Emir himself, moved to the Saudi Arabian resort of Taif and, from there, tried to organize resistance inside Kuwait itself. Iraqi reprisals, which involved considerable brutality, crushed the resistance by mid-November, with an estimated 7,000 Kuwaiti dead and a further 20,000 missing.

By the end of the year it had become clear that Iraq had systematically looted Kuwait of everything of value and had taken its spoils to Iraq.

The damage was estimated by the exiled government at $64,000 million, with damage to refinery plant alone estimated at $10,000 million. An indication of the scale of the damage was provided by the fact that gross fixed capital formation in Kuwait between 1970 and 1990 was $84,000 million in current price terms. The only construction undertaken by Iraq was to link Kuwait by a fresh-water canal to the Shatt al-Arab waterway and to build roads and a spur to link Kuwait into the Iraqi rail system. Kuwaiti oil production was seriously reduced as a result of the UN economic embargo, to between 50,000 and 100,000 b/d, and much of the oil produced—1 million tonnes—was used to flood defensive ditches along the frontline.

The government in Taif attempted to rally Arab and international support for the recovery of Kuwait. It provided $5,000 million towards the cost of the US-led military option and towards support for countries adversely affected by UN sanctions. It forgave Egyptian debts to Kuwait and offered interim financial support to exiled Kuwaitis, worth $1,500–2,000 million. This was done from the massive $8,000 million revenues received from Kuwait's investments abroad, worth between $100,000 million (book value) and $200,000 million (market value). The Emir also made a concession towards his opponents in the democracy movement during a meeting in Jeddah on 13–16 October, when he agreed to restore the 1962 constitution, once Kuwait had been liberated.

The other Arab Gulf states rallied behind Kuwait, with the UAE, which also contributed $2,000 million towards the cost of the US-led military force in Saudi Arabia, abandoning its traditional neutrality and condemning Iraq's invasion. Bahrain offered full support to Kuwait and 7,000 Kuwaitis took refuge there. Bahrain also accepted US, UK and French forces being stationed there, while establishing diplomatic relations with the USSR at the end of September and also with Czechoslovakia. Qatar adopted a similar policy at the end of September, the last Gulf Cooperation Council (GCC) state to do so, and also expelled 60 Palestinian families, together with 20 PLO officials, out of the 14,000 Palestinians resident in the state. This was apparently in retaliation for what it believed was PLO support for the Iraqi invasion, despite the fact that Palestinians in the Gulf deliberately condemned the invasion.

An indication of the profound changes wrought in the Gulf as a result of Iraq's actions was provided at the GCC summit in Doha in late December, when the member states proposed a new security arrangement for the Gulf which would include Iran. The GCC had originally been conceived at the start of the 1980s as a device to exclude both Iran and Iraq from security arrangements for the Gulf and to counter any Iranian threat. This new proposal was put forward by Oman, which was anxious for a peaceful solution to the crisis and had kept in touch with both Tehran and Baghdad. It was thus an indication that the GCC had at last come to terms with its own relative powerlessness.

The most profound domestic effect of the crisis on the GCC states was in their financial sectors. In the immediate aftermath of the invasion, all the banks in the Gulf suffered from serious runs on their deposits. In Bahrain deposits fell by 14.6 per cent during August, largely because most funds in the offshore and commercial sectors came from interbank funds ($44,000 million of the $68,500 million in the offshore sector, of which $38,000 million came from outside Bahrain—mainly from Kuwait—and was frozen as a result of the invasion). Qatar saw 15 per cent of its deposits leak away during August, while in the UAE deposits fell by 20 per cent. Some of the funds returned, particularly to Bahrain, towards the end of the year, but the outlook for Gulf banks continued to be poor.

In Bahrain the invasion also caused a downturn in the activities of the stock exchange, opened in 1989, and hindered the privatization process undertaken by the government. The government's attempt to revive the economy through industrialization also collapsed as a result of the invasion and the Balexco share offer due at the end of August had to be suspended. In Oman new financial institutions appeared during the year, with Banque Indosuez taking over the Union Bank of Oman and creating the Oman European Bank, while Gulf International created a new investment body, Gibcorp (Oman), and took a controlling interest in Oman Banking Corporation.

Other Gulf states were less seriously affected. Oman prepared a new five-year development plan, due to be published in January 1991, which was expected to emphasize the oil, infrastructure and power sectors, while also proposing extensive privatizations. On the anniversary of the accession of Sultan Qaboos in November, plans for a new Consultative Assembly were announced. This would replace the ten-year-old State Consultative Council. In the UAE there was an economic upturn during the first eight months of the year, but the economy then turned down despite increased oil revenues. The ruler of Dubai, Sheikh Rashid, died in October (see OBITUARY) and a new federal government was drawn up. Qatar ensured, through prudent financial management, that its economy contained enough slack to cope with the consequences of the Iraqi invasion of Kuwait.

Despite its financial problems, Bahrain did arrange finance for major projects. The $1,400 million Alba expansion, which would lead to aluminium production capacity of 460,000 tonnes per year by mid-1992, was financed two weeks before the invasion and generated a further $900 million worth of new contracts between June and November. Other projects were postponed or abandoned. In Oman new gas and power projects did go ahead, while in Qatar oil fields were upgraded and the all-important $1,300 million North Field gas development went ahead.

The first phase was due for completion in March 1991, but there was now doubt on the second and third stages. This was mainly because the GCC gas grid proposal had now been abandoned, as had a proposed LNG plant. Other associated projects—an aluminium smelter, methanol plant and petrochemical and fertilizer plants—were to go ahead. In the UAE the industrial and commercial recovery lasted until August, allowing a growth in municipal spending in Dubai and new public projects in Abu Dhabi.

Behind these developments lay the Gulf oil industry's response to the invasion of Kuwait. In Oman production was raised after August to 700,000 b/d, its maximum sustainable level. Windfall profits in Qatar in October from revenues of $330 million (compared with revenues in July of $150 million) guaranteed the prosperity of the economy, while production rose to 365,000–400,000 b/d by September from its 1989 level of 315,000 b/d. In the UAE oil revenues were 35 per cent higher in the last four months of the year than in the corresponding period of 1989. In Bahrain the Sitra refinery turned to processing 200,000 b/d of crude into qualities suitable for war use.

Chapter 4

SUDAN—LIBYA—TUNISIA—ALGERIA—MOROCCO—WESTERN SAHARA

SUDAN

CAPITAL: Khartoum   AREA: 2,500,000 sq km   POPULATION: 23,800,000 ('88)
OFFICIAL LANGUAGE: Arabic   POLITICAL SYSTEM: military regime
HEAD OF STATE AND GOVERNMENT: Lt.-Gen. Omar Hasan Ahmed al-Bashir, Chairman of Revolutionary Command Council (since June '89)
PRINCIPAL MINISTERS: Brig.-Gen. Zubir Mohammed Saleh (deputy premier), Ali Sahlul (foreign affairs), Brig.-Gen. Faisal Ali Abu Salih (interior), Abdul Rahman Mahmoud Hamdi (finance & economic planning), Brig. Ahmad Mahmud Hasan (justice)
INTERNATIONAL ALIGNMENT: NAM, Arab League, OAU, ACP, ICO
CURRENCY: Sudanese pound (end-'90 £1=Lsd22.12, US$1=Lsd11.46)
GNP PER CAPITA: US$480 ('88)
MAIN EXPORT EARNERS: cotton, agricultural products

THE increasing unpopularity of the military regime led to four unsuccessful coups by army officers either on active duty or retired. The Revolutionary Command Council (RCC) accused disaffected army officers and the alliance of trade unionists, professional associations, Sudan People's Liberation Army (SPLA) and banned political parties of complicity. In consequence, 40 army officers and soldiers were executed; others, including civilians, were either dismissed or imprisoned or pensioned off. General Fathi Ahmed Ali (commander-in-chief of the army until mid-1989) and his deputy joined the National Democratic Forum (NDF), an alliance of various political factions aiming to end the military regime.

The RCC continued its policy of detention, forced retirement, dismissal and pensioning-off of judges, trade unionists, doctors, academics, diplomats, directors of public sector banks and civil servants; such people were replaced by others who were either members of or sympathizers of the National Islamic Front (NIF). General Omar al-Bashir, Chairman of the RCC and head of state, emphasized the continuity of the Sharia laws and no return to civil laws, undertakings central to NDF politics.

Mounting discontent due to political oppression and serious economic decline led to demonstrations. Some political detainees, including the former Umma Party prime minister, Sayyid Sadiq al-Mahdi, and Sayyid Mohammed Othman al-Mirghani (leader of the Democratic Unionist Party), were released, but the arrest of political activists who opposed the regime continued. Amnesty International expressed concern over the condition of the detainees and criticized the government for holding prisoners without charge or trial under the state of emergency.

The civil war in the south continued and various attempts (in Nairobi, London and Kinshasa) to resolve the conflict between the SPLA and the RCC failed. An American proposal to deploy foreign troops to separate the SPLA and government forces was rejected by the RCC. The SPLA overran a number of garrisons and towns (some of which were retaken by government forces) and bombarded Juba, all with casualties. Relief workers were evacuated and Médecins Sans Frontières of Belgium left the south following the kidnapping of two doctors by the SPLA (although they were later released). The government set up a commission to investigate the killing of 214 southerners (the SPLA claimed that 2,000 had died) at the town of Jebelein by local Muslim militia. Mubarak al-Mahdi, an Umma politician and a former minister, joined the SPLA in its drive to topple the regime, as did several retired military officers.

The flow of southerners affected by the civil war continued and it was reported that 20,000 people fled from the region to Uganda to escape the fighting. Despite obstructions flights of relief supplies were resumed from Nairobi and Khartoum to Juba. American officials stated that the government had confiscated 40,000 tonnes of American grain intended for the south. The government appealed to the international community to implement the third phase of Operation Lifeline Sudan. Of the $120 million needed for relief supplies, $50 million had been raised by year's end.

The crisis in the Gulf created further difficulties for Sudan, which abstained from condemning Iraq's occupation of Kuwait at the Arab leaders' summit held in Cairo in August. General Omar al-Bashir held discussions with King Husain of Jordan and with President Saddam

Husain of Iraq, who gained Sudan's sympathy. Iraq and Sudan denied reports that Iraq had sent Scud missiles and fighter planes to Sudanese airfields. Some southern members of the RCC were critical of the regime's stance over the Kuwait invasion, and the SPLA issued a statement supporting Saudi Arabia's call for foreign military assistance. Egypt, Saudi Arabia and the Gulf states, as well as some Western countries, distanced themselves from Sudan because of its pro-Iraqi stance. Egypt's relations with the Sudan remained strained and it threatened to attack any Iraqi missile sites located in Sudan.

Sudan and Ethiopia continued to accuse one another of supporting rebel elements within their countries. Sudan accused Chad of aggression when its soldiers searching for Chadian dissidents occupied the towns of Geneina and Kutum. In return, Chad accused Sudan and Libya of supporting opposition groups who attacked Chadian border garrisons. Sudan's relations with Uganda were strained over a Sudanese fighter plane which bombed a location inside Uganda, and the NIF was accused of meddling in Uganda's internal affairs. The RCC thanked the Zaïrean government for the return of Sudanese soldiers who had crossed the border after being pursued by the SPLA. Sudan's political isolation and difficulties prompted the conclusion of an integration agreement with Libya in September intended to pave the way for a full merger; the reaction of the West and neighbouring countries was one of concern.

The US Agency for International Development wound up all its projects in accordance with its policy of banning military and economic aid to countries where a democratic regime had been overthrown by force. More serious was the IMF's declaration of Sudan as a defaulter nation since no payment had been made towards the $1,300 million owed to the Fund. Sudan became dependent for oil and money on Iraq, Libya and Iran. A measure towards reducing expenditure was the RCC decision to phase out 50,000 government employees at a saving of $130 million per year. Sudan received $170.6 million in loans from Japan, Saudi Arabia, OPEC and the US Development Programme for various projects and for a reconstruction programme in the areas affected by the 1988 flood. Saudi Arabia also agreed to release 217 million riyals for this programme.

The large influx of Ethiopian and Eritrean refugees led the Sudan government to seek help from the international community. The availability of food in the south and west deteriorated, and it was reported that nearly 6 million people would face starvation in Darfur, Kordofan and the east as a result of poor harvests due to lack of rainfall. Sudan needed 1.3 million tonnes of grain to reduce the risk of famine. In response to an appeal for help, 200,000 tonnes of grain were pledged by various organizations for rapid delivery to areas hit by drought and famine.

LIBYA

CAPITAL: Jaffra AREA: 1,775,000 sq km POPULATION: 4,200,000 ('88)
OFFICIAL LANGUAGE: Arabic POLITICAL SYSTEM: socialist 'state of the masses'
HEAD OF STATE: Col. Muammar Qadafi, 'Leader of the Revolution' (since Sept '69)
GOVERNMENT LEADERS: Maj. Abdul Salem Jalloud ('Libyan number two'), Abu Zaid Omar Dourda (sec.-gen. of General People's Congress), Omar Mustafa al-Muntassir (planning & economy), Ibrahim Mohammad Bashari (foreign affairs), Abdullah Salem al-Badri (petroleum), Farhat Sharnanah (economy & foreign trade)
INTERNATIONAL ALIGNMENT: NAM, Arab League, OPEC, OAPEC, AMU, OAU, ICO
CURRENCY: dinar (end-'90 £1=LD0.53, US$1=LD0.27)
GNP PER CAPITA: US$5,420 ('88)
MAIN EXPORT EARNERS: oil and gas

IN his speech to the Basic People's Congresses on 19 January Colonel Qadafi sharply condemned discontent over rising prices of food and consumer goods and the cost of health care and education. The Libyan leader's criticisms of Libyan consumerism were repeated at the General People's Congress (GPC, parliament) in early March. Although delegates demanded more subsidies, more free public services, wage rises in state-run organizations and no new duties or taxes, these were rejected by the executive. The bulk of foreign exchange was allocated to a number of major projects, notably the Great Man-Made River scheme, the Mlita power station and the Misurata steel complex, and it was made clear that consumer demand had to be held down. The import liberalization policy introduced over two years previously had proved popular, but had put heavy pressure on foreign exchange. The Congress reaffirmed that 'revolutionary legitimacy' was vested in Colonel Qadafi and adopted a resolution strongly criticizing 'negative phenomena' (indifference, opportunism, nepotism and economic mismanagement) in society. At an emergency session of the GPC held in camera on 17 March, Colonel Qadafi presented a 'revolutionary programme' aimed at 'destroying the consumer society and building a *jamahiriya* production society'.

Major changes in the General People's Committee (cabinet) occurred in early October. Abu Zaid Omar Dourda was appointed secretary-general, a post equivalent to prime minister, replacing Omar Mustafa al-Muntassir, who took over a new secretariat (ministry) combining economy and planning. The most surprising casualty was the petroleum secretary, Fawzi al-Shakshuki, a member of cabinet throughout the 1980s, who was replaced by Abdullah Salem al-Badri, former chairman of the National Oil Corporation (NOC). Said al-Zilitni, former chairman of the Libyan Arab Foreign Bank, was appointed governor of the Central Bank. Eleven new secretaries were appointed, and three new secretariats were created responsible for 'integration affairs' with Egypt, Sudan and the Maghreb. The mass mobilization and revolutionary guidance secretariat was abolished. The cabinet reshuffle was followed by radical changes in the organization of the oil sector. The role of the petroleum secretariat was greatly strengthened and the responsibilities of the NOC substantially reduced. All the oil companies now reported directly to the secretariat rather than to the NOC.

Colonel Qadafi attended the summit of heads of state of the Arab Maghreb Union (AMU) held in Tunis on 21–23 January. In spite of political tensions, notably over the Western Sahara conflict (see pp. 244–5), the final communique emphasized the members' commitment to achieving 'solidarity and integration'. But the emphasis on economic rather than political integration did not satisfy the Libyan leader, who saw the AMU as merely a step towards achieving his vision of pan-Arab unity. Against this background, Colonel Qadafi turned his attention to strengthening links with his eastern neighbours, Sudan and Egypt.

Relations with Egypt continued to improve. On 18–19 February Colonel Qadafi met President Mubarak of Egypt at Aswan. Economic relations were discussed as was the need for a united Arab approach to the establishment of a single European market in 1992. The head of the Libyan armed forces, Colonel Abu Bakr Yunis, visited Egypt on 15 January. At a meeting between Colonel Qadafi and the Chairman of the Sudanese Revolutionary Command Council, Omar Hasan al-Bashir, an agreement was signed on 6 March for the complete merger of the two countries within four years (see also p. 230). Colonel Qadafi visited Sudan on 20 October for the closing session of a national debate on Sudan's future. While Sudan's military leadership was anxious to secure economic and military aid from Libya, prospects for unity did not appear propitious, given the differences in the political systems of the two countries. On 23–24 March Colonel Qadafi hosted a meeting with the heads of state of Egypt, Sudan and Syria at Tobruk. The Libyan leader used the opportunity to press Egypt to break its relations with Israel. As no other members of the AMU were present, there was speculation that Libya might be trying to establish a political union with its eastern neighbours.

A meeting of the foreign ministers of Libya and Chad on 26 March in Libreville, Gabon, failed to resolve the dispute over the Aouzou Strip. Amidst renewed fighting between rebel and Chadian government forces near the Sudanese border, the Chadian Foreign Ministry accused Libya of assisting the rebels and trying to destabilize the country. On 27 April Chad claimed that some 2,000 Libyan-based troops were preparing to launch attacks across the border from Sudan. There was little doubt that Libya was supporting the rebels in order to put pressure on Chad to release the 2,000 Libyan prisoners of war still being held there. But it was thought unlikely that Libya would risk direct involvement in the fighting and thus jeopardize its improved relations with France. Following talks between Colonel Qadafi and President Hissène Habré of Chad in Rabat, Morocco, in late August, the Chadian Foreign Affairs

Minister, Achiekh Ibn Oumar, announced that the dispute over the Aouzou strip would be referred to the International Court of Justice at the Hague. The minister stated that both countries would continue to seek a political settlement to the conflict.

At a press conference for foreign journalists in Tripoli on 20 August, Colonel Qadafi condemned Iraq's invasion of Kuwait and its holding of foreign nationals. Iraq's action, he stated, had 'presented the region on a gold plate to American imperialism and its allies'. He said that Libya would support a naval blockade of Iraq if it were sanctioned by the UN, but made it clear that he was strongly opposed to the US using force to implement sanctions without the approval of the Security Council. Observers suggested that the Gulf crisis had placed Libya in a difficult position. On the one hand, it was opposed to the US military presence but on the other was anxious not to damage its improving relations with Egypt. Speaking at the 21st anniversary of the revolution in September, Colonel Qadafi stated that Libya would abide by the UN sanctions against Iraq but would not take part in any actions that would deprive the Iraqi people of food. Iraqi ships would be allowed to load food supplies from Libyan ports without charge. He proposed a peace plan to end the crisis that would allow Iraq to keep Bubiyan island and part of the Rumailah oilfield, in return for withdrawing from the rest of Kuwait.

Colonel Qadafi's statements on the Gulf crisis, which were seen in the West as increasingly supportive of Iraq, together with allegations in the Western press of sanctions-busting, put an end to any hopes that the European Community would lift its sanctions against Libya. In January President Bush extended US sanctions against Libya, which he accused of using and supporting international terrorism.

TUNISIA

CAPITAL: Tunis   AREA: 164,000 sq km   POPULATION: 7,800,000 ('88)
OFFICIAL LANGUAGE: Arabic   POLITICAL SYSTEM: presidential
HEAD OF STATE AND GOVERNMENT: Gen. Zayn al-Abdin Ben Ali (since Nov '87)
RULING PARTY: Constitutional Democratic Rally (RCD)
PRINCIPAL MINISTERS: Hamid Qarwi (Prime Minister), Habib Boulares (foreign affairs), Abdallah Kallal (defence), Abdelhamid Escheikh (interior), Mohammed Ghanouchi (economy & finance), Moncef Belaid (national economy)
INTERNATIONAL ALIGNMENT: NAM, Arab League, OAPEC, AMU, OAU, ICO
CURRENCY: dinar (end-'90 £1=D1.60, US$1=D0.83)
GNP PER CAPITA: US$1,230 ('88)
MAIN EXPORT EARNERS: tourism, oil and gas, phosphates, olive oil

IN his new year address President Ben Ali called for a meeting of the signatories of the 1988 National Pact setting out guidelines for Tunisia's political future after the removal of Habib Bourguiba (see AR 1988, pp. 235–7). This was seen as an attempt to revive the process of political reform. The two main legal opposition parties, the Mouvement des Démocrates Socialistes (MDS) and the Communist Party, together with the main Islamic group, el-Nahda, refused to participate. Nevertheless, the first meeting of the 'higher council' of the National Pact on 6 January, attended by only three small opposition groups together with trade union and employers' organizations, called for a revision of the electoral code and access to state-controlled television and radio, two of the main demands of the MDS and other main opposition parties.

A resurgence of unrest on the university campuses, the most important stronghold of the Islamic militants and a long-established battleground in Tunisian politics, came to a head in late February. After students occupied university buildings throughout the country, the security forces broke up the protests and made some 600 arrests; about half of those arrested were immediately sent to begin their national service with the army. In response, the Union Générale Tunisienne des Édudiants (UGTE), which was closely linked to el-Nahda, called a nationwide student strike which found widespread support, even among those students who did not normally follow the UGTE line. The rival leftist Union Générale des Étudiants de Tunisie (UGET) also called a two-day protest strike. The el-Nahda party issued a statement giving its full support to the students and condemning government actions. Its spokesman, Ali Laridh, was immediately arrested and the official newspaper, *La Presse*, accused el-Nahda of stirring up trouble and showing contempt for tolerance and democracy. By mid-March the government's tough stance had brought an uneasy calm to the campuses.

In a cabinet reshuffle in March President Ben Ali appointed former foreign minister, Abdelhamid Escheikh, to the Interior Ministry, a move seen as reinforcing the government's uncompromising attitude to the Islamic opposition. Ismail Khelil, the governor of the Central Bank and the architect of Tunisia's economic reform programme, replaced Mr Escheikh at the Foreign Ministry. The creation of a combined economy and finance portfolio placed control of economic policy firmly in the hands of the minister, Mohammed Ghanouchi. Significantly there were no changes at the Education Ministry, where Mohammed Charfi's liberal reform programme had been bitterly attacked by el-Nahda.

The government continued to underline its objection to mixing religion with politics and its refusal to give Islam a formal role in the country's political life. Although el-Nahda was given permission to publish its own newspaper in January, party leaders accused the police of threatening local printers to prevent its publication and the first issue did not appear until April. Some believed that President Ben Ali had decided to give el-Nahda access to the media to force the party to set out its programme in more detail and hopefully expose its lack of an effective strategy for Tunisia's economic and social problems. Some insight into the party's programme was given by spokesman Ali Laridh in *Le Temps-hebdo*. The party, he stressed, placed Islam above all else but was committed to democracy. In economic affairs, he advocated 'democratic socialism' with priority being given to agriculture and manufacturing and the phasing-out of tourism. Arabic should be used more widely in school syllabuses, laws guaranteeing women's rights should be reviewed by Islamic scholars and the veil should be obligatory for women. He opposed artificial methods of birth control.

President Ben Ali's main dilemma was that he wanted political reforms which left unchallenged Tunisia's pro-Western, secular values. By refusing to legalize el-Nahda, which remained the major opposition party, only the now-weakened secular parties were available to create a credible opposition to the ruling Rassemblement Constitutionnel Démocratique (RCD). This problem became acute with the approach of municipal elections which were originally to be held in May. After discussions in the higher council of the National Pact, certain amendments to the municipal electoral law were agreed, and later approved by the government. The new system gave 50 per cent of the seats in each constituency to the winning party (instead of 100 per cent), with the rest divided proportionally among all other lists receiving 5 per cent or more of the vote. The government also agreed to postpone the elections until June.

Nevertheless, the main opposition groups, which had called for full proportional representation, boycotted the elections and accused the ruling RCD of using state radio and television in its own interests. As a result the RCD faced opposition in only 19 of the country's 246 municipal councils and accordingly won control of all but one of the councils. Though observers detected little enthusiasm for the poll, the government claimed a turnout of almost 80 per cent. The opposition parties condemned the elections as a meaningless exercise and there were accusations that RCD activists had used threats and intimidation against voters in some constituencies.

The contrast with Algeria, where the Front Islamique du Salut won a stunning victory in municipal elections held two days after those in Tunisia (see p. 238), could not have been greater. In response to events in Algeria, the Tunisian authorities stepped up their tough line against el-Nahda and its supporters. *Al-Fajr*, the party's newspaper, was shut down for three months and a number of its supporters were arrested and imprisoned for criticizing the government. While the el-Nahda leader, Rachid Ghanouchi, bitterly attacked the government, calling for 'combat at all levels', spokesman Ali Laridh stressed that the party wished to avoid violent confrontation with the authorities and to defend democracy by peaceful means. President Ben Ali subsequently renewed contacts with leaders of the MDS and the communists in order to find a way of bringing them back into the process of democratic reform.

President Ben Ali took over as chairman of the Arab Maghreb Union (AMU) at its second summit held in Tunis on 21–23 January, giving a higher profile to regional affairs during the first half of the year. While political tensions were evident, agreement was announced on promoting integration through the removal of barriers to the movement of goods and citizens within the union. On 17 February, the union's first anniversary, the President outlined proposals to bring about greater practical measures for integration. At the third summit meeting held in Algiers in late July the five heads of state agreed to set up a full customs union by 1995 and to unify external tariffs by 1991. The summit called for stronger ties with the European Community. But in spite of a succession of meetings of follow-up committees, implementation of AMU decisions remained limited, and problems such as the choice of headquarters and a permanent secretary-general for the organization were unresolved.

In March President Ben Ali visited Cairo, the first visit by a Tunisian head of state in 25 years. No official mention was made of the future of the Arab League headquarters, but at a meeting of Arab foreign ministers a few days later agreement was reached in principle for the League's headquarters to return to Cairo, although its cultural section, the council of interior ministers and the Arab Broadcasting Union were to remain in Tunis. Chedli Klibi, the League's Tunisian secretary-general, resigned on 3 September. The League's headquarters formally returned to Cairo on 31 October, despite opposition from a group of North African states, supported by the pro-Iraqi League members.

In the Gulf crisis which followed Iraq's invasion and occupation of Kuwait on 2 August, President Ben Ali refused to attend the emergency Arab summit in Cairo and firmly condemned the deployment of foreign troops in the Gulf. His stand found favour with most opposition groups and at the popular level there were a number of pro-Iraqi demonstrations in Tunis. One of the largest was organized jointly by the ruling RCD, opposition parties, trade unions and human rights groups, revealing an unusual degree of political agreement. The crisis put el-Nahda in an uncomfortable position, because it received substantial financial support from the Gulf monarchies. Thus, while the party called for a *jihad* against American hegemony, it was careful to denounce Iraq's invasion of Kuwait.

On 28 August Ismail Khelil was replaced at the Foreign Ministry by Habib Boulares. No reason was given, but it was believed that he was opposed to the President's policy on the Gulf crisis. On 11 September Prime Minister Qarwi told parliament that Tunisia would follow the letter of the UN resolutions and on 22 September he led a delegation to Baghdad with a five-point peace plan. The main elements were the withdrawal of Iraqi forces from Kuwait, the replacement of Western with Arab forces in the Gulf, the release of all hostages, and settlements of Iraq's dispute with Kuwait and the Arab-Israeli conflict. Habib Boulares, the new Foreign Minister, actively supported an Arab solution to the crisis. The Economy and Finance Minister told parliament in October that the crisis would cost Tunisia at least $156 million during 1990, through losses in exports to Iraq and the loss of Kuwaiti investments and project finance.

ALGERIA

CAPITAL: Algiers   AREA: 2,400,000 sq km   POPULATION: 23,800,000 ('88)
OFFICIAL LANGUAGE: Arabic   POLITICAL SYSTEM: presidential
HEAD OF STATE AND GOVERNMENT: President Bendjedid Chadli (since Feb '79)
RULING PARTY: National Liberation Front (FLN)
PRINCIPAL MINISTERS: Mouloud Hamrouche (Prime Minister), Sid-Ahmed Ghozali (foreign affairs), Mohammed Saleh Mohammedi (interior), Ghazi Hidouci (economy), Ali Benflis (justice), Saddek Bousena (mines), Maj.-Gen. Khaled Nezzar (defence)
INTERNATIONAL ALIGNMENT: NAM, Arab League, OPEC, OAPEC, AMU, OAU, ICO
CURRENCY: dinar (end-'90 £1=DA23.18, US$1=DA12.00)
GNP PER CAPITA: US$2,360 ('88)
MAIN EXPORT EARNERS: oil and gas

THE year opened with the ruling Front de Libération Nationale (FLN) in complete disarray. By introducing a multi-party system after October 1988, the regime clearly hoped to reinvigorate the FLN, giving it new energy and enthusiasm. Other parties would be formed but, as they would be without traditions or a national role, it was assumed that the FLN would remain dominant. In March the National Assembly passed an amendment to the electoral law under which any party gaining an absolute majority of votes would receive only a proportionate number of seats instead of all the seats under the terms of the original law introduced in July 1989 (see AR 1989, p. 235). In a situation where no party had an absolute majority, the party winning most votes would take half the seats, with the rest distributed in proportion to votes received by all lists with at least 5 per cent of the total. While the government argued that these changes were necessary to do justice to the country's new democratic spirit, some observers argued that the FLN recognized that it was no longer the dominant party and that the original law might favour the Front Islamique du Salut (FIS), which had risen spectacularly to become the leading opposition party.

During the first half of 1990, in the run-up to communal and departmental elections in June, instead of reinvigorating itself the FLN was instead gradually deserted by its members, many of whom were attracted to other parties, or chose to stand as independents. Those who remained increasingly expressed contradictory views in public, thus undermining the party's credibility. Some FLN members, annoyed at not being chosen for the party's official lists in the municipal elections, chose to run instead for other parties. In some places the FLN was not even represented on the official lists because of rivalries between different 'clans' within the party. It was a vain hope that the FLN would regain the confidence of large sections of the population when it was responsible for the inefficient management of the country, marked by shortages, incompetence, clientalism and corruption. Particularly damaging were revelations in March by former Prime Minister Abdelhamid Brahimi that between 1979 and 1988 some $26,000 million was obtained by senior officials as bribes or commissions on the signing of major contracts with foreign companies—a sum greater than Algeria's external debt.

Popular discontent largely explained the spectacular rise of the FIS. It represented a vast socio-religious movement which had succeeded in uniting many of those opposed to the government, finding in Islam a powerful vector of opposition. The FIS leader, Dr Abassi Madani, consistently rejected responsibility for the acts of violence attributed to his organization which multiplied in the run-up to the June elections. However, it was clear that he did not control the base of the party, where the dominant influence was exercised by fiery imams who vied with one another in their denunciations of the regime. Foremost among them was Ali Belhadj, the young imam of Kouba quarter in Algiers (and Dr Madani's second in command) who had become the idol of the capital's youthful unemployed. In a country where three out of four Algerians were under 30 years of age and where unemployment affected particularly the young, the power of these young preachers was not to be underestimated.

The communal (municipal) and departmental (provincial) elections held on 12 June were the first multi-party elections held in Algeria since independence in 1962. They resulted in a dramatic defeat for the ruling FLN and a clear victory for the FIS. The FIS won 54 per cent of the popular vote nationally and took control of 853 of the 1,551 communal assemblies and 32 of the 48 *wilaya* (provincial) assemblies. The FLN in contrast received only 28 per cent of the popular vote and gained control of 487 of the communes and 14 of the *wilaya* assemblies. Independent lists took 106 communes and one *wilaya*, while the Rassemblement pour la Culture et la Démocratie (RCD) won 87 communes and one *wilaya*. The elections clearly revealed the weakness of the progressive secular opposition formations in a deeply conservative society. The once influential Parti de l'Avant-Guarde Socialiste, for example, did not win a single seat. Towns with more than 20,000 people (containing more than 75 per cent of Algeria's population) were almost entirely controlled by the FIS, including the four principal cities of Algiers, Oran, Constantine and Annaba. Its position was weaker in the smaller towns and in the countryside, where the FLN retained its main support. Irregularities certainly took place during the elections but they did not cast doubt on the principal results. Both President Chadli and the FIS leader declared that they were satisfied with the conduct of the elections (in which the abstention rate was probably considerably higher than the official figure of 35 per cent).

The local elections attracted unusually intense and often sensationalist international media coverage. Pre-election alarmist statements denouncing FIS militants by French TV and press, and by French right-wing politicians such as Jean-Marie Le Pen, merely served to weaken progressive opposition groups. The FIS was able to claim that 'democracy' and 'human rights' belonged to a 'foreign' culture and to condemn the secular opposition as 'allies of the West'. The FIS victory provoked an hysterical outburst from the French press, with headlines such as '*La révolution islamique à nos portes*'. Widespread fears were expressed that the victory would provoke a new wave of mass migration by the Algerian middle class to France, and there were demands for a strengthening of French immigration controls.

After its crushing defeat—the first electoral defeat of an Arab regime—the FLN tried to stress that while the results were not good they showed its serious commitment to the democratic option. Nevertheless, Prime Minister Hamrouche made it clear that the FLN must reform or die. In the elections the reformists in the party left the campaigning to the old-guard politicians. Their failure to achieve a victory for the FLN perhaps strengthened the reformists, but the scale of the FIS victory posed a serious threat to both the reformist and the traditionalist wings of the party. On 10 July it was announced that Mr Hamrouche and four cabinet ministers would leave the FLN politburo. While the Front's secretary-general stressed that the government remained an FLN administration, the move underlined the trend towards separating party and state. In a cabinet reshuffle on 25 July the army chief of staff, Major-General Khaled Nezzar, who was closely associated with the modernizing tendency within the army, was appointed Minister of Defence, a portfolio held by the President since 1965. The appointment strengthened the link between the military and the government.

On 29 July President Chadli announced that elections to the National Assembly, originally scheduled for 1992, would be brought forward to the first quarter of 1991. After its victory in the local elections the FIS had repeatedly called for the dissolution of the Assembly and early general elections. On 10 September the newly-appointed Defence Minister warned that the army might intervene if national unity was threatened in the elections. While the minister was careful to stress his respect for all parties, he urged the FIS to avoid excesses that might divide the national community.

On 3 October Rabah Bitat, one of the nine historic chiefs of the

Algerian revolution, resigned as president of the National Assembly (constitutionally the most senior politician after the President) in protest at the government's reforms, which he claimed were dismantling the public sector. Ex-premier Kasdi Merbah resigned from the FLN's central committee in early October and in November launched his own party, the Mouvement Algérien pour la Justice et le Développement. Mr Brahimi also resigned from the FLN central committee, while two FLN deputies quit the party to join ex-President Ahmed Ben Bella's Mouvement pour la Démocratie en Algérie. Since his return from exile in late September, Mr Ben Bella had tried to present himself as the only leader capable of bringing together a variety of political opinions. With groups splintering from the FLN, the party appeared to be fatally weakened. A realignment of the country's political forces was under way, some 30 parties having emerged since the introduction of a multi-party system.

Although the dominant opposition party, the FIS was not without its own internal problems. Dr Madani criticized some municipal councils for trying to impose Islamic values too quickly; nor did he rule out possible coalitions with other parties. Nevertheless, serious doubts remained about the party's real intentions concerning democracy and the role of the opposition. The party's second-in-command, Ali Belhadj, stated clearly that he did not regard 'democracy' as an Islamic concept. The FIS, moreover, did not have exclusive command over the Islamic movement, in which even more fundamentalist groupings were emerging to challenge it for support.

Despite the political upheavals and opposition from within the FLN, the government pressed on with its economic reform programme. Parliamentary approval was finally obtained in March for a new joint venture law to encourage foreign investment in both the public and private sectors. The law also allowed foreign banks and financial institutions to open branches in the country. More state-owned companies were freed from direct government control, and in August the previously closed domestic market was opened to approved international manufacturers and traders. Rumours that Algeria had decided to reschedule part of its debts were categorically denied by ministers. Higher oil prices resulting from the Gulf crisis were expected to bring an additional $1,400 million in oil revenues in 1990. Economy Minister Ghazi Hidouci announced on 3 October that the extra money would be used to clear arrears in payments, which he estimated at $600 million. In a series of positive economic statements Mr Hidouci indicated that the reform programme could now be speeded up and could be in place by the time of the 1991 parliamentary elections. Prime Minister Hamrouche spoke of making Algeria a market economy by January 1991: 'Algeria has an historic chance it must not miss to emerge from a planned economy and under-development.'

From August onwards foreign affairs were dominated by the Gulf crisis provoked by Iraq's invasion of Kuwait. While Foreign Minister Sid-Ahmed Ghozali initially emphasized that inherited colonial borders should be inviolable, he quickly turned to attacking American imperialism in the Gulf. After a visit to Baghdad on 25 August, Mr Ghozali was praised by Iraqi radio for his support. The crisis exposed the popular antagonism felt in Algeria, burdened by heavy debts, towards the wealthier Gulf sheikhdoms. Several big pro-Iraqi demonstrations took place. Some observers argued that the attractions of Saddam Husain's version of secular Arab nationalism had been exploited by the Algerian government to strengthen its position against the FIS, which was believed to receive financial support from Saudi Arabia. There were FIS demonstrations in several cities on 17 August against both Iraq's invasion of Kuwait and the Western military response.

MOROCCO

CAPITAL: Rabat AREA: 460,000 sq km POPULATION: 24,000,000 ('88)
OFFICIAL LANGUAGE: Arabic POLITICAL SYSTEM: monarchy
HEAD OF STATE AND GOVERNMENT: King Hassan II (since March '61)
RULING PARTIES: Constitutional Union heads coalition
PRINCIPAL MINISTERS: Azzedine Laraki (Prime Minister), Abdel Latif Filali (foreign affairs), Mohammed Berrada (finance), Driss Badri (interior & information) Moulay Mustapha Ben Larbi Alaiou (justice), Moulay Driss Alaoui M'Daghri (energy & mines)
INTERNATIONAL ALIGNMENT: NAM, Arab League, AMU, ICO
CURRENCY: dirham (end-'90 £1=DH15.53, US$1=DH8.05)
GNP PER CAPITA: US$830 ('88)
MAIN EXPORT EARNERS: phosphates, agricultural products, tourism

ON the occasion of his annual speech from the throne on 3 March, King Hassan announced a wide-ranging austerity programme to control a widening budget deficit. He stated that an increase in the price of oil, a sharp fall in phosphate product sales and salary increases awarded to civil servants were the main causes of the economic downturn. The King insisted that the government 'must reduce to the maximum [possible extent] all expenditure' and called for a year of 'wise and balanced austerity'. A committee of senior ministers was set up to coordinate the programme and ministries were told to cut their costs and to postpone investments. Mohammed Berrada, the Finance Minister, announced that revenues would be increased through higher customs duties, higher prices for non-sensitive goods and services provided by state monopolies but that there would be no new taxes or tax increases.

In early May the government devalued the dirham by some 10 per cent, the first ever devaluation to be publicly announced. At the same time, Finance Minister Berrada presented revised budget proposals for 1990 which proposed a reduction in the deficit from $792 to $680 million and a reduction in the investment budget by 16.4 per cent. It was announced that non-priority projects in agriculture, health, education, road-building and electricity would be cancelled, postponed or transferred to local authorities. These tough measures helped to ensure the approval of a standby loan of $131 million from the International Monetary Fund on 20 July.

On 20 May the first motion of no confidence in a Moroccan government since 1972 was defeated by 200 votes to 82 in the Chamber of Deputies, where the four pro-government parties—Union Constitutionelle (UC), Rassemblement National des Indépendants (RNI), Mouvement Populaire (MP) and Parti National Démocratique (PND)—commanded an absolute majority. Put forward jointly by the opposition Istiqlal, Union Socialiste des Forces Populaires (USFP), Parti du Progrès et du Socialisme (PPS) and Organisation pour l'Action Démocratique et Populaire (OADP), the motion attacked with unprecedented hostility the government's economic and financial policies and human rights abuses. It accused the government of waste and corruption and argued that its policies would raise the cost of living and increase unemployment. The motion appeared to mark the beginning of a breakdown in the so-called 'Saharan consensus' whereby opposition activity had been limited for some ten years in the name of national unity over Moroccan claims to the Western Sahara (see pp. 244–5).

Growing criticism of the government's economic policies was one of the factors which led King Hassan to carry out a limited cabinet reshuffle on 31 July. Moussa Saadi, the Minister of Tourism, was dismissed and replaced by Abdullah Kadri; Moulay Driss Alaoui M'Daghri was appointed Energy and Mines Minister in place of Mohamad Fettah, who became the new chairman of the Office Chérifien des Phosphates; and Rafiq Haddaoui was appointed to the new post of minister-delegate for relations with the Moroccan migrant community.

In the early part of the year there were scores of arrests of members of the Islamic fundamentalist Al-Adl Wal-Ihsaan Association, who were held for long periods before being charged with participation in an illegal organization and offences against public order. On 8 May some 2,000 demonstrators were arrested by police during a protest outside the court of appeal in Rabat where six leaders of the illegal association were being tried. The demonstration was one of the biggest ever staged by the Islamic fundamentalists.

The London-based Amnesty International, which published a report in February strongly criticizing the Moroccan government for persistent human rights violations, prepared a special document on the Al-Adl Wal-Ihsaan trials pointing to numerous allegations of irregularities. In a move to counter charges of human rights violations from within the country and abroad, King Hassan announced in May the creation of a 37-member consultative committee on human rights with representatives from government, political parties, the trade union movement and human rights organizations. Nevertheless, Amnesty International renewed its criticism of the Moroccan government in a report published on 21 November on the circumstances surrounding the 'disappearance' of hundreds of people from southern Morocco and the Western Sahara.

Morocco issued one of the strongest condemnations of Iraq's invasion of Kuwait in the Arab world. At the emergency summit of the Arab League held in Cairo on 10 August, Morocco voted for resolutions condemning the aggression and calling for an unconditional Iraqi withdrawal from Kuwait. Some 1,200 Moroccan troops were despatched to Saudi Arabia to join Egyptian and Syrian contingents to the multinational force defending the kingdom. In response, Moroccan diplomats accredited to Kuwait were forced to leave their embassy and were then refused permission by the Iraqi authorities to leave Baghdad. Morocco protested to Iraq about the detention of its diplomats and on 29 August two members of the Iraqi Baath party were expelled from Morocco after being accused of interference in the country's internal affairs.

In contrast to King Hassan's unambiguous stance on the Gulf crisis, there appeared to be a large measure of public support in Morocco for Iraqi leader Saddam Husain's version of Arab nationalism and his appeals to the Arab masses. On 14 October, for example, police dispersed several hundred demonstrators in Casablanca who were protesting against the military build-up in the Gulf and at US support for Israel. The UN embargo forced Morocco to find alternative sources of crude oil supplies (Iraq had traditionally supplied half of Morocco's oil imports). It also resulted in the loss of an important market for Moroccan exports—in 1989 exports to Iraq were worth $42 million—and of remittances from the 36,000 Moroccan workers in Iraq and Kuwait. In this delicate situation King Hassan was careful to stress the Arab League's mediating role and the purely defensive role of the Moroccan troops in Saudi Arabia. On 15 October Taha Yasin Ramadan, Deputy Prime Minister of Iraq, visited Rabat to discuss the Gulf crisis, but Moroccan Minister of State Moulay Ahmed Alaoui announced that his country's efforts to mediate had failed due to Iraq's total intransigence. In a live television broadcast on 11 November, King Hassan appealed to Arab leaders to attend an immediate summit conference to prevent war in the Gulf.

Relations with France deteriorated sharply after the publication in the summer of *Notre Ami le Roi* by Gilles Perrault, which was critical of King Hassan. Morocco claimed that the book, which received widespread publicity on French radio and television, was offensive and formed part of an 'anti-Moroccan campaign' in France. A major cultural festival, *Le Temps du Maroc*, which was to have been held in France to promote Morocco was cancelled. Tensions mounted when it was announced that the wife of the French President, Danielle Mitterrand, head of the human rights organization France-Libertés, planned to visit Polisario camps in Algeria. Her visit was eventually cancelled and in early November the French Foreign Minister, Roland Dumas, visited King Hassan to try to repair the damage to bilateral relations. Some observers argued that the Moroccan government, faced with growing criticism from the opposition parties and the prospect of tougher austerity measures following the rise in oil prices, found it useful to focus attention on the 'campaign of disparagement' by the former colonial power and away from domestic matters.

WESTERN SAHARA

CAPITAL: Al Aaiún AREA: 252,000 sq km POPULATION: 164,000 ('82)
STATUS: regarded as under its sovereignty by Morocco, whereas independent Sahrawi Arab Democratic Republic (SADR) was declared by Polisario Front in 1976

IN early March the executive committee of the Polisario Front repeated its willingness to cooperate with the UN and the Organization of African Unity (OAU) in the search for a settlement to the Western Sahara conflict, but again insisted on the withdrawal of Moroccan forces and administration from the territory before a referendum was held. UN Secretary-General Pérez de Cuellar visited the region at the end of March and held talks with King Hassan of Morocco, President Chadli of Algeria and Mohamed Abdelaziz, the Polisario leader and president of the Sahrawi Arab Democratic Republic. He announced that he was encouraged by the progress achieved in the negotiations and hoped that the referendum could be organized in 1990.

In early June Johannes Manz, Sr Pérez de Cuellar's special representative for the Western Sahara, presided over a meeting in Geneva of Saharan tribal chiefs nominated by Morocco and Polisario in order to verify the proposed electoral lists for the referendum. The meeting discussed the problems arising from using the 1974 Spanish census of the region as the basis for identifying eligible voters. Although the discussions were held as 'proximity talks', it was reported that contact between the two sides took place outside the formal meetings and that the important electoral lists were confirmed.

On 20 June the UN Secretary-General announced some of the details of the joint UN-OAU plan for the referendum. It called for a ceasefire 24 weeks before the referendum date, during which period the UN would take over the administration of the Western Sahara. A special UN peacekeeping force—the UN Mission for the Organization of the Referendum in the Western Sahara (MINURSO)—would supervise the progressive reduction of Moroccan military forces in the territory during the first 12 weeks of the ceasefire and assume control of the remaining Moroccan and Polisario forces. The UN force would ensure that all Sahrawis eligible to vote were able to return to the Western Sahara and it would also supervise the actual referendum. A request for the establishment of the peacekeeping force was submitted by Sr Pérez de Cuellar to the UN Security Council at the end of June. No detailed schedule for the referendum was announced, but Morocco demanded that the processes must be completed before its postponed general elections took place in late 1991. Bachir Mustapha Sayed, Polisario's second-in-command, announced in May that the referendum could take place 'towards the end of 1991'. On 9 July the UN Secretary-General hosted another round of proximity talks between Morocco and the Polisario Front in Geneva.

In a written report to the UN General Assembly in October, Sr Pérez de Cuellar stated that a solution to the Western Sahara conflict was well within reach and that he would soon produce a detailed report outlining the actual mechanics of a ceasefire and eventual referendum. Yet in spite of the Secretary-General's optimism and the preparation of a detailed UN plan, major problems remained unresolved. King Hassan criticized the UN plan, arguing that the peacekeeping force should play a more limited role with fewer controls over Moroccan forces in the Western Sahara. For Morocco the Western Sahara remained an integral part of its territory and the UN referendum was seen as merely a formality. This position was of course totally unacceptable to Polisario. Also important was Algeria's attitude towards the conflict, given the recent internal changes affecting Polisario's major supporter (see pp. 237–41).

VI EQUATORIAL AFRICA

Chapter 1

ETHIOPIA—SOMALIA—DJIBOUTI—KENYA—TANZANIA—UGANDA

ETHIOPIA

CAPITAL: Addis Ababa   AREA: 1,220,000 sq km   POPULATION: 47,400,000 ('88)
OFFICIAL LANGUAGE: Amharic   POLITICAL SYSTEM: people's republic
HEAD OF STATE: President (Lt.-Col.) Mengistu Haile-Maryam (since Feb '77)
RULING PARTY: Workers' Party of Ethiopia (WPE)
VICE-PRESIDENTS: Lt.-Col. Fisseha Desta, Lt.-Col. Berhanu Bayeh
PRINCIPAL MINISTERS: Hailu Yimenu (deputy premier, acting Prime Minister), Wole Chekol (deputy premier, economic affairs), Tesfaye Dinka (foreign affairs), Col. Tesfaye Wolde Selassie (internal affairs), Tekola Dejene (finance), Wondayen Mehretu (justice)
INTERNATIONAL ALIGNMENT: NAM, OAU, ACP, Comecon (observer)
CURRENCY: (end-'90 £1=Br3.96, US$1=Br2.05)
GNP PER CAPITA: US$120 ('88)
MAIN EXPORT EARNERS: coffee, agricultural produce

IN another bad year, President Mengistu Haile-Maryam's government lost control of the vital port of Massawa in Eritrea, and abandoned its 14-year commitment to marxism-leninism.

Fighting in Eritrea between government forces and the Eritrean People's Liberation Front (EPLF) resumed with an EPLF offensive in January, which culminated in mid-February with the capture of Massawa, the only major port serving highland Eritrea. Deprived of land or sea links with the rest of the country, an Ethiopian army of over 100,000 men in the area around the Eritrean capital of Asmara could only be supplied by air. Attempts to break out towards the coast were defeated in April and again in September. EPLF shelling of Asmara airport caused some civilian casualties, but it remained operational.

To the south of Eritrea, the Tigré People's Liberation Front (TPLF), which already controlled Tigré region, reported heavy fighting in Wollo and Gonder regions in March and April. It met increasing resistance from local government-armed militias, and withdrew from much of southern Wollo and Gonder. It also started to modify its previously rigid adherence to Albanian-style marxism-leninism, and private traders were permitted to operate in TPLF-held areas. Further south, the Oromo Liberation Front (OLF) captured settlements close to the Sudanese border in Welega region in January. By late in the year it had extended its operations further into Welega; and some OLF activity was also reported from Hararghe in the east of the country.

The peace talks which had opened between the government and both the EPLF and the TPLF broke down after the capture of Massawa, as the opposition movements scented the possibility of decisive gains on the battlefield, and raised their negotiating demands. Talks with the TPLF in Rome in March foundered over its insistence on including its ally, the Ethiopian People's Democratic Movement (EPDM). The EPLF refused to attend talks scheduled for Nairobi in April, until the government accepted its demand for UN observers; this was conceded in June, without eliciting any EPLF response. The government held talks in Yemen in April with smaller Eritrean groups, but these could achieve little in the absence of EPLF participation.

The Soviet Union continued to supply weapons to Ethiopia, at a level estimated by Western sources at US$750 million a year, though the Soviet government emphasized the need for reconciliation when Foreign Minister Tesfaye Dinka visited Moscow in March. The EPLF claimed that Israel was supplying cluster bombs and other weapons to Ethiopia, and two Libyan diplomats were expelled following a bomb explosion near the Israeli ambassador's apartment in Addis Ababa, shortly after he had presented his credentials on 23 March. The EPLF obtained arms from Iraq, and the gunboats which for the first time gave it a naval capability also seemed to have come from Arab sources.

Following Iraq's invasion of Kuwait in August, Ethiopia strongly supported the anti-Iraq alliance, its diplomatic profile being greatly enhanced by membership of the UN Security Council. A visit to Addis Ababa in November by US Assistant Secretary of State Herman Cohen signalled an improvement in relations. The EPLF's attitude was more ambivalent, although purported EPLF documents offering strong support to Saddam Husain appeared to be forgeries. In common with other insurgent movements, the EPLF was affected by loss of Arab aid and remittances, and the level of fighting declined towards the end of the year.

President Mengistu's announcement on 5 March of Ethiopia's abandonment of marxism-leninism was widely welcomed in the country, although nothing was subsequently heard of his proposal in the same speech to replace the Workers' Party of Ethiopia (WPE) with a Democratic Unity Party of Ethiopia (DUPE), which opposition groupings would be welcome to join. Though the WPE remained in being, it rapidly lost authority, especially in the countryside, where collective farms were abandoned, the government's villagization campaign ended, and the grain quotas previously enforced by the Agricultural Marketing Corporation were abolished. Peasants were given inheritance rights in the land they farmed. At the same time, the government retained firm control on central power. Twelve generals convicted of involvement in the attempted coup of May 1989 (see AR 1989, p. 242) were executed on 19 May, and a subsequent demonstration by university students—the first since the 1970s—was suppressed. The government's military recruitment methods aroused protest from human rights groups.

The EPLF's capture of Massawa, coupled with subsequent Ethiopian bombing of the port and destruction of food stocks, closed the major entry point for relief grain to famine areas of northern Ethiopia. From 20 March the government agreed to a food corridor through which grain was transported from the government-held port of Assab to TPLF-controlled areas of Tigré and Wollo. The EPLF shipped in food through Port Sudan, although some food intended for Eritrea was commandeered by the Sudanese government.

The harvest was good in much of Ethiopia, where peasant productivity was encouraged by agricultural reforms, but poor in parts of Hararghe and disastrous in the perennially drought-affected regions of Tigré and Eritrea. The threat of serious famine was averted, but by the end of the year relief agencies were once more sounding the alarm. Following long negotiations, an agreement to reopen Massawa for relief shipments was announced on 18 December, with the food to be equally shared between government- and EPLF-controlled areas.

SOMALIA

CAPITAL: Mogadishu   AREA: 638,000 sq km   POPULATION: 5,900,000 ('88)
OFFICIAL LANGUAGES: Somali & Arabic   POLITICAL SYSTEM: presidential
HEAD OF STATE: President (Maj.-Gen.) Mohammed Siyad Barre (since Oct '69)
RULING PARTY: Somali Revolutionary Socialist Party (SRSP)
PRINCIPAL MINISTERS: Mohammed Hawatie Madar (Prime Minister), Abdurahman Jama Barreh, deputy premier (finance), Abd al Qasim Salad Hasan (deputy premier, interior) Hussein Abdurahman Matan (justice, religious affairs), Brig.-Gen. Mohammad Siyad Morgan (defence), Ahmad Mohammad Adan Qaybeh (foreign affairs)
INTERNATIONAL ALIGNMENT: NAM, OAU, ACP, Arab League, ICO
CURRENCY: shilling (end-'90 £1=SoSh5060.53, US$1=SoSh2622.04)
GNP PER CAPITA: US$170 ('88)
MAIN EXPORT EARNERS: livestock, agricultural produce

PRESIDENT Mohammed Siyad Barre lost ground in an increasingly desperate struggle for survival. A series of governmental and constitutional changes failed to improve his position. The President dismissed the cabinet on 8 January but reappointed Prime Minister Mohammed Ali Samater, whose new cabinet, composed largely of junior technocrats, was sworn in on 17 February. This lasted only until its dismissal on 3 September, and a new Prime Minister, Mohammed Hawatie Madar, took office two days later. The President's half-brother, Abdurahman Jama Barre, returned as Minister of Finance, a post from which he had been removed the previous year in an attempt to improve the government's standing with international financial agencies. A new multi-party constitution was provisionally approved on 8 October, subject to a nationwide referendum 'if conditions in the country permit', an unlikely eventuality while the civil wars continued. Under it, the President stepped down as chairman of the previously sole permitted political organization, the Somali Revolutionary Socialist Party; his place was taken by his brother-in-law, Ahmed Sulayman Abdullah. In November the President's son, Brigadier Maslah Mohammed Siyad, was replaced as army commander by his son-in-law, General Said Hirsi Morgan.

A report prepared for the US State Department late in 1989 claimed that the Somali armed forces had 'purposely murdered' at least 5,000 civilians over the previous two years; the opposition Somali National Movement (SNM) had also engaged in widespread atrocities. The human rights group Africa Watch said in January that between 50,000 and 60,000 civilians had been killed since civil war erupted in May 1988. Over a hundred civilians died when troops fired into the crowd after hecklers interrupted a speech by President Siyad in a Mogadishu stadium in July. The United States suspended virtually all aid in protest at human rights violations in February. In June more than a hundred prominent Somalis, including the country's first President, Aden Abdullah Osman, published a 'Mogadishu manifesto' calling for the President's resignation, the disbanding of the security services, and the appointment of a transitional government pending democratic elections; many of the signatories were arrested, but later released following international pressure.

Loss of allies elsewhere pushed the regime into a rapprochement with radical Arab states. Iraqi arms reportedly reached Somalia in June, when President Siyad also visited Libya. When the Gulf crisis erupted in August, however, the government sided with the Arab League majority against Iraq. The crisis further damaged the economy, which was already badly affected by civil war.

In March government forces launched an offensive against the SNM in the north-west of the country, but by November most of the northern region outside the main cities was back in SNM hands. In August the Isaq-dominated SNM announced an alliance with the two other clan-based opposition movements, the Ogadeni Somali Patriotic Movement (SPM) and the Hawiye United Somali Congress (USC). Since USC support was concentrated in the area around the capital, Mogadishu, it was best placed to launch an attempt to overthrow the government. Heavy fighting between USC and government forces erupted in the city on 26 December, and by the end of the year the Siyad regime appeared to be on the brink of collapse.

DJIBOUTI

CAPITAL: Djibouti AREA: 23,000 sq km POPULATION: 370,000 ('87)
OFFICIAL LANGUAGES: Arabic and French POLITICAL SYSTEM: presidential, one-party state
HEAD OF STATE: President Hassan Gouled Aptidon (since '77)
RULING PARTY: Popular Rally for Progress (RPP)
PRINCIPAL MINISTERS: Barkat Gourad Hamadou (Prime Minister, planning & land development), Ismail Ali Youssouf (defence), Moussa Bouraleh Robleh (finance & economy) Moumin Bahdon Farah (foreign affairs), Khayreh Alaleh Hared (interior), Ougoute Hassan Ibrahim (justice, religious affairs)
INTERNATIONAL ALIGNMENT: NAM, OAU, ACP, Arab League, ICO, Francophonic
CURRENCY: (end-'90 £1=DF338.00, US$1=DF175.13)
GNP PER CAPITA: US$480 ('81)
MAIN EXPORT EARNERS: agricultural products

DJIBOUTI's attempts to insulate itself from the civil war in neighbouring Somalia were only partially successful. Violent clashes occurred among the 30,000 Somali refugees in the country, and the despatch of troops to seal the frontier in March aroused Somali government accusations of armed aggression. Djibouti applied for membership of the Gulf Cooperation Council, and in May an apparently unsolicited shipment of arms from Iraq was returned. French budgetary assistance continued despite the expiry of the previous aid agreement in 1989, but only on a year-by-year basis. Two exiled opposition movements, the Afar-based Front Démocratique de Liberation de Djibouti and the Issa-based Mouvement National Djiboutien pour l'Instauration de la Démocratie, agreed in February to form a common front as the Union des Mouvements Démocratiques.

KENYA

CAPITAL: Nairobi AREA: 580,000 sq km POPULATION: 22,400,000 ('88)
OFFICIAL LANGUAGE: Kiswahili POLITICAL SYSTEM: presidential, one-party state
HEAD OF STATE AND PARTY LEADER: President Daniel Arap Moi (since Oct '78)
RULING PARTY: Kenya African National Union (KANU)
PRINCIPAL MINISTERS: George Saitoti (Vice-President, finance), Wilson Ndolo Ayah (foreign affairs), Davidson Ngibuni Kuguru (home affairs), Zachary Onyonka (planning & national development)
INTERNATIONAL ALIGNMENT: NAM, OAU, ACP, Cwth.
CURRENCY: Shilling (end-'90 £1=Ksh46.29, US$1=Ksh23.98)
GNP PER CAPITA: US$370 ('88)
MAIN EXPORT EARNERS: coffee, tea, petroleum products, tourism

THE murder in February of Foreign Minister Robert Ouko, who had called for an investigation into government corruption, was followed by anti-government riots in Nairobi and Kisumu, western Kenya (his home area), revealing a strong undercurrent of opposition to the regime of President Daniel Arap Moi. A Scotland Yard detective submitted his report on the incident to the Attorney-General in September; it was not made public and there were suspicions of a government cover-up. Dr Ouko was succeeded by Wilson Ndolo Ayah, a Luo like his predecessor and a former minister of water and development.

The debate over whether Kenya should revert to a multi-party system heightened the political tension caused by Dr Ouko's death. Early in May two former cabinet ministers—Kenneth Matiba and Charles Rubia (both Kikuyu)—called for the immediate repeal of the 1982 constitutional amendment which had made Kenya a *de jure* one-party state. They pressed for the dissolution of parliament and the holding of multi-party elections; Mr Matiba, a wealthy businessman, also wanted the introduction of a free-market economy. An angry President maintained that a multi-party system would divide Kenyans on ethnic lines, while some of his officials said off the record that talk of multi-party democracy was a cover for an intended Kikuyu takeover (the Kikuyu having certainly lost power under his rule). He ordered the detention of both ex-ministers. Their arrest early in July, together with other multi-party advocates, and leaflets calling for armed insurrection distributed by the clandestine anti-government organization, Mwakenya, provoked four days of rioting, looting and vandalism in Nairobi and other towns in central Kenya; at least 20 people were killed.

Despite the use of the preventive detention weapon, pressure on the government from religious leaders and others to end the legal power monopoly of the Kenya African National Union (KANU) continued. In November the veteran politician and former Vice-President, Oginga Odinga, announced that he was launching a second party to 'safeguard democracy'. Such advocates of political liberalism received encouragement from the Nordic countries and the Bush administration in America. The President's response was to warn the churches not to dabble in politics and to insist that the real problems facing the country were the state of the economy, production and unemployment. He repeated his insistence that Kenya should remain a one-party state at a two-day KANU special delegates' conference held in Nairobi at the beginning of December to discuss the confidential findings of a 10-man review committee set up by the party in June. Though fundamental change did not emerge from this conference, it was expected that certain electoral rules of the party would be altered, the most important being the restoration of a secret ballot to nominate local candidates in place of the unpopular queueing system (see AR 1988, pp. 249–50). President Moi agreed that judges, the Attorney-General and Auditor-General should again enjoy security of tenure.

The death in a car accident in August of Alexander Muge, the Anglican bishop of Eldoret and a fearless critic of official repression and corruption, renewed suspicions of government involvement in the removal of its critics. The bishop had been threatened by politicians shortly before his death and the government subsequently yielded to demands by the church hierarchy for a public inquiry. In September the *Nairobi Law Monthly*, which voiced strong criticism of the government, was banned. Two months later Paul Joseph Ngei, a cabinet minister since independence in 1963, lost his government post and his seat in parliament on being declared bankrupt (which under the constitution disqualified him from holding office).

The 1990–91 budget, presented in June, emphasized tight fiscal discipline and export-led growth in order to meet the nation's large budgetary and external deficits. Professor George Saitoti, the Vice-President and Minister of Finance, introduced export incentives, announced the government's continued commitment to trade liberalization, and said that the Treasury would no longer automatically honour parastatal debt obligations. The Kenya National Shipping Line was launched in February, mainly to serve Kenya's external trade. Unemployment remained a serious problem: an estimated 2.5 million Kenyans—nearly 40 per cent of the work force and some 10 per cent of the total population—were out of work. Skirmishes followed the demolition in May of a Nairobi shanty-town, resulting, according to a leading clergyman, in eight deaths. The government denied that anybody was killed and charged three senior employees of *The Standard* newspaper with false reporting. At Egerton University, Nakuru, a student protest over a new assessment method resulted in a violent clash with riot police and the closure of the university on 17 September. The anti-poaching campaign continued.

Scientists of the Kenya Medical Research Institute reported the discovery of a drug named Kemron which, it was claimed, could alleviate the major symptoms associated with AIDS. In August the government announced that a Kemron plant was being established, with responsibility for developing the drug vested in the institute and companies in the United States and Japan. Some concern was expressed that this announcement would prejudice the national campaign against AIDS.

Full diplomatic relations were restored with Canada in March and with Uganda in August; a permanent joint ministerial commission was established with Uganda. In October diplomatic relations were broken off with Norway, an important aid donor, on the grounds that Norway was harbouring political dissidents who were conspiring to overthrow the government. This followed the arrest in Nairobi earlier that month on a charge of treason of Koigi wa Wamwere, a former minister who had sought refuge in Norway, where he had founded the Kenya Patriotic Front in 1986; three others, two of them lawyers, were charged with him. The break in diplomatic ties resulted in the suspension of Norwegian aid and technical assistance.

The government was involved in a year-long effort to reach a peace agreement between the Mozambican government and rebels belonging to the Mozambique National Resistance (Renamo). Pik Botha, the South African Foreign Minister, paid a surprise visit to Kenya at the end of November.

TANZANIA

CAPITAL: Dar es Salaam/Dodoma AREA: 945,000 sq km POPULATION: 24,700,000 ('88)
OFFICIAL LANGUAGES: Swahili & English
POLITICAL SYSTEM: presidential, one-party state
HEAD OF STATE AND GOVERNMENT: President Ali Hassan Mwinyi (since Nov '85)
RULING PARTY: Cham cha Mapinduzi (CCM)
VICE-PRESIDENTS: John Malecela (Prime Minister), Salmin Amour (President of Zanzibar)
PRINCIPAL MINISTERS: Stephen Kibona (finance), Ahmed Hassan Diria (foreign affairs), Augustine Lyatonga Mrema (interior)
INTERNATIONAL ALIGNMENT: NAM, OAU, ACP, Cwth.
CURRENCY: shilling (end-'90 £1=Tsh377.03, US$1=Tsh195.35)
GNP PER CAPITA: US$160 ('88)
MAIN EXPORT EARNERS: coffee, cotton, tropical foodstuffs

IN March President Ali Hassan Mwinyi dropped 7 ministers from his cabinet and reshuffled others in a bid to promote economic reform and fight corruption. In October he was re-elected President for a second five-year term, securing 95.5 per cent of the votes in a single-candidate poll. He created five new ministries and included six newcomers in his 26-member cabinet. Seventeen former ministers retained their portfolios, among them Stephen Kibona at finance (to which he had been appointed in March) and President Mwinyi himself at defence. A few important changes were made. John Malecela, a former high commissioner to the United Kingdom, took over as Prime Minister and First Vice-President from Joseph Warioba, who was switched to the local government portfolio. Benjamin Mkapa, former Minister of Foreign Affairs, and Ahmed Hassan Diria, former Minister of Information, exchanged portfolios. Idris Abdul Wakil, who had resigned unexpectedly in August, was succeeded as President of Zanzibar and Second Vice-President by Dr Salmin Amour.

In elections to the 241-seat legislature, which were held concurrently with the presidential poll, 33 MPs lost their seats to political newcomers; the defeated candidates included Paul Bomani, a former ambassador to the United States and Minister of State in the President's Office, and Major-General Muhiddin Kimario, regional commissioner for Dar es Salaam and an influential Minister of Home Affairs until March, when President Mwinyi had replaced him, criticizing his ministry for corruption.

Ex-President Julius Nyerere resigned as chairman of Chama cha Mapinduzi (CCM) at a special party congress held in Dar es Salaam in August and was replaced by President Mwinyi, with Rashidi Kawawa, Minister without Portfolio, as his deputy. In a keynote address, Mr Nyerere argued that Tanzania should be judged not by World Bank and IMF standards of economic performance but by the rise in Tanzania's literacy rate and life expectancy and the fall in the infant mortality rate. These were valid points, although the education sector was in dire straits and characterized by a sharp drop in primary school enrolment, while health administration was over-stretched, with 500,000 people reported to be infected with the AIDS virus. He attributed Tanzania's economic decline to the artificially low prices which the country had received for its exports rather than to failures in domestic policy. He also urged the party to resist Western demands for a more liberal political system, which would prove socially divisive (earlier reports having suggested that he was encouraging debate on the introduction of a multi-party system).

President Mwinyi argued that Western countries should not link the adoption of pluralist democracy to the assistance which they gave to African states. On the economic front, he moved steadily towards the adoption of a market economy through privatization measures and the introduction of more liberal investment laws—reforms welcomed by overseas aid-givers, including the Nordic countries, which the President visited in April. He gained popularity by making more consumer goods available in the shops. University of Dar es Salaam students were, however, disaffected and went on strike for three weeks in April. They pointed to deteriorating conditions and alleged that some administrators were corrupt; the government closed the university in May.

The 1990–91 budget, presented to the National Assembly in June, gave priority to overcoming chronic transport and communications problems that were impeding economic recovery; 42 per cent of government spending of Tsh 206,000 million was allocated to these sectors. In order to stimulate trade (a hefty deficit was anticipated in the 1990–91 financial year) the top income tax rate was cut by 10 per cent to 40 per cent, road tolls were abolished, and customs duty was reduced from 100 to 60 per cent. The crop marketing boards were to be overhauled and the possibility of reducing the large number of parastatals in the country, by merging viable and non-viable enterprises, was to be investigated. The Economic and Social Action Programme (ESAP), the successor of the Economic Recovery Programme (ERP), aimed to get inflation down from its present level of over 20 per cent to under 10 per cent by 1991–92.

A number of leading Zanzibaris, including the islands' former Chief Justice and Minister of Agriculture, were arrested in Zanzibar in June; no reason was given for the arrests. In September the Chinese, who completed building the now-profitable Tanzania-Zambia Railway (Tazara) in 1976, signed a further 10-year railway engineering, managerial and technological cooperation agreement with Tanzania and Zambia. They also undertook to build low-cost accommodation and a new broadcasting house in Zanzibar. A private firm, Zanzibar Marine Services, started a new express ferry service between Zanzibar, Dar es Salaam and Mombasa, while two local businessmen, in association with a US company, launched a new, privately-owned airline, Zanzibar Airways, to operate within East Africa. The port of Dar es Salaam was being expanded and rehabilitated with help from the International Development Association, which also supported a substantial educational project and provided credit to revitalize agriculture.

Up to 100 people died and some 142,000 were made homeless in the southern coastal area around Lindi and Mtwara in April in the worst floods for more than 50 years; army engineers helped to rebuild homes and reconstruct bridges.

UGANDA

CAPITAL: Kampala AREA: 240,000 sq km POPULATION: 16,200,000 ('88)
OFFICIAL LANGUAGE: English POLITICAL SYSTEM: presidential
HEAD OF STATE AND GOVERNMENT: President Yoweri Museveni (since Jan '86)
RULING PARTY: National Resistance Movement (NRM) heads broad-based coalition
PRINCIPAL MINISTERS: Samson Kisekka (Prime Minister), Eriya Kategaya (first deputy premier), Paul Semogerere (second deputy premier, foreign affairs), Crispus Kiyonga (finance) Ibrahim Mukiibi (internal affairs), Joshua Mayanja-Nkangi (planning & economic development), George Kanyeihamba (justice)
INTERNATIONAL ALIGNMENT: NAM, OAU, ACP, Cwth.
CURRENCY: shilling (end-'90 £1=Ush1,058.37, US$1=Ush548.37)
GNP PER CAPITA: US$280 ('88)
MAIN EXPORT EARNERS: coffee, cotton

EARLY in the year the National Resistance Council (NRC), the country's reconstituted legislature, extended the life of President Yoweri Museveni's broad-based government for five years beyond 1990, the year scheduled for the return of civilian rule (see AR 1989, p. 251). The constitutional committee consulted local resistance committees to collect views on the shape of a new constitution. Some instability persisted. One army officer (a former rebel commander) was shot dead as he tried to escape to Kenya and a number of other officers, also suspected of being involved in a coup attempt, were detained. In April Brigadier-General Moses Ali, Minister of Culture, Youth and Sports and a Finance Minister under ex-President Idi Amin, was arrested on a charge of sedition. The same month 40 rebels belonging to the Holy Spirit Movement (see AR 1987, p. 244) were killed in a clash with the army near Gulu.

However, the prospects for peace in former rebel areas improved. In July leaders of the Uganda Patriotic Democratic Movement, a 5,000-strong guerrilla force in northern Uganda, signed a peace accord with the government; the rebels were to be absorbed into the national army. Rebel activity declined, but non-partisan armed gangs still caused trouble. Early in the year a Verona Fathers missionary was killed and another missionary was wounded when gunmen ambushed their car in northern Uganda.

At the beginning of October Rwandan refugees deserted from the Ugandan army in which they were serving and invaded Rwanda in an attempt to overthrow the government of President Juvénal Habyarimana (see p. 281). The Rwanda Patriotic Front commander was Major-General Fred Rwigyema, a former deputy commander of Uganda's National Resistance Army (NRA) and a deputy defence minister until December 1989; he and most of the rebels belonged to the Rwandan Tutsi community, which had been ousted from power by the majority Hutu people in 1959. An embarrassed Uganda government tried to seal off the border between the two countries. The Uganda newspaper *New Vision* reported on 12 November that all non-nationals had been immediately retired from the NRA. On 20 November a border-post meeting between the two state Presidents helped to reduce tension.

The country remained dependent on the agricultural sector for economic growth: it accounted for almost 75 per cent of GDP, 40 per cent of government revenue and more than 90 per cent of exports, and employed 80 per cent of the working population. Receipts from the export of coffee, the mainstay of the national economy, fell sharply as a result of the rapid decline in the international price and worsened an already acute balance-of-payments crisis. The country had to import wheat, rice and sugar to meet its needs; the prospects for tea production were good and it was predicted that there would be a huge increase in cotton production over the 1989–90 season with the return of peace and security to most of the cotton-growing regions in the north and north east.

To turn prediction into reality the government offered incentives to cotton farmers. In his June budget statement Crispus Kiyonga, the Finance Minister, announced a 6 per cent increase in the producer price from 1 December, bringing it to more than double the level a year earlier. Cotton exporters were also allowed to exchange their foreign earnings on the newly-legalized open foreign exchange market. The government banned timber exports in an attempt to curb illegal felling, especially of hardwood trees like the rare mvule, and to protect the environment.

The International Development Association (IDA) provided a credit of $125 million to support Uganda's economic recovery programme.

Economic reforms projected included ending the monopoly of the state marketing boards and the introduction of liberalized trade and investment regulations designed to promote export diversification. The IDA also helped to finance a poverty-alleviation programme; those targeted included more than 500,000 orphans, victims of the prolonged civil war and the severe AIDS epidemic. The government began to sell off to nationals, or to foreign investors who had entered into joint ventures with Ugandans, unclaimed properties confiscated from the Asian business community by Idi Amin in 1972 (see AR 1972, p. 234). The two big Asian-owned sugar estates were back in production.

All foreign journalists and Ugandans working for foreign media organizations had to re-apply in writing for work permits following an incident involving the Zambian President during his visit in February. In April the government concluded a non-aggression pact with the Sudan, over 60,000 of whose nationals had sought refuge in Uganda. It dropped the remaining charge against Paulo Muwanga, vice-president in ex-President Milton Obote's second administration, and released him from remand prison. President Museveni was elected chairman of the Organization of African Unity in November.

The small colony of pygmies, living in the remote Ruwenzori mountains, faced extinction unless they consented to receive medical attention and made some changes to their life-style. The campaign to save the rare African mountain gorilla was showing signs of success, with an estimated one-third increase in their number (to some 450) over the past four years.

Chapter 2

GHANA—NIGERIA—SIERRA LEONE—THE GAMBIA—LIBERIA

GHANA

CAPITAL: Accra   AREA: 240,000 sq km   POPULATION: 14,000,000 ('88)
OFFICIAL LANGUAGE: English   POLITICAL SYSTEM: military regime
HEAD OF STATE: Flt.-Lt. Jerry Rawlings, Chairman of Provisional National Defence Council (since Dec '81)
PRINCIPAL MINISTERS: P. V. Obeng (Chairman of Committee of Secretaries), Obed Y. Asamoah (foreign affairs), Kwesi Botchwey (finance & economic planning) Mohamad Idrisu (defence), G. E. K. Aikins (justice)
INTERNATIONAL ALIGNMENT: NAM, OAU, ACP, Cwth.
CURRENCY: cedi (end-'90 £1=C661.70, US$1=C342.85)
GNP PER CAPITA: US$400 ('88)
MAIN EXPORT EARNERS: cocoa, gold, minerals

IN marked contrast to earlier years, the principal challenge to the government came in peaceful guise. A pro-democracy Movement for

Freedom and Justice (MFJ) was initiated in August (following its early origins in London) after a number of public meetings in Ashanti and the south. It was directed by Johnny Hanson, a former member of the ruling Provisional National Defence Council (PNDC). Helped by external pressure from Western donors, the MFJ reflected current demands, not only in Ghana, for multi-party politics and a democratic respect for civil rights. The specific demand was for a national referendum on the need to return the country to democratic civilian rule. However, when the movement attempted to hold an inaugural rally in Kumasi on 17 September the government ordered riot police to disperse the gathering. No explanation was offered for its action.

Meanwhile, Major Courage Quarshigah and others detained since 6 October 1989 after the alleged armed coup against the PNDC (see AR 1989, p. 253) continued to be held without trial under the 1982 preventive custody decree.

On a less sombre note, the country contrived to move away a little from the economic and financial plight of previous years. Inflation was still running at over 25 per cent, but good rains and harvests helped to offset a depressed cocoa price. Gold production increased at Konongo and Obuasi to almost 500,000 ounces for the year and was forecast to rise to 1 million per annum by the end of the decade. The balance-of-trade deficit for the year was estimated at a manageable US$250 million, although outstanding external debts were put at a massive $2,820 million.

The country was now mid-way through its three year 'enhanced structural adjustment facility' (November 1988–November 1991) provided by the IMF and multilateral donors to the tune of SDR 368.1 million. The harsh programme of restraint still required a national 'programme of action' (under the clumsy soubriquet of PAMSCAD) to 'mitigate the social costs of adjustments'.

The most dramatic aspect of external relations was Ghana's involvement in the ECOWAS attempt to impose an armed peace on Liberia (see pp. 264–5). Ghana was represented at the 13th ECOWAS summit in Banjul (28–30 May) and a strong contingent of its armed forces was despatched as part of the Nigerian-led peace-keeping force which landed in Liberia on 24 August. Ghanaian troops were then heavily engaged in the battle for control of the Springs Payne airfield close to Monrovia.

Memories of earlier political quarrels, and of previous 'prisoners of conscience', were recalled by the death in Accra on 8 July of Joe Appiah at the age of 71. A fierce opponent of Kwame Nkrumah in the 1950s and 1960s, Mr Appiah was a greatly respected lawyer and politician, known to a wider circle abroad through his marriage to Peggy, daughter of Sir Stafford Cripps, the former Labour Chancellor of the Exchequer in Britain.

NIGERIA

CAPITAL: Lagos   AREA: 924,000 sq km   POPULATION: 110,100,000 ('88)
OFFICIAL LANGUAGE: English   POLITICAL SYSTEM: military regime
HEAD OF STATE AND GOVERNMENT: President (Gen.) Ibrahim Babangida (since '85)
PRINCIPAL MINISTERS: Maj.-Gen. Ike Nwachuku (foreign affairs), Lt.-Gen. Sanni Abacha (defence), Alhaji Abubakar Alhaji (finance & economic planning), Jibril Aminu (petroleum resources), Prince Bola Ajibola (justice), Maj.-Gen. A. B. Mamman (internal affairs)
INTERNATIONAL ALIGNMENT: NAM, OAU, OPEC, ICO, ACP, Cwth.
CURRENCY: naira (end-'90 £1=N16.80, US$1=N8.71)
GNP PER CAPITA: US$290 ('88)
MAIN EXPORT EARNERS: oil and gas

'DRUG-BARONISH, inhumane, sadistic, deceitful, homosexually-centred and unpatriotic . . .' This somewhat bizarre litany of charges levelled over Radio Nigeria against the Babangida administration marked what was without doubt the most dramatic event of the year: the attempted coup during the early hours of 22 April. The coup leader, Major Gideon Ngwozor Orkar, from Benue state, claimed to represent the patriotic and well-meaning people of the middle belt and southern parts of Nigeria. Major Orkar declared that the Armed Forces Ruling Council (AFRC) had been dissolved and would be replaced by a more representative national ruling council. He also announced that the northern states of Bauchi, Bornu, Kaduna, Katsina and Sokoto would be excised from the federation until the rightful heir to the Sokoto sultanate had been installed. This last demand related to the highly controversial election of a new sultan in 1988 when the late sultan's son was passed over for someone who was widely regarded as a Babangida nominee (see AR 1988, p.260).

Despite the distinctly anti-northern tone of the attempt, it received negligible support in the south and soon collapsed. In the early afternoon of 22 April Army Chief of Staff Sanni Abacha announced that the President was safe and that most of the plotters had been arrested. Around five o'clock the President himself entered the press centre at Dodan barracks, confirming that the barracks had come under heavy bombardment and that his own presidential lodge had been severely damaged. It was estimated that 19 lives had been lost during the attempt, including that of the President's aide-de-camp, Colonel Usman Bello. A total of 377 suspects were arrested, including 177 civilians. The discovery of large quantities of ammunition and a number of new vehicles at the plotters' base some 15 kilometres from Lagos suggested that the attempt had been well-financed. There was a good deal of speculation that funds had been provided by wealthy businessmen incensed at the refusal of the national electoral commission (NEC) in 1989 to recognize the fledgling political parties they had bankrolled (see AR 1989, p. 256). In August 42 of the plotters, including Major Orkar, were executed, followed by a further 27 in September.

During the course of his Dodan address the President reaffirmed the AFRC's commitment to handing back power to a civilian government by 1992. In line with the transition programme, elections of party ward officers were held in May, whilst delegates to the first national party conventions since the unbanning of political activity in 1989 were selected in June. In July elections of state representatives were also held. Although the May ward elections were marred by poor planning and some violence, subsequent rounds proceeded in an orderly fashion. This was also the case with the national conventions, held at the end of July, at which the two government-sponsored parties elected their executive officers. However, concern was later voiced at the apparent tendency of the parties to express Nigeria's perennial and troublesome north-south division. Evidence of this was taken to be the selection by the National Republican Convention (NRC) of a Christian southern chairman, Chief Tom Ikimi, with the ultimate aim, under a zoning agreement, of fielding a northern presidential candidate. For similar reasons it was argued that the Social Democratic Party (SDP), the bulk of whose membership was in the south, had selected a northern chairman, Alhaji Babagan Kingibe.

Fears that north-south tensions would insinuate themselves into the December local government elections were intensified by the NEC's controversial decision to use the open ballot system. The fact that under this system voters were required to queue behind photographs of the candidate of their choice was seen as giving too much scope for harassment and intimidation. Despite these apprehensions the elections not only passed off peaceably but voting patterns failed to crystallize along north-south lines. The NRC made significant gains in alleged SDP strongholds in the south and vice versa. It seemed likely that a good deal of heat was taken out of the situation by an astute cabinet reshuffle in November. This reduced to ten the number of northern officers on the 23-man AFRC.

In his budget speech in January President Babangida admitted that the prospects for 1990 were only marginally better than in 1989. He also made clear that the slight improvement he anticipated would be achieved only if the world petroleum market held firm and if Nigeria were able to secure favourable debt rescheduling arrangements.

With regard to oil revenues, the Iraqi invasion of Kuwait in August and the subsequent steep rise in the price of oil seemed to amount to an unexpected bonus for debt-burdened Nigeria. Certainly with 1990 oil revenues set to exceed $12,000 million by December (nearly twice that estimated in the budget and 25 per cent higher than in 1989), and with this likely to rise to around $15,000 million in 1991, the future looked much brighter at the end of the year than at its beginning. However, there were a number of factors which together conspired to make this development not quite the windfall it first appeared.

Firstly, the transition to civilian rule would consume a sizeable proportion of the 1991 budget not only to finance elections but to allow the two political parties to function without becoming too dependent on wealthy businessmen. Secondly, 1991 would see the long-awaited census, which in a country of Nigeria's size would make heavy demands on public resources. Thirdly, and more immediately pressing, was the need to prop up the ailing naira, which by November had depreciated by about 60 per cent since the beginning of the year against sterling and the US dollar. Particularly hard hit was the manufacturing sector which was heavily dependent on imported inputs.

With regard to the estimated external debt of $32,000 million, the increase in oil revenue paradoxically weakened Nigeria's bargaining position with the Paris Club creditors. This was because the basic strategy of Finance Minister Alhaji Abubakar Alhaji was to seek concessionary repayment terms in view of Nigeria's 'poor nation' status (granted by the World Bank in 1988). President Babangida's official visit to Paris in March was in part aimed at persuading the French to use their influence to bring the Paris Club creditors round to this view. However, neither the French nor other creditor countries were noticeably won over to the idea that Nigeria should be granted the soft repayment terms conceded to other poor countries in Africa.

On the other hand, some progress was apparently made with the London Club of private creditors, who were owed some $5,000 million of the $32,000 million. Here the Finance Minister's strategy centred on a comprehensive buy-back arrangement. In August these negotiations seemed to have stalled, but by the end of October the London Club reportedly accepted the principle that Nigeria could buy back a proportion (estimated at 60 per cent) of its debts on the international secondary market, with the unbought portion to be converted into bonds. Despite this agreement Nigeria still needed to allocate one third of its oil revenue to debt-servicing.

The privatization programme claimed to be ahead of target in 1990, with over half of the 92 state enterprises earmarked for privatization already disposed of. However, the 1990 programme did not proceed as rapidly as in 1989, mainly for two reasons: firstly, because the smaller and more saleable ventures had already been sold off; and secondly, because the volume of capital available had already been depleted by previous sales. Accordingly, the chairman of the technical committee on privatization and commercialization, Dr Hamza Zayyad, admitted in June that recent share issues had been under-subscribed.

Nigeria's main external involvement in 1990 was its contribution to the ECOWAS force in Liberia combined with the problem of evacuating its citizens from that strife-torn country (see pp. 264–5). In June relations with Cameroon deteriorated over the death in mysterious circumstances of a prominent Nigerian businessman and the alleged harassment there of Nigerian nationals. However, in July Nigeria went ahead with a planned five-day exhibition in Yaoundé. Relations with Britain were slightly strained over Nigeria's reluctance to support the use of force against Iraq as well as its insistence on executing the April coup plotters. Nonetheless, the UK government in December announced an aid package of £25 million in support of Nigeria's structural adjustment programme, while President Babangida commiserated with Mrs Thatcher over her fall from power.

SIERRA LEONE

CAPITAL: Freetown   AREA: 72,000 sq km   POPULATION: 3,900,000 ('88)
OFFICIAL LANGUAGE: English   POLITICAL SYSTEM: presidential, one-party state
HEAD OF STATE AND GOVERNMENT: President Joseph Saidu Momoh (since Nov '85)
RULING PARTY: All-People's Congress (APC)
PRINCIPAL MINISTERS: Abu Bakar Kamara (First Vice-President), Salia Jusu-Sheriff (Second Vice-President), Abdul Karim Koroma (foreign affairs), Tommy Taylor-Morgan (finance), Sheka Kanu (planning & development), Ahmed Sesay (internal affairs), Abdulai Conteh (justice)
INTERNATIONAL ALIGNMENT: NAM, OAU, ICO, Cwth.
CURRENCY: leone (end-'90 £1=Le324.00, US$1=Le167.88)
GNP PER CAPITA: US$300 ('87)
MAIN EXPORT EARNERS: diamonds, coffee, cocoa

DESPITE several years of attempted institutional reforms and appeals to patriotic duty, President Joseph Momoh faced continued economic difficulties and found few takers for his 'constructive nationalism'. The new Finance Minister, Tommy Taylor-Morgan, was charged with putting the economy in order but could claim only limited success. Some recovery in the GDP was reported in the July budget and the decision to devalue the leone led to fresh discussions with the IMF in September, but the persistent problems of previous years remained: financial indiscipline and corruption in the public sector leading to enormous over-shooting in state expenditure; a widening trade gap resulting from poor export performance; an enduring parallel market; a weak agricultural sector and a fast decaying infrastructure, together with recurring currency shortages. Public morale and business confidence were further hit by the unexpected consequences of the civil war in neighbouring Liberia (see pp. 264–5). By late 1990 an estimated 250,000 refugees, returnees and transients made additional claims on Sierra Leone's scarce resources.

The ruling All-People's Congress was largely blamed for the economic situation. Public disenchantment led to calls, particularly from students, the legal profession and the press, for a return to multi-party politics. President Momoh, while not ruling out such a possibility, preferred to concentrate on economic recovery first. On several occasions he argued that economic and social circumstances were not ripe for the abandonment of single-party rule but he agreed to introduce minor reforms to the existing political system and to set up a constitutional review committee to look critically at the 1978 one-party constitution.

THE GAMBIA

CAPITAL: Banjul   AREA: 11,300 sq km   POPULATION: 822,000 ('88)
OFFICIAL LANGUAGE: English   POLITICAL SYSTEM: presidential democracy
HEAD OF STATE AND GOVERNMENT: President Sir Dawda Kairaba Jawara (since '70)
RULING PARTY: People's Progressive Party (PPP)
PRINCIPAL MINISTERS: Bakary Bunja Darbo (Vice-President), Omar Sey (external affairs), Saihou S. Sabally (economic affairs), Lamin Kiti Jabang (interior), Hassan Jallow (justice)
INTERNATIONAL ALIGNMENT: NAM, OAU, ACP, ICO, Cwth.
CURRENCY: dalasi (end-'90 £1=D14.60, US$1=D7.57)
GNP PER CAPITA: US$200 ('88)
MAIN EXPORT EARNERS: groundnuts and groundnut products

THE Gambia celebrated its 25th year of independence in a mood of continuing political and economic confidence. The possibility of the leading opposition group, the National Convention Party, merging or forming a coalition with the ruling People's Progressive Party was raised in talks between party leaders in September. Five years of austerity under the original Economic Recovery Programme and its successor, the Extended Structural Adjustment Programme (ESAP), continued to show results. According to the IMF, the leading external aid provider, strong growth and a substantial improvement in the balance of payments were recorded for 1989–90 and further gains were anticipated in the future. The groundnut harvest for 1989–90 was estimated to be up 20 per cent on the previous season, although tourism was expected to show a decline because of a drop in British visitors. Relations with Senegal were still to recover from the consequences of the break-up of the confederation in 1989 (see AR 1989, pp. 258–9, 262), but there was less evidence of harassment of Gambian traders and interference with cross-border trade.

The President, Sir Dawda Jawara, as current head of the Economic Community of West African States (ECOWAS), hosted the Banjul summit in May and spent much of the remainder of the year chairing the organization's Liberian ceasefire monitoring committee (ECOMOG). He not only helped bring about agreement among the quarrelling Liberian factions but also managed to restore unity among divided ECOWAS members.

LIBERIA

CAPITAL: Monrovia AREA: 97,750 sq km POPULATION: 2,400,000 ('88)
OFFICIAL LANGUAGE: English POLITICAL SYSTEM: presidential
HEAD OF STATE AND GOVERNMENT: Amos Sawyer, President of interim government
RULING PARTY: interim government backed by ECOMOG
PRINCIPAL MINISTER: Reginald Diggs (Vice-President of interim government)
INTERNATIONAL ALIGNMENT: NAM, OAU, ACP
CURRENCY: Liberian dollar (end-'90 £1=L$1.93, US$1=L$1.00)
GNP PER CAPITA: US$450 ('87)
MAIN EXPORT EARNERS: iron ore, rubber, coffee

THE December 1989 disturbances reported in Nimba county (see AR 1989, p. 260), a longstanding area of opposition to the brutal and corrupt rule of President Samuel Doe, turned into a country-wide insurrection in the course of the year. It was led by Charles Taylor, a man of uncertain moral standing and political leanings who had held a senior position in the Doe administration before fleeing the country in 1984 after being accused of embezzlement and who, though backed by Libya, claimed to be a 'worshipper of Reaganomics'. By mid-summer his insurgent National Patriotic Front (NPF) had reached the outskirts of the capital, Monrovia. Widespread atrocities, frequently along ethnic lines, by government and rebel forces alike, and a growing refugee problem, compelled the regional Economic Community of West African States (ECOWAS) to act. It established a five-nation ceasefire monitoring group (ECOMOG), comprising The Gambia, Ghana, Mali, Nigeria and Togo, together with representatives of two border states (Guinea and Sierra Leone). Its task was to try and put an end to the fighting, and to establish an interim administration acceptable to all sides, which would arrange new elections. Two lines of action were pursued simultaneously. Attempts were made to bring together at Freetown, Banjul and, finally, Bamako, representatives of all the warring groups and civilian political organizations and the Liberian Council of Churches, to try and elect an interim President and administration to replace the Doe government. In late August, moreover, it sent into Monrovia a multi-national military force charged with imposing a ceasefire.

Mr Taylor, controlling the largest rebel force and some 90 per cent of the country, opposed the ECOMOG presence and regarded it as an attempt by Nigeria to save the tottering Doe government and deny him victory. However, on 11 September forces loyal to Prince Yormie Johnson, a former army officer who had broken away from Taylor's NPF, captured and subsequently killed President Doe, while he was visiting the ECOMOG headquarters. President Doe's remaining followers, led by General David Nimley (later replaced by General Hezekiah Bowen), as well as Johnson's group, then agreed to support the ECOMOG presence. Mr Taylor, who claimed the interim presidency for himself, held out until the Bamako meeting in late November, when a ceasefire was established and the warring elements agreed to surrender their weapons to the ECOMOG forces. Dr Amos Sawyer, a long-time political opponent of the Doe government and former university professor and constitutional expert, was chosen to head an interim administration drawn from all political groups and geographical areas. Under ECOMOG military protection, Dr Sawyer and his transitional government returned to Monrovia in December to face a chaotic situation: over a million refugees, a bankrupt economy, a collapsed administration and the uncertain loyalty of the military warlords.

The USA, despite strong links with Liberia, limited its actions to cutting-off aid to Doe and evacuating its nationals by sea in June. It left it to ECOWAS to devise a regional solution to the crisis. In practice, this meant Nigeria's bearing the cost and providing the bulk of the intervention force of some 9,000 men. The ceasefire initiative for a time divided ECOWAS, with Burkina Faso and Côte d'Ivoire sympathising with Mr Taylor and criticizing the legality and objectives of ECOMOG.

Chapter 3

SENEGAL—GUINEA—MALI—MAURITANIA—CÔTE D'IVOIRE—
BURKINA FASO—NIGER—TOGO AND BENIN—CAMEROON—CHAD—
GABON AND CENTRAL AFRICAN REPUBLIC—CONGO—
EQUATORIAL GUINEA

SENEGAL

CAPITAL: Dakar   AREA: 196,000 sq km   POPULATION: 7,000,000 ('88)
OFFICIAL LANGUAGE: French   POLITICAL SYSTEM: presidential democracy
HEAD OF STATE AND GOVERNMENT: President Abdou Diouf (since '81)
RULING PARTY: Socialist Party (PS)
PRINCIPAL MINISTERS: Seydina Oumar Sy (foreign affairs), Medoune Fall (armed forces), Serigne Lamine Diop (justice), Famara Ibrahima Sagna (interior), Moussa Toure (economy, finance & planning)
INTERNATIONAL ALIGNMENT: NAM, ACP, ICO, Francophonie
CURRENCY: CFA franc (end-'90 £1=CFAF491.00, US$1=CFAF254.40)
GNP PER CAPITA: US$650 ('88)
MAIN EXPORT EARNERS: agricultural products and fish, chemicals

THE year was one of continued difficulties for Senegal. The economic rigours of structural adjustment were proving increasingly hard to maintain, and strained relations with neighbours, notably Mauritania, The Gambia and Guinea-Bissau, failed to improve. The serious problem with Mauritania, which had blown up in 1989 (see AR 1989, p. 261) amid mass expulsions of each other's nationals, continued to be tense in 1990, with a state of armed truce along the Senegal river, the border between the two countries. Peace-making efforts, involving particularly the OAU, failed to make progress.

Relations with Guinea-Bissau sank to a low point in May when there were four days of exchanges of cross-border artillery fire, causing a death toll of at least 17. This was followed by ministerial talks to work out methods of limiting border tensions, which increased after several serious incidents involving separatists in Senegal's southernmost province of Casamance, bordering on Guinea-Bissau. The authorities in Bissau denied any involvement with the separatists of the Mouvement des Forces Démocratiques de Casamance (MFDC), who had mounted a number of ambushes and grenade attacks on the Senegalese forces deployed to control the region. A military governor, retired General Amadou Dieng, was appointed in June because of the security situation, and was accused of mounting a reign of terror there. Amnesty International made serious charges of torture and other malpractices against Senegalese army units stationed in Casamance, where the death toll in various incidents through the year was reportedly over 100.

The Gambian government also denied any complicity with the Casamance separatists, even if relations between Senegal and The Gambia remained cool after the previous year's collapse of the Senegambian Confederation (see AR 1989, pp. 258–9, 262). The Senegalese finger was pointed more seriously at the Mauritanians, a suspicion reinforced after the Iraqi seizure of Kuwait. Senegal was strongly supportive of Kuwait and sent 1,000 troops to join the allied forces in Saudi Arabia, while Mauritania was sympathetic to Iraq, one of its principal sources of aid. These ripples from the Gulf caused the postponement of the Islamic summit planned for Dakar early in 1991, for which a large hotel/conference complex had been built in the Senegalese capital with Saudi/Kuwaiti support.

Although Senegal continued to be cited as a model for other African multi-party systems (the ruling party in Côte d'Ivoire even sent a delegation to study the Senegalese system), Senegal's own opposition politicians begged to differ. Still in dispute with the government over the electoral law, the coalition of most of the opposition parties decided to boycott the municipal elections at the end of November. While the ruling Parti Socialiste (PS) claimed 70 per cent voter participation, the opposition asserted it was less than 20 per cent.

GUINEA

CAPITAL: Conakry   AREA: 246,000 sq km   POPULATION: 5,400,000 ('88)
OFFICIAL LANGUAGE: French   POLITICAL SYSTEM: military regime
HEAD OF STATE AND GOVERNMENT: Brig-Gen. Lansana Conté, Chairman of Military Committee for National Recovery (since April '84)
PRINCIPAL MINISTERS: Maj. Jean Traoré (foreign affairs), Maj. Henri Tofani (defence), Edouard Benjamin (economy & finance), Bassirou Barry (justice), Capt. Mamadou Baldé (interior)
INTERNATIONAL ALIGNMENT: NAM, OAU, ACP, ICO, Francophonie
CURRENCY: Guinean franc (end-'90 £1=GF579.45, US$1=GF300.23)
GNP PER CAPITA: US$430 ('88)
MAIN EXPORT EARNERS: bauxite, oilseeds

THE wave of democratization which swept through much of francophone Africa did not leave Guinea untouched, even if the military government's 1989 commitment to return to civilian rule in five years (see AR 1989, p. 263) helped to mute the protest. There was an atmosphere of greater public debate, with more criticism of the government than in the days of Sekou Touré's dictatorship, which had ended with his death in 1984. There were also several teachers' and student strikes, and in October and November several students were killed in brutal repression of demonstrations in Conakry. A referendum in December massively approved a new draft constitution for civilian rule. For the five years prior to civilian rule, the country would be ruled by a National Transitional Council.

Guinea was also drawn into the Liberian conflict when it contributed 500 troops to the ECOMOG force constituted in August by the Economic Community of West African States, mainly from concern over Guinean nationals trapped and sometimes killed in the civil war.

MALI

CAPITAL: Bamako   AREA: 1,240,000 sq km   POPULATION: 8,000,000 ('88)
OFFICIAL LANGUAGE: French   POLITICAL SYSTEM: presidential, one-party state
HEAD OF STATE & PARTY LEADER: President Gen. Moussa Traoré (since '68)
RULING PARTY: Mali People's Democratic Union (UDPM)
PRINCIPAL MINISTERS: Django Cissoko (Secretary-General to Presidency), Ngolo Traoré (foreign affairs), Tienan Coulibaly (finance and trade), Souleymane Dembele (planning), Mamadou Sissoko (justice)
INTERNATIONAL ALIGNMENT: NAM, OAU, ACP ICO, Francophonie
CURRENCY: CFA franc (end-'90 £1=CFAF491.00, US$1=CFAF254.40)
GNP PER CAPITA: US$230 ('88)
MAIN EXPORT EARNERS: cotton, agricultural products

AFTER 22 years of military rule under President Moussa Traoré, signs of restiveness were not surprising. The influence of pro-democracy movements in a number of African countries made its way to Mali, where there was mounting pressure through the year for an end to the rule of the single ruling party, the Union Démocratique du Peuple Malien (UDPM). Although the party failed to pronounce immediately in favour of multi-partyism, it had to face the creation of an Alliance for Democracy in Mali (Adema), which by the end of the year was increasingly mobilized. There was evidence of an increase of independent newspapers, and hence of freedom of expression.

Concern grew during the year, however, over the increasing disaffection of the nomadic Touareg peoples in the northern part of the country and over tough military measures taken against them. In June a Touareg commando attacked Meneka in eastern Mali, killing 14 people, including the sub-prefect and his wife. Some 30 Malian soldiers were reported killed in a clash in the north in October, and there were indications of open revolt in large areas of Mali's Sahara regions. In August a summit of Algeria, Niger and Mali met to discuss the problem. At the end of the year there were talks on a truce. The disturbances took place against a background of new threats of drought because of poor rains.

MAURITANIA

CAPITAL: Nouakchott   AREA: 1,000,000 sq km   POPULATION: 1,900,000 ('88)
OFFICIAL LANGUAGES: French and Arabic   POLITICAL SYSTEM: military regime
HEAD OF STATE AND GOVERNMENT: Col. Moaouia Ould Sidi Mohamed Taya,
    Chairman of Military Council of National Salvation (since Dec '84)
PRINCIPAL MINISTERS: Hassiny Ould Didi (foreign affairs), Maj. Cheikh Ahmed Ould
    Baba (interior), Sow Adema Samba (justice), Sidi Mohamed Ould Boubaker
    (finance), Mouhamedou Ould Michel (planning)
INTERNATIONAL ALIGNMENT: NAM, Arab League, ICO, OAU, ACP, AMU, Francophonie
CURRENCY: ouguiya (end-'90 £1=UM152.12, US$1=UM78.82)
GNP PER CAPITA: US$480 ('88)
MAIN EXPORT EARNERS: iron ore, fish

THE pressures from the Arab world on Mauritania became stronger during the year. Even though the Western Sahara problem (see pp. 244–5) caused fewer problems in relations with two northern neighbours (Algeria and Morocco), the Gulf crisis brought its own problems. As a client state of Iraq, with connections in its army to the Baath Party, Mauritania was counted among the members of the Arab League more friendly to Iraq, although it did not actually support Saddam Husain's seizure of Kuwait. This in turn worsened the already difficult relations with Senegal to the south, strongly pro-Kuwait, and led to a new coolness in relations with anti-Iraq Morocco.

At the end of November a coup plot was announced in Nouakchott, in which some 60 people were arrested, mostly from the army and navy.

They were said to have confessed to have taken orders from Senegal, although this was denied in Dakar. Amnesty International, which had made regular charges that the ruling Moors were oppressing the black minority in southern Mauritania, suggested that the coup plot was a further pretext for harassing the minority.

CÔTE D'IVOIRE

CAPITAL: Abidjan   AREA: 322,000 sq km   POPULATION: 11,200,000 ('88)
OFFICIAL LANGUAGE: French   POLITICAL SYSTEM: presidential
HEAD OF STATE & GOVERNMENT: President Félix Houphouët-Boigny (since '60)
RULING PARTY: Democratic Party of Côte d'Ivoire (PDCI)
PRINCIPAL MINISTERS: Alassane Ouattara (Prime Minister, economy & finance), Amara Essy (foreign affairs), Léon Konan Koffi (defence), Emile Constant Bombet (interior), Jacqueline Lohoues Oble (justice)
INTERNATIONAL ALIGNMENT: NAM, OAU, ACP, Francophonie
CURRENCY: CFA franc (end-'90 £1=CFAF491.00, US$1=CFAF254.40)
GNP PER CAPITA: US$770 ('88)
MAIN EXPORT EARNERS: cocoa, coffee, timber

IT was a turbulent year, in which octogenarian President Houphouët-Boigny did well to survive in power, with a new five-year mandate in elections in October. The first part of the year saw a series of protests and demonstrations by different social groups, spearheaded by students and teachers but also involving trade unions and professional groupings. Although the background was one of mounting economic crisis, the demands were not just financial but also for a liberalization of the single-party regime. This duly came in May, when it was announced that party formation, technically possible under the constitution, would in fact be permitted. This took the heat off the regime, as nearly 20 groupings, some of them of a fairly ephemeral nature, were formed.

Alassane Ouattara, governor of the West African Central Bank, was brought in to coordinate an economic recovery programme. A short-lived programme of the Finance Minister, Moïse Koffi Komoé, which actually provided for salary cuts, was dropped (and his tenure of the office was equally short-lived). Mr Ouattara's plan, which involved substantial reforms, especially of the fund-raising sectors of the civil service such as customs, was felt to be making headway as the year concluded. In particular, it had the backing of the World Bank and the IMF, which had been in disaccord with Côte d'Ivoire for some three or four years.

In the presidential elections, despite multi-partyism, there was only one candidate standing against Mr Houphouët-Boigny, namely Laurent Gbagbo, a university teacher and leader of the Front Populaire Ivoirien (FPI). Although all the dice were loaded against him in that the whole governmental machine was behind the President, Mr Gbagbo was considered to have done well by obtaining 17 per cent of the poll against the incumbent's 83 per cent. Parliamentary and local elections before the end of the year recorded a similar pattern. However, a new slimmed-down government under Mr Ouattara as Prime Minister brought in new technocrats, and seemed to mark the end of the Houphouët era. The controversial £100 million basilica had been inaugurated at Yamoussoukro (the President's birthplace) in September (see also Pt. XIII, RELIGION). Thereafter, the aged leader was again the subject of speculation that he might retire soon, making way for his constitutional successor, Henri Konan-Bédié, who was re-elected as president of the National Assembly.

BURKINA FASO

CAPITAL: Ouagadougou   AREA: 275,000 sq km   POPULATION: 8,500,000 ('88)
OFFICIAL LANGUAGE: French   POLITICAL SYSTEM: military regime
HEAD OF STATE AND GOVERNMENT: Capt. Blaise Compaoré, Chairman of Popular
  Front (since Oct '87)
PRINCIPAL MINISTERS: Prosper Vocouma (foreign affairs), Thomas Sanon (economic
  promotion), Bintou Sanogo (finance), Frédéric Korsaga (planning), Antoine
  Komy Sambo (justice)
INTERNATIONAL ALIGNMENT: NAM, OAU, ACP, ICO, Francophonie
CURRENCY: CFA franc (end-'90 £1=CFAF491.00, US$1=CFAF254.40)
GNP PER CAPITA: US$210 ('88)
MAIN EXPORT EARNERS: cotton, agricultural produce

DESPITE continued reports that all was not well beneath the surface, Burkina's military leader, Blaise Compaoré, kept a firm hold on the country, while making a number of concessions to democratization. A commission was set up to prepare a new constitution. In the meantime, the government re-formed itself as the Popular Front, and invited other emerging political groupings to join it. Of ten parties formed by December, seven had joined the Front.

In the West African region Burkina became embroiled in the Liberian civil war (see pp. 264–5) as the principal backer of the rebel movement of Charles Taylor, who had spent his exile in Ouagadougou. Libyan arms for the rebels were said to have passed through Burkina, and members of the Burkina military reportedly supported the rebellion, despite considerable diplomatic pressures from neighbouring countries.

NIGER

CAPITAL: Niamey AREA: 1,267,000 sq km POPULATION: 7,300,000 ('88)
OFFICIAL LANGUAGE: French POLITICAL SYSTEM: military regime
HEAD OF STATE AND GOVERNMENT: President (Brig.) Ali Saibou (Since Nov '87)
RULING PARTY: National Movement for a Development Society (MNSD)
PRINCIPAL MINISTERS: Aliou Mahamidou (Prime Minister), Sani Bako (foreign affairs), Lt.-Col. Tanja Mamadou (interior), Wassalke Boukary (finance), Almoustapha Soumaila (planning), Ali Bandiere (justice)
INTERNATIONAL ALIGNMENT: NAM, OAU, ACP, ICO, Francophonie
CURRENCY: CFA franc (end-'90 £1=CFAF491.00, US$1=CFAF254.40)
GNP PER CAPITA: US$300 ('88)
MAIN EXPORT EARNERS: uranium, metal ores

ALTHOUGH there was evidence of unrest early in the year, the regime of President Ali Saibou was one of the last in French-speaking Africa to make concessions to multi-partyism. This was perhaps because even the establishment of a single-party structure had been very recent, following 16 years of military rule. The clashes in Niamey in February were also the result of the brutal suppression of a student march, which added to the Saibou regime's poor record in handling its student population. After the clashes all colleges and schools were closed, and relations between government and students remained bad through the year, as Niger became affected by the wave of democratic protests running through the region. In November President Saibou accepted a plan to instal multi-partyism recommended by a constitutional commission.

As the year ended shadows were cast by the probable effects of a new drought, as well as a new wave of discontent among the Touareg population in the north (see also p. 268). Nevertheless, Niger sent 500 troops to join the US-led forces gathering in Saudi Arabia and the Gulf.

TOGO AND BENIN

Togo
CAPITAL: Lomé AREA: 57,000 sq km POPULATION: 3,400,000 ('88)
OFFICIAL LANGUAGES: French, Kabiye, Ewe POLITICAL SYSTEM: one-party state
HEAD OF STATE AND PARTY LEADER: President Gnassingbe Eyadema (since '67)
RULING PARTY: Rally of the Togolese People (RPT)
CURRENCY: CFA franc (end-'90 £1=CFAF491.00, US$1=CFAF254.40)
GNP PER CAPITA: US$370 ('88)
MAIN EXPORT EARNERS: phosphates, cocoa

Benin
CAPITAL: Porto Novo AREA: 113,000 sq km POPULATION: 4,400,000 ('88)
OFFICIAL LANGUAGE: French POLITICAL SYSTEM: presidential
HEAD OF STATE: President (Brig.-Gen.) Mathieu Kerekou (since '72)
RULING PARTY: People's Revolutionary Party (PRP)
HEAD OF GOVERNMENT: Nicéphore Soglo, Prime Minister (since Feb '90)
CURRENCY: CFA franc (end-'90 £1=CFAF491.00, US$1=CFAF254.40)
GNP PER CAPITA: US$390 ('88)
MAIN EXPORT EARNERS: cotton, palm products

THE destinies of the two mini-states sandwiched between Ghana and Nigeria still appeared linked, even if they sometimes seemed to be moving in opposite directions. TOGO's President Gnassingbe Eyadema was one of the African continent's most fervent partisans of the single-party state, and was one of the last to start making concessions towards democratization. The ruling Rassemblement du Peuple Togolais (RPT), meeting early in the year, voted against any move to multi-partyism. Only after a violent demonstration in the capital, Lomé, early in October, in which four people were killed (according to official figures) was the establishment of a constitutional commission announced, amid suggestions that a multi-party system would be introduced in two to three years. A series of strikes and protests in different Togolese towns continued right up to the year's end.

Just across the border in neighbouring BENIN, however, the democratization process was very far advanced. After the protests and mass demonstrations of 1989 (see AR 1989, p. 267), spilling over into 1990, the crucial event was a National Conference in February, at which the multitude of different groups attending staged what President Kerekou called, in tears, a 'civilian coup d'état'. The groups voted to give themselves sovereignty, and proceeded to set up a constitutional committee and to make arrangements for a transitional government with substantial power, naming a former finance minister, Nicéphore Soglo, as Prime Minister. General Kerekou remained as President and commander-in-chief, but with limited power.

The main initiative for financial recovery came from Mr Soglo and his team, who went all out to drum up the kind of financial aid necessary to put the country on the road again. Although they had some success, the problems of rescuing a bankrupt economy remained enormous. In the meantime, a host of parties proliferated, and the new constitution took much longer to prepare and approve than had been envisaged. Finally held in December, a referendum showed overwhelming support for the new text. Its provisions included a prohibition on anyone over 70 standing for the presidency, which would thus exclude ex-Presidents Maga, Ahomadegbe and Zinzou, all still powerful figures in Benin. The next crucial step was the holding of presidential and parliamentary elections in 1991.

CAMEROON

CAPITAL: Yaoundé AREA: 475,000 sq km POPULATION: 11,200,000 ('88)
OFFICIAL LANGUAGES: French, English POLITICAL SYSTEM: presidential
HEAD OF STATE AND GOVERNMENT LEADER: President Paul Biya (since '82)
RULING PARTY: Cameroon People's Democratic Movement (RDPC)
PRINCIPAL MINISTERS: Jacques-Roger Booh-Booh (foreign affairs), Edouard Akame Mfoumou (defence), Simon Bassilekin (finance), Marcel Niat Nkifenji (planning), Adolphe Moudiki (justice)
INTERNATIONAL ALIGNMENT: NAM, OAU, ACP, ICO, Francophonie
CURRENCY: CFA franc (end-'90 £1=CFAF491.00, US$1=CFAF254.40)
GNP PER CAPITA: US$1,010 ('88)
MAIN EXPORT EARNERS: oil, cocoa, coffee, aluminium

IT was a critical year for Cameroon, in that all the original promise of the arrival of Paul Biya in power in 1982 became concentrated on the democracy movement. President Biya's original 'liberalization' had in any case proved extremely tepid, especially after the bloody failed coup attempt of 1984, but the new circumstances of 1990 offered a second chance. Initial attempts to form an opposition party (technically legal under Cameroon's constitution) were met with repression. A Douala lawyer, Maître Yondo Black, and colleagues were gaoled in April in connection with a meeting to form a party, although they were later amnestied. In May a meeting in Bamenda to launch a new party, the Social Democratic Front, was followed by a police shooting in which six people were killed. This provoked a strong emotional reaction, as it was the first time such repressive action had ever taken place in the English-speaking area of Cameroon.

Tensions increased when a prominent anglophone politician, John Ngu Foncha, resigned from an honorary post in the ruling Cameroon People's Democratic Movement (RDPC). The RDPC held a congress at the end of June which produced a number of measures designed to create a more liberal atmosphere, including eventually a phased transition to multi-partyism. These were framed as legislation which passed through the National Assembly before the end of the year. However, there were increasing signs, amid a greater atmosphere of press freedom than Cameroon had known since independence in 1960, that frustrations with the slow pace of change were mounting.

Although Cameroon had been subjected to less austerity than most other African countries, the population was still relatively feeling the pinch. Thus the modest windfall from the Gulf crisis, in the shape of increased oil prices, provided some welcome relief to Cameroon's economic planners.

CHAD

CAPITAL: N'djaména AREA: 1,284,000 sq km POPULATION: 5,400,000 ('88)
OFFICIAL LANGUAGES: French, Arabic POLITICAL SYSTEM: presidential
HEAD OF STATE AND GOVERNMENT: President (Col.) Idriss Deby (since Dec '90)
INTERNATIONAL ALIGNMENT: NAM, OAU, ACP, ICO, Francophonie
CURRENCY: CFA franc (end-'90 £1=CFAF491.00, US$1=CFAF254.40)
GNP PER CAPITA: US$160 ('88)
MAIN EXPORT EARNERS: cotton, agricultural products

IN a surprise twist over the first weekend in December, President Hissène Habré abandoned power in Ndjaména, fled to Cameroon and thence to asylum in Senegal. This followed the collapse of the Chad armed forces in the east of the country in the face of an invasion by 2,000 troops of the Mouvement Patriotique du Salut of Idriss Deby, a former close colleague of Habré's who had fled the country following an alleged coup plot in April 1989 (see AR 1989, p. 269). Colonel Deby used Sudan as a base and was supplied with arms and equipment by Libya; the invasion was nevertheless an operation that took military skill. The refusal of the French to listen to President Habré's request for assistance precipitated his departure. Though more than 1,000 French troops were present in Chad, they stayed in their barracks while Colonel Deby's men took the key eastern town of Abéché.

Colonel Deby proclaimed himself President and suspended the constitution which the Habré regime had just introduced. He also dismissed the parliament elected in July, although its speaker, Jean Bawoyeu Alingué (who had acted as head of state between President Habre's flight on 1 December and Colonel Deby's arrival the next day), became Minister of Agriculture. President Deby promised multi-partyism and released political prisoners, although it was later revealed that the outgoing presidential guard had killed 300 political prisoners before departing. Other brutal aspects of the eight-year Habré regime were also made public, such as his torture chambers.

The new regime also released Libyan prisoners of war: some 400 were sent home. Controversially, a further 700 who, it emerged, had been in training at a camp near Lake Chad run by the US Central Intelligence Agency were evacuated first to Nigeria, then to Zaïre, by the Americans. When the Libyans protested, President Deby denied having been consulted, but the action led to a sharp downturn in Chad's relations with Libya. The French, whose troops came in for accusations of complicity in the operation, said that it showed that the new President was 'his own man'. Although other Libyan allies, such as former Chadian leader Goukouni Oueddeye, denied that they were going to oppose the Deby regime, fighting between Chadians and Libyans was reported from the Tibesti area of northern Chad in December. Moreover, the issue of the Aouzou strip, claimed by both Chad and Libya, remained unresolved notwithstanding an agreement between the two sides in August to refer the matter to the International Court of Justice at The Hague.

GABON AND CENTRAL AFRICAN REPUBLIC

Gabon
CAPITAL: Libreville   AREA: 268,000 sq km   POPULATION: 1,100,000 ('88)
OFFICIAL LANGUAGE: French   POLITICAL SYSTEM: presidential
HEAD OF STATE AND GOVERNMENT: President Omar Bongo (since '67)
RULING PARTY: Gabonese Democratic Party (PDG)
CURRENCY: CFA franc (end-'90 £1=CFAF491.40, US$1=CFAF254.40)
GNP PER CAPITA: US$2,970 ('88)
MAIN EXPORT EARNERS: oil and gas, manganese

Central African Republic
CAPITAL: Bangui   AREA: 623,000 sq km   POPULATION: 2,900,000 ('88)
OFFICIAL LANGUAGE: French   POLITICAL SYSTEM: presidential, one-party state
HEAD OF STATE AND PARTY LEADER: President (Gen.) André Kolingba (since '81)
RULING PARTY: Central African Democratic Assembly (RDC)
CURRENCY: CFA franc (end-'90 £1=CFAF491.00, US$1=CFAF254.40)
GNP PER CAPITA: US$380 ('88)
MAIN EXPORT EARNERS: coffee, diamonds, timber

'THE wind from the east is shaking the coconut trees' was how President Bongo of GABON described the wave of democratic protest that swept across Africa in 1990. Gabon was one of the first countries affected, although it did not have a long history of militant political protest. A National Conference in April approved the setting up of a multi-party system, and parliamentary elections were held in September.

Because of massive malpractices, about one-third of the elections were cancelled, and held again at the end of October, producing a National Assembly in which the ruling party, the Parti Démocratique Gabonais (PDG), obtained a slender majority of 62 (including three affiliated independents) against a combined total for the opposition of 55 seats. Twenty of the latter went to the MORENA-Bucherons of Father Mba-Abessole, and 18 to the Parti Gabonais du Progrès (PGP) of Maître Agondjo-Okawe. There was some praise for the way President Bongo handled the situation, in spite of a serious outbreak of rioting in Port-Gentil in May following the death of an opposition parliamentarian. This had led to a brief French military intervention, supposedly to protect French citizens. It was reckoned that the new boom in oil prices following the Gulf crisis would further help President Bongo improve his position.

The regime of President André Kolingba in the CENTRAL AFRICAN REPUBLIC, in power since September 1981, suffered an unstable year, marked by a series of protests against one-party rule. Following serious violent demonstrations in the capital, Bangui, on 13 October, the ruling RDC held a congress at the end of the month. Contrary to expectations, this meeting did not approve the introduction of multi-partyism, but reasserted the single-party vocation of the RDC, claiming that a multi-party system would lead to 'civil war'. Observers expected protests from opposition groups to continue.

CONGO

CAPITAL: Brazzaville AREA: 342,000 sq km POPULATION: 2,100,000 ('88)
OFFICIAL LANGUAGE: French POLITICAL SYSTEM: presidential
HEAD OF STATE AND GOVERNMENT: President (Col.) Denis Sassou-Nguesso (since '79)
RULING PARTY: Congolese Party of Labour (PCT)
PRINCIPAL MINISTERS: Antoine Ndinga Oba (foreign affairs), Pierre Moussa (planning & economy), Edouard Ngakosso (finance), Alphonse Nzoungou (justice)
INTERNATIONAL ALIGNMENT: NAM, OAU, ACP, Francophonie
CURRENCY: CFA franc (end-'90 £1=CFAF491.00, US$1=CFAF254.40)
GNP PER CAPITA: US$910 ('88)
MAIN EXPORT EARNERS: oil and gas, timber

DESPITE its reputation as one of the most volatile countries of francophone Africa, the Congo was not in the vanguard of the democracy movement. It was only after mounting protest from both universities and trade unions, culminating in a national strike at the end of September which paralysed the country, that President Sassou-Nguesso announced immediate permission to create political parties and the calling of a National Conference. This formalized the new situation, as well as abolishing marxism-leninism as the credo of the ruling Parti Congolais du Travail (PCT) and de-linking party from state. By late November political parties had been formed right across the political spectrum.

EQUATORIAL GUINEA

CAPITAL: Malabo AREA: 28,000 sq km POPULATION: 336,000 ('88)
OFFICIAL LANGUAGE: Spanish POLITICAL SYSTEM: military regime
HEAD OF STATE AND GOVERNMENT: Col. Teodoro Obiang Nguema Mbasogo, President of Supreme Military Council (since Aug. '79)
PRINCIPAL MINISTERS: Capt. Cristino Seriche Bioko (Prime Minister), Santiago Eneme Owono (foreign affairs), Metanio Ebendeng Nsomo (defence), Miguel Edjang Angoue (economy, trade & planning), Silvestre Siale Sale Bileka (justice)
INTERNATIONAL ALIGNMENT: NAM, OAU, ACP, Francophonie
CURRENCY: CFA franc (end-'90 £1=CFAF491.00, US$1=CFAF254.40)
GNP PER CAPITA: US$410 ('88)
MAIN EXPORT EARNERS: cocoa, timber, coffee

AT the end of the year this former Spanish colony, consisting of the island of Malabo (formerly Fernando Po) and a mainland territory (Rio Muni) between Cameroon and Gabon, received President Babangida of Nigeria on an official visit. Some saw this as portending a switch in options. After independence in 1968 the country had first experienced 11 years of extreme isolation under the brutal Macias dictatorship, followed under the regime of Teodoro Obiang Nguema Mbasogo by rapprochement with Spain and opening up to France (including membership of the franc zone). The economic situation, although still very difficult, was said to be improving, even to the point of the World Bank considering investment in a scheme for the rehabilitation of cocoa plantations.

In June President Nguema was massively re-elected President as the sole candidate. To demands from exiled politicians for multi-partyism, the President expressed the view that it was not yet the right time. In September a report from Amnesty International said that torture was still 'accepted practice' and that a ban on its use existed 'only on paper'.

VII CENTRAL AND SOUTHERN AFRICA

Chapter 1

ZAÏRE—BURUNDI—RWANDA—GUINEA-BISSAU AND CAPE VERDE—
SÃO TOMÉ & PRÍNCIPE—MOZAMBIQUE—ANGOLA

ZAÏRE

CAPITAL: Kinshasa   AREA: 2,345,000 sq km   POPULATION: 33,400,000
OFFICIAL LANGUAGE: French   POLITICAL SYSTEM: presidential
HEAD OF STATE AND GOVERNMENT: President (Marshal) Mobutu Sese Seko (since '65)
RULING PARTY: Popular Movement of the Revolution (MPR)
PRINCIPAL MINISTERS: Lunda Bululu (first state commissioner), Selemani Muana Yile (deputy first state commissioner, economy, industry and trade), Mushobekwa Kalimba Wa Katana (foreign affairs), Adml. Marua Mudima (defence), Muyabu Nkulu (justice), Bompito Botomba (finance)
INTERNATIONAL ALIGNMENT: NAM, OAU, ACP, Francophonie
CURRENCY: zaïre (end-'90 £1=Z3,610.00, US$1=Z1,870.47)
GNP PER CAPITA: US$170 ('88)
MAIN EXPORT EARNERS: copper, other minerals, oil

HOWEVER autocratic the rule of President Mobutu Sese Seko, Zaïre could not be completely insulated from the winds of change blowing from Eastern Europe. The President was in the 25th year of his rule but his position was far from secure. He was confronted with the extent of his own unpopularity when he undertook a country-wide tour at the beginning of the year to conduct a 'national consultation on the general situation'. Many people spoke up freely or submitted written memoranda remarkable for their frankness. They called for an end to one-party rule and even for the President's resignation.

With his customary adroitness, the President went part of the way to meet these criticisms. In a long-heralded address to the nation on 24 April he announced that the ruling party, the Popular Movement of the Revolution (MPR), would lose its unique status under the terms of a new constitution to be worked out over a one-year transitional period. Henceforth, Zaïre would become a multi-party state, but apart from the MPR only two other parties would be allowed into the political arena. His own position as President would become one 'above politics' as 'arbitrator and last resort'; in what he described as his role as 'guarantor of national unity' he must not be subject to criticism or to the supervision of the legislature.

An extremely strict censorship made it impossible accurately to determine the extent of popular unrest, but there were brief reports of protracted strikes by civil servants, doctors and workers in the copper mining industry, while the universities were clearly centres of dissidence.

On the campus of the country's second largest university at Lubumbashi, the capital of Shaba province, one incident in May was so serious that it could not be kept from the outside world. Trouble started when students discovered police informers disguised as students and beat them up. A few days later a commando unit made up of men from the presidential guard was dispatched from Kinshasa to teach the students a ferocious lesson. On the night of 11–12 May the men, after cutting off the university's electricity, moved on to the campus and killed an uncertain number of students with bayonets, estimates ranging from 50 to 340.

In Belgium (the former colonial power) reports of this massacre provoked an immediate outcry and a demand for an international commission of inquiry, a demand which President Mobutu scornfully rejected. The Belgian government, whose relations with Kinshasa had been extremely strained in 1989 (see AR 1989, p. 273), then announced that it would freeze a new loan to Zaïre, to which the President replied by threatening to expel 700 aid workers. Meanwhile, relations with the United States steadily deteriorated. With the ending of the Cold War, Zaïre lost much of the strategic significance it had been deemed to possess by many influential Americans. There had long been a vociferous body of critics of President Mobutu in Congress, which in November rejected a request from the Bush administration for $3 million of military aid for Zaïre and required that all economic aid should be channelled through non-governmental organizations.

A further humiliation for President Mobutu in the field of international relations came from the Angolan government. Exasperated by what it regarded as Zaïre's double-dealing in continuing to allow UNITA rebels to be supplied from bases on Zaïrean territory while still professing to be a mediator in the Angolan civil war, Angola gradually made it known that it had no further use for President Mobutu's services.

After the 24 April announcement there was considerable activity among opposition groups. However, press restrictions on reports of their deliberations made it unclear how many new groupings would emerge and whether they would fit into the strait-jacket imposed by the President.

The year drew to a close with a serious downturn in the economy. Hyper-inflation set in: in October the exchange rate for the Belgian franc was 25 zaïres; four weeks later it was 60 zaïres. Civil servants abandoned their strike after their salaries had been doubled, but many of them, needing to find more gainful ways of earning a living, simply gave up coming to work. It was reported that the President was recruiting a detachment of South African mercenaries to strengthen his own security. On his increasingly rare visits to Kinshasa, he refused to spend a night on land, returning every evening to his yacht, which was moored upstream. Local wits took to calling him 'Noah': it was clear that the flood waters were steadily rising.

BURUNDI AND RWANDA

Burundi
CAPITAL: Bujumbura   AREA: 28,000 sq km   POPULATION: 5,100,000 ('88)
OFFICIAL LANGUAGES: French, Kirundi   POLITICAL SYSTEM: military regime
HEAD OF STATE AND GOVERNMENT: Maj. Pierre Buyoya, Chairman of Military Council for National Salvation (since Sept. '87)
CURRENCY: Burundi franc (end-'90 £1=FBu314.27, US$1=FBu162.84)
GNP PER CAPITA: US$240 ('88)
MAIN EXPORT EARNERS: coffee, tea

Rwanda
CAPITAL: Kigali   AREA: 26,300 sq km   POPULATION: 6,700,000 ('88)
OFFICIAL LANGUAGES: French, Kinyarwanda   POLITICAL SYSTEM: presidential, one-party state
RULING PARTY: National Revolutionary Movement for Development (MRND)
HEAD OF STATE AND PARTY LEADER: President (Maj.-Gen.) Juvénal Habyarimana (since July '73)
CURRENCY: Rwanda franc (end-'90 £1=RF229.34, US$1=RF118.83)
GNP PER CAPITA: US$320 ('88)
MAIN EXPORT EARNERS: coffee, tea, tin

In BURUNDI President Pierre Buyoya continued to press forward with his policy of allowing greater opportunities to the Hutu majority in a state that had always been dominated by its Tutsi minority (see AR 1988, p. 278, AR 1989, p. 274). For the first time examinations for entry into secondary school, which in the past had formed a barrier to Hutu advancement, could be described as fair and open. But this and other reforms failed to satisfy Hutu extremists, and aroused bitter indignation among Tutsi hardliners. On 13 August the most extreme Hutu group, known as Ubunwe and drawing its membership largely from Hutu refugees in Tanzania, attacked an army base in the south of the country. Another clandestine group, Palipehutu (Party for the Liberation of the Hutu People), began distributing tracts in the capital, Bujumbura. A third, more moderate, group called Frondebu (Burundi Democratic Front) was also formed. Responding to the 'wind from the east', a number of influential Burundians, Tutsi as well as Hutu, began calling for more democracy. But with the army firmly in Tutsi hands, there were clear limitations on the range of reforms a liberal-minded President could introduce.

In early September Pope John Paul II paid his first visit to RWANDA and Burundi. Addressing the diplomatic corps in Rwanda, he appealed for foreign aid 'to assist in the resettlement of those who have still not found a stable environment'. This was a clear reference to those Tutsi refugees, numbering several hundred thousand, who had left Rwanda in the early 1960s and also to the many Hutu who had fled from Burundi to escape the pogroms of 1972. Almost all these displaced persons had found refuge in neighbouring Uganda, Tanzania and Zaïre.

The serious political implications of this situation became apparent less than a month after the Pope's visit. On 1 October a group of Rwandans long resident in Uganda, and mainly but not exclusively Tutsi, launched an invasion of north-eastern Rwanda. This disrupted the political stability enjoyed by Rwanda since President Habyarimana came to power in 1973. The core of the invading force was made up of officers and men who had gained military experience with the guerrilla forces of Uganda's National Resistance Movement. Their leader, Major-General Fred Rwigyema, was an intimate friend of President Museveni of Uganda and had served for a time as deputy defence minister in Kampala, and his spirit of adventurous idealism had earned him the reputation of an African Ché Guevara. However, General Rwigyema was killed in the first days of fighting, and the invaders were unable to penetrate more than 50 miles into Rwanda. Following reports of clashes in the capital (Kigali) between rival factions of the Rwandan army, French legionnaires and Belgian paratroopers were flown in to protect European residents, while a detachment of soldiers also arrived from Zaïre to bolster the Rwandan army's resistance. At the beginning of November there was a flurry of diplomatic activity involving Rwanda's neighbours and the Belgian government, with agreement being reached on the need for a peacekeeping force under the auspices of the Organization of African Unity.

With a population density of 800 to the square kilometre (probably the highest of any country in sub-Saharan Africa) and with population growing at 3.7 per cent per annum, the Rwandan government constantly argued that it lacked the means to absorb refugees. Moreover, in spite of the country's rich soil, there were reports of famine in the south of the country due to declining yields from over-exploitation. Rwanda's economic problems were vastly increased by a fall in the price of coffee, the main source of export earnings. A shortage of foreign exchange meant less money to spend on much-needed artificial fertilizers. Politically, the regime had a reasonably good human rights record, but the President was accused of concentrating more and more power into the hands of family members. The situation at year's end looked confused and threatening.

GUINEA-BISSAU AND CAPE VERDE

Guinea-Bissau
CAPITAL: Bissau   AREA: 36,000 sq km   POPULATION: 940,000 ('88)
OFFICIAL LANGUAGE: Portuguese   POLITICAL SYSTEM: presidential
RULING PARTY: African Party for the Independence of Guinea and Cape Verde (PAIGC)
HEAD OF STATE AND GOVERNMENT: President (Brig.-Gen.) João Vieira (since '80)
CURRENCY: peso (end-'90 £1=PG1255.47, US$1=PG650.50)
GNP PER CAPITA: US$190 ('88)
MAIN EXPORT EARNERS: groundnuts, agricultural products

Cape Verde
CAPITAL: Praia   AREA: 4,000 sq km   POPULATION: 360,000 ('88)
OFFICIAL LANGUAGE: Portuguese   POLITICAL SYSTEM: presidential
RULING PARTY: African Party for the Independence of Cape Verde (PAICV)
HEAD OF STATE AND GOVERNMENT: President Aristides Maria Pereira (since July '75)
CURRENCY: Cape Verde escudo (end-'90 £1=CVEsc125.84, US$1=CVEsc65.20)
GNP PER CAPITA: US$680 ('88)
MAIN EXPORT EARNERS: cashew nuts, fish

RELATIONS between GUINEA-BISSAU and Senegal, strained for many years over a dispute about the demarcation of territorial waters, were given a new twist in May when a clash took place between border guards and Senegalese forces engaged in a hot pursuit of Casamance separatists (see p. 266). In November the country's first Vice-President, Colonel Iafai Camara, was reported to be under house arrest, accused of supplying arms to Casamance separatists. In September the central committee of the ruling PAIGC issued a document setting out the broad lines for a transition to a multi-party constitution.

In CAPE VERDE, President Aristides Pereira told a congress of the ruling PAICV at the end of July that he was giving up his position as party leader as a first step to ending 15 years of one-party rule. On 28 September the National Assembly revoked the clause in the constitution that guaranteed the PAICV's unique status and so set in motion changes designed to lead to free elections early in 1991.

In January Pope John Paul II visited Cape Verde which, with 90 per cent of the population baptized Roman Catholics, could claim to be the most Catholic country in Africa.

SÃO TOMÉ & PRÍNCIPE

CAPITAL: São Tomé   AREA: 965 sq km   POPULATION: 119,000 ('88)
OFFICIAL LANGUAGE: Portuguese   POLITICAL SYSTEM: presidential
RULING PARTY: Movement for the Liberation of São Tomé and Príncipe (MLSTP)
HEAD OF STATE AND GOVERNMENT: President Manuel Pinto da Costa (since July '75)
PRINCIPAL MINISTERS: Celestino Rocha da Costa (Prime Minister), Carlos da Graça (foreign affairs), Raul Bragança Neto (defence and security), Agapito Mendes Dias (economy and finance), Francisco Fortunado Pires (justice)
INTERNATIONAL ALIGNMENT: NAM, OAU, ACP
CURRENCY: dobra (end-'90 £1=Db291.08, US$1=Db150.82)
GNP PER CAPITA: US$490 ('88)
MAIN EXPORT EARNERS: cocoa, copra

KEEPING pace with the trend in other former Portuguese colonies, President Manuel Pinto da Costa announced that a referendum to endorse a multi-party constitution would be held on 22 August. The referendum gave a majority of 72 per cent in favour of abandoning one-party rule. Only 3.5 per cent opposed the change, the remainder of the electorate leaving ballot papers blank or failing to vote. With the government laying stress on the importance of tourism, the islands began to attract an increasing number of foreign visitors.

MOZAMBIQUE

CAPITAL: Maputo   AREA: 800,000 sq km   POPULATION: 15,900,000 ('90)
OFFICIAL LANGUAGE: Portuguese   POLITICAL SYSTEM: presidential
HEAD OF STATE AND GOVERNMENT: President Joaquim Chissano (since Nov '86)
RULING PARTY: Front for the Liberation of Mozambique (Frelimo)
PRINCIPAL MINISTERS: Mario da Graça Machungo (Prime Minister, planning), Pascoal Mocumbi (foreign affairs), Lt.-Gen. Alberto Joaquim Chipande (defence), Manuel António (interior), Abdul Magid Osman (finance), Ossmane Ali Dauto (justice)
INTERNATIONAL ALIGNMENT: NAM, OAU, ACP, Comecon (observer)
CURRENCY: metical (end-'90 £1=Mt 2,016.16, US$1=Mt1,044.64)
GNP PER CAPITA: US$100 ('88)
MAIN EXPORT EARNERS: sea food, cashew nuts, tea

IN 1989 the Frelimo government discreetly turned its back on its long-proclaimed ideology of marxism-leninism (see AR 1989, p. 277). In 1990 the process of change was taken further with the adoption of a new constitution that allowed for the transition from a one-party to a multi-party state.

The wide-ranging debate at many different levels of society which the government believed necessary before such fundamental changes could be legitimized began in January when President Joaquim Chissano unveiled the draft constitution at a public meeting in central Maputo. At this stage the President was clearly not in favour of a multi-party system. Six months later he had changed his mind after a national debate had shown that, while most people were still prepared to accept one-party rule, an appreciable minority wanted a multi-party democracy. At the end of July the Frelimo politburo agreed unanimously to accept a multi-party system. There followed a heated debate, first in the party's central committee, then in the National Assembly, before the new constitution was finally accepted at the end of November.

In drawing up the new constitution, the Frelimo leadership was reported to have been strongly influenced by the recent constitutional changes in Algeria (see AR 1989, pp. 234–5), a country with which many cadres had developed close ties during Mozambique's struggle for independence. The new constitution, a 74-page document, changed the country's name from 'People's Republic' to 'Republic of Mozambique', guaranteed freedom of the press and the right to strike, and established the independence of the judiciary and the separation of powers. Political parties would be legally registered and allowed to operate so long as they enjoyed the support of at least 100 people in each of the country's 11 provinces. Parties of a separatist, discriminatory or anti-democratic nature, or formed along ethnic or religious lines, were specifically forbidden. The country's economic order was defined as being based 'on the importance of labour, on market forces, on the initiative of economic agents, on the participation of all types of ownership and on action by the state as a regulator and promoter of economic and social development'.

The changes went almost all the way to meet the demands of the rebel National Resistance Movement (MNR, or Renamo), and President Chissano made a point of stressing that the MNR would be able to operate freely as a political party, provided that it laid down its arms. This statement was made at the end of July only two weeks after the first formal meeting between Frelimo and MNR representatives. The meeting had required months of patient mediation by the Kenyan and Zimbabwean governments and took place in the headquarters of a Catholic charity in Rome. After a number of further meetings, it was announced on 1 December that agreement had been reached on a partial ceasefire: Zimbabwean forces in Mozambique were to be withdrawn to the two railway lines connecting Zimbabwe with the sea, lines which the MNR pledged itself not to attack. Both sides also agreed not to disrupt the operations of aid agencies.

Even while these negotiations were taking place, the war continued with little abatement. In some areas the rebel forces were reported to have disintegrated into 'anarchic bands of teenage bandits who terrorize the peasants with torture, murder and rape'—a development which led observers to question whether the MNR leadership could ever impose a ceasefire on all those who claimed to be their supporters. In the central provinces government forces with strong backing from Zimbabwean contingents were reported to have achieved considerable success, regaining control of some of the most fertile areas. Further north, in Nampula province, a locally-organized militia known as Naprama cleared substantial areas of MNR guerrillas by purely peaceful means. Its leader, Manuel Antonio, claimed to have risen from the dead and to have acquired knowledge of a magic plant that conferred invulnerability against modern firearms. In the south, on the other hand, the rebels were strong enough to cause regular damage to the power lines carrying electricity to Maputo from South Africa. In February they derailed a train near the South African border and killed 66 passengers, many of them migrant workers returning from South Africa.

With pervasive insecurity hampering plans for economic recovery, the situation was rendered more desperate by a decline in the volume of international aid. In December a World Bank report estimated that half the country's 16 million people were facing starvation or serious deprivation. Distress was worst in remote rural areas, forcing many peasants to move into camps for displaced persons or to seek refuge in neighbouring Malawi, Zimbabwe or South Africa. But life was increasingly difficult in the major towns: rapid price rises—in part brought about by the IMF-inspired austerity programme (see AR 1987, p. 269)—led to unprecedented strikes in Maputo early in the year, affecting almost all salaried workers.

Exports, mainly prawns and cashew nuts, were worth $93 million in 1989 compared with $239 million in 1982. To exports could be added invisible earnings, such as port and rail dues and migrant workers' remittances. But the cost of servicing the country's debt was three times the value of its exports and invisible earnings, so that the country was facing a deficit on its current account of more than $1,000 million a year, which could be met only by aid inflows and debt relief. Thus in many ways Mozambique's situation in 1990 looked as appallingly bleak as ever. Free elections were due to be held in 1991. At the year's end the country's fate depended on the outcome of the negotiations between the government and rebels over a countrywide ceasefire.

ANGOLA

CAPITAL: Luanda   AREA: 1,247,000 sq km   POPULATION: 9,400,000 ('88)
OFFICIAL LANGUAGE: Portuguese   POLITICAL SYSTEM: presidential
HEAD OF STATE AND PARTY LEADER: President José Eduardo dos Santos (since '79)
RULING PARTY: Popular Movement for the Liberation of Angola—Workers' Party (MPLA-PT)
PRINCIPAL MINISTERS: Lt.-Col. Pedro de Castro Van-Dúnem 'Loy' (external relations), Kundi Paihama (security), Col.-Gen. Pedro Maria Tonha 'Pedalée' (defence), Augusto Teixeira de Matos (finance), António Henriques da Silva (planning), Zeferino Cassa Yombo (petroleum and energy), Fernando José França Van-Dúnem (justice)
INTERNATIONAL ALIGNMENT: NAM, OAU, ACP, Comecon (observer)
CURRENCY: kwanza (end-'89 £1=Kw58.23, US$1=Kw30.17)
GNP PER CAPITA: US$470 ('88)
MAIN EXPORT EARNERS: oil, coffee, diamonds

AT the end of 1989 the prospects for peace in a country that had been affected by war for close on three decades seemed as uncertain as ever. The hopes for peace inspired by the June 1989 'historic handshake' between President dos Santos and his arch-enemy, Dr Jonas Savimbi (see AR 1989, p. 279), had been dashed almost as soon as they had been raised. Early in 1990 MPLA and rebel Unita forces were engaged in some of the heaviest fighting of the 15-year-long civil war. But by the end of the year talks about a ceasefire had been resumed, and this time there seemed to be a reasonable chance of a successful outcome.

The main area of military operations was once again the centre and south-east of the country. Government forces, lavishly supplied with sophisticated Soviet weaponry but without the support of the Cubans, who were busy withdrawing from Angola, launched a massive attack on the key town of Mavinga. By early February the town was in government hands, although its strategically vital airstrip had been rendered unusable. With the onset of the rainy season in April, however, it proved impossible to send adequate supplies to MPLA forces in forward positions. Meanwhile, Unita was receiving a steady flow of American equipment air-lifted from Zaïre and so was strong enough to counter-attack and recapture Mavinga in early May. Both sides were reported to have suffered heavy casualties.

Many other parts of the country were also exposed to Unita guerrilla activity. In January Cuban soldiers were killed in an action north of Lobito; in retaliation, the Cubans, who had already withdrawn 31,000 of their 50,000 troops from Angola, halted further movements for several weeks. In the capital, Luanda, there were constant incidents involving urban guerrillas, while Unita was also active in the northern and central provinces. But the battering both sides had received in the battle for Mavinga led them once again to raise the issue of a ceasefire. This time there was to be no 'African diplomacy' as in 1989. President Mobutu, who had made no attempt to prevent the CIA from using the base of Kamina in western Zaïre to send military aid to Unita, was discredited as a mediator in the MPLA's eyes. Instead, the Portuguese government helped to bring the two sides together, the first of a series of meetings taking place in Portugal in June.

The two superpowers were also keenly interested in an Angolan ceasefire. A rare insight into Soviet thinking was provided by an article of exceptional frankness published in the Moscow weekly, *Literary Gazette*, in August. 'Why are we in Angola at all?', asked the writer, Vladislav Yanelis. The conflict had produced 'a caste of people for whom war is a means of self-assertion and prosperity'—a jibe at the MPLA elite and their 'luxurious villas'. Soviet equipment, much of it supplied free of charge (including 600 tanks and 60 fighter planes sent in 1989), was largely wasted through poor maintenance or theft. Soviet officers were exasperated with the cowardice and incompetence of the Angolan army and deeply wounded by the many slights and insults to which they were constantly exposed. An equally jaundiced view of the Angolan war came from a very different source. In a book published in South Africa, one of the best-known South African military officers, Colonel Jan Breytenbach, depicted Unita as a cowardly and ineffective movement constantly having to be rescued by the South African army. Critical voices were also to be heard in the US Congress over the aid supplied to Unita. After long debate the $60 million requested by the administration was only approved with the proviso that aid should cease once the two sides had agreed a ceasefire.

In December the Angolan situation was discussed at the meeting in Houston between the US and Soviet Foreign Ministers. Mr Shevardnadze later met Dr Savimbi in Washington, the first formal meeting between the Unita leader and a prominent member of the Soviet government. The Americans and Russians were reported to have drawn up a peace plan for Angola involving a ceasefire, free elections and a halt on arms supplies to both sides.

By this time the MPLA had come round, with evident reluctance among many party activists, to accept the necessity of abandoning one-party rule. The party's third congress, meeting behind closed doors in Luanda in December, voted for a two-stage reform of the constitution to inaugurate a multi-party system by April 1991.

The urgent need for a ceasefire was stressed in every report on the economic and social state of the country. There were reckoned to be close on 2 million people in southern Angola suffering from a famine brought about by a combination of drought and war. But attempts by United Nations and other aid agencies to bring relief were constantly hampered by bureaucratic obstruction, whether from government officials or from Unita agents in rebel-dominated territory. Another issue which deeply worried some observers was the widespread distribution of firearms, many of them left behind by the retreating Cubans. In these circumstances the chances of achieving a stable state of law and order, an essential precondition for effective development, seemed as doubtful as ever.

Chapter 2

ZAMBIA—MALAWI—ZIMBABWE—NAMIBIA—BOTSWANA—
LESOTHO—SWAZILAND

ZAMBIA

CAPITAL: Lusaka   AREA: 750,000   POPULATION: 7,600,000 ('88)
OFFICIAL LANGUAGE: English   POLITICAL SYSTEM: presidential
HEAD OF STATE AND GOVERNMENT: President Kenneth Kaunda (since Oct '64)
RULING PARTY: United National Independence Party (UNIP)
PRINCIPAL MINISTERS: Gen. Malimba Masheke (Prime Minister), Gen. Benjamin Mibenge (foreign affairs), Alex Shapi (security), Lt.-Gen. Hannaniah Lungu (defence), Gibson Chigaga (finance & planning), Gen. Kingsley Chinkuli (home affairs), Frederick Chomba (legal affairs)
INTERNATIONAL ALIGNMENT: NAM, OAU, ACP, Cwth.
CURRENCY: kwacha (end-'90 £1=K88.66 US$1=K45.94)
GNP PER CAPITA: US$290 ('88)
MAIN EXPORT EARNERS: copper, zinc, cobalt

FOR many Zambians, responding to the winds of change blowing both from South Africa and Eastern Europe, the year was one of political reawakening. President Kaunda, on the other hand, found himself faced with the most serious challenge to his authority in all his 26 years of rule. The year ended on a note of deep uncertainty about the country's political future.

The first sign of change came in late February when Nelson Mandela, recently freed from his long imprisonment, visited Lusaka, the headquarters of the South African ANC. His talk of freedom and democracy struck a responsive chord among Zambians restive under their President's mildly authoritarian rule and increasingly critical of his evident inability to bring any amelioration to the country's longstanding economic malaise. Sensing the new mood, the President made it known in May to the national council of the ruling United National Independence Party (UNIP) that a referendum on the issue of multi-party democracy would be held later in the year. He stressed, however, that he himself was strongly opposed to any deviation from one-party rule, and party activists began denouncing those pressing for change as 'drug-traffickers, misfits and malcontents'. At the same meeting the President also announced that some state-run enterprises would be privatized.

Privatization was one of the economic policies being urged on Zambia by the IMF and other donors of aid. So too was a gradual reduction of official subsidies on food. Accordingly, on 19 June the President announced a steep increase in the price of maize meal, most Zambians' staple food: the price of a 25 kg bag, enough to feed an average family for two weeks, rose from 114.50 to 269 kwacha. The impact of this increase on low-paid workers, many of whom could not expect to earn more than about 160 kwacha a week, was extremely painful. Inevitably, news of the increase led to panic buying, protest marches and threats of strike action. But the situation only took on a serious political dimension when on 25 June students of the University of Zambia in Lusaka, long a centre of dissidence, decided to stage a march on State House, the President's residence and office. The demonstration, in which the students were joined by shanty-town dwellers, turned into a riot after the march had been checked by the security forces. The rioters looted state-run shops in central Lusaka, from where the disturbances spread to some towns on the Copperbelt. By 29 June order had been restored and the university, which had been stormed by parliamentary forces, closed down. By then at least 27 people had been killed, some allegedly falling victim to vigilante groups of irate Indian shopkeepers. As a modest concession, the President announced that the referendum on multi-party democracy would be held on 17 October.

A strange twist to events occurred on the early morning of 30 June when listeners to Lusaka radio heard a young army officer announce—and repeat at regular intervals over four hours—that a military coup had taken place and the President overthrown. This announcement brought crowds out onto the streets in a mood of euphoric celebration, but their rejoicing, deeply indicative as it was of the President's unpopularity, was premature. It soon became apparent that the 'coup' was a complete fabrication, invented by a very small group of young soldiers. Nevertheless, the President was sufficiently alarmed by the incident to dismiss his army commander the next day and filled the vacant post of Defence Minister with a trusted appointee.

By early July calm had been restored, but UNIP's opponents felt the time was propitious to form themselves into a coherent organization, which took the name Movement for Multi-Party Democracy (MMD). Its first meeting in Lusaka was attended by former cabinet ministers, trade union leaders, businessmen, lawyers, academics and clergy. President Kaunda accused the advocates of pluralism of having 'unleashed the forces of hate' and announced that the referendum on multi-party democracy would be postponed until August 1991. But he tempered this apparent hardening with an amnesty under which all political prisoners, including those arrested for their part in the June disturbances, were released. Among those freed was Lieut.-General Christon Tembo, whose trial for high treason (see AR 1989, p. 283) was still in progress and whom some of the June demonstrators looked to as a leader to replace Mr Kaunda.

In September the President decided that it would not be necessary after all to hold a referendum on multi-party democracy. Instead, as members of the MMD had already pointed out, all that was needed was an amendment to the constitution. Accordingly, on 30 November the necessary legislation was unanimously passed by the Zambian parliament, and it was announced that elections would take place before October 1991. The year ended with President Kaunda confidently asserting that he 'enjoyed fighting' and with much speculation about the MMD's capacity to hold together. Political analysts reckoned that, of the country's nine provinces, five were anti-government, three neutral and only Eastern province a sure stronghold for UNIP.

By 1990 Zambia's official debt had reached $7,200 million, equivalent to $1,000 per capita, the highest figure for any country in sub-Saharan Africa. In July Zambia's creditors, meeting in Paris, agreed to provide $500 million in aid in the course of the coming year, $50 million more than the sum indicated at a preliminary meeting of donor countries in April. Donors were reported to have been encouraged by the Zambian government's willingness to allow multi-party elections.

MALAWI

CAPITAL: Lilongwe   AREA: 118,500 sq km   POPULATION: 8,000,000 ('88)
OFFICIAL LANGUAGE: English   POLITICAL SYSTEM: presidential, one-party state
HEAD OF STATE AND PARTY LEADER: President Hastings Kamuzu Banda (since '66)
RULING PARTY: Malawi Congress Party (MCP)
PRINCIPAL MINISTERS: Maxwell Pashane (without portfolio), Louis Chimango (finance), Robson W. Chirwa (trade & industry)
INTERNATIONAL ALIGNMENT: NAM, OAU, ACP, Cwth.
CURRENCY: kwacha (end-'90 £1=MK5.03, US$1=MK2.61)
GNP PER CAPITA: US$170 ('88)
MAIN EXPORT EARNERS: tobacco, tea, sugar

TOTALLY unmoved by the mood of change affecting so many African countries, Life President Dr Hastings Kamuzu Banda maintained his reputation as the continent's odd-man-out. In May the President, widely thought to be now in his nineties, reshuffled his cabinet, retaining four portfolios, including those of justice and external affairs, for himself. Under such a regime talk about political pluralism was clearly treasonable. Given the extremely rigorous censorship and the unwillingness of Malawians to talk freely, it was impossible for outsiders to gain an accurate notion of internal politics, which one internal critic described as being 'so Byzantine' that even Malawians could not understand what was happening. However, it was widely believed that more and more power was accruing to the President's 'official hostess', Cecilia Kadzamira, and her uncle, John Tembo.

Two highly critical reports on the state of human rights in Malawi appeared during the year. The first, issued by the US State Department, spoke of a deteriorating situation and referred to 'life-threatening conditions in prisons, lack of fair trials, interference with privacy, severe restrictions of freedom of speech and press, assembly and government and serious discrimination against northerners'. These allegations were repeated in a lengthy and detailed report issued by the human rights organization Africa Watch. The personality cult of President Banda was likened to that of Kim Il Sung in North Korea or of the late Nicolae Ceauşescu in Romania. The report gave details of a long series of political assassinations, one of the latest victims being Mkwaptira Mhango, a journalist and human rights monitor who died when his house in Lusaka was petrol-bombed in November 1989. Attention was drawn to an incident in Lilongwe in March in which 20 people, protesting against the failure of the authorities to investigate a particular murder, were shot dead by the police. No mention of this incident appeared in the local press and the country's one resident foreign correspondent had been expelled the previous month.

Another disturbing report, brought out with assistance from the Malawian government, was published by UNICEF. The report pointed out that Ethiopia was the only African country with levels of child malnutrition comparable to those in Malawi. Aid workers reported extraordinarily high levels of child mortality and of stunted growth among the survivors due to malnutrition. Such facts called in question the alleged success of Malawi's structural adjustment programme, which had won high praise from the IMF in the 1980s and been held up as a model for other African countries. New aid programmes stressed the need to ensure that aid, whether in the form of fertilizers, marketing facilities or credit, actually reached peasant farmers and small traders.

ZIMBABWE

CAPITAL: Harare   AREA: 390,000 sq km   POPULATION: 9,300,000 ('88)
OFFICIAL LANGUAGE: English   POLITICAL SYSTEM: presidential
HEAD OF STATE AND GOVERNMENT: President Robert Mugabe (since Dec '87, previously Prime Minister)
RULING PARTY: Zimbabwe African National Union—Patriotic Front (ZANU-PF)
PRINCIPAL MINISTERS: Simon Muzenda (Vice-President), Joshua Nkomo (Vice-President), Didymus Mutasa (senior minister, political affairs), Bernard Chidzero (senior minister, finance, planning & development), Nathan Shamuyarira (foreign affairs), Emmerson Munangagwa (justice), Richard Hove (defence)
INTERNATIONAL ALIGNMENT: NAM, OAU, ACP, Cwth.
CURRENCY: Zimbabwe dollar (end-'90 £1=Z$5.09, US$1=Z$2.64)
GNP PER CAPITA: US$650 ('88)
MAIN EXPORT EARNERS: tobacco, gold, cotton

As Zimbabwe entered its second decade of independence on 18 April, the last constitutional restraints imposed by the Lancaster House settlement of 1979 (see AR 1979, p. 257) fell away. A general election at the end of March produced a landslide victory for the ruling ZANU-PF party and set the scene for the establishment of a one-party state. At the end of the year Zimbabwe remained in theory a multi-party democracy, but President Mugabe and his ZANU-PF government appeared even more deeply entrenched than at its start.

The general election, the third since independence, was held on 28–30 March. ZANU-PF took 116 out of 120 contested seats. Two constituencies were won by the opposition Zimbabwe Unity Movement (ZUM), established in 1989 by former ZANU dissident Edgar Tekere (see AR 1989, p. 285), and one by the near-defunct ZANU-Ndonga party of Ndabaningi Sithole. Some 54 per cent of the electorate voted, with ZANU-PF winning just over 80 per cent of the votes cast. In the presidential contest held at the same time, President Mugabe polled 2,026,976 votes to Mr Tekere's 413,840. Mr Mugabe described his victory as an endorsement of the government's 'thrust for national unity'. The ZUM director of elections, Emmanuel Magoche, maintained that despite its poor showing the opposition had been able to 'expose the system to the ants for them to gnaw away at it'.

The election campaign was marred by outbreaks of violence and accusations of government intimidation. The most serious incident was the shooting, on 24 March, of the ZUM opponent of Vice-President Simon Muzenda in the Midlands constituency of Gweru. Also noticed, particularly by visiting journalists, was a spirit of 'widespread apathy' among voters. ZANU-PF election rallies were poorly attended, including that on 4 March in Rufaro stadium in Harare at which Nelson Mandela, on his first foreign visit since his release from prison in South Africa, launched the party's campaign. The smooth return to peace after the election was, however, a factor in the government's decision in July to revoke the state of emergency legislation, renewed as recently as 17 January. The legislation, continuously in force for 25 years, provided for indefinite detention without trial and had been so used by successive administrations.

The composition of the new 150-member House of Assembly reflected constitutional changes agreed in October 1989. With the abolition of the Senate, a proportion of that chamber was transplanted to the lower house. In addition to eight provincial governors and 10 members chosen by the traditional chiefs, 12 seats were filled by personal nomination of the President. Among this number were several members of the new cabinet, announced on 9 April. It included three white ministers, namely Denis Norman (transport and national supplies) and Chris Anderson (mines), both members of earlier post-independence cabinets, and Dr Timothy Stamps, a Harare general practitioner, who joined the government as Minister of Health. (Later in the year Mr Mugabe made a further high-ranking white appointment when Tony Gubbay was named Chief Justice following the retirement of Justice Enoch Dumbutshena.) Joshua Nkomo, leader of the opposition ZAPU party until its fusion with ZANU-PF in December 1989 (see AR 1989, p. 287), was reappointed senior minister in the President's office. On 6 August, following the passage of appropriate legislation, he was made a Vice-President, alongside Mr Muzenda.

The scale of ZANU-PF's parliamentary majority prompted moves towards major constitutional change. The Constitution of Zimbabwe Amendment (No 10) Bill, passed on 28 June, began the process of 'constitutional independence' from the Lancaster House restraints. However, Mr Mugabe's proposal to introduce one-party rule encountered opposition from the Catholic Commission for Justice and Peace which, in a major advertisement in the Harare *Herald*, argued that such a system 'ends up benefiting chiefly the people already entrenched'. Press reports in August suggested that a majority within the ruling party's own politburo also opposed the plan. Government statements later in the year deliberately distanced Zimbabwe from the failing model of East European single-party systems and stressed that a new political structure would not be imposed, but come about through popular vote.

Another controversial issue was that of land reform, a matter of increasing urgency in view of the rapid growth of the country's population. In November the government tabled a constitutional amendment empowering expropriation of land or buildings for resettlement at a 'fair' price and without resort to the courts. The clear intention was the nationalization of 13 million acres of farmland, much of it in white ownership, for redistribution to a million landless black peasants. But the dominating need for private investment, foreign and local, to provide jobs for the rising number of Zimbabwe's unemployed, was expected to take precedence over any expropriation policy.

As in previous years, the most articulate opposition to the government came from students at the University of Zimbabwe and from white-collar trade unions. A government ban on student participation in the workers' May Day celebration in Harare led to protests and to the denunciation, by the student representative council, of 'one-man one-party dictatorship'. A bill extending government control over the university was tabled on 12 October and led to campus demonstrations and pitched battles between students and police. Even the university vice-chancellor, Professor Walter Kamba, whose own powers were widened by the bill, appealed to the government to reconsider the legislation. Within the civil service, industrial action was firmly checked. In May a nationwide strike of schoolteachers, campaigning for improved salaries and conditions, led to the dismissal of 1,000 of the strikers. The dismissals were reversed, however, following an appeal to the High Court by the teachers' union.

The year saw a major redirection of the country's economy. Acknowledging that controls imposed since 1962 had progressively retarded economic growth, the senior Minister of Finance, Economic Planning and Development, Dr Bernard Chidzero, announced an economic reform policy concurrently with his budget speech on 26 July. Six weeks later he gave details of the first phase of trade liberalization, consisting of the removal of import controls on a limited range of commodities, a relaxation of price controls and markedly increased export incentives. The inevitable effect of these measures, together with the continued decline of the Zimbabwean dollar, and the increased costs of fuel occasioned by the Gulf crisis, was to push the rate of inflation above 25 per cent for the year. The 1990 budget was notable also for a commitment to reduce the country's budget deficit, running at more than 9 per cent of GNP. To this end Dr Chidzero announced plans for the ending of state subsidies to parastatals and a reduction in the size of the public service by 25 per cent over three years. The political administration remained overmanned, however, with 56 of the 150 MPs being either ministers, deputy ministers or provincial governors.

The 1989–90 rainy season was uneven, but satisfactory harvests in most areas provided food for those stricken by drought. Agriculture remained the greatest employer of labour and the highest earner of foreign currency. Increasing rural unemployment, however, resulted in a drift to the towns, leading to pressure on urban housing, the appearance of shanty dwellings and a sharp increase in the rate of urban crime. Crime against persons rose by 15 per cent in the year; property-related crime rose by 9 per cent. Car theft in particular reached epidemic proportions.

The incidence of AIDS continued to cast a shadow over the future of the country. In October the Minister of Health reported that an estimated 350,000 Zimbabweans were infected with the HIV virus, 17,500 of them suffering from full-blown AIDS.

NAMIBIA

CAPITAL: Windhoek AREA: 824,000 sq km POPULATION: 1,550,000 ('89)
OFFICIAL LANGUAGES: Afrikaans, English POLITICAL SYSTEM: presidential democracy
HEAD OF STATE: President Sam Nujoma (since March '90)
RULING PARTY: South West Africa Peoples' Organization (SWAPO)
PRINCIPAL MINISTERS: Hage Geingob (Prime Minister), Theo Ben Gurirab (foreign affairs), Peter Mueshihange (defence), Andimba Toivo ja Toivo (mines & energy), Hifikepunje Pohambe (home affairs), Ngarikutuke Tjiriange (justice), Otto Herrigel (finance)
INTERNATIONAL ALIGNMENT: NAM, OAU, SADCC, Cwth.
CURRENCY: South African rand (end-'90 £1=R4.94, US$1=R2.56)
GNP PER CAPITA: US$1,700 ('88)
MAIN EXPORT EARNERS: minerals

NAMIBIA, previously known as South West Africa, became independent on 21 March when the South African flag was lowered for the last time. A German possession until World War I, the country was Africa's last colony, and had been administered by South Africa under a League of Nations mandate. Its status after World War II was the subject of a long-drawn-out dispute between South Africa and the international community.

Independence, which came under the auspices of a United Nations peacekeeping force and transition team, followed a ceasefire in the protracted campaign of guerrilla insurgency fought by the South West Africa Peoples' Organization (SWAPO) against the occupying power. A liberal democratic constitution, providing for multi-party government, a bill of rights and an independent judiciary, was approved by the Constituent Assembly, elected in November 1989 (see AR 1989, p. 288).

Speaking in Windhoek at the independence ceremony, President F. W. de Klerk of South Africa said that Namibian independence marked the beginning of a new era for the whole southern African region. Namibia's first President, SWAPO leader Sam Nujoma, chose a pragmatic politician, Hage Geingob (48), who was chairman of the Assembly, to be the country's first Prime Minister.

President Nujoma, in his first speeches after independence, called for foreign and particularly South African investment in Namibia, stressing the need for rapid economic growth. He noted that the country had inherited a crippling debt of R 1,200 million from the previous administration. In July the Namibian chamber of commerce welcomed the budget presented by the Finance Minister, Otto Herrigel, as 'good and realistic'.

Pursuing an issue which could trouble relations with South Africa, Namibia's deputy Justice Minister, Vekuli Rokoro, accused Pretoria of lacking the political will to extradite to Namibia members of its clandestine special forces following the assassination of SWAPO lawyer Anton Lubowski. Mr Lubowski had been murdered at his own front door in circumstances suggesting political assassination. The case against an Irish mercenary, Donald Acheson, had to be dropped after two co-accused and four key state witnesses failed to appear. The High Court found there was insufficient evidence for the case to proceed.

Another issue between Pretoria and Windhoek which had yet to be resolved was the status of the port of Walvis Bay, a South African enclave which the United Nations had recognized as an integral part of Namibia.

Reports of banditry in the northern Ovambo region marred the first months of independence. There were clashes between police and former members of the pre-independence combatant groups who had failed to gain entry into the new Namibian Defence Force.

BOTSWANA

CAPITAL: Gaborone   AREA: 580,000 sq km   POPULATION: 1,200,000 ('88)
OFFICIAL LANGUAGE: English   POLITICAL SYSTEM: presidential democracy
HEAD OF STATE AND GOVERNMENT: President Quett Masire (since July '80)
RULING PARTY: Botswana Democratic Party (BDP)
PRINCIPAL MINISTERS: Peter Mmusi (Vice-President, local government & lands),
   Gaositwe Chiepe (external affairs), Festus Magae (finance & planning), Patrick
   Balopi (home & labour)
INTERNATIONAL ALIGNMENT: NAM, OAU, ACP, Cwth.
CURRENCY: pula (end-'90 £1=P3.60, US$1=P1.86)
GNP PER CAPITA: US$1,010 ('88)
MAIN EXPORT EARNERS: diamonds, copper-nickel, beef

BOTSWANA's economy continued to boom in 1990. In February the Bank of Botswana said the country's total export earnings had increased by 32 per cent in dollar terms in 1989 compared with 1988. The increase was ascribed to increased diamond exports. In his budget speech, the Minister of Finance and Planning, Festus Magae, disclosed the highest surplus yet recorded, but he warned that non-mineral revenues would for the first time in 10 years be insufficient to finance recurrent expenditures.

It was announced that the French motor company Peugeot was to invest $20 million in an assembly plant in Botswana, which would have the capacity to assemble 150 vehicles a week from kits shipped from France.

The 1990 summit of the Southern African Development Coordination Conference (SADCC) was held in August in Gaborone, marking the organization's tenth anniversary. The President of Botswana and chairman of the summit, Dr Quett Masire, delivered the keynote speech. The conference noted that a future democratic South Africa was expected to join the organization and to enhance regional efforts at arresting economic decline.

In the course of a state visit to newly-independent Namibia, Dr Masire announced that Botswana had plans for a rail link to Walvis Bay, once the status of this contested enclave had been resolved. He told a press briefing in Windhoek that good relations between Botswana and Namibia could be mutually beneficial. A road link to Gobabis in eastern Namibia was under construction.

As part of a campaign to build bridges between business in the region, the National African Chamber of Commerce and Industry (NAFCOC), an organization of black-owned South African concerns, was represented at Botswana's annual industrial trade show at Gaborone, displaying products manufactured by 14 black-owned South African firms.

LESOTHO

CAPITAL: Maseru AREA: 30,300 sq km POPULATION: 1,700,000 ('88)
OFFICIAL LANGUAGE: English, Sesotho
POLITICAL SYSTEM: monarchy, under military rule
HEAD OF STATE: King Letsie III (since Nov '90)
HEAD OF GOVERNMENT: Maj.-Gen. Justin Lekhanya, Chairman of Military Council (since Jan '86)
PRINCIPAL MINISTERS: Chief Evaristus Retselisitsoe Sekhonyana (finance), Tom Thabane (foreign affairs), Kgotsi Matete (interior), A. K. Maope (justice)
INTERNATIONAL ALIGNMENT: NAM, OAU, ACP, Cwth.
CURRENCY: maloti (end-'90 £1=M4.94, US$1=M2.56)
GNP PER CAPITA: US$420 ('88)
MAIN EXPORT EARNERS: diamonds, wool

IN February King Moeshoeshoe II was stripped of his powers by Lesotho's military ruler, Major-General Justin Lekhanya, and summarily deposed. This followed the king's refusal to approve changes in the administration which had been proposed by General Lekhanya.

Earlier, General Lekhanya had detained three members of the ruling Military Council, namely Colonel Thaabe Letsie (foreign affairs), Colonels Sekhobe Letsie and Khetang Mosoeunyane. Colonel Monyane Mokhantso, the Minister of Transport, was also held. The four men were believed to be supporters of King Moeshoeshoe. General Lekhanya said the action against them was aimed at ending insubordination in the military, preventing possible interference in judicial investigations and improving the conduct and coherence of Lesotho's foreign policy.

When King Moshoeshoe refused to accept the appointment of three new members of the Military Council to replace those in detention, General Lekhanya suspended the executive and the legislative powers of the king, who went into exile in Britain.

In his first public comment on the affair, King Moshoeshoe said that the close ties between the military regime in Maseru and the South

African government had led to attempts by the Lekhanya government to muzzle him because of his support for the South African liberation movements. He added that he believed his expulsion was prompted in particular by his insistence that General Lekhanya should step down during investigations into the latter's shooting of a student in 1988. Supporting the establishment of a commission of inquiry into corruption in government, he accused the military of frustrating efforts to establish democratic structures in Lesotho.

In July a Constituent Assembly was convened, including members of the opposition parties which had been banned by the military regime. In his speech to the Assembly, General Lekhanya indicated that the military were ready to return to their barracks after elections scheduled for 1992.

SWAZILAND

CAPITAL: Mbabane   AREA: 17,350 sq km   POPULATION: 735,000 ('88)
OFFICIAL LANGUAGE: English, Siswati   POLITICAL SYSTEM: monarchy
HEAD OF STATE AND GOVERNMENT: King Mswati III (since April '66)
PRINCIPAL MINISTERS: Obed Mfanyana Dlamini (acting Prime Minister), Sir George Mamba (foreign affairs), Sibusiso Barnabas Dlamini (finance), Senzenjani Tshabalala (interior), Zonke Khumalo (justice)
INTERNATIONAL ALIGNMENT: NAM, OAU, ACP, Cwth.
CURRENCY: emalangeni (end-'90 £1=E4.94, US$1=E2.56)
GNP PER CAPITA: US$810 ('88)
MAIN EXPORT EARNERS: sugar, agricultural products

PRIME Minister Obed Mfanyana Dlamini announced that he would seek a mandate from King Mswati III to investigate the possibilities for reform of the indirect electoral system. At a free-speech people's forum called by the king, this system was strongly criticized, notably on the grounds that people became members of parliament without their knowledge or participation. The system was also under attack at a symposium at the University of Swaziland at which the speakers included Dr Ambrose Zwane, who had not spoken in public since the suspension of the independence constitution in 1973.

In August the King's nephew, Prince Mfanasibili, was served with a detention order within minutes of being acquitted in the High Court on charges of treason. He was accused of plotting to overthrow the king, but the prosecution witnesses were described by the presiding judge as a 'parade of villains'. Observers attributed the prosecution to a royal (Dlamini) family power struggle.

Swaziland faced a new refugee problem when more than 7,000 people from the Natal province of South Africa fled across its borders from the violence which continued throughout the year between followers of the Inkatha movement and of the ANC/UDF alliance. There were already 80,000 refugees from Mozambique in Swaziland.

Chapter 3

SOUTH AFRICA

CAPITAL: Pretoria   AREA: 1,220,000 sq km   POPULATION: 34,000,000 ('88)
OFFICIAL LANGUAGES: Afrikaans and English   POLITICAL SYSTEM: presidential, under white minority rule (democracy for whites, partial representation for coloureds and Asians)
HEAD OF STATE AND GOVERNMENT: President F. W. de Klerk (since Sept '89)
RULING PARTY: National Party (NP)
PRINCIPAL MINISTERS: Roelof F. Botha (foreign affairs), Gen. Magnus A. Malan (defence), Gerrit van N. Viljoen (constitutional development), Barend J. du Plessis (finance), Gene Louw (home affairs), Kobie Coetsee (justice)
CURRENCY: rand (end-'90 £1=R6.58, US$1=R3.41)
GNP PER CAPITA: US$2,290 ('88)
MAIN EXPORT EARNERS: precious and base metals, minerals

THE movement away from apartheid which began in tentative fashion in 1989 (see AR 1989, pp. 292–6) gained momentum and appeared to become irreversible in 1990. President F. W. de Klerk unbanned the African National Congress (ANC), the Pan Africanist Congress (PAC) and the South African Communist Party (SACP), released Nelson Mandela from prison and began discussions with Mr Mandela and his colleagues to open the way to a negotiated settlement. By mid-year the ANC had agreed to suspend the armed insurgency against the Pretoria government which had begun in 1961. By the end of the year most of the obstacles to negotiation had been overcome. The stage seemed set for substantive negotiations to start in the first half of 1991. Yet it was evident that the transition from apartheid to non-racial democracy would be turbulent. As violent resistance directed against the state waned, there was a resurgence of factional violence in the black community and a disquieting incidence of right-wing terrorism on the part of die-hard whites. On all sides, it seemed, there were elements which would continue to rely on the use of force and would resist a negotiated settlement.

On 2 February President de Klerk, opening parliament, stunned conservative whites in not only unbanning the ANC and the PAC, which had been declared prohibited organizations at the time of the Sharpeville emergency in 1960, but in also removing the 40-year-old restrictions on the SACP. He declared a moratorium on executions, relaxed media and emergency regulations and announced the release of persons who had been gaoled on account of their membership of banned organizations. The season of violence was over, he said, and the time for reconciliation and reconstruction had come. He committed his government to work for a negotiated solution based on universal franchise and respect for human rights.

Then on 11 February Mr Mandela, a prisoner for 27 years, was released from Victor Verster prison at Paarl, and given an ecstatic welcome by a crowd of 50,000 gathered on the Grand Parade, Cape Town. His first speeches, in Cape Town and Soweto, calling for intensification of all forms of pressure on the South African government, were unfavourably received by the financial markets, which were disturbed by his apparent commitment to nationalization of the gold mines, banks and dominant financial institutions. Subsequent speeches and statements were more reassuring, suggesting that the ANC's economic policies would be more pragmatic than ideological, and accepting the need for rapid economic growth as a prerequisite of a more equitable distribution of wealth in South Africa.

Violence did not recede. As the old order of Verwoerdian apartheid collapsed, the long-running battle for political turf between Chief Mangosuthu Buthelezi's Zulu-based Inkatha movement and supporters of the pro-ANC United Democratic Front continued to take a fearsome toll of lives in Natal and in the self-governing territory of KwaZulu. On 25 February Mr Mandela addressed an appeal for peace to the belligerents, urging them to throw their weapons into the sea. In spite of his appeal, and similar calls by Chief Buthelezi, the violence continued unabated. There were insistent complaints that elements in the security forces were siding with the Inkatha impis.

There was also a disquieting measure of unrest and violence in the nominally independent homeland territories—the ramshackle showpieces in the constitutional legacy of apartheid. In Transkei a pro-ANC officer, General Bantu Holomisa, had already installed a military government after a coup and relations with Pretoria were deteriorating. In neighbouring Ciskei more than 50 people were killed, shops looted and factories destroyed in arson attacks as the unpopular President Lennox Sebe, seen as an upholder of the apartheid regime, was ousted. In Bophuthatswana five people were shot dead and many injured in clashes between police and dissidents in the township of Ga-Rankuwa. In a bloodless coup in Venda the defence force chief, Colonel Ramushwana, took over the leadership of the country. There was also violence and disorder in the self-governing territories of Lebowa and Gazankulu.

Meanwhile, preparations for the first top-level meeting between the ANC executive and the Pretoria government were going ahead, including the granting of amnesty to ANC leaders in exile to enable them to take part. Renewed clashes between police and people in the townships of the Vaal triangle prompted the ANC to call a halt to preliminary discussions after 18 people were shot dead and more than 400 were injured in police action against a protest march in Sebokeng near Vereeniging, south of Johannesburg. The ANC demanded an inquiry. Discussions were not resumed until President de Klerk had announced the appointment of a judicial commission to investigate the shootings. On 5 April Mr Mandela and President de Klerk agreed to go ahead with the proposed meeting on 2–4 May at Groote Schuur, near Cape Town.

Although available to President de Klerk much earlier, it was not until September that the report of the commission of inquiry was published. In it Mr Justice Goldstone upheld the ANC's complaints, castigating the police at Sebokeng as 'trigger-happy' and saying the officers in charge lacked discipline and coordination. He said the force used by the police was 'immoderate and disproportionate to any lawful object'. Of the 281 people shot, he said, 127 had been shot from behind. Only a few stones had been thrown and there was no credible evidence to suggest that the police could have been in fear of their lives or personal safety.

At the beginning of May formal talks about talks duly took place at Groote Schuur between delegations led by President de Klerk for the government and Mr Mandela for the ANC. Both sides hailed the meeting as successful. A joint working committee was set up to deal with the release of political prisoners and the return of exiles. The goal was to resolve difficulties about the definition of political prisoners and to meet criticism by the ANC that the return of exiles was being delayed by uncertainty over their status. The ANC agreed that it would work towards the resolution of violence and intimidation, from whatever quarter. The agreement was set out in a document which became known as the 'Groote Schuur minute'.

President de Klerk was now welcome in world capitals. Following the example of Mr Mandela earlier in the year, he set out on a nine-nation tour of Europe, lobbying for the removal of international sanctions against South Africa, just as Mr Mandela, in his turn, had lobbied for their retention. On 9 May Mr Mandela again set off on a political mission abroad, this time on a 12-day, six-country visit to African capitals. With both leaders abroad, violence continued on the home front. The joint government-ANC working group was due to present a draft agreement on the release of prisoners when 11 black protestors were shot dead at Thabong, near the Orange Free State mining town of Welkom. Mr Mandela warned President de Klerk that there could be no negotiations unless the country's police force was brought under control and the 'massacre of blacks' was ended.

Right-wing white resistance to President de Klerk's policy of negotiation was building steadily. On 14 April right-wing radicals had raided the Pretoria headquarters of the South African Air Force and made off with an arsenal of small arms, automatic weapons and ammunition; on 13 May more weapons were stolen from a South African Defence Force (SADF) armoury. In the following months two offices of President de Klerk's National Party (NP) were attacked with bombs, apparently planted by right-wingers, and there were other such incidents. Police posted a R50,000 reward for information leading to the arrest of right-wing activist Piet 'Skiet' Rudolph, a leader of the extremist Boerestaat Party who was suspected of involvement in bomb incidents. On 26 May Dr Andries Treurnicht, leader of the Conservative Party, largest of the white opposition parties, addressed a mass meeting of 60,000 ultra-rightists at the Voortrekker Monument, outside Pretoria, and declared that Afrikaner conservatives would, if necessary, use armed force to defend their right to a 'white fatherland'. In various conservative parts of the country, and notably at Welkom on the Free State goldfields, right-wingers were arming and forming vigilante groups under the leadership of the AWB (Afrikaner Resistance Movement) and other organizations, purportedly for self-defence. Two white mine employees and 14 black miners were killed in mid-May in an outbreak of inter-racial violence on the President Steyn gold mine at Welkom. On 9 June the Welkom offices of the (black) National Union of Mineworkers were damaged by a bomb.

Meanwhile, intense diplomatic activity continued over the sanctions issue, with Mr Mandela again travelling in Europe, Africa and North America to urge the international community, having come so far, to hold the line on sanctions until the ANC gave the word. At a London meeting in July Mr Mandela and Mrs Thatcher agreed to differ on the question of sanctions but exchanged views in a cordial atmosphere. Mr Mandela's US tour was described as a triumph. He was given a ticker-tape welcome in New York, addressed both houses of Congress and was entertained to lunch by President Bush. Yet he infuriated some sections of public opinion by making friendly references to the Palestine Liberation Organization, Yassir Arafat and Colonel Qadafi of Libya.

On 8 August the Pretoria government and the ANC leadership met again in formal session and recorded major progress. The most significant step forward at this meeting was the ANC's decision to suspend the 'armed struggle' and work for a climate favourable to negotiation. The agreements reached were set out in the so-called 'Pretoria minute'. The parties accepted the final report of the working group on the release of ANC-related prisoners and the granting of indemnity to exiles, adopting guidelines to be applied and setting up structures to consider individual cases. The date set for completion of the whole exercise was 30 April 1991. The ANC agreed that 'no further armed actions or related activities' by the ANC or its military wing would take place. The government agreed to continue its review of security legislation and its application to ensure free political activity.

However, it was clear at a post-conference press briefing that the ANC remained acutely concerned about police violence. Mr Mandela said it was evident that the government had not succeeded in restraining police actions. 'The government had either lost control of the police or the police are doing what the government wants them to do', he said. It appeared that the ANC in fact believed that the government had lost control of the police while the government, for its part, was by no means convinced that Mr Mandela could control the forces on his side. Yet the talks ended on a friendly note and were clearly a success, advancing the date of substantive negotiations.

Within weeks the process was in jeopardy again. In an outbreak of communal violence of unprecedented intensity in the black townships of the Transvaal, 500 people died in a matter of days. It appeared that the ANC-Inkatha power struggle was spreading north out of Natal with redoubled fury. But there was also evidence to suggest that a third force of mystery gunmen was deliberately stoking the flames of factional animosity, presumably in the hope of wrecking the chances of a negotiated settlement. Although both Chief Buthelezi and Mr Mandela called repeatedly for peace no meeting between them could be arranged as a signal to their followers to put away their weapons. Both seemed powerless to stop the violence and both lost considerable face as a result. Complaints of police partiality or the involvement of elements in the clandestine arm of the security forces on the side of Inkatha now became the key issue. A delegation of the South African Council of Churches led by Archbishop Desmond Tutu handed President de Klerk a bulky dossier containing allegations of misconduct by the security forces.

The question of the death squads was likewise unresolved. This was a legacy of the Botha presidency, when the clandestine arm of the security forces had appeared to enjoy a free hand in combating the ANC and its allies at home and abroad. There had been a series of mystery assassinations, car bombings and attacks on trade union and church premises. Public demand for an inquiry became irresistible after disclosures in the weekly journal *Vrye Weekblad*; a sustained investigation by the Johannesburg daily newspaper, *The Star*, left little doubt that something was seriously amiss. After hesitating for some months, President de Klerk appointed Mr Justice Harms to preside over a commission of inquiry, but its terms of reference were severely circumscribed, being limited to political killings on South African soil.

The inquiry did not bring much significant new information to light. Critical documentary records of an SADF undercover group—the quaintly-named Civil Cooperation Bureau (CCB)—became mysteriously unavailable when called for by the judge. Public opinion concluded that the inquiry was being frustrated by a well-orchestrated cover-up at a high level in the SADF. The commission exonerated the South African police of running death squads as such, although it pointed to criminal offences on the part of the police. The SADF, on the other hand, was severely criticized in the commission's report, which said that the CCB had contaminated the whole security arm of the state, ignoring orders by the SADF chief to cooperate with the commission and treating requests for information by parliament, the auditor-general and the commission itself with contempt. Mr Justice Harms conceded that his inquiry had failed to restore public confidence in the security arm of the state. Observers noted that the long list of assassinations of opponents of the Pretoria government, and other violent acts against liberals and radical individuals and organizations, remained unsolved and the perpetrators unpunished. There was dismay when President de Klerk accepted the Harms report and exonerated the Minister of Defence, General Malan, of political responsiblity.

In December both the de Klerk government and the ANC held meetings to take stock. The President and his cabinet withdrew to a Bushveld retreat for several days. Subsequent statements by President de Klerk indicated that the movement towards negotiation was on track as far as he was concerned. His end-of-the year message and other speeches expressed a determination to eradicate political violence. But confidence in his ability to do so had been shaken. The President was particularly concerned about violent intimidation directed at black policemen and black leaders running local government in the black townships. Although the ANC had launched a mass campaign to force the closure of the unpopular, inefficient and sometimes corrupt local councils, its leaders denied that the campaign included the illegal use of force and insisted on their right to mobilize electoral support in this fashion. When he received an honorary doctorate at the University of Cape Town in December, Mr Mandela appealed to ANC supporters to refrain from all kinds of violence.

The ANC gathering—a consultative conference held in Johannesburg—was the organization's first mass-based representative meeting on South African soil since its unbanning. The leadership was taken aback by the militancy of rank-and-file delegates and the outspoken criticism of the national executive committee. The ANC's ailing president, Oliver Tambo, had just returned after three decades in exile. He was well-briefed on changing international attitudes on sanctions against South Africa and, seeking to preempt a diplomatic setback, appealed for a reappraisal of the ANC's position on sanctions. This was brushed aside by the conference, which demanded that sanctions stay in place. While the conference was in session, the European Community, following an earlier unilateral decision by the Thatcher government in Britain, withdrew its ban on new investment in South Africa while retaining other sanctions for the time being. It was evident that international sanctions against South Africa were crumbling. Yet the conference was determined on having its own way and there was an insistence that the leadership should become more accountable to the ordinary membership. In spite of the militancy of the youth and other sections of the ANC's domestic constituency, the dominant figure at the conference was Mr Mandela, who reasserted his personal ascendancy in forceful interventions in the proceedings. In spite of reservations expressed from the floor, Mr Mandela insisted that he would continue his confidential meetings with President de Klerk in the interests of advancing the negotiation process.

At the end of the year the process was still on track but the country was in the grip of economic recession, with 30 or 40 per cent unemployment among the newly-urbanized black masses living in squatter settlements around the big cities. A quick constitutional settlement seemed imperative to restore investor confidence so that economic growth and development could be resumed. While constitutional agreement was seen as attainable in negotiation between the de Klerk and Mandela leadership groups, it was not yet clear how far they would be able to take their followers with them. It was likewise not clear how soon South Africa would outgrow political violence in favour of democratic government and respect for the law.

VIII SOUTH ASIA AND INDIAN OCEAN

Chapter 1

IRAN—AFGHANISTAN

IRAN

CAPITAL: Tehran AREA: 1,650,000 sq km POPULATION: 54,900,000 ('90)
NATIONAL LANGUAGE: Farsi (Persian) POLITICAL SYSTEM: Islamic republic
RELIGIOUS LEADER: Ayatollah Seyed Ali Khamenei (since June '89)
HEAD OF STATE AND GOVERNMENT: President (Hojatolislam) Hashemi Ali Akbar Rafsanjani (since July '89)
OTHER SENIOR LEADERS: Hossain Moussavi (presidential adviser), Hassan Ebrahim Habibi (Vice-President), Seyed Mohajerani (Vice-President, legal and parliamentary affairs), Massoud Roghani Zanjani (Vice-President, planning and budget), Reza Amrollahi (Vice-President, atomic energy), Mansour Razavi (Vice-President, state employment), Mehdi Manafi (Vice-President, environment), Hassan Ghafurifard (Vice-President, physical education), Ayatollah Mehdi Karrubi (Speaker of Majlis)
PRINCIPAL MINISTERS: Ali Akbar Velayati (foreign affairs), Gholamreza Agazadeh (oil), Abdollah Nouri (interior), Mohsen Nourbakhsh (economic affairs and finance), Hojatolislam Ismail Shostari (justice)
INTERNATIONAL ALIGNMENT: NAM, OPEC, ICO
CURRENCY: rial (end-'90 £1=Rls.124.80 US$1=Rls64.66)
GNP PER CAPITA: US$3.625 ('87)
MAIN EXPORT EARNERS: oil and gas, carpets

THE process of ending the Iran-Iraq war of 1980–88 began on Iraq's initiative in the immediate wake of its invasion of Kuwait on 2 August. By 16 August a formal statement had been issued by Iraq accepting Iranian conditions for a final peace, thereby conceding the Thalweg delimitation defined in the 1975 Algiers accord on the disputed boundary on the Shatt al-Arab waterway. All prisoners of war were to be released by both sides without condition. Iraq agreed to withdraw from all Iranian territory occupied during the war, following which the two former belligerents were to create a demilitarized zone along the entire length of the frontier. By end-1990 the only Iranian demand not conceded by the Iraqi government was war reparations, estimated at more than $300,000 million by Iran.

Iraq's invasion of Kuwait was condemned by the Iranian authorities, who promised to apply UN sanctions against Iraq by interdicting commercial goods (other than drugs and medicines) and banning imports of Iraqi oil. The Iranian Foreign Minister, Ali Akbar Velayati, stated that the geopolitical changes introduced into the Persian Gulf area by the Iraqi invasion of Kuwait were unacceptable to Iran; both he and President Hashemi Rafsanjani demanded the withdrawal of Iraq. Rapid deployment of US and allied armed forces in the Arabian peninsula and the Gulf in the second half of 1990 evinced a mixed response in Tehran. Iran's interests would be served by the expulsion of Iraq from Kuwaiti territory and so its spokesmen did not specifically complain about the allied military deployment except to criticize the government of Saudi Arabia for permitting non-Muslim troops on the same soil as the holy places of Mecca and Medina. Foreign Ministry sources, reinforced by the President and by a majority of Majlis deputies, made it clear that they wished for a rapid withdrawal of US and other foreign forces from the region once the crisis had been resolved.

Iranian relations with the United Kingdom were restored after a break of 20 months following a joint announcement in New York on 27 September by Mr Velayati and Douglas Hurd, the British Foreign Secretary. Iran made no concessions in the arrangement but the British side constrained the effect of the agreement by sending to Tehran a seven-man diplomatic group headed by a chargé d'affaires. Full normalization of links awaited a resolution of the Salman Rushdie affair (see AR 1989, pp. 35, 298, 493–4, 538), the release of Roger Cooper from prison in Tehran and the freeing of British hostages in Lebanon.

In the Middle East and North Africa Iran was active in developing relations with several countries. Diplomatic ties were restored with Tunisia in September; an economic cooperation council with Turkey and Pakistan was rehabilitated; and extended transport links were established with both Turkey and Oman. The Syrian President, Hafiz al-Asad, visited Tehran in September, improving bilateral relations and ensuring that Iran's restoration of peace with Baghdad did not adversely affect its alliance with Damascus. The Iranian authorities also maintained good relations with the USSR despite the crisis in Azerbaijan and the Soviet southern republics (see pp. 109–10). Some 160 Majlis deputies sent a letter to President Gorbachev on 23 January calling for even-handed treatment of Muslim subjects in the USSR. Spring saw the beginning of exports of natural gas to the southern USSR, and Iran continued to give general support to Soviet policies in Afghanistan. An Iranian delegation made formal contact with the European Community in Dublin on 16 May, though no agreements were reached at that time.

The year was one of marked internal political change. President Rafsanjani consolidated his position in October during the selection of candidates for the Council of Experts, which supervised the political system. The great majority elected to the 83-member Council were supporters of the President and of Ayatollah Khamenei, the country's religious guide; the more radical Islamic groups were left with little representation. The President also drew strength from the ending of the confrontation with Iraq on Iranian terms. In the second half of the year rising oil revenues gave the government a greater ability to import consumer goods for the populace and capital items for development. Organized political opposition declined perceptibly, as the Mujahideen Khalq rebels based in Iraq lost the support of the Iraqi regime. Some disquiet was felt concerning rapid population growth, estimated at more than 3 per cent in 1990, which brought total numbers to close to 55 million.

The northern Iranian provinces of Gilan and Zanjan were struck by a severe earthquake registering 7.3 on the Richter scale on 21 June. Possibly as many as 25,000 persons were killed and there was widespread damage to property, including the destruction of the towns of Majil and Rudbar. Entire villages in the higher Elburz mountain basins were wiped out. Rescue efforts were prompt and efficient in the larger towns, though some isolated village settlements went unassisted for some time. A remarkable circumstance arising from the effects of the earthquake was Iran's appeal for, and use of, foreign aid, which was donated generously in goods and services, particularly by the West. Opposition to acceptance of foreign material and personnel by radical Islamic groups was overcome by the arguments of the President, and the open-handedness of the international donors, in a way that much reinforced his standing in the country at large.

Oil production averaged 3.4 million barrels per day (b/d) in the January-June period, up by 9.2 per cent on the first half of 1989. The Iraqi invasion of Kuwait on 2 August caused the oil price to rise and gave the National Iranian Oil Company (NIOC) the opportunity to increase output to an average of approximately 3.1 million b/d for the year as a whole, including exports of 2.4 million b/d. Reconstruction of the war-damaged Kharg Island terminal was put in hand in June, while refinery building to add 450,000 b/d capacity began at Bandar Abbas and Arak. Some $2,000 million was allocated by the NIOC for the rehabilitation of the offshore oil zone and an ambitious programme to lift domestic consumption of natural gas was started. Iranian oil reserves were put at 92,900 million barrels.

A buoyant oil sector meant that Iran's general economic performance and prospects improved during 1990 as a whole despite a poor first six months in which inflation remained at more than 30 per cent, unemployment exceeded 2 million and the currency was devalued. Income from oil exports rose rapidly from mid-year and was expected to amount to over $20,000 million for the year as a whole. A campaign to increase non-oil exports had modest success and produced an income of some $1,000 million for the year.

Government spending rose on the strength of improved income, favouring investment projects in the oil and petrochemical industries and in electricity generation. Foreign exchange became more available to the bazaar and the private sector which, helped by a move away from state control of trade, enjoyed a good business year. Only agricultural production performed sluggishly, though individual farm incomes rose. Merchandise imports increased to an estimated $17,500 million, resulting in greater availability of goods in the market and ensuring adequate supplies of subsidized basic foods and medicines for the less-privileged portion of the population. A new five-year development plan was under formulation at the end of 1990, offering the prospect of better-ordered economic development in the future.

AFGHANISTAN

CAPITAL: Kabul   AREA: 650,000 sq km   POPULATION: 15,000,000 ('88 est.)
OFFICIAL LANGUAGES: Pushtu, Dari (Persian)   POLITICAL SYSTEM: presidential
HEAD OF STATE AND GOVERNMENT: President Mohammed Najibullah (since Nov '87, previously Chairman of Revolutionary Council)
RULING PARTY: Homeland Party
PRINCIPAL MINISTERS: Fazl Haq Khaleqiar (Prime Minister), Abdol Wahed Sorabi (deputy premier, planning), Abdol Wakil (foreign affairs), Maj.-Gen. Mohammed Aslam Watanjar (defence), Mohammed Hakim (finance), Raz Mohammed Paktin (internal affairs), Gholam Mahaynodin Darez (justice)
INTERNATIONAL ALIGNMENT: NAM, ICO, Comecon (observer)
CURRENCY: afghani (end-'90 £1=Af99.25, US$1=Af51.42)
GNP PER CAPITA: US$168 ('82)
MAIN EXPORT EARNERS: agricultural products

PRESIDENT Najibullah, who had survived in office despite the withdrawal of Soviet troops in 1989 (see AR 1989, p. 300), also surmounted an attempt by his Defence Minister to depose him by a coup in March. He responded by further broadening the political basis of his government and ending the entrenched constitutional status of the ruling People's Democratic Party of Afghanistan (PDPA), whose name was changed in June. Towards the end of the year UN-sponsored efforts to get substantive peace talks going with moderate elements within the anti-government mujahideen guerrilla movement appeared to make some progress in Geneva.

The coup attempt was mounted on 6 March by Lieut.-General Shahnawaz Tanay, who as Defence Minister had strong support in the armed forces, where his hard-line Khalq ('masses') faction of the PDPA opposed the more moderate line of the President's Parcham ('flag') wing. As many as 200 civilians and an unknown number of soldiers died in subsequent heavy fighting, before the rebels were crushed by loyal troops. Lieut.-General Tanay (with his family and close supporters) fled by helicopter across the Pakistan border, although he was later reported to have joined a mujahideen group inside Afghanistan. According to the Kabul regime, the coup attempt had been backed by the Pakistani secret service and also by the fundamentalist Hezb-e Islami mujahideen group led by Gulbuddin Hekmatyar.

The new Defence Minister, Major-General Mohammed Aslam Watanjar, was another Khalqi, and the divisions between the rival factions had subsided sufficiently by early May for President Najibullah to be able to lift the state of emergency which had been in force since the Soviet withdrawal. On 6 May a non-PDPA regional governor, Fazl Haq Khaleqiar, was appointed Prime Minister in succession to Sultan Ali Keshtmand (who was elevated to First Vice-President), the new government line-up containing a majority of independent or non-party ministers. Moreover, constitutional amendments adopted by a Loya Jirga (assembly of tribal leaders) on 28–29 May brought in a pluralist party system and deleted the references in the 1987 constitution to the PDPA's leading role. A month later a PDPA congress signalled the government's aspiration to national reconciliation by renaming the ruling formation the Homeland Party, of which President Najibullah was unanimously elected chairman.

In the guerrilla war mujahideen forces registered their first major success since the Soviet departure when the Hezb-e Islami captured the key town of Tarin Kot in central Afghanistan on 3 October. Fortified by this victory, Mr Hekmatyar then concluded a Pakistan-sponsored agreement with his main fundamentalist rival in the mujahideen, Ahmed Shah Massud of the northern-based Jamaat-e Islami. The so-called Islamabad accord set out a new strategy for overthrowing the Kabul government and envisaged the holding of elections in the 'liberated' northern provinces of Afghanistan early in 1991.

Faced with this militant challenge, the government stepped up its efforts to reach a peace settlement with the more moderate mujahideen groups. In November President Najibullah himself travelled to Geneva for UN-sponsored talks with undisclosed opposition representatives, a meeting which he described as 'a cornerstone' for ending the civil war. He also spoke positively about a 'new US attitude' to the conflict, apparently in reference to recent congressional moves to reduce US aid to the mujahideen. That the peace process remained delicate, however, was shown by the unwillingness of the principal moderate mujahideen leaders to confirm their participation in the talks.

In an interview with *The Independent* newspaper of London on 5 December, President Najibullah gave some details of the 'understanding' he claimed to have reached the previous month in Geneva, although he refused to name the opposition factions involved on the grounds that this would 'undermine' current contacts. He said that he had asked the guerrilla leaders to join a 'transitional council' which would enforce a total ceasefire and then steer Afghanistan towards democratic elections under UN auspices. Once a formal pact had been concluded, explained the President, UN advisers would be asked to ensure that 'no force interferes with the job of the transitional council', whose powers would 'surpass' those of his own government. In particular, the council would control both government and guerrilla forces and would distribute UN aid to the estimated 5 million refugees who would return to the country.

President Najibullah claimed in the same interview that his government had already made peace with two-thirds of the mujahideen military commanders, who were expected to agree a formal ceasefire on condition only that they could retain their militias until elections were held. However, objective observers took the view that with the militant Hezb-e Islami and Jamaat-e Islami groups both refusing any compromise with the Kabul regime, the prospects for a meaningful peace settlement remained problematical to say the least.

Chapter 2

INDIA—PAKISTAN—BANGLADESH—SRI LANKA—NEPAL—BHUTAN

INDIA

CAPITAL: New Delhi   AREA: 3,287,000 sq km   POPULATION: 815,600,000 ('88)
OFFICIAL LANGUAGES: Hindi, English   POLITICAL SYSTEM: parliamentary democracy
HEAD OF STATE: President Ramaswamy Venkataraman (since July '87)
RULING PARTIES: Janata Dal faction, with Congress (I) support
HEAD OF GOVERNMENT: Chandra Shekhar, Prime Minister (since Nov '90)
PRINCIPAL MINISTERS: Devi Lal (deputy premier, agriculture), V. C. Shukla (external
   affairs), Yaswant Sinha (finance), Subramanian Swamy (commerce, law & justice)
INTERNATIONAL ALIGNMENT: NAM, SAARC, Cwth.
CURRENCY: rupee (end-'90 £1=Rs34.30, US$1=Rs17.77)
GNP PER CAPITA: US$340 ('88)
MAIN EXPORT EARNERS: precious stones, textiles, tea, tourism

FOR many in India the year began with new hope, generated by a new government headed by a man, V. P. Singh, who had proclaimed and promised a new era of clean value-impregnated politics. The year ended with a different coalition government in office in New Delhi, the intervening months having in several respects been the most troubled and traumatic since independence in 1947. During the year India's many personalities frequently appeared to clash simultaneously: Hindu versus Muslim; upper caste versus lower; urban elites versus rural masses; peripheral peoples and territories versus heartland; South Asian preoccupations and tensions versus wider concerns and compulsions.

Caste and communal conflicts dominated the national scene, attaining greater significance even than threats of secession in Punjab, Kashmir and Assam and the dismal condition of the economy. In the second half of the year mounting caste strife, triggered by Mr Singh's belated decision to reserve more civil service jobs for lower castes and inflamed by the bitter Ayodhya controversy (see AR 1989, p. 303), combusted to produce spiralling violence and to force a change of the central government. Particular indications of the scale and range of turmoil included the extension of President's rule in Jammu and Kashmir (July) and in Punjab (April and October) and the imposition of President's rule in Assam (November) and Goa (December). In Assam government forces mounted 'Operation Bajrang' against would-be secessionists of the ULFA.

Internationally, it was a year of some moments of marked unease in Indo-Pakistan relations over Kashmir (see p. 317) but generally of mildly improving South Asian relationships. On the wider international scene, India watched warily as great changes took place throughout Eastern Europe and the Soviet Union—the latter having been one of India's closest diplomatic friends over the past 20 years or so. Otherwise, the most significant international negotiations for India were the continuing Uruguay Round of the GATT. India's interests and the chemistry of the GATT discussions cast the government as the prinicpal exponent of the case for concentrating on trade in goods, with the United States being the principal advocate that the negotiations should also integrally embrace the burgeoning world trade in services, patents and intellectual property. The Prime Minister of Japan, Toshiki Kaifu, visited New Delhi at the end of April. On 1 November India was elected as a non-permanent member of the UN Security Council for 1991.

India's politics were thrown into turmoil and deepening crisis from August onwards as politicians and citizens reacted angrily and often violently to the government's decision to implement the Mandal Commission's recommendations on the reservation of additional public sector jobs for members of lower castes. The commission, set up in 1978 and headed by B. P. Mandal, had reported to parliament in early 1982 and had called for 27 per cent of jobs in government services to be reserved for some 3,750 castes identified as socially or educationally backward classes (SEBCs). This allocation would be additional to the 22.5 per cent already reserved for scheduled castes and tribes. The Mandal commissioners pointed out that the SEBCs comprised over half of India's population, but the Supreme Court had ruled earlier that total reservations should not exceed 50 per cent of public service jobs. The Mandal report had been shelved by successive Congress (I) governments during the 1980s.

Mr Singh's announcement in early August that the Mandal recommendations were to be fully implemented triggered protests, demonstrations, acts of immolation and public unrest across the whole northern 'Hindu belt', from Gujarat in the west to Bihar in the east. In southern India, where the population was predominantly low caste, there was much support for the Prime Minister's proposal. By the end of September, however, an anti-Singh faction within the Janata

Dal had gathered around the Prime Minister's arch-rival, Chandra Shekhar. Further, Devi Lal, the controversial former deputy prime minister whose power base lay amongst the peasant farmers of Haryana and who had been dismissed from the cabinet in August, now seized the opportunity to rally opposition to the government. The Hindu revivalist Bharatiya Janata Party (BJP,) on whose parliamentary support the minority National Front government depended, also increasingly attacked Mr Singh's handling of the issue.

The controversy over implementing the Mandal report combined and combusted with mounting communal tensions arising from the 'temple-mosque' dispute at Ayodhya in Uttar Pradesh, where Hindu militants led by the Vishwa Hindu Parishad (VHP) sought to construct a temple on the site of the disused Babri Masjid mosque. In September the BJP leader, L. K. Advani, embarked on a much-publicized mass march to the site. His arrest in Bihar on 23 October was the occasion for the BJP to withdraw its support for Mr Singh's government, whose parliamentary strength then swiftly ebbed away. On 7 November it lost a vote of confidence in the Lok Sabha (lower house) by 346 votes to 142, with eight abstentions. Mr Singh resigned and was replaced by his old adversary, Chandra Shekhar, who secured the 'outside' support of Rajiv Gandhi's Congress (I) for the formation of a government by his small band of dissidents from Janata Dal.

On 16 November the newly-installed minority government passed its first parliamentary test by surviving a vote of confidence. It was the most politically diminutive administration ever to receive endorsement from an Indian parliament. On the day of the vote the new government comprised just two people with named offices, Chandra Shekhar himself and Devi Lal as his deputy. Five days later the Prime Minister had cobbled together more of his team, which consisted almost entirely of renegades from the Janata Dal party. The new government was swiftly sworn in by President Venkataraman on the morning of 21 November, shortly before Chandra Shekhar rushed off to the Maldives to attend a summit meeting of the South Asian Association for Regional Cooperation (SAARC).

The new 32-member government consisted of 13 full ministers, 15 ministers of state, and four deputy ministers. Among the prominent new ministers were V. C. Shukla, who had held several portfolios in early Congress regimes (and had leapt to international fame or notoriety during Mrs Gandhi's emergency of 1975–77) as well as A. K. Sen and Rao Birendra Singh, both veterans of the Congress era. Controversial figures in the second tier included Maneka Gandhi, the estranged sister-in-law of Rajiv Gandhi, and Sanjay Singh, a relation of V. P. Singh. The small Jharkhand Mukti Morcha party gained two representatives in the ministry. Half the Janata Dal breakaway MPs who had sided with Chandra Shekhar received ministerial positions, four of the new appointees being without previous ministerial experience at either central or state level. Few could have had much optimism about the longevity of the new government, which took office with the formal support of only 63 MPs in the 545-member Lok Sahha.

For the first time since independence India had acquired a Prime Minister who had never before held a government office—one who became the first to hold the portfolios of industry, home, defence and information simultaneously. Aged 63, Mr Shekhar had been described as 'an intellectual backwoodsman' and by other, less flattering, sobriquets. Until November 1990 he had seemed to be a perennial loser in Indian politics as well as one of its most complex and contradictory performers. Contemplative, often ill at ease on public occasions and possessed of a keen social conscience, he had served a spell in gaol during Mrs Gandhi's emergency rather than endorse her draconian measures. He was also, however, an ambitious politician who had been deeply resentful of the way he had been publicly out-manoeuvred when Mr Singh obtained the premiership after the November 1989 general election (see AR 1989, p. 304). On that occasion it had been agreed that Mr Shekhar would nominate Devi Lal for the post, but the former had not been told that there was a further agreement that the latter would nominate Mr Singh.

As regards political and economic orientation, Mr Shekhar had been an activist in the Indian socialist movement in his early days and had backed Mrs Gandhi's bank nationalization of 1969 after joining the Congress party. He was a recurrent critic of multinational corporations, of India's large business houses, of foreign investment and of anything that diminished Indian self-reliance. In July 1990 he had made a forthright attack on the mildly liberal industrial policy of the Singh administration, warning that deregulation would encourage industrial investment that would be irrelevant to 'social, economic and national priorities'.

At the end of the year the Indian government said that 890 people had been killed and nearly 4,000 injured in the 15 weeks of Hindu-Muslim riots provoked by the Hindu militant campaign against the Ayodhya mosque. The junior Interior Minister, Subodh Kant Sahay, reporting to parliament on some of India's worst communal violence since 1947, said that 332 people had died in the first two weeks of December alone. Also at the end of the year it was announced by Punjab's police chief that the government would be sending extra paramilitary forces to combat Sikh separatists in the area, after the most costly 12 months of the seven-year-old insurrection, during which more than 10,000 militants, security forces and innocent Hindus and Sikhs had been killed. Violence had spread through most parts of Punjab, with the militants' writ holding sway in many districts.

During the last week of December Simranjit Singh Mann, leader of the Akali Dal (the Sikhs' political party), met with the new Prime Minister, having been authorized by other leading Sikh factions to discuss the demand for a homeland. Mr Mann, himself a former police officer in Bombay and elsewhere, claimed that he now had the endorsement of the militants, all of whom were in hiding. Mr Shekhar had just announced that he was willing to consider an amendment to India's constitution in order to accommodate the Sikhs' aspirations. However, the Prime Minister faced the dual difficulty of leading a minority government without the necessary strength in parliament to amend the constitution and of there being no consensus among the main political parties on a settlement of the Punjab issue. It was widely predicted that the outcome of the Punjab talks was bound to affect movements for greater autonomy or independence in other Indian states, notably Kashmir. In this context, the Hindu fundamentalist BJP cautioned Mr Shekhar against giving in to the Sikh militants' demands for independence. The Prime Minister himself said that, while he was willing to consider an amendment of the constitution, any solution would have to be within its framework.

Severe winter weather, the worst for many years, swept across the whole of northern India during the last ten days of the year, causing some deaths and marooning whole villages and communities and leading to breakdowns in the supply of energy, raw materials and foodstuffs.

Among notable Indian personalities who died during the year were Mr M. P. Birla, one of the country's leading industrialists, who died in Calcutta on 30 July, aged 72; Mrs Vijaya Lakshimi Pandit, sister of Jawaharlal Nehru, who had had an active, distinguished and controversial political and diplomatic career in her own right, who died on 1 December at Dehra Dun, aged 90 (see OBITUARY); and Professor A. Appadorai, eminent author, political scientist and former head of the Indian School of International Studies, who died in New Delhi on 9 December, aged 88.

PAKISTAN

CAPITAL: Islamabad   AREA: 804,000 sq km   POPULATION: 110,400,000 ('90)
OFFICIAL LANGUAGE: Urdu   POLITICAL SYSTEM: nominal parliamentary democracy
HEAD OF STATE: President Ghulam Ishaq Khan (since Aug '88)
RULING PARTY: Islamic Democratic Alliance (Islami Jamhoori Ittehad), dominated by Muslim League
HEAD OF GOVERNMENT: Nawaz Sharif, Prime Minister (since Nov '90)
PRINCIPAL MINISTERS: Sahibzada Yaqub Khan (foreign affairs), Sartaj Aziz (finance & economy), Choudhry Shujat Husain (industries & interior), Hamid Nasir Chattha (planning & development)
INTERNATIONAL ALIGNMENT: NAM, ICO, SAARC, Cwth.
CURRENCY: rupee (end-'90 £1=PRs41.00, US$1=PRs21.24)
GNP PER CAPITA: US$350 ('88)
MAIN EXPORT EARNERS: cotton, textiles, rice

PAKISTAN's fragile experiment with democracy suffered a major shock in 1990 with the dismissal in August of Benazir Bhutto's Pakistan People's Party (PPP) government. In November an elected government was restored when Nawaz Sharif of the Islami Jamhoori Ittehad (IJI) took office, although doubts persisted both about the fairness of the polls and about the new Prime Minister's closeness to the army leadership. The repercussions of the Gulf crisis were felt both politically and economically, but tense relations with India did not quite deteriorate into armed conflict.

Ms Bhutto's hold on power had been tenuous from the very moment of her narrow victory in the November 1988 elections. By the beginning of 1990 she was trying to reconstruct her political base after only narrowly surviving a vote of no confidence in November 1989 (see AR 1989, p. 307). She resisted calls to build bridges with the IJI and its principal leader, Nawaz Sharif, and preferred instead to continue a policy of luring away members of the opposition with promises of positions and patronage. While this allowed the government to survive, it did little to quell the anxieties of the army leadership, senior bureaucrats and President Ghulam Ishaq Khan. Nor did it restrict the opposition's control of the Punjab. At the same time, high levels of violence persisted in Karachi and Hyderabad, reaching a peak in May when hundreds were killed.

On 6 August the President exercised his powers under the constitution, and dismissed the Bhutto government. In a speech to the nation he singled out two main issues. The first was the government's unwillingness to respect the federal structure of the constitution. This referred, for example, to a failure to call the Council of Common Interests, in which non-PPP forces would have been dominant. The President's second point was that the PPP government had become corrupt and ineffective. There was indeed some truth in these charges, although the government's record was not necessarily worse than its predecessors'. Observers also commented on anxieties in the army over increased civilian control.

The response to the President's action was more or less along party lines. While the core of the PPP felt outraged, the opposition parties welcomed it and argued strongly that it was justified both legally and morally. Ms Bhutto was succeeded as Prime Minister, pending fresh elections, by the head of the Combined Opposition Parties (COP) in the National Assembly, Ghulam Mustafa Jatoi, a veteran but relatively lightweight politician from Sind province. During his period in office a sustained effort was made to bring charges of corruption against Ms Bhutto, her husband and supporters. Her husband, Asif Zardari, was in fact arrested but contrary to some expectations she was not banned from contesting the elections.

The general elections were held on 24 October, followed by provincial polls three days later. Contrary to some predictions, the IJI and its allies won convincing victories in both contests. With the IJI itself winning 105 of the 206 parliamentary constituencies contested, the anti-PPP formations commanded a comfortable two-thirds majority in the new Assembly. The PPP could manage only 45 seats, mostly in the Bhutto home province of Sind; Ms Bhutto herself succeeded in retaining her local Larkana constituency but failed to win in a constituency outside Sind (where she had won in 1988). The pattern was repeated in the provincial elections, in which all four provinces (including Sind) returned anti-PPP majorities.

Opinions were divided among international observers as to whether the elections had been free of the rigging that had occurred in previous contests. The initial view was that they had been, but a team of French observers later suggested that some credence should be given to PPP claims of a selective and sophisticated IJI plan to target certain constituencies. Owing to the vagaries of Pakistan's electoral system, the PPP suffered its substantial defeat despite winning only 2 per cent less of the popular vote than it had in 1988. The party could also point to the way that popular support for Ms Bhutto appeared to have picked up in the last stages of the campaign. Nevertheless, if the PPP had provided more effective and forceful government when in power, it would have had a more plausible claim to an increased share of the vote. The IJI, by contrast, increased its vote by nearly 7 per cent. The turnout was no more than 50 per cent at the most, a sign perhaps of popular disillusionment with the whole political process.

After the elections were over it took a few days for the victors to decide who would be the new government leader. The two main contenders were Ghulam Mustafa Jatoi and Nawaz Sharif. The latter, who originally came to political prominence as a protegé of the late President Zia, emerged victorious and was sworn in as Prime Minister on 6 November. As well as representing, at 41, the younger generation, he was also the first Punjabi to have become an elected leader of the country. His cabinet contained a number of familiar figures from the past, including Ms Bhutto's Foreign Minister, Sahibzada Yaqub Khan, who thus provided important continuity in this critical area. By the end of the year Nawaz Sharif had succeeded in establishing control of the political situation, although a transport strike had already obliged him to cope with some of the ambiguities inherent in Pakistan's Islamicization programme.

Relations with India were tense throughout the year. The main issue was the situation in Kashmir, where India charged Pakistan with complicity in the local unrest and where Pakistan felt that India's treatment of the Kashmiris had been outrageous. Within Pakistan political competition between the PPP and IJI meant that both sides had to take strong pro-Kashmiri positions. During the year, however, regular diplomatic contacts with India succeeded in staving off military confrontation. In December talks at foreign secretary level led to progress on an agreement not to attack each other's nuclear installations.

Pakistan was badly affected by the Gulf crisis. Many thousands of its citizens were caught in Kuwait or Iraq and had to make difficult journeys to safety. Its economy was also hit by the increased price of oil and the sharp decline in workers' remittances. In line with its longstanding alliances it sent troops to Saudi Arabia, although it was careful to insist that they were not to come under US command. Despite cooperation over the Gulf crisis, Pakistan's relations with the USA were less easy than in the past, with Washington indicating that it was not entirely happy with the way the Bhutto government had been dismissed. Then at the beginning of October US aid was suspended because of the longstanding problem over Pakistan's nuclear programme, which failed to obtain the necessary White House certificate to Congress that it was entirely for peaceful purposes.

The economy, even before the impact of the Gulf crisis, was in some difficulty. While growth in the 1989-90 period was estimated at 5.2 per cent, the balance-of-payments deficit remained at a high level and reserves rarely covered more than a few weeks. Of equal importance was the size of the budget deficit, which despite strong pressure from the IMF was still at 6.8 per cent of GDP. The two largest items of government expenditure, making up 80 per cent of current expenditure, were defence and debt servicing. This latter included a large volume of domestic as well as foreign debt. To cope with the crisis the government had to cut back on a number of development projects. However, for political reasons it was not willing to accede to IMF pressure for sharp rises in administered prices except for those of petrol and oil.

BANGLADESH

CAPITAL: Dhaka   AREA: 144,000 sq km   POPULATION: 108,900,000 ('88)
OFFICIAL LANGUAGE: Bengali   POLITICAL SYSTEM: presidential
HEAD OF STATE: Shahabuddin Ahmed, acting President (since Dec '90)
INTERNATIONAL ALIGNMENT: NAM, ICO, SAARC, Cwth.
CURRENCY: taka (end-'90 £1=Tk66.50, US$1=Tk34.46)
GNP PER CAPITA: US$170 ('88)
MAIN EXPORT EARNERS: jute, fish

POLITICALLY, the year was dominated by various challenges to President Ershad's rule, culminating in his resignation in early December and the consequent rapid overthrow of the 'Ershad system'. This caused much uncertainty and further turmoil, as the main political interests and groupings manoeuvred and counter-manoeuvred in preparation for elections called for February 1991 by the newly-installed interim government.

The army's support had been critical for President Ershad's political survival since he seized power in 1982. When the military adopted an attitude of studious neutrality in the last quarter of the year, and especially from late November, the Achilles heel of his highly-personalized system of rule was revealed. Thereafter, the army remained in the wings as a latent but potentially potent factor for any future political brokerage which might become necessary. A new army chief of staff had been appointed at the end of August, namely Major-General Nuruddin Khan. He replaced Lieut.-General Atiqur Rahman, who had himself succeeded Lieut.-General Ershad (as he then was) in this key post in 1986.

As usual, relations with neighbouring India were of critical importance to Bangladesh. There were talks between the prime ministers of the two countries in late March in the Namibian capital of Windhoek, where they had both gone for Namibia's independence celebrations, and at the SAARC summit in Malé (Maldives) in November. Several rounds of bilateral talks also took place at official level, such as the 30th meeting of the Indo-Bangladesh joint rivers commission in New Delhi on 18–19 April.

The French President, François Mitterrand, arrived in Dhaka on 22 February on a three-day state visit. An agreement was signed whereby France would give Bangladesh 150 million francs in the next five years for pilot projects and studies for controlling floods. The two countries also renewed an earlier ten-year accord, due to expire in August, whereby France agreed to supply equipment and to train Bangladeshi experts for a nuclear reactor in Bangladesh described as being for 'peaceful use of nuclear energy'.

At a meeting held in Paris Bangladesh received aid pledges, totalling $1,800 million, from its aid donor group, who indicated that they would consider providing additional resources as the country implemented further reforms. This meeting took place against a background of some significant reported changes in the economy, which was showing signs of strong recovery, benefiting from rapid growth in food-grain production. But budgetary and balance-of-payments pressures had grown during the year too, and sustained economic recovery would depend on the resolution of these problems. Their seriousness was highlighted by the resignation of Finance Minister Wahidul Haq on 16 March and his replacement by Mohammed Abdul Munim, hitherto responsible for agriculture.

On 6 May President Ershad reshuffled his cabinet for the 63rd time since he came to power, but the adjustments were surprisingly few given that they were apparently intended to appease those who had been pressing for major government changes. On 22 May he announced that there would be nationwide presidential elections in 1991 and that he would seek a second five-year term as candidate of the ruling Jatiya Party (JP).

Parliament passed a constitutional amendment on 13 June, renewing the guarantee of at least 30 parliamentary seats for women for 10 years after the then scheduled 1993 elections. The opposition walked out in protest, complaining that this was another ploy by the JP to strengthen its hold on power, with the result that 226 MPs voted in favour and none against the bill. The original provision in the 1972 constitution had been designed to offset the disenfranchisement of women by reserving 30 seats for women for the next 15 years. The parliament ostensibly elected for a five-year term in 1988 had actually included three women parliamentarians elected directly along with their 297 male colleagues, to whom were later added 30 women effectively designated by the ruling party.

After weeks of mounting anti-government demonstrations, President Ershad declared a state of emergency on 27 November, the third emergency imposed by him since 1982. Immediately beforehand riots had erupted in Dhaka, following reports of the arrest of opposition leaders, including Sheikh Hasina Wajed, leader of the Awami League. The leader of the Bangladesh Nationalist Party (BNP), Begum Khaleda Zia, was reported to have escaped and gone into hiding. Turmoil continued, and on 6 December Ershad abruptly resigned and was succeeded by an interim government headed by Shahabuddin Ahmed as acting President.

In late December Abdul Kader ('Tiger') Siddiqi, the Bangladeshi revolutionary who had spent 15 years in exile in India, flew into Dhaka from Calcutta to a hero's welcome. Mr Siddiqi said he would not rest until the killers of the 'father of the nation', Sheikh Mujibur Rahman (assassinated in 1975), were brought to justice. He expressed hope that problems between India and Bangladesh would soon be solved and thanked Indians for the help given to him during his years of exile. He had returned home from self-exile on a travel permit issued by the Indian government, and was expected to stay in Bangladesh to contest the general elections scheduled for 27 February 1991, as an Awami League candidate.

A report issued by a UN environmental expert at the end of 1990 warned that Bangladesh was losing much of its wildlife, as part of a South Asia-wide process caused by illegal tree-felling, depletion of underground water, a high birth rate and natural disasters. Rhinoceros, yak and several species of monkeys were among the animals that had already disappeared; elephants, Bengal tigers, crocodiles, lizards, frogs, snakes and dozens of species of birds were on the endangered list. Up to 15 per cent of the country's present land area could be under water by the year 2030 because of the 'greenhouse effect' or global warming, and a consequential rise in the sea level.

By 1990 forests covered only 6 per cent of Bangladesh's 144,000 square kilometres of land area, whereas experts said that 25 per cent was needed to maintain the ecological balance.

SRI LANKA

CAPITAL: Colombo   AREA: 64,500 sq km   POPULATION: 16,600,000 ('88)
OFFICIAL LANGUAGES: Sinhala, Tamil, English
POLITICAL SYSTEM: presidential democracy
HEAD OF STATE AND GOVERNMENT: President Ranasinghe Premadasa (since Feb '89)
RULING PARTY: United National Party (UNP)
PRINCIPAL MINISTERS: Dingiri Banda Wijetunge (Prime Minister, finance), Harold Herath (foreign affairs), A.C.S. Hameed (justice), Festus Perera (home affairs)
INTERNATIONAL ALIGNMENT: NAM, SAARC, Cwth.
CURRENCY: rupee (end-'90 £1=SLRs76.00, US$1=SLRs39.38)
GNP PER CAPITA: US$420 ('88)
MAIN EXPORT EARNERS: tea, rubber, tourism

CIVIL war continued in the north and east but there was a return to relative normality in the rest of the country. Mass killings and expulsions of civilians were common and for much of the year government forces lost control of the city of Jaffna. The year ended on a more hopeful note with a ceasefire being announced by representatives of the Tamil Tigers (Liberation Tigers of Tamil Eelam—LTTE) from 31 December.

The gradual and then complete withdrawal of the Indian Peacekeeping Force (IPKF) from Tamil districts led to conflict between the LTTE and other Tamil groups which had enjoyed Indian support and taken part in the 1989 national and provincial elections (see AR 1989, p. 313). These latter groups, principally the Eelam People's Revolutionary Liberation Front (EPRLF) and the People's Liberation Organization of Tamil Eelam (PLOT), were soon pushed out of Jaffna and Vavuniya. On 1 March the EPRLF, which had been elected to control the North-East province, declared its 'independence' as the Free and Sovereign Democratic Republic of Eelam. But this lasted only a few days: on 11 March the chief minister, Varadaraja Perumal, and about 1600 EPRLF activists, fled to India. On 25 March the province was placed directly under the rule of its governor and on the same day the last Indian troops left Trincomalee, having lost over 1,100 dead since 1987. The Sri Lanka government seemed happy to talk with the LTTE, whose leader, Vellupillai Prabhakaran, emerged from hiding on 1 April after two-and-a-half years and gave a public press conference in Jaffna. The two sides negotiated on several outstanding issues, including the dissolution of the North-East provincial council, the rescinding of the sixth constitutional amendment prohibiting the advocacy of secession, the holding of new elections in the North-East and the laying down of LTTE arms.

This interim period of peace did not last long. On 7 May an EPRLF member of parliament, Sam Thambimuttu, was shot dead in Colombo. The government reopened talks with the EPRLF on 15 May, and on 30 May Amnesty International appealed to the Tigers to end their 'executions' of political opponents. The Tigers, as on previous occasions, would not surrender their arms and fighting broke out again on 11 June. Jaffna Fort, held by the Sri Lanka army, was besieged by the LTTE and eventually fell to them on 26 September. On 13 June 90 Sinhalese police were captured and killed by the Tigers in eastern Sri Lanka. Internecine conflict continued with the killing of 15 EPRLF members in Madras on 19 June, including a member of parliament, a former official of the North-East province and the party's general secretary. On 7 July the provincial council (whose members had mostly fled) was dissolved and the Provincial Councils Act was amended to simplify dissolution by the central government. On 23 July 11 members of parliament associated with the Eelam Revolutionary Organization of Students (EROS) resigned their seats in protest against the renewed warfare.

By August full civil war conditions had returned. There was a major rift between the Tigers, who controlled the main Tamil districts, and more moderate groups; the latter were increasingly forced to take refuge in Colombo or to go into exile in India, to which about 100,000 refugees had also moved. Relations between Tamils and Muslims deteriorated rapidly after the massacre of 120 Muslims at two mosques in Kattankudy on 3 August and 58 others at various eastern villages on 5 August. These massacres provoked retaliatory killings of Tamils by Muslims. By November thousands of Muslims had joined other refugees in fleeing from war zones, especially from the Mannar district in the north-west. Moderate Muslim and Tamil organizations attempted to reduce this tension by joint appeals that the government should protect civilians.

An army offensive against Jaffna was launched at the end of August. Further damage was done to the city after the fall of the fort to the Tigers and a consequent series of air raids. This led on 9 November to the destruction of the Jaffna hospital, which had been placed under the control of the International Committee of Red Cross. The most serious setback for government forces was the capture by the Tigers of the Mankulam Camp on 24 November, only five days after an indefinite curfew had been placed on the north. Plans to evacuate the entire Tamil population from this area were resisted, but by mid-September at least 931,000 people had already been displaced by warfare. By the end of the year some previously militant Tamil groups were actively assisting the government in fighting against the LTTE.

Under these conditions it was not surprising that Sri Lanka was regularly criticized for breaches of human rights and the collapse of public order. Although the universities were reopened in early January after a two-year closure, the deaths of many young people in violent circumstances continued. On 12 January the opposition Sri Lanka Freedom Party (SLFP) moved a parliamentary vote of no confidence on human rights. The government responded to similar criticism on 18 January when Foreign Minister Ranjan Wijeratne referred to Amnesty International as 'terrorists'. Public opinion was particularly shocked when the popular journalist Richard de Zoysa was abducted and murdered on 19 February. Charges against a police officer suspected of responsibility were dropped on 31 August for want of evidence, but the belief persisted that Mr de Zoysa had been a victim of one of the many vigilante squads in which police and military personnel were said to be involved. In an attempt to alleviate criticism the government set up an 'independent surrender committee' on 19 April to deal with those involved in the Janatha Vimukthi Peramuna (JVP) insurrection which had provoked many illegal killings in the Sinhalese south (see AR 1989, p. 313). Earlier in April, the SLFP and the United Socialist Alliance (USA) had boycotted the opening of parliament in protest against such killings, many of which, they claimed, had affected their own supporters.

As the war with the Tigers escalated, concern over the high level of civilian deaths resulted in Amnesty International launching a campaign on Sri Lankan civil rights on 19 September. On 23 October the European Community states also deplored Sri Lanka's human rights record, as did Canada in November. In the following month President Ranasinghe Premadasa appointed a special task force on human rights, while consideration was given to constitutional amendments to strengthen individual protection against arbitrary arrest.

Domestic politics at the parliamentary level remained relatively ineffectual, although parliamentary debates continued. In a major ministerial reshuffle on 30 March, Gamini Dissanayake was dropped from the cabinet after 13 years' service and Harold Herath became Foreign Minister. The economy was seriously affected by the civil war conditions, once again depressing the tourist trade, which had shown signs of reviving earlier in the year. The Gulf crisis forced about 100,000 Sri Lankans to return home and ended the important role which their remittances had played in the balance of payments. Donor countries voted aid of $1,000 million on 25 October but warned of the effects of the war and the Gulf crisis, noting that Sri Lanka had maintained a level of economic growth in excess of population increase.

NEPAL

CAPITAL: Kathmandu AREA: 147,000 sq km POPULATION: 18,000,000 ('88)
OFFICIAL LANGUAGE: Nepali POLITICAL SYSTEM: parliamentary democracy
HEAD OF STATE: King Birendra Bir Bikram Shah Deva (since '72)
HEAD OF GOVERNMENT: Krishna Prasad Bhattarai, Prime Minister (since April '90)
PRINCIPAL MINISTERS: Sahana Pradham (industry & commerce), Yog Prasad Upadhaya (home affairs), Nilam bar Acharya (justice), Devandra Raj Pandey (finance)
INTERNATIONAL ALIGNMENT: NAM, SAARC
CURRENCY: rupee (end-'90 £1=NRs57.77, US$1=NRs29.93)
GNP PER CAPITA: US$180 ('88)
MAIN EXPORT EARNERS: agricultural products, tourism

THIS was a year of political turmoil and of political change, actual and potential, for Nepal. When King Birendra, educated at Eton and Harvard, had ascended the throne in 1975, the Nepalese intelligentsia had hoped that he would introduce democratic reforms, inspired by his travels and schooling abroad. They had been mistaken. The king, who was 45 years old in 1990, was said by informed observers to have been dissuaded from any such move by the palace advisers clustered around him. Particularly influential in urging such advice was said to be his queen, Aishwarya, who came from the warrior clan of Rana. This clan had provided a virtually hereditary series of chief ministers, who had dominated their Nepalese 'god-kings' for more than a century, down to the early 1950s.

That the latter months of the year would see the inception of a new political order in Nepal, involving what appeared to be a great diminution of the king's prestige and authority, was not obvious in the preceding period. Throughout most of the year an image increasingly emerged, in strained interviews with opposition politicians and diplomats, of a ruler strangely aloof in his Kathmandu palace and rather easily swayed or manipulated by ambitious courtiers unwilling to relinquish their grasp on the kingdom's affairs.

In February a number of the many outlawed groupings began organizing pro-democracy strikes among doctors, pilots, lawyers and students. This unrest came to a head on 6 April, when 50,000 protesters marched towards the royal palace, throwing bricks and stones. Soldiers fired on them, killing at least 50 people. A curfew was imposed throughout the country, but the brutality of the security forces inflamed the discontent and the death toll mounted.

The curfew was lifted on 11 April, but a political breakthrough was not achieved until 19 April, when King Birendra appointed Nepal's first democratic government for 30 years. Committed to curbing the absolute powers of the monarchy and introducing a multi-party system, the new government was headed by K. P. Bhattarai (66) of the social democratic Nepal Congress Party and included representatives of the communist-dominated United Left Front (ULF). A month later the king announced a general amnesty for all political prisoners.

Drafting of a new constitution proceeded through the summer, encountering some last-minute difficulties when King Birendra attempted, unsuccessfully, to force through a version which preserved some of his exceptional powers. As formally promulgated on 9 November, the new text (which replaced the 1962 'panchayat' constitution) abolished the absolute powers of the monarchy and created a bicameral parliament, with multi-party elections to the 205-member (lower) House of Representatives being scheduled for May 1991. The monarch retained the right to declare a state of emergency in certain crisis conditions, but Prime Minister Bhattarai explained that ministerial and parliamentary approval would be required for such a step. In the capital, Kathmandu, thousands of Nepalese celebrated these dramatic political changes by tossing out into the streets photographs of the king and queen which earlier they had felt obliged to hang up in their shops and homes. The politicians' only ostensible, and ironical, concession was to retain the words of the Nepalese anthem, extolling the divine qualities of the monarch (who claimed to be the modern incarnation of the Hindu god Vishnu).

These domestic events dominated Nepal's year, but relations with India markedly improved following the strains of the previous year (see AR 1989, pp. 314–5). In both New Delhi and Kathmandu there was a determination to achieve some easement.

BHUTAN

CAPITAL: Thimphu   AREA: 46,500 sq km   POPULATION: 1,530,000 ('89)
OFFICIAL LANGUAGES: Dzongkha, Lhotsan, English   POLITICAL SYSTEM: monarchy
HEAD OF STATE AND GOVERNMENT: Dragon King Jigme Singye Wangchuk (since '72)
PRINCIPAL MINISTERS: Dawa Tsering (foreign affairs), Namgyel Wangchuk (home
   affairs), Sonam Chhoden Wangchuk (finance)
INTERNATIONAL ALIGNMENT: NAM, SAARC
CURRENCY: ngultrum (end-'90 £1=N34.30, US$1=N17.77)
GNP PER CAPITA: US$180 ('88)
MAIN EXPORT EARNERS: tourism, cement, timber

TWO trends were apparent in the landlocked Himalayan kingdom of Bhutan during 1990. Firstly, the government of King Jigme Singye Wangchuk continued to move away from its traditional international isolation, while at the same time seeking to increase its capabilities for self-reliance. Secondly, there were increasing manifestations of political expression amongst some Bhutanese, influenced in part by the democratic revolution in neighbouring Nepal (see pp. 324–5).

Bhutan continued to play an active role in the South Asian Association for Regional Cooperation (SAARC), having by end-1988 established formal relations with all the other six member states. Neighbouring India remained Bhutan's most important foreign partner, although in 1990 the New Delhi government, which had previously provided all the foreign assistance received by Bhutan for its five-year plans, decided to reduce its aid by about 50 per cent. This reflected the kingdom's success in generating more internal resources and also the beginning of new aid flows from other countries. Nevertheless, during an official visit to India by the king on 31 January–4 February, the two sides agreed to renew their free trade agreement for a further five-year period (1990–95). Trade between the two countries would continue to be transacted in Indian rupees or Bhutanese ngultrums (the two currencies officially being at par), while Bhutan for the first time permitted private participation in its international trade with third countries.

According to official trade figures, Bhutan's exports to India in 1989 were worth of the order of Rs 837 million and imports from that country some Rs 1,000 million, with the balance of trade thus continuing to be in India's favour. Whilst saying that India would sympathetically consider Bhutan's desire for more routes for trading, official Indian spokesmen pointed out that at present there were no customs and excise posts on the extra routes suggested by Bhutan.

That even remote, absolutist Bhutan could not remain immune from the worldwide challenge to undemocratic regimes was indicated by reports in September of major pro-democracy demonstrations in the southern part of the country. Apparently put down ruthlessly by government forces, with a death toll variously estimated at over 300 or less than ten, the demonstrations reportedly centred on the grievances of ethnic Nepalese, whose language and customs were under threat from the ruling Buddhist Drukpa community.

Chapter 3

MAURITIUS—SEYCHELLES, COMOROS AND MALDIVES—MADAGASCAR

MAURITIUS

CAPITAL: Port Louis   AREA: 2,040 sq km   POPULATION: 1,100,000 ('88)
OFFICIAL LANGUAGE: English   POLITICAL SYSTEM: parliamentary democracy
HEAD OF STATE: Queen Elizabeth II
GOVERNOR-GENERAL: Sir Veerasamy Ringadoo
RULING PARTIES: coalition of Mauritian Socialist Movement (MSM), Mauritian Militant Movement (MMM) and Organization of the Rodrigues People (OPR)
HEAD OF GOVERNMENT: Sir Aneerood Jugnauth (MSM), Prime Minister (since '82)
PRINCIPAL MINISTERS: Prem Nababsing (MMM/deputy premier, health), Beergoonath Ghurburrun (MSM/deputy premier, planning), Jean-Claude de l'Estrac (MMM/external affairs), Jayen Cuttaree (housing and justice)
INTERNATIONAL ALIGNMENT: NAM, OAU, ACP, Cwth., Francophonie
CURRENCY: rupee (end-'90 £1=MRs27·10, US$1=MRs14·04)
GNP PER CAPITA: US$1,800 ('88)
MAIN EXPORT EARNERS: sugar, textiles, manufactured goods, tourism

WHILE the traditional volatility of the Mauritian political scene continued in 1990, the island further consolidated its reputation as the regional economic star. Although it remained non-aligned in its foreign policy, Mauritius intensified its economic links with Britain and France, and became the hub of foreign investment and offshore banking initiatives in the Indian Ocean region. The political crisis which erupted in August over the issue of republican status raised fears that the island's export-oriented capitalist experiment and its privileged trading access to the European Community might be threatened.

Regional cooperation was a prominent theme of Mauritian external policy during 1990. In March two agreements were signed with Madagascar: one to enhance mutual understanding, and a second to improve customs liaison in the hope of combating smuggling and the drugs trade in the region. The two states also supported each other's territorial aspirations, including Mauritian claims to the Chagos Archipelago and Tromelin Island.

That the country's economic success demanded local expansion was evidenced by the Prime Minister's call in March for Mauritians to invest in Madagascar and the Comoros. This attempt to mitigate the consequences of virtually full employment—notably escalating labour rates harmful to the island's competitiveness—was also explained in terms of sharing the benefits of the country's economic experience with its neighbours.

The continuation of strict anti-inflationary policies was a top priority of the budget presented to parliament by Finance Minister Seetanah Lutchmeenaraidoo on 18 June. The inflation figure of 4·2 per cent remained unacceptably high. Fiscal policy for 1990-91 identified a target of 14 per cent in the growth of money supply and a 17 per cent limit on credit increases. Total recurrent expenditure and capital expenditure were calculated at MRs 9,000 million and MRs 2,600 million respectively. The budget made provision for water development and road improvement and facilitated the planned abolition of exchange controls. A reduction in interest rates for the Export Processing Zone (EPZ) was confirmed, as was the goal of strengthening agricultural production.

The embattled Prime Minister, Sir Aneerood Jugnauth, opted to shore up his governing coalition by seeking support from his erstwhile ally-turned-foe, the controversial Paul Bérenger and his Mauritian Militant Movement (MMM). This plunged the island into a political crisis which dominated the domestic scene in the second half of the year. An agreement between the Prime Minister's Militant Socialist Movement (MSM) and the MMM to adopt an Indian-style republican constitution, under which Queen Elizabeth II would give way to a president, was presented to parliament on 17 August. The crisis arose over Sir Aneerood's decision to offer Paul Bérenger the presidency in return for the MMM's political support. The decision provoked hostility within the majority Hindu community and not a little anxiety in business circles.

The bid to persuade parliament to amend the constitution collapsed when Sir Aneerood conceded that he lacked the required 75 per cent majority among MPs. The issue precipitated a split between the MSM and the junior government party, the Mauritius Labour Party (MLP), as well as dissension within the MSM itself. Following the dismissal or resignation of dissident MLP and MSM ministers, the Prime Minister was obliged to form a minority government. This latest round of political manoeuvering was concluded when the MLP joined the opposition, the MMM accepted the Prime Minister's invitation to join the government and Sir Aneerood reconstituted his cabinet on 25 September.

The second phase of the Mauritian economic development plan received a financial injection of $60 million from the United Nations Development Programme (UNDP). Mauritius also continued to attract finance and development aid from various sources, notably the European Community, and France. The Mauritian National Family and Population Council was the joint winner of the 1990 UN Population Award.

SEYCHELLES, COMOROS AND MALDIVES

Seychelles
CAPITAL: Victoria AREA: 454 sq km POPULATION: 68,000 ('88)
OFFICIAL LANGUAGE: Creole POLITICAL SYSTEM: presidential, one-party state
HEAD OF STATE AND PARTY LEADER: President France-Albert René (since June '77)
RULING PARTY: Seychelles People's Progressive Front (SPPP)
CURRENCY: rupee (end-'90 £1=SR9.50, US$1=SR4.92)
GNP PER CAPITA: US$3,800 ('88)
MAIN EXPORT EARNERS: tourism, copra, fish

Comoros
CAPITAL: Moroni AREA: 1,860 sq km POPULATION: 487,000 ('89)
OFFICIAL LANGUAGES: Arabic, French POLITICAL SYSTEM: presidential
HEAD OF STATE AND GOVERNMENT: President Said Mohammed Djohar (since Nov '89)
RULING PARTY: Union for Comorian Progress (UPC)
CURRENCY: CFA franc (end-'90 £1=CFAF491.00, US$1=CFAF254.40)
GNP PER CAPITA: US$440 ('88)
MAIN EXPORT EARNERS: vanilla, agricultural products, tourism

Maldives
CAPITAL: Malé AREA: 300 sq km POPULATION: 202,000 ('88)
OFFICIAL LANGUAGE: Divehi POLITICAL SYSTEM: presidential
HEAD OF STATE AND GOVERNMENT: President Maumoun Abdul Gayoom (since '78)
CURRENCY: rufiya (end-'90 £1=R18.37, US$1=R9.52)
GNP PER CAPITA: US$410 ('88)
MAIN EXPORT EARNERS: fish, coconuts, tourism

SEYCHELLES experienced a politically quiescent year in 1990, although demands for democratization and opposition to President France-Albert René's government continued to emanate from the Seychellois diaspora. While remaining firmly non-aligned in its foreign policy, the country gravitated towards a capitalist economic model, as the need to generate growth and sustain development became the government's chief preoccupation.

The Minister of Finance, James Michel, presented the 1990 budget to the People's Assembly on 30 December 1989; it provided for total expenditure of SR1,282 million, an increase of 38 per cent on the previous year. In an effort to balance the trade figures increases were announced on import taxes on alcohol, tobacco and luxury goods. Seychelles achieved a growth rate of 7 per cent in 1989, with tourism being the main source of that growth. However, as a result of the increased demand arising from improved air links and the buoyant tourist industry, imports reached a record level and exacerbated the trade deficit by 11 per cent. Moreover, debt servicing had become 'uncomfortably high', representing 19 per cent of GDP in 1990.

Government optimism about the general economic outlook was based partly on the anticipated roles of the private sector and foreign investment in revitalizing the economy, following the issuing of a long-delayed investment incentive code seeking to court would-be foreign investors. Its proposals included the encouragement of a variety of service industries such as offshore banking, insurance, marketing and engineering, full repatriation of invested capital and profits guaranteed to approved projects, and legal protection against nationalization without compensation. Other incentives facilitated the employment of expatriates, made labour laws more flexible and offered 99-year leases on industrial land.

The tourist sector remained the main foreign-exchange earner. According to the Central Bank's annual report published in May, the tourist trade had been an exceptional success, catering for 86,000 visitors in 1989. Revenue from tourism totalled SR515 million—19 per cent higher than in 1988—and the number of visitors was expected to rise to 100,000 in 1990. The opening of new air links with Paris and Kuala Lumpur confirmed Seychelles' intention to diversify its tourist clientele. A loan of F 33 million from the French Central Fund for Economic Cooperation for an air control centre underlined the significance of the tourist industry.

In July it was reported that a satellite communications programme, which was planned to become operational in 1991, would link the outlying islands with Mahé and other countries.

In a move designed to improve the government's relations with the Catholic Church, the first monthly meeting of a state-church coordination committee, established by President René, was held on 24 August.

In the COMOROS the year opened in an atmosphere of considerable unease following the November 1989 assassination of President Abdallah, (see AR 1989, p. 319–20). Early in January there were riots in the capital, Moroni, calling for a return to democracy, followed by an announcement by acting President Said Mohammed Djohar that presidential elections would take place in February. In the first attempt to hold them, polling was abandoned after a few hours, amid widespread allegations of rigging, and had to be rescheduled for 4 and 11 March. This time voting went off in reasonable order, the results giving victory to the acting President, as candidate of the ruling UPC, by over 60 per cent of the votes. A new government included two of the chief losing presidential candidates. Even so, in early April there were new disturbances in Moroni, organized by discontented opposition groups and calling for new elections. President Djohar later accused his principal rival, Mohammed Taki (who had obtained 9 per cent in the March election), of a 'destabilization attempt'.

Tensions subsequently subsided enough to permit a successful visit by President Mitterrand of France in June, as part of an Indian Ocean tour. After the disturbances, France had sent a military assistance team to advise on security matters. Increased economic aid and maintenance of democracy were also discussed, as was France's continuing presence on the island of Mayotte, in the Comoro group, which had voted to stay under direct rule from Paris after the Comoros became independent in 1974.

In September a Frenchman, one of the alleged assassins of President Abdallah, was arrested and sent for trial in Paris.

The repercussions of the 1988 coup attempt (see AR 1988, p. 327) continued to determine political developments in the MALDIVES during 1990. Following the Indian army's withdrawal from the islands (see AR 1989, p. 320), an Indo–Maldivian joint commission held its first meeting on 12 January in Malé. The session produced agreement on a number of issues which strengthened ties between the two states, including improved communications, abolition of the visa system and cooperation on development projects. However, while India continued to train the Maldives' security forces, President Gayoom rejected the need for a formal defence treaty with New Delhi.

In an address to a new session of parliament in February, President Gayoom spoke of the need for Maldivians to begin a new era of democracy and announced he would introduce legislation to share some presidential powers. The expansion of the President's Consultative Council from 15 to 55 members, the debate over the controversial article 38 of the Penal Code and the election of several reform-minded MPs encouraged the growing challenge to the traditional power-holders.

The movement towards cautious political reforms appeared to be reversed in April with the arrest of opponents of hardliners in the government. Thereafter, allegations of nepotism and corruption in government circles focused on the President's powerful brother-in-law, Ilyas Ibrahim, who was Minister of Defence, Trade and Industry, as well as deputy commander of the National Security Service (NSS). These tensions came to a climax on 30 May, when President Gayoom stripped his brother-in-law of his government posts and ordered an investigation into his activities. The episode culminated in the former minister's mysterious departure from the islands. Although the posts of Defence Minister and deputy commander of the NSS remained vacant, other members of the President's family retained their government positions.

MADAGASCAR

CAPITAL: Antananarivo   AREA: 587,000 sq km   POPULATION: 10,900,000 ('88)
OFFICIAL LANGUAGES: Malagasy, French   POLITICAL SYSTEM: presidential
HEAD OF STATE AND GOVERNMENT: President (Adml.) Didier Ratsiraka (since '75)
RULING PARTY: Vanguard of the Malagasy Republic
PRINCIPAL MINISTERS: Lt.-Col. Victor Ramahatra (Prime Minister), Jean Bemananjara (foreign affairs), Jean Robiarivuny (economy), Leon Rajaobelina (finance), Gen. Christopher Raveloson-Mahasampo (defence), Augustin Ampy Portos (interior), Joseph Bedo (justice)
INTERNATIONAL ALIGNMENT: NAM, OAU, ACP, Francophonie
CURRENCY: Malagasy franc (end-'90 £1=FMG2,581·25, US$1=FMG1,337·40)
GNP PER CAPITA: US$190 ('88)
MAIN EXPORT EARNERS: coffee, vanilla, cloves

THE 15-year-old regime of President Didier Ratsiraka seemed to be more and more in the good books of the West, from the Washington institutions to France and the USA. In the full throes of a Western-encouraged programme of structural adjustment, Madagascar found in April that the International Monetary Fund had included it for the first time on its list of 'good boys'—countries that had successfully implemented a reform programme. Although urban hardship continued, the righting of the economy was consolidated by a rescheduling of Madagascar's official debt by the Paris Club in June. There was also an interesting, and pioneering, 'environmental debt swap'—a programme for the protection of lemurs in return for 5 per cent of the country's commercial debt. Both France and the US also wrote off certain amounts of official debt.

Discontented elements found expression in a coup attempt in May, in which a commando of young armed men, not from the military, briefly seized the radio station and announced the overthrow of the Ratsiraka regime. It was rapidly suppressed, with an official death toll of six; but it left a bad taste on the eve of an official visit by President Mitterrand of France, having been accompanied by street anti-government demonstrations. In the event, the Mitterrand visit passed off without incident, although after it was over a French national, a member of the National Front in France, was also arrested. The trial of the participants in the attempted coup took place in December, and resulted in those responsible receiving mild sentences.

IX SOUTH-EAST AND EAST ASIA

Chapter 1

MYANMAR (BURMA)—THAILAND—MALAYSIA—BRUNEI—
SINGAPORE—INDONESIA—PHILIPPINES—VIETNAM—
KAMPUCHEA—LAOS

MYANMAR (BURMA)

CAPITAL: Yangon (Rangoon)　AREA: 676,500 sq km　POPULATION: 40,000,000 ('88)
OFFICIAL LANGUAGE: Burmese
POLITICAL SYSTEM: military regime with some democracy
HEAD OF STATE AND GOVERNMENT: Gen. Saw Maung, Chairman of State Law and
　Order Restoration Council and Prime Minister (since Sept '88)
PRINCIPAL MINISTERS: Rear-Adml. Maung Maung Khin (energy & mines), Maj.-Gen.
　Phone Myint (home & religious affairs), Maj.-Gen. Sein Aung (industry),
　Brig.-Gen. Able (trade, planning & finance)
CURRENCY: kyat (end-'90 £1=K11.58, US$1=K5.99)
GNP PER CAPITA: US$200 ('86)
MAIN EXPORT EARNERS: teak, rice, minerals

THE first multi-party general elections in Myanmar since 1962 were held in May under the auspices of the military State Law and Order Restoration Council (SLORC) government. Despite scepticism expressed in advance, and restrictions placed on candidates and campaign activities, the election was considered to have been 'free and fair' because the party most opposed to the army, the National League for Democracy (NLD), won 80 per cent of the 485 seats in the new People's Assembly, having received nearly 60 per cent of the popular vote.

The group thought to be closest to the army, the National Unity Party (NUP), a descendant of the defunct Burma Socialist Programme Party, gained only 10 seats on the basis of about 25 per cent of the vote. The NLD and the NUP came out of the election as the country's only national organizations. Most of the other seats were won by a variety of local and regional parties representing the diverse communities of the border states.

Though the elections revealed a widespread desire for political change, the military remained in power throughout the year and offered no promise to transfer power to a civilian government until a new constitution had been drafted. In the meantime, through a combination of legal restrictions and internal disputes among the aspirant legislators, the military was able to frustrate their ambitions. The resulting frustration led to several attempts to convene the legislature without official approval and the eventual establishment of a rump shadow government by several rebel groups in the border areas. The arrest of perhaps as many as 50 legislators, and the flight of others to avoid detention for violating military law, further limited the capacity of the civilian opposition to replace the military government on terms other than its own.

The continuation of military rule, and repeated allegations of violations of human rights, caused many major states, including Japan, the United States and the members of the European Community, to treat Myanmar much as a pariah state during the year. No significant bilateral aid was granted and the threat of an American trade embargo was held out.

Nonetheless, major Western oil corporations developed a close relationship with the government, from which they extracted a series of oil exploration contracts. As preparations for test drilling got under way, foreign investors, largely from other parts of South-East Asia, Korea and Hong Kong, began to develop joint ventures with government corporations.

Despite these new economic activities, inflation remained a major problem, as government expenditure grew much more rapidly than did revenues. Without foreign aid to offset the consequences of expanded spending, the government budget deficit reached 15 per cent of GDP in the fiscal year ending in March. An expenditure deficit of 10 per cent of GDP was budgeted for 1990–91.

Government spending was only one of the factors leading to an inflation rate estimated by some to be as high as 70 per cent. Another cause was the failure of the private sector to develop rapidly enough to ensure the smooth flow of goods to the market place at realistic prices, as the old state distribution system was wound down for all but government employees. Other inflationary pressures came from inadequate spares and raw materials, poor infrastructure and fuel shortages.

In terms of the government's long struggle with ethnic and communist insurgents, the year was marked by important dry-season military victories. The Karen National Union (KNU), the largest of these groups, suffered significant defeats and its hold over the smuggling routes into Thailand was largely destroyed. The smaller Mon guerrilla group was also dislodged from its strongholds, but the Kachin Independence Organization (KIO) remained effective in the far north.

The old Communist Party was militarily defunct during the year and its former heartland along the border with China came firmly under government control. Nonetheless, the government continued to argue that underground communists, as well as the ethnic autonomy movements, were in league with some of the civilian opposition, as demonstrated by the faltering establishment of a parallel government at the KNU headquarters in December.

The process of reform, accelerated after the political upheavals of mid-1988, continued in 1990 but without the speed the army government's critics demanded. The 'great changes' heralded in January by General Saw Maung, the SLORC Chairman, had not materialized in more than embryonic political forms by the end of the year.

THAILAND

CAPITAL: Bangkok   AREA: 513,000 sq km   POPULATION: 55,600,000 ('89)
OFFICIAL LANGUAGE: Thai   POLITICAL SYSTEM: parliamentary, under military tutelage
HEAD OF STATE: King Bhumibol Adulyade (Rama IX) (since June '46)
RULING PARTIES: Chart Thai (CT), Social Action (SAP), Democrat (DP), Rassadorn (RP), United Development (UDP) and Solidarity (SP) parties
HEAD OF GOVERNMENT: Maj.-Gen. Chatichai Choonhavan (CT), Prime Minister (since Aug '88)
PRINCIPAL MINISTERS: Subin Pinkayan (SAP/foreign affairs), Virabongsa Ramangura (ind./finance), Banharn Silpa-Archa (CT/interior), Police Lt.-Gen. Chamras Mangkalarat (CT/justice)
INTERNATIONAL ALIGNMENT: ASEAN
CURRENCY: baht (end-'90 £1=B47.00, US$1=B24.35)
GNP PER CAPITA: US$1,000 ('88)
MAIN EXPORT EARNERS: textiles, rice, tapioca, rubber, tourism

DOUBTS over the stability of Prime Minister Chatichai Choonhavan's coalition government dominated 1990. After a succession of scandals and conflicts, General Chatichai resigned on 8 December—but only after ensuring that he would be renominated by the major parties and then reinstated.

Strikes and threatened strikes in public-sector industries and a series of corruption scandals led to a parliamentary no-confidence debate on 18–20 July (broadcast live on television). The government easily defeated the motion by 220 votes to 38 after opposition MPs had walked out in protest. On 26 August there was a major cabinet reshuffle. Notable was Finance Minister Pramual Sabhavasu's move to the post of deputy prime minister and the replacement of long-serving Foreign Minister Siddhi Savetsila, who was felt to be generally hostile to rapprochement with Vietnam. Earlier, Air Marshal Siddhi had resigned as leader of the Social Action Party.

On 27 March Chaovalit Yongchaiyut tendered his resignation as commander-in-chief of the armed forces. The next day the Prime Minister appointed him as a deputy premier and Minister of Defence. To stifle accusations of corruption in the government, General Chaovalit was also put in charge of the counter-corruption commission. The deputy army commander, General Suchinda Krapayoon, was appointed as General Chaovalit's successor.

On 11 June, however, General Chaovalit resigned from the government over corruption allegations by Chalerm Yubamrung, a cabinet colleague. This prompted officers and their men to stage protests in their barracks, raising the spectre of a possible coup attempt. On 7 November General Suchinda publicly criticized the government and asked the Prime Minister to remove Captain Chalerm from the cabinet. General Chatichai announced a minor cabinet reshuffle on 22 November, but significantly kept Captain Chalerm in the cabinet. With both the Prime Minister and General Suchinda holding audiences with the King, rumours were rife. On 8 December General Chatichai resigned, only to be promptly renominated. The so-called 'Chatichai II' government excluded Captain Chalerm, who crossed to the opposition with his Muan Chon Party, while Solidarity joined the coalition, leaving the Prime Minister with a slightly reduced majority.

Chamlong Srimuang, leader of the 'clean' Palang Dharma Party, was re-elected as governor of Bangkok on 7 January; the following week his party won 184 out of 220 district seats in a Bangkok local election. The former commander-in-chief, General Chaovalit Yongchaiyut, launched the New Aspirations Party on resigning from the government. He said that it would not become involved in 'money politics' and that its accounts would be open to public scrutiny.

The economy was expected to grow by 9.9 per cent in 1990 (growth for 1989 having been revised upwards from 10.8 to 12.2 per cent). The rise in oil prices raised fears of spiralling inflation, which reached 7 per cent in October. There were also continued worries about the shortage of skilled workers and infrastructural bottlenecks, both of which threatened to undermine the export-led economic boom. In June and September respectively, Hopewell Hong Kong's $3,000 million road and rail scheme for Bangkok and Lavalin's $1,800 million mass transit system were approved by the cabinet. In October British Telecom and the Thai firm Charoen Pokphand were awarded a contract to install 3 million telephone lines over five years at a cost of almost $6,000 million.

In November the Prime Minister scrapped Decree 42, a restrictive press law which had been in force since the 1976 coup. By mid-year the Ministry of Public Health admitted to the seriousness of the AIDS problem, stating that 17,110 Thais had tested HIV positive; many AIDS workers believed the true figure to be over 100,000. In July the House of Representatives passed a controversial social security bill in the face of resistance from the army and the Senate. The system would be phased in over six years, with the government, employers and employees making contributions into a central fund. It would initially cover accident, death, disability, illness and maternity.

Foreign relations were generally overshadowed by domestic issues. However, the warming of relations with Vietnam continued. In late May the Vietnamese army commander, General Doan Khue, visited Bangkok, to be followed on 29 October by Foreign Minister Nguyen Co Thach, who held talks with the Prime Minister.

MALAYSIA

CAPITAL: Kuala Lumpur AREA: 132,000 sq km POPULATION: 16,900,000 ('88)
OFFICIAL LANGUAGE: Bahasa Malaysia POLITICAL SYSTEM: federal democracy
SUPREME HEAD OF STATE: Sultan Azlan Muhibuddin Shah of Perak (since April '89)
RULING PARTY: National Front coalition
HEAD OF GOVERNMENT: Dr Mahathir Mohamad, Prime Minister (since July '81)
PRINCIPAL MINISTERS: Abdul Ghafar Baba (deputy premier, development), Abu Hassan Omar (foreign affairs), Seri Najib Tun Razak (defence), Daim Zainuddin (finance), Seri Anwar Ibrahim (education), Hamid Albar (justice)
INTERNATIONAL ALIGNMENT: NAM, ASEAN, ICO, Cwth.
CURRENCY: ringgit (end-'90 £1=M$5.21, US$1=M$2.69)
GNP PER CAPITA: US$1,940 ('88)
MAIN EXPORT EARNERS: oil, palm oil, timber, rubber, tin

THE ruling Barisan Nasional (National Front) coalition was returned to office in elections on 20–21 October with a reduced majority in a federal parliament increased by three seats to 180 members. The victory was aided by a buoyant economy which registered a rate of growth of close to 10 per cent by the end of the year.

The elections were the most significant since independence because of the split which had arisen within the dominant United Malays National Organization (UMNO). Confronting a reconstituted UMNO, led by Prime Minister Mahathir Mohamad, was Semangat '46 ('Spirit of 1946'—the date of UMNO's formation) led by Tengku Razaleigh Hamzah, a former Minister of Trade and Industry. Semangat '46 had entered an electoral pact with Parti Islam (PAS) and the predominantly-Chinese Democratic Action Party (DAP) to pose a matching multi-racial challenge to the Barisan Nasional, of which UMNO was the principal component.

Only five days before polling Sabah's Chief Minister, Datuk Joseph Pairin Kitingan, announced that the ruling Parti Bersatu Sabah (PBS) was defecting from the Barisan Nasional to join the opposition coalition. In July the PBS had been returned to office in elections for the state assembly, after which charges were levelled that the federal government had intervened covertly on behalf of the Muslim opposition United Sabah National Organization (USNO).

In the event, the Barisan Nasional secured 127 seats in the federal parliament, thus retaining the two-thirds majority required to amend the constitution at will. However, Defence Minister Tengku Ahmad Rithauddeen and Science Minister Datuk Amar Stephen Yong lost their seats in Kelantan and Sarawak respectively. The Barisan Nasional won all the October contests for state assemblies with the notable exception of Kelantan where all seats, including those for the federal parliament, were secured by a coalition of PAS and Semangat '46.

At the end of October Dr Mahathir was returned unopposed as president of UMNO in elections at its general assembly. Also returned unopposed, as deputy president, was Deputy Premier Ghafar Baba. Heading the list of the three elected vice-presidents was Datuk Seri

Anwar Ibrahim, the Minister of Education, whose status in UMNO indicated the probable line of political succession. In November Dr Mahathir announced that Tengku Razaleigh would be investigated for corruption in connection with a bad loan made by a Hong Kong subsidiary of Bank Bumiputra while he was the minister responsible.

At the end of May eight Hong Kong nationals arrested in 1982 with heroin concealed in their suitcases were hanged, despite an appeal for clemency from the British government. Their execution was the biggest mass hanging ever in Malaysia. In July the acting senior assistant commissioner of police, Mohamed Said Awang, maintained that the mandatory death sentence for drug traffickers had not served as a deterrent.

In April plans were announced to build a naval base in Sabah to serve the defence needs of Malaysia's Borneo states. In December a contract was signed to purchase 28 Hawk trainer/attack aircraft from British Aerospace under the terms of a memorandum of understanding concluded in 1988. During the course of the crisis in the Gulf, Malaysia as a non-permanent member of the UN Security Council voted for all resolutions condemning Iraq and imposing sanctions. However, it was conspicuous in resisting US attempts to secure UN authorization for the use of force and also in seeking to link the resolution of the Gulf conflict with the Palestinian problem.

The death occurred on 6 December at the age of 87 of Tunku Abdul Rahman, the first Prime Minister of Malaya and later of Malaysia (see OBITUARY).

BRUNEI

CAPITAL: Bandar Seri Bagawan AREA: 5,765 sq km POPULATION: 241,000 ('88)
OFFICIAL LANGUAGES: Malay, English POLITICAL SYSTEM: monarchy
HEAD OF STATE AND GOVERNMENT: Sultan Sir Hassanal Bolkiah (since Oct '67)
PRINCIPAL MINISTERS: Prince Mohammed Bolkiah (foreign affairs), Prince Jefri
   Bolkiah (finance), Pehin Dato Haji Isa (internal affairs), Pengiran Bahrin (law)
INTERNATIONAL ALIGNMENT: ICO, ASEAN, Cwth.
CURRENCY: Brunei dollar (end-'90 £1=B$3.35, US$1=B$1.74)
GNP PER CAPITA: US$15,390 ('87)
MAIN EXPORT EARNERS: oil and gas

A report by UK Department of Trade and Industry inspectors on the takeover of House of Fraser (including Harrods) in 1985, released in March, concluded that the funds with which the Fayed brothers had acquired the retailing group accrued to them through 'association with the Sultan of Brunei'. A statement from the government of Brunei asserted that, if the Sultan's name or power of attorney had been used in connection with House of Fraser takeover, then it was 'totally without His Majesty's authority'.

Six political prisoners detained since the revolt in 1962 were released in January. In July it was revealed the Brunei had followed Singapore in offering the United States operational facilities for its armed forces.

SINGAPORE

CAPITAL: Singapore   AREA: 620 sq km   POPULATION: 2,600,000 ('88)
OFFICIAL LANGUAGES: Malay, Chinese, Tamil, English
POLITICAL SYSTEM: parliamentary
HEAD OF STATE: President Wee Kim Wee (since Aug '85)
RULING PARTY: People's Action Party (PAP)
HEAD OF GOVERNMENT: Goh Chok Tong, Prime Minister (since Nov '90)
PRINCIPAL MINISTERS: Lee Kuan Yew (senior minister), Ong Teng Cheong (deputy premier) Lee Hsien Loong (deputy premier, trade & industry), Wong Kan Seng (foreign affairs, community development), Richard Hu (finance), Shanmugam Jayakumar (home affairs & law), Suppiah Dhanabalan (national development)
INTERNATIONAL ALIGNMENT: NAM, ASEAN, Cwth.
CURRENCY: Singapore dollar (end-'90 £1=S$3.35 US$1=S$1.74)
GNP PER CAPITA: US$9,070 ('88)
MAIN EXPORT EARNERS: machinery & equipment, petroleum products, financial services, tourism

LEE Kuan Yew tendered his resignation as Prime Minister on 26 November after more than 31 years continuously in that office. It took effect on 28 November, when First Deputy Prime Minister Goh Chok Tong was sworn in as only the second Prime Minister in Singapore's history. Mr Lee did not give up politics but remained in the cabinet as Senior Minister, ranking in protocol directly after the Prime Minister. Ong Teng Cheong, incumbent Second Deputy Prime Minister, and Brig.-Gen. (Res.) Lee Hsien Loong were both appointed deputy prime ministers, with Mr Ong the senior in protocol rank but with Lee Hsien Loong nominated to deputize as Prime Minister whenever Mr Goh was out of the country. Lee Hsien Loong continued as Minister of Trade and Industry but relinquished the office of second minister of defence. The other significant cabinet change was the appointment of Brig.-Gen. (Res.) George Yeo as acting Minister for Information and the Arts, concurrently with the office of senior minister of state for foreign affairs.

In June Teo Soh Lung and Vincent Cheng, the last of 22 detainees originally arrested in 1987 for alleged involvement in a marxist conspiracy, were released conditionally. In July correspondents of the *Asian Wall Street Journal* and the *Far Eastern Economic Review* were refused permission to report an Asia-Pacific economic cooperation conference on the grounds that the two publications had tried repeatedly to engage in the domestic politics of Singapore. The ban provoked an unsuccessful protest by the US Secretary of State, James Baker.

At the end of August a bill was introduced in parliament providing for an elected President who would enjoy reserve veto powers over financial provision and senior public service appointments. In November parliament passed the Maintenance of Religious Harmony Bill, which established fines and imprisonment for those who heightened tension between members of different faiths. Also liable were those who incited others to defy, challenge or actively oppose secular government policies or who mobilized followers for subversion.

Soviet Prime Minister Nikolai Ryzhkov visited Singapore in February. China's Prime Minister, Li Peng, followed in August, paving the way for the establishment of diplomatic relations (on 3 October) despite Singapore's insistence that its armed forces would continue to make use of military facilities in Taiwan. Lee Kuan Yew visited China for a week from mid-October.

Brig.-Gen. Lee Hsien Loong, in his capacity as Second Minister of Defence, stated in March that a persuasive US presence in South-East Asia was required to avoid a power vacuum that others would scramble to fill. That view was reiterated by Lee Kuan Yew in May during a valedictory visit to Europe, including Britain. An agreement was signed on 13 November in Tokyo between Lee Kuan Yew and Vice-President Dan Quayle permitting enhanced use of military facilities in Singapore for US naval vessels and aircraft. Mr Lee subsequently paid a visit to Kuala Lumpur to brief Prime Minister Mahathir on the terms of the agreement.

In August there had been a hostile press response in both Malaysia and Indonesia to remarks by Goh Chok Tong, in the wake of the Iraqi invasion of Kuwait, that it was not enough for a country to be rich; it also had to be strong. Subsequently, the Singapore government firmly supported international efforts to secure Iraq's withdrawal from Kuwait.

INDONESIA

CAPITAL: Jakarta   AREA: 1,905,000 sq km   POPULATION: 174,800,000 ('88)
OFFICIAL LANGUAGE: Bahasa Indonesia
POLITICAL SYSTEM: presidential with army backing
HEAD OF STATE AND GOVERNMENT: President (Gen. retd.) Suharto (since '68)
RULING PARTY: Joint Secretariat of Functional Groups (Golkar)
PRINCIPAL MINISTERS: Lt.-Gen. (retd.) Sudharmono (Vice-President), Adml. (retd.) Sudomo (political affairs & security), Radius Prawiro (economy, finance, industry & development), Ali Alatas (foreign affairs), Gen. Rudini (internal affairs), Gen. Benny Murdani (defence & security), J. B. Sumarlin (finance). Lt.-Gen. (retd.) Ismail Saleh
INTERNATIONAL ALIGNMENT: NAM, ASEAN, ICO, OPEC
CURRENCY: rupiah (end-'90 £1=Rp3,670.92, US$1=Rp1,902.03)
GNP PER CAPITA: US$440 ('88)
MAIN EXPORT EARNERS: oil and gas

THE political atmosphere in Indonesia livened up during 1990 as speculation grew about who, if anyone, would succeed President Suharto when his fifth term ended in 1993. Discussion of the political future of the man who had dominated Indonesia for 25 years was highlighted by increasingly open expressions of concern about the alleged corrupt business practices of the President's children and worries about the financial activities of institutions owned by foundations he headed. The extent to which the President was aware of the new mood, or possibly encouraged it, remained unclear.

Because of the existing ban on open campaigning for the presidency prior to an election (and the indirect method by which the office was ultimately filled), succession discussions were clouded in ambiguity. However, central to the debate was the future political role of the army. The current army leadership was of a different generation from General Suharto, as were many of his civilian and ex-military critics. The army officer corps, concerned to preserve its influence in the making of government policy, began to project a more popular, pro-democratic image. Generational politics thus intersected with debates about how democratic the political future of the country should be.

Army efforts to eclipse the authority of General Suharto's hand-picked Vice-President, Lieut.-General (retd.) Sudharmono, demonstrated the strength of various elite rivalries. However, the President maintained his grip, as seen in the appointment of his brother-in-law, Major-General Wismoyo Arismunandar, as the commander of strategic forces in the capital. All of this suggested to observers that the army was struggling to maintain its authority while Golkar, the old army political party with which the Vice-President was identified, attempted to strengthen its own influence in an evolving political situation.

President Suharto continued to determine the national political agenda through his actions and statements. His call in January to leading businessmen, mostly Chinese, to donate 25 per cent of shares in their companies to their employees and cooperatives led to government action to force compliance while providing other benefits for less well-off businessmen and individuals. The President himself ensured that this programme got off to a good start by indicating that 10 per cent of the shares in Bank Duta and in a tea company owned by a Suharto-run foundation would be sold to cooperatives. Bank Duta later had to be rescued by the Central Bank because of major losses in foreign-exchange speculation.

Popular concern about the growing wealth of big businessmen and the increasing gap in income levels—both consequences of Indonesia's economic success of the 1980s—doubtless spurred the President to pressure the better-off to share their wealth. His concern for the wellbeing of the poorer sectors of society, as well as the strength of his own political leadership, were related points in his 16 August Independence Day speech to parliament. Seeming to endorse the recent move to more open politics, he called for a 'second national awakening' to start in 1993 (when his presidential term ended), but gave no clear signal as to his own intentions.

The more liberal atmosphere was tested by the emergence of an independent political group. Launched in Jakarta in November by the Institute for the Defence of Human Rights, a labour union called Setia Kawan was immediately declared illegal, but no other action was taken against it. Nor did public statements critical of the government lead to the arrest of individuals or the closure of newspapers. Only actions likely to cause religious discord suffered repression during the year.

The land conflicts which had led to armed clashes in rural areas in 1989 died out in 1990, but the year saw a continuation of armed clashes between anti-government bands and government troops in Aceh, on the northern tip of Sumatra. The armed insurgents appeared to be prompted by several demands, including a larger role for Islam in state policies and greater autonomy for the region. Banditry and smuggling also appeared to play a role. The simmering discontent which existed in East Timor province was largely underplayed by the government during the year.

Despite estimates of a lower rate of growth in 1990—perhaps 6.5 per cent as against 7.4 per cent in 1989—the Indonesian economy continued to perform well. Oil price rises assisted, but a broad range of economic activities also remained strong. Merchandise trade stayed well in the black. The largest macroeconomic issue remained inflation, with the money supply estimated to have increased by about 48 per cent over the year. To counter the effects of double-digit inflation, the authorities pushed up interest rates to 25 per cent for low rate corporate borrowers, thus dampening growth but having the desired deflationary effect.

Indonesia's foreign policy showed no change, except for the re-establishment of diplomatic relations with China, broken since the 1960s. Along with France, Indonesia continued to try to develop an international agreement which would facilitate an internal settlement of the Kampuchean question (see pp. 347–8). Foreign Minister Alatas could take some credit for progress on this score. The upheavals in the Gulf had little effect on Indonesia, despite it being the world's largest Islamic nation.

PHILIPPINES

CAPITAL: Manila AREA: 300,000 sq km POPULATION: 59,900,000 ('88)
OFFICIAL LANGUAGE: Filipino POLITICAL SYSTEM: presidential democracy
HEAD OF STATE AND GOVERNMENT: President Corazon Aquino (since Feb '86)
RULING PARTIES: principally People's Struggle (Laban) and United Democratic Organization (UDO)
PRINCIPAL MINISTERS: Salvador Laurel (Vice-President), Raul Manglapus (foreign affairs), Gen. Fidel Ramos (defence), Jesus Estanislao (finance), Franklin Drilon (justice), Guillermo Carague (budget), Peter Garrucho (trade & industry)
INTERNATIONAL ALIGNMENT: ASEAN
CURRENCY: peso (end-'90 £1=P51.00, US$1=P26.42)
GNP PER CAPITA: US$630 ('88)
MAIN EXPORT EARNERS: electrical goods, textiles, agricultural products, minerals

THE problems which had beset the Philippines for the past decade continued to plague the faltering government of President Corazon Aquino throughout 1990. She was faced with general dissatisfaction over the lack of government action, growing opposition from factions of an undisciplined army and from congressional rivals, and the simmering revolt of the communist New People's Army (NPA). That she nevertheless remained in office underscored the disarray of the various political forces struggling for power. Meanwhile, the future of the country's US bases and the continual decline of the country's economic fortunes remained unresolved.

If these man-made problems were not enough, the country was hit by natural and international calamities outside its control. A major earthquake in northern Luzon on 16 July caused the deaths of more than 400 persons and resulted in a reconstruction bill of many millions of dollars. Floods and typhoons lashed the country at other times during the year. The Gulf crisis contributed further to the problems of a faltering economy. The increase in oil prices forced an eventual doubling of domestic prices, and exacerbated a balance-of-trade deficit of about US$2,000 million by September. This deficit was further fuelled by the ending of hard-currency remittances from the tens of thousands of Filipinos who had worked in the Middle East prior to the Iraqi invasion of Kuwait.

Much of the political jockeying revolved around members of the political elite trying to position themselves to succeed Mrs Aquino if, as was expected, she chose not to run in the 1992 presidential election.

Defence Secretary Fidel Ramos was loyal to the President but developed no political base outside the bureaucracy. House leader Ramon Mitra acted like a candidate, as did Senate president Jovito Salonga. Mrs Aquino's most vigorous opponents, Senator Juan Ponce Enrile and her cousin, Eduardo Conjuangco (both close allies of former President Ferdinand Marcos), were threatened with legal action during the year but both managed to avoid judicial entanglement.

In the midst of these political rivalries, the traditional issue of Philippines nationalism, the country's relationship with the United States, came to the fore in the ongoing negotiations on the future of Subic Bay naval base, Clark air force base and other smaller US military installations. The bases became more important to the Americans during the year, as they were used as staging-points for forces en route to the Middle East. Nonetheless, the prospects that the Americans might actually give them up in ten years caused Philippines negotiators to back away from earlier demands for a prompt pull-out. By the end of the year it looked as if a compromise on the sovereignty question would again be reached, allowing the Americans to remain without any firm commitments as to the level of aid the US Congress would grant in exchange. However, the ultimate future of the bases would be determined by the Philippines Senate, where post-Aquino politics might determine the outcome as much as the issue of the American relationship itself.

The centrality of the American link with the Philippines was underscored in July when a New York court acquitted Imelda Marcos for wrongdoing in connection with the ownership of Manhattan property. But this was a mere detail in the efforts of the Aquino government to regain the estimated US$7,000 million which President Marcos was accused of having stolen while in office. Typical of the inability of the Aquino government to achieve its goals was the fact that less than 2 per cent of the Marcos fortune had been returned to the government by the end of 1990. Furthermore, despite the conviction of 16 military men for the 1983 assassination of the President's husband, Benigno Aquino, the central figures involved in ordering the murder remained at liberty.

While the government concerned itself with these issues of the past, it failed to make any significant advance in reforming the social and agrarian inequities which fuelled the continuing revolt of the NPA in the countryside. While the army spent much of its time trying to root out disloyal elements within its own ranks, the NPA maintained support amongst parts of the peasantry in large areas of the country. Warlord politics and the threat of rural violence and urban terrorism lay close to the surface of Philippine politics in 1990.

Throughout the year the army was repeatedly placed on full alert to forestall military coup attempts of the kind which nearly toppled Mrs Aquino's government in December 1989 (see AR 1989, pp. 332–3).

While none succeeded, dissent in the armed forces became organized around a new centre, the Young Officers Union (YOU), as well as in the Reform the Armed Forces Movement (RAM), which had played a role in bringing Mrs Aquino to power in the first place.

VIETNAM

CAPITAL: Hanoi   AREA: 330,000 sq km   POPULATION: 64,200,000 ('88)
OFFICIAL LANGUAGE: Vietnamese   POLITICAL SYSTEM: socialist republic
HEAD OF STATE: Vo Chi Cong, President of Council State (since July '87)
RULING PARTY: Communist Party of Vietnam (CPV)
PARTY LEADER: Nguyen Van Linh, CPV general secretary (since Dec '86)
PRINCIPAL MINISTERS: Do Muoi (Prime Minister), Gen. Vo Van Kiet (first deputy premier), Nguyen Co Thach (deputy premier, foreign affairs), Gen. Le Duc Anh (defence), Maj.-Gen. Mai Chi Tho (interior), Hoang Quy (finance), Pham Vam Kai (planning), Phan Hien (justice)
INTERNATIONAL ALIGNMENT: NAM, Comecon
CURRENCY: dong (end-'90 £1=D12,554.75, US$1=D6,505.05)
GNP PER CAPITA: n.a.
MAIN EXPORT EARNERS: coal, agricultural products, seafood

EVENTS in Vietnam were dominated in 1990 by efforts to reinvigorate the economy and how best to respond to the momentous changes in Eastern Europe and the USSR. At the 8th central committee plenum of the CPV in March there was heated, but inconclusive, debate between 'reformers' and 'conservatives'. The expulsion of outspoken reformist Tran Xuan Bach from the politburo suggested that the conservatives had won the day. Several portfolios were merged to streamline the council of ministers.

The year saw the imprisonment of prominent reformists in the south, further curbs on press freedom, and a decision to limit the number of Vietnamese studying in Eastern Europe and the USSR. All were interpreted as attempts to reduce the pressure for political reform.

After the 10th plenum on 1 December, the CPV released its Draft Platform for the Building of Socialism in the Transitional Period—only the second such document in 60 years. Commentators were unclear whether this, and an associated draft statement on economic planning, indicated a continuation of economic reform or a return to central planning. Both documents were to be debated at the next party congress scheduled for May 1991.

International business interest in Vietnam continued to grow, although the financial, physical and legal support infrastructures remained inadequate. The collapse in March of Hanoi's Thanh Huong perfume company and the subsequent failure of dozens of other cooperatives illustrated the weakness of the financial and banking systems. On 1 October a new banking law was introduced to deal with the crisis. In

July the foreign investment law was amended to give private individuals in Vietnam power to negotiate with foreign companies.

The economic necessity of cultivating fruitful relations with the West and the market economies of Asia was highlighted by the USSR's decision to halve its aid package and reduce exports of strategic goods such as fertilizers, steel and oil. A trade mission visited Taiwan in June (the first official contact since 1975), and a warming of relations with Thailand culminated in a meeting between Vietnamese Foreign Minister Nguyen Co Thach and the Thai Prime Minister in Bangkok at the end of October (see p. 336). In mid-November Indonesia's President Suharto visited Hanoi—the first visit by an ASEAN head of state since 1975—and signed an agreement on economic, technical and scientific cooperation. Premier Do Muoi was even reported as saying that Vietnam wished to join ASEAN.

More important, relations with China and the US showed signs of improvement. In June China's Deputy Foreign Minister for Asian affairs, Xu Dunxin, visited Vietnam—the highest level visit since 1979—and in September CPV leader Nguyen Van Linh and Prime Minister Do Muoi travelled to Chengdu for talks with the Chinese. In February Vietnamese and US officials met in Bali, and on 6 August further US-Vietnamese talks were held in New York, specifically on the Kampuchea issue (see p. 60). This led to a meeting between Foreign Minister Nguyen and US Secretary of State Baker in New York in October. The talks raised the possibility that relations between the two countries might be normalized, the US trade embargo lifted, and economic aid from the US resumed. However, at an IMF board meeting on 26 October the US and Japan blocked a move to formulate a structural adjustment programme for Vietnam.

By October inflation was running at 60 per cent (35 per cent in 1989) and the value of the dong had fallen sharply; at year's end the number of unemployed was estimated to be approximately 3 million. Hanoi imposed strict controls on foreign currency in an attempt to limit the import of consumer goods and control inflation. The agricultural sector continued to perform encouragingly. Exports of rice in the first six months of 1990 were 1.15 million tonnes. Offshore oil exploration intensified and in October the Vietnam News Agency announced that a Vietnamese-Soviet joint venture had discovered the country's largest offshore field, Dai Hung, containing an estimated 250–300 million barrels.

Two landmarks were the centenary of the birth of the late Ho Chi Minh on 19 May (marked with extensive celebrations) and the death on 13 October of veteran CPV official Le Duc Tho, who had been widely regarded as a figurehead of the 'old guard' conservative faction in the leadership (see OBITUARY).

KAMPUCHEA

CAPITAL: Phnom Penh AREA: 181,000 sq km POPULATION: 6,800,000 ('89)
STATUS: The Phnom Penh government of the Kampuchean People's Revolutionary Party (KPRP), headed by Heng Samrin, is not recognized by the UN majority, which recognizes the Coalition Government of Democratic Kampuchea (CGDK) headed by Prince Norodom Sihanouk.

THE Australian peace plan for Kampuchea was unanimously accepted in principle by the five permanent members of the UN Security Council in mid-January. Following heated talks in Jakarta (February) and Tokyo (June), and under mounting international pressure, the four competing Kampuchean factions accepted the proposal on 10 September in Jakarta. They agreed to set up a 12-member Supreme National Council (SNC) to occupy Kampuchea's UN seat in the run-up to UN-supervised elections. It was envisaged that the SNC would surrender most of its powers to the UN while a ceasefire and phased disarmament took place.

The plan's 18-month period of implementation would require a 5,500-strong UN-peacekeeping force with 2,000 UN-appointed officials, and would cost $1,300–$2,000 million. The framework for a comprehensive peace accord was agreed in Jakarta in mid-November and led to further settlements on issues such as the reconstruction of Kampuchea, its future neutrality and the repatriation of refugees.

Despite this flurry of activity, the animosity between the four factions and a hardening of positions by Vietnam, China and the USSR still threatened to derail the peace process. A meeting of the SNC in Paris in late December failed to agree on some key elements of the UN plan. Prior to the meeting Prince Norodom Sihanouk abolished the posts of SNC president and vice-president that he and Prime Minister Hun Sen were expected to fill.

On 24 January Prince Sihanouk, citing 'international hostility', resigned as President of the Coalition Government of Democratic Kampuchea (CGDK). He had resigned on a number of previous occasions. On 3 February he announced that henceforth the CGDK would be known as the National Government of Cambodia (NGC) in an effort to disassociate it from the 1975–79 Khmer Rouge (KR) government of Kampuchea. However, this did not prevent US Secretary of State Baker from announcing a dramatic change in US policy on 18 July. The US would no longer support the NGC while the KR was part of the coalition, he said, adding that the US would enter into direct discussions with Vietnam over Kampuchea. ASEAN Foreign Ministers meeting in Jakarta in late July concurred that this policy reversal would delay the peace process.

Throughout the year, confused reports emerged on the war in Kampuchea. Claims that the KR had made dramatic advances appeared to be exaggerated and there was a military stalemate at the onset of the dry season in November/December. In Phnom Penh itself there were indications that a power struggle was underway between hardliners, headed by president of the National Assembly, Chea Sim, and Hun Sen's moderates. On 21 June Phnom Penh radio announced that a coup attempt had been foiled in apparent reference to the arrest, in late May, of a number of senior army officers and officials who had tried to set up a rival political party. In July the KPRP central committee plenum postponed the party congress—due to begin in December—because of the 'severe problems afflicting the country'.

The announcement in mid-year that from 1991 Kampuchea would face a cutback in financial assistance from the USSR and Eastern Europe focused attention on the critical state of the economy. Moscow also said it would withdraw half its technical advisers. The war in the countryside forced many peasants off their land, and rice production was expected to be insufficient to meet the country's needs in 1991. The Kampuchean riel declined in value from $1:190 at the end of 1989, to a black market rate of $1:610 by November 1990. Inflation had accelerated to 10 per cent a month by July; the price of rice rose three-fold from the beginning of the year; and foreign investors were still very apprehensive about commiting resources in such a volatile political climate.

LAOS

CAPITAL: Vientiane AREA: 237,000 sq km POPULATION: 3,900,000 ('89)
OFFICIAL LANGUAGE: Laotian POLITICAL SYSTEM: people's republic
HEAD OF STATE: Phoumi Vongvichit, Acting President (since Dec '86)
RULING PARTY: Lao People's Revolutionary Party (LPRP)
HEAD OF GOVERNMENT AND PARTY LEADER: Kaysone Phomvihane, Prime Minister and LPRP general secretary (since Dec '75)
PRINCIPAL MINISTERS: Gen. Phoune Sipaseuth (deputy premier, foreign affairs), Gen. Khamtay Siphandon (deputy premier, defence), Saly Vongkhamsao (deputy premier, economy, planning & finance), Asang Laoli (interior), Kou Souvannamethi (justice)
INTERNATIONAL ALIGNMENT: NAM, Comecon (observer)
CURRENCY: new kip (end-'90 £1=KN1,323.08, US$1=KN685.53)
GNP PER CAPITA: US$180 ('88)
MAIN EXPORT EARNERS: minerals, timber, coffee, electricity

A draft text of the first constitution of the Lao People's Democratic Republic (LPDR) was published on 4 June in *Pasason*, the newspaper of the Lao People's Revolutionary Party (LPRP), 15 years after the revolution. The task of drawing-up the constitution had been given to the new People's Supreme National Assembly in March 1989. The text's 73 articles covered the legal, economic and political spheres and included a section on the rights and obligations of Lao citizens. The next party congress was scheduled for early 1991.

Further economic reforms were introduced during the year. In June the National Assembly met to discuss and pass five key economic laws encompassing contracts, the ownership of property, inheritance, the establishment of a national bank and court fees. In March the government asked the Asian Development Bank to prepare a master plan in order to improve economic efficiency and raise revenue.

On 2–3 August the Japanese Foreign Minister, Taro Nakayama, visited Laos, returning Premier Kaysone Phomvihane's visit to Tokyo in November 1989. Mr Nakayama's visit was the first by a Japanese cabinet minister since the creation of the LPDR in 1975. Japan became the largest non-communist aid donor to Laos following the signing of three economic aid agreements worth a total of $11 million. At the end of the year talks with the US laid the groundwork for the return of US Peace Corps volunteers to Laos. The talks in Vientiane represented the highest-level bilateral contact since 1975.

Chapter 2

CHINA—TAIWAN—HONG KONG—JAPAN—
SOUTH KOREA—NORTH KOREA—MONGOLIA

PEOPLE'S REPUBLIC OF CHINA

CAPITAL: Beijing AREA: 9,600,000 sq km POPULATION: 1,134,000,000 ('90)
OFFICIAL LANGUAGE: Chinese POLITICAL SYSTEM: people's republic
HEAD OF STATE: President Yang Shangkun (since April '88)
RULING PARTY: Chinese Communist Party (CCP)
PARTY LEADER: Jiang Zemin, CCP general secretary (since June '89)
POLITBURO STANDING COMMITTEE: Jiang Zemin, Li Peng, Qiao Shi, Song Ping, Li Ruihuan, Yao Yilin
CENTRAL MILITARY COMMISSION: Jiang Zemin, chairman (since Nov '89)
PRINCIPAL MINISTERS: Li Peng (Premier), Yao Yilin, Tian Jiyun and Wu Xueqian (vice-premiers), Qian Qichen (foreign affairs), Jia Chunwang (state security), Zou Jiahua (state planning commission), Wang Bingqian (finance), Cai Cheng (justice)
INTERNATIONAL ALIGNMENT: independent, orientated towards Third World
CURRENCY: yuan (end-'90 £1=Y10.06, US$1=Y5.21)
GNP PER CAPITA: US$330 ('88)
MAIN EXPORT EARNERS: oil, textiles, agricultural products, manufactured goods

THROUGHOUT 1990 the Chinese government was at pains to reiterate its continued commitment to the strategy of economic reform and opening-up, which had characterized domestic developments during the 1980s. It was, however, impossible to insulate the task of economic construction from the upheavals of 1989 (see AR 1989, pp. 337–41). There was renewed emphasis on the need for intensified ideological and political education in order to combat 'bourgeois liberalization' and maintain China's adherence to a socialist path. Vigorous efforts were also made to restore China's external image, so badly tarnished by the killings the previous year in Tiananmen Square. There was a gradual resumption of high-level contacts with Japan and West European countries, as well as with international organizations such as the World Bank and Asian Development Bank. By the end of the year there were also signs of improved relations with the United States—this last assisted by China's support for the American position on the Gulf crisis. Other important developments included the opening of diplomatic relations with Singapore and the resumption of ties with Indonesia.

On 11 January martial law restrictions, imposed on 20 May 1989, were lifted in Beijing and free access again allowed to Tiananmen Square. But the aftermath of the events of the previous year was still felt. There was tight security in the Chinese capital on the anniversary of the 'Tiananmen massacre', but minor disturbances were reported from the campus of Beijing University. Reports of the release of many of those arrested for their involvement in the earlier 'turmoil' were qualified by information that a large number remained in prison and that some had already been tried and received long gaol sentences as a result of their alleged crimes. In general the Chinese authorities sought to give an impression of tolerance and restraint, not least in the attempt to persuade more overseas Chinese students to return home.

One significant concession was the decision to permit China's most famous dissident, Fang Lizhi, and his wife (Li Shuxian) to leave China, ostensibly to receive medical care abroad, following six months of enforced shelter in the US embassy in Beijing. Meanwhile, the case of the former Chinese premier and party secretary, Zhao Ziyang, remained officially under investigation. Zhao himself was said to have retained his party membership and to be enjoying the same material privileges as before his dismissal in June 1989.

If such instances of leniency betokened the achievement of greater social stability, as was claimed by the authorities, it was clear that the general state of public order in China was far from satisfactory. In the first six months of 1990 more than one million criminal cases were filed (some 260,000 more than in the same period of the previous year) and a 25 per cent rise in major crimes was also reported. Economic crimes also remained serious. This was the background against which anti-crime campaigns were launched. The determination of the Chinese authorities to deal firmly with serious crime was evidenced by the execution in Guangzhou (Canton) in September of 65 people, who had been found guilty of murder, theft, arson, arms sales and 'hooliganism'.

The government work report, which Premier Li Peng delivered at the third session of the seventh National People's Congress (NPC) in March, set out the official view of China's domestic situation. His account of the upheavals of the previous 'unusual' year was a familiar rehearsal of the argument that they had constituted a 'counter-revolutionary rebellion', instigated by minority elements, who had been influenced by ideas of 'bourgeois liberalization' and abetted by hostile forces overseas. Li insisted that political conditions had since greatly improved and that social order had been restored.

Such remarks apart, it was noticeable that the main thrust of the Premier's report concerned economic issues. Li insisted that his government remained committed to the strategy of economic reform and opening-up to the outside world. But some of the shorter-term measures which he announced as part of the ongoing anti-inflationary programme of economic retrenchment pointed to a partial re-centralization of economic decision-making and planning.

It was clear from other sources that the Chinese economy in 1990 still faced serious problems, inherited from the immediate as well as the more distant past. The imposition of retrenchment was itself a recognition that the economic base could not support the rates of capital construction and levels of consumer demand which had made themselves felt during the 1980s. Excess aggregate demand also remained a problem. There was too much money in circulation, more than was required to support a realistic rate of economic growth. Meanwhile, accumulated internal debts stood at 800,000 million yuan, most of which was scheduled for repayment in the short term.

There were serious imbalances between, and within, individual sectors. Agriculture had shown itself unable to support the scale of recent industrial expansion. There was still a lack of coordination in the development of infrastructural, basic and processing industries. Energy, raw materials, communications and transport facilities were all in short supply. Poor efficiency and high material consumption also hindered overall economic advance.

In his contribution, Finance Minister Wang Bingqian spoke of China's 'grim' financial situation and admitted that it was proving difficult to implement the state budget. Retrenchment itself was a contributory factor, financial revenue being constrained by the slow-down in industrial growth and the failure of many enterprises to fulfil tax quotas and profit remittances.

Against the background of such deep-rooted difficulties, claims of the economic success of retrenchment policies were not wholly convincing, even though significant progress had undoubtedly been made in reducing the rate of price inflation (which official statistics showed as having fallen from 27 to 6 per cent between 1989 and 1990). Li Peng himself conceded that further effort was needed to cut aggregate demand even more. Meanwhile, more modest rates of economic and industrial expansion than had been experienced in the recent past were now called for: target rates for 1990 were, respectively, 5 and 6 per cent. In the industrial sector the focus of work during the year would be to improve the operation and management of industrial enterprises, especially those large and medium-scale state-owned units which generated such a large proportion of profits and taxes.

By contrast, in agriculture (whose lagging performance since 1984 had long been a source of concern) accelerated growth was looked for during 1990. Preliminary reports at the end of the year indicated that the planned 4 per cent increase in agricultural value-output had been fulfilled, and certainly the all-important grain harvest reached a new, all-time high (probably around 420 million tonnes). But with continuing population pressure, per capita grain output in 1990 was still almost 20 kilos below its previous peak level, and it had yet to be demonstrated that agriculture had at last attained a path of stable and sustained growth. Official comment in the face of the bumper harvest was deliberately cautious, urging concerted efforts by state and local governments, as well as by individual peasants, to break continuing bottlenecks.

At the beginning of the year China's foreign debt stood at US$41,300 million. Foreign exchange reserves had meanwhile risen to $17,000 million. Official sources insisted that China's debt-service ratio of 15 per cent was well within its repayment capacity, especially since medium- and long-term debts outweighed more immediate commitments. Meanwhile, it was also announced that from 7 November China's currency would be devalued by 9.57 per cent.

On 1 July China's fourth national census was held. Initial reports indicated a total population (excluding Taiwan) of some 1,134 million and a rate of natural increase in 1989–90 of 14.7 per thousand. The serious implications of China's underlying demographic profile were indicated in the revelation that the number of women at their fertility prime (between the ages of 20 and 29) had risen by 34.7 per cent during the 1980s. During the 1990s some 17 million new births were to be expected each year. Against this background, a new programme of population control was being formulated for the forthcoming eighth five-year plan (1991–95).

The long-awaited 7th plenum of the 13th CCP central committee finally took place in Beijing between 25 and 30 December. It considered drafts of the 1991–95 plan, and also of a 10-year programme designed to provide the framework of longer-term social and economic development. Delays in convening the meeting were widely interpreted as indicating differences amongst senior officials over the nature and direction of China's future developmental strategy. In the event, the concluding communique provided no details about the two economic plans. Earlier statements had predicted a shift away from excessive emphasis on physical growth indicators in favour of calls for economic restructuring, higher efficiency and better economic coordination in order to anticipate any further economic over-heating. Other priority areas were expected to include agriculture, infrastructure and basic industries. The overriding macroeconomic target remained the quadrupling of 1980 real GNP by the year 2000 and the simultaneous attainment of a 'fairly comfortable' standard of living for the majority of the population.

EXTERNAL RELATIONS. It was noticeable that for the first time in many years 1990 saw China's internal developments overshadowed by the attempt to strengthen its external relations. In part, this no doubt reflected the desire to restore an image badly tarnished by the killings in Tiananmen Square in June 1989. Significant new initiatives were, however, also in evidence.

The year saw the gradual resumption of high-level contacts with the West and Japan, although the degree of progress was not uniform. For example, the French government resumed its granting of loans to China as early as late-February. By contrast, not until November did the Japanese authorities authorize the release of the first part of the 810,000 million yen loan package which it had earlier negotiated with China. The delay reflected the Japanese government's insistence that certain political and humanitarian conditions had to be fulfilled before the first tranche of funds could be released.

The historical legacy of mutual suspicion and hostility which had characterized Sino-Japanese relations since the re-establishment of diplomatic relations in 1972 surfaced again in 1990. The installation by Japan of a lighthouse on Diaoyu island—claimed by China as part of its own territory—was interpreted as demonstrating Japanese 'expansionist mentality'. Later, a Foreign Ministry source warned that the adoption by the Japanese Diet of a bill designed to allow the dispatch of Japanese troops overseas (in this case to the Gulf) would be greeted with dismay from within China. (The bill was in fact later abandoned—see p. 364.)

But in the wake of the upheavals of 1989, it was China's relations with the United States which posed the greatest difficulties. The decision by the House of Representatives to override President Bush's veto of a bill extending the visas of Chinese students in the USA was condemned as interference in Chinese internal affairs. Similar comment was reserved for official US criticism of aspects of China's human rights record. There was, however, palpable relief that in May President Bush decided to extend China's most-favoured-nation trading status for a further year. Even so, the most concrete sign of rapprochement did not come until November, when the Chinese Foreign Minister, Qian Qichen, was welcomed in Washington for talks on bilateral and international issues with the President and Secretary of State Baker. The new warmth was no doubt partly the result of China's support for the American position on the Gulf crisis. In any event, the process was taken a step further the following month, when the US Assistant Secretary of State, Richard Schifter, travelled to Beijing for further discussions.

The restoration of high-level contacts between China and Britain was signalled by the visit to China during July of Francis Maude, the Foreign Office minister with special responsibility for Hong Kong. Both sides hailed the visit as a turning-point in bilateral relations, although it was noticeable that Chinese denunciations of some aspects of British policy towards Hong Kong (for example, the nationality package) did not diminish. China maintained that the British commitment to grant a right of abode in the UK to 50,000 Hong Kong families constituted a breach of earlier joint undertakings and warned that it would not recognize the scheme (see AR 1989, pp. 36, 342, 348). There was no sign of any softening in such attitudes during the visit to London in November of Vice-Foreign Minister Tian Zengpei, even if in other respects both sides spoke of continuing improvements in their relations.

In the face of the dramatic changes taking place in Eastern Europe, China's position remained one of non-interference and a pragmatic determination to maintain friendly ties with the new administrations. In October the Chinese President and Premier sent separate messages of congratulations to President von Weizsäcker and Chancellor Kohl on the occasion of German unification. Nevertheless, concern was also voiced at the likely emergence of a new economic superpower in Europe, and there were warnings that German unification was bound to lead to the collapse of the existing system of European security and to the development of a multi-polar world.

Nor were relations with the Soviet Union impeded by internal developments in that country, where the retreat from the single-party system was seen by China as a purely internal affair. The expansion of economic and other relations in recent years (trade having risen from $220 million to $3,200 million during the 1980s) showed how much China had to gain from improved bilateral relations, and high-level diplomatic, military and economic contacts again took place throughout 1990. The single most important event was the visit by Li Peng, accompanied by Qian Qichen and other senior officials, to the Soviet Union in the last week of April—the first prime ministerial visit since Zhou Enlai travelled to Moscow in 1964. The essential pragmatism of the two sides was apparent in a statement issued after Li's meeting with President Gorbachev, which stated that both parties agreed that there existed no universal formula for the implementation of socialist principles and that any continuing differences need not impede the development of bilateral relations. A number of agreements were signed, including one providing for long-term economic, scientific and technological cooperation; another set out the principles which should guide mutual troop reductions along their common border.

The year saw a number of important developments in China's relations with some of its immediate neighbours, as well as with South-East Asia. One of the most significant was the adoption by the NPC on 4 April of the Basic Law for the Hong Kong Special Administrative Region (SAR) after June 1997. In the light of widespread criticism of ambiguities in earlier drafts, official comment sought to anticipate continuing concern from Hong Kong quarters and insisted that the final revised version once and for all defined the nature of the post-1997 relationship between the central authorities in Beijing and those in the SAR. Hong Kong would enjoy a high degree of autonomy, even if the central government abrogated to itself responsibility for regional defence and foreign policy. The carefully-worded statement that 'democracy that suits Hong Kong's reality should gradually develop' was set in the more general context of the need for the future political structure of Hong Kong to accord with the fundamental principle of 'one country, two systems' and the maintenance of stability. The relationship between the executive and legislature in the SAC would be one of mutual regulation and coordination, even though ultimate power resided in the person of the Chief Executive, whose decisions would be accountable to Beijing. Agreement was also reached on the design of the SAR flag and emblem.

But if official Chinese reaction to the adoption of the Basic Law was one of optimism and confidence in the future, undercurrents of tension between China and Hong Kong were also evident during 1990. Senior government officials, including Deng Xiaoping himself, were said to have been angered by local hostility to PRC government policies and determined that Hong Kong should not become a base for subversion. There were attacks, too, on supposedly 'reactionary journals' in the colony and an unconfirmed report spoke of plans to exert more effective control over local media in the transitional period leading up to the transfer of sovereignty in 1997.

In October Chinese and South Korean officials agreed to establish, with immediate effect, trade offices in Seoul and Beijing. Some suggested that these would also serve as consular offices, although China continued to insist that such purely economic initiatives had no bearing on the absence of political relations between the two countries.

Despite continued criticism of Taiwan's 'flexible diplomacy' and rejection of the idea of 'one country, two govern' 'ents' as a basis for future reunification, Chinese officials continued to show an increasingly conciliatory attitude towards Taiwan. At the end of the year, President Yang Shangkun claimed that relations across the Taiwan Strait had grown closer and he proposed that negotiations for reunification should take place on the basis of the principle of 'one country, two systems'. He looked forward to Taiwan becoming another SAR within a single China, but enjoying even greater autonomy and privileges than had been granted to Hong Kong. Taiwan would be allowed to retain part of its armed forces and there would be no attempt to implant a new administration in Taipei. The Taiwan authorities' response to such overtures was, however, less than positive and there were many obstacles to be overcome before talks on reunification could begin. In the meantime, the most concrete evidence of closer bilateral ties was seen in the expansion of economic and inter-personal links.

On 1 July the Indonesian Foreign Minister, Ali Alatas, arrived in Beijing on the first visit by a senior government official since the suspension of ties in 1967. Two days later the two countries' Foreign Ministers signed a communique providing for the normalization of bilateral relations, which took effect from 8 August—the day on which Li Peng began a goodwill visit to Jakarta. Indonesia undertook to maintain its 'one China' policy, although China recognized that Jakarta's economic and trade links with Taiwan would continue. Subsequently, President Suharto paid a return visit to China.

Following his visit to Jakarta, the Chinese Premier travelled to Singapore for talks with his counterpart there, Lee Kuan Yew, prior to formal negotiations on the establishment of full diplomatic relations. These duly took place in Beijing in September, and the following month formal relations were established. There were even signs of a degree of rapprochement with Vietnam during 1990: a number of meetings took place in the second half of the year, involving senior Chinese and Vietnamese officials. However, differing views on the Kampuchea question in particular remained a serious obstacle to the normalization of relations.

As regards the Gulf crisis, from the outset China made clear its strong opposition to Iraq's invasion and occupation of Kuwait. In early UN General Assembly and Security Council debates, China supported the position of the United States and its allies. Its consistent stand was one of support for a political settlement through peaceful means, with full use being made of existing UN mechanisms. But while Chinese representatives joined UN colleagues in voting in favour of sanctions against Iraq, on 29 November they abstained from voting for resolution 678 authorizing use of 'all necessary measures' to resolve the crisis if Iraq had failed unconditionally to withdraw its troops by 15 January 1991. The Chinese decision was explained in terms of concern that the wording of the resolution was inconsistent with China's belief that the crisis must be resolved peacefully. Chinese officials added that resort to military action would have an adverse effect not only on the region but also on peace and security throughout the world.

TAIWAN

CAPITAL: Taipei AREA: 36,000 sq km POPULATION: 20,196,000 ('90)
OFFICIAL LANGUAGE: Chinese POLITICAL SYSTEM: presidential
HEAD OF STATE AND GOVERNMENT: President Lee Teng-hui (since Jan '88)
RULING PARTY: Kuomintang (KMT)
PRINCIPAL MINISTERS: Hau Po-tsun (Premier), Frederic Chien (foreign affairs), Vincent Siew (economic affairs), Wang Chien-hsuan (finance), Chen Li-an (defence)
CURRENCY: Taiwan dollar (end-'90 £1=T$52.35 US$1=T$27.12)
GNP PER CAPITA: US$6,053 ('88)
MAIN EXPORT EARNERS: textiles, plastic goods, electronics

AGAINST the background of a disappointing performance by the ruling Kuomintang (KMT) in the December 1989 elections to Taiwan's legislature and local governments (see AR 1989, p. 346), there was considerable intra-party manoeuvring in the approach to the indirect presidential election in March. In the event, Lee Teng-hui, who had been appointed to the presidency after the death of Chiang Ching-kuo in 1988, received the party's unanimous nomination as presidential candidate. His task was made difficult by the need to accommodate rival factions within the KMT, as well as to meet the potential threat posed by the Democratic Progressive Party (DPP). The DPP's strong showing in the 1989 elections had given it an influence out of all proportion to its miniscule status in parliament.

Lee showed himself to be quite skilful in side-stepping some of the potential opposition and was duly elected for a six-year term with 96 per cent of the votes in the National Assembly. His new cabinet reflected a realignment of power. His choice of the former Defence Minister, Hau Po-tsun, as Premier was regarded as a clever means of neutralizing rivals within the KMT. But there was also opposition to the appointment, Hau being regarded as a conservative, whose elevation might signal renewed military involvement in civil affairs. Other cabinet appointments included Chen Li-an as the new Defence Minister; Vincent Siew as Economic Affairs Minister; the replacement of Shirley Kuo as Finance Minister by Wang Chien-hsuan; and the appointment of Frederic Chien as Foreign Minister in place of Lien Chan.

Expectations that the President-elect would show more flexibility in pursuing relations with the mainland were in part borne out by his inaugural address, which looked towards closer economic and inter-personal links with Beijing. Proposed legislation, designed to provide a new framework for handling relations across the Taiwan Strait, also bore the hallmarks of a more conciliatory approach. Even so, President Lee continued to reject Beijing's advocacy of the principle of 'one country, two systems' as a basis for reunification, preferring to advance the rival concept of 'one country, two regions'. Further, his offer to abandon the three-fold policy of 'no contact, no compromise, no negotiations' was predicated on Beijing's agreement to renounce the use of force against Taiwan, to implement political and economic reform and to cease its attempt to isolate Taiwan in the international community.

An important institutional initiative was the establishment of a Foundation for Exchanges Across the Taiwan Strait. Notwithstanding its ostensibly independent status, much of its funding apparently derived from government sources and it remained answerable to the Premier and legislature through the government's Mainland Affairs Office. Its remit was deliberately administrative and non-political, the hope being that branch offices would eventually be opened in Hong Kong and major cities on the mainland.

Meanwhile, Taiwan's 'flexible diplomacy' achieved further success during 1990. Canada and Australia both agreed to upgrade their offices in Taipei, while Peru and Bolivia indicated their wish to strengthen relations. Nicaragua's decision to open diplomatic relations with Taiwan was a significant development, leaving only Mexico, amongst Central American countries, maintaining exclusive ties with Beijing. Economic pressure was also brought to bear on the Philippines in the hope of encouraging it to strengthen relations with Taiwan.

The distinction between direct and indirect trade with mainland China seemed effectively to have become redundant, even though legislation still provided for penalties against those engaged in direct economic relations. The rapid growth of such ties during the 1980s meant that at the end of the decade the value of two-way trade had reached US$2,700 million, while investment in China by Taiwanese entrepreneurs totalled $600 million. A slowing in the growth of both factors was, however, detectable in the second half of 1990.

The attraction of investment in the PRC emerged clearly when set against the increasingly severe shortages (and thus high costs) of both land and labour in Taiwan, as well as concern about the growing environmental cost of rapid industrial expansion. At the same time, the business sector continued to move new export-orientated industries to countries in South-East Asia.

Taiwan's foreign debt fell to $1,150 million in 1989 and was expected to fall below $1,000 million in 1990. Its debt-service ratio remained significantly below 1 per cent. Meanwhile, as of the end of June, foreign-exchange reserves stood at the remarkably high level of $63,630 million, and additional gold reserves were valued at $5,600 million.

At home there was some evidence of a slowing of industrial growth in 1990 and the expected rate of increase of GDP was 6 per cent—significantly less than the average annual growth record of recent years. The official unemployment rate was less than 2 per cent.

HONG KONG

CAPITAL: Victoria AREA: 1,068 sq km POPULATION: 5,700,000 ('88)
STATUS: UK dependency due to revert to Chinese sovereignty on 1 July 1997
GOVERNOR: Sir David Wilson
CURRENCY: Hong Kong dollar (end-'90 £1=HK$15.04 US$1=HK$7.79)
GNP PER CAPITA: US$9,600 ('88)
MAIN EXPORT EARNERS: manufactured goods, textiles, financial services

DOUBTS about the sincerity of Chinese government undertakings to uphold the provisions of the 1984 Joint Declaration on the future of Hong Kong, as well as anxieties about the British government's commitment to protect the interests of Hong Kong citizens, were apparent throughout 1990 (see also p. 355). Such misgivings were not appreciably allayed by the passing of the British Nationality (Hong Kong) Act 1990, nor by the endorsement by the Legislative Council of a Bill of Rights for the colony. The most dramatic evidence of the concern so widely felt was seen in a government forecast that the number of 'educated migrants' expected to leave Hong Kong in 1990 would be 62,000—13 per cent more than had originally been anticipated and 20,000 above the 1989 level.

Official high-level contacts with the mainland, suspended after the Tiananmen massacre of June 1989, were resumed in January, when the governor, Sir David Wilson, travelled to Beijing. He had discussions with senior government officials, including Premier Li Peng, Ji Pengfei (then still director of the State Council's Hong Kong and Macao Affairs Office) and Zhou Nan (newly-appointed head of the Hong Kong branch of Xinhua News Agency, Beijing's de facto embassy in Hong Kong). Both sides spoke of their wish to resume the earlier dialogue and cooperation. But while Li Peng claimed that the governor's visit had brought the sides closer together, Sir David's reference to a 'frank and direct' exchange of views suggested something less than cordiality and harmony.

Consultations between the British and Chinese authorities yielded agreement that the number of directly-elected members to the Hong Kong legislature should reach 20 by 1997 (one third of the total). This would be increased to 30 in the following decade. The British Foreign Secretary, Douglas Hurd, recognized that the implied pace of democratic advance was modest, but expressed the belief that it was in the interests of 'continuity' and suited objective conditions in Hong Kong. Such remarks confirmed some observers' suspicions that the British government was more interested in 'convergence' with Beijing than in protecting and promoting the interests of its own people.

Further details were made available of the nationality package, whereby passports would be made available to 50,000 Hong Kong households. In the first tranche, 43,500 documents were to be distributed, the rest being held back until closer to the transfer of sovereignty in 1997. There was a strong belief that civil servants, members of the business sector and the professions would be the chief beneficiaries of the scheme. Although greeted locally with some scepticism, the Nationality Bill was endorsed by both the Legislative and Executive Councils. So too was the Bill of Rights, drawn up in the wake of the 1989 political upheavals in China in an attempt to strengthen the civil liberties and legal rights of Hong Kong citizens.

Hong Kong's economic growth had slowed markedly since mid-1989. GDP growth in 1989 was a mere 2.5 per cent (against 7.3 per cent in 1988) and no significant improvement was expected during 1990. In the first half of 1990 domestic exports fell by 3 per cent over the same period of the previous year, whilst imports rose by the same proportion. Export performance in the British and American markets was particularly disappointing. Official forecasts originally looked forward to a small reduction in the rate of price inflation to 8.5 per cent, but such estimates were subsequently subject to upward revision.

Government policy was thought to be responsible, in part, for Hong Kong's disappointing economic performance and poor immediate prospects. Tax increases had allegedly pushed up prices, whilst official restrictions on labour immigration had a similar impact upon wages. Hong Kong's unemployment rate in 1990 was a mere 1.7 per cent. It was noticeable, too, that the size of the government sector was continuing to increase—public spending having risen from 15 to 17 per cent since 1987.

JAPAN

CAPITAL: Tokyo   AREA: 378,000 sq km   POPULATION: 122,600,000 ('88)
OFFICIAL LANGUAGE: Japanese   POLITICAL SYSTEM: parliamentary democracy
HEAD OF STATE: Emperor Tsugu no Miya Akihito (since Jan '89)
RULING PARTY: Liberal-Democratic Party (LDP)
HEAD OF GOVERNMENT: Toshiki Kaifu, Prime Minister (since Aug '89)
PRINCIPAL MINISTERS: Taro Nakayama (foreign affairs), Ryutaro Hashimoto (finance), Misoji Sakamoto (chief cabinet secretary), Eiichi Nakao (international trade & industry), Megumu Sato (justice)
INTERNATIONAL ALIGNMENT: OECD, security pact with US
CURRENCY: yen (end-'90 £1=Y261.75, US$1=Y135.62)
GNP PER CAPITA: US$21,020 ('88)
MAIN EXPORT EARNERS: transport and electronic equipment, other manufactured goods, financial services

AT the start of the year Japan was agog with developments in Eastern Europe. Prime Minister Toshiki Kaifu, who was only four months in office, set off for an 11-day tour of Europe in order to improve his image as an international statesman in view of the general election which was due during the year. The visit was originally planned to take in Poland and Hungary. The Japanese wanted to express their support for democratic reform in these countries and for the economic restructuring taking place after long years of rigid central planning. Mr Kaifu announced a billion-dollar assistance plan for Poland and Hungary and promised further investment missions. At other ports of call in Europe (Germany, Belgium, France, Britain, Italy and the Vatican), the Prime Minister explained Japan's policies towards reformist East European nations and stressed the importance of coordination on policy issues between Japan, the United States and European states. The Soviet Union was absent from Mr Kaifu's itinerary; but a visit to Mr Gorbachev was paid at the same time by Shintaro Abe, former secretary-general of the ruling Liberal-Democratic Party (LDP), when the question of the USSR returning the Northern Territories was again raised without success.

Mr Kaifu returned with an enhanced reputation as a significant international statesman and called a general election for 18 February. This was to be a vital contest because the LDP had lost its majority in the House of Councillors election in July 1989 (see AR 1989, p. 351), since when parliamentary affairs had been in disarray because a bill passed in the lower house could no longer be relied on to succeed in the upper. It was essential for him that the LDP should not lose its majority in the lower house, to which end steps had been taken to remove some of the criticisms commonly levelled at the corruption of party politics.

In the run-up to the election, the leader of the main opposition party, Takako Doi of the Japan Socialist Party (JSP), had a clear platform that she would abolish the unpopular 3 per cent consumption tax and would prevent the import of 'a single grain of rice'. The centrist parties failed to unite or to form a coalition with the left-wing parties on a joint platform to stop the LDP. When the election took place, the 74 per cent turnout of voters was one of the highest ever recorded. A total of 275 LDP candidates were elected to the 512-member lower house, in comparison with 300 at the previous election in 1986. The JSP, despite its success in 1989, could manage only a modest increase to 139 seats, while the centrist parties and the Communists on the whole fared badly.

The prediction of 1989 that political change was in the air for Japan had proved to be unfounded. Against the odds, the LDP party machine had been successful. The JSP, which had not led a government since 1947, could not offer the voters an experienced government team. Moreover, there were ideological differences within the party. So it was as much the weakness of the opposition as the strengths of the governing party that had given the LDP its further victory. One distinguished commentator speculated that the voters had seen the choice as lying between freedom and socialism and that socialism was out of fashion in the atmosphere of prosperity in 1990. But the opposition's dominance in the upper house continued. This meant that there was bound to be inter-cameral strife and inevitable difficulties in getting laws, especially on defence and trade protection, through both houses.

Mr Kaifu formed his second cabinet on 27 February, with Taro Nakayama continuing as Foreign Minister and Ryutaro Hashimoto being reappointed as Finance Minister. Once the new government had been set up, President Bush invited the Prime Minister to visit the US for discussions which were held at Palm Springs on 2–4 March. Part of the meeting was devoted to consideration of the US-Japanese Security Pact (which celebrated its 30th anniversary in 1990), but the main discussion was on trade and related topics. While the election campaign was in progress, the United States had not pressed the Structural Impediments Initiative (SII), a series of talks which had been proceeding between the two countries since September 1989. The underlying conception was that, if the US and Japan were to cure their trade frictions and rectify the vast Japanese surplus in bilateral trade running currently at $49,000 million per annum, the two countries would have to remedy structural weaknesses in each other's societies. Whereas the avowed intention was that the SII would be bilateral in its impact, it was widely believed that the old-fashioned distribution system in Japan was the prime target for change. The SII talks had got seriously behind schedule.

After the summit at Palm Springs there were high-level meetings of trade ministers and their officials, accompanied by lengthy discussions in the press. The two countries agreed on an interim report in April in which each side made recommendations about the structural changes needed in the other. In implementation of this, Japan relaxed controls on retail outlets in May 1990, a step which Washington had been recommending to cut away some of the protected status enjoyed by corner shops in Japan. Finally, after a last-minute hiccup in negotiations, a 'pact on economic reforms' was signed at the end of June in time for the world economic summit in July. The most difficult part of the negotiations had been to convince Japan to agree that public investment should be fixed at a set percentage of gross national product. Another last-minute difficulty was over the nature of the body which would monitor progress in what was inevitably a long-term prescription for reducing trade imbalance. Under the pact, processing of patent applications would be quicker; and Japan would conduct a study of corporate groupings (*keiretsu*). While the pact was saluted as 'historic', it was hardly binding and would not necessarily end Tokyo's surpluses or restrain American complaints. At the end of the year the Bush administration was still complaining of trade imbalances.

President Roh Tae Woo of South Korea paid a twice-postponed visit to Japan in May, the first visit by a Korean President since 1984. Serious friction arose over the terms of a formal apology which the Japanese were expected to make for their colonialist treatment of Korea in 1910–45. In the event, both Emperor Akihito and Prime Minister Kaifu made appropriate utterances regretting 'unfortunate' episodes in the past. In statements to the Diet and on television, the Korean President asked Japan to speed up technology transfers to his country and rectify the adverse balance of trade which had existed since the early 1960s. Some accords were signed dealing with visas, peaceful uses of atomic energy and maritime problems. Arrangements were made for follow-up discussions, including a trade mission and a two-day ministerial conference, which was held in November. The result was to improve the unsatisfactory legal status of Korean residents in Japan by ending the requirement that first- and second-generation Korean immigrants should be finger-printed as part of registration.

These developments were seen as helping to switch the focus of Korean-Japanese relations from the past to one aiming at future collaboration. In particular, it was in Japan's interest that the North-South conflict on the Korean peninsula—one of the remaining aspects of the Cold War in East Asia—should be resolved. Moreover, Japan recognized that as the former colonial power in Korea it had a responsibility to assist in the reconciliation. In November talks were held in Beijing to discuss ways of opening relations between Japan and North Korea.

An important initiative in the East Asian area was Japan's mediation over the longstanding Kampuchean dispute (see p. 347). Tokyo offered itself as the venue for talks which took place between the parties in June. Japan's involvement was partly diplomatic, as the organizer of the conference, and partly financial, in the sense that reconstruction of the economies of Indochina would be impossible without substantial aid from Japan. While the meeting was unsuccessful, some progress was made. It created an important precedent for Japanese diplomatic leadership on the western Pacific rim.

At the Houston meeting of the seven major industrialized powers in July, Prime Minister Kaifu took an independent minority line on two substantive issues. While the other nations retained the sanctions they had imposed on China since the 1989 Tiananmen Square incident, Japan held that China was too important for Asia to be penalized further and announced that it would resume its official loans to China. Regarding the Soviet Union, Japan objected to giving immediate direct aid, persisting with the view that it would not respond favourably to Soviet approaches until Moscow showed itself willing to undertake the return of the Northern Territories.

The year saw two impressive royal occasions. At the beginning of the year the engagement was announced of Prince Aya, the 24-year-old second son of the Emperor. In June he married Kiko Kawashima, a commoner and university friend, in a much-televised ceremony. More significantly, on 12 November the enthronement ceremony for Emperor

Akihito and Empress Michiko took place. The time-honoured ceremonial conducted in ancient costume was witnessed by a large international audience, including the Prince and Princess of Wales. On 22 November there followed the *daijosai*, the great food-offering ceremony, after the performance of which the Emperor emerged as the high priest of the Shinto religion. While the first of these ceremonies was not without controversy, the second generated particular criticism from left-wing and religious groups. According to the constitution, the state was obliged to refrain from religious activity. Since the Kaifu government agreed to fund the enthronement, its actions were challenged in the courts for their legality. Radical left-wing activists opposed to the imperial system were blamed for a number of bomb attacks on police dormitories, railway lines and other facilities associated with the enthronement. However, despite a great deal of media coverage in the preceding months, the ceremonies passed off without offence to the majority of the Japanese people.

When the Kuwait crisis blew up in August, the world waited to see whether Japan, which was heavily dependent on Gulf oil supplies and had a relatively large number of hostages there, would play a significant role. After some delay and not a little lobbying, Mr Kaifu announced a package of measures on 29 August: Japan would cooperate in the policy of economic sanctions against Iraq; give financial assistance for the Gulf peace-keeping efforts; offer emergency aid to the front-line states (Jordan, Egypt and Turkey); provide cargo aircraft and ships to transport non-military supplies to the multinational force; and send medical and technical personnel on a voluntary basis. But Japan decided to withdraw its diplomats from Kuwait and could not, under the terms of its post-war constitution, send troops beyond its main islands, even for a United Nations operation.

After considerable pressure from abroad and several visits by foreign dignitaries, the Kaifu cabinet proposed to amend the constitution to allow Japan to take part in international actions. After further discussions at the UN, Mr Kaifu visited five Middle Eastern countries to assess the situation (2–9 October), the first visit to the region by a Japanese prime minister for 12 years.

On his return he introduced, at an extraordinary Diet session (12 October–9 November), the UN Peace Cooperation Bill to permit the sending of a contingent of non-combatants to the Gulf. It was not well-received by public opinion, by some factions in the LDP and by the opposition JSP which was in a position to use its upper house majority to defeat the bill. Despite his large majority in the lower house, the Prime Minister did not put the bill to the vote, opting instead for a compromise proposal which might attract all-party support. However, action on this could not take place before spring 1991. While the Tokyo government identified itself with UN resolutions and was financially generous to the anti-Iraq cause, its attitude attracted considerable criticism both at home and abroad. But it was generally conceded that Japanese politics did not readily allow a quick response to a crisis and that the subject of defence and security was one of the most sensitive issues for the Japanese people.

In December another large-scale stock market scandal involving politicians came to the fore. Toshiyuki Inamura, a minister in the Nakasone cabinet of 1986–87, was alleged to have evaded about 1,700 million yen in taxes on stock market profits. While the Recruit scandal implicated a large number of politicians and officials, it was usually the officials who were charged. On this occasion a former minister was charged with having profited personally from substantial transactions.

Mr Kaifu carried out a root-and-branch reshuffle of his cabinet in the last week of the year. He retained only three ministers, including the holders of the foreign affairs and finance portfolios, but the changes did not appear to reflect any major departure in policy. The Prime Minister had been under some party pressure to ease back into office members who had had to resign over the Recruit scandal. In the light of the Inamura affair, he was able to resist this pressure and to bolster his standing in the party hierarchy. However, it could not be said that after 16 months in office he had yet established a strong and independent position, even though opinion polls showed him as being Japan's most popular prime minister on record.

SOUTH KOREA

CAPITAL: Seoul   AREA: 99,143 sq km   POPULATION: 42,380,000 ('89)
OFFICIAL LANGUAGE: Korean   POLITICAL SYSTEM: presidential
HEAD OF STATE AND GOVERNMENT: President Roh Tae Woo (since Feb '88)
RULING PARTY: Democratic Liberal Party (DLP)
PRINCIPAL MINISTERS: No Che Bong (Prime Minister), Lee Seung Yoon (deputy
    premier, economic planning board), Choi Ho Joong (deputy premier, unification),
    Yi Sangiok (foreign affairs), Ahm Eung Mo (home affairs), Yi Jong Gu
    (defence), Yi Jong Nam (justice)
CURRENCY: won (end-'90 £1=SKW1,380.15, US$1=SKW715.10)
GNP PER CAPITA: US$4,968 ('89)
MAIN EXPORT EARNERS: transport equipment, electrical machinery, footware, textiles

FOR the Republic of Korea (ROK) 1990 was a year of unparalleled success in terms of international diplomacy and international trade, whilst domestically it was a year of significant political problems. On the diplomatic front the ROK gained official recognition by all of the former eastern bloc countries of Europe except Albania. Political leaders and heads of state from these countries made visits to the republic during the year, including the visit of the President of Yugoslavia on 7–9 November and the President of Hungary on 14 November. Several high-level trade delegations also arrived, including one from the People's Republic of China in late October.

Formal relations with Czechoslovakia were announced on 22 March, with Mongolia on 26 March and with Romania in early April. By far the greatest coup was the formal recognition of the ROK by the Soviet Union on 30 September, following on from the dramatic summit meeting between Presidents Mikhail Gorbachev and Roh Tae Woo in San Francisco on 4 June. Informal recognition was extended to the ROK by the People's Republic of China through the signing of two agreements on trade and the effective creation of consular facilities on 20 October. Such events were one further indication of both the interest of the former communist bloc nations in the economic success of the ROK and the increasing international isolation of its communist rival to the north.

At a joint meeting of cabinet ministers from the ROK and Japan on 26–27 November in Seoul, the Japanese side agreed to withdraw the requirement that first and second Korean-Japanese should be fingerprinted—a sore point between the two governments for many years (see also p. 363).

Due to the change in the international diplomatic climate in favour of the ROK, there were three intra-Korean prime ministerial meetings in the autumn. The first was held on 4–7 September, when the Prime Minister of North Korea led an eight-member delegation to Seoul. During the talks the delegation met President Roh, who expressed a desire to meet the North Korean leader, Kim Il Sung. A return visit by a southern delegation to the North Korean capital took place on 16–19 October, when the then ROK Premier, Kang Yung Hoon, met President Kim. The latter agreed to visit the south if there were visible results from the intra-Korean premiers' talks. A third visit took place when the North Korean Premier again visited the south on 11–14 December.

In the middle of the December talks, the ROK President left for Moscow for talks with Mr Gorbachev. During this state visit (13–17 December) the USSR offered a formal apology for the Korean war and for the Soviet shooting-down of a Korean airliner in 1983. A Moscow declaration of 14 December pledged both sides to seek ways to lessen tensions on the peninsula and to create conditions for the unification of Korea. During his visit President Roh also met Boris Yeltsin.

The most startling domestic political development was the merger of two of the three major opposition parties, the New Democratic Republican Party (NDRP) and the Reunification Democratic Party (RDP), with the ruling Democratic Justice Party (DJP) to form the Democratic Liberal Party (DLP). Effectively in operation from February and commanding a massive majority in the National Assembly, the DLP was inaugurated on 9 May with a system of co-chairmen spreading the highest political authority amongst the various former party heads. The dominance of the new party led to the boycott of the Assembly by the remaining opposition parties from 28 May, although this impasse was resolved in the autumn. On 11 December the opposition and ruling parties agreed on a formula to hold the first elections for local officials.

Internally, President Roh was seen to be a 'weak' figure compared with the 'strong' leaders of the past, a perception which led to a lack of confidence in his government. His third cabinet reshuffle took place on 17 March, involving new appointments to 15 of the 27 ministerial posts. The Defence Minister was replaced for a second time on 8 October following an outcry over the revelation that the military intelligence had maintained surveillance of 1,300 opposition political figures. In a fourth cabinet reshuffle announced on 28 December, Kang Yung Hoon was replaced as Prime Minister by No Che Bong, while Choi Ho Joong, hitherto Foreign Minister, became Minister for Unification and also one of two deputy premiers.

NORTH KOREA

CAPITAL: Pyongyang   AREA: 122,370 sq km   POPULATION: 22,418,000 ('89)
OFFICIAL LANGUAGE: Korean   POLITICAL SYSTEM: people's republic
HEAD OF STATE AND PARTY LEADER: Kim Il Sung, President of Republic and KWP
   general secretary (since Dec '72 and June '49 respectively)
RULING PARTY: Korean Workers' Party (KWP)
PRINCIPAL MINISTERS: Yon Hyong Muk (Premier), Kim Yong Nam (vice-premier,
   foreign affairs), Choe Yon Nim (vice-premier, chairman of state planning
   commission), Vice-Marshall Oh Jin Wu (armed forces), Yun Ki Chong (finance)
CURRENCY: won (end-'90 £1=NKW1.87, US$1=NKW0.97)
GNP PER CAPITA: US$910 ('88)
MAIN EXPORT EARNERS: minerals and metal ores, metallurgical products, agricultural
   products

DURING 1990 North Korea found itself increasingly isolated and dependent upon China as its only major international supporter. Jiang Zemin, general secretary of the Chinese Communist Party, paid a visit to Pyongyang on 14–16 March. A return visit by the North Korean Premier to China took place on 23–28 November. Premier Yon met Jiang Zemin, Li Peng (the Chinese Premier) and President Yang Shangkun. Neither of these visits provided the kind of staunch support which the North Korean government had been seeking. A month before Premier Yon's visit, the Chinese government gave tacit recognition of South Korea by signing a consular treaty with the ROK.

Because of these diplomatic reverses, and undoubtedly because of behind-the-scenes pressure from both the Soviet Union and China, high-level North Korean representatives took part in a series of dramatic meetings with their counterparts from the south (see p. 366). The most positive diplomatic event of this year was the visit of Shin Kanemaru, a former deputy prime minister of Japan and representative of the ruling Liberal-Democratic Party (LDP), together with Tanabe Makoto of the opposition Japan Socialist Party. This visit, followed by a courtesy visit to the South, led to meetings in the autumn in Beijing between representatives of the Japanese and North Korean governments (see p. 363). It seemed likely that diplomatic relations between the two states would be established shortly.

MONGOLIA

CAPITAL: Ulan Bator   AREA: 1,565,000 sq km   POPULATION: 2,094,200 ('90)
OFFICIAL LANGUAGE: Halh (Khalkha) Mongolian   POLITICAL SYSTEM: people's republic with ruling communist party sharing some powers
HEAD OF STATE: Punsalmaagiyn Ochirbat (MPRP), Chairman of Presidium of People's Great Hural (Mar–Sept '90), President (since Sept '90)
DEPUTY HEAD OF STATE: Radnaasümbereliyn Gonchigdorj (SDP), Vice-President and Chairman of State Little Hural (since Sept '90)
RULING PARTIES: Mongolian People's Revolutionary Party (MPRP), in coalition with Social Democratic (SDP), National Progress (NPP) and Mongolian Democratic (MDP) parties
PARTY LEADER: Gombojavyn Ochirbat, MPRP general secretary (Mar–Apr '90), chairman (since Apr '90)
PRINCIPAL MINISTERS: Dashiyn Byambasüren (MPRP/Prime Minister), Davaadorjiyn Ganbold (NPD/chief deputy premier), Dambiyn Dorligjav (MDP/deputy premier), Choyjilsürengiyn Pürevdorj (MPRP/deputy premier), Tserenpiliyn Gombosüren (MPRP/foreign relations), Lt.-Gen. Shagalyn Jadambaa (MPRP/defence), Sed-Ochiryn Bayarbaatar (MPRP/trade & industry)
INTERNATIONAL ALIGNMENT: Comecon
CURRENCY: tugrik (end-'90 £1=T10.35, US$1=T5.56)
GNP PER CAPITA: US$550 ('89)
MAIN EXPORT EARNERS: livestock, agricultural products, copper ore

A series of hunger strikes and illegal rallies for democracy in the early weeks of 1990 eventually obliged the Mongolian leaders to give way to popular demands for radical reform. The removal of the statue of Joseph Stalin from in front of the state library near the centre of Ulan Bator was an early sign of their new flexibility. Encouraged by dissatisfaction with socio-political conditions following the collapse of communist regimes in Eastern Europe, new political movements challenged the self-proclaimed leading role of the ruling Mongolian People's Revolutionary Party (MPRP).

The main new political force to emerge was the Mongolian Democratic Union (MDU), headed by Sanjaasürengiyn Dzorig, which gave birth to the Mongolian Democratic Party (MDP) led by Erdeniyn Bat-Üül. The Democratic Socialist Movement (DSM) under Radnaasümbereliyn

Gonchigdorj and the Social Democratic Party (SDP) led by Bat-Erdeniyn Batbayar published a democratic reform platform like the MDP's and quickly established contacts with European social democrats. The New Progress Association (NPA) and the National Progress Party (NPP) chaired by Davaadorjiyn Ganbold pursued a more radical nationalist line. These new parties together with the Union of Students formed the core of the reform movement, although other political parties were established including the Free Labour Party, Buddhist Democratic Party and Green Party.

Faced with growing pressure for reform from within the party as well as popular demands for an end to one-party rule, MPRP general secretary Jambyn Batmönh and the politburo resigned in March. Protegés of former leader Yumjaagiyn Tsedenbal, those who resigned were closely linked in most people's minds with his 'bureaucratic dictatorship' and 'administrative command methods' which had caused the country's socio-economic 'stagnation' and subjugation to the Soviets. Gombojavyn Ochirbat, a former trade union leader, became the new MPRP general secretary, and new faces were brought into the politburo.

In April there were further demonstrations of protest, this time against official restrictions on the holding of rallies in public places. When an extraordinary congress of the MPRP was held the same month, only 18 former members were re-elected to the 91-member central committee. The politburo was renamed the presidium and the general secretary was redesignated chairman of the party. A session of the People's Great Hural (national assembly), also in April, removed references to the MPRP's 'leading role' from the constitution and adopted a new law on the holding of general elections. Jambyn Batmönh resigned the post of Chairman of the Presidium of the People's Great Hural (head of state) and was replaced by Punsalmaagiyn Ochirbat, an MPRP reformer who had been Minister of Foreign Economic Relations and Supply. Calling for a market economy in Mongolia, Mr Ochirbat declared that Mongolia too could be an Asian 'tiger' with high economic growth rates like South Korea, Hong Kong, Taiwan and Singapore.

At the same time, Dumaagiyn Sodnom was replaced as Chairman of the Council of Ministers (Premier) by Sharavyn Gungaadorj, hitherto Minister of Agriculture and Food Industry, while Dashiyn Byambasüren was promoted first deputy premier with the concurrent post of chairman of the State Committee for Socio-Economic Development. New chief directorates of state police and state security replaced the despised Ministry of Public Security.

Another session of the People's Great Hural in May adopted a law legalizing political parties. It also amended the constitution to institute the post of President and restore the State Little Hural (abolished in 1950), a standing legislature with 50 members elected by the Great

Hural, this time with proportional representation of political parties. Three-quarters of the Little Hural members had to be deputies of the Great Hural.

General elections to the new 430-deputy People's Great Hural took place in July in two stages: the candidates were first reduced to two per constituency, although many rural constituencies had only one MPRP candidate; the ballot for the final winners was held a week later. The MPRP, with 61.74 per cent of the vote, won 357 seats in the Great Hural, (84.6 per cent of the total) and the MDP, with 24.33 per cent of the vote, won 16 seats (3.8 per cent). The NPP received 6 seats, the SDP 4 and the Revolutionary Youth League 9; 39 other deputies were without affiliation.

At its first session in September the Great Hural elected Punsalmaagiyn Ochirbat to the new post of President. DSM Chairman Radnaasümbereliyn Gonchigdorj was elected Vice-President and *ex officio* concurrently chairman of the Little Hural. The post of chairman (speaker) of the Great Hural went to MPRP member Jambyn Gombojav, with two of his four deputies being from the NPP and SDP. Kinayatyn Dzardyhan, a Mongolian Kazakh, was made vice-chairman of the Little Hural. MDA coordinator Sanjaasürengiyn Dzorig, perhaps the best-known of the new democrats, was elected chairman of the Great Hural's parliamentary group. The MPRP had won 31 seats in the Little Hural, the MDP 13 and the NPP and SDP 3 each.

The Great Hural approved the nomination of Dashiyn Byambasüren (MPRP), a reformer in favour of a market economy, to the new post of Prime Minister. Formation of the new government was a slow process, however, each nomination being debated at some length in the Little Hural before a vote was taken. NPP chairman Davaadorjiyn Ganbold was appointed Chief Deputy Prime Minister, while MDP deputy coordinator Dambiyn Dorligjav and former deputy premier Choyjilsürengiyn Pürevdorj (MPRP) were approved as deputy prime ministers. The number of ministries was roughly halved to 11 new ones as well as a State Committee for Protection of the Environment.

James Baker paid an official visit to Mongolia at the beginning of August—the first by a US Secretary of State—but was obliged to cut the visit short because of the Iraqi invasion of Kuwait. However, agreements signed during the visit provided for the despatch of US Peace Corps units to Mongolia, the development of trade and simplification of diplomatic procedures. Mr Baker said that the USA would be prepared to grant Mongolia most-favoured-nation status as soon as it had satisfied itself with regard to Mongolia's emigration laws (which were under review). Mongolians would be given training in the USA in banking, management, agriculture, legislation and the 'development of democratic institutions'.

President Punsalmaagiyn Ochirbat paid an official visit to Beijing, the first by a Mongolian head of state, soon after his inauguration in May. A week later, accompanied by MPRP general secretary Gombojavyn Ochirbat, he flew to Moscow to meet President Gorbachev. In November 1990 President Ochirbat visited Tokyo, where Prime Minister Toshiki Kaifu responded positively to Mongolia's request for Japanese economic and technical aid.

Soviet First Deputy Premier Vladilen Nikitin said in Ulan Bator in July that bilateral trade would be switched to world prices in 1991. Mongolia would be given a better price for its exports, especially raw materials. However, Soviet investments in Mongolia would decline to R200 million in 1991–92, compared with R480 million in 1989 and R450 million in 1990. Moreover, from 1 January 1991 the upkeep of Soviet technical advisers in Mongolia was to become Mongolia's responsibility. Altogether the number of Soviet advisers had fallen by almost 50 per cent to just over 18,500, plus some 6,300 dependants, over the past two years. In Ulan Bator flats vacated by those going home were taken over by Mongolian squatters.

Although the Mongolians and Soviets agreed to review all treaties and contracts signed by the two sides since the Mongolian revolution of July 1921, Mongolia did not succeed in persuading the Soviets to reduce Mongolia's R 9,500 million debt to the USSR. Moscow agreed to postponement of repayments for ten years, but demanded interest payments in 1991–95. Prime Minister Byambasüren stated in September that Mongolia wanted more talks with a view to recalculating the debt. 'Some of the Soviet projects in Mongolia cost too much and are very inefficient', he said. Later there was disagreement between the sides over the hard-currency equivalent of the debt, the Soviets claiming a rate of US$1=R 2 and the Mongolians US$1=R 10.

In an open letter to President Gorbachev published in several Ulan Bator newspapers, the Mongolian writer Jambyn Pürev said of the Mongolian debt that for many years the Soviets had bought cheap from Mongolia and sold dear—R 50 for a Mongolian cow, R 20,000 for a Soviet combine harvester. The Soviet Union monopolized gold, silver, copper and tin mining in Mongolia, Mr Pürev went on, making the Mongolians 'economically dependent on one single country on its terms' and obliging them to 'hand over their raw materials at prices dictated by it'.

Meanwhile, several attempts were made during late 1990 to daub the Lenin monument in central Ulan Bator with red paint. This gave rise to a debate on Lenin's views on Mongolia and a defence of leninism in the MPRP press.

X AUSTRALASIA AND SOUTH PACIFIC

Chapter 1

AUSTRALIA—PAPUA NEW GUINEA

AUSTRALIA

CAPITAL: Canberra AREA: 7,687,000 sq km POPULATION: 16,500,000 ('88)
OFFICIAL LANGUAGE: English POLITICAL SYSTEM: federal parliamentary democracy
HEAD OF STATE: Queen Elizabeth II GOVERNOR-GENERAL: William Hayden
RULING PARTY: Australian Labor Party (ALP)
HEAD OF GOVERNMENT: Robert (Bob) Hawke, Prime Minister (since March '83)
PRINCIPAL MINISTERS: Paul Keating (deputy premier, treasurer), Gareth Evans (foreign affairs & trade), John Button (industry, technology & commerce), Ralph Willis (finance), Robert Ray (defence), Michael Duffy (Attorney-General)
INTERNATIONAL ALIGNMENT: ANZUS, OECD, Cwth.
CURRENCY: Australian dollar (end-'90 £1=A$2.50, US$1=A$1.29)
GNP PER CAPITA: US$12,340 ('88)
MAIN EXPORT EARNERS: minerals, meat and agricultural products, basic manufactures

THE Australian Labor Party (ALP) government of Prime Minister Bob Hawke was returned for a fourth term in March. The rest of the year saw a slump in Labor's popularity caused by economic crises based largely on the speculative legacy of the preceding decade. Corporate and individual business failures escalated, affecting not only private but public enterprises too. There was no shift in parliamentary power but support for the opposition Liberal (LP) and National (NP) parties rose in the opinion polls to well above the Labor level.

The national elections of 24 March were remarkable in several respects. The ALP was returned with its lowest percentage support since the 1930s, a result made possible by the preferential voting system attracting second preferences to Labor from a variety of Australian Democrat (AD), Green and other minority candidates. These candidates between them secured 17 per cent of the vote for the House of Representatives (lower house) and 19 per cent for the Senate (upper house). This support, which was nearly twice as high as in 1987 (see AR 1987, p. 345), returned the first independent to the House of Representatives since 1966 and increased minor party Senate representation to eight Democrats, one Green and one independent. Growing support for minor parties was accompanied by a decline in ALP lower house support from 45.8 per cent in 1987 to 39.4 per cent and of NP support from 11.5 to 8.4 per cent, the party's lowest proportion since 1955, placing them behind the Democrats for the first time. The LP vote rose only slightly above its level of the preceding three elections.

The elections were also remarkable in that three of the four major parties changed their leadership after the result. The familiar alternation between John Howard and Andrew Peacock for Liberal leadership was ended with Mr Peacock's resignation and his replacement at the beginning of April by John Hewson, a 43-year-old economics professor who had only served for three years in parliament. Like Mr Howard, he was from Sydney and represented the 'economic rationalist' or 'free market' wing of the party. The new NP leader, Charles Blunt (see AR 1989, p. 358), lost his northern New South Wales seat and was replaced by Tim Fischer, also from New South Wales. The NP lost its Senate leader, John Stone, who contested a Queensland lower house seat and was defeated. The AD leader, Janine Haines, also stood down from the Senate and was defeated in a Labor seat in Adelaide. She was replaced by Senator Janet Powell. There were no Labor leadership changes and no major party figures lost their seats. A very bad ALP result in Victoria was compensated for by gains in New South Wales and Queensland. The final results were:

	Representatives %	seats	Senate %	seats
ALP	39.4	78	38.4	32
LP	35.0	55	41.9	34
NP	8.4	14		
AD	11.3	-	12.6	8
Others	5.9	1	7.1	2

With a comfortable majority in the House of Representatives, the ALP was able, for the first time in its history, to form a fourth government. In the Senate it was dependent on negotiations with the Democrats on a number of issues.

The very weak showing for the ALP in Victoria, where it lost nine seats to the Liberals, reflected the collapse of support for the state government. State issues were also relevant in Queensland, where scandals surrounding the defeated NP government were still being revealed throughout the year (see AR 1989, p. 359–60). In Victoria, the second largest state and a banking and financial centre, the year began with a month-long Melbourne tramways strike which left abandoned trams in the city centre as a continuing reminder of the dispute over manning and a new, unworkable (and eventually abandoned) ticketing system. In January it was revealed that Tricontinental, the merchant banking arm of the State Bank, had lost A$900 million and that the bank was heading for its first loss in 148 years. At the state by-election for Thomastown on 3 February there was a swing of 24 per cent in a once safe Labor seat. On 22 February ministers assured shareholders in the private Pyramid building society that their investments were safe, which soon proved to be untrue when Pyramid closed its doors and share trading was ended in June. Financial disasters, coupled with the poor national election result for Labor, forced the resignation of state treasurer Rob Jolly on 30 March.

By April opinion polls were showing a dramatic decline in Labor support in Victoria and by June support for the premier, John Cain, had fallen to 26 per cent, the lowest since his triumphant election in 1982 (see AR 1982, p. 317). Mr Cain had personally guaranteed Pyramid shareholders against losses, but his popularity dropped to 20 per cent on 20 July and he resigned on 7 August. Mr Cain blamed disloyalty and bickering for his decision but it soon became clear that Victoria was in very serious financial straits in both the public and the private sectors. He was replaced by Joan Kirner, the second woman premier in Australian history after Carmen Lawrence, elected in Western Australia on 12 February in rather similar circumstances of financial crisis and ALP dissension.

On 26 August an agreement was reached for the Commonwealth Bank to take over the Victoria State Bank for A$2,000 million. The State Bank, mainly through its Tricontinental dealings, had bad debts of A$2,700 million, which would have consumed its entire capital. The Commonwealth Bank, in a decision which caused some controversy within the ALP, was to sell 30 per cent of its assets to the private sector to finance the arrangement. On 28 August Mrs Kirner announced the establishment of a royal commission into Tricontinental. Two days later a state budget was introduced which cut 8,000 public sector jobs and sold off A$1,000 billion of public assets. While these policies went far towards solving the immediate financial crisis, Victoria's economy began to show serious signs of depression, with rising unemployment, towards the end of the year.

Apart from these crises in the public sector, there was continuing instability in some major private corporations. The Bond Corporation continued to survive (see AR 1989, p. 360) through a series of complex arrangements, but Alan Bond was arrested and charged on 6 December over his 1987 rescue bid for the Rothwell's finance company. The end of the year saw two of the three commercial television networks and the oldest and second-largest print media corporation (Fairfax) in the hands of the receiver and being prepared for sale. Companies which also got into very serious difficulties included Adelaide Steamship, whose shares slumped on 1 December, and the brewing giant Elders-IXL.

Corporate Australia lost one of its best-known entrepreneurs with the death of Robert Holmes à Court on 4 September. His companies had been making a recovery from previous crises and their control passed to his widow. Australia's richest man, Kerry Packer, suffered a severe heart attack while playing polo on 7 October but made a quick recovery and also survived the surrounding corporate decline, being well placed for control of various media. Less fortunate was George Herscu, of the failed Hooker Corporation, who was gaoled on 7 December for bribing former Queensland minister Russell Hinze, whose own trial was delayed as he was suffering from cancer. Also gaoled, in May, was Tasmanian businessman Edmund Rouse, for attempting to bribe a Tasmanian Labor politician in the aftermath of the close state election of the previous year (see AR 1989, p. 359).

In other similar developments, three former National Party ministers in Queensland were gaoled for a variety of financial misdemeanours while in office. On 30 November Perth businessmen Laurie Connell and Dallas Dempster were arrested and charged in connection with the Rothwell's collapse. Mr Connell denounced his arrest and raids on his home and offices as 'disgraceful and political' on 3 December. Other former entrepreneurs were charged at the end of the year in connection with Rothwell's and the Spedley Group. By the end of the year the speculative boom of the 1980s was looking quite battered, with the individual and corporate rich in crisis and the Commonwealth Treasurer, Paul Keating, eventually admitting in December that Australia was in recession. The only benefit of all this was a lowering of interest rates from the record high levels of 1989 and a decline in inflation.

The tarnished reputation of Australian business prompted various attempts to improve and control matters. The most important was the creation of an Australian Securities Commission (ASC), to take full powers from 1 January 1991, replacing the previous National Companies and Securities Commission (NCSC). However, the powers of the ASC, under the Commonwealth Australian Securities Commission Act and the Corporations Act (both of 1989), were held to be unconstitutional by the High Court on 8 February, on the grounds that the constitution allocated company registration to the states. The ASC was meant to operate from 1 July but this was delayed by a series of complex manoeuvres as the federal government tried to secure state agreement to refer their powers. Agreement was reached on 4 May, but subject to states amending their laws. The conservative majority in the Western Australia legislative council took the opportunity to obstruct the decision of the lower house, despite the general agreement of all other states, business and the national Liberal Party. It did not renege from this opposition until December. Despite difficulties over compensation to the States and staffing questions, the transition from the NCSC to the ASC was effected between July and January, under the chairmanship of Tony Hartnell. It was expected that the new arrangements would be much more effective in creating uniform company law and supervision.

The ALP, forming the government of the country and in five of the six states, was obliged to inspect its basic principles, which it did without serious disruption at a special conference on 24 September. This sought to depart from traditional Labor policy in encouraging the privatization of federal agencies in aviation and telecommunications. It resolved that the international airline Qantas would remain in public ownership at a level of 51 per cent control, but that the domestic Australian Airlines could be completely sold. The telephone and telecommunications monopoly Telecom would remain publicly-owned but be forced to compete with a private network based on the sale of the Aussat satellite system, which would be entitled to use the existing Telecom networks for a fee. Service to remote and rural areas was to be maintained. Other government business enterprises were to operate on a fully commercial basis. Funds resulting from the sale of public assets would be used for national economic development and for achieving social justice goals. The sobering experience of state Labor governments with failed business enterprises, and the general intellectual acceptance of competitive markets, made it relatively easy for the party leadership to amend the platform in a direction permitting such privatization, despite nearly a century of commitment to public ownership by the Australian labour movement.

A special premiers' conference in October endorsed the 'new federalism', replacing tied grants by block grants to the states and extending their responsibilities in welfare areas where there was felt to be undue overlap and duplication. This, like the emphasis on deregulation, privatization and market forces, marked a shift towards approaches previously identified with the conservative parties. Airline deregulation became effective on 31 October, a long pilots' dispute having ended in mid-March with the defeat of their union.

The year saw the celebration of the 75th anniversary of the landing at Gallipoli on 25 April, with the Prime Minister accompanying a party of the few remaining veterans to the site in Turkey. On 6 June the federal government extended asylum to 20,000 Chinese students resident in Australia, but this was modified on 12 June, when their residence rights were limited to four years pending political changes in China. Immigration numbers dropped off, partly in response to the perceived state of the economy, and regulations concerning refugee status were tightened. The new Aboriginal and Torres Strait Islander Commission (ATSIC) came into being and its first elections were held in November. In October the ruling Country-Liberal administration was returned in the Northern Territory in an election in which the powers of ATSIC and aboriginal land rights were major issues. Australia failed in its bid to secure the 1996 Olympic Games for Melbourne. In August the government gave full support to the UN blockade of Iraq by sending two frigates and a supply ship to the Gulf.

On 30 September Patrick White died at the age of 78. He won the Nobel Prize for literature in 1973 and was widely regarded as Australia's leading writer (see OBITUARY).

PAPUA NEW GUINEA

CAPITAL: Port Moresby AREA: 463,000 sq km POPULATION: 3,700,000 ('88)
OFFICIAL LANGUAGES: Pidgin, Motu, English
POLITICAL SYSTEM: parliamentary democracy
HEAD OF STATE: Queen Elizabeth II
GOVERNOR-GENERAL: Sir Kingsford Dibela
RULING PARTIES: coalition headed by Pangu Pati
HEAD OF GOVERNMENT: Rabbie Namaliu, Prime Minister (since July '88)
PRINCIPAL MINISTERS: Ted Diro (deputy premier, public services), Michael Somare (foreign affairs), Arnold Marsipal (defence), Paul Pora (finance & planning), Matthew Bendumb (home affairs), Bernard Narakobi (justice)
INTERNATIONAL ALIGNMENT: Cwth., ACP
CURRENCY: kina (end-'90 £1=K1.83, US$1=K0.95)
GNP PER CAPITA: US$810 ('88)
MAIN EXPORT EARNERS: copper, coffee, palm oil, cocoa

THE secession crisis on the island of Bougainville continued to dominate the political and economic environment in 1990 (see AR 1989 pp. 361–2). The rapid escalation of the guerrilla campaign against the central government led, in March, to a precipitate withdrawal of government forces from the island, leaving it under the effective control of the rebel Bougainville Revolutionary Army (BRA). One consequence of this was a disorganized (and evidently inebriated) attempt by the national police commissioner and controller of the state of emergency on Bougainville, Paul Tohian, to mount a coup against the government in Port Moresby. The challenge was wholly unsuccessful, receiving only limited support from sections of the police and none at all from the army. To the surprise of many accustomed to the traditionally-relaxed response to high-level wrong-doing, however, Commissioner Tohian was charged with treason.

In May the BRA declared an independent republic in Bougainville. The new 'state' failed to secure any recognition abroad and the government in Port Moresby responded with a blockade of supplies. After a number of false starts, the two sides agreed to talks on the neutral ground of New Zealand naval vessels off Bougainville. Despite claims of a breakthrough following the first round of talks, no concrete proposals for a settlement emerged. The BRA lacked organizational cohesion, and the nature and identity of its leadership were difficult to discern. Such a situation made viable agreements virtually impossible. By the end of the year the government had reimposed its blockade and had occupied the offshore island of Buin.

The crisis—and the contingent loss of revenue from the giant Panguna copper mine—continued to have a major impact on the national economy. Massive cuts were imposed on the hitherto relatively high levels of public spending and, in January, the kina was devalued by 10 per cent. Emergency economic aid was sought and secured from Australia. One effect of this stringency was a worsening of Papua New Guinea's chronic crime problem. More positively, however, the 'infection' of Bougainville did not, as many had feared, spread into the other largescale mining projects being developed around the country. The longer-term prospects for the mineral sector remained relatively bright.

Parliamentary politics remained volatile during 1990. In April Ted Diro, the 'disgraced' former Foreign Minister and leader of the Papuan block of MPs, completed his reintegration into the higher levels of government when he was appointed Deputy Prime Minister (see AR 1989, p. 362). In July the Namaliu government survived a no-confidence vote. The victory was, however, tainted by reports that several ministers had been bribed to give up their posts in order to free portfolios for wavering backbenchers. This was a disappointment to those who saw Mr Namaliu as one of the less corruptible of national politicians and provoked a huge student-led public protest outside the parliament building.

In November, after the successful passage of the annual budget, Mr Namaliu suspended parliament until late in the following year, thus pre-empting further no-confidence votes. The move, while extraordinary in constitutional terms, had little practical importance, since the legislative and supervisory functions of the national parliament were anyway distinctly limited.

Chapter 2

NEW ZEALAND

CAPITAL: Wellington   AREA: 270,000 sq km   POPULATION: 3,300,000 ('88)
OFFICIAL LANGUAGE: English   POLITICAL SYSTEM: parliamentary democracy
HEAD OF STATE: Queen Elizabeth II
GOVERNOR-GENERAL: Dame Catherine Tizard
RULING PARTY: National Party (NP)
HEAD OF GOVERNMENT: Jim Bolger, Prime Minister (since Oct '90)
PRINCIPAL MINISTERS: Don McKinnon (deputy premier, external relations & trade), Ruth Richardson (finance), Warren Cooper (defence), Paul East (Attorney-General), Doug Graham (justice)
INTERNATIONAL ALIGNMENT: ANZUS (suspended), OECD, Cwth.
CURRENCY: New Zealand dollar (end-'90 £1=NZ$3.28, US$1=NZ$1.69)
GNP PER CAPITA: US$10,000 ('88)
MAIN EXPORT EARNERS: meat and meat products, wool, dairy products

THE dominant event of the year was the spectacular defeat of the Labour government in an October general election. Mike Moore's Labour Party saw its parliamentary strength halved to only 29 seats in the newly-elected 97-member House of Representatives. Seven ministers lost their seats, as did the Speaker, his deputy, four junior ministers, and both whips. The National Party (NP) led by 55-year-old Jim Bolger, a King Country farmer, registered only a slight increase of support to reach 48 per cent of the vote, but third parties such as New

Labour and the Greens took 16 per cent (but only one seat), benefiting from a massive defection by traditional Labour voters. Compared with the 1987 general election, the Labour Party sustained a punishing 13 per cent cut in its share of the total vote.

Labour was defeated so heavily because it lost touch with its core support by following economic policies that failed to generate jobs, growth, or confidence in the country's future. Three years of unrelieved political infighting within government ranks also took its toll at the ballot box. This occurred between those favouring continuing deregulation, tight control of the money supply and the sale of state assets, and those endorsing a return to Labour's traditional welfare and state intervention policies. In a desperate manoeuvre barely eight weeks before the election, the cabinet deposed sitting Prime Minister Geoffrey Palmer, replacing him with the more ebullient Mike Moore.

One of Mr Moore's first initiatives was getting an agreement with the trade unions to restrict wage increases to 2 per cent during the following year, although with allowances for productivity improvements. The Reserve Bank agreed that if the unions could agree to small wage increases this would curb inflation and enable the bank to pursue an easier monetary policy. Although regarded as a positive measure, this so-called growth agreement was seen as coming too late to assist Labour's chances of returning to office.

The election occurred in a bleak economic environment characterized by faltering growth, a deteriorating international trading outlook, unemployment at 206,000 and rising, a large balance-of-payments deficit, and a growing internal budgetary crisis. During the campaign both major parties were vague about how they would deal with these problems, because their internal divisions over economic policy were wider than those between them. In March the Labour government made a controversial agreement with the Reserve Bank to operate monetary policy so as to achieve an annual rate of inflation of 0–2 per cent by December 1992. For many Labour Party activists that target was too severe in its likely generation of further unemployment and public-sector retrenchment.

The 0–2 per cent inflation guideline was accepted by Mr Bolger and colleague Ruth Richardson (duly appointed Finance Minister) as appropriate for 1993, but attacked by other NP figures such as former Prime Minister Sir Robert Muldoon and the high profile Maori affairs spokesperson, Winston Peters.

Mr Moore tried to distance himself from the deregulation and monetarism of Labour's former finance minister, Roger Douglas, but could not do so entirely without further jeopardizing frail party unity. In a July budget, Finance Minister David Caygill had sought to provide a financial surplus and give the business community confidence that controls on public spending would help to ease interest rates.

Although the annual rate of inflation was kept to 5 per cent, the cost of 90-day bills never fell below 13 per cent before the election. The Labour government's attempts to forestall an internal deficit were based on its controversial continuation of state asset sales into private ownership. This gave it returns from the disposal of State Insurance, the Shipping Corporation, the Tourist Hotel Corporation, and various printing, film, and energy interests. Easily the biggest deal occurred in June when Telecom was sold for NZ$4,500 million to Bell Atlantic and Ameritech of the United States.

The Labour government indicated that asset sales returns would be used for spending on education and to relieve international debt. This programme was controversial, however, not least because it was directed by Richard Prebble who returned to the cabinet on 31 January as Minister of State Enterprises, having been sacked by former Prime Minister Lange in 1988 (see AR 1988, p. 367).

Once in office, Prime Minister Bolger faced an awesome array of difficulties. One of his first steps was to inject NZ$620 million of public money towards a capital restructuring of the ailing Bank of New Zealand. The government repealed Labour's 1990 legislation facilitating pay equity for women. Committed to deregulation of the labour market, the new government then removed award coverage and arbitration settlement procedures and introduced voluntary unionism. Representing a massive revision of industrial relations, these measures effectively ended the state's role as a protector of union rights.

But within weeks of gaining office, the new government backtracked over other pre-election promises such as additional funding for higher police numbers, relief for pensioners by the removal of the existing surcharge on the guaranteed retirement income, and spending to curb unemployment. In December, and following a quickly-established review of all public spending, the government launched a full-scale assault on the welfare state. The long-established family benefit was abolished, with other benefit levels slashed in welfare cuts designed to halve a projected internal deficit of NZ$5,000 million by 1993. Health and prescription charges were increased and cuts made in pre-school education.

The country's economic difficulties were compounded by the oil price rises that followed Iraq's invasion of Kuwait in August. The December breakdown of the long-running GATT Uruguay round, leaving the European Community's damaging common agricultural policy essentially intact, was regarded as ominous by the primary export sector. Declining real returns for key exports compounded existing market access difficulties for New Zealand. Some relief occurred in December with the conclusion of major dairy produce sales to the Soviet Union and Iran.

For the Labour government an important foreign relations concern was the sponsorship of a protocol formula for inclusion in the existing Antarctic Treaty, providing for a permanent ban on mining and effective environmental preservation of the continent. Resisted by the United Kingdom and Japan, this initiative made some progress at an Antarctic Treaty consultative parties meeting held in Chile.

The incoming government decided in December to commit military transport and medical units to the Gulf following UN Security Council Resolution 678 (see DOCUMENTS). This was an attempt to improve relations with the United States following the breakdown of security relations between the two countries over Labour's ban on nuclear-propelled or armed vessels entering New Zealand. Before the general election the National Party had changed its position by indicating that it would not repeal 1987 legislation formalizing that ban.

In May the Labour government released an official report on New Zealand's relations with the South Pacific. Although the government tabled the report's recommendations on environmental policy before the South Pacific Forum meeting in July, it did not act on a suggestion to resume high-level contacts with the military-backed regime in Fiji. However, the Foreign Minister in the Bolger administration, Don McKinnon, met with Prime Minister Ratu Sir Kamisese Mara of Fiji and indicated that New Zealand would recommence use of Fiji's facilities for air surveillance in the South Pacific. Mr McKinnon added that any resumption of military assistance could only occur once Fiji held elections under its new constitution (see p. 383).

Before it was defeated, the Labour government introduced legislation restricting smoking in indoor environments, eliminating the promotion and advertising of tobacco products, and creating a health sponsorship council. Port and transport reforms were also completed. In August, the government announced policy guidelines aimed at a 20 per cent reduction in carbon dioxide emissions in the following 15 years, and a similar reduction in solid waste streams by 1993.

When parliament was prorogued the outgoing government left incomplete its Resource Management Bill (see AR 1989, p. 365), although the National Party did not say that it would drop the bill. By contrast, the incoming government's Minister for Maori Affairs, Winston Peters, indicated his lack of support for the Waitangi Tribunal's assumption of mandatory powers.

The year was remarkable for the scale of detected fraud in financial operations. After months of detailed investigations, the serious fraud office produced information that resulted in the arrest of leading figures in the collapsed Equiticorp conglomerate. Their alleged conspiracy to defraud involved a massive NZ$500 million dollars, arising from Equiticorp's purchase of New Zealand Steel from the government and related transactions.

The year also saw a visit by Queen Elizabeth II, as part of the 1990 sesquicentennial celebrations of the Treaty of Waitangi. Other notable events included the ordination of New Zealand's first woman bishop and the appointment of its first woman governor-general, Dame Catherine (Cath) Tizard.

Chapter 3

SOUTH PACIFIC

Fiji
CAPITAL: Suva AREA: 18,375 sq km POPULATION: 732,000 ('88)
OFFICIAL LANGUAGES: Fijian, Hindi POLITICAL SYSTEM: presidential republic
HEAD OF STATE: President Sir Penaia Ganilau (since Nov. '87)
HEAD OF GOVERNMENT: Sir Kamisese Mara, Prime Minister (since Dec '87)
CURRENCY: Fiji dollar (end-'90 £1=F$2.83, US$1=F$1.46)
GNP PER CAPITA: US$1,520 ('88)
MAIN EXPORT EARNERS: sugar, agricultural products, tourism

New Caledonia
CAPITAL: Nouméa AREA: 19,000 sq km POPULATION: 158,000 ('88)
STATUS: French overseas territory

Solomon Islands
CAPITAL: Honiara AREA: 28,000 sq km POPULATION: 303,000 ('88)
OFFICIAL LANGUAGE: English POLITICAL SYSTEM: parliamentary democracy
HEAD OF STATE: Queen Elizabeth II
HEAD OF GOVERNMENT: Solomon Mamaloni, Prime Minister (since March '86)
GOVERNOR-GENERAL: Sir George Lepping
CURRENCY: Solomon Islands dollar (end-'90 £1=SI$5.05, US$1=SI$2.61)
GNP PER CAPITA: US$630 ('88)
MAIN EXPORT EARNERS: timber, copra, fish, tourism

Vanuatu
CAPITAL: Port Vila AREA: 12,000 sq km POPULATION: 147,000 ('88)
OFFICIAL LANGUAGES: English, French, Bislama
POLITICAL SYSTEM: parliamentary democracy
HEAD OF STATE: President Fred Timakata (since Jan '89)
HEAD OF GOVERNMENT: Fr Walter Lini, Prime Minister (since '83)
CURRENCY: vatu (end-'90 £1=VT216.50, US$1=VT112.18)
GNP PER CAPITA: US$840 ('88)
MAIN EXPORT EARNERS: copra, agricultural products, tourism

Kiribati
CAPITAL: Tarawa AREA: 1,000 sq km POPULATION: 67,000 ('88)
OFFICIAL LANGUAGE: English POLITICAL SYSTEM: parliamentary democracy
HEAD OF STATE AND GOVERNMENT: President Ieremia Tabai (since '79)
CURRENCY: Australian dollar (end-'90 £1=A$2.50, US$1=A$1.29)
GNP PER CAPITA: US$650 ('88)
MAIN EXPORT EARNERS: copra, phosphates, tourism

Tuvalu
CAPITAL: Fongafale AREA: 26 sq km POPULATION: 8,700 ('88)
OFFICIAL LANGUAGES: Tuvaluan, English
POLITICAL SYSTEM: parliamentary democracy
HEAD OF STATE: Queen Elizabeth II GOVERNOR-GENERAL: Toalipi Lati
HEAD OF GOVERNMENT: Bikenibeu Paeniu, Prime Minister (since Sept '89)
CURRENCY: Australian dollar (end-'90 £1=A$2.50, US$1=A$1.29)
GNP PER CAPITA: US$680 ('81)
MAIN EXPORT EARNERS: copra, tourism

Western Samoa
CAPITAL: Apia   AREA: 2,830 sq km   POPULATION: 159,000 ('88)
OFFICIAL LANGUAGES: Samoan, English   POLITICAL SYSTEM: monarchy
HEAD OF STATE: Susuga Malietoa Tanumafili II (since Jan '62)
HEAD OF GOVERNMENT: Tofilau Eti Alesana, Prime Minister (since April '88)
CURRENCY: tala (end-'90 £1=ws$4.37, us$1=ws$2.26)
GNP PER CAPITA: US$640 ('88)
MAIN EXPORT EARNERS: cocoa, copra, agricultural products, tourism

American Samoa
CAPITAL: Pago Pago   AREA: 197 sq km   POPULATION: 37,000 ('88)
STATUS: unincorporated territory of USA

Niue
CAPITAL: Alofi   AREA: 250 sq km   POPULATION: 2,700 ('88)
STATUS: self-governing associated territory of New Zealand

Tonga
CAPITAL: Nuku'alofa   AREA: 750 sq km   POPULATION: 100,000 ('88)
OFFICIAL LANGUAGES: Tongan, English   POLITICAL SYSTEM: monarchy
HEAD OF STATE: King Taufa'ahua Tupou IV (since Dec '65)
HEAD OF GOVERNMENT: Prince Fatafehi Tu'ipelehake, Prime Minister
CURRENCY: pa'anga (end-'90 £1=T$2.50, us$1=T$1.29)
GNP PER CAPITA: US$830 ('88)
MAIN EXPORT EARNERS: agricultural products, tourism

French Polynesia
CAPITAL: Papeete   AREA: 4,200 sq km   POPULATION: 186,000 ('88)
STATUS: French overseas territory

Belau
CAPITAL: Koror   AREA: 500 sq km   POPULATION: 8,500 ('86)
STATUS: republic with US commonwealth status

Marshall Islands
CAPITAL: Dalap-Uliga-Darrit   AREA: 200 sq km   POPULATION: 41,000 ('88)
STATUS: free association with US

IN FIJI a new constitution was promulgated in July. As widely expected, it placed predominant power in the hands of the Fijian Council of Chiefs, who were given authority to appoint a President for a five-year term and 24 Fijians to a 34-member Senate. A House of Representatives was proposed comprising (i) 37 seats for Fijians, although through a form of representation discriminating against urban Fijians (whose votes were decisive in electing the Bavadra government toppled by the military in 1987); (ii) 27 seats for Indians; and (iii) six for other races. The opposition indicated that it would boycott elections contested under the proposed constitution, which was also attacked as discriminatory by legal and human rights groups internationally. Relations with India worsened, the Indian mission in Suva being closed by Fiji on the grounds that India was interfering in domestic politics and blocking Fiji's return to the Commonwealth.

In NEW CALEDONIA Paul Neaoutyine returned from a period of political limbo when he was elected president of the Kanak Socialist Liberation Front. Representatives of the pro-independence Front made progress at the South Pacific Forum in gaining regular access to its meetings to present their views. In May the French government reached an agreement with a Franco/Japanese consultancy for a feasibility study on the technical and commercial prospects for a free port zone in the north of the main island.

In the SOLOMON ISLANDS Prime Minister Mamaloni outwitted his rivals when he resigned from his ruling Alliance Party in October to form a government of national unity. He then sacked five of his former Alliance cabinet colleagues, replacing them with four key opposition figures and a backbencher. Among the new appointees was former Prime Minister Sir Peter Kenilorea, who accepted responsibilities for foreign relations.

In VANUATU Father Walter Lini conducted a November reshuffle of his cabinet. He took over the foreign relations portfolio from Donald Kapolkas as well as adding energy to his responsibilities. At the UN General Assembly, and with specific reference to US chemical weapons destruction on Johnston Atoll, Father Lini said the South Pacific should not become a permanent toxic waste disposal centre.

At international conferences on the environment and climate change held in Stockholm and Geneva respectively, representatives from KIRIBATI (Peter Timeon) and TUVALU (Prime Minister Paeniu) warned about the dangers of greenhouse warming and climate change to their low-lying atoll countries.

In WESTERN SAMOA legislation was passed in December giving all adults the right to vote. The right to stand for election remained restricted to *matai* title holders. This followed narrow approval for universal suffrage in an October referendum.

In AMERICAN SAMOA Governor Peter Coleman surprised the US government by saying that the territory would seek autonomy from the United States, although not full independence.

In NIUE 82-year-old Premier Robert Rex withstood a challenge to his leadership following an April election which saw the formation of an action group to contest the leadership.

In TONGA Akilisi Pohiva's reform group, demanding greater accountability from the ruling nobles and monarchy, won six of the nine seats allocated to commoners in a February election for the country's 33-member Assembly.

FRENCH POLYNESIA received a visit from President Mitterrand, who indicated that the territory, now enjoying greater internal autonomy, would receive further economic assistance from France, but would face continued nuclear weapons testing by France. A study conducted by American scientist Norman Buske revealed that radioactivity from French nuclear testing at Muroroa Atoll was leaking into the sea within six years of each detonation.

In BELAU electors failed for the seventh time in seven years to reach the 75 per cent required under the territory's constitution to alter its constitutional ban on nuclear weaponry and permit the United States to introduce nuclear weapons into the country. The United States again maintained that it was unwilling to accept any compact of free association not allowing it to station nuclear weapons in Belau.

The people of Enewetak Atoll in the MARSHALL ISLANDS filed a class action suit contending that the United States had failed to compensate them adequately for the damage to the islands from 43 nuclear weapons tests.

Throughout Polynesia widespread destruction and the loss of seven lives occurred in February in the wake of Cyclone Ofa. The worst devastation in living memory occurred in Western Samoa, with Niue, Tokelau and Tuvalu also sustaining serious damage.

XI INTERNATIONAL ORGANIZATIONS

Chapter 1

THE UNITED NATIONS AND ITS AGENCIES

IT was a momentous year for the United Nations. For the first time in its often turbulent history, it achieved the near-miracle of having 12 potentially controversial Security Council resolutions on the Gulf crisis passed without recourse to the veto by any of the five permanent members (China, France, the United Kingdom, the USSR and the USA). This was due, in part, to the euphoria following the almost complete thawing of the Cold War between the USA and the USSR. From August until the end of the year the UN was given the opportunity of playing the role always envisaged by its founding fathers: that of a world authority reacting positively within the terms of its charter to the blatant aggression of one member state against another.

The invasion of Kuwait by Iraq on 2 August presented the UN with an almost classic scenario of how to deal with an explosive situation capable of producing a third world war. The year ended with the UN still holding the ring as the last resort for the future of global justice and peace. As the Secretary-General, Javier Pérez de Cuellar, emphasized in his UN day message on 24 October: 'What is being tested is nothing less than the organization's capacity to establish the rule of law in international relations and its consistency in applying its principles.'

45th GENERAL ASSEMBLY. The Assembly began its 45th session on 18 September and elected Guido de Marco of Malta as its president. In his opening address, Mr de Marco stated that, despite the ending of the Cold War, events in the Middle East had brought about the realization that there were still serious problems which continued to pose threats to the world's political, economic and social development. Apart from the Gulf crisis, the people in Palestine, Cyprus and Lebanon were all looking to the UN for just and peaceful solutions.

In his annual report to the General Assembly, the Secretary-General said the world was experiencing a period which contained 'both the aspects of hope and the countenance of dangerous unrestraint'. In one major segment of world affairs 'a political change of phenomenal character' had occurred. However, in large parts of the globe the scene continued to be one of 'simmering resentments, violent collisions and at best a precarious peace'. During 1990 the UN had had remarkable success in conducting a variety of operations aimed at managing peaceful transitions in societies troubled by conflicts. He referred specifically to Namibia and Central America, adding that encouraging progress continued to be made towards resolving the problem of Western Sahara and that a solution to the conflict in Kampuchea might be within reach. On the problem of development, Sr Pérez de Cuellar said the distortions in the international economy were reflected in the crisis of the least-developed countries, most of which were in Africa.

The Assembly elected five non-permanent members to the Security Council to serve in 1991: Austria, Belgium, Ecuador, India and Zimbabwe (replacing Canada, Colombia, Ethiopia, Finland and Malaysia). The election of Namibia and Liechtenstein brought the total UN membership to 160 states.

FINANCE. According to figures published in 1990, member states owed the UN over $402 million in outstanding contributions, of which $300 million was owed by the United States. Moreover, the peacekeeping budget was $346 million short of sums received in 1989.

POLITICAL QUESTIONS

IRAQ-KUWAIT. Immediately after the invasion of Kuwait by Iraq, the Security Council convened an emergency meeting just before dawn on 2 August New York time. In a unanimous vote (Yemen did not participate), the Council adopted resolution 660 demanding the immediate and unconditional withdrawal of the Iraqi forces from Kuwait (see DOCUMENTS for texts of the main Security Council resolutions on the Gulf crisis).

Addressing the Council, Mohammed A. Abulhasan of Kuwait said the problem must be solved by peaceful means, not by force. The situation was a test for the Council and was important to the peace and security of all nations, particularly those which were small and insecure. Sabat Talat Kadrat, speaking for Iraq, insisted that the matter was an internal affair which should not have been brought before the Council. The US delegate, Thomas R. Pickering, said his country had made it clear that it would stand 'shoulder to shoulder with Kuwait in this time of crisis'. The UN Secretary-General declared that the events were of the 'gravest consequence' to the UN and its member states, and urged that the Council should await the outcome of discussions taking place in Cairo between the ministers of the Arab League.

Four days later the Council adopted resolution 661 with two abstentions (Cuba and Yemen), calling on the international community to impose mandatory economic sanctions against Iraq. On 9 August resolution 662 unanimously declared Iraq's annexation of Kuwait to be 'null and void'.

In the meantime, negotiations were going on behind the scenes in New York among member states trying to produce solutions to lessen the tension and achieve a compromise. For his part, the Secretary-General said he was proud of the way in which the Council had dealt with the problem. In less than eight days it had produced three resolutions which were evidence of the responsibility of its members. With regard to the Soviet Union's suggestion that the Military Staff Committee of the Security Council should become involved, he said it was an interesting idea which deserved full consideration but it was for the Council to decide. He described the US troop movements in the Gulf as 'parallel' to the decisions of the Council.

Another unanimous resolution (664), adopted on 18 August, demanded that Iraq 'permit and facilitate' the immediate departure of all third-country nationals from Iraq and Kuwait. A further resolution (665) of 25 August, on which Cuba and Yemen abstained, called on member states to use 'measures commensurate to the specific circumstances' to halt all maritime shipping going to Iraq. The Security Council had set up a committee to monitor the implementation of sanctions against Iraq and on 13 September by resolution 666 (Cuba and Yemen against) requested the Secretary-General urgently to seek information from the relevant UN and other humanitarian agencies on the availability of food in Iraq and Kuwait and inform the sanctions committee of his findings. Three days later another unanimous resolution (667) condemned aggressive acts perpetrated by Iraq against diplomatic premises and personnel in Kuwait. On 24 September, by resolution 669, the Security Council decided unanimously to authorize the sanctions committee to examine requests for assistance under article 50 of the charter and recommend appropriate actions.

Meanwhile, at Kuwait's request, an item entitled 'Iraqi aggression and the continued occupation of Kuwait in flagrant violation of the UN charter' was given priority consideration in the General Assembly. As a result, many top-ranking delegates gave their governments' views on the crisis during the general debate, in most cases entirely predictably.

The British Foreign Secretary, Douglas Hurd, said the chances of a more secure world order depended directly on the success of the international coalition in reversing the occupation of Kuwait. Calling for a new and serious attempt to resolve the complex of Middle East disputes, including Palestine, he said there was also a need for a new security structure.

President Bush of the United States forecast that in the aftermath of Iraq's unconditional departure from Kuwait there would be opportunities for both countries to settle their differences and for all the states in the region to settle the conflict that divided the Arabs from Israel. He reiterated his country's support for sanctions and cited the improved relationship between the United States and the Soviet Union as critical to the emergence of a stronger United Nations.

The Soviet Foreign Minister, Eduard Shevardnadze, asserted that the

Security Council must have the means to enforce its decisions and have a mechanism for preparing and coordinating such action. It should begin by reactivating the work of the Military Staff Committee. He also proposed that the Security Council should set up an expert group to consider ways to deal with 'unconventional situations' arising from the mass taking of hostages and cases of blackmail involving particularly dangerous and destructive weapons.

The Emir of Kuwait, Shaikh Jabir al-Ahmad al-Jabir as-Sabah, told the Assembly that the fate of a people, of a nation, was in its hands. Iraq's aggression against his country had been part of a scheme to seize the entire state by force despite internationally-recognized agreements between the two countries. Rape, terror and torture ruled the day in Kuwait and there were daily reports of massacres, looting and mass destruction of property. Prince Saud al-Faisal, the Saudi Arabian Foreign Minister, said the presence of friendly forces on Saudi territory was temporary, 'in response to our request' and for defence only.

For Iraq, Sabah Talat Kadrat said that the 'Western imperialist alliance under the leadership of the United States' was conducting a large-scale campaign of disinformation. He added that King Husain of Jordan had sought to convene a summit meeting on 4 or 5 August to be attended by Iraq, Saudi Arabia, Egypt, Yemen and Jordan to deal with the situation in the Gulf within an Arab framework. Two days after the scheduled date of that meeting, American forces had landed in the Arabian peninsula; this showed that it was the United States which had 'put the Arab mechanism out of action'.

The delegates of Italy, Norway, Sweden, Argentina, Brazil and Cyprus were among those who supported the Security Council's resolutions, while Iran, although condemning Iraqi aggression, maintained that lasting peace and security in the 'volatile' Gulf could be provided only by the countries of the region. Jordan, too, while not recognizing the Iraqi decision to annex Kuwait by force, said that efforts to solve the crisis within a regional context had not been given sufficient opportunity and support. Central American and African delegates tended to ignore the subject, as did Taro Nakayama, the Japanese Foreign Minister.

Back in the Security Council, the Secretary-General was asked to implement the recommendations contained in the sanctions committee's report on Jordan, and to undertake immediate technical, financial and material assistance to that country. This was in response to the Jordanian government's request for relief, under article 50 of the charter, from what was described as the 'dramatic' impact of the imposed sanctions.

On 25 September the Security Council, by resolution 670 (Cuba voting against), instituted an air embargo against Iraq and Kuwait. On 29 October it adopted resolution 674 (Cuba and Yemen abstaining), demanding that Iraq stop taking third-country nationals hostage in Iraq and Kuwait. The Council further expressed its 'trust' in the Secretary-General to make available his good offices and pursue appropriate diplomatic efforts in order to reach a peaceful solution to the crisis on the basis of previous Council resolutions.

In accordance with resolution 674, the Secretary-General took the initiative to invite 20 'eminent persons' to meet at the Paris headquarters of UNESCO on 17 November to discuss informally the consequences of the Gulf crisis for the world economy. Responding to questions from the press on the effect of UN sanctions, Sr Pérez de Cuellar said they had already 'started to produce the effect the Security Council desires', but it was not possible to say how much more time was needed for them to be effective. The UN Military Staff Committee held informal consultations on the situation in the Gulf with particular reference to the implementation of the embargos contained in resolutions 661, 665 and 670. The consultations were attended by the most senior military officers ever to be present at such meetings.

On 28 November, the Security Council unanimously adopted resolution 677 condemning Iraq for destroying the civil records maintained by the legitimate government of Kuwait. The next day it authorized member states 'to use all necessary means' to uphold and implement resolution 660 and all subsequent relevant resolutions, 'unless Iraq withdraws from Kuwait by 15 January'. Resolution 678 was sponsored by Canada, France, Romania, the Soviet Union, the UK and the USA and adopted by 12 votes in favour to two against (Cuba and Yemen) with one abstention (China). Addressing the Council after the vote, the Secretary-General said that the resolution envisaged 'at least 45 days of earnest effort to achieve a peaceful solution of the crisis'.

As the year ended four non-aligned members of the Security Council—Colombia, Cuba, Malaysia and Yemen—submitted a peace plan to the Council, proposing that a UN peacekeeping force oversee the withdrawal of Iraqi troops from Kuwait. The four countries stated that the Council could 'serve the cause of peace no better than to work collectively to avoid the outbreak of war'.

ISRAEL-PALESTINE. Throughout the year the perennial conflict between Israel and the Palestinians in the West Bank and the Gaza Strip was scarcely ever off the UN agenda. Claims and counter-claims by both sides, starting in February with the attack on a tourist bus near Cairo in which many Israeli civilians were killed or wounded (see p. 204), culminated on 20 December in a unanimous Security Council resolution calling on the Secretary-General to monitor and observe the situation of Palestinian civilians under Israeli occupation. During the interim months all UN-sponsored efforts to diffuse the situation were in vain. The tension was exacerbated by the mounting casualties in the *intifada* campaign and attacks on the offices and personnel of the UN Relief and Works Agency (UNRWA).

The main events were as follows. In March UNRWA complained about the continued curfew in the occupied territories and the closing of the universities. The following month the Secretary-General told journalists who were inquiring about the situation in the Old City of Jerusalem that he had refrained from commenting while awaiting the decision of Israel's high court concerning new Jewish settlements in the Christian quarter. Two days of violence on 21–22 May resulted in ten deaths in the Gaza Strip, while 600 wounded were treated in UNRWA hospitals and local clinics. All the agency's educational, health and relief services came to a halt.

Following the precedent set in 1988, the Security Council met in Geneva on 25–26 May, at the request of Bahrain on behalf of the Group of Arab States, 'to consider the crime of collective murder committed by Israel against the Palestinian people'. Yassir Arafat, chairman of the PLO, said the Council must shoulder its responsibility to protect the lives of Palestinian men, women and children and put an end to the occupation. Israel must be made to comply with UN resolutions and not consider itself to be outside the scope of international law. For Israel, Benjamin Netanyahu said the Council had not been convened to advance peace but to retard it; he added that the meeting was an attempt to violate international law and to encroach on Israel's right to govern the occupied territories.

In June the Secretary-General decided to send Jean-Claude Aime as his personal representative on a visit to Israel and the occupied territories, after receiving Israel's assurance that it was prepared to receive the mission. Later in the month Sr Pérez de Cuellar issued a statement that he hoped a way would soon be found for the US government to resume its dialogue with the PLO, since the UN was an organization committed to the furthering of peace through dialogue.

In the report of his mission on 22 June–1 July, M. Aime stated that he had had wide-ranging discussions with Palestinians in Jerusalem, Gaza, Nablus, Bethlehem, Jericho and Ramallah. The principal concern conveyed at those meetings was the Palestinians' profound feeling of vulnerability resulting from lack of protection not only for the residents of towns and villages but also those living in refugee camps. In addition, they were deeply concerned about the need to ensure their basic human and economic rights. Their grievances had been conveyed to the Israeli authorities who were urged to take the necessary steps to redress them.

On 8 October further bloodshed occurred in Jerusalem when Israeli troops fired on demonstrators at the Temple Mount, killing at least 17 Palestinians (see pp. 198, 203). A week later the Security Council unanimously adopted resolution 672, condemning the acts of violence committed by the Israeli security forces. The Council called upon Israel to abide scrupulously by its legal obligations under the 1949 Fourth

Geneva Convention on the protection of civilians in time of war, which the Council understood applied to Jerusalem. The Council welcomed the Secretary-General's decision to send another mission to the region and asked for a report before the end of the month. On 24 October the Security Council deplored the Israeli government's refusal to accept the Secretary-General's mission and unanimously adopted resolution 673, expressing grave concern at the continued deterioration of the situation in the occupied territories. The Council urged the Israeli government to reconsider its decision and insisted that it permit the mission to proceed.

In spite of Israel's continued refusal, the Secretary-General submitted his report on 1 November in which he reiterated Israel's obligation to abide by international law and stressed that Israeli cooperation was essential for any measure of protection for the Palestinians. They had expressed the need for an impartial presence, properly mandated by the UN, to provide them with a credible sense of protection. The determination of the Palestinians to persevere with the *intifada* was evidence of their rejection of the occupation and their commitment to exercise their legitimate political rights including self-determination.

At the same time, the UNRWA commissioner-general, Giorgio Giacomelli, introduced the agency's report to the General Assembly. It said that the situation in the occupied territories, together with the Gulf crisis, was increasing the demand for the agency's services, with the result that serious financial difficulties were being experienced. In addition, UNRWA was continually meeting difficulties such as harassment, beatings and detentions of staff in the performance of its duties. The representative of Israel described the report as biased and unbalanced.

At a meeting of the Security Council on 7 November, the observer for Palestine, Nasser al-Kidwar, asked for an international observer force to monitor Israel's compliance with the Geneva Convention and Council resolutions. The representative of Israel, Yoram Aridor, said the convention did not apply to territories which had been illegally occupied by Jordan when Israel entered them. On 16 November four non-aligned members of the Council—Colombia, Cuba, Malaysia and Yemen—sponsored a draft resolution which would have deployed UN military observers in the occupied territories to monitor the situation of Palestinian civilians. The draft was recirculated on 5 December with the appointment of a UN ombudsman taking the place of the UN observers proposal and calling for an international peace conference to negotiate a settlement in the Middle East.

On 20 December the Security Council requested the Secretary-General to monitor and observe the situation of the Palestinian civilians. It also unanimously adopted a resolution calling upon the high contracting parties to the 1949 Fourth Geneva Convention to ensure respect by Israel for its obligations under the convention. It further requested the Secretary-General to develop the idea of convening a meeting of those parties to discuss measures that might be taken and to submit a progress report to the Council by the first week of March 1991, and every four months thereafter.

The General Assembly also called for the convening of an international peace conference on the Middle East and reaffirmed the principles for the achievement of comprehensive peace in that region. These included withdrawal of Israel from occupied Arab territories; guaranteed security arrangements for all states in the region; resolving the problem of the Palestinian refugees and guaranteeing freedom of access to holy places and religious buildings and sites. The president of the Assembly said he would visit Palestinian refugee camps in Jordan and the occupied territories early in 1991. The visit would permit the president to see at first hand the conditions faced by those living in the camps and personally to express to them the support and concern of the General Assembly. It would be the first such visit ever made by an Assembly president.

KAMPUCHEA. In unanimously adopting resolution 668 on 30 September, the Security Council welcomed the formation by the parties to the Kampuchea conflict of a supreme national council (see also p. 347) and urged the members to elect a chairman as soon as possible. It also endorsed the settlement framework which included the suggested transfer of temporary control of the country to the UN. But by the end of the year no chairman had been elected, so that the permanent members of the Security Council called for a speedy reconvening of the Paris international conference on Kampuchea in order to adopt the comprehensive agreement. It was hoped that this would lead to the rapid deployment of a UN operation to supervise elections in Kampuchea.

NAMIBIA. Following independence (see p. 295), Namibia became a member of the UN at a special session of the General Assembly in April. As a result, the UN Council for Namibia was dissolved, since it had fulfilled its mandate. The Assembly requested that the Secretary-General should continue to provide the necessary resources to complete the programme activities for 1990 as approved earlier by the Council. The UN Fund for Namibia would continue under the custody of the Secretary-General and the Assembly established the UN trust committee to serve as trustee.

WESTERN SAHARA. The Security Council on 27 June expressed its full support to the Secretary-General in his mission of good offices on how best to implement the peace plan for Western Sahara (see p. 244). It would include a referendum for self-determination for the people which would be organized by the UN, in cooperation with the Organization of African Unity (OAU); the extension of the suspension of military operations; and direct dialogue between Morocco and the Polisario Front, under the auspices of the Secretary-General. The Security Council also unanimously adopted a resolution approving a report by the Secretary-General containing the text of settlement proposals as accepted by both parties.

FALKLAND ISLANDS. The General Assembly deferred until its next session the question of the Falkland Islands (Malvinas) after receiving a report from the UN special committee on decolonization which urged the UK and Argentina to resume negotiations aimed at finding a peaceful solution to the sovereignty dispute. The committee regretted that the implementation of the General Assembly resolution had not yet begun, but support was expressed for the Secretary-General's renewed mission of good offices.

CYPRUS. Referring to a 'general deterioration' of the atmosphere and frustration because of the lack of progress in talks between the two sides (see p. 191), the Secretary-General reported to the Security Council on 12 July on his recent good offices mission in Cyprus. It was important, he said, that the leaders of the Cypriot and Turkish communities should meet with him again to try and negotiate an overall agreement. In a further report in November he said that the negative atmosphere previously referred to still persisted, and he renewed his appeal to both parties to lend him their full cooperation in his mission.

SOUTH AFRICA. The UN special committee against apartheid called on the UK government not to destroy world unity against apartheid through 'premature unilateral action' in relaxing sanctions against the South African regime. In June senior UN officials went to South Africa on a fact-finding mission. They met a wide cross-section of the community and supported the view that the apartheid system must be ended 'through negotiations'. Nelson Mandela visited the UN on 22 June and the Secretary-General described the occasion as 'a landmark in the organization's long involvement in the struggle by the people of South Africa against the apartheid system'. Mr Mandela said he believed that the South African President, F. W. de Klerk, and his colleagues were people of integrity and would abide by decisions arrived at in the course of negotiations (see pp. 299–305).

DISARMAMENT. The UN Conference on Disarmament, which began its meetings in Geneva in July, agreed to re-establish its ad hoc committee on a nuclear-test ban. Ian R. Kenyon (UK) said his government's position was that in the interests of defence needs it would have to continue to rely on nuclear arms and on conducting underground tests. Later, at the General Assembly, the UK, together with France and the US, voted against a resolution calling on the Secretary-General to submit a study for next year's Assembly on the possible reallocation of military resources to civilian activities that would protect the environment. The same three countries also voted against a resolution urging all nuclear-weapon states to discontinue all nuclear-test explosions.

OTHER UN ACTIVITIES AND AGENCIES

DRUGS. The 'world ministerial summit to reduce demand for drugs and to combat the cocaine threat' was held in London from 9–11 April. Organized by the UK government in association with the UN, the conference aimed to increase international commitment to reduce demand for all drugs and to find ways in which international cooperation could most effectively combat the production and trafficking of cocaine.

Opening the conference, Mrs Thatcher said that mankind faced two most serious problems in the growing threat to the environment and in the abuse of hard drugs and the social evils they brought. The UN Secretary-General told the conference that the drug problem required a global response which only the UN could effectively provide. The years 1991–2000 had been declared the UN Decade against Drug Abuse.

WORLD ECONOMY AND TRADE. A new *World Development Report*, the first major study of the world's poor in a decade, was issued by the World Bank (IBRD) in July. It stated that poverty was likely to decline in the year 2000, except in sub-Saharan Africa. In the coming decade the IBRD would concentrate more consistently on ridding the world of poverty by following a comprehensive two-part strategy: generating better income-earning opportunities for labour, and disseminating new terminologies in order to increase the capacity of the poor to respond to those opportunities. The report called for increased aid to those countries which were seriously committed to the reduction of poverty. Cutting military expenditure in the industrialized countries by just 10 per cent would pay for a doubling of aid.

However, according to an update of the *World Economic Survey 1990*, prospects for the world economy had worsened considerably. The report stated that the economic trend in the developing countries and in Eastern Europe appeared worse than expected, and would probably be further worsened by the Gulf crisis. Efforts were being made to strengthen the functioning of the international economy in the multilateral trade negotiations under the Uruguay Round in GATT, but the talks had fallen dangerously behind schedule.

HUMAN RIGHTS. During a six-week session in Geneva, the UN Commission on Human Rights reported that for the first time a commission representative had been allowed into Iran to observe the situation there. While welcoming the Iranian government's cooperation, the commission expressed concern following complaints about unlawful executions, torture and among other things, imprisonment beyond the period specified in the sentencing. The commission also strongly deplored foreign military intervention in Panama and called on Cuba to provide information about the situation in that country. Israel was condemned for continued violations of human rights in southern Lebanon, but no action was taken regarding human rights in Iraq and China.

POPULATION. At a press conference in London on 15 May the UN Population Fund reported that the 1990s would see the greatest growth in human numbers of any decade on record. The agency predicted that the world's population, which stood at 5,300 million, would increase by another 100 million by the end of the century.

ENVIRONMENT. Speaking at the second World Climate Conference in Geneva, the executive director of the UN Environment Programme (UNEP), Mostafa Tolba, said scientific estimates of a rise in global temperature of up to 3°C by the end of the next century might be conservative. He warned that only dramatic reductions of emissions of greenhouse gases would forestall global catastrophe (see also Pt. XIV, Ch. 3, ENVIRONMENT).

ANTARCTICA. The General Assembly requested the Secretary-General to prepare two reports for submission to the next Assembly in 1991. The first was a comprehensive study on the establishment of a UN-sponsored station in Antarctica; the second was on the state of the environment in the Antarctic.

UNESCO. The possibility of the UK returning to UNESCO was discussed when Timothy Sainsbury, parliamentary under-secretary at the Foreign Office, had talks with the director-general, Federico Mayor, in Paris on 28 February. The next day, at a meeting with the House of Commons foreign affairs committee, Professor Mayor outlined the reforms he had initiated, explaining that UNESCO had concentrated its resources on fewer programmes with more action and less research. The most notable change had been in the field of communications, where a free flow of information had to be guaranteed.

CHILDREN. The 72 heads of state who attended the 'world summit for children' at UN headquarters in New York on 29–30 September signed a 'world declaration on the survival, protection and development of children', committing themselves to a 10-point programme to protect the rights of children and improve their lives. A plan of action for implementing the declaration was also adopted.

FAMINE AND REFUGEES. The Food and Agriculture Organization, the World Food Programme, the UN Disaster and Relief Office, UNICEF and the High Commission for Refugees were all engaged throughout the year in trying to cope with famine or near-famine conditions in Africa and, following the outbreak of the Gulf crisis, in housing and feeding the waves of refugees who fled to Jordan, Iran, Turkey and Egypt. All the agencies were stretched beyond their normal commitments and had to appeal for emergency donations to carry on their work.

The High Commissioner for Refugees, Thorvald Stoltenberg of Norway, resigned from his post on 2 November to become his country's Foreign Minister. He was succeeded by Mrs Sadako Ogata of Japan.

Chapter 2

THE COMMONWEALTH

THE extraordinary events in Eastern Europe, the Soviet Union and the Gulf—none of which directly involved the Commonwealth—provided a dramatic backdrop to the fullscale assessment of the Commonwealth role in the 1990s and beyond which the 1989 summit in Kuala Lumpur had decided should be carried out (see AR 1989, p. 381). In a sense, the timing was fortunate because the changed world that was emerging would require new Commonwealth responses.

The group of ten leaders chosen to appraise the Commonwealth's future, known as the 'high-level appraisal group' (HLAG), set up a team of senior officials, chaired by the secretary-general of the Malaysian Ministry of Foreign Affairs, Datuk Nik Kamil Jaffar, to do the detailed work. The officials met in London in March and August and in Kuala Lumpur in November. The Group sought the views of a wide variety of non-governmental organizations (NGOs), as well as governments. Following a number of NGO meetings and seminars, numerous papers were submitted. The ten leaders would put their conclusions to the heads of government meeting in Harare in 1991.

For the Commonwealth 1990 was a quietly positive year that started with the successful 14th Commonwealth Games in Auckland (24 January–4 February). They were held without any of the boycotts over South Africa that had marred the event in earlier years and a record number (nearly 3,000) of athletes took part. Afterwards, outgoing Secretary-General Shridath Ramphal set up a working party on strengthening

Commonwealth sport, chaired by Roy McMurtry of Canada. It aimed to help sportspeople improve their performance, make better facilities available and enable more countries to host the Games. There was anxiety that previous Games venues, except in one case (Jamaica), had always been in developed countries.

On 27 February a group of Commonwealth leaders met Nelson Mandela in Lusaka only 16 days after his release from prison. Dr Mahathir Mohamad, Prime Minister of Malaysia, chaired the meeting, which was attended by the Canadian Foreign Minister, the Commonwealth front-line presidents, and representatives from Nigeria and Australia. Later, Mr Mandela briefed a meeting of the Commonwealth committee of foreign ministers on southern Africa in Abuja, Nigeria, on 15–17 May.

In July the new Commonwealth Secretary-General, Chief Emeka Anyaoku of Nigeria, hosted a dinner in London for Mr Mandela. It was attended by business executives involved in South Africa, a pointer to changing relations at a time when sanctions were still being maintained. Soon afterwards Chief Anyaoku convened an expert group to help define the priorities for education, training and work experience to be met if blacks were to take their proper place in South African society. For the first time a Commonwealth expert group contained two South African members.

On 21 March the Commonwealth acquired its 50th member, namely Namibia. The offer of membership had been laid on the table by heads of government at their Jamaica summit in 1975. Now, on independence day (see p. 295), it took up that offer. The Commonwealth had helped Namibia in many ways in the months leading to independence, notably in constitution-drafting, setting up a foreign ministry, restructuring the civil service and assisting through the Commonwealth Fund for Technical Cooperation.

Shridath Ramphal retired as Secretary-General on 30 June after serving three five-year terms. During farewell visits many Commonwealth countries conferred on him their highest honours. His departure coincided with the 25th anniversary of the founding of the secretariat.

One of his successor's first actions was to set up, at Prime Minister Mahathir's request, a Commonwealth observer group for the elections held in Malaysia on 20–21 October (see p. 337). The group of 12, from 10 countries and led by former Foreign Minister Dudley Thompson of Jamaica, decided that the electors had been able 'to freely express their choice' in accordance with Malaysian law. The full report, released later by the Malaysian government (which had funded the exercise), referred to 'imperfections' concerning the voters' roll and unequal access of the opposition parties to the mainstream media. The Malaysian operation was the first carried out after the 1989 summit decision to make the strengthening of democracy a Commonwealth objective at a time when the international climate seemed favourable. In statements immediately after taking office Chief Anyaoku stressed this role and also highlighted the importance of NGOs and the need to improve human rights.

Increasing concern about human rights within the Commonwealth led to the launching of a Commonwealth 'human rights initiative' (CHRI), sponsored by five NGOs representing trade unionists, journalists, doctors and lawyers. A group of distinguished persons chaired by the former Canadian Foreign Minister, Flora MacDonald, met in London, Wellington and New Delhi to prepare a report for heads of government. An official working group also reviewed cooperation on human rights and submitted a report in mid-year. The year was notable for an increasing realization of the importance of the Commonwealth's NGO network. In Sydney the Commonwealth Foundation convened a conference of 70 representatives of professional associations—the first of its kind. Its 36 recommendations included called for the foundation to facilitate better contacts with governments and plans for NGOs to become more self-reliant.

Another first was a meeting of Commonwealth ministers of science and technology in Malta (15–16 November). The focus was on the widening gap in science between North and South and the need for closer collaboration between governments in applying science and technology to development problems. The first meeting was also held in November of a newly-set-up Commonwealth 'consultative group on technology management'.

Two imaginative Commonwealth projects were launched in the Caribbean. For one Guyana set aside a million acres to be preserved as virgin forest where plant and animal species could be studied. The aim was an international centre for research and training in management of tropical rain forests. The second project was the first comprehensive oceanographic survey of the Caribbean Commonwealth countries' exclusive economic zones. Some 60 scientists worked in a survey ship loaned by the Indian government.

Other major Commonwealth meetings in 1990 included those of law ministers (Auckland, 23–28 April); finance ministers (Port of Spain, 19–20 September); ministers responsible for women's affairs (Ottawa, 8–12 October); and education ministers (Barbados, 29 October–2 November).

Chapter 3

THE EUROPEAN COMMUNITY

THE turbulent course of world events largely determined developments in the European Community (EC) in 1990. In the first half of the year the main issues were German unification and the progress of democracy in Eastern Europe. In the second six months it was the Gulf crisis, the GATT talks and the economic collapse of the Soviet Union which preoccupied the Community. These events influenced and sometimes overshadowed the preparation of inter-governmental conferences on economic and monetary union and on political union which formally began in Rome on 15 December.

GERMAN UNIFICATION. The Community found its own frontiers extended with the formal incorporation of the five *Länder* of the German Democratic Republic into the Federal Republic (see pp. 149–55), the EC's population thus rising from 320 million to 336 million people. At the beginning of the year this had seemed a distant prospect, but the pace accelerated despite the apparent misgivings of some member countries.

It was such misgivings which Chancellor Kohl tried to allay in a visit to Brussels in March, when he underlined the need for German unification to take place under 'a European roof' and called for greater progress in European integration. Germany was not, he said, proposing to act like an elephant in a china shop or to establish a fourth Reich. The Chancellor and President Mitterrand of France then addressed a letter to their fellow EC heads of government calling for moves towards European political union at the special European Council called by the Irish presidency in Dublin in April. At this summit it was agreed that German unification could be achieved without changing the EC treaties. It was to be brought about by assimilation rather than by negotiation. As soon as the GDR became part of the Federal Republic, it would become part of the European Community as well.

In practice this meant transitional measures for the introduction of policies such as farming policy, financial help to be provided from EC funds, and a full opening-up of trade between the ex-GDR and the other member countries from the moment of unification. A heavy burden of legal work was needed to achieve this, proposed by the European Commission in August, reviewed by the European Parliament and adopted by the Council of Ministers within a few weeks. Economic, monetary and social union between the two parts of Germany took place on 1 July 1990, the full unification following on 3 October. Most of the financial burden of unification was assumed by Germany's taxpayers. The net cost to the Community budget was estimated at about 500 million ecu a year, the balance between 2,000 million ecu in expenditure and 1,500 million in revenue.*

---

*At end–December 1990 1 ecu=£0.71 or US$1.36.

EASTERN EUROPE. The European Commission continued to act as coordinator for channelling assistance to the countries of Eastern Europe on behalf of the Group of 24 developed countries (G-24), which held a series of meetings in Brussels during the year. The so-called PHARE programme, introduced in 1989 to help Poland and Hungary, was extended to the other East Europeans whose revolutions had taken place towards the end of that year. The Community allocated 500 million ecu to the PHARE programme, including 180 million to Poland, 91 million to Hungary, 24 million to Bulgaria, 35 million to Yugoslavia and 30 million to Czechoslovakia. This was for a range of projects, including the importation of agricultural inputs, environmental improvement schemes and industrial restructuring programmes. Substantial loan capital was also made available from the EC lending institutions.

The main concern at the end of the year was the deteriorating balance-of-payments and credit situation of the East European countries, especially Czechoslovakia and Hungary, because of the Gulf crisis. The European Council agreed in Rome in December that additional financing might be provided beyond that available from the international financial institutions (such as the IMF). Existing commitments were honoured for balance of payments assistance to Hungary.

During the course of the year the Community began negotiations with Hungary, Poland and Czechoslovakia with a view to concluding 'Europe agreements' to come into effect at the beginning of 1992. These were designed to bring about a new type of relationship, both political and economic in nature, which would help the process of change in the countries concerned. All three countries saw these agreements as a stage on the way to joining the Community: the Hungarian Prime Minister, Jozsef Antall, said in July that he hoped his country could join by 1995. The practical effect of each agreement would be to ensure industrial free trade, to align the partners' legislation more closely to EC law, to develop economic and cultural cooperation and to set up a regular political dialogue between the parties. The basic timetable for these talks was agreed in December so they could begin in substance at the start of 1991.

Long-term economic agreements had already been negotiated with Hungary (1988) and Poland (1989) and 10-year agreements were concluded with Czechoslovakia and Bulgaria in 1990. A trade and cooperation agreement was negotiated with Romania, but its signature was held up because of doubts as to human rights in that country. As from October 1990 all quantitative restrictions on imports from the East European countries into the Community were removed.

SOVIET UNION. The deteriorating political and economic situation in the Soviet Union gave increasing cause for concern, with conflicting views as to whether it was more important to bolster President

Gorbachev's position or to see real reform first. Mr Gorbachev's helpful view of German unification encouraged those who favoured rapid assistance to support the President, while the sceptics like Britain saw this as pouring money down the drain.

Substantial bilateral help was given during the year by individual member countries (more than 1,100 million ecu from Germany alone), but this was largely linked to troop withdrawals. At the June meeting of heads of government in Dublin it was agreed to make no immediate commitment to EC help, but to commission a report on the situation in the Soviet Union with recommendations for action. This foreshadowed a similar decision at the world economic summit of the major industrialized countries in Houston shortly afterwards.

Commission President Jacques Delors presented the EC report to the European Council in Rome on 14 December. The decision taken there by Community leaders was to provide food aid to the USSR amounting to 750 million ecu, of which 250 million ecu would be given under the 1990 farm budget and the balance as a medium-term loan. Technical assistance would also be provided under a practical programme linked to specific projects to a value of 400 million ecu in 1991 and a further sum in 1992, to be released in tranches. The European Commission was asked to explore with the Soviet authorities the idea of a major agreement which would include a political dialogue and cover all aspects of economic and cultural cooperation.

The 10-year agreement on trade, economics and commerce, signed at the end of 1989, came into force on 1 April 1990. It provided for the progressive abolition of the Community's quantitative restrictions on Soviet exports by the end of 1995 and a range of measures to facilitate commercial cooperation in areas such as mining, agriculture, environmental protection and energy. The joint committee set up to oversee the operation of this agreement had its first meeting in May and M. Delors visited Moscow in July.

THE GULF CRISIS. The Community's capacity to act as one in world affairs was most sorely tested in the aftermath of Iraq's invasion of Kuwait. In the implementation and application of sanctions there was complete solidarity; substantial assistance was given for repatriation of refugees and for helping those countries neighbouring Iraq. There was some discrepancy between words and deeds in dealing with the hostage question; and a wider divergence on the advisability of using force to dislodge Saddam Husain from Kuwait. However, the Community did maintain a consistent line in arguing for a Middle East peace conference to be held after Iraq's withdrawal, which would discuss among other matters the plight of the territories occupied by Israel.

The immediate reaction of the 12 EC states to the invasion of Kuwait on 2 August was a declaration calling for Iraq's unconditional withdrawal. This was followed two days later by a meeting of foreign ministers in Rome which gave support to UN resolution 660 (see DOCUMENTS) and imposed an immediate embargo on purchases of oil and oil products from Kuwait and Iraq, a freezing of assets of the two countries and an arms embargo. By 8 August legislation had been adopted to apply the UN sanctions on all trade, which was subsequently extended to include services. The importance of effective sanctions was repeatedly recognized by the Community.

In the months following the invasion, as refugees streamed from Iraq, the Community became deeply involved in the problem of repatriation, especially from Jordan. About 100 million ecu, primarily from EC budget sources, was allocated, representing about 30 per cent of the total international aid provided. This was spent on medical aid, shelter and food for 400,000 people in Egypt and 150,000 in Jordan for a period of four months and the repatriation of about 38,000 Egyptians and 91,000 people from Asia. The Community agreed in principle that 1,500 million ecu should be provided for Egypt, Jordan and Turkey in 1991, of which 500 million was expected to come from the EC budget.

At a special European Council held in Rome (27–28 October) there was a further call for Iraq's withdrawal and condemnation of its holding of hostages, with a commitment not to send government representatives to Baghdad to negotiate their release. A number of senior politicians nonetheless made the journey, some of them with apparent connivance by their governments (see p. 217).

The defence aspects of the crisis were outside the scope of EC decision-making—a fact which would have its lessons for the discussion on political union (see below) and there was no coordination at Community level of the military commitments to be made by member states. There were differences of view on the advisability of using force. Germany and Belgium were reluctant to go along with an American view, whereas the UK and the Netherlands saw no alternative to military action relatively soon if Iraq did not withdraw. One major concern of the French—which sent forces to the Gulf—was to distance themselves from the US position while recognizing the possible need for military intervention.

The major difference between the Community and the United States was over whether an international conference on the Middle East (in particular concerning the occupied territories) could play a part in finding a solution to the Gulf crisis. While insisting on prior Iraqi withdrawal, the Twelve underlined their own commitment to such a conference in the conclusions of the December Rome summit. In this communique there was a further call for a complete withdrawal from Kuwait and support for action by the UN Secretary-General; relief at the decision to release all foreign hostages but deep concern at Iraq's failure to withdraw and at the destructive nature of its occupation of Kuwait.

In the same communique the Council expressed its dismay 'at the continuing lack of clear prospects for a solution to the Arab–Israeli conflict and to the Palestinian problem' and criticized aspects of Israeli policy.

ECONOMIC AND MONETARY UNION. On 1 July there began the first stage of the proposed three-stage programme towards economic and monetary union (EMU), as agreed 12 months before at the Madrid European Council (see AR 1989, pp. 388–9, 545–8), and work intensified with a view to the inter-governmental conference scheduled to begin in Rome in December. The British had already expressed their opposition to plans for EMU and had put forward their own ideas for the 'hard ecu', a currency which would be introduced in parallel with existing currencies and would be run by a monetary fund, but not necessarily leading to a single European currency (certainly not, in the view of the then British Prime Minister, Mrs Thatcher). At a meeting in Milan in the summer, the then UK Chancellor, John Major, explained these ideas and seemed to draw a degree of support from his Spanish opposite number.

In August the Commission put forward its ideas for stages two and three. It proposed that stage two should begin on 1 January 1993 and stage three after a relatively short transitional period. During the second stage the European System of Central Banks (Eurofed) would be set up and currency values would be fixed. A Community economic policy would prohibit monetary financing of public deficits and excessive budget deficits would be avoided. The aim of monetary policy would be price stability.

The British government continued to underline its hostility to EMU, but took an important political and economic decision on 6 October, when it announced that the pound sterling would join the exchange rate mechanism (ERM) as from 8 October, with a commitment to keeping the currency within a 6 per cent margin of movement above or below the ERM basket. The central rate against the Deutschmark at that moment was DM 2.95=£1.

The Italian presidency had called a meeting of the European Council in Rome (27–28 October) in order to discuss assistance to the USSR and other foreign affairs issues and there were suggestions that this meeting was unnecessary. According to some commentators this stung the Italian government into a change of plan, pushing the preparation of the two inter-governmental conferences (scheduled for December) to the top of the agenda. The summit was short and dramatic. The final communique talked of guidelines agreed by 11 member states on plans for EMU, so isolating the UK and leaving Prime Minister Thatcher not only isolated but ignored—one significant link in the chain of events which led to Mrs Thatcher's downfall (see pp. 36–41).

President Mitterrand and Chancellor Kohl had already talked of 1 January 1994 as the right date to begin the EMU second phase and this was agreed at the summit by everyone except the British. The 11 heads of government agreed that monetary union should be managed by a new institution formed by national central banks and a central body, whose prime task would be to ensure price stability. The new organization would be independent. Before the second stage began, the single market programme should be completed, a new treaty ratified, the independence of the members of the new institutions should be guaranteed and member states would have renounced the financing of budget deficits by monetary means. Within three years of the beginning of the second stage the Commission and the new institution would report to the Council on the functioning of the second stage in order to prepare a decision about stage three.

The inter-governmental conference began its deliberations in Rome on 15 December, with a view to holding regular sessions in the first half of 1991. As governments got down to detailed talks, so their initial negotiating positions pointed up the differences. Germany was keen to insist on the discipline of the Eurofed, but had reservations as to the long-term role of the ecu. The French, on the other hand, wished to see the development of the ecu and Finance Minister Pierre Bérégovoy saw certain virtues in the British ideas for a hard ecu. He stressed in a news conference that 12 national parliaments must ratify the new treaty. It was governments, he said, and not the European Commission which would pilot this legislation through parliaments.

POLITICAL UNION. Work on the inter-governmental conference on political union was not so far advanced as that on EMU, although the conference was due to begin on the same day—15 December 1990. A wide range of issues was on the table, including the need to introduce greater democracy, partly by strengthening the European Parliament and partly by giving national parliaments a bigger role; improving the working of the institutions and including the principle of 'subsidiarity' into the treaty whereby the EC would renounce taking measures on issues best left to local, regional or national decision; and foreign policy, security and defence. This last area of discussion took on a special importance in the light of developments in the Gulf and in Eastern Europe and the Soviet Union. There was very little scope for Community action in the security and defence fields and existing provision in foreign affairs were inadequate. The end of the Cold War in Europe would certainly require a rethink of defence and security issues as the role of NATO diminished and ideas were developing during the year to incorporate into the EC treaty some provisions covering security (see Pt. XII).

GATT. The negotiations on the Uruguay Round were due to be concluded at the week-long session in December in Brussels. The

Community had put its general proposals on the table at the mid-term review in 1989, but more specific policy papers were expected from the negotiating partners during the final year of talks. The Community accordingly tabled its ideas on tariff reductions (an average cut from 5.44 per cent to 3.86 per cent in the EC tariff level), on services (principle of equal national treatment but not mirror-image reciprocity) and on the general linkage between the 15 major issues in the negotiations.

It was clear from an early stage, however, that there was a fundamental difference of approach between the two main protagonists in the talks, the European Community and the United States. The American position was forcibly expressed at the world economic summit at Houston in July, when US negotiators implied that the talks could only succeed if there were a commitment to a drastic cut in levels of support for agriculture in Europe. The European position was to accept 'substantial and progressive reduction' in agricultural support, but nothing approaching that demanded by the Americans, and to stress the global nature of the negotiations.

In October the European Commission agreed with some difficulty on a draft negotiating text for agriculture. This was presented to the Council of Ministers by Ray MacSharry, EC Commissioner responsible for agriculture. It envisaged a 30 per cent reduction in the level of support and protection for farm products. This was for the period 1986–96 and therefore took account of some cuts already introduced. Several agriculture ministers, especially from Germany and France, had reservations about these proposals, and it was November before general agreement could be obtained.

The difficulty with which these modest proposals were agreed, combined with the absolutist American approach, did not bode well for a conclusive December negotiation. Despite some last-minute modifications in the EC position, the final session in Brussels resulted in a standoff between the EC and the United States and, on 7 December, an adjournment of the talks until mid-January.

THE SINGLE MARKET. The routine business of agreeing legislation for the internal market continued. Transitional measures were agreed abolishing the payment of VAT at frontiers, which was expected to cut the number of documents required by 50–60 million; the system for EC control of mergers came into effect; the Council agreed on the next steps towards air transport liberalization; and further progress was made on agreeing the 1992 legislation on industrial trade and services.

Chapter 4

OECD—COMECON—NON-ALIGNED MOVEMENT

ORGANIZATION FOR ECONOMIC COOPERATION AND DEVELOPMENT

TIES with countries in Eastern Europe claimed much OECD attention, as experts discussed the mechanics of conversion to market economy structures. In June a 'centre for cooperation with the European economies in transition' was set up at the OECD headquarters in Paris, while in late November an OECD conference joined in the warnings that large-scale Western aid could be vital to stabilize the turbulent process of transition. Meanwhile, the OECD invented a new acronym in its relations with the newly industrializing countries of South-East Asia; no longer labelled as NICs, they were now 'dynamic Asian economies', or DAEs.

Within its existing membership of 24, the OECD embraced the opposing camps in the deadlocked GATT Uruguay Round of trade talks. The divisions, particularly on agriculture, were too wide to paper over at the annual OECD ministerial meeting in Paris on 30–31 May. The USA wanted a specific commitment to reduce farm supports and subsidies; this was resisted by European Community countries and Japan, and the eventual communique spoke only of 'urgent steps to reform agricultural policy' with the long-term goal of a 'market-oriented trading system'. The OECD executive council, at a special session on the problems of the trade talks in October, urged lamely 'that all participants, and the OECD countries in particular, should be ready to make the requisite moves to complete the round'.

On 3–4 December the annual high-level meeting of the OECD's development assistance committee (DAC) focused on 'participatory development', environmental sustainability, and slowing population growth where it was too high for sustainable development. Concern for Eastern Europe should not obscure the high priority of Third World development; rather, the end of the Cold War should allow concerted effort on 'meeting the interlinked challenges of defeating poverty, stemming population growth and preserving the environment'. DAC's annual statistics published in May showed its members providing $46.5 million in official development assistance (ODA) in 1989, and a world total of $51.3 million (bilateral and multilateral). This was less than in 1988, but total net resource flows to developing countries were assessed as up by some 4.5 per cent to $109 million.

The OECD's *Employment Outlook* on 12 July recorded falling unemployment in member states in 1989 for the sixth successive year. Persistent structural long-term unemployment, however, needed to be addressed through structural policies. Estimates for 1990 unemployment rates were that they would remain constant at 6.4 per cent overall; countries well above this average were France (9.3), Denmark (9.3), Turkey (10.9), Italy (12.2), Ireland (14.9 but falling) and Spain (16.1 but falling).

The semi-annual OECD *Economic Outlook* was published in June and again on 20 December, when the slowing of growth had become clear. The OECD global GNP growth figure of 3.4 per cent in 1989 would fall to 2.8 per cent in 1990 (6.1 per cent in Japan, 4.2 per cent in Germany and only 1 per cent in the USA) and to 2 per cent in 1991. Oil price increases were affecting short-term prospects both for growth and for controlling inflation. There was no change in the OECD recommendation for tight monetary policy to control inflation, and for the determined reduction of budget deficits. The report pointed to Japan, Germany and France as the most successful in balancing monetary and fiscal policies in the 1980s, and thus as best placed to weather a stormier economic climate.

COUNCIL FOR MUTUAL ECONOMIC ASSISTANCE (COMECON)

IT was remarkable that the CMEA (Comecon) survived the whole of 1990, which opened with new governments in Eastern Europe calling for its abolition. Its 45th Session, originally scheduled for the summer of 1989, took place on 9–10 January in Sofia, all six East European administrations having meanwhile changed. Each member, save the Cuban and Vietnamese, was represented by its Prime Minister and all resolved to abolish two of the organization's key functions—multilateral economic cooperation and the coordination of plans—in favour of bilateral negotiation among members, and consequentially to reduce the size of the Comecon secretariat.

A special committee was established 'to consider member countries' proposals on crucial aspects of cooperation within the CMEA framework and to elaborate draft basic documents as soon as possible'. It was chaired by a succession of Hungarian ministers, because by virtue of the cyrillic alphabetical order the chairmanship of the CMEA Executive Committee was currently vested in Hungary and three meetings were set up, all in Moscow, in February, June and November. In advance of each session the representatives of Czechoslovakia, Hungary and Poland—the most market-based economies—met in Prague to concert their policy. The June meeting of the committee was effectively also a meeting of the Executive Committee and instituted an expert group to draft a new statute for a replacement organization, names for which were discussed.

The variant recommended when the committee reported (in time for an Executive Committee scheduled for 3 January 1991, which would in turn prepare for the 46th Session) was 'Organization for Economic Cooperation', deliberately echoing that of the OECD, which was taken as the most appropriate model. The draft statute, by comparison with that of the CMEA, made no mention of socialism but, rather, committed all members to 'market principles' (which all except Cuba had already applied to their domestic economies) and to integration with the world economy. The proposed successor organization, which would require only about one-third of the CMEA's staff, would have 'consultative advisory functions'. All nine remaining members would be eligible to join, but new members would have to be European. Finland and Yugoslavia would have special status and Austria and Germany were likely to be invited, at least as associate members.

Although the German Democratic Republic ceased to be a separate CMEA member on its unification with the Federal Republic in October, the latter government promulgated in December special arrangements, effective from 1 January 1991, to replace the settlements, hitherto made with CMEA members by the five eastern *Länder* in transferable roubles. Both the transferable rouble and bilateral trade agreements lost their validity after 31 December, but 40 per cent of eastern *Länder* trade was with the USSR. To ease transition to convertible currency payments, Soviet export earnings (some DM 6,000 million annually) from sales of oil, natural gas and raw materials to enterprises in those *Länder* would be earmarked for Soviet purchases from enterprises in those *Länder*, which would enjoy government export guarantees.

Two other membership issues remained open. Firstly, the third meeting of the special committee had to be postponed because of an unexpected proposal from some of the western USSR republics, notably the Ukraine, that they should participate in their own right. This matter remained unresolved at the end of the year. Secondly, the three less-developed CMEA non-European members had until the reorganization been beneficiaries of a 'special integrated programme for the multilateral cooperation of the European CMEA members with Vietnam, Cuba and Mongolia'. Although trade and assistance between these countries and other members would be bilaterally negotiated from 1 January 1991, the three states requested special preferences. Moreover, Cuba dissociated itself from the special committee's draft commitment to 'market principles'.

The Sofia recommendation to liquidate the CMEA instrument of mutual payment (the transferable rouble) from 1 January 1991 involved numerous formal measures by member governments. Ministers of finance met as the 50th session of the Permanent Commission of Finance and Currency in Prague on 16–18 January and set out the requirements. The USSR notified other members in June that all payments from 1991 would be in convertible currency, but stated that it wished to preserve a role for the agent of that currency, the International Bank for Economic Cooperation (IBEC). Czechoslovakia was the first (in March) to cancel adherence to the Karlmarxstadt agreement on inter-member exchange rates and all had abrogated it by the end of the year.

Bilateral discussions were conducted on the rate at which transferable rouble balances were to be translated into convertible currency, the USSR being the biggest debtor. It conceded quite favourable rates to its East European creditors, since it stood to see its estimated $7,000 million deficit with those six countries in 1990 transformed into a surplus of some $8,000 million in 1991, due to movements in world prices, especially for oil and gas. In at least one case, Hungary, the USSR postponed any actual payment for five years and in another, Mongolia, deferred receipt until 2000.

Because of the switch to convertible currency, official CMEA transport tariffs were to be withdrawn from 1 January 1991. Bulgaria, Czechoslovakia, the former GDR, Poland, Romania and the USSR concluded a new 'international transport tariff' (MTT) for rail freight in November, but the Hungarian railways opted for a separate tariff (denominated in Swiss francs). The former agreement remained valid for the Asian members.

The Permanent Commission for Standardization (meeting in Jadwisin, near Warsaw, on 17–19 January) resolved to withdraw from the CMEA and constitute itself as an independent regional standardization agency, applying such norms as those of the European Commission or the International Organization for Standardization.

The CMEA International Institute for the Economic Problems of the World Socialist System (MIEPMSS in its Russian abbreviation) prepared a new niche for itself. At a meeting of academic institutions from six member states and the CMEA Secretariat in Kiev on 17–19 April it created an International Association for the Promotion of Economic Development and Cooperation, 'to cooperate in solving problems in the transition to a market system'. The CMEA Secretariat looked to its own future by establishing in June an International Centre of Scientific and Technical Information in Moscow. Its director, Aleksandr Butrimenko, said that hitherto CMEA information services had been restricted to members but would now be commercially available to business. Participation in the new centre was open and North Korea had become a founding member.

Finally, with the prospective elimination of the military functions of the Warsaw Treaty Organization, the CMEA Permanent Commission for the Defence Industry received, on Polish initiative at its meeting in Moscow on 20 December, a resolution that it be abolished; obligations already contracted would be respected, provided that their execution was profitable for the enterprises and research institutes concerned.

This was the first formal revelation that the commission existed; from its secret creation in 1957 it had never been listed by CMEA or its sessions reported.

As the CMEA in its traditional form disintegrated, the attraction of the European Community (EC) was still further enhanced for the emerging market economies of Eastern Europe. The CMEA role did not entirely vanish. A fourth joint session of the Secretariat (led by Stefan Zawodzinski, deputy secretary) and the EC Commission (led by John Maslen, the relevant departmental director) was eventually held in Moscow on 12-13 June. It agreed steps to harmonize foreign trade and retail price statistics and discussed possible cooperation in environmental protection and economic forecasting.

The EC Commission had been accorded the leading role in assessing the needs of the newly-marketizing countries by the G-7 summit in Paris in July 1989 (see AR 1989, pp. 383-4), initially of Hungary and Poland but from December of other East European states too. In February the European Council requested the Commission to formulate a policy whereby the existing 'first generation' bilateral cooperation agreements with European CMEA members would be replaced by 'second generation' longer-term association agreements. Association would not automatically lead to Community membership, although that would not be excluded when the time came. All CMEA members also participating in the Conference on Security and Cooperation in Europe (CSCE) subscribed to a CSCE declaration adopted in Bonn on 11 April and incorporating commitment to a normal market economy.

The two banks of the CMEA group, the IBEC and the International Investment Bank (IIB), concluded their transactions in transferable roubles, but the director of the latter's board, Albert Belichenko, stated that more than 80 per cent of the 5,800 million transferable rouble credits made since the IIB's foundation was in convertible currency. It stood ready to participate in the joint financing of investment projects with the European Bank for Reconstruction and Development (EBRD), constituted in March and to begin operations in April 1991 from headquarters in London (see also Pt. XVIII, Ch. 2).

NON-ALIGNED MOVEMENT

NO major meetings of all the members of the Non-Aligned Movement (NAM) took place in 1990, but the organization had sufficient complexity that it nevertheless made a significant input to world politics during the year. After the Iraqi invasion of Kuwait the Yugoslavs, acting in their capacity of chairing the Movement, immediately reacted on 2 August with a statement 'denouncing recourse to force' and describing the move as 'aggression'. Despite Iraq's membership of the Movement, the

August meeting of the NAM Coordinating Bureau also demanded Iraq's withdrawal and the restoration of Kuwaiti sovereignty. In September the Yugoslavs convened a meeting in Belgrade of the foreign ministers of Yugoslavia, India and Algeria, to explore the possibility of a peaceful settlement to the crisis, but they concluded there were no realistic prospects of an initiative succeeding. At a plenary meeting of the NAM foreign ministers in New York on 3 October strong support was given to the UN Security Council resolutions (see pp. 387–90 and DOCUMENTS), with the Iraqis also being asked to allow a mission from the International Committee of the Red Cross to visit Kuwait. However, the meeting reacted against the moves towards war by expressing 'deepest concern over the increasing danger of further escalation which might lead to a military conflict'.

In the period from October to December four Non-Aligned members of the Security Council (Colombia, Cuba, Malaysia and Yemen) worked together as a distinct caucus group. They sought a 'political solution by peaceful means' for the Gulf crisis, submitting a plan for a UN force to supervise an Iraqi withdrawal from Kuwait. They also lobbied hard for the Security Council to convene a Middle East peace conference and establish a UN presence in the Israeli-occupied territories. In reaction to their failure on both issues they took the unusual step of initiating a debate in the General Assembly on the Security Council's annual report. Both the Malaysians and the Colombians complained of the 'dictatorship of the permanent members'. At the end of December the Yugoslav Foreign Minister, Budimir Loncar, went to Baghdad and met President Saddam Husain, but with no more success than the many others who appealed to the Iraqi President.

On 11 March the NAM Committee of Nine on Palestine, consisting of the foreign ministers of Algeria, Bangladesh, Cuba, India, Palestine, Senegal, Yugoslavia, Zambia and Zimbabwe, met in Tunis. They supported the Palestinian *intifada* and argued that the right of Jewish people to emigrate from the Soviet Union should not be at the expense of the Palestinians. The main hope then seemed to be that US influence on Israel would lead to a 'fruitful Palestinian-Israeli dialogue'.

At the end of the Movement's ninth summit in Belgrade in September 1989 Dr Julius Nyerere, President of the South Commission, had announced the formation of a Group for South-South Cooperation and Consultation, which came to be known as the Group of 15. The group initially consisted of 13 NAM members: Algeria, Argentina, Egypt, India, Indonesia, Jamaica, Malaysia, Nigeria, Peru, Senegal, Venezuela, Yugoslavia and Zimbabwe. Two non-members, Brazil and Mexico, were subsequently invited and agreed to join the group. Their first summit meeting was held 1–3 June 1990 in Kuala Lumpur. Their discussions were seen as occurring in the context of 'structural changes taking place in the world economy' that required a global response.

They emphasized the persistence of the debt problem and its link with the Uruguay Round trade negotiations.

A dozen specific proposals were endorsed for cooperation on trade, debt and development. The proposals included the establishment of a steering committee from Malaysia, Venezuela and Senegal, to operate between the annual summits. The intention of the Malaysians was that this should lead to the formation of a permanent 'secretariat of the South', but the Yugoslavs were still firmly resisting the explicit desire of nearly all the major leaders of developing countries to form such an institution.

Later the same month on 25–26 June, the third ministerial meeting of the Mediterranean Non-Aligned Countries was held in Algiers. Their main concern was that the CSCE process should be extended to cover the Mediterranean region and that the North African countries should be participants in any new collective security system. They also wished to see a reduction in military arsenals and foreign fleets, as well as the dismantling of bases in the region.

The South Commission produced its final report, *The Challenge to the South*. This was a radical, but well-researched and carefully argued, document. Not only did it set out the traditional position on North-South interdependence and South-South 'collective self-reliance', but it also updated the arguments, for example by taking on board global environmental interdependence and by advocating realistic institutions for South-South cooperation. The genuinely new dimension of the report was an analysis of failures within the South: lack of popular participation in politics, excessive centralization, corruption, militarization, neglect of rural development, discrimination against women and inadequate priority for population planning. The Commission concluded that there must be a reorientation to 'people-centred development', with the 'priority goal of first meeting the basic needs of the mass of the people'.

Upon becoming independent, Namibia joined the Non-Aligned Movement. There was no increase in the number of members, however, because the South West Africa People's Organization had been a full member since 1978. Indeed, the subsequent merger of the two Yemens reduced the Movement to a total of 101 members.

Chapter 5

COUNCIL OF EUROPE—EUROPEAN FREE TRADE ASSOCIATION—
NORDIC COUNCIL

COUNCIL OF EUROPE

THE then Prime Minister of Hungary, Miklós Németh, was speaking about his country and its economic difficulties when he told the Parliamentary Assembly of the Council of Europe on 24 January: 'We are aware that basically it is up to us to resolve our problems. The specific historical situation only offers an opportunity; it will not act instead of us. We are also aware that a long process full of unknown and non-predictable difficulties is yet to come and sacrifices will have to be made.' By the end of the year these words read as a remarkably prescient summary of the events of 1990.

The Council of Europe had devoted much of its attention in recent years towards fostering relations with the countries of central and eastern Europe, and 1990 was seen as a year for optimism, consolidation and opportunity in this area. The deliberations of both the Assembly and the Committee of Ministers reflected a sense of their concern not to let the possibilities of the moment slip away, but equally to meet the expectations to which they felt that their past work had given rise amongst the former communist countries of Europe. The 'conclusions from the chair' document, summing up the deliberations of the Committee of Ministers after a special meeting convened in Lisbon on 23–24 March, noted that these countries 'regard the Council of Europe as symbolizing the ideas and values to which they have aspired for many years'. It was agreed to strengthen and widen programmes of assistance in order to take account of the growing number of requests for assistance, their urgency, and the increase in the number of states interested.

The ministers were firm in their assertion that there could be no lowering of the standards required for membership of the Council of Europe. All central and eastern European countries except Albania held observer or special guest status at the beginning of the year. By its end, Hungary had acceded in a ceremony on 6 November in the Palazzo Barberini in Rome; Poland's accession awaited only the holding of free and fair elections; Czechoslovakia (officially the Czech and Slovak Federal Republic) and Yugoslavia had applied for membership; and contacts had been made with Bulgaria and Romania. Meanwhile, all non-member countries, including the Soviet Union, were acceding to increasing numbers of Council of Europe conventions.

The Parliamentary Assembly was addressed by several of the leaders of the emerging democracies, each presenting the problems faced by their own country in the context of wider events. But if Mr Nemeth articulated the realization that problems existed, and Tadeusz Mazowiecki (then Poland's Prime Minister) posed the questions that arose from that realization, it was President Václav Havel of Czechoslovakia who suggested where the answers lay. In a speech combining politics, philosophy and poetry, he outlined the political, economic, civic and security structures for his vision of the new Europe.

Few would have disputed the Council of Europe's claim to have a special role in the fields of political, legal, social and cultural cooperation, and hence its ability to contribute to the third basket of the CSCE process. The Committee of Ministers sought the right to be represented officially at CSCE summit meetings, which was achieved by the Paris session in November. The Council of Europe was also represented at the Copenhagen conference on the human dimension of the CSCE in June. The Parliamentary Assembly argued that a vital tier in the architecture of the new Europe had been overlooked, but 'by virtue of its wide field of competence and expanding membership' it was the best placed organization to supply the 'missing' parliamentary dimension. To this end, the Assembly invited all CSCE countries to participate in a debate in Strasbourg on 26–27 September. Only the US Congress, due to the coinciding budget crisis and its longstanding attachment to the North Atlantic Assembly, did not participate. The final resolution called for continuous parliamentary involvement in the CSCE process through an Assembly of Europe, based on the Parliamentary Assembly of the Council of Europe.

In other developments during 1990, a Commission for Democracy through Law was established under Council of Europe auspices with the aim of studying the legal cultures of democratic countries, while the European Centre for Global Interdependence and Solidarity also began work following up the 1988 North-South campaign.

On the legal front, Caroline Cossey of Britain failed in her attempt in the European Court of Human Rights to have her changed sex legally recognized.

EUROPEAN FREE TRADE ASSOCIATION

FOR EFTA the year ended with optimism on the planned European Economic Area (EEA). This unfamiliar acronym was the new title which EFTA and the European Community (EC) had given during the year to what they had hitherto been calling the European Economic Space (EES), effectively a single market embracing the seven EFTA members and the 12-member EC.

A foreign ministers' meeting with the EC in Brussels on 19 December, postponed from earlier in the month when the position appeared highly problematic, issued a joint declaration which was presented as a breakthrough on the EEA. Efforts would be intensified to complete an EEA treaty for signature by mid-1991, allowing 18 months for ratification so that the agreement could be effective in time for 1 January 1993. On the key contentious issue—how decisions would be taken when EC policy would effectively determine the rules for the whole EEA—an EEA council would be created to set 'general political guidelines'. Consisting of ministers from EFTA and EC countries and members of the European Commission, its work would be complemented by a joint committee of experts, from EFTA and EC countries. This formula would make it possible for EFTA to play its part in 'decision-shaping', without breaching the EC refusal to accept participation by non-members in its decision-making *per se*.

Substantive areas where further negotiation was needed included the application of environmental, health and safety standards where current EFTA rules were more stringent than those of the Community. Also difficult were the details of fishing policy, especially in view of Iceland's heavy dependence on fish, and the applicability of free movement of labour, whose implications in terms of immigration were of particular concern to the Swiss. On competition policy, EFTA was to set up a watchdog body of its own, with powers similar to those of the European Commission in this sphere.

It remained clear that the value of the EEA concept was regarded differently by different EFTA members. Austria, Sweden and perhaps also Norway and even Finland could regard it as a staging-post on the road to potential full EC membership (for which Austria had applied already, while Sweden's parliament approved on 12 December the government's decision to make an application in 1991—see pp. 172–3). For Iceland and for Switzerland/Liechtenstein, it might prove a more durable framework for their relationship as non-members of the EC, while the idea of the EEA as an 'outer gate' or 'ante-chamber' appealed to some EC officials as a means of structuring relations with some of the Mediterranean and East European countries.

The negotiations with the EC had dominated the annual EFTA heads of government meeting, held in Gothenburg (Sweden) on 14 June, just six days before the first of the year's six full meetings in Brussels of the EC-EFTA high-level negotiating group. The summit ended with celebrations of EFTA's 30th anniversary, and the early years were again remembered, but in more sombre mood, with the death on 27 November of Sir Frank Figgures, who had been the first secretary-general of EFTA in 1960–65 (see OBITUARY). On the organizational side the EFTA Council chairmanship passed on 1 July from Sweden to Switzerland; ministers met informally in Geneva on 22–23 October and held their annual autumn meeting there on 13–14 December; and on 31 May the

Council approved a budget for the year July 1990 to June 1991 which was up by almost 20 per cent to 27 million Swiss francs. This included cooperation projects with the EC (notably the TEDIS trade electronic data interchange system), but was also to cover increases in the EFTA secretariat and the greater volume of work associated with the EEA negotiations.

Relations with European countries to the east provided the other main theme of 1990 for EFTA, as the architecture of a 'common European home' came under serious practical consideration. The mid-year Gothenburg meetings included the signature on 13 June of joint declarations of cooperation with Czechoslovakia, Hungary and Poland, which were followed through with the first meetings of the respective joint committees, in Budapest on 27–28 September, in Geneva on 25 October (Poland), and in Geneva again on 16 November (Czechoslovakia).

The EFTA-Yugoslavia joint committee, meeting in Belgrade in February, received Yugoslavia's application for EFTA membership, and by the time of its November meeting in Berne the committee was ready to agree on full negotiations starting on 17 December. Yugoslavia was to become a member in January 1992, but with some trade preferences still applicable in a transitional period thereafter.

NORDIC COUNCIL

THE 38th session of the Nordic Council met in Reykjavik between 26 February and 2 March. It adopted 33 recommendations for action by the Council of Ministers, representing the governments of the five Nordic countries (Denmark, Finland, Iceland, Norway and Sweden).

The Council called for the preparation of joint Nordic programmes in the areas of regional policy, linguistic cooperation, youth unemployment, the rights of Nordic citizens in other Nordic countries, sea and air pollution, the working environment, and the development of environmentally-friendly technology, waste disposal and recycling.

The Council recommended the establishment of a Nordic Environment Financing Corporation to invest in East European projects of environmental interest to the Council's member states. Other environmental recommendations included greater cooperation to develop environmentally-friendly agricultural methods, ratification of the Basle Convention controlling the international transportation of dangerous waste materials, and Nordic support at the United Nations for a proposal that the industrial countries should devote a proportion of their GNP to support global environmental cooperation.

The Council called on the Council of Ministers to ensure the continued development of a Nordic regional policy within the context of efforts to bring about closer European integration. It asked the five governments to lay down guidelines for the work of the Nordic Research Council during 1990–92. Other recommendations included an increase in the lending limits of the Nordic Investment Bank, the mutual recognition of higher academic and vocational qualifications, the establishment of a Nordic art and culture centre in Nuuk (Greenland), the holding of a Nordic cultural festival in 1992, the establishment of an institute for toxicology, harmonization of arms legislation, the encouragement of greater support for sexual equality by the UN specialized agencies, and a study with policy proposals of the situation of homosexuals in the Nordic states. Lastly the Council called for ratification of the UN convention on children's rights and a Nordic programme to implement its terms.

In their debates members addressed the questions of Nordic cooperation in a post-Cold-War Europe and the role of the Nordic Council in a future European Economic Area (EEA) linking the EFTA and European Community (EC) countries (see also pp. 415–6). Left-wing socialist and centre (agrarian) party groups, opposed to far-reaching adaptation to the imminent EC single market, urged the further development of Nordic cooperation, perhaps even with supra-national elements, as a counterweight or alternative to the EEA. Conservative group speakers accepted a reduced role for the Nordic Council in economic questions, but saw a continued role for a reformed organization. For example, Carl Bildt, leader of Sweden's opposition Moderate Party, suggested that the Nordic Council might become the basis for the Nordic component of the planned parliamentary cooperation between EFTA parliaments and the EC parliament. Social democratic speakers such as Gro Harlem Brundtland (Norway) and Mats Hellström (Sweden) argued for the voluntary introduction of supra-national elements in Nordic cooperation before it was forced on them by the EEA treaty.

Following the sessions these questions were examined by an organization committee established to review the whole Nordic Council structure and propose ways of making it more effective. The committee's report was published in October and contained many proposals. It recommended revising the 1962 Helsinki agreement to permit more than one session per year, majority voting in the Council of Ministers, greater influence on the budget for the Council itself, and permitting the presidium and committees to initiate proposals. International affairs would at last be brought formally within the Nordic Council's competence by treaty revision and the creation of a council of foreign ministers. The presidium would assume responsibility for coordinating the Nordic Council's international activities. The EEA treaty should contain a clause, modelled on article 233 of the Treaty of Rome, recognizing the existence and continuation of Nordic cooperation based on the Helsinki agreement. These and other committee recommendations would be debated by the Council at its 1991 session.

Chapter 6

AFRICAN CONFERENCES AND ORGANIZATIONS—
SOUTH ASIAN ASSOCIATION FOR REGIONAL COOPERATION—
SOUTH EAST ASIAN ORGANIZATIONS—SOUTH PACIFIC
REGIONAL COOPERATION—LATIN AMERICAN
ORGANIZATIONS—CARIBBEAN ORGANIZATIONS

AFRICAN CONFERENCES AND ORGANIZATIONS

AFRICA held its customary round of meetings for the most part before the outbreak of the Gulf crisis, which might have exposed potential divisions, even if most African countries, as members of the United Nations, condemned the Iraqi invasion of Kuwait with varying degrees of enthusiasm. The oil producers hoped to say as little as possible while discreetly obtaining benefit from the windfall of higher oil prices. Non-oil producers were alarmed at the prospect of more expensive oil. Only the North African countries, and to some extent the Islamic African countries, were more involved in the Gulf situation.

Prior to the Gulf crisis the preoccupations of the continent were more with continuing economic crisis and the movement for democracy, influenced by developments in Eastern Europe and in South Africa. The summit of the 51-member Organization of African Unity (OAU), held in Addis Ababa on 9–11 July, approved a declaration on 'the political and socio-economic situation in Africa and the fundamental changes taking place in the world'. Apart from developments in Eastern Europe, the leaders took into account 'the movement from confrontation to cooperation in East-West relations', as well as Western Europe's steady move towards monetary and political union, the increasing global tendency towards regional integration, the establishment of trading blocs and advances in science and technology. They felt that there was a threat of the marginalization of the African continent unless these challenges were adequately met.

The OAU declaration expressed full awareness of the link between democracy and development, conceding that a 'political environment which guarantees human rights and the observance of the rule oı ıaw will ensure high standards of probity and accountability, particularly on the part of those who hold public office'. Committing themselves to 'further democratization', the leaders reaffirmed the right of African countries to determine 'in all sovereignty their system of democracy on the basis of their socio-cultural values'. Thus did they duck a commitment to multi-partyism. At the same time, they expressed concern at 'an increasing tendency to impose conditionalities of a political nature for assistance to Africa'. This was a perhaps inevitable response to a number of earlier statements from such people as the president of the World Bank, Barber Conable, and British Foreign Secretary Douglas Hurd, to the effect that the time had come for democratic strings to be tied to aid.

The summit document also reaffirmed established OAU positions on such issues as apartheid, the African economic crisis, debt, the unjust international economic order, the urgency of continental integration and collective Third World action on international economic issues such as commodity prices. Optimistically, moves to establish an African common market by the year 2000 were also approved, and it was hoped that a treaty to that effect would be ready for endorsement at the 1991 summit due to be held, exceptionally out of Addis Ababa, in the new Nigerian capital of Abuja.

Attended by 25 heads of state the 1990 summit unanimously chose Uganda's President Yoweri Museveni as OAU chairman in succession to Egyptian President Husni Mubarak. The post was normally held for one year. In his acceptance speech, President Museveni spoke of the problems caused for Africa by the 'inequities of the international system', adding that the lack of continental integration exacerbated the negative impact of the world economy on Africa. After dwelling at length on the bad effects of foreign interference in Africa, he said it was the right of every African to enjoy democracy and dignity. All forms of dictatorship and violation of human rights should be opposed, but each country should decide its exact forms of political organization.

President Sam Nujoma was welcomed into the ranks of African leaders with the admission of Namibia as the OAU's 51st member. The vice-president of the African National Congress of South Africa, Nelson Mandela, whose release earlier in the year had been widely welcomed by OAU member states, addressed the summit to a rapturous reception. Former President Julius Nyerere of Tanzania addressed the summit as chairman of the South Commission, whose report set out ways in which countries of the 'South' (i.e. the developing countries) could improve their mutual cooperation (see also p. 413). Ministers meeting before the summit considered the vexed question of $50 million arrears owed by member states, the equivalent of two years' annual budget.

The meeting also considered reports from the committee set up to reconcile Senegal and Mauritania (which was said to have contained the dispute and prevented it from escalating) and from another on the Chad-Libya situation. This subsequently met at head of state level in Rabat, without substantial result, under the auspices of King Hassan of Morocco. The Western Sahara question, in which the OAU had been deeply involved to the point of admitting the Sahrawi Arab Democratic Republic (SADR), was also considered, even though Morocco had still not formally resumed its membership; however, the referendum which the OAU and the UN had called for had still not been held by the end of the year (see p. 244).

Many other institutions and regional groupings in Africa were also affected by the problem of arrears in subscriptions, a reflection of the desperate financial state of many African countries. Those dependent on the OAU, like the Supreme Council for Sport in Africa and the Pan-African News Agency, were especially badly hit; but significant regional groupings such as the Economic Community of Western African States (ECOWAS), the Economic Community of Central African States (CEEAC) and the Preferential Trade Area (PTA) all had to consider non-payment of subscriptions at their respective summits.

The newest large regional grouping on the continent, the Arab Mahgreb Union (AMU), formed in 1989 (see AR 1989, pp. 238, 240), was still enjoying its first élan, setting up a number of institutions in the banking and customs sectors. It also seemed determined to face the challenge of differences arising from the Gulf crisis. The PTA, at its summit in November, appealed for increased aid for Africa because of the hardship higher oil prices caused to non-oil producing African economies. The Southern African Development Coordination Conference (SADCC) admitted Namibia, but seemed to be facing an identity crisis arising from the changing regional situation, since its vocation had been very much to reduce dependence on South Africa.

The effects of Africa's internal conflicts spilled over into regional groupings concerned in theory only with economic matters. The heads of state of ECOWAS, meeting in Banjul at the end of May, were obliged to consider the Liberian civil war (see p. 264). They cautiously set up a mediation committee to bring together the 'warring factions', which, at its first meeting in August, decided to send a peace-keeping force, the ECOWAS Monitoring Group (ECOMOG), to Liberia. This survived a row about the circumstances of the capture (and subsequent death) of President Doe outside its headquarters in September. By the end of the year it had supervised the establishment of a transitional government under President Amos Sawyer. An emergency summit in Bamako at the end of November gave its blessing to the ECOMOG, and to continued efforts to bring the factions together, without formally endorsing the Sawyer government. The Liberian operation, while it led to calls for a possible revision of the organization's treaty, obscured the fact that implementation of the practical aspects of ECOWAS integration was still very slow. Funding a peace-keeping force was an added burden for an organization already in financial difficulties.

Africa's main economic structure, the African Development Bank, continued to represent a solitary success story. The annual assembly in Abidjan in May demonstrated the bank's skill in keeping its non-African shareholders (especially European and North American) sweet. The bank's president met with the secretary of the UN Economic Commission for Africa and the OAU secretary-general at the end of the year, in the first of planned regular tripartite summits.

Leaders of French-speaking African states and others went to the French resort of La Baule in June for the 16th Franco-African summit. The question of the movements for democracy in Africa was inevitably on the agenda. President Mitterrand hinted that there would be linkage between aid and democratic performance, producing the oracular phrase 'no democracy without development; no development without democracy'. Of the 35 delegations present, that of Uganda was a newcomer.

SOUTH ASIAN ASSOCIATION FOR REGIONAL COOPERATION

THE fifth summit meeting of SAARC was held in Malé, capital of the Maldives, on 21–23 November. This summit had originally been scheduled to take place in Sri Lanka during 1989, as part of the agreed process whereby SAARC met annually by rotation in each of its seven member countries. The Sri Lankan government had refused, however, to host the meeting whilst Indian troops remained on its soil (see AR 1989, pp. 406–7) and withdrawal was not completed until March (see p. 321). Thereafter, given Sri Lanka's claims and the desire of the Maldivian government to host a SAARC summit in the 25th anniversary year of its independence, there was some talk of two summits within the year. In the event, only one transpired, it being agreed that the sixth summit would be held in Sri Lanka in 1991.

Such was the scale and pace of political change in South Asia in the 18 months preceding the Malé meeting that only three of the seven heads of state or government present (President Ershad of Bangladesh, the King of Bhutan and host President Gayoom of the Maldives) had been at the previous summit; moreover, President Ershad was to be deposed from power within a fortnight of his visit to the Maldives (see p. 320). The Prime Ministers of India, Pakistan, Sri Lanka and Nepal respectively were thus all novitiates on SAARC's summit stage. They met in a new conference hall completed just in time for the summit, which was preceded by three days of conferring at ministerial and senior bureaucratic levels.

Predictably, the summiteers reaffirmed their commitment to the purposes and principles of SAARC. According to their 27-paragraph final communique, which they labelled the Malé Declaration, they 'renewed their resolve to intensify cooperation under [SAARC's] aegis in pursuit of their common objectives' and to extend the activities of SAARC with respect to economic cooperation, biotechnology, environmental issues and tourism. They also called for 'expeditious enactment of enabling measures for the implementation of the SAARC regional convention [agreed in 1988] on the suppression of terrorism'.

The leaders recalled the usefulness of their first ministerial meeting on international economic issues held in Islamabad in 1986, and agreed that a second such ministerial meeting should be held in India in 1991 'to review the outcome of the [GATT] Uruguay Round and to coordinate positions at international conferences, including the 1992 UN Conference on Environment and Development. They welcomed moves towards a comprehensive nuclear test ban treaty and praised the initiative of the Maldives at the UN in urging special attention for 'the protection and security of small states'.

The Malé summit described recent developments in the Gulf as 'the most unfortunate aberration from the present trend of detente, cooperation and peaceful settlement of disputes'. While emphasizing the need for a peaceful solution of the issue, the leaders called for 'immediate and unconditional withdrawal of Iraqi forces from Kuwait and the restoration of its legitimate government'. They also stated that the crisis already had 'dealt a severe blow to their economies' and called for 'massive international assistance to compensate the loss suffered by them due to a sharp decline in remittances, setback to their exports and severe strain on their balance-of-payments position imposed by increased oil prices'.

SOUTH-EAST ASIAN ORGANIZATIONS

THE decision taken by the United States in July to withdraw its support from the Khmer Rouge-led Kampuchean rebel government at the UN and to enter into dialogue with Vietnam came as an immense shock to the six ASEAN countries (see also pp. 346–7). As usual, the Kampuchean imbroglio, and in particular the US bombshell, dominated the annual ASEAN foreign ministers' meeting, the organization's 23rd, held in Jakarta (Indonesia) in July. The new US position led to a closing of ASEAN ranks, with little evidence of the internal bickering over Kampuchea which had surfaced in Brunei in 1989. In a terse final communique the six claimed that the US move would 'set back the search for a comprehensive political solution to the problem'. The USA and Vietnam also came under attack for their continued opposition to the forcible repatriation of Indo-Chinese boat people.

ASEAN economic ministers held their 22nd annual meeting in Indonesia in October. The ministers amended the terms of the planned ASEAN industrial joint-venture (AIJV) to include allowing non-ASEAN investors to hold up to 60 per cent of equity. The ministers also adopted a new plan for common effective preferential tariffs on selected industrial products 'to facilitate the free flow of goods within ASEAN'.

The eighth ASEAN-EC meeting took place in Sarawak early in the year amidst ASEAN concerns over possible changes in the relationship with the EC after 1992. The Europeans attempted to assuage ASEAN fears by suggesting that, as highly competitive traders, the six would in all likelihood benefit from a more open European market after 1992. However, the EC also raised ominous questions about the ASEAN members' continued status as 'developing countries', given their favourable balance of trade with Europe. Relations between the two groupings deteriorated late in the year after the EC threatened to ban imports of tropical forestry products.

The question of American military bases in Asia remained a source of intra-ASEAN tension. Malaysia, and to a lesser extent Indonesia, expressed concern at a November agreement which provided for increased US use of Singapore's military facilities. However, unease did not threaten to frustrate Singaporean efforts to promote an innovative economic 'growth triangle' involving itself, Johore state in Malaysia and Riau province in Indonesia. Meanwhile, negotiations between Washington and the Philippines over the future of Clark air base and Subic naval base remained effectively deadlocked, with Manila continuing to insist that it would take over the bases when the current agreement expired in 1991 (see p. 344).

Differences also emerged within ASEAN over attitudes towards the Asia-Pacific Cooperation Council (APEC), the embryonic 'Pacific Rim grouping' launched by Australia in late 1989 (see AR 1989, p. 408). Malaysia, in particular, appeared cautious of the initiative, whilst Singapore was the most enthusiastic of the six. Such caution seemed hardly warranted, however, when the second ministerial meeting of the 12-member APEC in July turned out to be a hesitant affair, with no concrete results. Solemn promises were made to conduct 'urgent reviews' of negotiating positions to facilitate a breakthrough at the deadlocked GATT Uruguay Round negotiations. Members also set themselves the task of finding an acceptable formula to bring the 'three Chinas' into the fold. Other countries openly expressing interest in joining the group included the Soviet Union, Vietnam, Papua New Guinea, Mongolia, Chile, Ecuador, Mexico and Peru.

Resolutions adopted at the 46th session of the UN Economic and Social Commission for Asia and the Pacific (ESCAP), held in Bangkok in June, called for a strengthening of support for the Commission's population programme and for a regional plan of action to deal with urbanization. Other resolutions called for 'education for all' in the region, for the integration of women in all aspects of development and increased foreign investment in the region's least developed countries. One of the papers prepared for the conference called for a modified Marshall Plan for the ESCAP region, contending that Japanese surplus capital should be used to restructure the Asian and Pacific economies just as the United States had done for post-war Europe.

A report prepared by ESCAP in December predicted a slowing of economic growth rates of developing and newly industrializing nations in the ESCAP region during 1991 as a result of the effects of the Gulf crisis, recession in the United States and the deadlock in the GATT talks.

SOUTH PACIFIC REGIONAL COOPERATION

AT the July South Pacific Forum (SPF) meeting held in Vanuatu, heads of government welcomed Japan's decision to stop drift-net fishing in the region a year ahead of a date stipulated in UN General Assembly resolution 225 of 1989, but called for stricter controls over 'purse seiner' (deep encirclement) methods of fishing. There was a call on France to expand its educational and development assistance to the indigenous Kanak people of New Caledonia, and the meeting established a monitoring group to assess that territory's progress towards self-determination.

The most prominent issue before the meeting concerned American destruction of chemical weapons on Johnston Atoll. It was declared that the Pacific should not be used as dumping area for the disposal of hazardous materials including chemical weapons, that Johnston Atoll should be closed down once current operations had been completed, and that early discussions with the United States on the issue should commence. (In Hawaii in October President Bush subsequently met with representatives from 11 Pacific Islands states, nine of whom were heads of government; he indicated that the United States did not plan to use Johnston Atoll beyond the programme of activities already announced.)

Most isolated in the SPF debate over Johnston Atoll was Australia. The leak of a foreign affairs cable at the Vanuatu meeting, spelling out the tactics decided between the Americans and Australians to 'manage' the Forum debate by not releasing relevant scientific reports on the facility, provoked resentment from other delegations, particularly Nauru.

The South Pacific Commission (SPC) held its annual conference in Nouméa in October. The key issues included cooperation in health and how best to combat the spread of AIDS, progress on establishing an autonomous South Pacific Regional Environmental Programme (SPREP) following ratifications by France and Western Samoa, and, after extensive debate, the deferral of a decision on rebuilding or relocating SPC headquarters.

LATIN AMERICAN ORGANIZATIONS

AFTER many years of hesitation, Canada became the 33rd member of the Organization of American States (OAS) on 13 November, when it signed the Charter in a brief ceremony at the OAS headquarters in Washington. An OAS observer since 1972, Canada had previously stated that it did not see any military obligation as stemming from its full membership. In the course of the year other developments indicated a new responsiveness of the USA to some, at least, of its neighbours' problems.

On 15 February the Presidents of Bolivia, Colombia, Peru and the USA met at the Colombian Caribbean port of Cartagena to sign the Cartagena declaration, pledging their governments to more strenuous efforts to combat the illegal traffic in cocaine, with increased US financial assistance. In view of the strong popular hostility to what was widely seen as the imperialist designs of the USA, and the possible threat posed by Colombia's drug syndicates, the meeting took place under conditions of strict security.

A summit meeting of the Andean Pact countries held in Cuzco (Peru) on 22–23 May took further steps towards the integration of the sub-region and ensuring free trade in goods by 1995 by the creation of an Andean presidential council. The meeting resolved to formulate a common position on the debt issue for submission to a ministerial meeting of the Latin American Economic System (SELA), of which the USA was not a member. President Alan Garcia Pérez of Peru complained that the USA was emphasizing a military approach to the elimination of illegal drugs production at the cost of the crop substitution programmes called for at Cartagena. However, President Jaime Paz Zamora of Bolivia (who had been successful in obtaining a considerable increase in US aid to his country to some $33 million) said that US intentions would have to be taken on trust—a position strongly supported by the Venezuelan President, Carlos Andrés Pérez. In the event, Sr Garcia's successor, President Alberto Fujimori, subsequently rejected a proposed $35.9 million US aid package for Peru (see p. 84).

The Group of Rio, meeting in Mexico DF on 30–31 March, agreed to expel Panama from the Latin American Group of 8 (G-8) countries, calling at the same time for popular consultation, without external interference, to determine the legitimacy of the government of President Guillermo Endara. The meeting also condemned the invasion of Cuban airspace by the US-sponsored TV Martí. At a meeting in Dublin on 10 April with the foreign ministers of the European Community (EC), Group representatives advocated institutionalization of their joint relationship and that of the EC with the Latin American Association for International Development (ALADI). At a further meeting in Budapest on 12 April with representatives of the East European countries, joint agreements were reached to increase political, economic, cultural, scientifc and technological exchanges between the two regions.

On 27 June President Bush announced an Enterprise for the Americas Initiative, aimed at Latin America and the Caribbean and based on the premise that trade, not aid, was the route to continued peace and prosperity in the region. He proposed a new investment fund to promote free trade, the free market and privatization. To this fund the USA would contribute $100 million and Europe and Japan equivalent sums. The Inter-American Development Bank (IDB) would also make available sums of up to $300 million to promote free market conditions favourable to foreign (mainly US) investment. Preferential trade benefits would be extended to any state that reduced trade barriers with the long-term aim of creating a western hemisphere free trade zone. Steps would at the same time be taken to reduce the region's aggregate debt of some $12,000 million to the USA on condition that the states concerned accepted IMF and World Bank terms.

The Presidents of Colombia, Ecuador and Venezuela, with representatives of Bolivia and Peru, welcomed the US initiative at a two-day conference in Bogotá on 4–5 August. They issued an Andean Declaration, which in turn called on the USA to eliminate non-tariff barriers currently affecting some 50 per cent of imports from Latin America and re-emphasized the need to address the debt issue. At Caracas on 11–12 October the Group of Rio welcomed the Bush initiative, but called for the restructuring of existing regional institutions and a policy of regional energy self-sufficiency.

CARIBBEAN ORGANIZATIONS

INTERESTING parallels developed in 1990 between the global, regional and sub-regional concerns of Caribbean states in relation to the interests of small nations within broader trading and political relationships. Tensions emerged between the 13-member Caribbean Community and Common Market (CARICOM) and the USA, within CARICOM itself and within its regional offshoot, the Organization of Eastern Caribbean States (OECS).

The CARICOM states reacted unenthusiastically both to the US proposal in June of an Enterprise for the Americas Initiative based on a pan-American free trade zone, and more particularly to the Bush administration's efforts to discuss the initiative on a country-by-country basis rather than through CARICOM. The main preoccupations in CARICOM were the potential impact on preferential trading arrangements with the European Community, and the effects of exposure to duty-free US imports. The USA renewed its 1983 Caribbean Basin Initiative in August; the new package (CBI-2) retained the duty-free treatment of many exports of the 22 beneficiary countries, but there were no new concessions on sugar quotas or textiles.

The annual CARICOM heads of government meeting opened in Kingston, Jamaica, on 31 July, with Trinidad & Tobago represented by its

Foreign Minister, since its Prime Minister was being held hostage in an attempted coup (see p. 95). The member states condemned the attempt, which led to discussions on a common CARICOM security policy. Four states (Antigua & Barbuda, Barbados, Jamaica and St Vincent & the Grenadines) contributed troops to a temporary force invited in when the Trinidadian government regained control on 2 August.

The Kingston summit restored the momentum of Anglo-Caribbean economic integration with an accord to phase the introduction of a common external tariff (CET) over one year from the original deadline of 1 January 1991 (see AR 1989, p. 411), except for Montserrat, which would accede on 1 January 1994. (The misgivings of the smaller tariff-protected Eastern Caribbean states, voiced at a CARICOM ministerial meeting in April, were highlighted by an Antiguan request in November for a postponement of the CET because of domestic economic problems and the Gulf crisis.) Other measures agreed in Kingston included cross-listing by the region's three stock exchanges from 1991, the harmonization of investment incentives, and progress towards a common currency by 1995. Passport and work permit requirements within CARICOM were to be eliminated from 1991, with a common passport from 1993.

The CARICOM summit admitted two UK dependent territories, the British Virgin Islands and the Turks & Caïcos Islands, as associate members; Mexico and Venezuela (which were providing oil on concessionary terms) became observers. A renewed application from Haiti was left on the table, as was one from the Dominican Republic, which had alienated the Windward states by exporting bananas to Europe.

The seven OECS heads of government, meeting in Dominica in May and in Grenada in September, reached agreements on a common travel area and on the development of trade with the French islands of Guadeloupe and Martinique. The four Windward members (Dominica, Grenada, St Lucia, and St Vincent & the Grenadines) further agreed to convene a joint constituent assembly to prepare for unification referendums in mid-1991. The Leeward members (Antigua & Barbuda, Montserrat and St Kitts & Nevis) had endorsed the principle of unification in 1987, but saw less urgency in the project. It was also resisted by a regional Standing Committee of Opposition Parties (SCOPE), formed to counter the conservative government parties represented in the Caribbean Democratic Union (CDU).

The West Indian Commission, a 15-person 'think tank' launched by CARICOM in November 1989, held its first 'strategy meeting' in April. The Commission was to travel through the region to 'consult intensively with the people' on regional development beyond 1992, including the expansion of CARICOM beyond the English-speaking states. The Caribbean Tourism Organization (CTO) met in October with its private-sector associate, the Caribbean Hotel Association

(CTA), to discuss the industry's problems, including the worldwide downturn in tourist air traffic, outdated facilities, competition from other destinations and fragmented marketing. The Caribbean Development Bank (CDB), which obtained its fifth loan-and-credit package from the World Bank and IDA in mid-1990, identified its current priorities as infrastructural development and post-hurricane reconstruction.

XII DEFENCE AND ARMS CONTROL

THE year was one in which the prospects for peace in Europe resulting from the revolutions of 1989 in Eastern Europe were enhanced by a major conventional arms reduction agreement and by measures to develop the Conference on Security and Cooperation in Europe (CSCE) into a new pan-European security framework. It was also a year in which the United States and the Soviet Union continued making progress towards a more harmonious and cooperative relationship, in spite of continuing American concerns over the future of the Soviet Union and the failure in 1990 to reach an accord on strategic arms reductions.

These positive trends in Europe and in superpower relations were, however, largely overshadowed by the crisis in the Gulf precipitated by the Iraqi invasion of Kuwait on 2 August and the resultant major confrontation between Iraq and the United States. This crisis simmered through the rest of 1990, as the United States adopted a strategy of coercive diplomacy and, in its largest deployment of military forces since the Vietnam war, sent over 400,000 troops to the region.

The initial and rapid deployment of US forces to Saudi Arabia certainly provided a major deterrent to an Iraqi incursion. As these forces were joined by those of some of the major European allies, especially France and Britain, it was still not clear that Iraq would depart from Kuwait. The United Nations, in a show of great-power cooperation that was virtually unprecedented, imposed economic sanctions on Iraq. There was general agreement, however, that sanctions could take up to 12 months to work and 1990 ended without there being any clear-cut resolution of the Gulf crisis.

GERMAN UNIFICATION AND STABILITY IN EUROPE

IN Europe itself 1990 was dominated by the achievement of German unification and by the preparations for the November summit of the 34-nation CSCE, at which major arms reduction and confidence-building measures were signed.

The German unification process went much faster and with fewer difficulties than had been expected, even though it was closely linked with developments in NATO and with the negotiations on conventional force reductions that had been underway since 1988. The framework for the negotiations on German reunification was provided by the 'two-plus-four' talks—consisting of the governments of both East and West Germany and the four occupying powers from World War II (the United States, the Soviet Union, Britain and France). Although in the first half of the year it appeared that these talks would stall on the issue of whether or not a united Germany should remain a member of NATO, President Gorbachev proved far more flexible on this issue than expected.

Mr Gorbachev's flexibility was made much easier by developments in NATO itself. At a meeting of the NATO defence planning committee on 21–22 May, the alliance declared that, since the Warsaw Treaty Organization (WTO) no longer posed a military threat, NATO should review its military strategy and reduce its readiness requirements. The positive nature of NATO's response to the developments that had taken place in Eastern Europe was underlined even more dramatically at the NATO heads of state and government meeting in London on 5–6 July. At the end of the summit, NATO issued the London Declaration on a Transformed North Atlantic Alliance, which started from the premise that Europe had 'entered a new, promising era' and that, as a consequence, the alliance had to adapt. As part of this process of adapting NATO to the new Europe, President Gorbachev and leaders of the central and eastern European countries were invited to address the North Atlantic Council. This was accompanied by a more substantial step, as the governments of the Soviet Union, Czechoslovakia, Hungary, Poland, Romania and Bulgaria were invited to establish regular diplomatic liaison with NATO. In addition, the declaration reaffirmed NATO's commitment to establishing 'an entirely different quality of openness in Europe', to be achieved through agreement on 'open skies' and other confidence-building measures. It was also announced that, as Soviet troops left Eastern Europe, NATO would field smaller and more mobile forces relying increasingly on multinational corps; it would also scale back readiness and would reduce its forward deployments, relying more on the ability to build up larger forces if they were needed.

In some ways the most striking aspects of the London Declaration were those statements dealing with nuclear weapons—an issue on which there were differences of approach in that Washington and Bonn wanted to go further than London and Paris in minimizing the role of nuclear weapons in post-Cold War Europe. The result was a document which was very obviously an uneasy compromise. Although the declaration stated that there would be reduced reliance on nuclear weapons and that they would be truly 'weapons of last resort', at the insistence of the British and French it also acknowledged 'that there are no circumstances in which nuclear retaliation in response to military action might be discounted'. Similarly, while the alliance committed itself to the elimination of all nuclear artillery shells from Europe, the declaration also stated that NATO would maintain for the foreseeable future 'an appropriate mix of nuclear and conventional forces, based in Europe and kept up to date where necessary'. This ambivalence led some to contend that the announced changes were little more than a declaratory shift and that nuclear weapons had always been weapons of last resort. There was something to this argument—but the fact that NATO had publicly announced its reduced reliance on nuclear weapons was symbolically very important.

Another significant feature of the London Declaration was the emphasis placed on the CSCE and its role in the evolving European security framework. The declaration proposed that the CSCE should establish regular consultations at a high level, a schedule of two-year review conferences, a small secretariat and a Centre for the Prevention of Conflict. The significance of this endorsement was that the CSCE was, in effect, accepted as complementary to NATO rather than as a rival security organization for post-Cold War Europe.

Although the London Declaration contained its share of ambiguities and pieties, NATO had clearly begun the process of adapting to the end of the Cold War in Europe. The most immediate significance of the declaration, however, was its impact on the negotiations on German unification. In effect, the declaration made it much easier for Mr Gorbachev to accept continued German membership in a NATO that was less worrisome to the Soviet Union than in the past. At a meeting on 16 July between Chancellor Kohl of West Germany and Mr Gorbachev—which suggested that 'two-plus-four' had in effect become 'one-plus-one'—the Soviet leader consented to continued German membership of NATO. The two leaders also agreed that Soviet forces would remain in the eastern part of Germany for an interim period of four or five years. During this period Germany would assist with the building of housing and barracks in the Soviet Union for these forces, thereby facilitating their eventual withdrawal. It was also agreed that, after unification, non-German NATO forces would not be deployed in the territory of what was formerly the German Democratic Republic (see also pp. 151–2).

There were two broad views on the Soviet decision to accept a united Germany in NATO. The first was that Chancellor Kohl, by holding firm for NATO membership, had forced Mr Gorbachev to accept Western terms. The other was that Herr Kohl had effectively emasculated NATO, sacrificing the alliance on the altar of German reunification. This more critical assessment, however, seemed somewhat harsh given that the movement towards German unification and the London Declaration were part of a more general trend towards demilitarization in Europe.

CONVENTIONAL ARMS CONTROL AND THE CSCE STRUCTURE

ALTHOUGH the trend towards European force reductions had been evident in the late 1980s, it accelerated significantly during 1990. In July, for example, the British government—which remained the most sceptical of all West European governments about the changes in the

Soviet Union—announced that its forces in Germany would be reduced by 50 per cent over the next five years. Other NATO members also revealed that force levels would be reduced and that troop contingents would be withdrawn from Germany. More immediately important than the unilateral cuts, however, were the negotiations on conventional armed forces in Europe (CFE), which took place in the framework of the CSCE process but included only the members of the two alliance systems. These talks had made considerable progress during 1989, and although there were one or two setbacks during 1990 they culminated in the CFE agreement signed at the Paris summit in November.

In January 1990 there were several developments which improved the prospects for the CFE talks, including a US retreat from its earlier emphasis on the need for stringent and intrusive verification procedures—proposals which had upset its allies more than the Soviet Union. Even more important, in his State of the Union address, President Bush proposed that Soviet and American troops in central and eastern Europe be reduced to 195,000 on each side. This superseded the President's proposal at the NATO summit of June 1989 for ceilings of 275,000 for the United States and the Soviet Union. Although administration spokesmen subsequently insisted that the US military presence in Western Europe did not depend solely on a Soviet presence in Eastern Europe, the Bush initiative received the support of the NATO allies and, for the most part, was greeted enthusiastically by the Soviet Union. On 13 February Washington and Moscow agreed informally upon a common ceiling of 195,000 ground and air personnel on foreign territory in the central zone in Europe, with an added proviso that the United States should be permitted to deploy an additional 30,000 troops elsewhere on the continent. While this highlighted the growing convergence of Soviet and American approaches to the new European security situation, manpower was not formally included in the negotiations. Moreover, in the formal talks there were still substantial problems and disagreements.

One of the problems was that the negotiations were no longer taking place between two cohesive blocs. Events in Eastern Europe, in particular, had complicated the talks. This was evident when Hungary, without Soviet approval, proposed a ceiling on troops stationed outside national territory and called for the withdrawal of all Soviet troops from its soil by the end of 1991. More serious than these complications were the continued substantive differences, especially the dispute over aircraft limits, which continued to bedevil the talks for several months. Perhaps most important of all, however, was the linkage between CFE and the German problem. When the sixth round of the negotiations opened in Vienna on 15 March it became clear that the Soviet Union was holding up progress because it first wanted the German issue settled in the two-plus-four framework. At this stage there were also differences over what should be done with equipment removed from Europe, with NATO pressing for total destruction of equipment and most of the WTO countries wanting to allow some conversion to civilian uses. Although progress was made on verification and information exchange, it appeared for several months that the talks were being stalled. Even a visit to Moscow on 16–19 May by US Secretary of State James Baker did little to restore the momentum to the negotiations. Nevertheless, the commitment to an agreement by the end of the year was reaffirmed at the Washington summit between Presidents Bush and Gorbachev that took place from 30 May to 2 June, at which some progress was made on the outstanding issues.

On 14 June, at the Vienna negotiations, an informal agreement was reached on the limits on tanks and armoured combat vehicles. Although aircraft limits continued to be a problem—and there was also substantial disagreement over the extent to which single countries should be limited—progress was made on other issues. A big step forward was taken when, at their 16 July meeting, Chancellor Kohl and Mr Gorbachev agreed that the Bundeswehr in a united Germany would have no more than 370,000 troops. Not only did the agreement on German force levels highlight the linkage that had developed between the two-plus-four negotiations and the CFE talks, but it also made it possible for the participants to move towards final agreement in CFE.

Real momentum did not develop until late September when the two negotiating teams met in New York, along with Mr Baker and Mr Shevardnadze, the Soviet Foreign Minister. At this meeting NATO agreed to permit conversion of 750 tanks and 3,000 armoured vehicles in the European part of the Soviet Union. By 5 October it was announced that agreement had been reached on most of the outstanding issues. Yet there were major differences between the Soviet Union and its East European allies over the allocation of the forces that would be allowed under the CFE ceilings, the so-called entitlements question. In fact, the Hungarian CFE negotiator noted that there were few joint Eastern proposals and that differences within the WTO were greater than within NATO. These differences were aired at a meeting of the WTO disarmament commission on 9–10 October, but were resolved in a further meeting of the commission on 26–27 October, leading to signature of a formal agreement by foreign ministers on 3 November. Although some of the detail remained to be worked out, the way was prepared for the CFE agreement to be signed in Paris on 19 November. Prior to this, on 6 November, it was agreed that there would be four groups in Vienna after the summit: (i) a joint consultative group, envisaged as the CFE oversight body dealing with information exchange; (ii) CFE-1A, which would handle residual issues as well as matters to do with aerial inspections and manpower; (iii) the CFE-2 mandate talks; and (iv) the talks on confidence- and security-building measures (CSBMs).

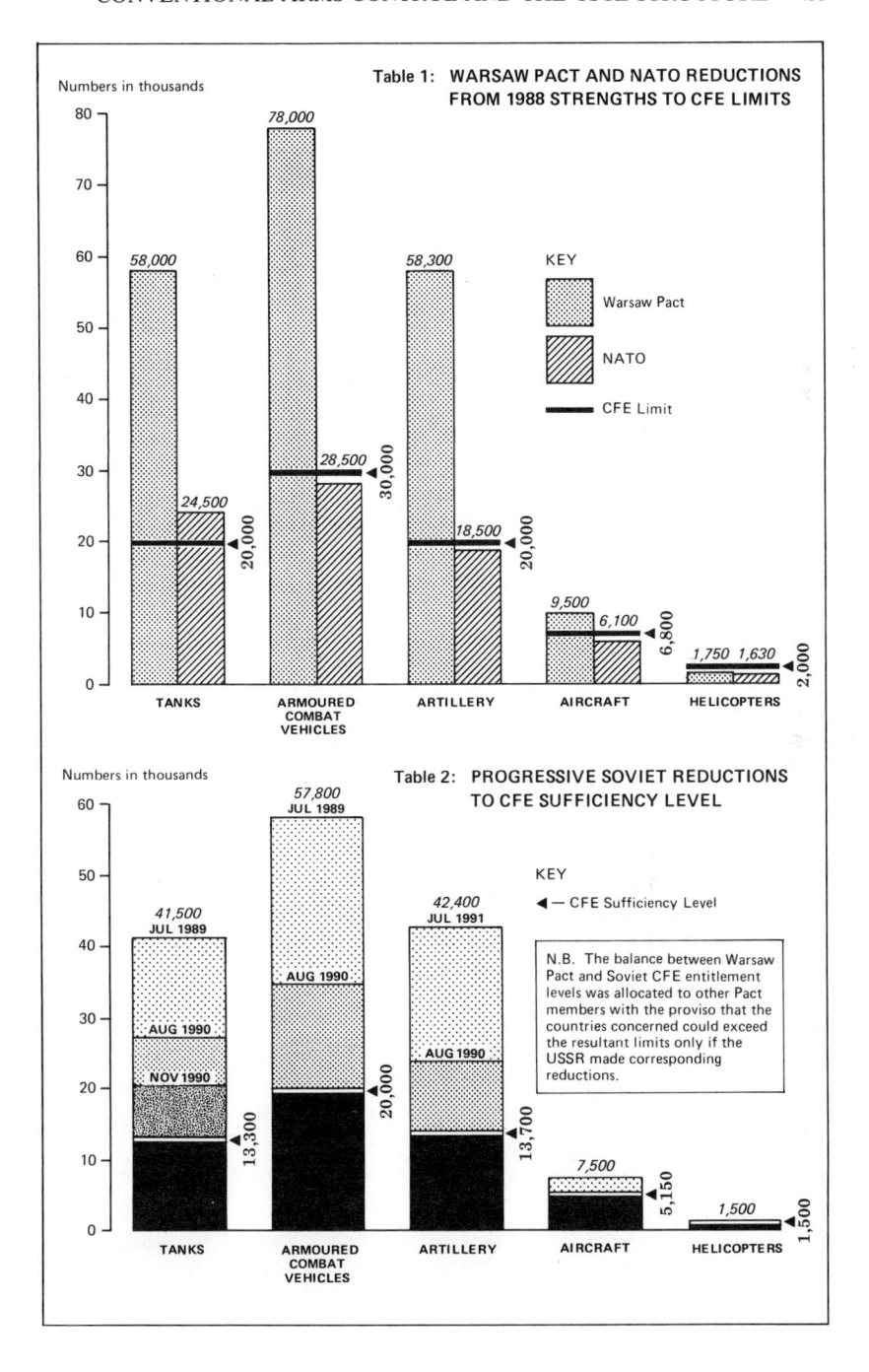

CONVENTIONAL ARMS CONTROL AND THE CSCE STRUCTURE 435

Table 1: WARSAW PACT AND NATO REDUCTIONS FROM 1988 STRENGTHS TO CFE LIMITS

Numbers in thousands

KEY
- Warsaw Pact
- NATO
- ◀ CFE Limit

	Warsaw Pact	NATO	CFE Limit
TANKS	58,000	24,500	20,000
ARMOURED COMBAT VEHICLES	78,000	28,500	30,000
ARTILLERY	58,300	18,500	20,000
AIRCRAFT	9,500	6,100	6,800
HELICOPTERS	1,750	1,630	2,000

Table 2: PROGRESSIVE SOVIET REDUCTIONS TO CFE SUFFICIENCY LEVEL

Numbers in thousands

KEY
- ◀ — CFE Sufficiency Level

N.B. The balance between Warsaw Pact and Soviet CFE entitlement levels was allocated to other Pact members with the proviso that the countries concerned could exceed the resultant limits only if the USSR made corresponding reductions.

	JUL 1989	AUG 1990	NOV 1990	JUL 1991	CFE Sufficiency Level
TANKS	41,500				13,300
ARMOURED COMBAT VEHICLES	57,800				20,000
ARTILLERY				42,400	13,700
AIRCRAFT				7,500	5,150
HELICOPTERS				1,500	1,500

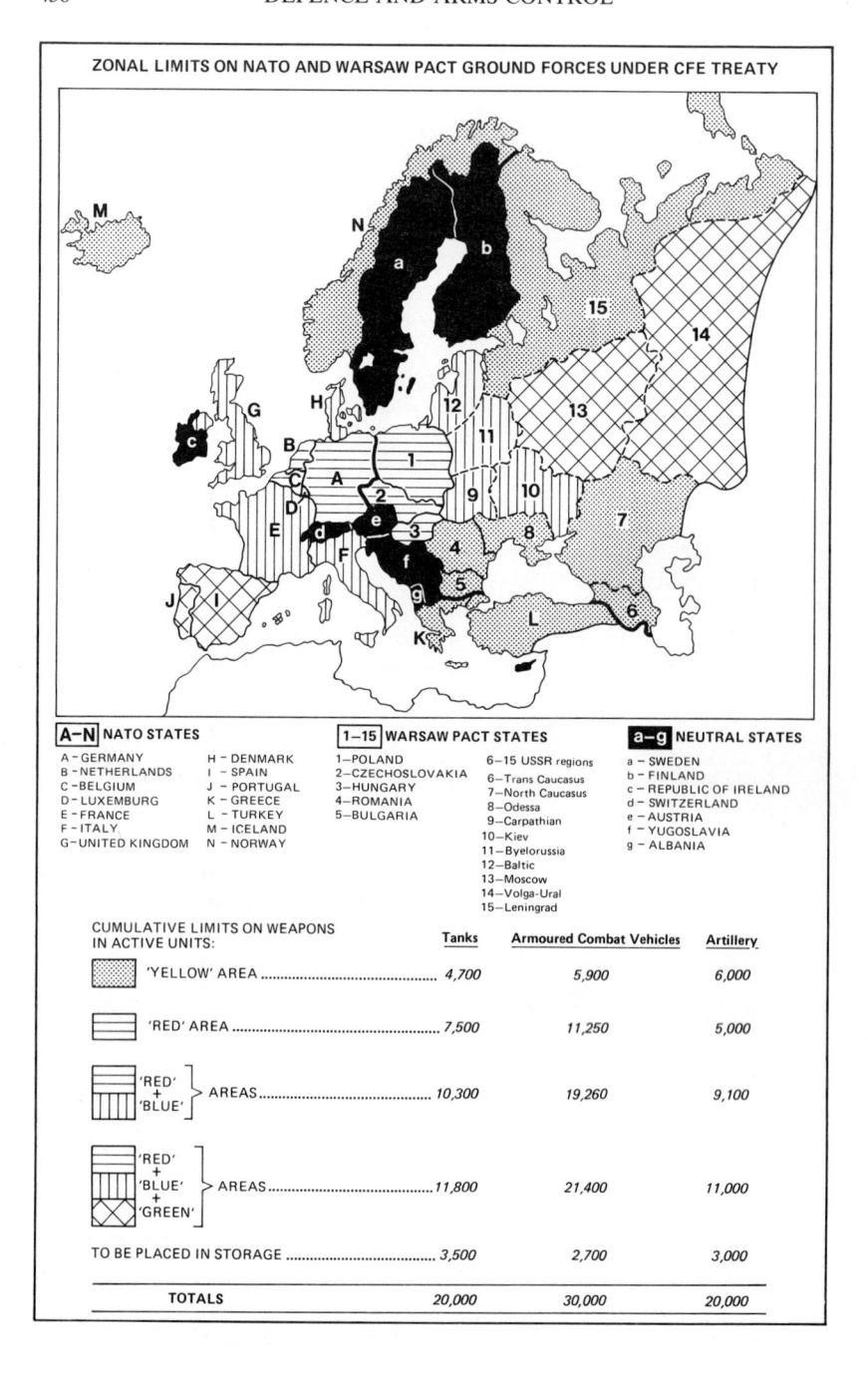

ZONAL LIMITS ON NATO AND WARSAW PACT GROUND FORCES UNDER CFE TREATY

A–N NATO STATES

- A – GERMANY
- B – NETHERLANDS
- C – BELGIUM
- D – LUXEMBURG
- E – FRANCE
- F – ITALY
- G – UNITED KINGDOM
- H – DENMARK
- I – SPAIN
- J – PORTUGAL
- K – GREECE
- L – TURKEY
- M – ICELAND
- N – NORWAY

1–15 WARSAW PACT STATES

- 1 – POLAND
- 2 – CZECHOSLOVAKIA
- 3 – HUNGARY
- 4 – ROMANIA
- 5 – BULGARIA
- 6–15 USSR regions
- 6 – Trans Caucasus
- 7 – North Caucasus
- 8 – Odessa
- 9 – Carpathian
- 10 – Kiev
- 11 – Byelorussia
- 12 – Baltic
- 13 – Moscow
- 14 – Volga-Ural
- 15 – Leningrad

a–g NEUTRAL STATES

- a – SWEDEN
- b – FINLAND
- c – REPUBLIC OF IRELAND
- d – SWITZERLAND
- e – AUSTRIA
- f – YUGOSLAVIA
- g – ALBANIA

CUMULATIVE LIMITS ON WEAPONS IN ACTIVE UNITS:	Tanks	Armoured Combat Vehicles	Artillery
'YELLOW' AREA	4,700	5,900	6,000
'RED' AREA	7,500	11,250	5,000
'RED' + 'BLUE' AREAS	10,300	19,260	9,100
'RED' + 'BLUE' + 'GREEN' AREAS	11,800	21,400	11,000
TO BE PLACED IN STORAGE	3,500	2,700	3,000
TOTALS	**20,000**	**30,000**	**20,000**

The CFE agreement itself (see map and diagrams on pp. 435–6) limited the number of weapons in Europe from the Atlantic to the Ural mountains. Tanks were limited to 20,000 apiece for NATO and the WTO—a figure which meant marginal cuts for NATO and very substantial cuts for the Warsaw Pact states. Armoured combat vehicles were to be limited to 30,000 per alliance, which had little impact on NATO but required massive cuts by the Soviet Union and its erstwhile allies. For artillery pieces the figures were set at 20,000, for helicopters 2,000 and for combat aircraft 6,800. In all cases the cuts required were hugely asymmetrical, with the Soviet Union and the WTO states having to reduce forces substantially and NATO in some instances not having to reduce at all. For the other Eastern Europe states the reductions were also very substantial, especially in tanks and artillery. For NATO, in contrast, the only real reductions were in tanks and helicopters. As well as the overall limits, there were also zonal limits and limits on individual nations. Manpower was not formally included as part of the agreement, but the ceilings of 370,000 German troops and 195,000 Soviet and American troops in the central region were presented as accompanying deals. It was agreed, moreover, that more formal limits on manpower would be sought in the CFE-1A negotiations.

In the aftermath of the CFE accord there were some major discrepancies in the Soviet data—and some question as to whether the treaty would be ratified by the US Senate in 1991 unless these problems were dealt with. Even with these potential problems, the agreement was of major significance. In 1988 the first set of East-West talks on cutting forces in Europe, the mutual and balanced force reduction (MBFR) negotiations, had been wound up after failing to reach agreement over a 15-year period. Seen against this background of always difficult and often sterile negotiations, the CFE treaty was remarkable. It achieved what NATO had never been able to do through its own efforts, namely conventional military parity. Equally important, the agreement included a substantial and intrusive verification regime which would add to the mutual transparency and confidence that were becoming increasingly salient features of the European security system. The CFE agreement was also a major symbol of the end of the Cold War in Europe and it highlighted the continuing trend towards demilitarization. Yet there was also a sense in which CFE had become somewhat less relevant as a result of the political changes that had taken place in Europe during 1989 and 1990. The agreement codified the military balance in Europe at a time when this balance no longer had the same relevance or importance as in the past. Moreover, the trend in force levels was so clearly downwards that although the CFE restrictions provided ceilings it was very obvious that they would not provide a floor on force levels. As part of a continuing attempt to redefine force levels and security relations after the Cold War, however, the CFE agreement was clearly of considerable importance. It not only prepared the way for follow-on negotiations but was also part of a package of agreements at the Paris summit that marked the beginnings of the creation of a new security framework in Europe.

At the Paris summit the 34 states of Europe also completed a CSBM agreement, known as the Vienna Document 1990, which went well beyond the Stockholm accord of 1986 in terms of constraining military exercises and exchanging information. It was agreed that there should be prior notification of manoeuvres involving at least 13,000 troops or 300 battle tanks, or amphibious or air assaults involving 3,000 troops or more. There was also to be observation of manoeuvres involving 17,000 troops or more and of amphibious or airborne assaults with over 5,000. For activities involving more than 40,000 troops two years' notice had to be given. Each state also had to accept at least three inspections per year on its territory, while there was provision for consultation and cooperation regarding unusual or unscheduled military activities.

The third document concluded at the Paris summit was a declaration of non-aggression between NATO and the Warsaw Pact. The fourth, the Charter of Paris for a New Europe (see DOCUMENTS), moved in the direction highlighted in the London Declaration. A Conflict Prevention Centre was established in Vienna, a small secretariat was set up in Prague, an office of free elections was based in Warsaw, and it was agreed that there would be a Council of the CSCE consisting of regular meetings at foreign minister level. The Conflict Prevention Centre had a broad but somewhat hazy mandate. Its task was to assist the Council in reducing the risk of conflict. In the initial stages this was to be accomplished by supporting the implementation of CSBMs such as exchanges of information, and through mechanisms for cooperation regarding unusual military activity or hazardous military incidents. It was also stated, however, that the Centre could assume other functions and that these initial rather modest tasks were not meant to provide a restrictive mandate.

Although some of the agreements and institutions established at the Paris summit were rather modest, it was clear that the event not only marked the end of the Cold War in Europe but, insofar as it also placed the constraints on German military power within a broader political framework, was in some respects a substitute for the peace treaty that was never signed with Germany after World War II. By establishing very clear principles on which security relations in Europe were to be conducted, the summit also pointed the direction for post-Cold War Europe. It was clear, though, that this was only the beginning of what would be a long process.

Although the Paris summit did not create a new pan-European security system, the moves towards a new European security order based on the framework provided by the CSCE inevitably raised questions about the future of NATO. These questions were even more insistent because of the effective dissolution of the Warsaw Pact. Most commentators had agreed that one consequence of the events of 1989 would be the dissolution of the Soviet-dominated military organization. Yet the speed and ease with which this process developed during 1990 was very striking. The Soviet Union, of course, was anxious to maintain at least the vestiges of its bloc and consequently adopted a flexible approach. On 30 January President Gorbachev stated that the WTO was 'the most essential element of stability on the European continent' but also made clear that it was being 'developed from the military-political into a political-military alliance'. In March Mr Shevardnadze said that Soviet interests were best served not by a *cordon sanitaire* of dubious regimes but by neighbouring free, democratic and prosperous states, open both to the West and to the East. This was reflected in a joint statement by the Warsaw Pact foreign ministers on 7 June. The Soviet Union agreed that a commission should work on the transformation of the WTO to 'a treaty of sovereign states with equal rights formed on a democratic basis'. This would help to stabilize a Europe of nations 'wishing to live in mutual harmony without artificial barriers and ideological hostility'.

Some of the WTO states were prepared to go along with this in order to prevent the Soviet Union from becoming isolated. They were strongly in favour of turning the pact into a political alliance whose major role would be in disarmament negotiations. At the same time, they regarded this as a temporary measure and saw the WTO as something that would be superseded by an all-European security framework. The most restive of the central and eastern European states was Hungary. In June the Hungarian National Assembly voted overwhelmingly to begin negotiations on leaving the WTO; in August the Hungarian Prime Minister, Mr Antall, stated that Hungary would leave the WTO military organization by the end of 1991. In September the German Democratic Republic, as part of the final moves towards German unification, formally left the WTO. The Czechoslovak government, however, made clear that it wanted to remain a member in order to influence the direction of the organization in the new Europe. For their part, the Poles indicated that they wanted to leave the military structure, even though this structure was effectively being dismantled. On 5 November the Soviet Union revealed that it was preparing to disband the WTO supreme command and staff in Moscow. On 20 November, at the Paris CSCE summit, the Hungarian Prime Minister announced that the Warsaw Pact countries had agreed to dissolve the military elements of the alliance and transform it into a purely political organization.

Although the effective disintegration of the WTO and the achievement of conventional parity called into question the role and rationale of NATO, the many uncertainties about the future of the Soviet Union militated in favour of a prudent approach. Alliance strategy was reformed and readiness and force levels were reduced, but the essential elements of the political and military infrastructure, and the links between Western Europe and the United States, were maintained intact.

STRATEGIC ARMS LIMITATION TALKS

THE uncertainties over the future of the Soviet Union were underlined by the strategic arms limitation (START) negotiations, in which the Soviet military increasingly seemed to be playing a major role. This was one reason why, in spite of progress towards the creation of a post-Cold War security framework in Europe, the superpowers were less successful in 1990 in reaching agreement on strategic arms control. At the start of the year it was hoped that there would be broad agreement on most of the outstanding issues in the START negotiations before the planned June summit between Presidents Gorbachev and Bush, and that the superpowers would then be able to sign an agreement before the end of the year. In the event this did not occur, even though in February both sides agreed that the START negotiations should also include preliminary discussions about START II.

Part of the problem was that there were major asymmetries in force structures. Soviet and American strategic forces were structured very differently, with the Soviet Union having the main elements of its force in inter-continental ballistic missiles (ICBMs) and the United States placing more emphasis on the sea-launched variety (SLBMs). This asymmetry was one of the issues which had made agreement so elusive even though the superpowers had agreed in principle to reduce their forces by 50 per cent. Another problem was that each side was concerned about key elements in the other's armoury for which it had no equivalent. The United States, for example, remained concerned about the heavy Soviet missile, the SS-18, while the Soviet Union was anxious about US sea-launched cruise missiles (SLCMs), demanding limits on conventional as well as nuclear SLCMs. In addition, there were differences over the permissible ranges of air-launched cruise missiles (ALCMs).

Some of the differences were eased in May during Secretary Baker's visit to Moscow, when he agreed that ALCM limits should be set at 600 kilometres—the United States having initially wanted a 1,500-kilometre limit. There was also agreement that, although the SLCMs would not be covered in the treaty, the United States and the Soviet Union would exchange binding declarations of the number of nuclear SLCMs with ranges over 600 kilometres that they intended to deploy: as long as the START agreement was in effect, this number would be 880.

On Mr Baker's return to the United States, he was severely criticized by conservatives for the concessions he had made. The issue of heavy-missile modernization also continued to cause concern in some

US quarters. Further progress was made, however, at the Washington summit (30 May–2 June), where it was agreed that there would be sub-limits on mobile missile warheads. On 1 June Presidents Bush and Gorbachev also signed agreements on peaceful uses of atomic energy and new protocols to the Peaceful Nuclear Explosions Treaty and the Threshold Test-Ban Treaty. Although both of these treaties had been signed during the 1970s, they had never been ratified. With agreement on a new set of verification rules, all doubts were dispelled and the treaties were subsequently unanimously approved by the US Senate on 25 September. At the summit itself, the two leaders also initialled a joint statement outlining many of the limits they had agreed to in START.

Although the US-Soviet summit gave impetus to the negotiations, the problems were highly technical and complex. The outstanding issues included limits on ICBM development, defining new types of missiles, phasing of reductions, numbers of ICBM warheads, and verification, especially of rail-mobile ICBMs. An additional issue was whether or not the Soviet Backfire bomber should be subject to specific limits. For their part, the Soviets also insisted that, while they were prepared to accept the American commitment to supply Britain with Trident submarines, this should be the last agreement of its kind, since it was a means of circumventing the treaty. In response, the United States argued that existing patterns of cooperation should be allowed to continue. In early August START negotiator Richard Burt stated that, if the United States was compelled to choose between START and the 'special relationship' with Britain, it would choose the latter. By September enough issues were still unresolved for it to be clear that there would not be a START agreement during 1990.

There were several reasons for this. One was the sheer complexity of the issues, resulting partly from the asymmetries in force posture. Another was the fact that from the early months of 1990 onwards the Soviet military exerted pressure against further concessions, clearly believing that the Soviet Union was moving too far and too fast in arms control with the United States. A third reason was that during 1990 the arms control agenda was somewhat overloaded, while for the Soviet Union in particular the CFE agreement clearly took priority. Moreover, after August the top-level decision makers, especially in the United States, were increasingly preoccupied with the crisis in the Gulf. Nevertheless, the year ended on a reasonably good note in the START talks with both the Backfire issue and the non-circumvention issue resolved.

In short, 1990 was a good year for arms control. At the end of the year it was clear that there had been remarkable progress in consolidating the gains of 1989 and in enhancing security and stability in Europe. Yet events in the Gulf underlined the fact that the end of the Cold War did not mean an end to international conflict.

WESTERN EUROPEAN UNION AND THE GULF CRISIS

AN important aspect of the Gulf crisis which dominated the international agenda from early August was the European response, in particular the role of the Western European Union (WEU), consisting of France, Britain, Germany, Italy, the Benelux countries, Spain and Portugal. Even before the Gulf crisis, the WEU was considering measures intended to give it a larger role in the evolving European security system. In April 1990 the members of the organization agreed to strengthen consultation between the military and political wings, to hold talks with the East Europeans and to consider the establishment of an agency to verify arms accords by satellite. Consideration was also given to the idea of a multinational force, with the Federal Republic of Germany and Italy supporting this and Britain and France against it. Although there was no agreement on the creation of such a force, the Gulf crisis became the occasion for the WEU to enhance its role as the primary institution for dealing with challenges to West European security, whether emanating in Europe or elsewhere.

The WEU was in a strong position to respond to the Gulf crisis because of its earlier experience when it coordinated West European naval activity in ensuring free passage through the Gulf during the Iran-Iraq war. It also recognized the importance of some kind of European response in order to pre-empt American criticisms that its NATO allies were not doing enough—something that could weaken the trans-Atlantic linkage which, even after the Cold War, remained important. The importance of the WEU, as pointed out by its secretary-general, was that it provided a framework for concerted European action and for cooperation between the Europeans and the United States.

Although the initial consultations on the Gulf crisis took place within NATO, it was the WEU that took the initiative in coordinating the European response. On 21 August WEU foreign and defence ministers met in Paris and agreed 'joint specific guidelines' covering areas of operations, definition and performance of mission, exchange of information, logistic support, and coordination of deployments for the commitment to the Gulf. On 27 August the various chiefs of defence staff met to give practical effect to these guidelines for operations in the Gulf. On 8–9 September a naval conference to discuss enforcing the embargo was held in Bahrain, with the WEU presidency acting as co-chairman. In substantive terms, the WEU nations provided over 30 vessels to help with the embargo.

The naval dimension, of course, was only one element in response to the crisis in the Gulf. Britain and France were contributing both ground and air forces, while Italy was deploying air power to the region. On 18 September a WEU ministerial meeting decided to enlarge the scope of the military activities beyond naval forces and agreed to 'extend the coordination at present operating in the maritime field to ground and air forces and, within this framework, to identify the forms that these new deployments will take to seek to ensure that they are complementary, to harmonize the missions of member states' forces and to pool their logistical support as required'. Although coordination of land forces was to be accomplished primarily on a tripartite basis between France, Britain and the United States, the WEU initiative was important both in symbolic and in practical terms.

Yet the role of the WEU did not go unchallenged. Meeting in Venice on 7 October, the European Community (EC) foreign ministers, largely under the impetus of Italy as current EC chairman, began to discuss the need for the Community to take on a more direct role in defence matters. It was subsequently proposed that the EC treaty framework should incorporate article 5 of the Brussels Treaty on which the WEU was based. This article stated that in the event of an armed attack against one of the parties, the others would provide aid and assistance. The WEU response, however, was to oppose any notion that its activities should be integrated into the Community, contending that 'it would be absurd to abolish these institutions in favour of a Community that has no powers in such matters'. Indeed, at the end of the year, although the European Community had by then held an inter-governmental conference on European political union (see p. 405), the WEU seemed to be emerging as the main locus of a European defence identity that would help to balance the United States in the NATO framework and provide a greater sense of self-reliance in Western Europe.

At the end of 1990 many of the uncertainties over the future European security architecture had been eliminated. Yet what appeared to be emerging was not necessarily a tidy structure. NATO remained intact, although with a clearly diminished reliance on nuclear weapons and with a less central role; the CSCE had started to develop some institutional basis for moving towards a genuine pan–European security framework; and moves were being made towards the emergence of a more cohesive West European defence identity. There were many unresolved issues, especially about the relationship, and indeed the compatibility, of Atlantic, West European and pan-European structures. Even so, the outlines of a post-Cold War security system in Europe based on something of a hybrid structure were discernible. Given that it was only 12 months since the monumental changes in Eastern Europe had occurred, to get even this far was a very considerable achievement. Yet at the end of the year, the most pressing questions were not about European cooperation but about the prospects for war and peace in the Gulf. The Cold War was over, but regional conflict was at the forefront of the international security agenda.

XIII RELIGION

RELIGIOUS FREEDOM. Relaxation of oppressive laws and practices increased throughout Eastern Europe and in differing degrees across the world. In the USSR 4,500 congregations had been registered since 1988, bringing the total to 17,000. Christenings increased from 16.4 per cent of births in 1985 to 46.4 per cent in 1989, with smaller growths in religious weddings and funerals. On 26 September the Supreme Soviet, by 341 votes to 1, gave outline approval to a law allowing freedom of religion, curbing propagation of atheism and permitting religious activity even in the armed forces. On 14 October St Basil's Cathedral in the Kremlin saw its first liturgy since 1918. The funeral of Patriarch Pimen on 6 May was attended by government representatives, who paid tribute to him as a 'true spiritual pastor of the faithful' (see OBITUARY). On 7 June he was succeeded as Patriarch of Moscow and All Russia by Mikhailovich Aleksi (61), Metropolitan of Leningrad and Novgorod, a non-Russian of Baltic German descent, one of the few men of his generation to have had formal theological education and an open supporter of government reformist policies.

Islam had been persecuted as vigorously as Christianity in the USSR, and as recently as 1986 Mikhail Gorbachev had called it an 'enemy of progress and socialism'. This approach changed and tolerance accelerated. The main Muslim secondary school (*madrasseh*) in Bukhara increased its intake by 50 per cent, and Tashkent opened its first Islamic courses for girls. From 84 mosques in Uzbekistan before 1989, there were now 300, and numbers grew from 15 to 50 in Kirghizia, five to 30 in Turkmenia, 17 to 40 in Tadjikistan and 37 to 70 in Kazakhstan. Donations for building poured in from Pakistan, Saudi Arabia and Libya, and increasing numbers of pilgrims—1,525 in 1990—went to Mecca.

In Romania, in May, László Tökés became Protestant Bishop of Oradea (see AR 1989, p. 426), but his life was threatened by ultra-nationalist Romanians. In August he was severely injured in a traffic accident in Hungary, and one of his closest associates, Pastor Culcsi, was found dead. Bishops László Papp and Gyula Nagy, who had collaborated with the Ceauşescu regime, both resigned in March; another time-server, Orthodox Patriarch Theoctist, retired to a monastery in January but was reinstated in April despite opposition. Chief Rabbi Moses Rosen was also criticized for previous conduct but claimed to support the new administration. The Orthodox Church handed back the cathedral and seminary at Blaj in central Romania to the Greek Catholic Church.

In Bulgaria 64 per cent were claimed to be Christian, mostly Orthodox, but religious leaders had supported the previous government and on 20 July six members of the Holy Synod admitted committing 'personal, direct and indirect transgressions'. They had opposed an Independent Committee for the Defence of Religious Rights, organized by Fr Hristofor Subev, which had mass support. At Easter he held a public liturgy in Sofia for the first time in four decades. Many mosques were reopened in Bulgaria, but there were strikes and mass protests against Islamic Turks who had previously been forbidden to use their own language and Islamic names.

Albania was the only country in the world where all religion had been forbidden since 1947, although 70 per cent were Muslims, and mosques and churches were closed or destroyed. However, on 8 May the Deputy Premier announced that the law banning religious propaganda was being repealed. Some churches and mosques were returned to their owners; Mass was celebrated in public at Shkodr in northern Albania on 15 November, attended by 10,000 Catholics and some Muslims; and Christmas festivities were held publicly in the capital.

Pope John Paul II paid his first visit to Czechoslovakia in April. He warned of the dangers of Western materialism, stressing the role of the church in uniting nations, and announcing a synod of bishops from all over Europe. Welcomed by President Havel with full honours, the Pope paid tribute to those who had suffered under persecution. The deadlock over the appointment of bishops (see AR 1988, p. 436) was solved and eight new bishops were accepted.

Even in Mongolia, where 75,000 monks had been executed under communist rule and only four religious buildings left standing, a thaw began. Ganden monastery in Ulan Bator was crowded with worshippers and plans were made to revive rituals, rebuild monasteries and republish texts. Buddhist lamas were prominent supporters of democracy, the partial advent of which enabled bibles to be imported in limited numbers. In China, however, religious activity was restricted and four house-churches in Canton were closed in February. In Tibet religious ceremonies required government approval; when troops occupied Buddhist monasteries monks and nuns walked out in protest. In Communist-ruled Vietnam, only three of the 40 churches in Ho Chi Minh City (formerly Saigon) were closed by order, but church leadership was increasingly elderly. Young people were attracted to rapidly-growing house-churches led by junior pastors and lay activists.

In present or formerly marxist African states freedom of religion was guaranteed by constitutions. Church schools and hospitals were nationalized, but in Benin and Guinea-Bissau religious personnel either continued to operate them or were active in church instruction outside school hours. In Mozambique, although politicians were officially marxists, most had been educated in mission schools and civil war brought concerted action for relief work. The Christian Council of Mozambique cooperated in food distribution and rehabilitation of refugees, providing clothing, farming tools and seeds. Temporary hospitals and schools replaced those destroyed and churches initiated peace talks between warring factions.

CHURCH DEBATES. On 1 September a new Council of Churches for Britain and Ireland replaced the British Council of Churches, including 34 churches of the main denominations together with Roman Catholic and black-led churches for the first time. But one result of such a loose federation seemed to be lack of a single voice, notably over the question of a 'just war' in the Gulf. Six Anglican bishops denounced war as 'a mortal sin' but the Bishop of Oxford, Rt Rev Richard Harries, asserted 'the possibility that this war could be just'. In November the retiring Archbishop of Canterbury, Dr Robert Runcie (a former tank commander and holder of the Military Cross), called for talks with Iraq and more time for sanctions; he said that 'a year of sanctions would be far cheaper in every way than even a very short war', but accepted that 'though war is only rarely just, it can be justifiable'. Roman Catholic bishops in the USA, by 249 votes to 15, declared that there was a 'clear presumption against war' and demanded a 'vigorous pursuit of non-violent solutions'.

The Pope scored an own goal, declared a Catholic theologian, when the Vatican in June issued an *Instruction on the Ecclesial Vocation of the Theologian*. This product of the Congregation for the Doctrine of the Faith, headed by Bavarian Cardinal Joseph Ratzinger, required 'religious submission of will and intellect' from theologians, declaring that democratic standards 'cannot be purely and simply applied to the church'. There were protests from many liberal theologians and a Tübingen Declaration 'For Freedom in the Church' from 22 theologians, following an earlier objection by 196 theologians meeting at Cologne.

The papal hard line continued in the appointment of conservative bishops in Vienna and Cologne (see AR 1988, p. 438), and also at Chur (Switzerland), where the elevation in June of Bishop Wolfgang Haas disregarded previously-agreed procedures of Swiss cantons. In October a closed synod of all Roman Catholic bishops in Rome discussed the priesthood, without being allowed to consider priestly marriage, despite recent sex scandals among clergy in Canada and the USA. The trend of vocations was said to be 'positive', with increases in Asia and Africa offsetting large decreases in Europe. There were 16,505 fewer priests in the world than a decade earlier. The Pope agreed to the ordination of married men in Brazil as long as they lived with their wives 'as brother and sister', a ruling criticized as degrading the sacrament of marriage.

The largest cathedral in the world was consecrated by Pope John Paul II on 9 September at Yamoussoukro in Côte d'Ivoire, dedicated to Our Lady of Peace. The controversial basilica, built at the instigation of President Houphouët-Boigny, was larger than St Peter's in Rome, though in similar style, and had cost an estimated £100 million in one of Africa's poorest countries (see p. 270).

The appointment of Dr Cahal Daly, Bishop of Down and Connor, as Roman Catholic Archbishop of Armagh and Primate of All Ireland in succession to Cardinal Tomás O Fiaich (who died on 8 May—see OBITUARY), was welcomed by Catholics and Protestants alike. Dr Daly (73) had close relations with Anglicans and free churches, and criticized both the violence of the IRA and some reactions of the security forces. The synod of the Anglican Church in Ireland voted in May to allow women to become both priests and bishops, but the first two women ordained agreed not to celebrate communion in England to avoid confrontation.

In November the Dutch Reformed Church in South Africa accepted a 'confession of sin' on behalf of 'the Afrikaner people as a whole' for its role in the apartheid system. In Kenya, on 15 July, Anglican Bishop John Okullu denounced the government for dictatorship. His fellow-bishop, Alexander Muge, was threatened with death and was killed in a road accident in August, giving rise to accusations of murder. In January two nuns were killed by Contra rebels in Nicaragua.

ANTI-SEMITISM. Racial and religious attacks on Jews, which had blackened Europe during the Nazi period, began to appear again. In May Jewish graves were desecrated at Carpentras, France, and the body of a recently-buried man was impaled on a parasol. Painting of swastikas on graves and synagogues was reported from Rambouillet and Strasbourg, from Germany, Sweden and Italy, and from Manchester, Leeds, Luton and Edmonton in England. In Eastern Europe and several Soviet cities nationalist groups tried to foment anti-Jewish pogroms.

Councils of Christians and Jews sought to bring tolerance, and Cardinal Basil Hume of Westminster condemned 'depraved acts'. But some leaders spoke differently, notably Cardinal Jozef Glemp of Poland, who referred to Jews as instigators of 'anti-polonism'. Anti-semitic accusations were made during the Polish presidential elections, but were not condemned by the successful candidate, Lech Walesa, until after the first round of voting. The Polish bishops deferred till the following January a letter to be read in all churches stressing that the church was 'rooted in the Jewish people and Jewish faith'. Yet the numbers of Jews remaining in Eastern Europe were very small: 6,000 in Poland (from 3,500,000 in 1939); 400 in East Germany (from 503,000); 12,000 in Czechoslovakia (from 357,000); 23,000 in Romania (from 800,000); and 100,000 in Hungary (from 725,000).

Racial and religious tensions were fuelled in October in Jerusalem when at least 17 Arabs were shot dead by Israeli troops on the Temple

Mount (see pp. 198, 203). The disturbances followed a rumour that Gershon Solomon, Jewish extremist leader of the Temple Mount Faithful, was going to lay a cornerstone for a new Jewish temple on the site of the Muslim Dome of the Rock. This led to rioting in which stones were thrown from the Mount onto thousands of Jews praying at the Western Wall for the festival of Sukkot (Tabernacles).

On 6 November Rabbi Meir Kahane, whose Kach movement sought to expel all non-Jews from Israel, was assassinated in New York. Although Jewish religious parties in Israel took a comparable hard line, opinion polls indicated that well over half of all Israelis favoured the principle of 'territory for peace' and the Palestinians' right of self-determination. They were supported by many Jews in Europe and the USA.

ISLAMIC TENSIONS. The Salman Rushdie affair (see AR 1989, pp. 428–9, 493–4, 538) rumbled on, the Indian-born novelist remaining in hiding under police guard. On 6 February his Herbert Read memorial lecture was read on his behalf by dramatist Harold Pinter. In this Mr Rushdie declared that 'religious faith, profound as it is, must surely remain a private matter', whereas 'literature is the one place in any society' where we can hear 'voices talking about everything in every possible way'.

On 9 April the Queen's Bench divisional court dismissed an application by Abdul Hussain Choudhury for a summons for blasphemous libel against Mr Rushdie and his publishers, since English law against blasphemy concerned Christianity only. In July a Pakistani film *International Guerrillas*, featuring Mr Rushdie as villain and his fictional death by lightning, was banned by the British Board of Film Classification. On 24 December Mr Rushdie broadcast an appeal, declaring his faith in Islam and disavowing anti-Muslim sentiments in his book. He promised that there would be no paperback edition of his novel or further translations, as long as there were objections to it, and said that he believed that this was 'the beginning of the end' of the death threat against him. In Iran, however, religious leader Ayatollah Ali Khamenei rejected this repentance and declared that the *fatweh* against Mr Rushdie was a 'divine ruling' and irrevocable. Diplomatic relations between Britain and Iran had been soured by this affair, but they were restored after the Foreign Secretary wrote in August that 'the British government had nothing to do with the publishing of *The Satanic Verses* . . . Islam is one of the world's great religions, with a proud history and long traditions. We have the greatest respect for it and its values.'

On 2 July at least 1,500 pilgrims in Mecca died in a tunnel from the city to a hill outside. King Fahd observed that 'had they not died there, they would have died elsewhere, and at the same predestined moment'. In the Gulf crisis there were calls for *jihad* (holy war) against the USA, notably in Jordan and Yemen, where the Muslim Brotherhood urged volunteers to fight for Iraq and opposed King Fahd's alliance with other Arab and Western forces. President Saddam Husain of Iraq called on 'all Arab and Muslim masses wherever they are [to] save Mecca and the Tomb of the Prophet from occupation . . . by the spears of the Americans and the Zionists'.

Moves towards fuller application of Islamic law were felt from Pakistan to Sudan, in the latter case causing a revival of the seven-year war between the mainly Muslim north and the mainly Christian south (see p. 229). In Algeria the shock victory of the Front Islamique du Salut in municipal and provincial elections brought moves for the 'moralization' of public life, including banning the sale of alcohol, strict fasting during Ramadan, and restriction on the mixing of men and women in public places (see pp. 238–9).

ASIAN TROUBLES. On 30 October thousands of saffron-robed Hindus filled the streets of Ayodhya, vowing to rebuild the temple of Rama at the Babri mosque (see AR 1989, p. 430). The leader of the militant Hindu Bharatiya Janata Party (BJP) was arrested, but demonstrators climbed on the roof of the mosque and erected a Hindu flag. The new year festival of Divali was overshadowed by religious tensions, and in November Muslims and Sikhs in New Delhi joined together to fight Hindus, after the burning of the Sikh holy book. Muslim separatists in Kashmir clashed with security forces, while the Hindu BJP vowed that the integrity of India would be protected at all costs.

In January monks in Burma were arrested for disruptive activities and retaliated by refusing religious services for military personnel. This boycott appeared to end in October when six large monasteries in Mandalay were surrounded by troops and gave in to an ultimatum; in Rangoon, however, there were demonstrations and two monks were killed.

On 11 November Emperor Akihito of Japan began the Shinto rituals of enthronement, amid public criticism of expenditure and fear from other religions, Buddhist and Christian, of implied change from the separation of religion and state accepted after World War II (see p. 364). The enthronement was paid for by the government, but rituals of the Great Festival on 22 November were the responsibility of the imperial budget. After a night devoted to the imperial ancestor, the Sun Goddess Amaterasu Omikami, Akihito emerged as the 125th emperor of Japan.

BOOKS OF THE YEAR. Massive biblical commentaries appeared with *Saint Luke* by C. F. Evans, *James* by J. B. Adamson, and *Jude* by R. Bauckham. In *Jesus Christ in Modern Thought*, J. Macquarrie, former professor of divinity at Oxford, dismissed the virgin birth and gave alternative views of the resurrection. In *Gorbachev, Glasnost and the Gospel*, M. Bourdeaux, director of Keston College, charted the survival and renewal of religion behind the former Iron Curtain. N. O. Hatch wrote on *The Democratization of American Christianity* and P. Vallely examined difficulties of Third World debts in *Bad Samaritans*. E. P. Sanders continued studies of Judaism and early Christianity in *Jewish Law from Jesus to the Mishnah*. Among several books on survival and assimilation, P. F. Jones wrote on *The Jews of Britain* and Yisrael Gutman edited *The Jews of Poland between Two World Wars*. C. Novak wrote of *Jewish-Christian Dialogue*, a theme continued by M. Braybrooke in *Time to Meet*. Anton Wessels, in *Images of Jesus*, studied perceptions of non-European cultures and N. Robinson wrote on *Christ in Islam and Christianity*. A. C. Graham crowned a life's work with *Disputers of the Tao* and *Studies in Chinese Philosophy and Philosophical Literature*.

XIV THE SCIENCES

Chapter 1

SCIENCE AND MEDICINE

ASTRONOMY AND SPACE RESEARCH. After cumulative delays of more than seven years and several last-minute postponements, the US space shuttle *Discovery* finally blasted off at 12.34 GMT on 24 April, carrying the Hubble space telescope into orbit. The optical telescope was the largest, most expensive and, it was hoped, most rewarding scientific instrument ever to be placed in orbit. Its central curved mirror was 2.4 metres in diameter. Weighing 11 tons, the whole satellite was 13.3 metres in length and 4.3 metres in diameter, the maximum that could be fitted in to the shuttle's cargo bay. When astronaut Steve Hawley used the remote manipulator arm to swing the telescope gently out of the shuttle's cargo hold and to release it into orbit, astronomers rejoiced.

But before very long it became clear that something had gone devastatingly wrong. The telescope that had been expected to see stars, without the blurring effect of the Earth's atmosphere and with a resolution ten times better than the best obtainable on the ground, was producing only blurred images. It transpired that one of the telescope's two focusing mirrors had been ground and polished in an erroneous way, creating spherical aberration, so that rays of light coming from stars, entering the telescope and reflected from the mirrors, were not brought together perfectly at a point. Instead, the rays met at several different points, providing only fuzzy images.

In November an official investigating team concluded that the error had stemmed from what it called the same 'management climate' that had led to the explosion that destroyed the space shuttle *Challenger* in 1986 (see AR 1986, pp. 48–9, 399, 402). A technician's error in assembling a mirror-polishing device, at the workshops of the company which had made the mirror, was the immediate cause of the problem. But the report said that programme managers were also to blame, for choosing quality control tests which enabled the error to pass unnoticed.

By no means all of the telescope's ability to perform useful work was lost, however. Its ability to analyse the colours of light from very distant stars, thus providing valuable clues to very early stellar evolution, was unaffected. Moreover, computer enhancement techniques, developed to sharpen up pictures of planets sent back by spacecraft, enabled sharper images of stars than any produced by ground-based telescopes to be obtained. But astronomers had to resign themselves to waiting three years for the Hubble space telescope to produce its planned performance. That was the shortest timescale for another shuttle flight to ferry up a new camera, which would contain an extra lens or mirror able to correct the fault, as if the telescope had donned a pair of spectacles.

Meanwhile, astronomers at the University of Illinois (USA), led by Professor Laird Thompson, were developing ways to improve the performance of ground-based optical telescopes to the point where they could match or even out-perform the Hubble telescope. Their work involved calculating the precise distorting effects of the Earth's atmosphere and then electronically subtracting these from pictures produced by terrestrial telescopes. The unresolved question at the end of the year was whether such developments would render the fitting of 'spectacles' to Hubble pointless by the time it was possible to send up a shuttle crew to act as opticians.

Radio astronomers using the 64-metre dish at Parkes in New South Wales (Australia), which had been fitted with a very sensitive receiver taken from the US Greenbank radio telescope following its disastrous collapse, provided the first really detailed radio survey of the southern hemisphere. They located over 50,000 radio sources, six times as many as in previous radio surveys of the southern sky. At the end of the year astronomers were sorting this vast amount of new data into different categories of objects.

The Venus probe named *Magellan*, launched in May 1989, went into orbit around the planet in August. The probe was intended to make a radar map of up to 90 per cent of the surface of Venus (whose permanent cloud cover made optical mapping impossible). But the radar mapping was afflicted by several problems. First a stray cosmic ray damaged part of the probe's computer memory. Then a wrong command from ground control pointed its transmitting aerial away from Earth, while another control problem caused the spacecraft to wobble while surveying the planet and thus to produce blurred pictures. Nevertheless, *Magellan* returned good clear radar pictures of much of Venus, including images of great lava flows and volcanic cones, indicating violent volcanic activity. Also revealed was a formation like a rift valley, indicating terrestrial-type geological activity.

The *Galileo* space probe, which had also been launched in 1989 and had already circled Venus, sped back past Earth at only 1,000 kilometres distance on 8 December. This was part of a remarkable trajectory, in which the spacecraft was using the gravitational attraction of Venus and Earth (with another fly-past of the Earth planned) to achieve sufficient speed to travel to Jupiter, its real target, arriving in 1995. The first fly-by of Earth was used to take pictures of our own planet and the far side of the Moon, with instruments otherwise used only to survey the other planets of the solar system.

In January the US space shuttle *Columbia* brought safely back to Earth a big satellite called the 'long duration exposure facility' (L-DEF), which had been used to expose potential space construction materials as well as organic matter (including shrimp eggs and tomato seeds) to radiation in space, unprotected by the Earth's atmosphere, for a full six years. This was five years longer than originally planned. The long delay in returning L-DEF to Earth was one of many consequences of the *Challenger* disaster in 1986. Preliminary findings showed that the Earth was circled by far more microscopic particles of burnt rocket fuel and flakes of rocket paint than had been thought, suggesting that such pollution might prove a major hazard to sensitive instruments on future astronomical satellites.

In the first week of December *Columbia* orbited Earth with a crew of seven, who used an elaborate set of telescopes to observe ultra-violet and X-rays from distant objects. At the same time, four Russian cosmonauts and a Japanese journalist (whose sponsors had paid $30 million for his flight) were together for a few days in orbit in the Soviet space station *Mir*. The journalist filed several unsurprising reports from space and conducted experiments on the behaviour of tree frogs in weightless conditions. The main significance of his presence was the evidence it provided of the determination of the Soviet space agency Glavcosmos to make space activities pay. He returned to Earth with two of the cosmonauts, who had been replaced as the station's long-term crew by the two who had gone up with him.

Data returned from the US 'cosmic background explorer' (COBE) satellite, launched in November 1989, deepened the mystery of how stars and galaxies had come into being. Surveying cosmic background radiation from the very early universe with instruments far more sensitive than any deployed earlier, COBE found it to be perfectly smooth and featureless. The unanswered and increasingly puzzling question was: how had the discontinuities which developed into stars and galaxies evolved from such a totally featureless background?

PHYSICS. Scientists continued to work towards the commercial exploitation of high-temperature superconductors, i.e. materials able to conduct electricity without resistance at temperatures well above absolute zero. On 24 May a report in *Nature* described how a team at the Centre for Superconductivity in Texas had produced a bar of high-temperature superconducting material, measuring 5 cm long by 0.5 cm wide and 0.3 cm deep and made of yttrium barium copper oxide, using a continuous manufacturing process for the first time. This was also the first time anything more than a thin film of small particles of such a material had been manufactured.

British ICI scientists developed a means of shaping high-temperature superconductors into required shapes, by making the material into a powder, mixing it with polymers and solvents, extruding it to form a wire, bending the wire into any required shape, and then burning off the non-superconducting materials while at the same time fusing the particles of superconducting material into a solid mass. A component made in this way was used in a medical scanner, the first commercial use for high-temperature superconductors.

Dr Richard Friend and colleagues at Cambridge University (UK) developed and tested an electrically-conducting plastic that behaved sufficiently like the silicon materials used in electronic components to make possible the future development of flat-screen television sets and computer terminals. There were hopes of developing the material—known as poly p-phenylene vinylene, or PPV—not only into flat TV screens but also into transistors able to process optical signals in the way that electronic components processed electrical signals. It even seemed that it might be possible to shape single molecules of PPV into molecular transistors able to process optical signals.

In December *Science* (the journal of the American Association for the Advancement of Science) named diamond as its 'molecule of the year' for 1990, in recognition of advances in techniques for making synthetic diamond. These had for the first time made cheap, large-scale production of the material a realistic hope. The most significant of the advances was made by the US General Electric Company, which succeeded in making synthetic diamond containing 99.9 per cent of one isotope of diamond (C12) compared with 99 per cent in natural diamond. This improved isotopic purity gave the new synthetic diamond drastically improved properties. General Electric scientists were astonished when they found that it conducted heat 50 per cent more effectively than the previous best performance, and that their new material was five times more resistant to damage by high-powered lasers than the best natural diamond. The ability of synthetic diamond to conduct heat away from electronic components was making it possible to miniaturize such components still further. Many other new uses for synthetic diamond—in jet engine nozzles and as thin films protecting windows and lenses, for example—were also envisaged.

BIOLOGICAL SCIENCES. Several reports suggested that it might be possible to extend the human life span. Thus Professor Michael Rose of the University of California at Irvine claimed, at a meeting of the Royal Society in London, that humans could be enabled to live twice as long as at present. He based his claim on work on fruit flies, which had shown that by selecting the longest-lived flies and breeding only from them, and by subjecting flies to stresses of shortage of food and water, it was possible to produce flies that lived 80 per cent longer than normal.

In a separate series of experiments, Dr John Sheppard and Dr Walter

Gehring of Basle University prolonged the lives of fruit flies by up to 40 per cent by adding extra genes to fertilized fly eggs, which then developed normally. The gene added was for a protein, EF-1 Alpha, known to be naturally present in large quantities early in life but to decline with age. The healthy part of the flies' life cycle, rather than their decrepit old age, was the part that was prolonged.

Meanwhile, clinical trials of the effects of human growth hormone on elderly men showed that it greatly improved the ratio of muscle to fat, and the thickness of healthy skin, returning these to the state they had been in ten or 20 years before. Those responsible pointed out that growth hormone had no effect on the ageing of the brain and nervous system. Others said that the fact that so much had emerged so quickly about how to reverse some effects of ageing in both men and animals must give hope that drugs or forms of gene therapy able to prolong healthy human life might be developed in the not too distant future.

The discovery of the exact location of the gene responsible for male sex in humans and mammals was reported in *Nature* on 19 July. One target for the researchers was to find ways to use genetic engineering to insert the male gene on both sex chromosomes of female cattle. This would make it possible to produce, when required, offspring that would be 100 per cent male beef cattle rather than the natural 50-50 male/female split.

A research group at the University of Sydney in Australia, building on work by Chinese scientists, took a major step towards the target of creating wheat and other cereal crops able to fix nitrogen from the air just as legumes such as peas and beans did. Professor Yanfu Nie of Shandong University (China) had earlier succeeded in making the roots of wheat plants form nodules like those of legumes, by treating them with a herbicide known as 2,4-D. The Australian group, headed by biologist Dr Ian Kennedy, used similar techniques to create nodules on wheat and sweet potato. Dr Kennedy infected the nodules with a bacterium, azospirillum, which was capable of fixing nitrogen like the rhizobium bacteria found in legumes. Some experiments suggested that this could be done with great efficiency, although the results still awaited confirmation at the end of the year. The importance of the research lay in the fact that nitrogen-fixing cereals and other crops, especially tropical crops, would release farmers from the need to buy large quantities of expensive fertilizers.

MEDICINE AND AIDS. There were two major advances in the use of drugs to combat tropical parasitic diseases. On 30 November the World Health Organization (WHO) agreed to support the large-scale use of the drug Ornidyl against African sleeping-sickness (trypanosomiasis). The drug, made by the US pharmaceutical company Marion Merrell Dow, had already been nicknamed the 'resurrection drug' by doctors who had seen its effects on patients whose brains had been invaded by the disease-causing parasites and who were comatose and near death. Ornidyl had been shown to be able to restore most such patients to perfect health. Its chemical name was alpha difluoromethylornithine (DFMO) and it worked by preventing parasites from making new proteins, thus making it impossible for them to evade attack and destruction by the immune system of the infected person. The drug was expected to become generally available in West Africa in the first half of 1991. It was also showing promise against other diseases caused by trypanosome parasites, namely leishmaniasis and Chagas disease.

More good news came in the campaign against another major tropical parasitic disease, onchocerciasis, also known as river blindness. A team from the Centre for Preventive Ophthalmology at Johns Hopkins University in Baltimore (USA) showed that the drug Ivermectin could on its own completely eliminate the disease in all but the most severely infected areas. The team gave Ivermectin once a year to everyone at risk in an area in Liberia where onchocerciasis was endemic. After only two years the prevalence of infection in five-year-old children was reduced by 21 per cent, and by 45 per cent in 7-to-12-year-old children. Analysis of these results strongly suggested that the drug could completely eliminate river blindness within a few years in the whole of Latin and Central America and in most areas of West and Central Africa.

The AIDS epidemic continued to rage uncontrollably through much of Africa. A WHO report, published in October, said that after years of decline there was now an explosive AIDS-related increase in tuberculosis (TB) occurring in large areas of Africa. The new epidemic was occurring among AIDS patients who had contracted TB early in life but whose infection had been kept under control until the weakening of their immune systems by AIDS. The WHO report described the increase in TB, with which 3 million AIDS patients in Africa were infected, as a parallel epidemic to that of AIDS. Professor Keith McAdam of the London School of Tropical Medicine, who led the team responsible for the report, described the findings as 'horrific'. He said there was clear need to shift public health resources to the use of drugs to eliminate TB in AIDS patients, before their symptoms became severe and to prevent them infecting others.

In Britain 20 healthy volunteers were vaccinated against AIDS with a British-made vaccine developed by Drs Sue and Alan Kingsman at Oxford University's department of biochemistry. The vaccine was made from whole virus particles nicknamed pseudoviruses, developed from structures found in yeast cells which closely mimicked the structure of human immune virus particles. Another vaccine developed at the microbiological research centre at Porton Down was shown, in tests on monkeys, to protect completely against the entry of an AIDS virus into white blood cells. This was a major step forward, since scientists had been pessimistic about preventing the virus from entering cells, although more confident that it could be prevented from travelling from cell to cell, once initial infection had taken place. The results, published in December, led the leading medical journal *The Lancet* to say, in an editorial, that there was now optimism about the development of a vaccine able to prevent and even perhaps to cure AIDS. Other tests, of another vaccine made from a single coat protein of the virus, showed that chimpanzees could be completely protected.

Studies by the UK National Cancer Research Institute compared the progress of women with breast cancer who had received conventional treatment with that of others who had also received alternative therapies at the Bristol Cancer Health Centre. These showed that cancer was nearly three times as likely to spread to other parts of the body in the women receiving alternative therapy, and that women whose cancers had already spread were twice as likely to die if they had received alternative therapies. Whether these findings were due to some harmful effect of one or another alternative therapy, or to physical or psychological differences between the women in the two groups, was unclear at the end of the year. Doctors agreed that there was a need for more research to discover the reason for the findings.

Fears that humans might have contracted bovine spongiform encephalopathy (BSE), also known as 'mad cow disease', grew with the discovery that the condition could be spread from cattle to another mammalian species, namely mice. While stringent measures had been adopted to prevent the possibility of such transmission, it was still possible that undiscovered infection in cattle might have been passed unknowingly to humans consuming brain or nervous tissue from infected cattle. Concern was further increased by the finding of symptoms of apparent spongiform encephalopathy in at least one pet cat, which might have acquired the disease by eating infected pet food. In December the death of an antelope in London Zoo from spongiform encephalopathy, almost certainly contracted from its mother, raised fears that the same thing could happen in cattle, conceivably leading to human infection.

A major problem in countering BSE was the fact that the causative agent of the disease was an abnormal form of the prion protein, produced by an abnormal form of the prion gene. The protein appeared to contain no nucleic acid (i.e. no DNA or RNA), unlike any other known living organism or infective agent. However, experiments by Dr Stanley Prusiner in the USA, reported in December, showed that this extraordinary disease agent could be investigated by transplanting part of the human immune system into so-called 'transgenic' mice, and then seeing if these part-human mice could be made to develop spongiform encephalopathy from infection with abnormal prion protein taken from cattle. The results of these experiments were awaited with some trepidation by the medical community.

A new method of contraception approved by the US Food and Drugs Administration (FDA) was the first to obtain FDA endorsement in 30 years. The Norplant method consisted of six capsules the size of matchsticks, which were implanted under the skin in a woman's arm under local anaesthetic and gradually released synthetic sex hormone, as used in contraceptive pills, into a woman's body. Already widely tested in 41 nations, Norplant prevented contraception for as long as five years with 99 per cent efficiency and no serious side effects. Its long-acting format was seen as a major advantage.

The first authorized human gene therapy was approved by the US government with the aim of treating the most severe form of skin cancer (melanoma) and a very rare disease of the immune system in children. The first child patients were undergoing treatment by the end of the year. Melanoma was being treated by strengthening natural resistance to cancer by introducing extra genes for a natural anti-cancer agent, tumour necrosis factor, into white cells of the patients' immune system. The children's disease was being treated by inserting healthy versions of the defective genes into bone marrow, to try to compensate for defective genes causing fatal defects in the immune system. The first patient to be treated in this way, a four-year-old girl, was making good progress at the end of the year.

NOBEL PRIZES. The 1990 Nobel Prize for chemistry was awarded to Professor Elias James Corey of Harvard University (USA), for developing better techniques for synthesizing organic chemicals and natural substances. He had invented the technique called 'retrosynthetic analysis', in which chemists worked backwards from the complex structure of a wanted compound step-by-step to simpler compounds until they arrived at a cheaply and easily available material, after which they used the same, synthetic, steps in the reverse direction, to make the target compound.

The Nobel Prize for medicine was awarded jointly to two US doctors, Joseph Murray of the Brigham and Women's Hospital of Boston and Donnall Thomas of the Fred Hutchinson Cancer Research Centre in Washington DC, for their pioneering work on kidney and bone marrow transplants respectively. Dr Murray had led the team which had carried out the world's first kidney transplant in 1954, and had later pioneered the use of whole body radiation and later of drugs to prevent rejection. He had also carried out the world's first series of transplants between non-identical donors and recipients. Dr Thomas had developed techniques for transplanting bone marrow to treat leukaemia and other conditions to the point where the procedure could be used routinely.

The Nobel Prize for physics was awarded jointly to Dr Jerome

Friedman, Dr Henry Kendall and Professor Richard Taylor of Stanford University in California, for work which had revealed that inside protons and neutrons (the sub-atomic particles forming atomic nuclei) were smaller particles, named quarks. They obtained the evidence for the existence of quarks by using the linear accelerator at Stanford to bombard protons and neutrons, revealing the outlines of quarks inside them.

Chapter 2

TECHNOLOGY

EXCITEMENT continued to abound about developments at the leading edge of the computing industry and related fields, so that singling out any particular theme of the year might appear over-subjective or idiosyncratic. However 1990 saw particular progress towards multimedia, built upon market and technical developments related to optical storage technology. For several years, the industry enthusiasts had been making dramatic predictions about the advent of multimedia and its effect in the realm of education, information and entertainment. Ugly neologisms, such as 'edutainment' and 'infotainment' were coined, although in retrospect it was surprising only that such hybrid words had not appeared much sooner, given that philosophers since Aristotle (and no doubt before) had placed emphasis upon the importance of combining instruction with pleasure.

OPTICAL MEDIA. Digital recordings of musical performances on compact discs were already familiar to consumers. The same laser-based technology applied to data other than sound patterns made its public debut as the CD-ROM (compact disc with read-only memory) around 1985. For reasons which included the higher density of storage afforded by such optical media compared with magnetic storage, CD-ROM was quickly recognized as a technology which could facilitate multimedia applications—that is, applications permitting combinations of the written word, sound, graphics, animation, high-resolution still photographs and moving pictures. Indeed, some basic standards were agreed by major industry players at an early stage, including the High Sierra agreement of 1986. Subsequently, a number of variants appeared, including CD-I (CD interactive), CD-ROM-XA (extended architecture) and, in 1990, CDTV (Commodore dynamic total vision), as manufacturers and developers sought to find the precise ingredients for a product which would emulate in the realm of education, information and entertainment the success which CD audio had already enjoyed.

The year did not see the hoped-for massive explosion in CD-ROM take-up by consumers, but there were clear signs of substantial progress with reasonable expectations that it could be sustained in coming years. Statistics produced for the Optical Publishers' Association in the United States by the specialist consultancy Infotech showed that the number of installed CD-ROM drives worldwide more than tripled in 1989 to 544,500 (from 168,000). Compared with the number of CD audio players, this figure was small, but undoubtedly reflected more than a temporary phenomenon. Furthermore, it was also evident that the 'chicken and egg' stage had been passed, for figures included in *The CD-ROM Directory* issued by TFPL Publishing of London in December 1990 showed that the number of CD-ROM or other optical format publications available 'in print' rose from 816 in 1989 to 1,522 in 1990. It was generally believed that a surge in available material for use would further fuel sales of CD-ROM drives; indeed, Infotech predicted 6 million units by 1992.

Another interesting development, interpreted as a further indicator of imminent CD-ROM market growth, was the appearance in Japan in mid-1990 of the Sony Data Discman. Weighing around one pound and with a keyboard and flip-up LCD (liquid crystal display) screen able to show 10 lines of 15 characters, this device played three-inch compact discs capable of storing over 200 megabytes of data. Sony stated its intention to seek arrangements with a number of publishers in order to be able to offer a range of data discs before launching the product outside Japan. The contents of typical discs would tend to be reference material, such as foreign language dictionaries, encyclopedias, the Bible and other basic texts.

In addition to being relevant to CD-ROM growth, the advent of the Data Discman fitted into another manifestation of computer miniaturization, namely the development of the so-called hand-held electronic book (HEB). Hitherto, such devices had mostly been either 'dedicated'—meaning a unit encapsulating only one work or collection of works—or had interchangeable 'plug'-in' chips. Thus the arrival of a small optical disc drive opened up new possibilities.

MULTIMEDIA. The TFPL directory referred to above classified 193 titles in 1990 as 'multimedia' compared with only 40 in 1989, almost a five-fold increase. Nevertheless, the most elusive element for multimedia perfection still presented some problems, although significant progress was made in 1990. 'Full-motion video' (FMV) was already achievable using a portion of the screen, but full-screen FMV was more difficult because of the need for very high rates of data transfer. The commitment of the Dutch electronics company Philips and Sony, who had jointly developed CD-I, not to launch the product commercially until full-screen FMV was available had already caused delay. By the end of 1990, the third quarter of 1991 was the latest forecast for its appearance.

Meanwhile, other approaches were being pursued. In November 1990 the US chip manufacturer Intel, which had already developed a technology known as DVI (digital video interactive), capable of compressing and decompressing moving video in real time in conjunction with CD-ROM or any other digital storage medium, announced the i750 video processor, consisting of an 82750PB pixel processor together with an 82750DB display processor. Furthermore, Intel indicated that in quantities of 1,000 or more the unit cost would come down to £62, a level which would permit the i750 to be included in equipment manufacturers' products at affordable prices. Whether DVI would undermine CD-I remained to be seen, but there was a suggestion that DVI would be more orientated towards professional applications and CD-I more towards consumer markets.

An arguably more pragmatic approach was adopted by Commodore, the US microcomputer manufacturer, which produced prototypes of its CDTV product during the second half of the year, for commercial launch in early January 1991. The product was capable of playing CD audio discs and multimedia CDTV discs in the same drive and connected to a standard domestic television set to display text, still pictures and motion video. Full-screen FMV was not incorporated, as Commodore took the view that it was not essential initially and that the product could be successful with partial-screen FMV, the full-screen capability coming in a later model. An important feature of the CDTV player was that it had similar dimensions and a similar appearance to the modules of a standard home music centre and could be stacked with it. Such physical convenience and compatibility in a domestic environment appeared to be a good portent and fitted in well with predictions of industry commentators that the convergence of technology would lead to something like a home 'infotainment' centre, incorporating familiar devices like television and telephone with newer technology.

An interesting by-product of the spread of CD-ROM and related technology was an increase in activity on publishers' rights. Technology companies like Philips, Sony and Commodore recognized that their product would only sell beyond the enthusiast market if there were a sufficient supply of material on disc to use with the new devices. Hence, such companies were seen to undertake some disc preparation themselves and to encourage others, including traditional publishing companies, to do so by providing technical support or joint venture funding. Since traditional publishers frequently already held much suitable material in machine-readable form, it was inevitable that they should be approached either to participate directly by publishing on disc themselves or at least to license others to use material originally compiled for print publication.

TRAFFIC AND VEHICLE SYSTEMS. While the driverless vehicle was still only practical in relatively circumscribed situations, as in automated warehouses, developments took place in 1990 which in the long run could bring such vehicles closer to day-to-day reality. One interesting example was the launch in the first half of the year of the TravelPilot vehicle navigation system by the German company Bosch, known for its Blaupunkt in-car entertainment products. The system consisted of digital cartographic data held on CD-ROM in the car, together with direction finding and distance measuring apparatus which allowed present position or destination to be displayed on screen when the vehicle was stationary. Discs were made available for several West European countries.

Another system, AVIC-1, was launched in mid-year by Pioneer Electronic, the Japanese electronics company. Using satellite communications rather than an in-vehicle CD-ROM, this system calculated the car's location and transmitted appropriate cartographic data, which could be displayed on screen at five different levels of detail. A slightly different approach was taken by the UK company General Logistics' Trafficmaster, whose system was launched later in the year. Traffic sensors mounted on motorway bridges provided drivers with frequently-updated information on slow-moving traffic, average speeds and lengths of tail-backs. Information was displayed on an LCD screen with an audible alerting signal.

RESEARCH AND DEVELOPMENT. In April 1990 the Commission of the European Community (EC) gained final approval from the Council of Ministers for a third R&D 'framework programme', covering the years 1990–94. A total budget of 5,700 million ecu was allocated for this programme, of which the largest portion (39 per cent) was for information and communications technologies. In the meantime, major activities were progressing under continuing EC programmes, such as ESPRIT (European Strategic Programme for Research in Information Technology) and RACE (Research and Development in Advanced Communication in Europe). An interesting experiment, within the context of the IMPACT (Information Market Policy Actions) programme, was conducted by the German company AEC working with ECHO (European Commission Host Organization). The experiment was an audiotex service providing Community information such as ecu exchange rates and employing spoken menus and speech recognition technology to permit the user to navigate through the database.

The year also saw important progress, within the forum of the International Telecommunication Union (ITU), on a number of standards relating to high-definition television (HDTV). The 17th plenary assembly of the International Radio Consultative Committee (CCIR), one of the permanent organs of the ITU, was held in Düsseldorf in May-June and unanimously adopted five recommendations (i.e. standards) considered to be a major step towards the unification of world television production systems. Nevertheless, strong fractious influences persisted, since Europe, Japan and the United States continued to pursue separate lines of development, designed to favour indigenous industry.

CHIP TECHNOLOGY. International Business Machines (IBM), the US computer manufacturer, claimed in February that it had already produced in small quantities a 16-megabit DRAM (dynamic random access memory), with four times the storage capacity of the 4-megabit DRAMs which had been the most powerful up to that time. IBM predicted that the 16-megabit DRAM would be in high-volume production within two years. At about the same time, there were indications that serious efforts were being undertaken to produce the next generation of chips after the 16-megabit DRAM, with IBM and Siemens (the German technology company) signing an agreement for the joint development of a 64-megabit DRAM. This trans-Atlantic collaboration was taken to reflect the fact that the development costs of each successive generation of chips had increased by around 50 per cent, but was frowned on in some European quarters because of the key role played by Siemens in JESSI (Joint European Sub-micron Silicon Initiative). The advent of the 64-megabit DRAM was variously predicted by industry experts for between 1995 and 1998.

In another development, Signetics (based in the United States, but owned by the Philips conglomerate) reported that it had successfully completed research into a new type of chip, referred to as the LIFE (long instruction format engine) chip. It was claimed that LIFE chips were able to perform more simultaneous tasks than other available microprocessors and offered better performance characteristics than RISC (reduced instruction set computer) chips.

OLFACTORY TECHNOLOGY. One of the more unusual projects of the year was the development of a hand-held sniffer by the University of Manchester Institute of Science and Technology (UMIST) in the UK. By pumping air over a series of sensors and analysing chemical patterns, the device was able to detect truffles. Whilst the invention would clearly have important practical applications, it was encouraging to know that not all research was driven by sheer utilitarianism and that the finer elements of life were not totally forgotten.

Chapter 3

THE ENVIRONMENT

WHILE scientists reached broad agreement during 1990 on the reality and the scale of the threat of global warming, the year also saw a split emerge between scientists and many political leaders on the issue. Scientists tended to demand action to limit the pollution leading to warming and argued that such action was cost effective; political leaders failed to agree on pollution limitation goals.

The long-awaited final report of the Intergovernmental Panel on Climate Change (IPCC), released in the summer, predicted that if no action were taken to curb the emission of 'greenhouse gases' then average global temperatures would rise by between 1.4 and 2.8 degrees centigrade by the year 2030. Some 10 million people would have to be evacuated from low coastal areas of East Anglia, Bangladesh and the Netherlands as oceans rose, largely due to expansion caused by warming, and many other low-lying coastal areas would be affected. The report was important not only for the numbers it contained, but also because it was an international scientific statement that pollution-driven global warming actually existed.

Despite the IPCC certainty, the 137 governments participating in the second World Climate Conference in Geneva in early November (see also p. 396) failed to agree on emission standards for carbon dioxide (CO_2), the main greenhouse gas. They did sign an agreement recognizing that global warming was a reality and pledging to take steps to limit it. Hopes for this limitation were pinned on a global convention on climate change to include legally-binding protocols on emission standards for greenhouse gases, which governments agreed to begin negotiating in February 1991. They hoped to have an agreement ready for signing at the 1992 UN Conference on Environment and Development (UNCED) in Brazil.

At the Geneva conference, the EC, Japan, Australia and other European nations advocated a freeze on CO_2 emissions at present levels by the year 2000. The United States, the Soviet Union and Saudi Arabia opposed the setting of firm targets. Scientists at the conference said in a statement that 'nations should now take steps towards reducing sources and increasing sinks of greenhouse gases'. They pointed out that 'technically feasible and cost-effective opportunities exist to reduce CO_2 emissions in all countries'.

Similar lines of division continued throughout the year. In May 32 European nations plus the United States and Canada assembled in Bergen (Norway) for a regional meeting to prepare for the 1992 UNCED. Most governments represented called for a stabilization of CO_2 emissions at present levels by the year 2000. The USA, the Soviet Union and the

UK argued that targets should not be set until the climate conference in November.

In mid-April the Bush administration held a Washington conference on climate change, attended by delegates from 17 governments. President Bush told the gathering that further research was needed before action could be taken. The French Secretary of State for the Environment, Brice Lalonde, joined several other foreign delegates in accusing the US government of inviting them to listen but not to participate. In November several prominent US scientists complained that, despite the President's call for more research, funding for climate research was actually being cut by the US and other governments.

The temperature averages of 1990 added to the circumstantial evidence of global warming, in that it was the hottest year since records were first kept. The next five hottest years all occurred in the 1980s.

Toward the end of 1990 first the rains, then the grain harvests, failed across most of the African Sahel region. The US Climate Analysis Centre reported in October that rainfall was three-quarters of normal in the western Sahel but less than half the norm in eastern Sudan and northern Ethiopia. From Ethiopia and the Sudan in the east, across to Mauritania, Mali and Burkina Faso in the west, drought and pest damage had produced harvests as low as those of 1984–85, which led to regional famine conditions. Estimates at the end of the year suggested that as many as 12 million people in Sudan and Ethiopia alone would suffer famine. Poor harvests in 1989 meant that food reserves were low or non-existent.

The renewed—or continuing, depending on one's point of view—drought prompted speculation among climatologists over whether Sahelian drought was linked to global warming. According to Jean Palutnik of the climate research unit at the University of East Anglia (UK), 'more and more climatologists' were coming round to this view 'as the drought persists from year to year'. Some pointed to the fact that many years which had been among the warmest globally—such as 1983, 1987 and 1990—were associated with dryness and hotter than normal weather in the Sahel.

In June 98 governments agreed, in London, to strengthen the Montreal protocol on protecting the ozone layer, pledging to phase out chlorofluorocarbons (the industrial chemicals known as CFCs) by the year 2000. Japan, the Soviet Union and the USA had opposed a European call for a phase-out by 1997. The governments also agreed, despite initial US reluctance, to establish a global fund—initially $160 million, with scope for additional money as more Third World nations signed on—to help developing nations transfer to more expensive alternatives to CFCs. The EC countries agreed in December to phase out all CFC production by the year 1997.

The Washington-based World Resources Institute published a report in conjunction with the United Nations which showed that tropical forests were being lost at a rate about 50 per cent higher than that revealed by the last global UN forests survey (in 1980). It said that each year some 16–20 million hectares were being cleared. There were about 885 million hectares of such forests remaining. In January a conference in Brazil on rain-forests and global warming, attended by rain-forest countries, issued a statement agreeing that forest conservation was 'of crucial importance for global climatic stability', but called upon industrialized nations to reduce their own emissions of greenhouse gases.

In March the third international North Sea Conference, at The Hague, agreed to reduce by half or more the levels of pollution from the 37 worst pollutants. Levels of lead, mercury, cadmium and dioxin were to be cut by at least 70 per cent by 1995. On the final day of the conference, the UK upset other governments by declining to agree not to dispose of radioactive wastes under the seabed. It said that it had no plans to do so, but wanted to keep the option open.

In September the British government published a 300-page White Paper on the environment, the first government document to put all environmental concerns into one strategy (see p. 35). It disappointed environmental groups by being largely a survey of ongoing commitments and plans. It contained little new, and rejected the imposition of 'carbon taxes' or other new fiscal measures to combat global warming over the 'next few years'. But it did pledge to promote increased energy efficiency and the generation of electricity from renewable sources (solar, wave, wind, etc.).

The EC issued two directives on the release and contained use of genetically-modified organisms. The one on release into the environment required member states to 'avoid adverse effects on human health and on the environment'. The EC also issued a directive obliging all public authorities holding information on the environment to make it available upon request, subject to certain exclusions.

In January, at a Moscow meeting of 700 religious leaders and parliamentarians from some 30 countries, Soviet leader Mikhail Gorbachev called for an 'international Green Cross' to aid nations with ecological problems. He also proposed the creation of a UN force of 'green berets' to intervene in ecological disasters.

The year 1990 saw an outpouring of popular and media attention for the environment. Earth Day 1990 occurred on 22 April, 20 years after the original Earth Day in 1970. Inspired by US groups, the day saw worldwide demonstrations, celebrations and mass tree-plantings. In May most of the television networks of Western Europe cooperated to produce a week of environment and development programmes under the title *One World Week*. In Britain the BBC had previously joined forces with environment and development groups to produce relevant literature to be sent to viewers.

The shark emerged as one of the most talked about, and perhaps most unlikely, 'endangered species' of 1990. While recreational shark fishing declined slowly in the United States, commercial fishing increased rapidly. Shark meat fillets joined shark fin soup as a delicacy in restaurants. The US National Marine Fisheries Service published a plan to limit the catch of 38 different kinds of sharks in key areas off the southern United States.

Rocket fuel leaked into the White Sea of the Soviet Arctic in late April or early May, killing 100,000 seals and millions of other marine animals, according to Soviet press reports and Soviet naval sources. At least one-third of sea life in the White Sea appeared to have died, in what the Soviet newspaper *Izvestia* called 'an ecological tragedy of huge proportions'.

The year opened with a 300 sq km oil slick, released by a series of explosions on the Iranian super-tanker *Kharg-5*, moving toward the coast of Morocco, although it later dispersed with little damage. The Exxon Corporation admitted that 500,000 gallons of heating oil had been spilled into New York harbour after a pipeline was hit by an Exxon-owned vessel on new year's day. Several bird sanctuaries were affected.

The year closed with much press speculation on the possible environmental effects of a war in the Gulf. King Husain of Jordan told the World Climate Conference that the environmental impact of a war would be 'swift, severe and devastating'. Experts warned that major fires in the Kuwaiti oilfields could burn for months and change the climate in the region, producing cooler weather and disrupting the monsoon rains on the Indian sub-continent. Others argued that a major oil slick was a more likely result of the conflict, and noted that the Gulf was shallow and slow to clean itself. Several experts pointed out that the threatened Gulf conflict was the first in which the environmental effects had been discussed in advance of any fighting.

XV THE LAW

Chapter 1

INTERNATIONAL LAW—EUROPEAN COMMUNITY LAW

INTERNATIONAL LAW

THE International Court of Justice (ICJ) did not decide on the merits of any contentious case in 1990, but proceedings continued in five of the seven cases carried over from 1989. After the change of government in Nicaragua, proceedings in its cases against Honduras and the USA were postponed. One new case was brought to the Court: Libya and Chad separately instituted proceedings to settle the course of their frontier. They had agreed on 31 August 1989 that the dispute should be resolved by negotiation and that if no firm solution was reached within a year the question should be referred to the ICJ (see AR 1989, p. 230–1). The willingness of two developing states to submit such a longstanding and serious dispute to the Court illustrated the growth in its activity and prestige in recent years.

In another case arising out of a boundary dispute (see AR 1989, p. 448), Guinea-Bissau requested the Court to indicate provisional measures. Guinea-Bissau alleged that the Senegal navy had boarded foreign vessels in the course of an unjustified supervision of the contested maritime area and had escorted them to its ports for trial. It argued that the area remained contested because the arbitral award determining their maritime boundary was null and void, and requested the ICJ to indicate 'that parties shall abstain in the disputed area from any action of any kind whatever during the Court proceedings.' On 2 March the Court, by 14 votes to 1, dismissed this request. It followed earlier cases in holding that in a request for provisional measures the Court ought to satisfy itself that there was a prima facie basis for its jurisdiction on the merits of the case. The Court found that the declaration of the parties under article 36(2) of the ICJ Statute provided this basis. However, another requirement was that the purpose of such an award should be to preserve rights that were the subject of the dispute in the judicial proceedings. Here the Court said that the issue before it in this case was the validity of the arbitral award, which did not involve the Court in deciding on the respective rights of the parties in the contested maritime areas. Accordingly, the Court refused to indicate provisional measures.

In another exercise of its incidental jurisdiction the Court decided on the application made by Nicaragua on 17 November 1989 to intervene in the boundary case submitted to a chamber of the Court by El Salvador and Honduras (see AR 1987, p. 440). Nicaragua's object in seeking to intervene was to protect its legal rights in the Gulf of Fonseca and adjacent maritime areas and to inform the Court of the nature of its legal rights. Nicaragua argued that the full Court should decide on its application to intervene. Because it was not a party to the agreement between El Salvador and Honduras to submit their boundary dispute to a chamber of the Court and had not taken part in the formation of the chamber, Nicaragua said that principles of equity and equality demanded that the full Court should exercise its incidental jurisdiction. However, the Court held, by 12 votes to 3, that it was for the tribunal seized of a principal issue to deal also with any subsidiary issue, so a chamber formed to deal with a particular case should therefore deal not only with the merits of a case but also with the incidental proceedings. Accordingly, Nicaragua's application to intervene was decided by the chamber of the Court on 13 September.

Under article 62 of the ICJ Statute the state seeking to intervene was required to show that it had 'an interest of a legal nature which may be affected by the decision in the case'. The dispute between El Salvador and Honduras concerned several distinct legal issues: their land frontier, the legal situation of certain islands in the Gulf of Fonseca, the legal status of the waters of the Gulf and the possible determination of a maritime boundary in and outside the Gulf. The chamber found that Nicaragua had no legal interest in the first two issues but accepted that the question whether the Gulf of Fonseca was a condominium affected Nicaragua as well as El Salvador and Honduras. As regards the question of delimitation, Nicaragua had not brought any evidence to show that it might have a legal interest in any maritime areas which might be affected by any possible delimitation line between El Salvador and Honduras. Accordingly, the scope of Nicaragua's right to intervene was limited to those aspects of the dispute in which it had a legal interest.

This was the first case in the history of the ICJ in which a state was given permission to intervene under article 62. The chamber, therefore, in a unanimous decision, made it clear that the intervening state did not become a party to the proceedings. It also made an important ruling on a matter that had been controversial since the French nuclear tests case (see AR 1974, pp. 411–2) when it rejected El Salvador's argument that for Nicaragua to intervene it must show a valid jurisdictional link between Nicaragua and the parties to the case. Such a requirement would unduly restrict the right to intervene under article 62.

On 15 November Judges Robert Jennings (UK) and Gilbert Guillaume (France) were re-elected as members of the Court. Andrés Aguilar Mawdsley (Venezuela), Raymond Ranjeva (Madagascar) and Christopher Weeramantry (Sri Lanka) were elected as from 6 February 1991.

The repercussion of the blowing-up of the *Rainbow Warrior* (see AR

1985, p. 313–14) continued. France and New Zealand submitted to an arbitration tribunal (consisting of Eduardo Jiménez de Aréchaga, Kenneth Keith and Jean-Denis Bredin) their dispute over the implementation of the UN Secretary-General's ruling of 6 July 1986. This ruling, accepted by France and New Zealand in agreements concluded on 9 July 1986 (see AR 1986, p. 325), provided that the two French agents responsible for the attack on the *Rainbow Warrior* were to be transferred to a French military establishment on the island of Hao for a period of three years and were not to leave the island without the consent of both governments.

The main question put to the tribunal was whether France had acted illegally in removing the two agents from the island and in refusing to return them. To justify its actions France pleaded *force majeure* and distress, relying on the general law of state responsibility as set out in the International Law Commission's draft articles. New Zealand argued that the applicable law was the law of treaties. In a controversial ruling, the tribunal accepted the French argument in principle. But on the merits of the case it found that although the initial removal of one of the French agents from the island without New Zealand's consent was justified by his serious illness, France's subsequent refusal to return him to Hao was not lawful. The failure to obtain the consent of New Zealand to the removal of the other agent when she became pregnant was also unlawful.

However, the tribunal found that the obligation to keep the French agents on Hao was for a fixed period ending on 22 July 1989 and that France's breach of its obligations also ended on that date. As regards remedies, the tribunal said that New Zealand had suffered moral, political and legal damage but held that in the particular circumstances a declaration of breach was itself an appropriate satisfaction for New Zealand. Because France's obligations had ended on 22 July 1989, the tribunal would not order the return of the two agents to Hao. But the tribunal recommended the establishment of a fund to promote friendly relations between the citizens of the two states and that France should make an initial contribution of $2 million to this fund.

Two important UN treaties entered into force. The 1988 Convention against Illicit Traffic in Narcotic Drugs and Psychotropic Substances, providing for a wide range of measures to counter the global operations of drug-trafficking organizations (including confiscation of proceeds and extradition) entered into force on 11 November. The 1989 Convention on the Rights of the Child (see AR 1989, pp. 377–8) came into force on 2 September after an unprecedented first year response during which it was signed by 61 states.

In the European system for the protection of human rights there were some important procedural developments. Protocol No 8 to the European Convention on Human Rights entered into force on 1 January.

This was designed to speed up proceedings before the Commission and Court, its most important provision being for the division of the Commission into two chambers. Protocol No 9 was opened for signature on 5 November and would enter into force when ratified by 10 states. It empowered individuals to bring admitted cases before the Court, thus representing important improvement in the position of individual victims of human rights violations. Turkey accepted the jurisdiction of the European Court of Human Rights on 22 January.

EUROPEAN COMMUNITY LAW

IF 1989 saw the pace of Community law quicken, 1990 saw it quickening yet faster. At the same time new elements, often finding their origin in President Gorbachev's *perestroika* to the east, began to appear; and with them came a promise that legal developments, which hitherto had been linear (faster or slower movement towards or away from greater integration), would thenceforth become much more complex. Partly this was a result of the implosion of Europe. The comfortable conceptual simplicity of states being either members or non-members of the European Community (EC)—a situation hardly disturbed by a couple of ancient association agreements (Greece and Turkey), a half-dozen free trade agreements, and special privileges for the ex-colonies (Lomé), none of which caused the Community or its Court of Justice more than 30 seconds distraction from its own internal concerns—was suddenly replaced by awareness that Europe no longer stopped at the Community's frontiers. Europe had indeed become whole again; and the Community, if it was to retain its idealistic credibility, would need to work out structures of relationship, not only with the Nordic and Alpine countries, but also with the Eastern states and possibly even, it was challengingly suggested, with the constituent republics of the Soviet Union. Work was begun, but in nearly every case it was not concluded before the year's end. To that extent it was a year of change and preparation rather than accomplishment, only the 1992 legislation programme being predictable (see also pp. 404–5).

As part of this gathering together of Europe, for which the Community was now sufficiently mature to act as the natural nucleus, special trade treaties were drafted with the Eastern states; and for the central three (Poland, Hungary and Czechoslovakia) association agreements were negotiated as a half-way house to possible full membership. The German Democratic Republic (GDR) did not even have to contemplate such procedures since, as a result of its accession to the Federal Republic of Germany (FRG) in October (see pp. 146–55), it automatically became part of the Community, with EC law directly applicable to it at the same time as its reception of FRG law. In practice, however, it was not so simple either internally (where an overlapping of FRG and GDR law to a limited extent continued) or as regards Community law, where special transitional measures had to be taken.

The negotiation with EFTA on a quasi-membership arrangement through what was now rebaptized the European Economic Area (EEA) made good progress; but completion was postponed to mid-1991, the main issues outstanding at the year's end being fisheries and whether the EFTA countries should have any place at all in Community law-making (see pp. 415–6). In any case, the hope that conclusion of the EEA would head off new applications for full membership was shown up as vain when the Swedish parliament voted in December to authorize the government to apply to join the Community. In the south formal applications to join were also made by both Malta and Cyprus; while Andorra entered into a free trade agreement, which came into force as 1990 ended.

In the field of internal constitutional law, the major developments were likewise set in motion but not completed. The two intergovernmental conferences (IGCs)—on economic and monetary union and on political union—were both started in December, accompanied by a flurry of proposed draft amending treaties. At the same time the term 'subsidiarity'—a loose concept aimed unconvincingly at replicating the division of legislative power within federal systems—entered the debate as a means of assuaging the worries of those who increasingly feared the lack of effective democratic control of the prospective union.

Unexpectedly, the Commission formally requested the Council to approve an application for the Community as such to adhere to the European Convention on Human Rights. The desirability of such a step was shown by the text of the Schengen Agreement, finally released after its signature in June. This treaty, concluded between five of the original six EC members (with a sixth, Italy, joining in November), included far-reaching rules on aliens control, trans-border police powers and a major inter-linked police and aliens computerized database (the 'Schengen information system'). While strictly speaking it was not an EC text, and indeed was specifically made subordinate to Community law, there was no doubt that its rules were being closely followed in the parallel Trevi negotiations taking place in similar secrecy between all 12 EC member states. The issue by the Commission of a draft directive on money laundering, which although formally part of the Community's banking law required member states to adopt criminal procedures of considerable sensitivity, merely emphasized how the Community was beginning to move into areas of law which involved the liberties of the citizen. Indeed, the concept of Community citizenship itself was increasingly being raised and was the subject of a long and carefully prepared report by the Federal Trust which was adopted in time for submission to the IGCs in December. Of longer term constitutional concern was the future of the European Coal and Steel Community, which would reach the end of its 50-year life in 2002. Should it be extended or abolished or absorbed into the European Economic Community? The Commission, which clearly preferred the last alternative, produced a discussion paper to bring the issue into a wider arena in good time.

The European Court of Justice (ECJ) did not escape these structural trends. Having the previous year been supplemented by a junior tribunal, the Court of First Instance (CFI), which would hopefully take some of its case load off its shoulders, it promptly found itself saddled with two more sources of jurisdiction and the prospect of a third. The revised Community Patent Convention, adopted at the end of the previous year, contained elaborate provisions for judicial intervention, with wide powers of reference to the ECJ. Then during 1990 a special protocol was signed to the Rome Convention on choice of law in contract, which likewise gave powers of reference to the ECJ. Additionally, the function of the ECJ in interpreting the future EEA treaty was one of the more important issues to be settled in those negotiations.

By the year's end the Court did not seem any nearer to solving its problems: it was still averaging some 2½ years to deal with direct actions and 1½ years for references from national courts (compared with six to eight months for references in the 1970s). Likewise, the delay in publishing its judgments was still 20 to 24 months after their delivery. An attempt by the Court's president to cut through this problem by not translating the less important judgments was unacceptable to the member states. They therefore granted the Court an extra one million ecu per annum to provide additional translation resources, in return for which the Court would drop the innovation from January 1992—although the preceding three years (1989–1991) would still be reported only selectively.

The CFI began issuing judgments during the year and clearly indicated its intention to adopt its own style. By the year's end it had gained sufficient self-confidence to produce a document for the IGCs in which it proposed considerable extension of its functions. However, in spite of producing draft rules in June, it had still not acquired its own rules of procedure by December and was having to continue using those of the ECJ as a temporary substitute.

The Commission too was experiencing problems in publishing competition decisions and followed the ECJ in adopting a selective approach. Only those decisions which it was statutorily required to publish would be translated and put in the *Official Journal*. Others were merely announced and transcript copies made available to those who specially requested them. Although this problem became apparent earlier in the year it was exacerbated by the entry into force of the Mergers Regulation (4064/89) in the autumn after its rules of procedure (regulation 2367/90) and guidelines had been promulgated in July/August. That was immediately followed by a surge of applications for clearance to which the Commission, which had set up a special mergers task force, responded with admirable promptness. Among its other decisions was one in which, having found that ICI and Solvay had operated a cartel in soda ash, it imposed higher fines than ever before (£12 million and £20 million respectively). In another case it found that the terms on which the UK government had sold the Rover Group constituted state aid contrary to article 92 EEC and required the government to obtain repayment of £44.4 million from the purchaser, British Aerospace.

The Court performed a dramatic *volte face* when it deliberately overruled its 1974 decision in the *Café HAG* case and held that sequestration of the Belgian subsidiary of HAG after World War II did after all break the link between it and its German ex-parent for trade mark purposes (*CNL-Sucal* v. *HAG AG*). It also, as expected, confirmed that, if the English courts thought it proper to disapply the Merchant Shipping Act 1988 pending a ruling by the ECJ on its compatibility with Community law, they should do so notwithstanding any procedural rules to the contrary.

Chapter 2

LAW IN THE UNITED KINGDOM

THE *Courts and Legal Services Act*, embodying the most fundamental changes in the legal system and the legal profession for many decades, received the royal assent on 1 November. Its principal effects were to provide for the reallocation of business between the High Court and county courts and the introduction of procedures designed to expedite litigation and to reduce its cost; to permit solicitors and non-lawyers to gain wider rights of audience in the courts; to remove the monopoly on conveyancing and probate work formerly held by solicitors; and to allow (in limited circumstances) litigation to be conducted on a contingent fee basis. Other changes of significance in the operation of the legal system included the extension to the county court of the power to make an award of provisional damages[1], the removal of the exclusion of some classes of hearsay evidence in cases involving children[2], the making of provision for evidence in criminal cases to be received by a live television link[3], and an important decision of the House of Lords on alternative verdicts[4]. Substantial alterations in the rules requiring corroboration of evidence were foreshadowed by a Law Commission working paper[5].

The European Court of Justice, acting on a reference from the House of Lords, ruled that an interim injunction might be awarded to stay the operation of regulations made under a UK statute if there was a seriously-arguable case that the regulations infringed the applicant's rights under directly applicable European Community legislation[6]. On further reference back to the House of Lords, an injunction was awarded[7]. In a case concerning the powers of the Secretary of State to fix a local authority's budget and hence reduce the level of community charge ('poll tax'), the House of Lords refused to allow judicial review on the grounds that the powers had not been exercised in bad faith or in breach of procedural requirements[8]. The Court of Appeal held that haemophiliacs claiming damages for negligence against the Department of Health after they had been infected by contaminated blood were entitled to discovery of documents relating to the formulation of government policy on the importation of blood products[9].

The rights of individuals against public bodies were further strengthened by the *Access to Health Records Act*; and Sir Nicolas Browne-Wilkinson held that documents which had been properly seized by the police in the course of a criminal investigation could not be made available to a party in related civil proceedings[10], notwithstanding that there were no express limitations in the Police and Criminal Evidence Act restricting the purposes for which such documents could be used. On the other hand, the House of Lords took a more conservative approach in upholding the conviction for contempt of court of a journalist who had refused to reveal the source of information which had been passed to him in breach of an obligation of confidentiality[11].

The House of Lords continued to underscore the increasingly limited scope of the tort of negligence. In *Caparo Industries plc* v. *Dickman*[12], it was held that accountants owed no duty of care towards potential investors in a company whose accounts they had audited; subsequently the Court of Appeal provided more explicit guidance on the scope of the accountants' duty of care to investors[13]. The House of Lords took a similar restrictive attitude to the liability of builders and local authorities in respect of defectively-constructed buildings[14], formally overruling their earlier decision in *Anns* v. *Merton London Borough*[15], and to the liability of parties to a contract who were aware that the agent of another party might be acting wrongfully[16]. A more liberal approach was visible in personal injury cases: brothers and sisters of the victims of negligent injuries were held to be entitled to recover damages for nervous shock suffered by seeing a live television transmission of the accident[17]; and a police authority was held liable for the suicide of a prisoner held on remand[18], although it was stressed that the standard of care imposed should take account of all the circumstances[19].

The problems of post-divorce settlements attracted considerable attention. In *Clutton* v. *Clutton*[20] the Court of Appeal reiterated the need to ensure that both parties were treated fairly in the distribution of family assets, even though the need to provide a home for the wife and children was the primary concern. In *Re Citro*[21], however, it was stated that the interests of a trustee in bankruptcy would normally prevail over those of an innocent wife and children. In *Delaney* v. *Delaney*[22] the Court of Appeal held that where the parties had very limited resources it was necessary to take into account the availability of state benefits in assessing the appropriateness of making an order for the payment of maintenance. The more general risk that the costs of supporting divorced wives and their children might in fact fall on the state, notwithstanding the existence of a maintenance order, was dealt with by section eight of the *Social Security Act*, which provided that the Department of Social Security might itself take steps to enforce the order. In a White Paper, *Children Come First*[23], the government announced its intention of introducing further legislation to ensure that the cost of maintaining children in single-parent families should be met so far as possible by absent fathers rather than by public funds. Almost simultaneously the Law Commission presented proposals for radical reform of the law of divorce[24], designed to ensure that the financial and other consequences of the breakdown of a marriage had been fully determined before a divorce was granted. The related issue of the abduction of children by one parent in derogation of the custody or access rights of the other parent was considered by both the House of Lords[25] and the Court of Appeal[26]. The European Court of Human Rights upheld the ruling of the English courts denying the validity of the marriage of a transsexual[27] (see also p. 415).

The long-established rule that a husband could not be guilty of the rape of his wife came under attack. In a case heard in the Sheffield Crown Court[28], Simon Brown J. ruled that the so-called marital exception did not represent English law; the question was referred to the Law Commission, which produced a working paper outlining the arguments for the amendment of the law in line with this ruling[29]. The Court of Appeal heard four separate cases concerning the mental element in statutory offences against the person[30]; two of these, reaching opposite conclusions, were heard by differently-constituted courts on the same day. The final result was described by the court, imploring the intervention of the House of Lords, as practically unworkable and theoretically objectionable. Two statutes of major importance for the criminal law were enacted. The *Computer Misuse Act* introduced new offences of obtaining unauthorized access to computer programmes and making alterations to computer programmes without permission. The *Human Fertilization and Embryology Act* clarified the law on abortion formerly contained in the Abortion Act 1967 and the Infant Life (Preservation) Act 1929. It introduced a 24-week period within which abortion would normally be allowed, and extended the circumstances within which an abortion might be permitted beyond this period.

After a trial lasting 113 days, Ernest Saunders and other defendants were given substantial sentences after conviction on offences of fraud and conspiracy committed in connection with the takeover by Guinness of the Distillers Group in 1986[31] (see p. 22). The Court of Appeal refused to uphold a prison sentence on a young mother convicted of assisting shoplifters; the trial judge was rebuked for his intemperate criticisms of the Lord Chief Justice[32]. The Queen's Bench divisional court confirmed that the crime of blasphemy protected only the Christian religion, refusing to permit a prosecution in respect of Salman Rushdie's book *The Satanic Verses*[33]. The conviction of three Irish people for conspiracy to murder the Secretary of State for Northern Ireland was quashed on the grounds that the publicity given during the trial to the views of the intended victim and others that the defendants' right to silence should be abolished had irredeemably prejudiced a fair trial[34]. The trial of a shipping company for manslaughter after the 1987 Zeebrugge ferry disaster collapsed after the judge ruled that a corporation could only be guilty of this offence in a very narrow range of circumstances[35].

In two cases of great importance for conveyancers and mortgagees, *Lloyds Bank* v. *Rosset*[36] and *Abbey National Building Society* v. *Cann*[37], the House of Lords considered whether the mortgagee of registered land was bound by the rights of a person in occupation of the land at the time when the mortgage was registered, though not at the time when the mortgage was completed. It was held that no overriding interest was created in favour of a person whose occupation commenced only after the completion of the mortgage, in essence ensuring the worth of the security taken in the common domestic mortgage. In addition, in *Rosset*, the House of Lords held that in the absence of an express agreement an equitable interest in property would normally only be conferred on a person who had made a direct financial contribution to the purchase.

The *Employment Act* introduced further regulation to the operation of trades unions, strengthened the existing requirements to hold a ballot before taking industrial action, and put more obstacles in the way of unofficial strikes. The law relating to discrimination in employment and elsewhere continued to develop, largely under the influence of decisions of the European Court of Justice. Of particular importance was the decision of the House of Lords in *James* v. *Eastleigh Borough Council*[38], holding that sexual discrimination was established by proof of nothing more than that 'but for' the complainant's gender he or she would have been treated differently.

The jurisdiction of the English courts over international commercial transactions was clarified by the *Contracts (Applicable Law) Act*, ratifying the Rome Convention of 1980 between the member states of the European Community. The principles underlying Mareva injunctions were further developed, after very protracted litigation, by the Court of Appeal in *Derby* v. *Weldon (No 6)*[39]. In the latest stage of the litigation stemming from the collapse of the International Tin Council in 1986, the Commercial Court laid down the rules according to which damages for the breach of a contract for the sale of goods should be calculated in such abnormal market conditions[40].

1   SI 89/2426; SI 89/2467
2   *Children (Admissibility of Hearsay Evidence) Order*
3   *Crown Court (Amendment) Rules; Criminal Appeal (Amendment) Rules*
4   *R* v. *Maxwell* [1990] 1 All ER 801
5   Law. Com. Working Paper 115: 'Corroboration of Evidence in Criminal Trials'
6   *Factortame Ltd and others* v. *Secretary of State for Transport* [1990] New Law Journal 927; cf [1989] 2 All ER 692
7   *Factortame Ltd and others* v. *Secretary of State for Transport (No. 2)* [1990] New Law Journal 1457
8   *R* v. *Secretary of State for the Environment, ex parte Hammersmith and Fulham London Borough Council and others* [1990] 3 All ER 589
9   *Re HIV Haemophiliac Litigation* [1990] New Law Journal 1349
10   *Anchor Brewhouse Ltd* v. *Jaggard, The Times*, 5th December
11   *X Ltd* v. *Morgan Grampian Ltd*; *Re Goodwin* [1990] 2 All ER 1
12   [1990] 2 WLR 358
13   *James McNaughton Paper Group Ltd* v. *Hicks Anderson & Co, The Times*, 2 October; see too *Morgan Crucible Co plc* v. *Hill, The Times*, 2 November
14   *Murphy* v. *Brentwood District Council; Department of the Environment* v. *Thomas Bates & Son* [1990] 3 WLR 414
15   [1977] AC 728
16   *Banque Financière de la Cité SA* v. *Westgate Insurance Co Ltd* [1990] 2 All ER 947
17   *Jones and others* v. *Chief Constable of South Yorkshire* [1990] New Law Journal 1717
18   *Kirkham* v. *Chief Constable of Greater Manchester Police* [1990] 3 All ER 246
19   *Knight* v. *Home Office* [1990] 3 All ER 237
20   *The Times*, 13 November
21   [1990] 3 All ER 952
22   [1990] 2 FLR 457
23   Cmnd. 1264
24   Law. Com. 192, 'Ground for Divorce'.
25   *C* v. *S (minor: abduction: illegitimate child)* [1990] 2 All ER 961
26   *Re H (minors: abduction: jurisdiction)* [1990] New Law Journal
27   *Cossey* v. *United Kingdom, The Times*, 17 October
28   *R* v. *C* [1990] New Law Journal 1497
29   Law. Com. Working Paper 116, 'Rape Within Marriage'
30   *DPP* v. *K* [1990] 1 All ER 331; *R* v. *Spratt* [1990] Criminal Law Review 797; *R* v. *Savage* [1990] Criminal Law Review 709; *R* v. *Parmenter* [1990] New Law Journal 1231
31   See [1990] New Law Journal 1217
32   *The Times*, 17 January
33   *R* v. *Chief Metropolitan Magistrate, ex parte Choudhary* [1990] New Law Journal 702
34   *R* v. *Cullen and others, The Times*, 1 May
35   [1990] New Law Journal 1496
36   [1990] 1 All ER 1111

37 [1990] 1 All ER 1085
38 [1990] 2 All ER 690
39 [1990] 3 All ER 263; see also [1990] 3 All ER 161, [1990] 3 All ER 762
40 *Shearson Lehman Hutton Inc* v. *Maclaine Watson & Co Ltd (No 2)* [1990] 3 All ER 723

Chapter 3

LAW IN THE UNITED STATES

A few significant developments in 1990 presaged the spread of liability for clean-up of the environment. The Clean Air Act raised standards for emissions by industrial firms and consumer goods, including vehicles[1]. The legislation required utilities and industrial concerns to modify plants emitting pollutants into the air, oil companies to reduce air polluting elements in petrol and automobile makers to improve car engines. A federal appellate court held that a lender to a firm liable for environmental clean-up could itself be held liable even though such lender had not taken title, through foreclosure, to the property for which clean-up was required, or operated such property[2]. Previously, lenders' liability for clean-up costs had been predicated on ownership, which had been acquired through foreclosure. The lender's liability was based on his active supervision of the borrower's affairs. The California supreme court, following decisions in other jurisdictions, held that an insurer might be liable to indemnify the insured under its general liability policy for environmental clean-up costs incurred by the insured[3].

Anti-trust law, which under the Reagan administration was not actively prosecuted to curb mergers and acquisitions, received a boost from the Supreme Court, which held that state attorneys-general could individually prosecute violations of such laws. As a result, state officials might take an interest in mergers and acquisitions in their jurisdiction, and firms proposing an acquisition or merger might also have to obtain clearance from state officials[4].

The courts considered the right to life in several contexts. The Supreme Court held that a person had a right to have life-supporting systems disconnected, but that a state, by legislation, might require clear and convincing evidence that such a choice had been made[5]. The decision was expected to increase the use of 'living wills' whereby individuals stipulated in advance their choice not to be connected to life-supporting systems. The Supreme Court also held that health-care professionals who performed abortions on minors were not required to get parental consent if there was no procedure for obtaining a decision from a court; however, it was stipulated that they must wait for 48 hours, after notifying parents, before performing the abortion[6]. In another case considered by pro-life groups as pivotal to their campaign to protect foetuses against experiments, including experimental fertilization techniques and genetic screening, a federal district judge held invalid, as an unwarranted interference with a woman's right to privacy, an Illinois law making it illegal to conduct an 'experiment on a foetus unless such experimentation is therapeutic to the foetus'[7]. Implicitly recognizing that potential parents were entitled to control conception and, to some extent, birth, courts in Kansas and Massachusetts allowed parents to recover damages for 'wrongful birth' of a child. In one case, it was ruled that the physician had a duty to advise the parents of tests by which they could ascertain non-correctable gross deformities and, accordingly, decide to avoid conception or abort birth. In the other, a sterilization, carried out for financial reasons, had been unsuccessful in preventing pregnancy[8].

Protection of children from abuse was raising vexing questions for the courts. A New York court held unenforceable a surrogate parent agreement (whereby a surrogate mother, for $10,000, agreed to conceive, give birth to and surrender the child for adoption) on the grounds that it was violative of state laws against trafficking in children and permitting payments in connection with adoption[9]. The Supreme Court upheld a state law allowing children, testifying as witnesses in abuse cases, to give testimony on closed-circuit television[10]. A Wyoming criminal court convicted a father of rape of his ten-year-old daughter, committed in 1962 but reported by her for the first time in 1990. The father pleaded guilty, and his daughter provided the only evidence[11]. Statutes had been enacted in several states allowing individuals to report at any time their abuse as children, even long after the event had occurred, although the conviction in Wyoming was not based on such a statute. A decision was awaited in the California courts on whether insurers of parents could be made liable under their policies for abuse by parents of their children[12].

In a few highly controversial cases the courts readdressed some old issues in the area of freedom of expression. A federal law, which Congress enacted to overturn the 1989 Supreme Court decision striking down a law banning flag-burning (see AR 1989, pp. 459–60), was held invalid by the Supreme Court as restrictive of free expression[13]. A New York city regulation prohibiting begging and 'panhandling' in the subway system was upheld by the courts, and the Supreme Court declined to review the lower court decisions[14]. A federal district court issued an injunction against the enforcement of the Helms Amendment prohibiting the use of 'indecent' speech over the telephone and directed towards the growing industry in verbal pornography by telephone, ruling that the law was too vague and violative of free speech[15]. Another federal court held invalid a law requiring adults who desire to hear sexually-explicit messages to obtain an access code to receive such messages, on the ground that the procedure 'chilled' both the rights of callers and the message services to communicate and listen to such communications[16].

No major developments occurred in the criminal law. The Supreme Court held that random sobriety checks of automobile drivers did not violate such drivers' right to be free from unreasonable search and seizure[17]. That Court also held that an appeals court, reviewing a decision imposing the death sentence upon a convicted person, might re-weigh all the relevant evidence and reach the same conclusion, even though the jury which initially imposed that sentence failed to do so properly[18].

[1] Public Law 101–476
[2] Marcus and Felsenthal, 'Lender May be Liable for Client's Clean-up' *Wall Street Journal*, 29 May 1990
[3] *AUI Ins. Co. v. Superior Court*, 33 Cal.3d 807 (1990)
[4] *California v. American Stores Co.*, No. 89–258
[5] *Cruzan v. Missouri Department of Health Services*, No. 88–1505
[6] *Hodgson v. Minnesota*, No. 88–1125
[7] Hilts, 'Federal Judge Throws Out Law Barring Foetal Research', *New York Times*, 28 April 1990, p. 7
[8] *Arche v. US Department of the Army*, 798 P.2d 477 (Kan.1990); *Burke v. Rivo*, 1 March 1990 (Mass.)
[9] Matter of Adoption of Paul, 550 N.Y.S.2d 815 (N.Y.Fam.Ct.1990)
[10] *Maryland v. Craig*, No. 89–478
[11] 'Courts Begin to Respect Memory of Child Abuse', *New York Times*, 8 January 1991, p. 3
[12] *J. C. Penny Casualty Ins. Co. v. M.K.*, California Supreme Court, No. S010524
[13] *US v. Eichman*, No. 89–1433
[14] *Young v. New York City Transit Authority*, 10 May 1990 (C.A.2 N.Y.1990); No. 90–591
[15] *American Information Enterprises Inc. v. Thornburg*, 724 F. Supp. 1255 (S.D.N.Y.1990)
[16] *Fabulous Associates Inc. v. Pennsylvania Public Utility Commission*, 16 February 1990 (C.A.3 Pa.1990)
[17] *Michigan Department of State Police v. Sitz*, No. 88–1897
[18] *Clemons v. Mississippi*, No. 88–6873

XVI THE ARTS

Chapter 1

OPERA—MUSIC—DANCE/BALLET—THEATRE—CINEMA—
TELEVISION & RADIO

OPERA

IN London the year was dominated by the death of one world-famous soprano and the retirement of another: Dame Eva Turner died at the age of 98 in June (see OBITUARY), while Dame Joan Sutherland made her final stage appearance on 31 December. The revival of *Turandot* which opened the Royal Opera's 1990–91 season at Covent Garden, when the protagonist was sung by Dame Gwynneth Jones (who had learnt the role from Dame Eva), was dedicated to the memory of the Lancashire-born soprano, herself a magnificent exponent of Puccini's icy princess. Sutherland had made her last complete operatic appearance on 2 October at the Sydney Opera House as Marguerite de Valois in Meyerbeer's *Huguenots*, but at Covent Garden on New Year's Eve she took part, together with mezzo Marilyn Horne and tenor Luciano Pavarotti, in the party scene of Johann Strauss's *Die Fledermaus*; after a duet with each of her fellow-guests, Dame Joan ended an association of nearly 40 years with the Royal Opera by singing 'Home, Sweet Home'.

Other events at Covent Garden included new productions of *Prince Igor* (Borodin), *The Cunning Little Vixen* (Janáček), *Guillaume Tell* (Rossini) and *Siegfried*, latest instalment in Götz Friedrich's production of Wagner's *Ring*. A visit by Kent Opera to Covent Garden in February with an acclaimed staging of *King Priam*, in honour of Michael Tippett's 85th birthday, was cancelled since the company had ceased to exist following the withdrawal of Arts Council funds. The only celebration of Sir Michael's birthday in London, therefore, was a Promenade concert of *The Ice Break* at the Albert Hall, although his most recent opera *New Year* received its British premiere at Glyndebourne.

The Glyndebourne season opened with a highly controversial staging of *Die Zauberflöte* by American director Peter Sellars, who set Mozart's magic opera in the Californian drug-culture of the 1960s and cut all the dialogue. Though the first-night audience was outraged, later many people found the production full of interest, particularly when it was taken on tour.

English National Opera (ENO) began the year with an admired

new staging of Verdi's *Macbeth*, followed by the premiere of Robin Holloway's *Clarissa*, based on the novel by Samuel Richardson, which was politely received. Undeterred by its perennial cash crisis, ENO, having made an enormously successful tour to the USSR, then embarked on a season of twentieth-century opera, to which was added a leavening of Mozart in honour of the coming bicentenary of his death. Productions of Berg's *Wozzeck* and Debussy's *Pelléas et Mélisande* won universal approval, but a double bill of Delius's *Fennimore and Gerda* with Puccini's *Gianni Schicchi* was less popular.

British regional companies were equally adventurous in their repertoires: Welsh National premiered John Metcalf's *Tornrak*, a legend set largely in the Canadian Arctic among the Inuit people; Opera North scored a splendid double with first British performances of Verdi's *Jérusalem* (the French version of *I Lombardi*) and of Nielsen's *Maskerade*; Scottish Opera (SO)offered a thrilling production of Verdi's *Forza del destino* in its original version as well as the premiere of Judith Weir's *Vanishing Bridegroom*, based on three Highland Scottish folktales; this also achieved a London performance during SO's three-day visit to Covent Garden, when the other opera performed was Berlioz's epic *Les Troyens*.

In Paris *Les Troyens* was the first production at the new Opéra Bastille, still not completely finished. Later, operas staged included Janáček's *Katya Kabanova*, Verdi's *Otello* and, in anticipation of 1991, *Le nozze di Figaro*. Other theatres to mount Mozart productions were La Scala, Milan, where Riccardo Muti conducted *La clemenza di Tito* in March and opened the new season on 7 December with *Idomeneo*. The Salzburg Festival also chose *Idomeneo*, while the Metropolitan, New York, staged a new *Don Giovanni*, directed and designed by Franco Zeffirelli. The first new production of the 1990–91 season at the Met, however was not of Mozart, but of Rossini's *Semiramide*.

During the year, New York City Opera gave the first staged New York performances of Janáček's *From the House of the Dead* and of Schoenberg's *Moses und Aron*. Lyric Opera Chicago opened its autumn season with Gluck's *Alceste*, in which Jessye Norman scored a triumph; Lyric also gave the first local performance of Dominick Argento's *Voyage of Edgar Allen Poe*. San Francisco staged Massenet's *Don Quichotte* for the first time while Santa Fe presented the US premiere of Siegfried Matthus's *Judith*.

Among other festivals, Brighton offered the State Opera of Poznan in the British premiere of Penderecki's *Schwarze Maske*; Aldeburgh paid tribute to Aaron Copland on his 90th birthday with *The Tender Land*; Aix-en-Provence staged Rameau's opera-ballet *Les Indes galantes* in spectacular fashion; Almeida and Harrogate gave the premieres of, respectively, Gerald Barry's *Intelligence Park* and Wilfred Joseph's *Alice in Wonderland*; the Bolshoi Opera brought Prokofiev's *Betrothal in a Monastery* to Edinburgh; Wexford produced two unjustly-neglected operas, Leoncavallo's *Zazà* and Nicholas Maw's *Rising of the Moon*.

It was too soon to assess the effect of the reunification of Germany on the country's many opera houses. In Berlin the Deutsche Oper premiered Hans Werner Henze's first large-scale opera for many years, *Das verratene Meer*, adapted from Yukio Mishima's novel, *The Sailor who Fell from Grace with the Sea*, and directed by Götz Friedrich. At Hamburg Maxim Shostakovich conducted the first local performance of his father, Dmitry Shostakovich's opera, *Lady Macbeth of Mstensk*. In Vienna Harry Kupfer used all the vast resources of the State Opera for his production of Bernd Alois Zimmermann's multi-media work, *Die Soldaten*. At Oslo, Antonio Bibalo's new setting of *Macbeth* scored a tremendous success at its first performance.

Deaths during 1990 included the American composer Leonard Bernstein and the Italian composer Luigi Nono (see OBITUARY). Among singers who died were the German soprano Ilse Hollweg; the Australian tenor Ronald Dowd; the French baritone Martial Singher; the German soprano Erna Berger (see OBITUARY); the British soprano Elizabeth Harwood; the Czech tenor Vilem Pribyl; the Australian baritone Arnold Matters; the German soprano Helena Braun; the British tenor Richard Lewis; the American soprano Eleanor Steber and the American tenor John Alexander.

MUSIC

THERE were competing claims in different countries for the hand of music in 1990. Many saw the city of Glasgow as the focal point of the year's musical achievement, since it was the 'European City of Culture, 1990', a fact which resulted in greatly increased artistic activity of all kinds. On the other hand, the Kurt Weill Foundation declared 1990 to be 'Kurt Weill Year'; starting with a 4-month festival in Düsseldorf (January-April) this spread to include numerous performances worldwide, and took in most of Weill's output. This concept, it must be said, was not so far-fetched as it might appear, and had more to it than merely the partisan promotion of a nationalist German composer with marxist leanings; rather it had to do with the identity of the new Germany, just emerging from the momentous political changes in Eastern Europe.

Meanwhile from the Soviet Union came another claim, that 1990 should be designated 'Tchaikovsky Year'. Not only was it the 150th anniversary of that composer's birth, but it was the centenary of his crowning achievement, the opera *The Queen of Spades*. In Russia too, at a time of great political and ethnic unrest, music was seen as the great unifying factor. Indeed the Soviet Minister of Culture, Nikolai

Gubenko, himself an artist and former theatre director, saw his task as nothing less than the preservation of Soviet culture in all its ethnic guises. The city of Moscow, and its renowned Tchaikovsky Competition, was a prime focus for performers; and the Moscow Festival aimed to bring together musicians from numerous other countries; so the current trends in pop, jazz and early music were inevitably much in evidence.

But the true Slav culture, sustained by the traditions of the Orthodox Church, was perhaps chiefly celebrated in the Ukrainian city of Kiev. Here the terms folk-song and folk-culture assumed fresh meaning as the festival was announced by the great bells of the ancient cathedral of S. Sophia. British music was represented chiefly by the English National Opera, whose oddly-assorted repertoire, heard also in Moscow and Leningrad, consisted of Verdi's *Macbeth*, Britten's *The Turn of the Screw* and Handel's *Xerxes*. The Handel opera, attended in Kiev by Mrs Thatcher, introduced Soviet audiences to something totally new—the counter-tenor voice (that of Christopher Robson). It made him the hero of the moment and was the first time such singing had been heard at the Bolshoi Theatre.

At Munich the Second International Biennale, masterminded by Hans Werner Henze, included no fewer than 19 world premieres in its three-week span. There were workshops for music-theatre, music-teaching, and 'participation'; there were also five special commissions, among which the strongest impression was made by Hans-Jürgen von Bose's *63:Dream Palace*, which drew its eclectic idiom from a multiplicity of different sources. The festival also made a speciality of Marionette Theatre, to which David Lang made a notable contribution with his *Judith and Holofernes*.

Spoleto, in Charleston, South Carolina, saw a new opera, *Hydrogen Jukebox*, by the minimalist Philip Glass, based on poems by Allen Ginsberg. Of all the trends in the 1980s, the acceptance of minimalism by audiences was both the most surprising and the most dramatic. Its origin lay partly in a reaction against the complexity of previous avant-garde works—such as those of Stockhausen, whose music was not so much to the fore in 1990; the key to its wide acceptance lay partly in its accessibility to the ordinary listener. In this new work Glass combined his familiar repetitive patterns with visual elements, such as slide and film projections; moreover the subject was not abstract or semi-mythical as before (see AR 1981, p. 423) but the social problems facing America at the beginning of the 1990s. In this sense Glass could be seen as a successor to Kurt Weill, whose music also had a strong popular dimension.

The year was one of consolidation rather than fresh achievement. Those trends which were apparent at the beginning of the 1990s had appeared gradually over the previous decade: a progressive concern with early music; an increase in the hold of pop/rock music over young and mass audiences; a disenchantment with the complexities of avant-garde music of the 1960s and 1970s, and a corresponding reaction in favour of easier idioms; finally a mistrust of those who pronounced on matters of aesthetic standards which had ceased to exist. There was a levelling-down of music's status to that of a commercial product. The listener seeking enlightenment about a new work would find that his sources contradicted each other.

One of the least desirable trends in Britain in the 1980s was the gradual decline of the Arts Council, from being a somewhat idealistic organization for the funding of the arts throughout the country, to becoming one which used public money to promote its own events. The bizarre prejudices reflected by this trend came to a head in 1990 with the funding of a Black Music Centre in London.

No abrupt new reputations were made in the year; rather were existing ones enhanced, sometimes controversially. The Soviet composer Alfred Schnittke, for example, was much to the fore. He was heard in Glasgow, at the Barbican (February/March), and was featured at the Huddersfield Contemporary Music Festival (November/December). That doyen of radicals John Cage also had a good year, featuring in two avant-garde festivals: at the Almeida (June) his *Europeras 3 and 4* was first heard, and at the Glasgow Musica Nova (September) a retrospective of his work was mounted, and a new piece, *Scottish Circus*, introduced. The 33rd Warsaw Autumn Festival witnessed a spectacular return to his native Poland, after 36 years in exile, by Andrzej Panufnik. His music unfortunately was not sufficiently avant-garde for the audience, who seemed in two minds about the nature and purpose of their festival. During the years of political and artistic isolation, it had been a lifeline with the radical and innovative West; but in 1990—what? Shostakovitch's *Rayok*, a satire on Stalin, proved a hit; *Alax* by Xenakis, unquestionably avant-garde, was a highlight; the ubiquitous Schnittke's *Symphony 5*, and Szymanowski's *Four Liturgical Pieces*, were successful if not sensational; Reich's *Drumming* had by this time assumed '20th century classic' status. But Panufnik's music fell uncertainly between different stools, even if his personal reception was cordial.

The biggest single challenge in 1990 remained the problem of performing contemporary music successfully alongside the vast repertoire of the established classics. In America the practice of 'residency' with an orchestra had become established in the 1980s, with hugely beneficial results. Joan Tower for example, winner of the 1990 Grawemeyer Award for her work *Silver Ladders*, had been resident with the St Louis Symphony; the most active of all living composers, John Harbison, whose successes in 1990 included his *Double Concerto* for brass, choir and orchestra, and his *Viola Concerto*, was resident in Pittsburgh and Los Angeles. Such links with the concert platform not only gave the composer invaluable access to fellow-professionals, but replaced confrontation with cooperation.

Something of the same principle applied in Australia and New Zealand, where, perhaps as a result of the Australian bicentenary of 1988, composers suddenly found themselves in demand. The premieres of Peter Sculthorpe (*Earth Cry* and *Second Guitar Concerto*) led the way to a host of lesser known hopefuls—Carl Vine, Roger Covell, Martin Wesley-Smith, Keith Humble. In New Zealand the simplicity of Maori and Pakaha folk-idioms was invoked by Douglas Lilburn (*Music Sea Changes* and *Sings Harry*) as well as by Edwin Carr (*Makariri-Koanga*).

A desire for accessibility to the listener was felt by composers worldwide. In England it took the form of a somewhat self-indulgent romanticism, as shown in Holloway's *Clarissa* and Maw's *Odyssey*. In America it took the form of 'traditional folk music' in the hands of Michael Smith (*The Grapes of Wrath*) and Stephen Sondheim (*Sunday in the Park with George*). The incorporation of folk and church melodies greatly strengthened the idiom of Arvo Pärt, while his fellow-Estonian, the late Eduard Tubin, pursued a similar path with comparable success. In 1990 he earned posthumous recognition with the issue of seven compact discs (CDs) of his music—a unique case of a composer's work being rescued by the record industry.

Generally speaking the record industry proved a barometer of public taste in 1990. The endless stream of familiar classics, American music, early music, opera, stage musicals, and the re-issue on CDs of legendary performances from the past, such as RCA's recordings of Toscanini, made up the year's work. The death of Leonard Bernstein led to the issue of 25 CDs by Deutsche Grammophon, taken from concerts given by him since 1977.

The pop/rock world saw in 1990, as Dr Ben Green has said, a grassroots swing to the 1960s, as a reaction against the primitive repetition of rap, dub and sampling techniques that produced such derivative plagiarisms as *Ice Baby*. Record companies released a gamut of original back-material. Paul McCartney undertook a massive world tour, playing new material and, for the first time, reprising songs by The Beatles. He played some 102 concerts to 2,742,000 people, and established a world record for a stadium concert, in Rio de Janeiro, where his audience numbered 184,000.

Madonna, whose songs reflected a paradoxical mixture of Catholic symbolism and overt sexuality, continued to shock with her *Blond Ambition* tour. Although the media revelled in displaying their moral outrage, others began to suspect that a more subtle message transcended other imagery, in such songs as *Like a Prayer* and *Vogue*. Since 1983 she had sold some 30 million records, and in America her run of sixteen consecutive Top Five singles broke the Beatles' earlier record. As for other new material in 1990, the Prefab Sprout album, *Jordan–The Comeback*, moulded such diverse themes as the Gospels, the Beach Boys and Atlantis into a tightly-produced lyrical disc whose originality shone out strongly from the darkness of the rest of the year's offerings.

Among those who died in 1990 were the two foremost American composers Aaron Copland and Leonard Bernstein, the cellist Paul Tortelier, the singer Dame Eva Turner and the Italian composer Luigi Nono (see OBITUARY).

BOOKS OF THE YEAR. *Brahms* by Malcolm Macdonald; *Gustav Holst* by Michael Short; *The Apollonian Clockwork on Stravinsky* by Louis Andriessen and Elmer Schonberger; *Gesualdo* by Glenn Watkins; *Rachmaninov* by Barrie Martyn; *Rock Music* by Peter Wicke; *Berlioz* by D. Kern Holoman.

DANCE/BALLET

THE year was memorable for fine performances of fine ballets, superb dancing in both the classical and contemporary fields, the exhilarating presence of Soviet dancers as guests with both American and British companies—and a woeful record of new choreography.

The Royal Ballet (RB) at Covent Garden, continuing its celebrations of the 60th birthday of Sir Kenneth MacMillan, gave more performances of his *Prince of the Pagodas*—in which Nina Ananiashvili and Alexei Fadeyechev of the Bolshoi Ballet tackled their first MacMillan choreography with notable success—and revivals of such beautiful and poignant works as *Gloria* and *The Song of the Earth*. In his *Romeo and Juliet*, the French ballerina and star, Sylvie Guillem, a permanent guest artist with the RB, danced a sensitive Juliet and came the nearest yet to integrating fully with the company. Full evening ballets, including Makarova's staging of *La Bayadère*, continued to dominate the repertory (and the box office) but gave opportunities to many dancers in the major roles. The young generation of RB dancers being nurtured by director Anthony Dowell fulfilled his faith: Darcey Bussell, Viviana Durante, Deborah Bull, Dana Fouras, Errol Pickford, Bruce Sansom and Stuart Cassidy all made great progress. Other welcome guests from abroad were Altynai Asylmuratova and Konstantin Zaklinsky from the Kirov in Leningrad, and Laurent Hilaire from the Paris Opéra.

The RB had one magnificent acquisition for the repertory in Balanchine's *Stravinsky Violin Concerto*, immaculately staged and very well danced; and one harbinger for early 1991 when MacMillan made the Farewell pas de deux from *Winter Dreams* for Darcey Bussell (his *Pagodas* heroine) and Irek Mukhamedov, formerly a hero of the Bolshoi Ballet and now a member of the RB—resident in London and on a five-year contract.

Two new ballets, David Bintley's *The Planets* (Holst) and Ashley

Page's *Bloodlines*, were near-disasters—both choreographically undistinguished and overwhelmed by powerful but omnipresent designs by, respectively, Ralph Koltai and Deanna Petherbridge. There was some concern about the state of the Ashton repertory and a lot of concern about musical standards. When conductors such as Mark Ermler and, supremely, Bernard Haitink took charge the orchestra responded to them. By the end of 1990 neither of the RB companies had a musical director.

Sadler's Wells Royal Ballet, under that name, had a triumphant tour of New Zealand but its finest hour came in October when, re-named the Birmingham Royal Ballet (BRB) and relocated in Birmingham, the company took up residence in that city. The city council had financed the new buildings behind the Hippodrome theatre, specifically designed for a dance company, to the tune of over £4 million. While London continued to moan about the lack of a dance house, Birmingham acted. The company, which danced Balanchine choreography so well, added another of his works to the repertory for this first season—Stravinsky's *Symphony in Three Movements*. The BRB also had fine stagings of *Swan Lake* and *The Sleeping Beauty*, which looked so well on the big Hippodrome stage, and succeeded in sustaining a more varied repertory of triple bills than did the considerably larger troupe at Covent Garden. The initial October season was followed at Christmas by a new production of *The Nutcracker* by Peter Wright, designed by John Macfarlane, which was sold out before it even opened. Wright's master-minding of the whole operation of relocation had been superb. The move to Birmingham, to a permanent regional base for Britain's national ballet, was the most significant event in its history since Dame Ninette de Valois took her Sadler's Wells Ballet into the Royal Opera House, Covent Garden, in 1946.

English National Ballet (formerly Festival Ballet) sacked its director Peter Schaufuss and appointed in his stead the Hungarian Ivan Nagy—who had a distinguished career as a dancer with American Ballet Theatre and had since worked in Cincinnati. The year was one of confusion and transition. Nagy engaged many new dancers—hardly any of them English—and the London summer season was saved by guest artists Eva Evdokimova and Trinidad Sevillano returning to the company to give superb dramatic readings of, respectively, Tatiana in *Onegin* and the title role in *Anastasia*.

Rambert Dance Company acquired another masterwork by Merce Cunningham, *Doubles*, together with its simple, beautiful designs by Mark Lancaster. In other works Rambert leaned too far towards fashion. The trend in fashion design, so well begun by Victor Edelstein in *Rhapsody in Blue*, was pushed too far by John Galliano (for Ashley Page's *Currulao*) and English Eccentrics (for Richard Alston's *Dealing with Shadows*). London Contemporary Dance Theatre by the end of the year had not found a successor to Dan Wagoner (who was returning to New York) but he had left the company in wonderful dancing shape, dominated by the young generation. In Kim Brandstrup they had a choreographer of real potential—and a tour to Russia was an immense success.

Among smaller companies, Lloyd Newsom of DV8 followed his *Dead Dreams of Monochrome Men* (which had won many international television awards) with *If Only . . .* , in which Wendy Houstoun was outstanding. Adventures in Motion Pictures, Rosemary Butcher, The Cholmondeleys, and Laurie Booth maintained a faithful following although statistics showed that attendances at contemporary dance companies were smaller than at the ubiquitous 'classics' in the ballet repertory. Dance Umbrella once again provided a showcase for new work while at The Place Theatre John Ashford had created a true dance house. In seasons like Spring Loaded, Indian Summer and The Turning World he welcomed innumerable groups, from home and overseas, to show their wares. In the regions, the Derngate in Northampton presented Miami City Ballet; Bradford presented the Alvin Ailey Dance Theatre (still superb, even after the loss of its founder); and Glasgow showed the Stuttgart Ballet in John Neumeier's *A Streetcar Named Desire*.

Pride of place among visiting companies, however, went to the Kirov Ballet, which brought a conventional repertory but a galaxy of new talent. Larissa Lezhnina, Yulia Makhalina, Veronika Ivanova and Yelena Pankova; Alexander Lunyov, Kirill Melnikov and Igor Zelensky all seemed poised to inherit the great roles (many of which they already danced). The Kirov corps de ballet remained peerless in the world today.

American Ballet Theatre (ABT), celebrating its 50th anniversary, came to the London Coliseum for an all too short week. Still sustained by the work Baryshnikov did for the company before he left, the company was in fine form. *Drink To Me Only With Thine Eyes* gave London first sight on stage of a large-scale Mark Morris work (his *Hidden Soul of Harmony* television programme had introduced other beautiful choreography and the man himself) and confirmed his international reputation as one of the most important creators of today. A surprise and a delight was the way in which Farouk Ruzimatov, from the Kirov, gave an outrageous but irresistible comedy performance as the Peruvian in Massine's *Gaieté Parisienne*. (He left the ABT later in the year to return to Leningrad).

In the United States, New York City Ballet sustained its high level of performance and its School of American Ballet acquired new, residential premises in New York. The Paul Taylor Dance Company continued to produce new work—as did Martha Graham at the age of 96! The San Francisco Ballet staged a new *Sleeping Beauty* and the Tulsa

Ballet revived Fokine's *Paganini*. In Oakland, an ambitious and lively reconstruction was achieved of the 1920s Cocteau ballet for Diaghilev, *Le Train Bleu*.

Merce Cunningham showed no sign of reducing his choreographic output or of any decline in creativity, although he now restricted his actual stage performances. He took his company to India for a tour of enrichment for both dancers and audiences. In Paris, Patrick Dupond made a good start as director of the Paris Opéra Ballet, succeeding Nureyev. MacMillan produced his *Manon* there and for the first time enjoyed the success that had previously eluded him in Paris. The Royal Danish Ballet, still under the direction of Frank Andersen, reconstructed an old Bournonville ballet, *The Lay of Thrym*, through the researches of Elsa Marianne von Rosen and Allan Fridericia. The Queen of Denmark agreed to design a new production of Bournonville's *A Folk Tale* for the next season.

Losses sustained by the dance world included Boris Kochno, poet, ballet librettist and one time secretary to Serge Diaghilev; Dame Peggy van Praagh, dancer, teacher and architect of the Australian Ballet (see OBITUARY); Margaret Craske, eminent teacher and guardian of the precepts of Maestro Cecchetti; Ashley Lawrence, internationally-renowned conductor for ballet; Angus McBean, doyen of photographers; Professor K. H. Taubert, great authority on historical dances; Robin Duff, president of Scottish Ballet; Alfonso Catá; director of the Ballet du Nord at Roubaix; and Mama Lu Parks, saviour of the Lindy Hop.

BOOKS OF THE YEAR. *A Century of Russian Ballet, Documents and Eyewitness Accounts, 1810–1910* by Roland John Wiley; *World Ballet and Dance, Volume I* edited by Bent Schønberg; *Folk Dance of Europe* by Nigel Allenby Jaffé; *The Black Tradition in American Dance* by Richard A. Long; *Soviet Choreographers in the 1920s* by Elizabeth Souritz; *Ballets Suédois* by Bengt Hager.

THEATRE

FROM year to year different plays by Shakespeare dominate the repertory. After 1988, the year of *The Tempest*, and 1989, the year of *Hamlet*, it was the turn of *King Lear* in 1990, when both the National Theatre (NT) and the Royal Shakespeare Company (RSC), as well as Kenneth Branagh's Renaissance Theatre Company, chose to mount productions of Shakespeare's greatest tragedy. The RSC's version was the first to be seen; but, saddled with elegantly-clinical stage design, it was about as far removed from the spirit of this poetic and turbulent drama as it is possible to be, and with Lear played (by John Wood) as an actorish bully, casually modern in diction and never in any danger of going mad, it was easily eclipsed by its two rivals.

At the NT, Brian Cox's Lear appeared completely demented from the very first scene, in a production by Deborah Warner which in all other respects dealt intelligently and sensitively with the play. By far the most impressive of the three Lears was Richard Briers in Kenneth Branagh's touring production for his own Renaissance Company. Briers made the tempest in the king's mind as real as the storm outside, his very being smelled of mortality, and at the end he slipped away from life easily but most affectingly. The company did almost equally well by Shakespeare with *A Midsummer Night's Dream* in which Branagh, a moving Edgar in *King Lear*, clearly enjoyed himself as that quintessential directorial figure, Peter Quince.

During the year, surveys, polls and reports on the state of the theatre continued to proliferate and to send out their conflicting messages. Subsidized theatres throughout the country went on complaining of the inadequacy of public funding, and even some commercial managements began to clamber aboard that particular bandwagon. A report by the Policy Studies Institute produced the not very startling information that Shakespeare remained the most frequently performed playwright in Great Britain, followed closely by Alan Ayckbourn and Arthur Miller. According to the same report, annual attendance figures for West End theatres increased from 8.1 million at the beginning of the decade to 10.9 million in 1990.

Revivals dominated the year. These included not only such well-known but infrequently-performed classics as Ibsen's *When We Dead Awaken*, Pirandello's *Henry IV* or Molière's *Tartuffe*, but also a number of obscure yet enjoyable pieces such as Lope de Vega's *Punishment Without Revenge*, enterprisingly staged at the tiny Gate Theatre, Corneille's *The Illusion*, and Isaak Babel's *Marya*, both at the Old Vic where Jonathan Miller's idiosyncratic guiding hand would surely be missed in 1991. (Dr Miller resigned as the Old Vic's artistic director when his season was truncated at short notice by the theatre's owner and backer.) One or two very fine plays from the earlier years of the twentieth century were revived, plays from the era when 'well-made' was not a term of denigration. Terence Rattigan's *Flare Path*, at the adventurous King's Head Theatre, stood up well, and London could have done with more J. B. Priestley and Noël Coward than *Time and the Conways* (Old Vic) and *Private Lives* (Aldwych), the former play dominated by Joan Plowright, and the latter giving Joan Collins a chance to demonstrate that she could articulate the elegant wit of Coward as effectively as the anodyne dialogue of the TV soap opera in which she had been imprisoned for several years.

The revival of *Tartuffe*, a production mounted by the NT's education department for touring, proved to be an exotic collector's item. Adapted by Jatinder Verma as a piece of Hindi theatre, and performed by an all-Asian cast, it was set in 17th-century India at the time of the Mogul

Emperor Aurangzeb, and opened with the arrival at the emperor's court of a French traveller, for whose delectation a performance of Molière's play is staged. This asiaticised Molière, a serendipitous blend of cultures and styles, worked extremely well, for the play's theme of hypocrisy preying on gullibility was universal, and by no means confined to Molière's own century.

The NT's only Shakespeare production, apart from *King Lear*, was *Richard III*, turned into a fashionable attempt to drag the bard kicking and screaming into the twentieth century. Richard Eyre's staging alienated those who took *Richard III* seriously, not as one of Shakespeare's greatest plays but as a splendid piece of poetic melodrama, a superb concerto for solo actor and company, and a highly entertaining example of Shakespearian comic-strip history. In his performance of the title-role, Ian McKellen's characterization contrived to encompass a large number of well-known people. His Richard became Adolf Hitler in black shirt and jackboots, or possibly Doctor Strangelove, the actor's arm taking unilateral action in a Nazi salute. Joyce Redman's Duchess of York moved sartorially from the style of the present Queen Mother to that of Queen Mary. George V was present, too, in the person of Brian Cox's Buckingham. Sadly, few of these contemporary references made much sense.

For its Christmas attraction, the NT commissioned from Alan Bennett a new adaptation of Kenneth Grahame's *The Wind in the Willows*, already highly popular on the stage in the A. A. Milne version, *Toad of Toad Hall*. Bennett sprinkled a few grains of verbal sophistication over Grahame's whimsical story while Mark Thompson's decor made spectacular use of the resources of the Olivier Theatre's stage.

The NT fared rather poorly with new plays. Its best by far was David Hare's *Racing Demon*, concerned with the problems facing a team of priests in a south London parish whose dwindling congregation consisted largely of Jamaicans. The fierce debate within the Church, as seen by Hare, was between humanists and fundamentalists. Some of Hare's ecclesiastical jokes, though old, were funny; his clergymen tended to be much wittier and more eloquent than their counterparts in real life. David Edgar's *The Shape of the Table*, one of several plays thrown up by recent events in Eastern Europe, consisted entirely of meetings at which an unspecified country's new constitution was being hammered out. An example of theatrical politics rather than political theatre, it attempted half-heartedly to suggest that what failed in Eastern Europe was not a political system but simply the fallible human beings who ran it.

In strong contrast to this was Brian Friel's *Dancing at Lughnasa*, a sensitive evocation of childhood in Ireland, which fell uncomfortably between the two genres of novel and play. Athol Fugard's *My Children! My Africa!* was hardly a play at all, but a dramatised tract, using as its theme the relationship between an amiable, foolish, Europeanized black teacher and his teenage protegé whom the teacher's methods, irrelevant and dictatorial, inevitably drive into the clutches of militants.

Once in a While the Odd Thing Happens by Paul Godfrey was a twee exercise in biographical theatre, dealing with events in the life of Benjamin Britten, spanning the later stages of the composer's friendship with W. H. Auden and the beginnings of his relationship with Peter Pears, the tenor for whom Britten wrote so much of his later music. Godfrey's characters were conceived as poetic ciphers who sometimes talked in a verse bordering on doggerel but who for the most part restricted themselves to an opaque utterance striving all too obviously, but in vain, for significance.

Tony Harrison's *The Trackers of Oxyrhynchus* told the story of two British papyrologists who, scrabbling about in the desert in 1907, discovered fragments of a satyr-play by Sophocles. Harrison incorporated the fragments into his fantasy in which he used Sophocles to support a theory about the modern division between high and low art. His verse seemed hastily written, and his own production of his play was not only highly pretentious but also made tendentious use of the plight of the homeless living in cardboard cartons only a few hundred yards from the theatre.

By far the most interesting new play presented by the National Theatre—new at least to Great Britain—was Arthur Miller's crypto-autobiographical *After the Fall*. His most parochially American play to date, it offered as its narrator a man whose obsession with his own moral purity, whose agonies of conscience, and even whose verbosity were presented as those of Everyman, though they were all too clearly no more than the attributes of an extremely self-absorbed Arthur Miller. But the play could hardly have been more impressively staged than by Michael Blakemore, and its cast was exemplary, James Laurenson investing the narrator with a welcome charm and Josette Simon brilliantly portraying Wife No 2's descent into drugs, drink and viciousness.

This was Terry Hands' last full year as artistic director of the RSC and in February it was announced that a successor, Adrian Noble, had been found from within the company. A distinct cut above the average RSC director, Noble was certainly competent and, equally important, respectful in his attitude to Shakespeare. Given Noble's known dislike of the Barbican Theatre, the company's London base, it was likely that Terry Hands was being somewhat disingenuous in stating that an inadequate Arts Council grant was the reason for the RSC's decision to withdraw from the Barbican for four months in the winter. It might well be that Noble insisted on a move away from that venue as one of his conditions for accepting the post.

The RSC's final production at the Barbican was *Moscow Gold*, a dutiful plod through recent Soviet history by Tariq Ali and Howard

Brenton. Earlier in the year it had mounted a dismal and disspirited production (by John Caird) of *As You Like It* and, having had some success in previous years with plays by Gorky, had scraped the bottom of the Gorky barrel to come up with *Barbarians*, an unwieldy piece of mock-Chekhov. Stratford fared better with a delightful staging of *Love's Labour's Lost* by Terry Hands, beautifully designed by Timothy O'Brien, and *Richard II* in which Alex Jennings (excellent, earlier in the year, as Hjalmar in Peter Hall's commercial production of Ibsen's *The Wild Duck*) brought the complex character of King Richard to life more completely than any of his predecessors in recent years.

The commercial theatre fared better than the subsidized companies in the matter of new plays. There were, admittedly, a large number of pointless imports, mainly from the United States, among them *Other People's Money*, a simple piece about the attempts of a Wall Street corporate raider to take over a small family-run firm in New England, and *Vanilla*, an embarrassingly unfunny slice of social satire, directed (surprisingly) by Harold Pinter. A. R. Gurney's trite *Love Letters* failed to find an audience, but Alan Ayckbourn's latest play, *Man of the Moment*, a stinging comedy about the false values of the news media, represented Britain's finest serious-comic dramatist at somewhere very near his best.

Simon Gray returned to the West End with *Hidden Laughter*, his best new play for years. He was well served by his cast, especially by Peter Barkworth's virtuoso performance as an engagingly agnostic Church of England vicar. Gray and Ayckbourn wrote comedies, while Ray Cooney's genre was that of farce. Verbal wit might not be Cooney's forte, but hilarious situations certainly were, and *Out of Order* exploited a huge number of them, with Donald Sinden and Michael Williams proving (not for the first time) to be superb farceurs.

Dreadful musicals are always to be found in abundance, and 1990 produced at least four. In tactful chronological order, they were Anthony Burgess's *A Clockwork Orange* (Burgess was not responsible for its vapid score), Petula Clark's *Someone Like You*, *Bernadette* by Gwyn and Maureen Hughes, and Stephen Schwartz's romp through the Old Testament, *Children of Eden*. Much better were two Stephen Sondheim shows new to Britain, *Sunday in the Park with George* and *Into the Woods*, though both were flawed by their librettist, James Lapine. By far the most enjoyable musical was *Five Guys Named Moe*, which Clarke Peters concocted around the music of Louis Jordan, a black American entertainer of the forties. It opened at the Theatre Royal, in the London suburb of Stratford East, but soon moved to the West End.

NEW YORK THEATRE. Though the influential critic of the *New York Times* described Andrew Lloyd Webber's *Aspects of Love* as the most boring musical of the season, it survived, whereas 'the second most boring musical', *Shogun*, did not. Musicals dominated the Broadway scene as usual, but the most unusual of them, *Falsettoland* by William Finn and James Lapine, which dealt with AIDS, originated in an Off-Broadway theatre. One of its highlights was a barmitzvah in the hospital room of a man dying of the disease. Towards the end of the year, *Buddy*, a show about the rock musician Buddy Holly which was so successful in London, seemed unlikely to repeat that success in New York.

The number of new plays to be seen on Broadway was depressingly low, but four of them were of compensatingly high quality. From London came Maggie Smith in Peter Shaffer's delightful *Lettice and Lovage*, but the other three plays were by American playwrights. John Guare's *Six Degrees of Separation* was a gentle comedy about race, class, money, imagination and much else, with Stockard Channing in the leading role; *The Piano Lesson* was the latest in August Wilson's series of plays about life for black Americans in the twentieth century; and *Prelude to a Kiss* dealt sympathetically and movingly with love and death. Encouragingly, all of these plays were still running at the end of the year, though at any given moment there were always too many dark theatres on Broadway.

CINEMA

THE year 1990 was the second most successful in the history of Hollywood—at least as far as box-office returns were concerned. But if quality rather than popularity was the criterion, no such record could be claimed. The world's most dominating film culture produced few outstanding movies. And it would certainly be true to say that, in this, the rest of the world followed suit. It was not so much a bad year for films as rather a predictable one during which commercial considerations seemed to come first, possibly the entertainment parallel to the consumer society.

It was predictable, for instance, that Hollywood's major companies would look at the huge receipts gathered up throughout the world by *Batman* in 1989 and instruct their film-makers to go and do likewise. The result was a series of expensive and expansive epics that got in each other's way at the box-office and eventually failed to do the same scale of business. *Dick Tracy, Total Recall, Back to the Future III, Die Hard II, Gremlins II, Robocop II, Days of Thunder* and others, mostly clinging to the coat-tails of previous successes, were finally beaten in the popularity stakes by two much smaller scale romantic fantasies, *Pretty Woman* and *Ghost*, and also by the independently-made children's film *Teenage Mutant Ninja Turtles*. Added to this, the 1990 Academy Award for Best Film went not to an expensive production but to Bruce Beresford's touching but lightweight *Driving Miss Daisy*, the story of a cantankerous old Jewish woman and her black chauffeur in the racist South of the sixties. None of these films could be accorded the status of works that would live very long in the memory, but Warren Beatty's *Dick Tracy* at least had the benefit of superb production values and Paul Verhoeven's *Total Recall*, starring the monolithic Arnold Schwarzenegger, leavened its violence with some real imagination in its making.

The outstanding quality inherent in the American cinema, however, was provided by Oliver Stone's *Born on the Fourth of July*, a striking Vietnam parable which proved that Tom Cruise, playing the crippled and disillusioned veteran Ron Kovic, was an actor as well as a star; Woody Allen's *Crimes and Misdemeanours*, in which Allen attempted very successfully to marry a serious theme with good ironic comedy; and perhaps most of forcibly of all by Martin Scorsese's *GoodFellas*, a chilling but superbly directed and played gangster film culled from the director's own memories of his streetwise New York youth.

These and a few other films such as David Lynch's *Wild At Heart* (the Cannes Festival winner), an equally brilliant follow-up to the audacious *Blue Velvet*, Danny DeVito's *War of the Roses*, a black and brackish comedy about the institution of marriage, and Whit Stillman's *Metropolitan*, a debut of some distinction about the hopes and fears of youth, proved beyond question that America could still make films that treated its audiences like adults rather than overgrown children.

But if Hollywood was still clearly alive and well, most of Tinsel City was no longer owned by Americans. Only Paramount, Walt Disney and Warner Bros now remained in American hands. In 1990, Giancarlo Parretti, an Italian entrepreneur, bought up the financially-embarrassed remains of MGM/UA, and a Japanese conglomerate, Matsushita Electric Industries, subsumed Universal by acquiring its parent company MCA. No one could forecast what the results of this wholesale change of ownership were likely to be. But they might not be very dramatic until Hollywood ceased to make hit films. And that day clearly had not arrived yet.

Hollywood's dominance of other world markets, which it surely deserved as a well-oiled story-telling factory, hype-merchant and creator of stars, had finally awoken the European cinema, including that of Britain, to the dangers of such cultural domination. As yet, there was more rhetoric than action. But the formation of a European Film Society in an attempt to publicize European cinema with a set of European Film Awards (first mounted in Berlin in 1988) was at least a first step. There were other plans afoot, from both within and outside the EEC, to create more favourable conditions for the financing and exhibition of other than Hollywood films. There was a general determination to do something before the once state-subsidized film-producing centres of Eastern Europe were totally destroyed and there were still such animals as genuinely Hungarian, Polish and Czech films.

The hope was that co-production would finally be the answer, but not of 'Euro-pudding movies' so much as national films of some international appeal. No one expected such productions to beat Hollywood at its own game. It was thought certain, however, that a substantial minority of film-goers would not want their own film cultures to die from neglect. In Britain for instance, which had a disastrous year for film production owing largely to a chronic lack of investment, a deputation of prominent members of the industry met the Prime Minister, Mrs Thatcher, to plead if not for subsidy then at least some form of bait with which to hook investors. The meeting was pronounced a success, Mrs Thatcher lending a sympathetic ear for the first time for a decade, but her resignation left a promising situation looking less tenable, particularly during a period of recession.

Even so, British films that were produced gained their share of awards. Daniel Day-Lewis won the Best Actor Oscar for his performance as the palsy victim in *My Left Foot*, and Kenneth Branagh won the Best European Actor award as *Henry V* in his own version of the Shakespeare play. The film itself won the prize for the Best Young European Film. Added to that, several other British films did well in the US market, including Michael Caton Jones' *Memphis Belle*, produced in Britain with an American cast by David Puttnam, Peter Greenaway's *The Cook, the Thief, His Wife and Her Lover* and Jonathan Lynn's comedy *Nuns on the Run*. It was also cheering that just under 100 million people went to the cinema in Britain during the year—the best figure for a decade. The worst figure was 70 million in 1985. This, however, was more a reflection of the success of American films rather than of home product.

In France, considered to be the strongest European nation cinematically, 70 million customers had been lost during the same period. But the situation was still more favourable as far as production was concerned since the French government protected its film industry lovingly. It made at least one international success during the year—Jean Paul Rappeneau's *Cyrano de Bergerac*, in which Gérard Depardieu played Rostand's long-nosed hero almost to perfection. Otherwise, the French cinema ticked over rather than covered itself with glory, and it was noted with some concern that, even in France, America now controlled 60 per cent of the product shown in the cinemas. The figure was around 98 per cent for Britain.

Both Germany, now united, and Italy, had graver difficulties, though Italy's *Porte Aperte* (Open Doors) won the European equivalent of the Best Film Oscar and Guiseppe Tornatore's *Cinema Pardiso* won the Hollywood Oscar for Best Foreign Film. There were signs that the long deterioration in the Italian cinema had been halted by some promising work from younger directors. Scandinavia, also beset with money problems, produced very little of real note, though Aki Kaurismaki, the prolific young Finnish director, continued to add to his reputation with *The Match Factory Girl* and a film made in Britain, *I Hired a Contract Killer*. The other young European director to prosper internationally was Pedro Almodovar of Spain whose *Tie Me Up, Tie Me Down!* proved a box-office success much further afield than Spain. The Soviet cinema, free of previous constraints but also short of funds, continued to produce some internationally admired films, including the oddly titled *Lie Still, Die, Revive* and *The Asthenic Syndrome*, both of which won Festival awards.

Other countries and continents came up with one or two films of special merit, without suggesting that their industries were prospering. Canada contributed *Jesus of Montreal* by Denys Arcand, the most successful French-Canadian film ever, and African film was graced by Idrissa Ouedraogo of Burkina Faso whose fine *Yaaba* was followed at the Cannes Festival by the equally impressive *Tilai*. Both these films were supported with European money but were totally African in style and outlook. The first Sino-Japanese co-production for many years, *Jou Dou*, was one of the year's most admired films from the East.

From India, *Shaji's Piravi (The Birth)*, was deservedly sold to many countries, and was followed by Adoor Gopalakrishnan's *The Walls*, also from the southern state of Kerala and an equally good example of what is known as the Parallel Indian Cinema. Satyajit Ray, India's best-known film-maker, followed his Ibsen adaptation, *Enemy of the People*, with *Branches of a Tree*, a family saga made with French funds and co-produced by Gérard Depardieu. After six years of inactivity owing to illness, he was now making a third film in his home state of Bengal.

Few offerings from the Chinese cinema reached the West, largely because of political problems. A few quality Latin American films surfaced at film festivals, suggesting that the financial constraints and political problems of much of that continent were not now as insuperable as during much of the eighties. But the sad fact remained that only the American cinema really prospered during the year, finding enough money occasionally to help an outstanding world figure such as Akira Kurosawa of Japan whose *Dreams*, a group of short stories on the general state of the world, unfortunately proved one of his lesser works. This is a situation about which nobody was happy, since there was now hardly a country in the world that did not make films but only a very few who could be confident of the outcome. Only India's vast commercial output could beat Hollywood in its own territory.

Among notable performers who died during the year were Greta Garbo, Capucine, Sammy Davis Jr, Aldo Fabrizi, Ava Gardner, Paulette Goddard, Rex Harrison, Jill Ireland, Arthur Kennedy, Silvano Mangano, Barbara Stanwyck, Terry-Thomas, and Max Wall. Film-makers included Dimitri De Grunwald (producer), Michael Powell, Martin Ritt, Jim Henson and V. Shantaram. (For Garbo, Davis, Fabrizi, Gardner, Goddard, Harrison, Stanwyck, Wall, Powell and Henson, see OBITUARY.)

TELEVISION & RADIO

IN broadcasting it was the year of CNN—Ted Turner's Cable News Network. When it was launched in 1980 the 24-hour-a-day television news channel based in Atlanta, Georgia, was called 'Chicken Noodle News'. Its performance in the Gulf crisis enabled it to put such disparaging nicknames behind it.

In the hostage crisis in Iraq, when President Saddam Husain for a time flaunted a 'human shield' policy, the most memorable image was carried live on CNN. It was the Iraqi leader's counter-productive attempt to present a human face by going on television with a rather frightened little boy called Stuart Lockwood from England. But CNN's role in the Gulf crisis was much more fundamental than that. Sir David Nicholas, chairman of Britain's Independent Television News (ITN), said CNN's coverage had become a 'diplomatic weapon' in the crisis. President Bush and President Saddam Husain were simultaneously watching each other's moves live through the medium of satellite television. According to one report, a CNN team was even allowed to fly in an American F-15 warplane and film its radar and weapons system, so that an obvious message on military might could be sent to Iraq. The Iraqi President in turn sent back news of his 'human shield', until that policy was abandoned at the end of the year.

CNN ended 1990 with its power and influence at a new high. The same could not be said of all broadcasting and media organizations, as some of the more grandiose hopes for the expansion of the electronic media came up against financial reality and the worst advertising recession for more than a decade. The most dramatic symptom of the new sense of reality was the unexpected merger of Britain's satellite television rivals, British Satellite Broadcasting (BSB) and Rupert Murdoch's Sky Television, after weeks of secret talks.

The two groups had spent hundreds of millions of pounds striving for pre-eminence, if not outright victory in the satellite television battle. In the early hours of 3 November they decided that 50 per cent each of a potentially profitable venture was more interesting than separate businesses facing serious losses for the foreseeable future. As Frank Barlow, chief operating officer of Pearson (one of the main BSB shareholders), put it: 'Two bad businesses will make one marvellous business.' Together the two groups had so far invested a total of £1,250 million, most of it by BSB.

At the time of the merger Sky Television claimed to be in 1.6 million homes in the UK and Ireland, via individual dishes and cable television networks, but was still losing £10 million a month. After technical delays BSB had finally launched its five-channel service in April. By the beginning of November the service could be seen in 750,000 homes, although only 120,000 of that total got pictures direct through diamond-shaped 'squarials'. For the BSB investors the crunch point was approaching, there being no chance of meeting the Christmas target of 400,000 installed 'squarials'. The view was taken that there was a 'window of opportunity' to get a good deal with Mr Murdoch, who was himself under pressure from his bankers to reduce his debts of more than $7,000 million.

In financial terms the deal was a merger between near equals. In terms of programme style, technology and staff, it was a complete takeover by Sky. The merger also marked the effective end of BSB's sophisticated D-MAC technology and the triumph of the simpler PAL standard used by Mr Murdoch. By the end of the year, according to Continental Research, a total of 1,278,000 homes were receiving satellite channels direct from space.

The merger caused a fierce regulatory row. The BSB partners had not told the Independent Broadcasting Authority (IBA) of their plans and the latter threatened to cancel the BSB licence on the grounds that it had been breached by the merger. More seriously, the IBA hinted that it had the power to refuse a 'non-domestic' satellite licence for the new merged company British Sky Broadcasting, to broadcast from the Astra satellite system used by Sky. In the end, a deal was struck under which BSkyB would continue to broadcast on both the BSB and Astra satellites for up to two years (so that no-one would lose their service). In the meantime, the IBA would look for new uses for the BSB satellites—probably specialist services such as education or television for ethnic minorities. A fully-combined five-channel service was planned for April 1991 after the launch of a second Astra satellite, which would also double the number of satellite television channels available in the UK to 32.

The Cable Authority completed its work by awarding cable television franchises covering 60 per cent of the country, and the body was rolled up into the new Independent Television Commission (ITC), successor to the IBA. A large majority of the franchises went to American cable and telephone companies. The cable companies were given a further boost by the government's review of the telecommunications 'duopoly', under which they were likely in future to be able to run their own telephone services in competition with British Telecom and Mercury Communications. It was less clear how quickly the vast investment needed to cable Britain would be forthcoming.

The government's Broadcasting Bill, nearly five years in the planning, finally reached the statute book, much modified from the original green and white papers which had promised a substantial opening-up of commercial broadcasting in the UK to market forces. The concept that commercial television licences would in most cases be awarded to the highest bidder survived the parliamentary passage of the bill. But significant changes were accepted by the then Home Office minister responsible for broadcasting, David Mellor. Obligations to provide religious and children's programmes were written into the bill. Moreover, the government made explicit, what it always claimed was implicit, that a bid of exceptional quality could be preferred over the highest cash offer.

The method of financial bidding was also simplified under the bill. Instead of having to make a bid to cover the 10 years of the franchise, bidders would have to make an offer only for the first year, with the sum payable to the Treasury in later years being simply indexed to retail prices. More importantly, the ITC felt that the government had given it considerable discretion in drawing up the rules of the new franchises (to be awarded in 1991 and to begin in January 1993). It used this discretion to draw up programme guidelines for bidders, incorporating obligations little different from those facing the ITV companies at the moment.

There was general agreement that a very ideological draft bill had been greatly improved during its passage by realistic compromise. In television, apart from the principle of highest bids, a number of contentious issues remained, however. One was the ending of the list of 'protected' sporting events, such as the FA Cup Final and Wimbledon, which had to be available to all the nation. In future, a minority satellite channel would be able to buy exclusive broadcasting rights to such events. Also controversial was the decision to force the ITV companies to sell off a majority stake in their wholly-owned subsidiary, the ITN news organization. Most controversial of all, under the prompting of peers such as Lord Wyatt, the government wrote into the bill details of what should be included in a code of broadcasting impartiality, requiring the ITC to 'take account of' due impartiality on 'major matters'. Lord Thomson of Monifieth, a former chairman of the IBA, criticized the ITC's acceptance of the final version of the government's rules as 'profoundly mistaken', and warned that the ambiguity involved would lead inevitably to litigation.

The pressure to get costs down in order to fight off opposition bids led to hundreds of job losses in the ITV system. The BBC also came under intensified financial pressure when the government decided to question the licence fee's link with the retail price index. Consultants Price Waterhouse carried out a rapid study for the Home Office and all the signs were that the 1991 BBC licence fee would be significantly below inflation. However, the principle of the licence fee would be maintained at least until the renegotiation of the BBC's royal charter in 1996.

Even without the new squeeze on the licence fee, the BBC had already made it clear that 1,400 jobs would have to go to save £75 million a year by 1993 to pay for the move towards 25 per cent independent programme production and to improve pay for remaining staff. The corporation also said it planned to launch a new service—BBC Select—in September 1991, although delay seemed likely because of the recession. This would be made up of a wide range of subscription services broadcast in scrambled form over normal transmitters in the middle of the night. Special services were planned for doctors, farmers and lawyers, minority groups such as the Irish and Asians, and film or yachting enthusiasts.

Commercial radio began its long-planned expansion during the year. More than 20 stations were set up even before the new Radio Authority opened for business on 1 December. The new authority said it would advertise nearly 30 new local radio licences in 1991, but the main excitement would be competitive tenders for two of the planned three new national commercial radio networks. The government made it known that it favoured one of the new national stations being 'non-pop' and another largely speech-based. Meanwhile, the BBC launched a new national radio channel—Radio 5— to handle sport, education and some current affairs.

In the USA, following the completion of the $13,000 million Time-Warner merger, to create the largest media company in the world, there were further Japanese inroads into the entertainment industry. Matsushita, the Japanese consumer electronics company, paid $6,100 million for MCA, the Hollywood film and television company. The deal meant that four of the seven major US studios were now under foreign ownership. Commercial pressure on the US networks continued, with CBS forecasting a fourth-quarter loss.

In December the first high-definition television sets with sharper, wider pictures went on sale to the Japanese public, but queues were not expected. The sets cost around £15,000 each and the special-format broadcasts were transmitted for only one hour a day. Companies in both Europe and the USA were trying to develop rival high-definition television systems.

In France Canal-Plus, the pay television service based mainly on films and sport, continued to prosper. In 1990 the company reached its target of 3 million subscribers, declared profits of around $160 million and was expanding into other European countries, including Germany, through joint ventures. By contrast, technical problems with France's high-power television satellite system, TDF1 and TDF2, persuaded the government not to invest in a third satellite. Instead, France planned to join with other European countries under the Eutelsat organization to launch three new medium-power satellites, probably by the mid-1990s.

Overall, one of the most remarkable aspects of the year in broadcasting was the continued launch of new private channels. In Spain three new commercial channels got going and began to change the face of Spanish broadcasting. One of the three, Tele-5, was launched on 3 March and beat the Spanish national broadcaster with its inauguration programme. In November the channel took a 40 per cent share of the Spanish audience with the American drama *Twin Peaks*. Half-a-dozen new channels were launched in Japan, covering everything from sports and movies to music, and new pay-channels arrived in Italy and New Zealand. In the USA new television channels planned for 1991 included one devoted entirely to courtroom coverage and another to science fiction. Even more interestingly, a company in Washington state announced in October that it would use techniques of digital compression to squeeze 20 channels into a single satellite transponder. The Skypix service announced that it would be able to offer 80 film channels, making it the equivalent of 'a video shop in the sky'.

As Steven Ross, chairman of Time-Warner, put it in a lecture at the Edinburgh television festival in August, the age of media abundance first predicted 20 years ago had nearly arrived. While there was still some way to go, the television revolution was sweeping everything in its path 'toward both an ever-increasing interdependence of peoples and an ever-greater participation by the individual'.

Chapter 2

ART—ARCHITECTURE—FASHION

ART

IT wasn't boom, it was bust—or so the headlines called the state of the market in the autumn of 1990. Sotheby's and Christie's, the big players, announced substantial redundancies. The *New York Times* simply proclaimed in November that 'the exuberance of the eighties is gone'. Lord Carrington, chairman of Christie's, was reported as saying: 'The bread and butter are there. It's the jam we don't know about.' In *The Independent* newspaper in December, Geraldine Norman reported that 'investors who once inflated the market have now driven it into recession'. Sotheby's own art index, for example, had indicated that prices for Impressionist paintings had risen by 155 per cent between 1987 and 1989; modern paintings (the first half of the 20th century) by 122 per cent; and contemporary art (post-1950) by an unprecedented 195 per cent. It could not go on: and it did not; but Mrs Norman considered that those who were not investors would still be buyers and players, in the less fashionable parts of the market. Even so, the world's most expensive painting was purchased on 15 May by the Japanese tycoon Ryoei Saito, who bought Van Gogh's portrait of *Dr Gachet* at Christie's New York for £49.5 million. Later the same week Mr Saito also bought Renoir's *Au Moulin de la Gallette* at Sotheby's New York for £46.5 million, the second highest sum ever paid for a painting sold at auction.

Despite these particular records everyone piled in to say the greedy 1980s were over. The euphoria over political events in Eastern Europe clouded a little as the complications of extraordinary cultural ramifications began to become apparent. How were the German museums to attempt some form of rationalization, particularly in what had been East and West Berlin? How would the Eastern bloc in general face up to the dismantling of government backing of cultural institutions? In the West, however, it was exhibition business as usual, with a glorious year for shows, gallery refurbishments, and new installations of existing collections.

Glasgow was European City of Culture in 1990, and the resulting enormous cultural programme had several bonuses for the visual arts. The Burrell initiated a significant series of exhibitions, mostly concerned with art near the end of the 19th century and culminating in a fascinating exhibition of The Age of Van Gogh: Dutch Painting 1880–95. The McLellan Galleries in the centre of Glasgow were restored to their original Victorian function as working art galleries, but opened to enormous controversy with a South Bank–sponsored British Art Show; this was promoted as the most innovative and interesting contemporary British art, but many commentators found it both dreary and pretentious. Julian Spalding, the controversial head of the Glasgow art galleries, riposted with a show called The Great British Art Show, and a nice, acrimonious time was had by all.

Edinburgh had a wonderful year, too, although 1990 ended with rumours flying about the imminent closure of the Fruitmarket, which had had a superb—and unique—showing of the showing of the sculpture of Max Ernst during the festival. Pride of place went to the remarkable Cézanne and Poussin: The Classical Vision of Landscape, a major exhibition at the National Gallery in Edinburgh, which compared the landscapes of the 17th and 19th century masters of the French School, after Cézanne's oft-quoted remark that he wished to re-do nature after Poussin. Whatever spectators thought of the thesis, many beautiful paintings were gathered together for the occasion, again unique to Edinburgh. Moreover, Edinburgh reported a huge surge in attendances: double the figures recorded in 1980, 100,000 more than 1989, for a total of 808,803.

The Dutch painter Vincent van Gogh (1853–90) had an international season for the centenary anniversary of his self-inflicted death. The Netherlands hosted a major exhibition from March until 29 July, the actual date of his demise, with drawings at the Kröller Müller,

Otterlo, and paintings at the Rijksmuseum Van Gogh. Admission was only by pre-bought ticket, and a complicated system of international ticket purchase was initiated. The Rijksmuseum Van Gogh had, all in all, a scintillating year, following up the retrospective with a show devoted to Émile Bernard, and finally Van Gogh and Modern Art, a fascinating exploration of Van Gogh and his near contemporaries, such as Kandinsky. The other major event in Holland's art year was an inclusive showing of El Lissitzky, from Russian and Dutch sources in the main, at the van Abbe museum, Eindhoven, and the great Frans Hals retrospective, seen in Haarlem after its mammoth debut at the Royal Academy.

The Royal Academy, indeed, surprised everyone, including themselves. Long plagued by severe financial problems, they saw themselves into the black. The showing of Monet in the '90s: the Series Paintings (seen previously in 1990 at the Boston Museum of Fine Art and the Art Institute, Chicago) attracted over 650,000 visitors, and was also the first time advance ticketing for exhibitions had been instituted in Britain. Total attendances at the Royal Academy were over 950,000 in the 1989–90 season (autumn to autumn), an increase of 21 per cent over the previous year. The last three months of 1990 saw an influx of an unprecedented number of visitors: 609,556, to be exact.

The real news for London was the rejuvenation of the Tate, by the simplest yet most subtle of means. The director appointed in 1988, Nicholas Serota, simply rehung the whole gallery in a sequence of changing displays. The whole was inaugurated under the title Past Present Future and opened in January by the then Prime Minister, Mrs Thatcher. About 15 per cent of the Tate's collections were always out on loan. Even with the Tate Gallery Liverpool and proposed extensions (announced in 1990) of the Tate at St Ives—for which plans were already drawn up and architects appointed—and at Norwich, only a small proportion of the total could be on view (as of 1990 there were approximately 17,500 works in the collection, exclusive of Turner). Moreover although there were strengths, there were also serious gaps, the School of Paris among them: the Tate's holdings of, say, Matisse, were strikingly inadequate compared with Paris and New York. The new cyclic rehanging, unprecedented in a major museum, made the Tate more a sequence of changing exhibitions than a museum.

Contemporary British art did well: the sculptor Anish Kapoor, representative of Britain at the Venice Biennale, carried off a major prize there; an exhibition of his drawings was held at the Tate. Stanley Spencer's *Crucifixion* made £1,320,000 at auction (Sotheby's May 1990), the record for a modern British painting.

Refurbishment proceeded apace. From Dublin's National Gallery and the National Museum of Wales to Birmingham's Barber Institute, museums were re-installing their permanent collections to enhanced effect. Much of the Royal Collection that the public normally did not see, from the Grand Corridor at Windsor Castle, went walk-about to half a dozen museums in the course of the year, culminating in an exhibition of 60 paintings from Canaletto and Gainsborough to Landseer, at the National Museum of Wales. The Courtauld Galleries finally moved in the spring to newly-restored galleries at Somerset House in the Strand; the display and hanging were adversely criticized.

Meanwhile, the Victoria and Albert, after the much-reported difficulties of 1989 (see AR 1989, pp. 484–5), seemed very much on course with the opening of the long awaited Nehru Gallery of Indian Art 1550-1900, described by the *Financial Times* as 'an out-and-out success, an exemplary marriage of scholarship and imaginative, articulate design'. Some 5 per cent of the Indian collection was now on display. Education was also a priority, the director, Mrs Estève-Coll, having been quoted as saying that 'the museum is a primary educational resource'.

Perhaps the most beautiful exhibition of the year was the largest-ever devoted to Velasquez. The 50 or so paintings in the permanent collection of the Prado in Madrid were joined by international loans, including the Rokeby *Venus* from London's National Gallery. And when *Venus* came home in the early summer, she was joined by the unprecedented loan, as a thank-you, of two Goyas, the naked *Maja* and the clothed *Maja*, which were hung with the *Venus* as Goya had always hoped they would be. The National Gallery continued to upgrade its galleries and to put on other excellent exhibitions in the year, including Art in the Making: Impressionism.

New York and Washington both excelled as well in 1990. Exhibitions of note included Velasquez as well as 30 Centuries of Mexican Art at the Metropolitan. New York's Museum of Modern Art put on the controversial but popular High and Low, which attempted to look at the relationships between popular and high art. Washington had a revelatory exhibition of the paintings of Van Dyck, as well as the great Titian exhibition, which was also shown at the Doge's Palace in Venice. Also in Italy, the magnificent restoration, which took nine years and was sponsored by Olivetti, of the Brancacci Chapel in Florence opened to the public, to great acclaim. The original 15th-century frescoes by Masolino, Masaccio and Filippino Lippi, painted over a period of 60 years, were considered crucial components of the birth of Renaissance art; in the course of restoration, previously–unknown frescoes behind the baroque altar had been discovered.

Paris saw the massive Art et Publicité (Art and Advertising) show at the Pompidou, and yet another view of the protean Picasso in a major exhibition of the French state's acquisition (in lieu of taxes) of 400 works by Picasso from the estate of his widow, Jacqueline, shown at the Grand Palais in the autumn.

America continued its unenviable record of litigation over art, in particular controversies about censorship in art. The Robert Mapplethorpe controversy (see AR 1989, pp. 486–7) rumbled on. Dennis Barrie, director of the Contemporary Arts Centre in Cincinnati, Ohio, appeared in court in September on criminal charges over seven allegedly obscene photographs which were part of a Mapplethorpe exhibition shown at the Centre. It was the first time in the USA that a museum director had been so charged; and in the course of a ten-day trial the museum argued for the artistic value of the images. As Mr Barrie himself put it in a subsequent interview: 'The jury were all ordinary working-class people not usually interested in art; they found the pictures lewd and difficult, but our experts convinced them that the photographs were art, and that art doesn't have to be pretty. The jury acquitted us in two hours.' Issues of artistic freedom and censorship continued to be hotly debated in America, with the National Endowment for the Arts in the firing line.

In Britain the debate on the purpose of the museum continued, with issues to do with marketing, admission charges, the place of curators and scholarship being ventilated frequently in the media. The Royal Society of Arts hosted a one-day international conference on the issue in October, with the Science Museum, the Natural History Museum and the Victoria and Albert questioned about what some saw as their populist marketing stance to the detriment of scholarship.

There were some intriguing newcomers in the autumn to the art media. *The Art Newspaper* made its debut in London, edited by Anna Somers Cock, formerly the editor of *Apollo*; and *The Journal of Art*, edited in New York by the art historian and critic Barbara Rose, also began appearing in London. Both were competing for a small but specialized and economically-powerful readership.

By the end of the year commercial galleries, particularly some in London and New York dealing with contemporary art, were reported to be in severe financial difficulties. Nevertheless, London itself boasted a tiny new quartier in art, with the senior gallery Annely Juda moving to Dering Street (at the top of New Bond Street) in June and opening with a major retrospective of the Russian contructivist sculptor Naum Gabo. The avant garde gallery Maureen O Paley also moved to Dering Street in the late autumn.

Throughout the year the commercial art market was in difficulties, and the public sector was painfully under-financed; but the public, in terms of what could be seen on public view, was in spite of everything magnificently served.

Deaths announced in 1990 included those of the painters Aubrey Williams, Rodrigo Moynihan (see OBITUARY) and Tadeusz Kantor, the photographers Norman Parkinson, Roman Vishniac, Lotte Jacobi and Hans Namuth, and the critic and writer Peter Fuller.

ARCHITECTURE

AFTER the construction boom of the late-1980s, the architectural events of 1990 were overshadowed by a sudden slump, especially in commercial property. By December the influential Building Employers' Confederation was describing it as the 'worst recession ever'. No major architectural practice went into liquidation, but there were few new commissions, and a survey by the Association of Consultant Architects revealed that one in five architects in private practice lost their jobs during the year. As banks and funding institutions lost confidence in development, several exciting schemes had to be shelved, including modernist Richard Rogers' £800 million shopping and leisure complex in the Royal Docks, east London.

The recession also damaged hopes that entrepreneur John Broome could revive his ambitious plan to turn Battersea power station on the south bank of the Thames into a £280 million fun park, a scheme designed by Renton Howard Wood Levin. English Heritage warned Broome he would be served with an emergency repairs notice to protect the interior of the listed 1930s power station, now roofless and battered by the weather. Meanwhile, other consultants drew up alternative proposals. Max Hutchinson, president of the Royal Institute of British Architects (RIBA), designed an exhibition centre for architecture and building, while building consultant Peter Kreamer suggested the complex could be turned into a rubbish-burning facility.

After the storm of controversy over the architectural views expressed in his 1989 book, *A Vision of Britain*, the Prince of Wales kept a low-profile in 1990. In April, he hosted a private lunch at Sandringham to launch an initiative promoting his architectural views in Eastern Europe. The Prince's summer school, which took students from around the world to Oxford and Rome, promoted a return to the 'traditional principles' upon which architecture was based 2,500 years ago. The course was oversubscribed, and another was planned for 1991. Meanwhile, the Prince's model development of Poundbury, outside Dorchester, Dorset (see AR 1989, p. 489), had to be redesigned for a second time, following the slump in the housing market and opposition from county council planners to the layout of the roads. Relations between the Duchy of Cornwall and masterplanner Leon Krier became strained by the autumn, with Krier at one point threatening to resign.

Despite the Prince's reluctance to speak out, the quality of building design remained firmly on the political agenda. In December, architects elected as the next RIBA president Richard MacCormac, described as a 'romantic pragmatist', who pledged to campaign for architectural quality rather than professional self-interest. The backlash began against US architectural practices working in the UK, many of which had scooped the most lucrative design commissions of the late-1980s. In March,

Royal Fine Art Commission chairman, Lord St John of Fawsley, said the invasion of American architects was threatening London with a 'rash of quite unsuitable buildings'.

Among those Americans under fire were Kohn Pedersen Fox, for a giant £500 million commercial development at Broomielaw, Glasgow, and SOM, whose office scheme at Blackfriars in London was described as 'overbearing' by the Ancient Monuments Society. Most of the opprobrium was reserved for Swanke Hayden Connell (SHC), hired as masterplanners for the redevelopment of Spitalfields market in East London, following the resignation of Richard MacCormac. In April Tower Hamlets council said: 'The reason this scheme is lousy is that the architecture is lousy.' The height and bulk of the designs were also attacked by the Royal Fine Art Commission and conservationists such as the Georgian Group. The Environment Secretary, Chris Patten, ordered that the fate of the proposals should be determined at a public inquiry in 1991. Desperate to avoid the lengthy delays of an inquiry, the Spitalfields Development Group told SHC to redesign their scheme, but this failed to appease the conservationists. One conservation group, Save Britain's Heritage, commissioned post-modern architect Terry Farrell to prepare an alternative masterplan. The only American architect to triumph was Cesar Pelli, whose 800 ft tower at Canary Wharf in London's docklands—the second tallest in Europe—was topped out in November, amid a fanfare of publicity.

At Waterloo station, a design battle raged over proposals by P&O to build huge office blocks above the new Channel Tunnel terminal. *Building Design*, the weekly architectural newspaper, mounted a successful campaign to persuade P&O and architects RHWL to think again. It argued that piercing the glass roof of the terminal would destroy the integrity of modernist architect Nicholas Grimshaw's clarity. In December, P&O agreed not to build above the terminal.

Arts Council chairman Peter Palumbo had a mixed year in his long-running campaign to win approval to demolish Victorian buildings at Poultry in the City of London, and replace them with a new building by James Stirling. In April the Court of Appeal overturned a High Court decision to approve the Stirling scheme, arguing that in his original approval the then Environment Secretary, Nicholas Ridley, had failed to give adequate reasons for departing from stated government policy not to allow demolition of listed buildings unless every effort had been made to preserve them. Palumbo was then granted leave to appeal to the House of Lords, but suffered a setback when Ridley's successor, Chris Patten, refused to defend Ridley's decision.

Outside London, Conservative MPs voiced mounting concern that the quality of some of Britain's best towns and cities was being threatened by ugly new buildings. More than 100 lobbied Mr Patten to persuade him to include strict new aesthetic controls on architects in the forthcoming planning bill. Mr Patten refused, on the grounds that design quality could not be enshrined in legislation, but said the standard of design must improve. In his last act as Environment Secretary (before Michael Heseltine took over in November), he ordered a review of the department's hated Marsham Street slab block offices, with demolition as an option.

Mr Patten's strong line on design quality opened up the government to accusations of hypocrisy when three government departments chose the design-and-build construction method to procure their new regional headquarters. The Royal Fine Art Commission and RIBA president, Max Hutchinson, argued that constraints of cost and construction time would restrict the architect's freedom to design great public buildings. The government refused to back down, and by the end of the year work had started on the first, a 40,000 sq m complex in Leeds for the departments of health and social security.

Money and public patronage of design was also at the centre of a battle over the proposed East London River Crossing, the most important new bridge over the Thames this century. Stanhope Properties were so disappointed by the Department of Transport's box-girder design for the bridge that they commissioned a stunning alternative from the Spanish architect/engineer Santiago Calatrava. But at a public inquiry, the department refused to consider Calatrava's single-arch design because, it alleged, the costs would be nearly double.

Architectural competitions also continued to be shrouded in controversy in 1990. The most heated arguments surrounded the apparently obscure Dulwich Picture Gallery ideas competition in south London. Prompted by falling workloads, a record 367 architects entered. Three unknown architects were named as winners and told to work up their scheme, but after violent anti-modernist protests by architectural 'fogeys' in the national press the gallery told them not to proceed, although it later relented. Undeterred, the competition's sponsor, *Country Life* magazine, launched another ideas competition—for a monument to Thatcherism.

Despite the controversy, modernist architects won a clean sweep of the honours for design in 1990. Dutch architect Aldo van Eyck won the Royal Gold Medal, while Indian Charles Correa collected the International Union of Architects' gold medal. The Italian, Aldo Rossi, won the Pritzker prize. In April, Norman Foster's Willis Faber Dumas headquarters in Ipswich was voted 'the finest work by a British designer anywhere in the world'.

FASHION

THE start of a new decade saw fashion being pulled in all directions. Rules were broken. Sporty parkas looked city chic, hard tailoring went soft, shorts competed with short skirts as the new suit silhouette, a colour explosion came close to banishing black, and leggings were worn with everything. Telling quotes from the world's top fashion designers reflected the new uncertainty. Karl Lagerfeld, the man behind the phenomenally successful Chanel label remarked: 'The dressy look in fashion doesn't look young and modern any more. Fashion is finished with skirt lengths.' And Italian designer Gianni Versace said, 'We are redefining chic all over again. In this new world short is classic and prints and colour are fashion.'

The world of couture had more of an influence on high-street fashion than ever, partly due to the new couture customer profile being one of a younger woman, and partly because of a new breed of young couturiers at the helm of couture houses who had opted for a more modern simplicity without losing any of the luxury. The star of the couture was Claude Montana, who received rapturous applause with his second collection for Lanvin, after a disappointing first. His circular swinging trapeze coats with cinched waists and draped hoods in vibrant oranges, lemons and limes were breathtaking. The message coming out of Paris was: Go for colour, put some swing in your skirts and coats but put them over skinny leggings.

Spring swept in on a wave of sixties nostalgia and with it came the revival of the shift dress, swingy trench coats, pale tights, wide headbands, sixties wigs, and lots of black and white. Rifat Ozbek, the designer who showed exotic colours the previous summer, went for an all-white collection this time round, with sporty shorts, bomber jackets, oversized shirts and cropped tops. He also flaunted white with silver sequins and silver metallic, producing a decidedly racy look. The fashion fraternity called it New Age, and we all gave up our blue jeans for white ones.

Prints also packed a punch, as the original Puccis, all swirling psychedelic patterns in lilacs and greens, pinks and oranges, purples and yellows, heralded a thousand copies on everything from a silk shirt to a pair of briefs. Clash with dash was the look to go for, as Emilio Pucci, that aristocratic Florentine who dressed stars such as Elizabeth Taylor and Jacqueline Kennedy Onassis in the sixties, revived his original prints. For fashion victims Pucci was the latest designer label to covet, be it the real thing or a fabulous fake mass-market copy. In a not very good year for fashion retailing, it was left to bright colour and bold prints to put a little life into flagging sales. But with all this looking back to the sixties there was one vital ingredient that gave fashion its own nineties look. Stretch Lycra ensured that fashion's 'must have' basics—leggings, bodies, and catsuits—had the necessary cling.

The summer was having a heatwave in every way, as for once soaring temperatures matched the mood of the clothes. Tropical colours, cool creams or classic seafaring navy reworked with a touch of brass buttons or gold braid for that top-deck look provided classics with a twist. By the autumn we had got used to a lot of colour and it turned up in delicious warm pastels like peach, rosy pink and lemon, or bold and bright in Navaho plaids and stripes. Fringing was a popular trim, on wraps, jackets, and, for the junior market, skirts and body-cling dresses.

The jacket of the year was the parka, now glamorous in washed silks and peachy suedes, fake fur hoods and pale colours. Paired with the sharper line of ski pants the winter uniform was complete. The influential American designers continued along the path of paring down minimalism, with cashmere turtle necks, silk sarong skirts, slimline flannel trousers, and simple wrap and tie dresses all giving a luxurious but understated look to daywear. Elsewhere designers worked with lush and plush textures to give an opulent air to winter evenings. Brocades, velvets, tapestry, satins, metallics and quilting combined with rich bronze, purple and red looked exotic. Party pieces veered from the simplicity of the little black slip dress, to the dressed-up mood of lavish jewels worked into sweaters and jackets.

The controversial designer Vivienne Westwood, who gave fashion Punk, the Pirates and the New Romantics, was named British Designer of the Year, an accolade many thought long overdue. Norman Parkinson, fashion photographer and photographer to the royal family died aged 76, and Erté, the eminent stage and fashion designer, died aged 97 (see OBITUARY).

Chapter 3

LITERATURE

As the year ended two literary grandes-dames, who practised in contrasting genres, appeared on the front pages. The crime-writer P. D. James was appointed a life peer; the breathtakingly-productive romantic novelist Barbara Cartland was created a dame. Miss Cartland promptly announced the imminent publication of her 500th book. However, this brief distraction for the new year honours did nothing to diminish the story which had dominated the publishing world just as it did in 1989: despite strenuous efforts, on one side at least, the Rushdie affair seemed no nearer a resolution.

On 14 February Salman Rushdie marked a sombre anniversary—that of the *fatweh*, condemning him to death, pronounced by Ayatollah Khomeini for allegedly blaspheming Islam in *The Satanic Verses* (see AR 1989, p. 493-4). In a 7,000-word essay for a Sunday newspaper Rushdie, who said he had remained uncharacteristically silent 'because I felt that my voice was simply not loud enough to be heard above the clamour of the voices raised against me', expressed his repugnance at the exploitation of his case by bigots and racists. He wrote that he had found it bewildering to learn how 'millions upon millions of people' had been willing to judge the novel—which he described as 'a migrant's-eye view of the world'—and its author without having read it. He regretted that offence was taken when none was intended; but in an accompanying interview he said: 'I honestly believe there isn't a sentence I can't justify.'

Rushdie's defence was made from the latest of many safe-houses, where he had lived under 24-hour Special Branch protection. His by-then estranged wife, the American novelist Marianne Wiggins, had disclosed that within the first five months they had slept beneath 56 separate roofs. The international security operation, heavily focused on his publishers, the Viking Penguin group, had already cost several million pounds. Not everyone was sympathetic: the Conservative politician Norman Tebbit proclaimed Rushdie 'an outstanding villain . . . perhaps the world's richest multiple renegade'. There was furious debate about whether or not the paperback edition should appear.

By the autumn, however, Rushdie had begun to take tentative steps back into society—a process which coincided with the publication in September of a new work of fiction. *Haroun and the Sea of Stories* was written for his son, Zafar, and described a child in a Far Eastern city who redeemed his father, a professional storyteller. This modern fairy tale was favourably received in reviews which for once were allowed outside the conventional ghetto afforded children's literature. Rushdie appeared on television and radio and, most dramatically, arrived with his 'minders' at a Hampstead bookshop, where he signed copies of *Haroun* for bewildered browsers and passers-by. Just before Christmas he declared that he had espoused Islam and that there would be no paperback of *The Satanic Verses* nor any further translations. Some of his supporters were angered by an apparent volte-face, but there was reconciliation with some Muslim leaders in Britain. Their Iranian masters remained unimpressed. The *fatweh* prevailed (see also Pt. XIII, RELIGION).

Early in the year the novelist's predicament inspired a number of analyses, most accessibly Malise Ruthven's *A Satanic Affair*. The devastating consequences of Middle East strife in Lebanon were laid bare in Robert Fisk's *Pity the Nation*, a formidably-documented impression of the country's benighted beauty; while in *Tribes with Flags* Charles Glass gave a vivid account of his captivity and escape in Beirut. A collection of articles by Amos Oz, *The Slopes of Lebanon*, explored the struggle for Israel's soul. As the Iraqi occupation of Kuwait presented the very real threat of world war, Judith Miller and Laurie Mylroie explained the background authoritatively in *Saddam Hussein and the Crisis in the Gulf*.

Elsewhere, Allister Sparks's *The Mind of South Africa* provided a valuable complement to the release of Nelson Mandela; Rian Malan subjected his native country to a far harsher examination in *My Traitor's Heart*. In South America a callous disregard for the welfare and rights of the jungle-dwellers, and for the global ecological balance, was exposed by Andrew Revkin's *The Burning Season*. Inevitably, however, the most prolific source of current-affairs material was Eastern Europe, where change was so fast and so profound that newsdesks, never mind publishers, found it hard to keep pace. Prominent among assessments through Western eyes were David Selbourne's *Death of the Dark Hero: Eastern Europe 1987–90*, Zbigniew Brzezinski's *The Grand Failure: the Birth and Death of Communism in the Twentieth Century* and Christopher Hope's tragi-comic *Moscow! Moscow!*. Robert Conquest updated his monumental 1968 history, *The Great Terror*.

Personal testimonies were recorded by Timothy Garton Ash in *We the People*, by Francine du Plessix Gray in *Soviet Women: Walking the Tightrope*, by Susan Richards in *Epics of Everyday Life*, and in *The Other Russia*, recollections of escape and exile assembled by Norman Stone and Michael Glenny, the outstanding translator, who died in the summer. *Against the Grain*, the autobiography of the radical Moscow politician Boris Yeltsin, provided further testimony to Glenny's skill. Andrei Sakharov, the heroic reformer, left some impressive *Memoirs*. Vitali Vitaliev, one of the commentators galvanized by Gorbachev's glasnost policy, produced a work unthinkable even three years earlier, *Special Correspondent: Investigating in the Soviet Union*. The defector Oleg Gordievsky collaborated with the Cambridge historian Christopher Andrew on *KGB*. And the thriller-writer John Hands watched in wry amusement as events caught up with the plot of his *Perestroika Christi*.

For the second year running the committee of the Nobel prize for literature showed a preference for the Spanish-speaking world, by giving its 87th award to the 76-year-old Mexican poet, critic and diplomat Octavio Paz. In Paris the judges of the Goncourt took a leaf out of a *roman d'amour* by favouring *Les Champs d'Honneur*, a first novel by 38-year-old Jean Rouaud, who showed no inclination to abandon his newspaper kiosk in the 19th arrondissement for a full-time writing career. M. Rouaud's book, a nostalgic vision of French rural sensibility, considered the legacy of two world wars on a family in the south-west. The Prix Médicis went to Jean-Noel Pancrazi's *Les Quartiers d'Hiver*, an alienating study of the habitués of a homosexual bar in Paris; the Prix Fémina to Perrette Fleutiaux's gigantic family saga, *Nous Sommes Eternels*.

In London the most imaginative addition to a crowded milieu was the Encore Award, founded by the Society by Authors for a best second novel. The inaugural prize was shared by Peter Benson's *A Lesser Dependency* (Macmillan) and Paul Watkins's *Calm at Sunset, Calm at*

Dawn (Hutchinson). Little controversy attended the more lucrative and 'hyped' awards. Dillons, the bookselling chain vociferously opposed to the net book agreement, put the six titles shortlisted for the Booker prize on sale at a discount, but had to back down when publishers obtained a court injunction. A. S. Byatt's *Possession: a Romance*, about a quest by a pair of contemporary academics for the true story of a love affair between two Victorian poets, won both the Booker and the Irish Times/Aer Lingus international award for fiction, totalling more than £40,000.

On each occasion *Possession* was challenged by John McGahern's *Amongst Women*. This exquisite chamber piece, about an ageing former IRA hero, his three daughters and his second wife, won the Irish Times Irish fiction award and the Hughes Irish fiction award. Brian Moore, no stranger to the Booker shortlist, also set his expertly-crafted thriller, *Lies of Silence*, in Ireland. Mordecai Richler, a fourth Booker contender with his rumbustious *Solomon Gursky Was Here*, had the consolation of the Commonwealth Writers' prize. The others on a shortlist remarkable for the fact that none of the authors was younger than 50 were Penelope Fitzgerald, with *The Gate of Angels*, and Beryl Bainbridge, with *An Awfully Big Adventure*. It was no secret that Colm Toibin's *The South*, again with an Irish setting, narrowly missed inclusion; but there was surprise at the omission once more of William Boyd, whose *The New Confessions* had seemed a certainty in 1987 and whose new book, *Brazzaville Beach*, set in an East African chimpanzee research station, no less so in 1990.

The South African winner of the 1983 Booker, J. M. Coetzee, was likewise much championed for his harrowing *Age of Iron*, which took the form of a letter from a dying former classics teacher to her daughter. It was rewarded with the Sunday Express fiction prize, worth £20,000. The fiction category of the Whitbread was won by Nicholas Mosley's *Hopeful Monsters*, the story of a German Jewess's love for an Englishman, which one critic described as 'a scripture for our times'. Hanif Kureishi's *The Buddha of Suburbia* won the category for first novel; Peter Dickinson's *AK*, that for children's novel. V. S. Pritchett was given the W. H. Smith award for *A Careless Widow and Other Stories*. To mark his 90th birthday in December, Sir Victor released two volumes of essays, *Lasting Impressions* and *At Home and Abroad*, and his *Complete Short Stories*. Coincidence or not, the short story experienced something of a revitalization in 1990—witness the list below—with outstanding collections from William Trevor (*Family Sins and Other Stories*) and Alice Munro (*Friend of My Youth*).

Kingsley Amis, awarded a knighthood in June, revealed more melancholy and less spleen in *The Folks That Live on the Hill*. Margaret Forster retold the Brownings' story in *Lady's Maid*, and Mary Wesley supplied another cut-glass vignette of upper-middle-class English society in *A Sensible Life*. Allan Massie further demonstrated his versatility in *The Hanging Tree* and Peter Vansittart wrote richly of Rome at the beginning of its decline in *The Wall*. Peter Levi, biographer of Pasternak, also completed Cyril Connolly's literary mystery, *Shade Those Laurels*, and proved it had stood the test of time.

Most of the year's best fiction came from abroad. John Updike magisterially completed his Harold C. Angstrom sequence with *Rabbit at Rest*; Richard Ford plangently conjured small-town America in *Wildlife*, and Nicholson Baker gave a virtuoso meditation on happiness in *Room Temperature*. Nadine Gordimer displayed her customary commitment in *My Son's Story*. The Dane Henrik Stangerup memorably depicted the crack-up of a wayward writer in *The Seducer*. Ivan Klima told of a writer-turned-roadsweeper in *Love and Garbage*. Several critics chose Rosetta Loy's gem, *The Dust Roads of Monferrato*, as their novel of 1990; others were infected by Oscar Hijuelos's energetic recreation of Cuban-American clubland in *The Mambo Kings Play Songs of Love*. However there was a chorus of disappointment for *Vineland*, the first work for 17 years from the arch-recluse Thomas Pynchon; Mickey Spillane resuscitated Mike Hammer after 19 years and fared no better with *The Killing Man*. Alberto Moravia's 25th novella, *Journey to Rome*, appeared shortly before his death in September (see OBITUARY) and achieved, as ever, a delicate erotic balancing act. But no novel in Europe caused a fuss on the scale of *American Psycho*, by Bret Easton Ellis, a member of New York's erstwhile 'Brat Pack'. Said to be a catalogue of shopping and killing, it was dropped by his publisher, Simon & Schuster, on grounds of taste, and bought by Knopf.

The most eagerly-awaited biography of 1990 was Peter Ackroyd's *Dickens*, with which Christopher Sinclair-Stevenson launched his glittering list as an independent publisher. The fortunes of the house in its attempt to break the conglomerate mould were watched as intently as were its authors. Ackroyd's book fulfilled expectations as a commanding account of a prodigious life, but was marred by a running dialogue between the writer and his appreciative subject.

Dickens duly failed to win the biography category of the Whitbread prize, where the victor was Ann Thwaite's *A. A. Milne*, a portrait which left Hilary Spurling, for one, thinking of 'nothing so much as Eeyore and his pricked balloon'. Mrs Spurling was herself responsible for one of the outstanding lives: *Paul Scott* showed most movingly how the author of the *Raj Quartet* was a man of black despair. The prolific A. N. Wilson wrote fervently of a bluff Christian apologist in *C. S. Lewis*, and Alan Judd's *Ford Madox Ford* earned wide praise for his compassionate treatment of the author of *The Good Soldier*. Deirdre Bair dealt intelligently with 'Sartre's girlfriend' in *Simone de Beauvoir*, while Claire Tomalin was more elegant in *The Invisible Woman*, her story of Charles Dickens's intimate, Nelly Ternan. Ray

Monk's *Ludwig Wittgenstein* was a scintillating intellectual biography of the philosopher/iconoclast. Donald Thomas and Richard Mullen successfully evoked the 18th and 19th centuries in their respective studies of *Henry Fielding* and *Anthony Trollope*. Carole Angier brought off a risky marriage of biography and criticism in *Jean Rhys*.

The other blockbusting biography of 1990 was Philip Ziegler's official *King Edward VIII*, a massively convincing dissection of an ultimately wretched, unprepossessing figure. No less definitive would prove Jean Lacouture's *De Gaulle*, the first volume of which arrived in translation with an author's note of displeasure that the publisher intended to combine volumes two and three. Anthony Howard was both eloquent and fair in (Richard) *Crossman: the Pursuit of Power*, and Francis Wheen displayed an irresistible sardonic relish as he gave full exposure to *Tom Driberg: His Life and Indiscretions*. Steven Naifeh and Gregory White Smith's *Jackson Pollock* was not for the squeamish. A new volume of *The Dictionary of National Biography* was criticized not for its contents but for its jacket, which carried likenesses of Diana Dors, Eric Morecambe and David Niven to the exclusion of R. A. Butler, Sir Douglas Bader and Arthur Koestler.

In a moderate year for autobiography one of the agreeable surprises came from the chairman of the Booker judges, Sir Denis Forman, whose *Son of Adam* recalled a Dumfriesshire childhood. India was the backdrop for M. M. Kaye's *The Sun in the Morning*, Berkshire for Richard Adams's *The Day Gone By* and Bukovina for Gregor von Rezzori's *The Snows of Yesteryear*. Light relief was abundant in *Yours, Plum*, the letters of P. G. Wodehouse edited by Frances Donaldson. Sir Anthony Quayle's posthumously-published, rugged *A Time to Speak* was the best showbusiness memoir. Most exhilarating of all was the second batch of 'confessions' in Anthony Burgess's *You've Had Your Time*.

A modest tremor was felt in the corridors of literary scholarship when Gary Taylor, the co-editor of the Oxford Shakespeare, contended in *Reinventing Shakespeare* that the Bard was overrated. More localized was the upheaval when a notice by Auberon Waugh of Anthony Powell's collected reviews in *Miscellaneous Verdicts* caused the Daily Telegraph's eminent principal critic to resign.

Proof positive that the English language was at least in one safe pair of hands came from Derek Walcott, the West Indian poet, celebrating his sixtieth birthday with his finest work to date, *Omeros*, an epic of the sea, at once autobiographical and mythological, stunningly sustained over great length. The contentious Mr Waugh, believing that English poetry is 'in a sorry state', attempted a rescue by compiling *The Literary Review Anthology of Real Poetry*.

In history, two books shone through, Peter Gwyn provided a sumptuous portrait of Thomas Wolsey in *The King's Cardinal*; Jonathan

Sumption had the reviewers looking forward impatiently to the second volume of his *The Hundred Years' War*. David Cannadine stirred the blue blood with his survey of *The Decline and Fall of the English Aristocracy*. The 50th anniversary of Dunkirk went relatively unnoticed compared with the bombardment of titles commemorating the Battle of Britain. There was an inspiring account of heroism in occupied France in Claude Morhange-Bégué's *Chamberet*. Helmuth James von Moltke's *Letters to Freya* afforded first-hand witness to the battles of a German intelligence officer against the persecution of minorities by his superiors. *A Mother's War* was an unself-pitying memoir by a German aristocrat whose life became a nightmare after her father was executed for his part in the bomb plot against Hitler.

It was heartening to find this area of publishing, if anything, on the increase. Less so, the obsession with tycoons, whose biographies proliferated like never before. Journalism had a good year between hard covers. Tom Pocock wrote a good life of the late Alan Moorehead, two of whose intrepid kindred spirits, the reporter Clare Hollingworth and the photographer Don McCullin, produced compelling memoirs, respectively, *Front Line* and *Unreasonable Behaviour*. *The Soccer War* was a powerful collection by the Polish journalist Ryszard Kapuscinski; *The Last Paragraph*, a fitting tribute to David Blundy, killed on assignment in Central America. Duff Hart-Davis compiled a delightful history of the Telegraph newspapers in *The House the Berrys Built*, while Peter Chippindale and Chris Horrie veered between disgust and hilarity in their account of The Sun, *Stick It Up Your Punter!* Both Michael Green and Nicholas Garland had the same famous headline in mind when they chose as their titles *Nobody Hurt in Small Earthquake* and *Not Many Dead*.

Apart from Moravia, among those figures from the world of books who died in 1990 were: the novelist Rosamond Lehmann (at 89), the versifier Patience Strong (83), the historian A. J. P. Taylor (84), the creator of *The One Hundred and One Dalmatians* Dodie Smith (94), and the American novelist Irving Wallace (74). Both Patrick White, who won the Nobel Prize in 1973, and Lawrence Durrell had works of non-fiction published within weeks of their deaths at 78—the former, *Patrick White Speaks*, a collection reflecting his ambivalent fascination with his native Australia; the latter, *Caesar's Vast Ghost*, a homage to Durrell's adopted Provence. None of the above, however, could claim the influence of Roald Dahl, after Enid Blyton the most popular children's author of the century. Shortly before his death, at 74, he donated the manuscript of a new book to an auction in aid of the Dyslexia Institute: it was sold for more than £300,000. (For Lehmann, Taylor, Smith, White, Durrell and Dahl, see OBITUARY).

Ironically, the most lively literary row in Britain during the year revolved around the interpretation of a clause in Philip Larkin's will regarding the destruction of his diaries and other writings. Like the Rushdie affair, it remained unsettled.

Among interesting new books published during the year were:

FICTION. *The Folks That Live on the Hill* by Kingsley Amis (Hutchinson); *War Fever* by J. G. Ballard (Collins); *An Awfully Big Adventure* by Beryl Bainbridge (Duckworth); *Room Temperature* by Nicholson Baker (Granta); *Three Novels* by Nina Berberova (Chatto); *Brazzaville Beach* by William Boyd (Sinclair-Stevenson); *Brief Lives* by Anita Brookner (Cape); *Possession: a Romance* by A. S. Byatt (Chatto); *Look at It This Way* by Justin Cartwright (Macmillan); *Shade Those Laurels* by Cyril Connolly, concluded by Peter Levi (Bellew); *Age of Iron* by J. M. Coetzee (Secker); *The Greek Interpreter* by Max Davidson (Hodder); *AK* by Peter Dickinson (Gollancz); *The Gate of Angels* by Penelope Fitzgerald (Collins); *Nous Sommes Eternels* by Perrette Fleutiaux (Gallimard); *Wildlife* by Richard Ford (Collins Harvill); *Lady's Maid* by Margaret Forster (Chatto); *Constancia and Other Stories for Virgins* by Carlos Fuentes (Deutsch); *Malachy and His Family* by Carlo Gebler (Hamish Hamilton); *My Son's Story* by Nadine Gordimer (Bloomsbury); *The Other Side* by Mary Gordon (Bloomsbury); *The Last Word and Other Stories* by Graham Greene (Reinhardt); *Perestroika Christi* by John Hands (Simon & Schuster); *Richard's Feet* by Carey Harrison (Heinemann); *The Mambo Kings Play Songs of Love* by Oscar Hijuelos (Hamish Hamilton); *Visiting Cards* by Francis King (Constable); *Love and Garbage* by Ivan Klima (Chatto); *The Buddha of Suburbia* by Hanif Kureishi (Faber); *The Sixth Day and Other Tales* by Primo Levi (Michael Joseph); *The Dust Roads of Monferrato* by Rosetta Loy (Collins Harvill); *Flashman and the Mountain of Light* by George MacDonald Fraser (Collins Harvill); *The Innocent* by Ian McEwan (Cape); *Amongst Women* by John McGahern (Faber); *The People and Uncollected Stories* by Bernard Malamud (Chatto); *The Hanging Tree* by Allan Massie (Heinemann); *Lies of Silence* by Brian Moore (Cape); *Journey to Rome* by Alberto Moravia (Secker); *Hopeless Monsters* by Nicholas Mosley (Secker); *Friend of My Youth* by Alice Munro (Chatto); *The World of Nagaraj* by R. K. Narayan (Heinemann); *Lantern Slides: Short Stories* by Edna O'Brien (Weidenfeld); *Les Quartiers d'Hiver* by Jean-Noel Pancrazi (Gallimard); *The Complete Short Stories* by V. S. Pritchett (Chatto); *Vineland* by Thomas Pynchon (Secker); *The Last World* by Christoph Ransmayr (Chatto); *Going Wrong* by Ruth Rendell (Hutchinson); *Solomon Gursky Was Here* by Mordecai Richler (Chatto); *Les Champs d'Honneur* by Jean Rouaud (Editions du Minuit); *Haroun and the Sea of Stories* by Salman Rushdie (Granta); *Four Bare Legs in a Bed and Other Stories* by Helen Simpson (Heinemann); *Symposium* by Muriel Spark (Constable); *The Killing Man* by Mickey Spillane (Heinemann); *The Seducer: It is Hard to Die in Dieppe* by Henrik Stangerup (Marion Boyars); *Journey of a Lifetime and Other Stories* by Gillian Tindall (Hutchinson); *The South* by Colm Toibin (Serpent's Tail); *Family Sins and Other Stories* by William Trevor (Bodley Head); *Rabbit at Rest* by John Updike (Deutsch); *The Wall* by Peter Vansittart (Peter Owen); *The Storyteller* by Mario Vargas Llosa (Faber); *A Sensible Life* by Mary Wesley (Bantam); *Escapes and Other Stories* by Joy Williams (Collins Harvill).

POETRY. *Selected Poems* by Anna Akhmatova (Collins Harvill); *Unauthorised Versions: Poems and Their Parodies* edited by Kenneth Baker (Faber); *Collected Poems 1937–1971* and *The Dream Songs* by John Berryman (Faber); *Selected Poems, 1990* by D. J. Enright (OUP); *Selected Poems* by John Heath-Stubbs (Carcanet); *Greenheart* by Alan Jenkins (Chatto); *Collected Poems* by Norman MacCaig (Chatto); *Collected Poems* by Edwin Morgan (Carcanet); *Collected Poems* by J. Enoch Powell (Bellew); *Counterpoint* by R. S. Thomas (Bloodaxe); *Omeros* by Derek Walcott (Faber); *The*

Literary Review Anthology of Real Poetry edited by Auberon Waugh (Ashford, Buchan & Enright); *Self-Portrait with a Slide* by Hugo Williams (OUP).

LITERARY CRITICISM. *Mother Tongue: the English Language* by Bill Bryson (Hamish Hamilton); *Ancient Cultures of Conceit: British University Fiction in the Post-War Years* by Ian Carter (Routledge); *The Life and Times of the English Language: the History of Our Marvellous Native Tongue* by Robert Claiborne (Bloomsbury); *Waugh's World: a Guide to the Novels of Evelyn Waugh* by Iain Gale (Sidgwick); *Novelists in Their Youth* by John Halperin (Chatto); *The Cambridge History of Russian Literature* edited by Charles A. Moser (CUP); *Miscellaneous Verdicts: Writings on Writers 1946-1989* by Anthony Powell (Heinemann); *Haydn and the Valve Trumpet* by Craig Raine (Faber); *The State of the Language* edited by Christopher Ricks and Leonard Michaels (Faber); *Reinventing Shakespeare: a Cultural History from the Restoration to the Present* by Gary Taylor (Hogarth).

BIOGRAPHY. *Dickens* by Peter Ackroyd (Sinclair-Stevenson); *Jean Rhys* by Carole Angier (Deutsch); *Simone de Beauvoir: a Biography* by Deirdre Bair (Cape); *As Thousands Cheer: the Life of Irving Berlin* by Laurence Bergreen (Hodder); *The Dictionary of National Biography 1981-1985* edited by Lord Blake and C. S. Nicholls (OUP); *The Reign and Abdication of Edward VIII* by Michael Bloch (Bantam); *Wilde's Devoted Friend: a Life of Robert Ross 1869-1918* by Maureen Borland (Lennard); *Vladimir Nabokov: the Russian Years* by Brian Boyd (Chatto); *Clever Hearts: Desmond and Molly MacCarthy—a Biography* by Hugh and Mirabel Cecil (Gollancz); *Octavia Hill: a Life* by Gillian Darley (Constable); *William Gerhardie: a Biography* by Dido Davies (OUP); *Ronald Searle* by Russell Davies (Sinclair-Stevenson); *Charles Ricketts: a Biography* by J. P. G. Delaney (OUP); *Best of Friends* by Julian Fane (Sinclair-Stevenson); *One Man in His Time: the Life of Lieutenant-Colonel N. L. D. ('Billy') McLean DSO* by Xan Fielding (Macmillan); *Emily Brontë: a Chainless Soul* by Katherine Frank (Hamish Hamilton); *Newman and His Age* by Sheridan Gilley (Darton, Longman & Tod); *Good and Faithful Servant: the Unauthorized Biography of Bernard Ingham* by Robert Harris (Faber); *Proust: a Biography* by Ronald Hayman (Heinemann); *Serious Pleasures: the Life of Stephen Tennant* by Philip Hoare (Hamish Hamilton); *Crossman: the Pursuit of Power* by Anthony Howard (Cape); *Ford Madox Ford* by Alan Judd (Collins); *De Gaulle: the Rebel 1890-1944* by Jean Lacouture (Collins Harvill); *Norma Shearer: a Life* by Gavin Lambert (Hodder); *Stalin: the Glasnost Revelations* by Walter Laqueur (Unwin Hyman); *Boris Pasternak* by Peter Levi (Hutchinson); *A Good German: Adam von Trott zu Solz* by Giles MacDonogh (Quartet); *Saddam Hussein* by Faoud Matar (Highlight); *D. H. Lawrence: a Biography* by Jeffrey Meyers (Macmillan); *Allan Ginsberg: a Biography* by Barry Miles (Viking); *Ludwig Wittgenstein: the Duty of Genius* by Ray Monk (Cape); *Anthony Trollope: the Victorian in His World* by Richard Mullen (Duckworth); *Jackson Pollock: an American Saga* by Steven Naifeh and Gregory White Smith (Barrie & Jenkins); *Louise Brooks* by Barry Paris (Hamish Hamilton); *Boris Pasternak: the Tragic Years 1930-60* by Evgeny Pasternak (Collins Harvill); *Alan Moorehead* by Tom Pocock (Bodley Head); *Luchino Visconti: the Flames of Passion* by Laurence Schifano (Collins); *Paul Scott: a Life* by Hilary Spurling (Hutchinson); *Mrs Humphrey Ward: Eminent Victorian, Pre-eminent Edwardian* by John Sutherland (Clarendon Press/OUP); *Henry Fielding* by Donald Thomas (Weidenfeld); *A. A. Milne: His Life* by Ann Thwaite (Faber); *The Invisible Woman: the Story of Nelly Ternan and Charles Dickens* by Claire Tomalin (Viking); *James Baldwin: Artist on Fire* by W. J. Weatherby (Michael Joseph); *Tom Driberg: His Life and Indiscretions* by Francis Wheen (Chatto); *C. S. Lewis: a Biography* by A. N. Wilson (Collins); *Woolley of Ur: the Life of Sir Leonard Woolley* by H. V. F. Winstone (Secker); *King Edward VIII: the Official Biography* by Philip Ziegler (Collins).

AUTOBIOGRAPHY AND LETTERS. *The Day Gone By: an Autobiography* by Richard Adams (Hutchinson); *Bury My Heart at W. H. Smith's* by Brian Aldiss (Hodder); *Basingstoke Boy: the Autobiography* by John Arlott (Collins Willow); *An Immaculate Mistake: Scenes from Childhood and Beyond* by Paul Bailey (Bloomsbury); *As It Was: Pleasures, Landscapes and Justice* by Sybille Bedford (Sinclair-Stevenson); *The Crooked Timber of Humanity: Chapters in the History of Ideas* by Isaiah Berlin (Murray); *Recollections and Reflections* by Bruno Bettelheim (Thames & Hudson); *No Other Choice* by George Blake (Cape); *Music Sounded Out* by Alfred Brendel (Robson); *The Rags of Time: a Fragment of Autobiography* by William Buchan (Ashford, Buchan & Enright); *You've Had Your Time: Being the Second Part of the Confessions of Anthony Burgess* (Heinemann); *The Play of the Eyes* by Elias Canetti (Deutsch); *Memoirs of a Libel Lawyer* by Peter Carter-Ruck (Weidenfeld); *My Dear Max: the Letters of Brendan Bracken to Lord Beaverbrook 1925–1958* edited by Richard Cockett (Historians' Press); *Past Tense: the Cocteau Diaries Volume Two* by Jean Cocteau (Methuen); *Where I Fell to Earth: a Life in Four Places* by Peter Conrad (Chatto); *From Early Life* by William Cooper (Macmillan); *Walled Gardens: Scenes from an Anglo-Irish Childhood* by Annabel Davis-Goff (Barrie & Jenkins); *Yours, Plum: the Letters of P. G. Wodehouse* edited by Frances Donaldson (Hutchinson); *Don't Shoot the Yanqui: the Life of a War Cameraman* by Erik Durschmied (Grafton); *Rebel with a Cause: the Autobiography of H. J. Eysenck* (W. H. Allen); *Son of Adam* by Denis Forman (Deutsch); *A Place for Us* by Nicholas Gage (Bantam); *Not Many Dead: Journal of a Year in Fleet Street* by Nicholas Garland (Hutchinson); *Through a Window: Thirty Years with the Chimpanzees of Gombe* by Jane Goodall (Weidenfeld); *Nobody Hurt in Small Earthquake* by Michael Green (Heinemann); *Reflections* by Graham Greene (Reinhardt); *A Sparrow's Flight: the Memoirs of Lord Hailsham of St Marylebone* (Collins); *Engaging Eccentrics* by David Herbert (Peter Owen); *A Sort of Clowning: Life and Times 1940–1950* by Richard Hoggart (Chatto); *Front Line* by Clare Hollingworth (Cape); *Finding Connections* by P. J. Kavanagh (Hutchinson); *The Sun in the Morning: Being the First Part of Share of Summer* by M. M. Kaye (Viking); *Loopy: an Autobiography* by George Kennard (Leo Cooper); *Unreasonable Behaviour* by Don McCullin (Cape); *My Traitor's Heart: a South African Exile Returns to Face His Country, His Tribe, and His Conscience* by Rian Malan (Bodley Head); *Chamberet: the True Story of a Jewish Family in Wartime France* by Claude Morhange-Bégué (Peter Owen); *Master of None: an Autobiography* by J. E. Morpurgo (Carcanet); *Vladimir Nabokov: Selected Letters 1940–1977* edited by Dmitri Nabokov and Matthew J. Bruccoli (Weidenfeld); *Hanging On: Diaries December 1960–August 1963* by Frances Partridge (Collins); *At Home and Abroad: in Celebration of V. S. Pritchett's Ninetieth Birthday* and *Lasting Impressions* by V. S. Pritchett (Chatto); *A Time to Speak* by Anthony Quayle (Barrie & Jenkins); *A Mother's War* by Fey von Hassell (Murray); *Letters to Freya 1939–1945* by Helmuth James von Moltke (Collins Harvill); *The Snows of Yesteryear: Portraits for an Autobiography* by Gregor von Rezzori (Chatto); *A Particular Kind of Fool* by Noel Whitcomb (Quartet); *Up the Down Escalator* by Glyn Worsnip (Michael Joseph).

HISTORY. *The Long Gray Line: the American Journey of West Point's Class of 1966* by Rick Atkinson (Collins); *Napoleon and Josephine: a Love Story* by Theo Aronson (Murray); *Caligula: the Corruption of Power* by Anthony A. Barrett (Batsford); *The Decline and Fall of the English Aristocracy* by David Cannadine (Yale); *The World War 1939–45: the Cartoonists' View* by Roy Douglas (Routledge); *Signals of War* by Lawrence Freedman and Virginia Gamba-Stonehouse (Faber); *The King's Wife: Five Queen Consorts* by Robert Gray (Secker); *The King's Cardinal: the Rise and Fall of Thomas Wolsey* by Peter Gwyn (Barrie & Jenkins); *Redcoats and Rebels: the War for America 1770–1781* by Christopher Hibbert (Grafton); *The Virgin Queen: the Personal History of Elizabeth I* by Christopher Hibbert (Viking); *British Intelligence in the Second World War, Vol 4—Security and Counter-Intelligence* edited by F. H. Hinsley and C. A. G. Simkins (HMSO); *The Great Game: on Secret Service in High*

LITERATURE

Asia by Peter Hopkirk (Murray); *Mary Tudor: a Life* by David Loades (Blackwell); *The Roman Empire of Ammianus* by John Matthews (Duckworth); *Chronicle of the Second World War* edited by Derrik Mercer (Longman); *The People's Peace: British History 1945–1989* by Kenneth O. Morgan (OUP); *An Uncertain Hour: the French, the Germans, the Jews, the Klaus Barbie Trial and the City of Lyon 1940–45* by Ted Morgan (Bodley Head); *I Have Sind: Charles Napier in India 1841–1844* by Priscilla Napier (Michael Russell); *Himmler: Reichsfuhrer-SS* by Peter Padfield (Macmillan); *The Lost King of England; the East European Adventures of Edward the Exile* by Gabriel Ronay (Boydell & Brewer); *The Hundred Years' War: Vol I—Trial by Battle* by Jonathan Sumption (Faber); *Petain's Crime: the Full Story of French Collaboration in the Holocaust* by Paul Webster (Macmillan); *On a Darkling Plain: an Account of the Nigerian Civil War* by Ken Saro-Wiwa (Saros).

CURRENT AFFAIRS. *KGB: the Inside Story of Its Foreign Operations from Lenin to Gorbachev* by Christopher Andrew and Oleg Gordievsky (Hodder); *The Grand Failure: the Birth and Death of Communism in the Twentieth Century* by Zbigniew Brzezinski (Macdonald); *The Great Terror: a Reassessment* by Robert Conquest (Hutchinson); *Soviet Women: Walking the Tightrope* by Francine du Plessix Gray (Doubleday); *A Marriage of Inconvenience: the Persecution of Ruth and Seretse Khama* by Michael Dutfield (Unwin Hyman); *Pity the Nation: Lebanon at War* by Robert Fisk (Deutsch); *We the People: the Revolution of '89 Witnessed in Warsaw, Budapest, Berlin & Prague* by Timothy Garton Ash (Granta); *Tribes with Flags: a Journey Curtailed* by Charles Glass (Secker); *Moscow! Moscow!* by Christopher Hope (Heinemann); *The Soccer War* by Ryszard Kapuscinski (Granta); *The Last Paragraph: the Journalism of David Blundy* edited by Anthony Holden (Heinemann); *Saddam Hussein and the Crisis in the Gulf* by Judith Miller and Laurie Mylroie; *The Slopes of Lebanon* by Amos Oz (Chatto); *In the Beginning* by Irina Ratushinskaya (Hodder); *The Burning Season: the Murder of Chico Mendes and the Fight for the Amazon Rain Forest* by Andrew Revkin (Collins); *Epics of Everyday Life: Encounters in a Changing Russia* by Susan Richards (Viking); *A Satanic Affair: Salman Rushdie and the Rage of Islam* by Malise Ruthven (Chatto); *Memoirs* by Andrei Sakharov (Hutchinson); *Death of the Dark Hero: Eastern Europe 1987–90* by David Selbourne (Cape); *The Mind of South Africa: the Story of the Rise and Fall of Apartheid* Allister Sparks (Heinemann); *The Other Russia* edited by Norman Stone and Michael Glenny (Faber); *Special Correspondent: Investigating in the Soviet Union* by Vitali Vitaliev (Hutchinson); *Against the Grain: an Autobiography* by Boris Yeltsin (Cape).

MISCELLANEOUS. *Our Age: Portrait of a Generation* by Noel Annan (Weidenfeld); *Singular Encounters* by Naim Attallah (Quartet); *Inside the British Army* by Anthony Beevor (Chatto); *The Identity of France: Volume II—People and Production* by Fernand Braudel (Collins); *The Thesaurus of American Slang* edited by Robert L. Chapman (Collins); *Stick It Up Your Punter! The Rise and Fall of The Sun* by Peter Chippindale and Chris Horrie (Heinemann); *Sweet Waist of America: Journeys around Guatemala* by Anthony Daniels (Hutchinson); *The Lives and Times of Ebenezer Scrooge* by Paul Davis (Yale); *Caesar's Vast Ghost: Aspects of Provence* by Lawrence Durrell (Faber); *The English Town* by Mark Girouard (Yale); *Writers in Hollywood 1915–1951* by Ian Hamilton (Heinemann); *Blood, Class and Nostalgia: Anglo-American Ironies* by Christopher Hitchens (Chatto); *The House the Berrys Built* by Duff Hart-Davis (Hodder); *Nothing If Not Critical: Selected Essays on Art and Artists* by Robert Hughes (Collins Harvill); *The Lord Chamberlain's Blue Pencil* by John Johnston (Hodder); *Euthanasia: the Good Death* by Ludovic Kennedy (Chatto CounterBlasts); *The Penguin Book of Lies* edited by Philip Kerr (Viking); *Debrett's Peerage and Baronetage 1990* edited by Charles Kidd and David Williamson (Macmillan); *The End of Nature* by Bill McKibben (Viking); *The Scots Thesaurus* edited by Iseabail Macleod (Aberdeen

UP); *The Oxford Book of Humorous Prose* edited by Frank Muir (OUP); *India: a Million Mutinies Now* by V. S. Naipaul (Heinemann); *Life after Life: Interviews with Twelve Murderers* by Tony Parker (Secker); *Hunting Mister Heartbreak* by Jonathan Raban (Collins Harvill); *My Learned Friends* by Adam Raphael (W. H. Allen); *The Oxford Book of Marriage* edited by Helge Rubinstein (OUP); *Dust of the Saints* by Radek Sikorski (Chatto); *A Slight Case of Libel: Meacher v. Trelford and Others* by Alan Watkins (*Duckworth*).

XVII SPORT

ASSOCIATION FOOTBALL. The World Cup finals in Italy ended with West Germany as deserving champions, but with the competition tarnished by the style and low standard of the play and by poor refereeing. The event was brilliantly staged by the host nation and breathlessly watched by millions, yet irretrievably flawed by Argentina's final performance, which climaxed much unsatisfactory and unsporting behaviour on the field. Among the spectators, in contrast, there were relatively few disturbances, not least because of massive Italian police deployments at sensitive locations.

'Fair play' was the advance slogan, yet the disciplinary record was twice as bad as in any previous championship. The referees had been ordered to be strict, but 16 players sent off and 164 booked reflected styles of play which did little credit to the game. Defending champions Argentina had by far the worst record of any nation and saved their most shameful display for the final. They started without four first-choice players, who were suspended for previous misdemeanours, and added two more red cards to their collection and several yellows as well, including a second booking for their fading star, Diego Maradona.

Argentina reached the final only as a result of penalty shoot-outs against two superior teams, namely Yugoslavia in the quarter-final and Italy in the semi-final. From the start they ruined the final as a spectacle by total concentration on defence in a tactical ploy aimed at survival for yet another penalty shoot-out. It was indeed a penalty, coolly taken by Andreas Brehme of West Germany, that defeated them, but this one had been dubiously awarded five minutes before the end of full time. By then Argentinian substitute Pedro Monzon had already been sent off, and Gustavo Dezotti soon followed. No wonder the Argentinian team was whistled from the field, their day of shame being later compounded as the country's President, Carlos Menem, tried to excuse his team by making a verbal attack on the referee. Certainly the refereeing overall was of unusually poor standard, but Argentina at least got what they deserved.

By contrast, England not only won the fair play award for the team with the best disciplinary record, but never indulged in the play-acting by which some players, West Germany's included, tried to win penalties or to get opponents booked. England did indeed have some good fortune in their early games, notably in beating Cameroon 3–2 in the quarter-final, but none at all in losing the semi-final to West Germany in a penalty shoot-out and the play-off for third place to Italy. These two matches were judged two of the best and most sporting in the competition, with England playing delightful attacking football and scoring two remarkable goals through Gary Lineker and David Platt, who together with Paul ('Gazza') Gascoigne were among the great successes of the tournament. Lineker was honoured by FIFA with a £20,000 award as the most sporting player in the finals, an achievement which did much to restore the international good name of English football after the troubles of recent years.

Inevitably, there were other fine individual performances and attractive matches. Cameroon gave the tournament a splendid start by beating the holders Argentina. Sadly, they also set the pattern of foul-play, getting two men sent off in that opening match. Thereafter they gave a great stimulus to African football by winning their group and then beating Colombia, before going out to England in extra time in a match which they could have won with their exceptional ball skills.

Egypt also surprised many with the quality of their football, drawing with the disappointing Dutch team and also with Ireland, before a narrow defeat by England eliminated them. The form of such teams indicated the levelling of standards worldwide, with Europe and South America no longer so far ahead of the rest as they once were. There were great individual performances from two Italians, Salvatore Schillaci and Roberto Baggio. The former came on as substitute to score the goal which beat the USA and went on to become the tournament's highest individual goal-scorer with six in total. Baggio was a close rival as Italy's star, with his dazzling dribbles and brilliant goals. For West Germany, captain Lothar Matthaus typified the team with his professional expertise, his driving determination and goal-scoring flair.

Scotland turned in another of their standard World Cup performances, having qualified for the tournament for the fifth successive time but then failing yet again at the first hurdle. Ireland, in contrast, were runners-up to England in their first-round group (a drawing of lots putting them ahead of the Dutch, who had also drawn all three matches); the team then beat Romania in a penalty shoot-out, before losing a closely-fought quarter-final to Italy. Ireland's highly effective English manager, Jack Charlton, was such a good spokesman for Irish football and became such a popular figure that he was made an honorary Irishman. On his way home he was presented with a fly-fishing rod and promptly departed to Alaska to enjoy a relaxing session at his favourite sport.

In the domestic 1989–90 season, Liverpool were again the outstanding English team, winning the League championship and reaching the semi-final of the FA Cup. Their conquerors in the latter competition were the London side Crystal Palace, who drew 3–3 with Manchester United in the Wembley final, only to lose the replay to Lee Martin's goal.

The start of the new season in the autumn was noteworthy for the readmission of English clubs into two of the three European competitions, five years after the 1985 Heysel Stadium tragedy which had caused them to be banned. However, a continuing ban on Liverpool (the English team involved in that disaster) kept them out of the European Champions Cup.

RUGBY UNION. The five-nations championship was dominated by Scotland and England, both sides having convincing wins over France, Wales and Ireland. Against Ireland England's Rory Underwood scored a record 19th try and there were several more to come. Captain Will Carling was also a major influence and against Wales scored one of the best tries of the season. Everything turned on the final match between Scotland and England at Murrayfield, with both the Grand Slam and the Calcutta Cup at stake. It was not just a contest between two outstanding teams, but also one between outstanding coaches. Ian McGeechan and Roger Utley had jointly masterminded the Lions win in Australia, but on this occasion McGeechan and his Scottish team proved superior. The Scottish captain, David Sole, ensured that his pack more than matched the formidable one from which England's successes had stemmed. Gavin Hastings was also prominent and set up the decisive try.

The New Zealand All Blacks lost an international at last, after remaining unbeaten for 52 matches. They were defeated by Australia 21–9 in the final game of a three-match series, having won the previous two. The Argentinians surprisingly drew a series with England in Argentina, only to lose by a massive margin in a return encounter at Twickenham. To add to their depression the team's 51–0 defeat was the first time that their most famous player, Hugo Porta, had failed to score in an international. The young Argentine prop-forward, Frederico Mendes, was sent off for knocking out Paul Ackford. In happier mood, the Barbarians celebrated their centenary with the free and flowing rugby so enjoyed by the spectators. Wasps won the English League, while Bath beat Gloucester in the Pilkington Cup final.

RUGBY LEAGUE. In the first of a three-match series in England, Great Britain at last beat the Australians (19–12). But Mal Meninga, the Australian captain, then played a leading part in setting up a narrow victory in the second game and a more decisive one in the third, to ensure that Australia retained the Ashes as usual. Ellery Hanley and Martin Offiah were outstanding for the British team. Hanley also shone as Wigan won the Regal trophy for the fifth time and then completed the double with a Challenge Cup win at Wembley. Former Welsh union star Jonathan Davies was inspirational for Widnes, who took the Premiership title.

BOXING. As always, boxing's talk and action centred on the American heavyweights. Undisputed champion Mike Tyson was headline news as the world's most feared fighter, of whom his manager, Don King, remarked: 'If Mike was a pier 6 brawler he'd be hard to sell, but he surgically discombobulates his opponents.' Yet going into the ring in Japan as odds-on favourite, an ill-prepared Tyson was himself 'discombobulated' by James 'Buster' Douglas. The Tyson camp inevitably tried to cry foul, but even Mr King could not persuade many people to overlook the fact that his man had been knocked out cleanly. A few months later Douglas himself failed to train properly for a fight and lost the heavyweight crown to an impressive Evander Hollyfield. By year's end his tenure of sport's most lucrative title (although not necessarily to the pugilists themselves) was under challenge from former champion George Foreman, making a middle-aged comeback, and more ominously from Tyson himself, who appeared to have recovered his fearsome power.

Mark Breland (USA) became an impressive champion by demolishing former middle-weight title-holder Lloyd Honeyghan of Britain. Chris Eubank fought fellow-Briton Nigel Benn for the WBO version of the middle-weight title, scoring an impressive win in a ferocious contest that lived up to all its advance publicity.

COMMONWEALTH GAMES AND ATHLETICS. The Commonwealth Games were staged in New Zealand and lived up to their title of the 'friendly' games. There were many outstanding performances. In track and field England won more than 50 medals, including 16 golds. Steve Backley confirmed his standing as the world's best javelin thrower and Tessa Sanderson made it an England double by winning the women's event. Indeed, British athletes gave a foretaste of their later success in the European championships. Linford Christie won the 100 metres in 9.93 seconds and Marcus Adam just beat John Regis in the 200 metres to set a new Games record of 20.1 seconds. Peter Elliott comfortably won the 1,500 metres, while Colin Jackson of Wales set another Games and European record by winning the 110 metres hurdles in 13.08 seconds. In other events, Australia's swimmers dominated in the pool, winning 21 gold medals between them. For England Adrian Moorhouse equalled the world record in the 100 metres breaststroke, as he was to do again later in the year. There were medals galore for England, particularly in the judo events.

By the time the European athletic championships were held in Split, Yugoslavia, Backley had set a world javelin record, lost it to Jan Zelazny, then regained it with the first-ever throw beyond 90 metres. At Split his first throw was good enough to win and his final distance of 87.56 metres set a new record for the event. Britain dominated the men's track events, as East Germany did the women's. In all, Britain's athletes won nine gold medals, which left Britain second to East Germany overall. Yvonne Murray (3,000 metres) scored the only victory for the women, but Britain's men won every event from 100 to 800 metres. In the 100 and 200 metres Christie and Regis each took a gold and a bronze. In the 400 metres Roger Black, restored from an injury which seemed to have ended his career, was again the winner, while Tom McKean took gold in the 800 metres. Peter Elliott was favourite to win the 1,500 metres, but in his heat he was pushed over and left sprawled on the track. A controversial decision to reinstate him in the final did him no favours, as he and Steve Cram were beaten into fourth and fifth places respectively. In the hurdles Jackson just beat Tony Jarrett, while Kriss Akabusi won the 400 metres hurdles and broke a British record which had stood for 22 years. The British 4 × 400 metres relay team ended the championships in style, with Black some 15 metres clear.

The French 4 × 100 metres relay team had earlier set the only world record of the games, their 37.80 second run leaving Britain's fancied four a yard behind.

CRICKET. As one star set, two rose. In July the New Zealand all-rounder Richard Hadlee retired with a record 431 wickets and 3,124 runs in Test cricket. Honoured with a knighthood, Sir Richard finished in style with a fine performance in his final Test against England. By the year's end a young Pakistani, Waqar Younis, had made such dramatic impact that the Deloitte rankings listed him the world's best bowler, while India's 17-year-old Sachin Tendulkar had saved a Test against England with a brilliant century.

England's performance improved as Graham Gooch took over the captaincy from David Gower for the West Indies tour. The first Test was won by fine bowling from Angus Fraser and Devon Malcom, on a ground where West Indies had not lost for 35 years. The second was washed out, and rain and Desmond Haynes's delaying tactics deprived England of victory in the third. But with Gooch and Fraser by now injured, West Indies won the next two and the series.

In England better pitches and smaller seams on the balls brought a spate of runs. Gooch broke the record for the highest total of Test runs in an English summer and led England to wins against New Zealand and India. The New Zealand series depended on the result of the final Test, in which the batting of Gooch and Mike Atherton plus the bowling of Malcolm and Eddie Hemmings ensured victory for England despite Hadlee's 5 for 58 in the second innings.

The first Test against India proved decisive. This Lord's match belonged to Gooch, who scored 333 in the first innings and a racing 123 in the second, more runs than anyone had previously scored in a single Test. Having himself taken a wicket and some good catches, Gooch finished the game in style by throwing down the wicket for a run-out. For the Indians there was a magical century from their captain, Mohammad Azaharuddin, and the follow-on was avoided when Kapil Dev hit Hemmings for four successive sixes. For the rest of the series batsmen dominated two ordinary attacks, with Tendulkar saving the second Test after India were on the verge of defeat. India then had the chance to square the series at the Oval after making England follow-on 266 runs behind. But Gooch and Atherton again launched the innings with a century partnership, during which Gooch passed Bradman's record to end with more than 1,000 runs in the series. An elegant unbeaten 157 from David Gower ensured a draw and a second series win for England. The euphoria was short-lived. The winter tour found England struggling again against Australia and losing the first two Tests by wide margins.

Pakistan confirmed their standing as a top Test team by beating New Zealand 3–0, then drawing a three-match series with the dominant West Indies. The New Zealanders were destroyed by Younis, who took 29 wickets at 10.86 runs apiece, while batsman Shaoib Mohammad averaged 169. Younis was again a destructive force against West Indies. At a lower cricketing level, 17 of the countries which had not yet achieved Test status, including the USA, took part in the fourth ICC Trophy competition staged in the Netherlands. Zimbabwe came through to win for the third successive time, beating the host country in the final.

Mike Gatting's England career was finally ended when he led a 'rebel' tour to South Africa, where it aroused so much opposition that it was aborted early. After abuse abroad, Gatting had applause at home as he captained Middlesex to win the county championship. Lancashire were kings of the one-day game, winning both the Benson & Hedges Cup and the NatWest Trophy. A sad finale to the season was the death of Sir Leonard Hutton, former captain of Yorkshire and England (see OBITUARY).

GOLF. Greg Norman was top of the USA PGA Tour money list and Ian Woosnam headed the European Volvo order of merit, but Nick Faldo was the master of the majors and the golfing superstar of 1990. For the second successive year Faldo's consistency and coolness in a crisis brought him the coveted green jacket of the US Masters championship at Augusta. Ray Floyd seemed set to win, until Faldo began holing long putts to catch him over the final holes and to force a play-off, as in the previous year. Again Faldo's opponent missed a chance to take the title at the first extra hole and again Faldo triumphed at the next, hitting his second shot to the middle of the green after Floyd had pulled his into the water. Until Faldo, only Jack Nicklaus had ever won two successive US Masters.

The British Open saw Faldo at his devastating best. By the third round he was paired with Norman as joint leader. Going round in nine strokes less than the Australian, he wiped him out of contention and went on to win by five strokes from Payne Stewart and Mark McNulty. Faldo's success owed much to his rapport with his coach, David Leadbetter, and with his caddy, Fanny Sunesson. That combination nearly won another major as well. In the US Open only the occasional uncharacteristic lapse when chipping and a final putt which mysteriously stayed out of the hole prevented Faldo being involved in a play-off. Instead, Hale Irwin became the oldest winner of the title (beating Mike Donald) and for good measure had a follow-up victory in the Buick Classic. For Faldo there was American recognition of his special status when he was nominated the US PGA's player of the year, an award no other non-American had won since its inception in 1948.

For Norman, who headed the Sony world rankings until being overtaken by Faldo, this was a year of mixed fortunes. The pluses were his $1,165,477 earnings on the US PGA tour, his chipping in for an eagle at the play-off hole to win the Doral Ryder Open, and his sinking of a 279-yard shot for an albatross in the Australian Open. The minuses were his poor form in the majors, including missing the cut in the Masters, and being beaten by a stroke in the Nestlé Invitational, when Robert Gamez holed his 7-iron shot to the last green. For Seve Ballesteros the balance-sheet was less even. His disappointing season included a solitary win in the Renault Open in Baleares. As compensation he achieved his first tournament hole-in-one in the second round of the Monte Carlo Open, which Woosnam won with a final round of 60, a record for the course. By contrast, fellow-Spaniard José-Maria Olazabal had another fine season, finishing third in the Volvo order of merit and picking up a further $337,837 on the US PGA tour.

Ireland defeated England in the final of the Nations Cup at St Andrews, while the Germans Bernhard Langer and Torsten Giedeon won the World Cup in Orlando, Florida. With Australia's Wayne Grady winning the US PGA championship, Norman the leading money-maker in America, and Woosnam of Wales continuing the recent British domination of the Suntory World Matchplay championship, America no longer rated as the superpower of golf. However, there was no disputing the US PGA's nomination of Tom Watson as the outstanding player of the 1980s. Tom Kite also became a record money-spinner when he won the St Jude Classic, taking his overall earnings past $6 million. However, Wayne Levi was the leading American of the year, with four wins and earnings of over $1 million, putting him second behind Norman.

MOTOR SPORT. Another explosive Grand Prix season was marred by serious accident and bitter controversy. Again Brazil's Ayrton Senna was at the centre of the action and the recriminations, and again it was his rivalry with Alain Prost of France which provoked the collisions on and off the track. Senna was still smarting from his previous year's defeat by Prost in the drivers' championship (see AR 1989, pp. 508–9), and from the official reprimand which he received for dangerous driving.

This time it was Senna who won, but the manner of final victory did nothing for his reputation.

The decisive incident on Japan's Suzuka track, which put himself and Prost out of the race, summed up Senna's bewildering mixture of brilliance and recklessness. It also rekindled his sordid feud with Prost. Senna, reasonably enough, had complained that his pole position, so hardly won, was on the dirty side of the track, while Prost's second qualifying place had given him the clean side. The officials refused to make any change. Prost duly got the better start, and a furious Senna drove into his back at the first corner. Both cars ran into the sand-trap, which at least saved those behind from a horrendous multiple pile-up. It also ensured victory in the drivers' championship for Senna. A few weeks earlier, he and Prost had appeared to end their 18-month-long antagonism with a much-publicized handshake. That brief truce ended as Senna hit Prost's Ferrari so hard that the rear wing snapped off.

'The world championship is for sport, not war', said an outraged Prost. 'I don't give a damn what Prost says', riposted Senna, adding: 'Tactically speaking, Prost made a mistake, knowing I was going for the gap. I always do.' Prost's Ferrari team was equally incensed. A commission of inquiry was set up after Suzuka. Ferrari wrote to the FIA president threatening to withdraw from the 1991 championship if no satisfactory action was taken on safety and driver conduct. There had been other worrying accidents, too, with Britain's Derek Warwick lucky to escape from a spectacular crash at Monza and Martin Donnelly very badly injured during practice before the Spanish Grand Prix at Jerez. Alessandro Nannini of Italy was another to end up in hospital, but his injuries were the result of a helicopter crash.

Prost's failure to get any points at Suzuka meant the championship was already decided in Senna's favour before the final race in Australia, which was celebrated as the 500th in the Grand Prix series. Britain's Nigel Mansell harried Senna so relentlessly that the latter was forced to juggle with his brake balance to keep ahead; this led to gearbox failure and retirement on the 62nd lap. The latter stages of the race were enlivened by a stirring battle between Mansell and Nelson Piquet (Brazil); Piquet just held on for his second successive victory, while Mansell narrowly failed to record his second win of the season.

TENNIS. The season had a predictable start, with Ivan Lendl (Czechoslovakia) and Steffi Graf (Germany) winning the singles events in the Australian Open. But later the season proved to be very open indeed, with no fewer than eight players winning Grand Slam events.

After 66 consecutive victories, Graf lost a match at last—sadly for her in her home country—as 16-year-old Monica Seles of Yugoslavia won the final of the German Open. With domestic problems leading to a loss of form, Graf was beaten again by Seles in the final of the

French championship, in which 13-year-old Jennifer Capriati (USA), the youngest person ever to play on the professional circuit, reached the semi-final. Graf lost out again at Wimbledon, where she defeated Capriati but lost to Zena Garrison (USA). Garrison also knocked out Seles to reach the final, where Martina Navratilova (USA) recorded her ninth Wimbledon win. The US Open was won by Gabriela Sabatini (Argentina).

Lendl's number one status was lost to the Swede, Stefan Edberg, who beat him in the Wimbledon semi-final before meeting Boris Becker (Germany) in the final for the third successive year. Edberg's skill and all-round ability overcame Becker's impressive power, as it had Lendl's.

America continued to produce a wealth of tennis talent in the men's game as well as the women's. Andre Agassi (USA) was favourite to win the French championship, but was defeated in the final by the Ecuadorian Andrés Gómez. America later won the Davis Cup, beating Australia 3–2 in the final, while the Grand Slam Cup in Munich became an all-American affair. In the tournament the leading multi-millionaire of tennis, Ivan Lendl, let slip another couple of million dollars when he lost in straight sets to the unfancied David Wheaton (USA). With Edberg falling in the first round, an American quartet contested the semi-finals, with Wheaton matched against Brad Gilbert and Michael Chang against Peter Sampras, who had won the US Open. In the final 19-year-old Sampras added this most lucrative prize to his growing collection.

THE TURF. A legend's triumphant return provided racing's most remarkable story, as 54-year-old Lester Piggott returned to the track after a five-year absence. Having served a prison sentence for tax evasion, the most outstanding jockey of modern times found fulfilment again in the saddle. After Vincent O'Brien had persuaded him to ride in a veterans' race, his undimmed master status was rapidly confirmed as he came second on his first real ride and had eight winners within a fortnight. Asked if he had changed his style, the taciturn Piggott replied: 'It's still the same—one leg each side of the horse.'

The most remunerative winner of the 5,142 he had ridden so far in his career came in America. At Belmont Park Piggott forced Royal Academy ahead of Itsallgreektome in the last few strides of the Breeders' Cup Mile to win a purse of £279,503. The colt had been sired by Nijinsky, a Derby winner 20 years earlier with Piggott riding. Britain's Willie Carson, riding the European champion sprinter Dayjur, had lost out unluckily in the previous race, the Breeders' Cup Sprint, when his excitable horse had leapt a shadow on the track to lose by a neck from Safely Kept. That was a rare mishap for Carson, in a season in which he became only the fourth jockey to have ridden 3,000 winners and had a double success on Salsabil in the 1,000 Guineas and the Oaks. Pat Eddery was again outstanding with over 200 wins, including the Derby on Quest For Fame. Quest's trainer, Roger Charlton, completed an unusual double in that his horse Sanglamore had won the French Derby at Chantilly three days earlier.

The people's favourite jumper, Desert Orchid, was beaten into third place in the Cheltenham Gold Cup, which was won by 100–1 outsider Norton's Coin. However, 'Dessie' came back to form to win the Irish Grand National and finished the season with a runaway success in the King George VI Chase at Kempton. Trainer Martin Pipe and jockey Peter Scudamore continued their run of winners (224 for Pipe, 170 for Scudamore). The Grand National had a stirring finish when Mr Frisk held off Durham Edition to win by a length. Jockey Marcus Armytage said afterwards: 'All my life I had wanted an excuse to punch the air, and I almost fell off doing it.' With Armytage firmly in the saddle, Mr Frisk again held off Durham Edition to win the Whitbread Gold Cup.

OTHER NOTABLE ACHIEVEMENTS. In the Whitbread Round the World Race the Australian yacht *Steinlager 2* won every leg. But the performance of Tracy Edwards and the all-female crew of *Maiden* won much acclaim as they proved outstanding in their class. In snooker 21-year-old Stephen Hendry of Scotland came as close to perfection as was possible, taking over from Steve Davis as the world's number one. For courage it was hard to better Louise Aitken-Walker, the Scottish winner of the Ladies World Rally championship. In Portugal her car spun off the track, slid down a cliff and into a lake. Despite her narrow escape from death, this merely strengthened her determination to win the title.

AMERICAN ASPECTS. The San Francisco 49ers confirmed themselves as the American football team of the decade with an overwhelming 55–10 defeat of the Denver Broncos in Super Bowl XXIV. Quarter-back Dan Merino masterminded the rout, which so humiliated Denver that they won only three of their first eleven games in the new season, while the 49ers continued in invincible form. The Oakland 'As' had seemed as dominant in winning the baseball World Series the previous year and in their form throughout the season. They were expected to have another clean sweep against the Cincinnati Reds, in the World Series, but this time it was Oakland who were out-played.

America's Greg Lemond won the prestigious Tour de France cycle race for the third time and Paul Lim recorded the only perfect nine-dart finish ever achieved in a world darts championship, although it was England's unfancied Phil Taylor who beat Eric Bristow in the final to become world champion. Atlanta was chosen to host the 1996 Olympics, as this once-amateur event became increasingly commercialized. The

United States was also due to host the World Cup soccer finals in 1994, but the performance of its team in Italy did little to generate interest. With the organizers having problems in booking the requisite stadia during the baseball season, Germany and Italy were hopefully informing FIFA that they stood ready to take over should America withdraw.

XVIII ECONOMIC AND SOCIAL AFFAIRS

Chapter 1

POLAND AND EASTERN EUROPE

THE main economic event of the year was the collapse of communism in Eastern Europe. This was accompanied by attempts to dismantle the centrally-planned economic system in order to replace it with Western-style free markets. However, with the exception of Poland—which opted for a 'big bang' solution—and East Germany (which could rely on huge financial support from West Germany), progress was very patchy.

The USSR, the biggest economy, was facing possible collapse as it struggled to make changes in a piecemeal way while its constituent regions were trying to break away from central authority (see pp. 109–11). The country admitted to a 5 per cent (unplanned) contraction of output in 1990 even before it had agreed transitional policies which would, almost inevitably, bring even sharper shocks. In Hungary gross domestic product contracted by 5 per cent against a background of accelerating inflation. The country's problems were exacerbated by a severe drought in the summer, sharp increases in energy prices (now having to be paid in hard currency to the USSR) and a reluctance to devalue. Czechoslovakia was slow to liberalize because of fears of the social costs involved. It was planning a similar policy to the Poles, though on a smaller scale, involving devaluation and the removal of price controls within a year.

Poland decided to implement all the unpopular measures in one 'big bang' starting at the beginning of January. This was one of the most remarkable economic experiments ever carried out anywhere. The country was virtually turned into an economic laboratory in which a series of measures which might normally have been applied over a period of years were destruction-tested during a few months. For instance Britain took ten years to get inflation down from 10.3 to 7.7 per cent. Poland tried to reduce an inflation rate of over 1,000 per cent in 1989 to single figures (on a monthly basis) in a few months. Most of the soaring subsidies—which swallowed nearly a third of all budget spending—were swept away at a stroke. While Britain was debating the merits of an independent central bank, Poland announced one in January, accompanied by a vast privatization programme. Poland also made the zloty convertible with the US dollar overnight and raised coal prices by 700 per cent and road transport fares by 250 per cent. As part of the programme, wage increases were reduced from 80 per cent of prices to only 30 per cent, thereby entailing a savage cut in living standards for people who were among the poorest in Europe.

Within six months the Polish experiment was outwardly very successful, though at considerable social cost. Decades of long queues at shops and petrol stations disappeared, having been priced out of the market place. Instead of merely reducing the huge budget deficit (equivalent to 8 per cent of the economy), the government produced a budget surplus of 6 to 7 per cent of GDP in the first six months, thanks to the removal of subsidies. Inflation tumbled from almost 80 per cent a month to 3.4 per cent in June, though it rose later in the year because of a relaxation of incomes policy, coupled with the effects of higher world energy prices. The once-almighty dollar had been dethroned and the black market rate almost eliminated. In January almost 70 per cent of money in circulation was dollars. By June the proportion had fallen to 40 per cent as confidence in the domestic currency revived. Instead of the traditional trade deficit, the economy was boasting its biggest trade surplus for 40 years. Hard currency exports rose from $500 million in 1989 to $11,500 million in 1990. The problem was that the financial targets had been met at a far greater contraction of industrial output (30 per cent) and living standards (also 30 per cent) than had been planned. This was even more worrying than the leap in unemployment from nil to 600,000, which had been expected as the inevitable cost of moving into a market economy.

This was probably the sharpest economic contraction ever experienced by a non-third-world nation in such a short time. The whole economy contracted by 15 per cent in the first half of the year, though at a slower rate in the second half. Some economists, such as Jeffrey Sachs (an adviser to Solidarity), claimed that the 31.8 per cent drop in the index of real wages in 1990 greatly overstated the underlying fall in living standards. They argued that higher prices merely removed the excess demand in the goods markets, thereby reversing the exceptional rise in real wages of the previous two years when there had been too much money chasing very few goods. It was also pointed out that if wages were measured in dollars (now fully convertible with the zloty) then there was a rise from an average of $91 per month in December 1989 to $164 in December 1990.

Under pressure from rapidly falling living standards and the prospect of presidential elections (which saw Lech Walesa come to power—see p. 118), the government eased policy in the second half of the year. It started to spend its unexpected budget surplus on a range of measures, including unemployment relief and increased spending on public works such as hospitals, and on a relaxation of the worst rigours of the incomes policy. This helped to mitigate the impact of the policies, but it was clear at the end of the year that Mr Walesa would need all his political skills to prevent the pent-up grievances of the population from exploding.

Poland was pushing hard to get Western banks and governments to ease the burden of its $44,000 million external debts, which it was unable to service in any meaningful way. These debts were built up by the former communist regime, and the government was hoping that the West would write off much of the burden. However, the attentions of the West were distracted from August onwards by the even greater problems arising from Iraq's invasion of Kuwait. By the end of the year many of the good intentions which Western countries had professed towards Eastern Europe were being diluted because of an economic slow-down at home and growing political problems abroad.

Chapter 2

THE INTERNATIONAL ECONOMY

THE world's industrialized nations grew by 2.8 per cent in 1990, according to the 24-nation OECD, compared with 3.4 per cent in 1989. Although the outcome for 1990 was much as predicted a year earlier, the distribution of growth was different, with the United States growing much more slowly than anticipated (1 per cent against 2.3) and Japan growing faster than expected (6.1 per cent against 4.5). West Germany, whose unification with East Germany was not on the cards in the autumn of 1989 when the OECD made its predictions for 1990, expanded by 4.2 per cent compared with forecasts of 3.2 per cent. This marked the eighth year of economic growth above 2.5 per cent in the OECD area and was achieved with a slow-down in unemployment growth (from 6.4 to 6.2 per cent) and with inflation remaining unchanged at 4.3 per cent despite the mid-year boost to oil prices triggered by the threat of war in the Gulf. World trade (the average of growth in import and export volumes) slowed down to 5.1 per cent after a 7.0 per cent increase in 1989.

Once again the lion's share of increased prosperity went to the countries of the Pacific Basin, which continued to outpace the rest of the world (see AR 1989, pp. 515–7). Japan, China, Taiwan, Indonesia, Malaysia, the Philippines, Singapore, South Korea and Thailand all recorded growth rates of between 5 and 10 per cent. Eastern European countries experienced negative growth as they struggled with the birth pangs of transition to capitalism (see previous chapter). In South America the most dramatic event was Brazil's attempts to cure hyper-inflation under its new young President, Fernando Collor de Mello. In March the administration announced the most draconian economic adjustment in the country's history, which included freezing the cash in many of the nation's bank accounts. By the end of the year the monthly rate of inflation had come down from an astronomic 80 per cent to a still-unsustainable 20 per cent (see also pp. 77–8).

Among developing countries Africa fared worst, suffering a decline in per capita incomes for the 12th year running. The continent had to absorb an increase in its oil bill of $2,700 million at a time when the goodwill of Western nations was distracted by the emergence of democracy in Eastern Europe and the threat of war in the Gulf. During the year Africa's aggregate external debt rose by 4.7 per cent to $272,000 million, almost equal to the region's gross domestic product (GDP) and three times the value of export earnings. The one redeeming feature was that, for only the third time in 20 years, agricultural output grew faster than population.

In order to expedite structural change in Eastern Europe, governments in the West agreed to set up the European Bank for Reconstruction and Development (EBRD), with a capital of $13,000 million. Based on an idea by the French politician Jacques Attali (its first president), it was intended to supplement the work of the World Bank and other international bodies in stimulating new investment projects in Eastern Europe. With headquarters in London, the EBRD was scheduled to begin operations in April 1991.

MONETARY POLICIES. Monetary policies differed quite considerably in response to domestic requirements, ranging from reductions in interest rates in the United States (to stave off the recession) to increases in both Japan (to bear down on inflation) and in West Germany (to contain the pressures of unification with East Germany and upward pressure on the money supply). Interest rates were eased in France at the end of October, but only by one quarter per cent as France struggled to maintain its new-found monetary virility against the strong German model. Interest rates were reduced by 1 per cent in the United Kingdom as a kind of political gesture to accompany entry into the exchange rate mechanism of the European Monetary System on 8 October (see pp. 33, 404). Interest rates also fell in Italy and Canada, reflecting favourable inflation trends in both countries.

There was concern during the year about the indebtedness of banks, particularly in the United States, where the consequences of excessive corporate debt had to be met, and in Japan, where the surge in equity prices (partly financed by the easy loans accompanying financial liberalization) reversed itself in 1990 with a fall of around 40 per cent.

Fiscal policy was loosened among OECD countries for the first time for many years mainly because of the gathering recession in the United States and some other countries. The 18 leading economies recorded a total budget deficit (excess of spending over income) equivalent to 1.6 per cent of GDP in 1990 compared with 1.1 per cent in 1989. This interrupted an improving trend apparent every year since 1985, when the deficit was 3.3 per cent of GDP. Since that time the main improvements had come from Japan (which turned a 1 per cent deficit into a 3 per cent surplus) and the UK which turned a 2.7 per cent deficit into a small surplus. The biggest swing came from Norway whose surplus was reduced from 10.4 per cent of GDP to 2.5 per cent.

INTERNATIONAL TRADE. The growth in the volume of world trade slowed down to 5.1 per cent in 1990 compared with 7.0 per cent in 1989. Exports within the OECD area grew by 5.2 per cent against import growth of 5.6 per cent. Exports to countries outside the OECD area were only 3.1 per cent against imports of 5.3 per cent. The OECD area's current-account deficit with the rest of the world worsened during the year from $50,000 million to $85,000 million. Improvements in the US deficit were offset by reduced trade surpluses in West Germany and Japan. OPEC countries turned a $2,000 million deficit into a surplus of $14,000 million, while Latin America deteriorated by $3,000 million to $6,000 million thanks to higher oil prices. Although the US had the largest deficit, this was due to the size of the economy. As a percentage of the economy, a number of countries had much worse deficits, including Switzerland (4.3 per cent), Canada (2.6 per cent), Finland (4.4 per cent), Greece (4.7 per cent), New Zealand (4.4 per cent) and Australia (6.0 per cent).

The talks aimed at lowering barriers to trade held under the auspices of the General Agreement on Tariffs and Trade (GATT) were adjourned in December, with the European Community being unable to agree to the extent of reduction in agricultural subsidies which the US demanded (see pp. 66, 405–6).

THE NOBEL PRIZE FOR ECONOMICS. The 1990 prize, worth $364,000, was awarded jointly to three academics from the United States for their pioneering research into the theory of corporate finance and financial markets. They were Professor Harry Markowitz of New York's City University, regarded as the founder of modern investment theory; Professor William Sharpe of Stanford, who helped to forge the capital asset pricing model; and Professor Merton Miller, a specialist in financial economics.

Chapter 3

THE ECONOMY OF THE UNITED STATES

IN the economic sphere 1990 would be remembered as the year in which the longest peacetime recovery on record finally came to an end. The economy expanded by under 1 per cent compared with 2.5 per cent in 1989 and 4.5 per cent in 1988. By the final quarter of 1990 the economy was contracting at an annualized rate of over 3 per cent with no sign of an early recovery. Eight years of strong, uninterrupted growth—during which the debt-ridden US economy seemed at times to be defying gravity—finally caught up with reality (see also pp. 55–8).

Inflation grew slightly during 1990 from 4.5 to 5.4 per cent (as measured by the private consumption deflator) or from 4.1 to 4.2 per cent (as measured by the GDP deflator). The main cause of the increase was the rise in oil prices triggered by the threat of a war with Iraq over its occupation of Kuwait. However, there was also an increase in 'core' inflation (excluding food and energy) from 4 to 5 per cent.

The United States entered the recession with its financial system in unusually poor health. In the private sector some of the nation's richest and most famous financiers—including Michael Milken, the pioneer of 'junk bonds'—were disgraced as the ballooning debts of the eighties claimed their victims. In the public sector the budget deficit on the newly-agreed definitions (i.e. excluding the social security surplus and expenditures of the Resolution Trust Corporation) was expected to reach $250,000 million in fiscal 1991 rising to $264,000 million in 1992. There was still a long way to go before eliminating it completely as required by law. Unemployment rose for the first time in nine years, from 5.3 to 5.5 per cent as the growth-recession took its toll.

OUTPUT AND EMPLOYMENT. The tightish monetary policy of 1988-89 and the increasing debt problems of the private sector combined to depress the growth of output in 1990. Once again, the main engine of growth was exports, thanks to the comparative weakness of the dollar. Exports grew by 5.8 per cent against import growth of 3.3 per cent, which was sufficient to reduce the current-account deficit—the third successive reduction—from $110,000 million to $104,000 million. Government spending rose by almost 3 per cent, but private consumption was up by barely 1 per cent. Private fixed investment was static, a rise of 1.5 per cent in non-residential investment being offset by a 4.1 per cent reduction in residential investment—mainly because of the effects of the indebtedness of the private sector. Industrial production rose by less than 1 per cent (against 3.3 and 5.7 per cent in 1989 and 1988 respectively).

A combination of flat employment and depressed output led to an acceleration in unit labour costs from 3 per cent in a year in 1989 to 4 per cent in the third quarter of 1990. Wage increases, as measured by average earnings, rose by a comparatively modest 3.6 per cent in the year to November, the lowest annual rise among the top 12 industrial nations including Japan.

GOVERNMENT POLICY. As the year progressed there was a mild, but consistent, easing of monetary policy in an attempt to prevent the slowdown in activity from developing into a serious recession. The Federal Reserve's policy of engineering slight reductions in interest rates, evident in the second half of 1989, was continued in the new year with falls in the federal funds rate in July, October and November. This helped to keep the dollar at a 'competitive' level, thereby boosting export prospects while not stoking up inflation too much. The success of the Fed's tightrope walk between inflation and recession was particularly important in 1990 because of the extreme fragility of the financial system, suffering as it was from the collapse of the junk bond market, the exploding debts of the Savings and Loans (S&L) institutions, the de-rating of the credit-worthiness of major banks and the collapse of property prices.

At the end of October Congress approved a fiscal package designed to reduce the federal budget deficit by a total of $492,000 million over the following five years. But even after these cuts the budget deficit was still expected to rise in 1991 and 1992. This was in spite of an about-turn on tax increases by President Bush, who had been elected to office on a 'no tax increases, read my lips' ticket. It was a far cry from previous plans under the administration of President Reagan to eliminate the deficit entirely by 1993. During the year the eventual cost of rescuing the S&L institutions was raised from estimates of $100,000 million at the end of 1988 to as high as $500,000 million.

The easing of monetary conditions was reflected in the growth of the money supply. The narrow measure of money was growing at 4.2 per cent a year at the end of 1990 (compared with 0.4 per cent a year earlier). However, the wider measure of money was expanding at only 1.4 per cent annualized—the slowest of any large industrialized nation.

Chapter 4

THE ECONOMY OF THE UNITED KINGDOM

THE British economy expanded by less than 1 per cent in 1990 compared with growth of 1.8 per cent in 1989 and 4.3 per cent in 1988. This ended eight years of uninterrupted expansion which had seen growth of 3 per cent a year since the nadir of the previous recession in 1981, or just over 2 per cent since the Conservatives were returned to power in 1979. The economy had continued to expand during the first half of 1990, fed by resilient consumer expenditure, rising exports and continuing investment. During the second half of the year the cumulative effect of two years of high interest rates, a stronger pound and rising inflation took their toll as investment—particularly by manufacturing industry—sagged and consumer expenditure slowed down.

The major economic event of the year was Britain's entry into the exchange rate mechanism (ERM) of the European Monetary System which, for the best part of a decade, the goverment had promised to join 'when the time is ripe'. The time became ripe on Monday 8 October when Britain finally entered the European club pledging to keep the value of the pound within 6 per cent of a central range of European currencies (see also pp. 33, 404). In the case of the key Deutschmark, this meant keeping within a range of DM 2.7780 and DM 3.1320. The entry announcement was accompanied by a 1 per cent reduction in interest rates, to 14 per cent.

OUTPUT AND EMPLOYMENT. Unemployment rose by 211,000 to 1,850,000 in the year to December in response to the growing recessionary forces. The long fall in unemployment which had characterized the boom years came to a halt in March at 1,606,600 or 5.6 per cent of the workforce. Thereafter, it rose every month until December (6.5 per cent of the workforce) with no obvious end in sight. In the nine months to September the number of people with jobs continued to rise by almost 400,000 to 23,261,000. This consisted of an extra 460,000 (mainly female part-time jobs) offset by a 78,000 decline in (mainly male) manufacturing jobs.

Industrial production in the three months to December was running 1.5 per cent lower than the previous quarter and also 3 per cent below a year earlier. This included a 3 per cent fall in manufacturing which, in turn, included a 4 per cent drop in engineering and a 4 per cent fall in output by the metals industry. As a result of all this the total output of the economy, which had been growing at an annual rate of 2.5 per cent in the first half of the year, was thrown into reverse with negative (annualized) growth of 2.5 per cent being recorded in the second half of the year.

COSTS AND PRICES. The strong inflationary pressures of 1989 continued in 1990. The underlying increase in average earnings, reacting partly to earlier monetary laxness, edged up from 9.5 per cent at the beginning of the year to 10.25 per cent in July before falling back to 9.75 per cent at the end of the year. The new factor was that the impressive productivity increases of previous years (which had offset the high cost of labour to manufacturers) disappeared during 1990. Wages and salaries per unit of output, which had fallen to only 2 per cent at the start of 1988, had risen to 10 per cent by the third quarter of 1990 in manufacturing industry and over 12 per cent throughout the whole economy.

The natural response to such a sharp rise in unit costs—especially now that the UK was part of the fixed exchange rate system of the ERM—might have been to reduce wage increases. But, as in the recession of 1980-81, employers found it much easier to shed manpower than to tackle the unions head-on over wages. In the 12 months to November Britain had easily the highest inflation rate (9.7 per cent) among the Group of 7 leading industrialized countries. The next worst was Italy with 6.5 per cent followed by the United States with 6.3 per cent. The inflation rates of its nearest rivals, France and Germany (3.0 and 3.6 per cent respectively), provided a measure of the task ahead for the UK if it was to bring its labour costs in line with those of other members of the ERM.

GOVERNMENT POLICY. Monetary policy during the year continued to be aimed at correcting what the governor of the Bank of England described as the 'insufficiently restrictive' policies of 1987 and 1988, when interest rates were allowed to fall prematurely. The maintenance of high interest rates (notwithstanding the 1 per cent 'political' reduction which accompanied entry into the ERM in October) appeared to be having a dampening effect on the growth of the money supply by the end of the year. In the six months to December the expansion of the narrow MO measure of money (largely cash in circulation) was down to an annual rate of only 0.7 per cent—implying a sharp contraction after allowing for inflation. Broad money growth, which had remained stubbornly high for some years, also started contracting in real terms by the end of the year. The year-on-year growth of bank and building society lending also slowed down sharply towards the end of the year, as the high interest rate regime finally induced people to moderate their spending habits, at least temporarily.

Entry into the ERM was preceded by a five-month period in which the value of sterling increased by 8 per cent against other currencies. This gave rise to worries that sterling had been nailed into Europe's fixed exchange rate system at a rate which could injure industrial competitiveness, but the government regarded it as an essential move in the fight to curb inflation.

The March budget was the first and, as it turned out, the only one to be introduced by John Major as Chancellor. The budget did not add much to the squeeze in fiscal terms, but that was partly because there was so much deflation happening outside the budget, from the introduction of the community charge (poll tax) to higher council rents and mortgage interest charges. One of the main features of the budget was the announcement of TESSAs (tax-exempt savings schemes), enabling people to put aside up to £9,000 free of tax as long as they kept it in a special account for five years. The budget forecast of a financial surplus of £7,000 million evaporated during the year, as unemployment rose and concessions on the poll tax hit Exchequer revenues. This spoiled the government's aim of reducing the national debt further, but the UK ended the year in a much better fiscal position than most of its competitors. Norman Lamont became the new Chancellor when Mr Major was elected Prime Minister in November (see p. 42).

EXTERNAL TRADE. The current-account deficit was reduced from £20,000 million in 1989 to £16,000 million in 1990, the fifth consecutive year of deficit. This was a rather modest improvement considering that the country had suffered over 30 months of high and rising interest rates. However, there were some encouraging longer-term trends discernible. The export improvement which had been apparent at the end of 1989 continued during 1990. In November export volume was 6.5 per cent above a year earlier compared with a rise in import volume of only 0.5 per cent. This appeared to reverse, at least temporarily, Britain's long-term propensity to import significantly more than it exported. However, a large part of the reduction was clearly due to the decline in consumer spending, which could easily be reversed once the economic brakes were taken off. There were also worries that the sharp rise in the value of the pound prior to entry into the ERM, coupled with the slow-down in world trade, might hit the improving trend of exports.

The trade deficit continued to be financed disproportionately by short-term 'hot' money as opposed to the traditional flows of long-term capital. The high rates of interest which had to be paid to attract these funds to the UK helped to reduce the balance on 'invisibles' still further. As recently as 1988 the UK had sported a surplus of £6,100 million on invisible items like tourism and banking. By October and November 1990 this surplus had disappeared altogether.

Chapter 5

ECONOMIC AND SOCIAL DATA

The statistical data on the following pages record developments from 1985 to the latest year, usually 1990, for which reasonably stable figures were available at the time of going to press. Year headings 1985 to 1990 are printed only at the head of each page and are not repeated over individual tables unless the sequence is broken by extending series of figures over a longer period than elsewhere on the page.

Pages to which the point is relevant include a comparative price index, allowing the current-price figures to be adjusted in accordance with changing values of money.

Unless figures are stated as indicating the position at the *end* of year, they should be taken as annual *totals* or *averages*, according to context.

Tables 2, 3, 4 and 5. Statistics which are normally reported or collected separately in the three UK home jurisdictions (England and Wales, Scotland, and Northern Ireland) have been consolidated into UK series only to show general trends. As the component returns were made at varying times of year and in accordance with differing definitions and regulatory requirements, the series thus consolidated may therefore be subject to error, may not be strictly comparable from year to year, and may be less reliable than the remainder of the data.

Symbols: — = Nil or not applicable .. = not available at time of compilation.

Sources

A. **THE UNITED KINGDOM**
   GOVERNMENT SOURCES
   Annual Abstract of Statistics: Tables 1, 2, 3, 4, 5.
   Monthly Digest of Statistics: Tables 1, 11, 17, 18, 23, 24, 25.
   Financial Statistics: Tables 9, 11, 12, 13, 14, 15, 16, 26.
   Economic Trends: Tables 6, 7, 8, 9, 11, 26.
   Social Trends: Tables 2, 3, 4, 5, 10.
   Department of Employment Gazette: Tables 19, 20, 21, 22.
   Housing and Construction Statistics: Table 5.
   ADDITIONAL SOURCES
   National Institute of Economic and Social Research, *National Institute Economic Review*: Tables 6, 7, 8.
   United Nations: *Monthly Bulletin of Statistics*: Table 1.
   The Financial Times: Tables 13, 15.

B. **THE UNITED STATES**
   GOVERNMENT AND OTHER PUBLIC SOURCES
   Department of Commerce, *Survey of Current Business*: Tables 27, 28, 29, 30, 31, 32, 37, 38, 40.
   Council of Economic Advisers, Joint Economic Committee, *Economic Indicators*: Tables 30, 36.
   Federal Reserve Bulletin: Tables 33, 34, 35.
   ADDITIONAL SOURCES
   A. M. Best Co.: Table 35.
   Insurance Information Institute, New York: Table 35.
   Monthly Labor Review: Tables 38, 39.
   Bureau of Economic Statistics, *Basic Economic Statistics*: Table 39.

C. **INTERNATIONAL COMPARISONS**
   United Nations, *Annual Abstract of Statistics*: Tables 41, 42.
   UN, *Monthly Bulletin of Statistics*: Tables 41, 42, 44.
   World Bank, *World Development Report*: Table 41.
   IMF, *International Financial Statistics*: Tables 41, 43, 45, 46, 47, 48, 49.
   OECD, *Main Economic Indicators*: Table 42.
   International Institute for Strategic Studies, *The Military Balance*: Table 50.
   OECD, *Labour Force Statistics*: Table 51.

ECONOMIC AND SOCIAL DATA

A. THE UNITED KINGDOM

SOCIAL

1. Population

	1985	1986	1987	1988	1989	1990
Population, mid-year est. ('000)	56,618	56,763	56,930	57,065	57,236	..
Crude birth rate (per 1,000 pop.)	13·3	13·3	13·6	13·8	13·6	..
Crude death rate (per 1,000 pop.)	11·8	11·6	11·3	11·4	11·5	..
Net migration ('000)	+59	+37	+2	−21	+44	..

2. Health

Hospitals:						
staffed beds, end-year ('000)	421·2	409·9	388·7	372·9	362·5	..
waiting list, end-year ('000)(1)	803	831	806	828	827·0	841·6
Certifications of death ('000)(2) by:						
ischaemic heart disease	181·9	176·8	173·6	171·0	173·4	..
malignant neoplasm, lungs and bronchus	40·1	39·4	39·4	39·4	39·6	..
road fatality	5·5	5·5	5·4	5·1	5·5	..
accidents at work (number)	659	537	525	610	..	..

(1) From 1988, March.
(2) Great Britain.

3. Education

Schools ('000)	36·1	35·6	35·4	35·2	34·9	..
Pupils enrolled ('000) in schools	9,544	9,385	9,246	9,101	9,203	..
maintained primary(1)	4,624	4,521	4,550	4,599	4,024	..
maintained and aided secondary	4,244	4,080	3,902	3,701	3,551	..
assisted and independent	605	607	619	635	641	..
Further education: institutions (number)	4,975	3,627	3,252	3,356	3,508	..
full-time students ('000)	594	608	624	633	646	..
Universities	46	46	46	46	46	..
University students ('000)	305	310	316	321	334	..
First degrees awarded (number)	72,209	70,912	71,817	73,756	..	..
Open University graduates ('000)	8·1	8·0	8·0	8·0	..	..

(1) Including nursery schools.

4. Law and Order

Police ('000)						
Full-time strength(1)	134·3	135·3	136·2	137·3	138·0	..
Ulster, full-time strength	8·3	8·2	8·2	8·2	8·3	..
Serious offences known to police ('000)(2)	4,085	4,324	4,437	4,241·7	4,419·4	..
Persons convicted, all offences ('000)(2)	2,144	2,118	1,779	1,777	..	..
Burglary or robbery(3)	76	63	61·4	54·5	49·6	..
Handling stolen goods/receiving, theft	219	187	180	167	138	..
Violence against person	48	44	49	64	57·1	..
Traffic offences	1,111	1,120	795	774	760	..
All summary offences	1,503	1,542	1,202	1,204	1,224	..
Prisons: average population ('000)	53·6	54·3	56·4	57·1	55·41	..

(1) Police full-time strength: Great Britain only. (2) Because of differences in juridical and penal systems in the three UK jurisdictions, totals of offences are not strictly comparable from year to year: they should be read only as indicating broad trends. (3) Specific offences: England, Wales and N. Ireland.

Overall price index (1985=100)	100·0	102·7	107·9	115·1	123·6	133·3

	1985	1986	1987	1988	1989	1990
5. Housing						
Dwellings completed ('000)						
by and for public sector(1)	43	35	34	30	30	31
by private sector	154	167	178	185	177	153
Homeless households ('000)(2)	91	112	118	123	134	..
Housing land, private sector,						
weighted ave. price (£/hectare)	190,450	243,749	327,538	479,843	..	..
Dwelling prices, average (£)(3)	33,188	38,121	44,220	54,280	53,205	..

(1) Including government departments (police houses, military married quarters, etc.) and approved housing associations and trusts. (2) Accepted by local authorities as in priority need. (3) Of properties newly mortgaged by building societies.

PRICES, INCOME AND EXPENDITURE

6. National Income and Expenditure
(£ million, 1985 prices)

	1985	1986	1987	1988	1989	1990
GDP(1), expenditure basis	306,849	317,987	332,033	345,618	351,422	353,313
income basis(2)	305,262	326,963	358,028	400,778	437,742	..
output basis (1985=100)	100·0	103·0	107·7	112·4	114·5	115·3
average estimate (1985=100)	100·0	103·9	108·7	113·8	116·2	117·6
Components of gross domestic product:						
Consumers' expenditure	215,267	227,757	241,382	257,918	271,707	277,787
General government						
consumption	73,995	75,398	76,346	76,678	76,897	..
Gross fixed investment	60,283	61,293	66,894	75,680	79,355	..
Total final expenditure	453,124	471,744	498,028	527,040	546,382	..
Stockbuilding	569	689	1,051	3,578	3,501	..
Adjustment to factor cost	49,521	51,893	55,164	56,890	59,098	..

(1) At factor cost. (2) Current prices, £ 000 million.

7. Fixed Investment
(£ million, 1985 prices, seasonally adjusted)

	1985	1986	1987	1988	1989	1990
Total, all fixed investment	60,283	61,478	67,329	77,302	81,048	80,126
Dwellings	11,928	12,798	13,697	14,472	14,402	13,255
Private sector	48,043	49,124	55,934	66,700	69,050	..
manufacturing	8,735	8,489	9,949	11,404	12,415	11,738
other	39,308	40,635	45,985	55,296	56,624	..
Government and public corporations	12,240	12,347	11,395	10,602	11,998	..

8. Personal Income and Expenditure
(£ million, seasonally adjusted, current prices unless otherwise stated)

	1985	1986	1987	1988	1989	1990
Wages, salaries and forces' pay	168,837	183,131	198,525	221,178	246,028	..
Current grants	46,791	50,920	52,498	53,896	56,835	..
Other personal income(1)	61,595	68,453	74,843	85,556	94,797	..
Personal disposable income	239,781	260,884	280,071	315,787	352,097	378,079
Real personal disposable income(2)	241,362	252,286	261,301	276,628	291,266	300,356
Consumers' expenditure	217,023	239,535	264,120	296,165	324,348	..
Personal savings ratio(3)	9·5	8·2	5·7	4·1	5·0	..

(1) From rent, self-employment (before depreciation and stock appreciation provisions), dividend and interest receipts and charitable receipts from companies. (2) At 1985 prices. (3) Personal savings as % of personal disposable income.

Overall price index (1985=100)	100·0	102·7	107·9	115·1	123·6	133·3

UNITED KINGDOM STATISTICS

9. Government Finance(1)
(£ million)

	1985	1986	1987	1988	1989	1990
Revenue(2)	139,548	151,305	158,801	174,457	191,371	205,485
taxes on income	48,513	52,442	52,464	58,459	63,015	71,030
corporation tax	8,341	10,708	13,495	15,734	18,537	21,495
taxes on expenditure	53,340	57,687	63,881	69,780	77,190	81,455
value added tax	18,534	19,329	21,377	24,067	27,328	29,483
taxes on capital(3)	1,757	2,356	3,034	3,733	4,118	4,014
Expenditure(4)	151,978	159,776	168,829	177,754	184,592	205,034
net lending(5)	−1,706	−2,119	−3,918	−5,231	−5,354	..
Deficit(−) or surplus	−12,430	−8,471	−9,343	−3,297	+6,891	+582

(1) Financial years ended 5 April of year indicated. (2) Total current receipts, taxes on capital and other capital receipts. (3) Capital gains, capital transfer tax, estate duty. (4) Total government expenditure, gross domestic capital formation and grants. (5) To private sector, public corporations, and overseas.

10. Public Expenditure
(£ billion, constant prices)

	1985	1986	1987	1988	1989	1990
Health and personal social services	24·1	24·2	25·1	26·2	27·0	..
Social security	48·9	50·5	52·6	52·3	49·9	..
Education	20·9	20·6	21·8	22·5	22·7	..
Housing	5·4	4·7	4·5	4·4	3·2	..
Defence	21·1	20·9	20·5	20·2	19·1	..
Law and order	7·7	7·5	8·0	8·4	8·8	

11. Prices and Costs (index 1985=100)

	1985	1986	1987	1988	1989	1990
Total UK costs per unit of output(1)	100·0	102·7	107·9	115·1	123·6	133·3
Labour costs per unit of output	100·0	104·8	108·8	116·0	126·0	..
Mfg. wages/salaries per unit of output	100·0	104·5	106·1	108·9	114·4	125·2
Import unit values	100·0	95·7	98·2	97·5	103·2	107·1
Wholesale prices, manufactures	100·0	104·3	108·3	113·2	118·9	125·9
Consumer prices	100·0	103·4	107·7	113·0	121·8	133·3
Tax and prices	100·0	101·9	104·5	107·5	115·0	124·5

(1) Used as 'Overall price index' on all pages of UK statistics.

FINANCIAL

12. Monetary Sector(1)
(£ million, amounts outstanding at end of period)

	1985	1986	1987	1988	1989	1990
Notes and coins in circulation	12,071	12,824	13,592	14,755	15,362	15,189
M_0(2) (average)	14,425	15,159	15,894	16,377	17,312	18,209
M_2(3)	147,028	168,882	187,104	213,678	234,814	253,411
M_4(4)	225,293	261,073	303,753	357,218	424,017	474,932
Deposits						
domestic	140,403	173,802	210,720	252,108	336,108	..
overseas	415,995	493,401	474,211	511,672	610,069	..
Domestic lending						
private sector	167,676	206,555	250,782	318,763	432,941	471,505
public sector	19,212	18,102	17,021	15,153	15,140	14,705
Overseas lending	403,275	479,735	460,772	483,726	566,377	544,621

(1) Institutions recognized as banks or licensed deposit-takers, plus Bank of England banking dept. and other institutions adhering to monetary control arrangements. (2) M_0= Notes and coins in circulation plus banks' till money plus bankers' balance with Bank of England. (3) M_2= Notes and coin plus sterling retail deposits with banks and building societies. (4) M_4= Notes and coin plus all sterling deposits held with UK banks and building societies.

Overall price index (1985=100)	100·0	102·7	107·9	115·1	123·6	133·3

550   ECONOMIC AND SOCIAL DATA

	1985	1986	1987	1988	1989	1990
13. Interest Rates and Security Yields(1)						
(% per annum, end of year)						
Treasury bill yield	11·17	10·69	8·37	12·91	14·63	13·44
London clearing banks base rate	11·50	11·00	8·50	13·00	15·00	14·00
2½% consols, gross flat yield(2)	10·11	9·47	9·31	9·12	9·22	10·84
10-year government securities(2)	11·06	10·05	9·57	9·67	10·18	11·80
Ordinary shares, dividend yield(2)	4·47	4·01	3·50	4·32	4·24	5·03
Interbank 3-month deposits	11·91	11·25	8·87	12·94	15·13	14·03
Clearing bank 7-day deposits	7·86	6·92	3·58	5·97	6·59	5·11

(1) Gross redemption yields, unless stated otherwise. For building societies see Table 16. (2) Average during year.

14. Companies
(£ million unless stated)

Total income	73,102	67,696	80,794	93,185	103,269	106,692
Gross trading profit in UK	57,205	51,987	61,470	70,136	72,169	70,506
Total overseas income	8,715	7,997	11,386	14,343	18,257	20,828
Dividends on ord. shares	6,354	8,381	11,060	14,669	19,001	21,972
Net profit	32,524	30,617	37,907	42,239	33,091	28,814
Companies taken over (number)	474	842	1,527	1,499	1,336	778
Total take-over consideration	7,090	15,363	16,486	22,742	27,054	7,920
Liquidations (number)(1)	14,895	14,405	11,439	9,427	10,456	14,951
Receiverships (number)(1)	6,772	7,155	6,994	7,717	8,138	12,058

(1) England and Wales.

15. The Stock Market
(£ million, unless otherwise stated)

Turnover (£000 mn.)	390·5	646·3	1,757·5	1,602·8	1,627·3	1,655·0
ordinary shares (£000 mn.)	105·6	181·2	496·1	405·2	564·6	..
New issues, less redemptions (value)	4,500	8,519	15,256	7,141	7,863	2,829
Government securities	9,232	7,169	5,425	−266	−14,113	..
Local authority issues(1)	−566	−202	−177	−34	−11	−35
UK companies	5,110	8,971	15,433	7,175	6,827	2,637
FT ordinary share index (1935=100)(2)	1,004·64	1,287·11	1,600·01	1,448·73	1,781·41	1,749·4
FT-Actuaries index (750 shares)(3)	631·95	782·10	1,025·07	931·67	1,110·29	1,092·4
Industrial, 500 shares	692·02	858·57	1,133·51	1,019·76	1,221·71	1,199·1
Financial, 100 shares	475·31	590·05	725·37	679·99	763·45	761·6

(1) Includes public corporation issues. (2) Average during year. (3) 1962=100.

16. Building Societies

Interest rates (%): end year:						
Paid on shares, ave. actual	8·71	8·14	6·51	8·38	9·96	10·06
Basic rate	7·00	5·99	4·02	5·59	6·57	5·77
Mortgages, ave. charged	13·01	12·32	10·34	12·75	14·44	14·34
Basic rate	12·75	12·30	10·30	12·77	14·42	14·48
Shares and deposits, net (£ min.)	7,462	6,592	7,561	13,214	7,735	6,562
Mortgage advances, net (£ min.)	14,711	19,541	15,390	24,737	24,041	24,090

Overall price index (1985=100)	100·0	102·7	107·9	115·1	123·6	133·3

	1985	1986	1987	1988	1989	1990
17. Industrial Production (Index, average 1985=100, seasonally adjusted)						
All industries	100·0	102·2	105·8	109·6	110·0	109·3
Energy and water	100·0	105·0	103·9	99·3	89·8	88·6
Manufacturing industries	100·0	100·9	106·6	114·2	119·0	118·5
Food, drink and tobacco	100·0	100·8	103·2	105·3	105·4	106·6
Chemicals	100·0	101·8	109·0	114·1	119·2	117·9
Metal manufacture	100·0	100·3	108·5	122·0	124·8	121·9
Engineering and allied	100·0	99·1	103·9	112·6	120·3	119·8
Textiles	100·0	100·8	103·9	102·1	98·4	96·2
Intermediate goods	100·0	103·6	106·4	107·9	104·2	102·9
Consumer goods	100·0	101·5	106·8	112·4	114·7	114·6
Paper, printing, publishing	100·0	104·2	114·3	126·4	..	..
Construction	100·0	103·3	111·4	119·5	124·5	..
Crude steel (million tonnes)	15·7	14·8	17·4	18·9	18·7	..
Man-made fibres (million tonnes)	0·33	0·29	0·27	0·28	0·27	..
Cars ('000)	1,048	1,019	1,143	1,227	1,299	..
Motor vehicles, cars imported ('000)(1)	1,064	1,054	1,041	1,250	1,310	1,140
Commercial vehicles ('000)	266	229	247	318	327	..
Merchant ships(2) completed ('000 gr.t)	225	106	247	31	106	..

(1) Including imported chassis. (2) 100 gross tons and over.

18. Energy

Coal, production (mn. tonnes)	94·1	108·1	104·4	104·1	101·1	92·9
Power station consumption (mn. tonnes)	73·9	82·6	86·2	82·5	80·6	..
Electricity generated ('000 mn. kwh.)	279·8	282·4	282·7	288·4	292·9	..
by nuclear plant ('000 mn. kwh.)	49·7	47·5	44·8	51·7	59·3	..
Natural gas sent out (mn. therms)	19,047	19,246	19,814	18,655	18,590	..
Crude oil output ('000 tonnes)(1)	127,200	127,200	123,600	114,375	91,800	91,600
Oil refinery output (mn. tonnes)(2)	69·8	69·2	67·7	72·3	73·0	..

(1) Including natural gas liquids. (2) All fuels and other petroleum products.

LABOUR

19. Employment
(millions of persons, in June each year)

Working population(1)	27·59	27·86	28·21	28·26	28·50	28·59
Employed labour force(2)	24·41	24·59	24·68	25·92	26·75	27·34
Employees: production industries	5·84	5·66	5·54	5·59	5·55	5·55
Manufacturing	5·26	5·13	5·04	5·12	5·10	5·09
Transport and communications	1·30	1·33	1·33	1·35	1·34	1·33
Distributive trades	3·41	3·49	3·29	3·32	3·41	3·19
Education and health	2·97	3·01	2·91	3·09	3·18	3·28
Insurance, banking, financial	1·97	2·06	2·30	2·44	2·64	2·81
Public service	1·88	1·93	1·98	2·02	1·96	1·66
Total employees	21·47	21·54	21·82	22·10	22·23	22·69
of whom, females	9·52	9·66	9·93	10·16	10·53	10·99

(1) Including registered unemployed and members of the armed forces. (2) Including employers and self-employed.

Overall price index (1985=100)	100·0	102·7	107·9	115·1	123·6	133·3

552   ECONOMIC AND SOCIAL DATA

	1985	1986	1987	1988	1989	1990
20. Demand for Labour						
Average weekly hours worked, manufacturing industry, men over 21(1)	43·0	42·7	43·5	43·5	43·4	..
Manufacturing employees:						
Total overtime hours worked ('000)(2)	11,940	11,720	12,680	13,976	13,380	..
Short time, total hours lost ('000)(2)	416	485	364	249	302	..
Unemployment, excl. school-leavers, adult students (monthly ave. '000)(3)	3,163	3,107·2	2,822·3	2,294·5	1,795·5	1,664·6
Percentage of working population	11·3	11·2	10·1	8·1	6·4	5·9
Unfilled vacancies, end-year ('000)	162·1	188·8	235·0	238·3	195·4	128·7
Job schemes average ('000)(4)	725	820	925	..	..	..

(1) October. (2) Great Britain. (3) Seasonally adjusted. (4) Numbers supported on employment or training schemes.

21. Industrial Disputes

Stoppages (number)(1)(2)	887	1,053	1,004	770	664	588
Workers involved ('000)(3)	643	538	884	759	730	237
Work days lost ('000), all inds., services	6,402	1,920	3,546	3,702	4,068	1,880

(1) Excluding protest action of a political nature, and stoppages involving fewer than 10 workers and/or lasting less than one day except where the working days lost exceeded 100. (2) Stoppages beginning in year stated. (3) Directly and indirectly, where stoppages occurred; lay-offs elsewhere in consequence are excluded.

22. Wages and Earnings

Average earnings index (1985=100)						
Whole economy	100·0	107·9	116·3	126·5	138·0	151·4
Manufacturing	100·0	107·7	116·3	126·2	137·2	150·2
Average weekly earnings(1)(2)						
Men						
Manual	163·6	174·4	185·5	200·6	217·8	237·2
Non-manual	225·0	244·9	265·9	294·1	323·6	354·9
All occupations	192·4	207·5	224·0	245·8	269·5	295·6
Women						
Manual	101·3	107·5	115·3	123·6	134·9	148·0
Non-manual	133·8	145·7	157·2	175·5	195·0	215·5
All occupations	126·4	137·2	148·1	164·2	182·3	201·5
Average hours(3)	40·4	40·4	40·4	40·6	40·7	40·5

(1) In all industries and services, full time. (2) April. (3) All industries and services, all occupations, men and women over 18 years.

23. Productivity
(Index of output per head 1985=100)

All production industries(1)	100·0	105·0	110·1	112·9	112·9	..
Manufacturing	100·0	103·0	109·7	115·8	119·8	120·0
Minerals	100·0	107·8	115·3	129·8	134·1	..
Metal manufacture	100·0	112·6	131·8	154·7	168·3	..
Engineering	100·0	102·5	107·6	115·3	122·0	..
Textiles	100·0	100·6	104·8	101·8	100·6	..
Chemicals	100·0	104·7	114·8	119·5	124·7	..

(1) Excluding extraction of mineral oil and natural gas.

Overall price index (1985=100)	100·0	102·7	107·9	115·1	123·6	133·3

UNITED KINGDOM STATISTICS

TRADE

24. Trade by Areas and Main Trading Partners

(£ million; exports fob; imports cif)	1985	1986	1987	1988	1989	1990
All countries: *exports*	78,416	72,810	79,848	81,475	93,771	103,882
All countries: *imports*	84,697	85,662	94,023	106,412	121,888	126,135
E.E.C.: *exports*	38,226	34,943	39,415	40,932	47,540	55,071
E.E.C.: *imports*	41,474	44,506	49,555	55,785	63,807	65,955
Other Western Europe: *exports*	7,420	6,962	7,621	7,412	7,987	9,041
Other Western Europe: *imports*	12,025	11,864	12,884	13,943	15,155	15,745
North America: *exports*	13,310	12,065	12,992	12,623	14,437	14,973
North America: *imports*	11,703	9,994	10,781	12,899	15,929	16,751
Other developed countries: *exports*	3,792	3,614	4,046	4,496	4,519	4,824
Other developed countries: *imports*	6,379	6,861	7,283	8,505	8,514	8,414
Oil exporting countries: *exports*	5,957	5,494	5,223	5,021	5,831	5,575
Oil exporting countries: *imports*	2,782	2,062	1,700	2,087	2,313	2,974
Other developing countries: *exports*	7,924	7,644	8,549	8,630	11,185	12,189
Other developing countries: *imports*	8,451	7,770	9,284	10,471	13,557	13,855
Soviet Union and E. Eur.: *exports*	1,587	1,727	1,571	1,623	1,473	1,480
Soviet Union and E. Eur.: *imports*	1,894	1,865	2,099	2,039	1,781	1,797
Balance of trade in manufactures	−6,314	−5,812	−8,254	−9,961	−19,567	−13,722

25. Terms of Trade
(Index 1985=100)

Volume of exports(1)	100·0	103·8	109·2	112·0	117·3	125·3
manufactures	100·0	103·1	111·3	118·9	132·1	142·4
Volume of imports(1)	100·0	106·9	114·3	130·1	140·9	144·6
Unit value of exports(1)	100·0	90·5	94·3	94·7	101·3	106·9
manufactures	100·0	102·0	106·0	110·0	116·0	120·0
Unit value of imports(1)	100·0	95·7	98·2	97·5	103·2	107·1
Terms of trade(2)	100·0	94·6	96·0	97·1	97·9	99·5

(1) Seasonally adjusted: Overseas Trade Statistics basis. (2) Export unit value index as percentage of import value index, expressed as an index on the same base.

26. Balance of Payments
(£ million: current transactions seasonally adjusted; remaining data unadjusted)

Exports (f.o.b.)	77,988	72,678	79,421	80,772	92,792	102,754
Imports (f.o.b.)	80,178	81,141	89,594	101,587	116,632	120,706
Visible balance	−2,190	−8,463	−10,174	−20,815	−23,840	−17,952
Invisible balance	+5,465	+8,509	+7,475	+6,154	+4,217	+5,119
Current balance	+3,275	+46	−2,699	−14,661	−19,623	−12,794
Direct investment overseas(1)	−8,456	−11,728	−19,033	−20,760	−19,164	..
Portfolio investment overseas(1)	−19,436	−23,072	+3,326	−9,898	−37,779	..
Bank lending abroad(1)	−21,835	−53,840	−50,322	−19,267	−27,482	..
Direct investment in UK(2)	+3,865	+4,945	+8,508	+8,990	+15,848	..
Portfolio investment in UK(2)	+8,733	+9,365	+14,194	+11,794	+12,066	..
UK overseas bank borrowing(2)	+29,461	+63,966	+52,814	+33,844	+41,770	..
Net change in assets/liabilities	−7,429	−10,107	−3,301	+4,966	+4,341	..
Balancing item	+4,268	+10,148	+7,696	+10,052	+16,509	..
Official reserves, end of year	10,753	14,776	23,490	28,589	23,966	..

(1) − = increase, + = decrease. (2) − = decrease, + = increase.

Overall price index (1985=100)	100·0	102·7	107·9	115·1	123·6	133·3

B. THE UNITED STATES

27. Population	1985	1986	1987	1988	1989	1990
Population, mid-year est. (mn)	239·28	241·60	243·77	246·3	248·8	249·6
Crude birth rate (per 1,000 pop.)	15·7	15·5	15·7	15·9	..	..
Crude death rate (per 1,000 pop.)	8·7	8·7	8·7	8·8	..	..

28. Gross National Product
('000 million current dollars)

Gross national product	4,015	4,232	4,524	4,881	5,233	..
Personal consumption	2,629	2,797	3,011	3,235	3,471	..
Gross private domestic investment	642	659	700	750	774	..
Net exports, goods and services	−77·9	−97·4	−112·6	−73·7	−47·7	..
Government purchases	819	870	925	969	1,036	..

29. Government Finance
('000 million dollars, seasonally adjusted)

Federal government receipts	789	828	911	972	1,044	..
from personal taxes(1)	346	361	406	413	460	..
Federal government expenditure	986	1,034	1,074	1,117	1,195	..
Defence purchases	259	278	295	298	302	..
Grants to state/local govts.	100	107	103	111	119	..
Federal surplus or (−) deficit	−196·9	−206·8	−161·3	−145·8	−145·9	..
State and local govt. receipts	581·8	626·3	656·1	701·6	741·8	..
from indirect business tax(1)	278·5	298·4	314·0	336·7	358·2	..

(1) Includes related non-tax receipts on national income account.

30. Balance of Payments
(millions of dollars)

Merchandise trade balance	−122,148	−145,058	−159,500	−127,215	−113,248	..
Balance on current account(1)	−112,687	−133,252	−143,700	−126,548	−85,161	..
Change in US private assets abroad(2)	25,951	97,953	86,364	81,544	57,390	..
Change in foreign private assets in US(2)	131,012	186,011	172,847	180,417	117,177	..

(1) Includes balance on services and remittances and US government grants other than military.
(2) Includes reinvested earnings of incorporated affiliates.

31. Merchandise Trade by Main Areas
(millions of dollars)

All countries: *exports* (f.o.b.)	215,935	224,361	252,866	322,245	360,465	..
All countries: *imports* (f.o.b.)	338,083	368,700	424,082	440,940	475,329	..
Western Europe: *exports*	56,015	60,664	69,718	87,995	98,475	..
Western Europe: *imports*	77,454	89,074	99,934	100,515	102,301	..
Canada: *exports*	55,390	56,984	59,814	70,862	79,746	..
Canada: *imports*	70,394	70,315	71,510	80,921	89,408	..
Latin America						
exports	30,788	30,877	31,574	43,624	48,825	..
imports	46,109	41,426	44,371	51,421	57,438	..
Japan: *exports*	22,145	26,361	28,249	37,732	43,673	..
imports	65,653	80,764	88,074	89,802	93,455	..

| *Dollar purchasing power (1982–84=100)* | 92·8 | 91·3 | 88·0 | 84·6 | 80·7 | .. |

32. Merchandise Trade by Main Commodity Groups
(millions of dollars)

	1985	1986	1987	1988	1989	1990
Exports:						
Machinery and transport equipt.	94,278	95,289	108,596	135,135	148,780	..
Motor vehicles and parts	19,364	18,365	24,632	29,430	..	..
Electrical machinery	12,489	13,630	16,637	10,857	..	..
Food and live animals	19,268	17,303	19,179	26,415	29,724	..
Chemicals and pharmaceuticals	21,759	22,766	26,381	32,300	36,485	..
Imports:						
Machinery and transport equipt.	137,264	166,240	182,807	201,938	205,761	..
Motor vehicles and parts	55,740	57,990	87,479	89,991	..	..
Food and live animals	18,649	22,395	22,224	21,771	20,685	..
Petroleum and products	49,607	39,838	46,724	41,813	49,624	..
Iron and steel	11,223	8,900	9,178	12,579	..	..

33. Interest Rates
(per cent per annum, annual averages, unless otherwise stated)

Federal Funds rate(1)	8·10	6·80	6·66	7·57	9·21	..
Treasury bill rate	7·49	5·98	5·82	6·69	8·11	..
Government bond yields: 3–5 years	9·64	7·19	7·68	8·26	8·55	..
Long-term (10 years or more)	10·75	8·14	8·39	8·85	8·49	..
Banks' prime lending rate(2)	9·93	8·33	8·22	9·32	10·87	..

(1) Effective rate. (2) Predominant rate charged by commercial banks on short-term loans to large business borrowers with the highest credit rating.

34. Banking, money and credit
('000 million dollars, outstanding at end of year, seasonally adjusted)

Money supply M1(1)	620·1	725·4	752·3	790·2	794·8	..
Money supply M2(2)	2,563	2,808	2,910	3,072	3,222	..
Money supply M3(3)	3,196	3,491	3,677	3,918	4,045	..
Currency	167·7	180·4	196·4	211·8	221·9	..
Deposits of commercial banks	1,772·5	2,018	2,009	2,121	2,268	..
Advances of commercial banks	1,617·2	1,807	1,899	2,021	2,206	..
Instalment credit	517·8	571·8	613·0	667·3	716·6	..
Motor vehicle contracts	209·6	246·1	267·2	290·4	290·8	..
Mortgage debt	2,290	2,597	2,943	3,154	3,524	..

(1) Currency plus demand deposits, travellers cheques, other checkable deposits. (2) M1 plus overnight repurchase agreements, eurodollars, money market mutual fund shares, savings and small time deposits. (3) M2 plus large time deposits and term repurchase agreements.

35. Insurance
($ million, unless otherwise stated)

Property-liability, net premiums written	144,186	176,552	193,246	202,015	207,800	217,600
Automobile(1)	61,334	73,386	81,199	86,379	..	..
Underwriting gain/loss(2)	−24,794	−15,913	−9,624	−11,168	−19,300	..
Net investment income(3)	19,508	21,924	23,960	27,723	30,500	..
Combined net income(3)	−5,286	+6,012	+14,335	+14,900	+11,200	..
Annual rate of return (%)(4)	3·8	13·1	12·8	13·2	8·4	..
Life insurance, total assets, end-year	825,901	937,551	1,044,459	1,166,870	..	..

(1) Physical damage and liability, private and commercial. (2) After stockholder and policy-holder dividends and premium rebates. (3) Property, casualty. (4) Per cent of net worth.

| Dollar purchasing power (1982–84=100) | 92·8 | 91·3 | 88·0 | 84·6 | 80·7 | .. |

ECONOMIC AND SOCIAL DATA

36. Companies(1) ('000 million dollars)	1985	1986	1987	1988	1989	1990
Net profit after taxes	87·7	83·1	115·6	154·8	136·5	..
Cash dividends paid	45·5	46·0	49·5	57·1	65·2	..

(1) Manufacturing corporations, all industries.

37. The Stock Market
(millions of dollars, unless otherwise stated)

Turnover (sales), all exchanges	1,199,420	1,705,124	2,284,166	1,584,106	1,844,768	..
New York Stock Exchange	1,023,179	1,448,235	1,983,311	1,377,711	1,576,899	..
Securities issued, gross proceeds	356,372	395,217	389,437	368,000	..	..
Corporate common stock	36,242	58,852	65,835	45,485	..	..
Stock prices (end-year):						
Combined index (500 stocks)(1)	211·28	242·17	247·08	277·7	353·4	330·22
Industrials (30 stocks)(2)	1,537·73	1,895·95	1,938·83	2,168·6	2,753·2	2,633·7

(1) Standard and Poor Composite 1941–43=10. (2) Dow-Jones Industrial (Oct. 1928=100).

38. Employment
('000 persons)

Civilian labour force(1)	115,460	117,841	119,850	121,666	123,869	..
in non-agricultural industry	103,967	106,433	109,229	111,796	114,142	..
in manufacturing industry	19,314	18,995	19,112	19,403	19,612	..
in agriculture	3,179	3,165	3,210	3,175	3,199	..
unemployed	8,312	8,243	7,410	6,695	6,528	..
Industrial stoppages(2) (number)	54	69	46	40	51	..
Workers involved ('000)	324	533	174	118	452	..

(1) Aged 16 years and over. (2) Beginning in the year. Involving 1,000 workers or more.

39. Earnings and Prices

Average weekly earnings per worker						
(current dollars): mining	519·9	525·81	530·85	539·3	562·39	..
contract construction	464·1	466·75	479·68	493·1	506·72	..
manufacturing	386·0	396·01	406·31	418·4	429·27	..
Average weekly hours per worker						
in manufacturing	40·5	40·7	41·0	41·1	41·0	..
Farm prices received (1977=100)	128·0	123·0	127·0	138·0	146·0	..
Wholesale prices (1982=100)	103·1	100·2	102·8	106·9	112·2	..
Fuels and power	91·4	70·2	70·2	66·7	72·9	..
Consumer prices (1982–4=100)	107·6	109·7	113·7	118·4	124·0	..
Food	105·7	109·1	113·6	118·3	125·22	..
Dollar purchasing power (1982–84=100)(1)	92·8	91·3	88·0	84·6	80·7	..

(1) Based on changes in retail price indexes.

40. Production

Farm production (1977=100)	118·0	111·0	110·0	99·0	..	..
Industrial production (1977=100)	123·8	125·1	129·8	137·2	141·7	..
Manufacturing	126·4	129·1	134·7	142·8	148·1	..
Output of main products and manufacturers						
Coal (million tons)	886·1	886·0	915·2	946·3	971·2	..
Oil, indigenous (000 barrels/day)	8,934	8,727	8,347	8,159	..	..
Oil refinery throughput (000 barrels/day)	13,690	14,522	14,626	13,708	..	..
Natural gas ('000 mn. cu. ft.)	16,395	16,791	17,155	..	..	..
Electricity generated ('000 mn. kwh)	2,470	2,487	2,572	2,704	2,781	..
Steel, crude (million tonnes)	88·3	81·6	89·1	99·9	97·9	..
Aluminium ('000 tonnes)	3,499	3,036	3,343	3,944	4,030	..
Cotton yarn ('000 running bales)	12,988	9,438	14,359	14,985	11,884	..
Man-made fibres (millions lbs.)	8,121	8,447	8,921	9,119·7	.. ..	..
Plastics/resins (millions lbs.)	36,583	38,415	32,295	..	..	..
Motor cars, factory sales ('000)	8,002	7,516	7,085	7,105	6,808	..

C. INTERNATIONAL COMPARISONS

41. Population and GDP, Selected countries

	Area '000 sq. km.	Population (millions) mid-year estimate 1987	1988	Gross Domestic Product(1) US $ mins(2) 1988	1989
Argentina	2,767	31·10	31·5	89,660	..
Australia(3)	7,687	16·20	16·51	246,990	282,970
Belgium	31	9·92	9·91	152,524	156,853
Canada	9,976	25·90	26·01	486,495	550,351
China	9,561	1,080·7	1,088·41	376,535	422,485
Denmark	43	5·13	5·11	107,482	104,702
France	552	55·63	59·91	949,235	956,443
Germany, West (incl. W. Berlin)	249	61·17	61·3	1,201,800	1,189,149
India (incl. India-admin. Kashmir)	3,287	787·50	815·6	237,450	..
Irish Republic	70	3·60	3·6	32,546	33,940
Israel (excl. occupied areas)	22	4·37	4·4	41,878	..
Italy	301	57·35	57·41	828,872	865,826
Japan	378	122·09	122·6	2,858,884	2,833,734
Kuwait(4)	18	1·87	2·0	20,025	23,082
Netherlands	34	14·66	14·8	228,286	223,690
New Zealand(4)	270	3·28	3·3	38,187	..
Norway	324	4·19	4·2	91,183	90,894
Portugal	92	10·25	10·3	40,766	..
Saudi Arabia	2,200	12·61	14·0	75,292	..
South Africa	1,220	32·60	34·0	88,501	90,577
Spain	505	38·83	39·0	340,098	380,005
Sweden	450	8·44	8·4	178,882	189,423
Switzerland	41	6·54	6·6	193,193	177,150
Turkey	781	52·60	53·8	70,598	80,423
USSR	22,403	281·71	285·0	1,026,700	..
UK	244	56·93	57·1	807,473	831,672
USA	9,372	243·93	246·3	4,497,200	5,163,200

(1) Expenditure basis. (2) Converted from national currencies at average exchange rates. (3) Years beginning 1 July. (4) Years beginning 1 April.

42. World Production
(Index 1980=100)

	1985	1986	1987	1988	1989	1990
Food(1)	114·0	115·0	116·0	117·0	..	..
Industrial production(2)	108·5	112·0	116·3	122·3	100·4	..
Crude petroleum, nat. gas	79·0	82·6	83·1	87·6	92·2	..
Manufacturing	112·8	115·8	120·6	127·1	131·9	..
Chemicals	114·8	119·3	125·2	133·2	137·5	..
Paper, printing, publishing	115·8	119·9	126·6	133·4	138·2	..
Textiles	102·5	106·1	109·2	110·5	112·6	..
OECD	108·9	110·1	113·4	120·1	125·4	..
EEC(3)	103·5	105·4	107·6	111·6	115·7	..
Developing market economies(4)	119·2	129·6	139·7	150·8	159·1	..
Caribbean, C. & S. America	102·0	109·8	117·3	121·6	127·0	..
Asia(5)	144·7	160·5	178·2	200·5	212·6	..
France	99·0	101·0	104·0	108·1	112·0	..
Germany, West	105·0	107·0	107·0	111·2	117·0	..
Italy	96·9	99·0	103·0	108·1	113·0	..
UK	108·1	110·0	113·0	118·0	119·0	..
Japan	118·0	118·0	122·0	133·5	142·0	..
Sweden	109·0	110·0	114·0	115·1	120·0	..
USSR	120·2	126·1	130·9	134·0	136·0	..

(1) Excluding China. (2) Excluding China, N. Korea, Vietnam, Albania. (3) Community of Twelve. (4) Manufacturing. (5) Excluding Japan and Israel.

43. World Trade(1)
millions of US dollars. Exports f.o.b., imports c.i.f.

	1985	1986	1987	1988	1989	1990
World(1): exports	1,804,000	2,003,200	2,364,800	2,688,500	2,891,200	..
imports	1,881,100	2,059,100	2,424,800	2,767,600	2,983,500	..
Industrial Countries: exports	1,255,900	1,462,500	1,712,300	1,987,900	2,126,300	..
imports	1,360,200	1,357,200	1,794,300	2,067,500	2,238,800	..
USA: exports	213,144	217,307	250,405	322,426	363,812	..
imports	361,627	387,081	424,081	459,542	492,922	..
Germany, West: exports	183,913	243,327	294,168	323,326	341,231	..
imports	158,490	191,084	228,346	250,473	269,702	..
Japan: exports	177,139	210,757	228,631	264,856	273,932	..
imports	130,505	127,553	150,496	187,378	209,715	..
France: exports	101,674	124,948	148,534	167,787	179,397	..
imports	107,768	129,402	158,475	178,857	192,986	..
UK: exports	101,248	106,989	131,239	145,166	152,344	..
imports	108,957	126,330	154,454	189,339	197,730	..
Other Europe: exports	422,211	506,658	599,656	665,620	708,673	..
imports	452,020	529,520	645,564	697,462	767,342	..
Australia, NZ, S. Afr: exports	44,983	46,956	55,238	63,401	68,757	..
imports	43,350	45,156	51,923	62,194	71,550	..
Less Developed Areas: exports	525,247	510,286	624,644	700,550	764,900	..
imports	521,191	521,891	607,561	700,110	744,750	..
Oil exporters: exports	148,450	117,300	132,020	..	..	..
imports	105,220	93,400	91,370	104,790	..	..
Saudi Arabia: exports	27,481	20,085	26,975	23,738	..	..
imports	23,622	19,112	24,345	21,784	..	..
Other W. Hemisphere: exports	63,354	57,324	60,491	73,919	79,281	..
imports	52,636	52,148	59,742	59,937	..	..
Other Middle East(2): exports	15,731	14,972	15,700	..	..	..
imports	28,219	32,004	44,588	..	..	..
Other Asia: exports	158,710	174,856	261,002	323,255	358,187	..
imports	187,251	191,547	260,308	337,460	377,212	..
Other Africa: exports	26,822	28,889	31,509	..	..	..
imports	27,393	29,971	31,002	..	..	..

(1) Excluding trade of centrally planned countries (see Table 47). (2) Including Egypt. (3) Unweighted average of IMF series for US$ import and export prices in developed countries.

World trade prices (1985=100)(3)	100·0	111·0	111·8	112·6	111·4	..

44. World Trade of Centrally Planned Countries
(millions of US dollars)

	1985	1986	1987	1988	1989	1990
European(1): exports	174,834	193,765	211,451	221,591	195,998	..
imports	165,899	184,546	195,686	210,877	194,358	..
USSR: exports	87,201	97,336	107,772	110,541	109,212	..
imports	82,578	88,906	96,033	107,242	114,550	..
China: exports	27,343	30,942	39,542	47,540	43,220	..
imports	42,491	42,904	43,392	55,251	48,840	..
Total: exports	204,894	227,722	254,252	273,108	250,922	..
imports	212,101	223,588	246,055	274,104	261,367	..

(1) Except Yugoslavia and Albania.

INTERNATIONAL COMPARISONS

45. Prices of Selected Commodities
(Index 1985=100)

	1985	1986	1987	1988	1989	1990
Aluminium (Canada)	100·0	110·5	150·4	244·7	187·4	157·5
Beef, All origins	100·0	97·3	110·8	116·9	119·2	119·0
Copper, wirebars (London)	100·0	96·7	125·7	183·4	200·9	187·8
Cotton, Egyptian (L'pool)	100·0	95·9	99·4	133·2	176·4	183·0
Gold (London)	100·0	115·9	140·8	137·8	120·2	..
Newsprint New York	100·0	97·9	106·4	112·7	109·6	..
Rice, Thai (Bangkok)	100·0	96·7	105·7	138·7	147·3	131·9
Rubber, Malay (Singapore)	100·0	106·3	129·8	156·2	127·8	114·0
Soya Beans, US (R'dam)	100·0	92·9	96·1	135·2	122·5	110·0
Sugar, f.o.b. (Caribbean)	100·0	149·3	166·7	251·4	315·9	308·6
Tin, spot (London)	100·0	56·3	60·3	63·3	75·5	53·7
Wheat (US Gulf Ports)	100·0	84·6	83·1	106·9	124·6	99·8
Wool, greasy (Sydney)	100·0	92·0	132·9	219·5	201·5	..

46. Consumer Prices, Selected Countries
(Index 1985=100)

	1985	1986	1987	1988	1989	1990
Argentina	100·0	190·0	440·0	1,948	61,933	..
Australia	100·0	109·0	118·0	127·0	136·6	..
France	100·0	102·5	105·9	108·8	112·6	..
Germany, West	100·0	99·8	100·1	101·2	104·0	107·0
India	100·0	108·7	118·3	129·4	137·4	..
Japan	100·0	100·6	100·7	101·4	103·7	..
South Africa	100·0	118·6	137·7	155·4	178·2	..
Sweden	100·0	104·2	108·6	114·9	122·2	..
UK	100·0	103·4	107·8	113·0	121·8	133·4
US	100·0	101·9	105·7	109·9	115·2	121·5

World trade prices (1985=100)	100·0	111·0	111·8	112·6	111·4	..

47. Industrial Ordinary Share Prices
(Index 1985=100) end of year

	1985	1986	1987	1988	1989
Amsterdam	100·0	128·7	129·2	119·7	151·4
Australia, all exchanges	100·0	134·8	193·4	164·6	176·6
Canada, all exchanges	100·0	111·0	131·5	121·8	140·1
Germany, West, all exchanges	100·0	135·2	124·5	104·0	133·0
Hong Kong (31 July 1968=100)(1)	1,752	2,568	2,292	2,687	2,836
Johannesburg	100·0	128·0	188·0	148·0	207·0
New York	100·0	126·2	159·2	147·6	178·2
Paris	100·0	153·3	177·6	162·1	234·9
Tokyo	100·0	132·9	196·4	213·9	257·8
UK	100·0	124·1	163·8	147·6	176·5

(1) Hang Seng index for Hong Kong Stock Exchange only: last trading day of year.

48. Central Bank Discount Rates
(per cent per annum, end of year)

	1985	1986	1987	1988	1989	1990
Canada	9·49	8·47	8·75	8·75	12·46	12·82
France	9·50	9·50	9·50	9·50	10·25	10·25
Germany, West	4·00	3·50	2·50	3·50	6·00	6·00
Italy	15·00	12·00	12·50	12·50	13·50	12·50
Japan	5·00	3·00	2·50	2·50	3·75	6·00
Sweden	10·50	7·50	7·50	8·50	9·50	11·00
Switzerland	4·00	4·00	2·50	3·50	6·00	6·00
UK	11·50	11·00	8·50	13·00	15·00	14·00
USA (Federal Reserve Bank of N.Y.)	7·50	5·50	6·50	6·50	7·00	7·00

49. Exchange Rates
(Middle rates at end of year)

Currency units per US dollar — per £

	1986	1987	1988	1989	1990	1989	1990
Australia (Australian dollar)	1·5049	1·3897	1·1694	1·2655	1·2965	2·0413	2·500
Belgium-Luxembourg (franc)	40·41	38·00	37·26	35·60	30·95	57·40	59·75
Canada (Canadian dollar)	1·381	1·300	1·1907	1·1585	1·1605	1·8675	2·2400
China (yuan)(1)	3·722	3·722	3·697	4·7001	5·1974	7·5790	9·9011
France (franc)	6·425	5·342	6·057	5·7850	5·0855	9·3300	9·8200
Germany W. (Deutschmark)	1·940	1·574	1·773	1·6915	1·4950	2·7275	2·8850
Italy (lire)	1,351	1,165	1,306	1,268·0	1,128·0	2045·0	2,177·0
Japan (yen)	159·9	121·3	124·9	143·80	135·65	231·75	261·75
Netherlands (guilder)	2·191	1·772	2·002	1·9116	1·6865	3·0825	3·2550
Portugal (escudo)	146·1	129·0	146·2	149·58	134·05	241·20	255·30
South Africa (rand)	2·184	1·988	2·379	2·5480	2·5635	4·1088	4·9373
Spain (peseta)	131·9	107·75	113·18	109·40	95·55	176·00	183·70
Sweden (krona)	6·780	5·785	6·125	6·1925	5·6250	9·9850	10·8650
Switzerland (franc)	1·6230	1·2755	1·5022	1·5425	1·2750	2·4875	2·4600
USSR (rouble)(1)	0·6783	0·591	0·603	0·6132	0·5655	0·9889	1·0774
UK (£)(2)	1·4768	1·8785	1·8090	1·6125	1·9300	..	..

(1) Official fixed or basic parity rate. (2) US dollars per £.

50. Defence Expenditure

Expenditure or budget (US$ mn.)

	1986	1987	1988	1989	$ per capita 1989	% of GNP 1989
France	28,459	34,530	35,950	35,088	628	3·7
Germany, East	8,948	11,626	12,750	..	..	..
Germany, West (inc. W. Berlin)	28,248	34,244	33,654	33,654	549	2·8
Greece	2,418	2,972	2,470	..	..	..
Iran	5,904	8,956	9,900	..	..	..
Israel	5,560	5,136	5,710	..	..	..
Japan	20,930	25,422	28,850	28,015	228	0·99
Saudi Arabia	17,930	16,235	13,570	..	..	..
South Africa	2,340	3,294	3,410	3,773	111	4·2
Sweden	3,832	4,429	4,780	4,560	536	2·4
Turkey	2,770	2,890	2,660	2,877	53	3·8
USSR(1)	19·06	20·5	20·5	..	..	..
UK	27,344	31,774	34,490	34,111	596	4·1
USA	281,102	288,433	288,600	302,294	1,218	5·9

(1) Official budget, Roubles '000 mn.

51. Employment and Unemployment

Civilian Employment ('000)

	1984	1985	1986	1987	1988
USA	105,005	107,150	109,597	112,440	114,968
Japan	57,660	58,070	58,530	59,110	60,110
W. Germany	24,828	25,000	25,267	26,626	26,825
France	20,978	20,916	20,949	21,018	21,179
UK	23,739	24,065	24,434	24,755	25,555
EEC(1), Employment by Sectors (%)					
Agriculture	8·7	8·7	8·2	7·7	7·4
Industry	33·5	33·7	33·3	32·9	32·5
Services	57·8	57·7	58·5	59·4	60·1
Unemployment (%)					
OECD	8·1	8·0	7·9	7·5	6·9
EEC	10·9	11·1	11·2	10·8	10·2
USA	7·4	7·1	6·9	6·1	5·4
Japan	2·7	2·6	2·8	2·8	2·5
UK	11·1	11·5	11·6	10·4	8·3

(1) Community of Twelve.

XIX DOCUMENTS AND REFERENCE

UN SECURITY COUNCIL RESOLUTIONS ON GULF CRISIS

Printed below are the operative passages of the series of resolutions adopted by the UN Security Council in light of the Iraqi invasion of Kuwait on 2 August 1990 and subsequent developments. A feature of the decisions was that none of the Council's permanent members (China, France, the USSR, the UK and the USA) exercised their right of veto over any of them. The 10 non-permanent members in 1990 were Canada, Colombia, Côte d'Ivoire, Cuba, Ethiopia, Finland, Malaysia, Romania, Yemen and Zaïre. (Texts supplied by the UN Information Office, London.)

RESOLUTION 660

Adopted on 2 August 1990 unanimously but with Yemen not participating in the vote.

The Security Council,
   Alarmed by the invasion of Kuwait on 2 August 1990 by the military forces of Iraq,
   Determining that there exists a breach of international peace and security as regards the Iraqi invasion of Kuwait,
   Acting under Articles 39 and 40 of the Charter of the United Nations,
   1. Condemns the Iraqi invasion of Kuwait;
   2. Demands that Iraq withdraw immediately and unconditionally all its forces to the positions in which they were located on 1 August 1990;
   3. Calls upon Iraq and Kuwait to begin immediately intensive negotiations for the resolution of their differences and supports all efforts in this regard, and especially those of the League of Arab States;
   4. Decides to meet again as necessary to consider further steps to ensure compliance with the present resolution.

RESOLUTION 661

Adopted on 6 August 1990 by 13 votes to none, with Cuba and Yemen abstaining.

The Security Council, . . .
   1. Determines that Iraq so far has failed to comply with operative paragraph 2 of resolution 660 (1990) and has usurped the authority of the legitimate government of Kuwait;
   2. Decides, as a consequence, to take the following measures to secure compliance of Iraq with operative paragraph 2 and to restore the authority of the legitimate government of Kuwait;
   3. Decides that all states shall prevent:
   (*a*) The import into their territories of all commodities and products originating in Iraq or Kuwait exported therefrom after the date of this resolution;
   (*b*) Any activities by their nationals or in their territories which would promote or are calculated to promote the export or transshipment of any commodities or products from Iraq or Kuwait; and any dealings by their nationals or their flag vessels or in their territories in any commodities or products originating in Iraq or Kuwait and exported therefrom after the date of this resolution, including, in particular, any transfer of funds to Iraq or Kuwait for the purposes of such activities or dealings;
   (*c*) The sale or supply by their nationals or from their territories or using their flag vessels of any commodities or products, including weapons or any other military equipment, whether or not originating in their territories but not including supplies intended strictly for medical purposes, and, in humanitarian circumstances, foodstuffs, to any person or body in Iraq or Kuwait or to any person or body for the purposes of any business carried on in or operated from Iraq or Kuwait, and any activities by their nationals or in their territories which promote or are calculated to promote such sale or supply of such commodities or products;
   4. Decides that all states shall not make available to the government of Iraq or to any commercial, industrial or public utility undertaking in Iraq or Kuwait, any funds or any other

financial or economic resources and shall prevent their nationals and any persons within their territories from removing from their territories or otherwise making available to that government or to any such undertaking any such funds or resources and from remitting any other funds to persons or bodies within Iraq or Kuwait, except payments exclusively for strictly medical or humanitarian purposes and, in special humanitarian circumstances, foodstuffs;

5. Calls upon all states, including states non-members of the United Nations, to act strictly in accordance with the provisions of this resolution notwithstanding any contract entered into or licence granted before the date of this resolution . . . .

RESOLUTION 662

Adopted unanimously on 9 August 1990

The Security Council, . . .
Gravely alarmed by the declaration by Iraq of a 'comprehensive and eternal merger' with Kuwait, . . .

1. Decides that annexation of Kuwait by Iraq under any form and whatever pretext has no legal validity, and is considered null and void;
2. Calls upon all states, international organizations and specialized agencies not to recognize that annexation, and to refrain from any action or dealing that might be interpreted as an indirect recognition of the annexation;
3. Further demands that Iraq rescind its actions purporting to annex Kuwait . . . .

RESOLUTION 664

Adopted unanimously on 18 August 1990.

The Security Council, . . .

1. Demands that Iraq permit and facilitate the immediate departure from Kuwait and Iraq of the nationals of third countries and grant immediate and continuing access of consular officials to such nationals;
2. Further demands that Iraq take no action to jeopardize the safety, security or health of such nationals;
3. Reaffirms its decision in resolution 662 (1990) that annexation of Kuwait by Iraq is null and void, and therefore demands that the government of Iraq rescind its orders for the closure of diplomatic and consular missions in Kuwait and the withdrawal of the immunity of their personnel, and refrain from any such actions in the future . . . .

RESOLUTION 665

Adopted on 25 August 1990 by 13 votes to none, with Cuba and Yemen abstaining.

The Security Council, . . .

1. Calls upon those member states cooperating with the government of Kuwait which are deploying maritime forces to the area to use such measures commensurate to the specific circumstances as may be necessary under the authority of the Security Council to halt all inward and outward maritime shipping in order to inspect and verify their cargoes and destinations and to ensure strict implementation of the provisions related to such shipping laid down in resolution 661 (1990);
2. Invites member states accordingly to cooperate as may be necessary to ensure compliance with the provisions of resolution 661 (1990) with maximum use of political and diplomatic measures, in accordance with paragraph 1 above;
3. Requests all states to provide in accordance with the Charter such assistance as may be required by the states referred to in paragraph 1 of this resolution;
4. Further requests the states concerned to coordinate their actions in pursuit of the above paragraphs of this resolution using as appropriate mechanisms of the Military Staff Committee and after consultation with the Secretary-General to submit reports to the Security Council

and its Committee established under resolution 661 (1990) to facilitate the monitoring of the implementation of this resolution . . . .

RESOLUTION 666

Adopted on 13 September 1990 by 13 votes to 2 (Cuba and Yemen).

The Security Council, . . .
1. Decides that in order to make the necessary determination whether or not for the purposes of paragraph 3 (c) and paragraph 4 of resolution 661 (1990) humanitarian circumstances have arisen, the Committee [set up under that resolution] shall keep the situation regarding foodstuffs in Iraq and Kuwait under constant review;
2. Expects Iraq to comply with its obligations under Security Council resolution 664 (1990) in respect of third state nationals and reaffirms that Iraq remains fully responsible for their safety and well-being in accordance with international humanitarian law including, where applicable, the Fourth Geneva Convention;
3. Requests, for the purpose of paragraphs 1 and 2 of this resolution, that the Secretary-General seek urgently, and on a continuing basis, information from relevant United Nations and other appropriate humanitarian agencies and all other sources on the availability of food in Iraq and Kuwait, such information to be communicated by the Secretary-General to the Committee regularly;
4. Requests further that in seeking and supplying such information particular attention will be paid to such categories of persons who might suffer specially, such as children under 15 years of age, expectant mothers, maternity cases, the sick and the elderly;
5. Decides that if the Committee, after receiving the reports from the Secretary-General, determines that circumstances have arisen in which there is an urgent humanitarian need to supply foodstuffs to Iraq or Kuwait in order to relieve human suffering, it will report promptly to the Council its decision as to how such need should be met;
6. Directs the Committee that in formulating its decisions it should bear in mind that foodstuffs should be provided through the United Nations in cooperation with the International Committee of the Red Cross or other appropriate humanitarian agencies and distributed by them or under their supervision in order to ensure that they reach the intended beneficiaries;
7. Requests the Secretary-General to use his good offices to facilitate the delivery and distribution of foodstuffs to Kuwait and Iraq in accordance with the provisions of this and other relevant resolutions;
8. Recalls that resolution 661 (1990) does not apply to supplies intended strictly for medical purposes, but in this connection recommends that medical supplies should be exported under the strict supervision of government of the exporting state or by appropriate humanitarian agencies.

RESOLUTION 667

Adopted unanimously on 16 September 1990.

The Security Council, . . .
1. Strongly condemns aggressive acts perpetrated by Iraq against diplomatic premises and personnel in Kuwait, including the abduction of foreign nationals who were present in those premises;
2. Demands the immediate release of those foreign nationals as well as all nationals mentioned in resolution 664 (1990);
3. Further demands that Iraq immediately and fully comply with its international obligations under resolutions 660 (1990), 662 (1990) and 664 (1990) of the Security Council, the Vienna Conventions on diplomatic and consular relations and international law;
4. Further demands that Iraq immediately protect the safety and well-being of diplomatic and consular personnel and premises in Kuwait and in Iraq and take no action to hinder the diplomatic and consular missions in the performance of their functions, including access to their nationals and the protection of their person and interests;
5. Reminds all States that they are obliged to observe strictly resolutions 661 (1990), 662 (1990), 664 (1990), 665 (1990) and 666 (1990);

6. Decides to consult urgently to take further concrete measures as soon as possible, under Chapter VII of the Charter, in response to Iraq's continued violation of the Charter, of resolutions of the Council and of international law.

RESOLUTION 670

Adopted on 25 September 1990 by 14 votes to 1 (Cuba).

The Security Council, . . .
1. Calls upon all states to carry out their obligations to ensure strict and complete compliance with resolution 661 (1990) and, in particular, paragraphs 3, 4 and 5 thereof;
2. Confirms that resolution 661 (1990) applies to all means of transport, including aircraft;
3. Decides that all states, notwithstanding the existence of any rights or obligations conferred or imposed by any international agreement or any contract entered into or any licence or permit granted before the date of the present resolution, shall deny permission to any aircraft to take off from their territory if the aircraft would carry any cargo to or from Iraq or Kuwait other than food in humanitarian circumstances, subject to authorization by the Council or the Committee established by resolution 661 (1990) and in accordance with resolution 666 (1990), or supplies intended strictly for medical purposes or solely for UNIIMOG;
4. Decides further that all states shall deny permission to any aircraft destined to land in Iraq or Kuwait, whatever its state of registration, to overfly its territory unless:

(*a*) The aircraft lands at an airfield designated by that state outside Iraq or Kuwait in order to permit its inspection to ensure that there is no cargo on board in violation of resolution 661 (1990) or the present resolution, and for this purpose the aircraft may be detained for as long as necessary; or

(*b*) The particular flight has been approved by the Committee established by resolution 661 (1990); or

(*c*) The flight is certified by the United Nations as solely for the purposes of UNIIMOG;
5. Decides that each state shall take all necessary measures to ensure that any aircraft registered in its territory or operated by an operator who has his principal place of business or permanent residence in its territory complies with the provisions of resolution 661 (1990) and the present resolution;
6. Decides further that all states shall notify in a timely fashion the Committee established by resolution 661 (1990) of any flight between its territory and Iraq or Kuwait to which the requirement to land in paragraph 4 above does not apply, and the purpose for such a flight;
7. Calls upon all states to cooperate in taking such measures as may be necessary, consistent with international law, including the Chicago Convention, to ensure the effective implementation of the provisions of resolution 661 (1990) or the present resolution;
8. Calls upon all states to detain any ships of Iraqi registry which enter their ports and which are being or have been used in violation of resolution 661 (1990), or to deny such ships entrance to their ports except in circumstances recognized under international law as necessary to safeguard human life;
9. Reminds all states of their obligations under resolution 661 (1990) with regard to the freezing of Iraqi assets, and the protection of the assets of the legitimate Government of Kuwait and its agencies, located within their territory and to report to the Committee established under resolution 661 (1990) regarding those assets;
10. Calls upon all states to provide to the Committee established by resolution 661 (1990) information regarding the action taken by them to implement the provisions laid down in the present resolution;
11. Affirms that the United Nations Organization, the specialized agencies and other international organizations in the United Nations system are required to take such measures as may be necessary to give effect to the terms of resolution 661 (1990) and this resolution;
12. Decides to consider, in the event of evasion of the provisions of resolution 661 (1990) or of the present resolution by a state or its nationals or through its territory, measures directed at the State in question to prevent such evasion;
13. Reaffirms that the Fourth Geneva Convention applies to Kuwait and that as a high contracting party to the convention Iraq is bound to comply fully with all its terms and, in particular, is liable under the convention in respect of the grave breaches committed by it, as are individuals who commit or order the commission of grave breaches.

RESOLUTION 674

Adopted on 29 October 1990 by 13 votes to none, with Cuba and Yemen abstaining.

The Security Council, . . .
1. Demands that the Iraqi authorities and occupying forces immediately cease and desist from taking third-state nationals hostage, mistreating and oppressing Kuwaiti and third-state nationals and any other actions, such as those reported to the Security Council and described above, that violate the decisions of this Council, the Charter of the United Nations, the Fourth Geneva Convention, the Vienna Conventions on Diplomatic and Consular Relations and international law;
2. Invites states to collate substantiated information in their possession or submitted to them on the grave breaches by Iraq as per paragraph 1 above and to make this information available to the Security Council;
3. Reaffirms its demand that Iraq immediately fulfil its obligations to third-state nationals in Kuwait and Iraq, including the personnel of diplomatic and consular missions, under the Charter, the Fourth Geneva Convention, the Vienna Conventions on Diplomatic and Consular Relations, general principles of international law and the relevant resolutions of the Council;
4. Also reaffirms its demand that Iraq permit and facilitate the immediate departure from Kuwait and Iraq of those third-state nationals, including diplomatic and consular personnel, who wish to leave;
5. Demands that Iraq ensure the immediate access to food, water and basic services necessary to the protection and well-being of Kuwaiti nationals and of nationals of third states in Kuwait and Iraq, including the personnel of diplomatic and consular missions in Kuwait;
6. Reaffirms its demand that Iraq immediately protect the safety and well-being of diplomatic and consular personnel and premises in Kuwait and in Iraq, take no action to hinder these diplomatic and consular missions in the performance of their functions, including access to their nationals and the protection of their person and interests and rescind its orders for the closure of diplomatic and consular missions in Kuwait and the withdrawal of the immunity of their personnel;
7. Requests the Secretary-General, in the context of the continued exercise of his good offices concerning the safety and well-being of third-state nationals in Iraq and Kuwait, to seek to achieve the objectives of paragraphs 4, 5 and 6 above and in particular the provision of food, water and basic services to Kuwaiti nationals and to the diplomatic and consular missions in Kuwait and the evacuation of third-State nationals;
8. Reminds Iraq that under international law it is liable for any loss, damage or injury arising in regard to Kuwait and third states, and their nationals and corporations, as a result of the invasion and illegal occupation of Kuwait by Iraq;
9. Invites States to collect relevant information regarding their claims and those of their nationals and corporations, for restitution or financial compensation by Iraq with a view to such arrangements as may be established in accordance with international law;
10. Requires that Iraq comply with the provisions of the present resolution and its previous resolutions, failing which the Security Council will need to take further measures under the Charter;
11. Decides to remain actively and permanently seized of the matter until Kuwait has regained its independence and peace had been restored in conformity with the relevant resolutions of the Security Council . . . .

RESOLUTION 677

Adopted unanimously on 28 November 1990.

The Security Council, . . .
1. Condemns the attempts by Iraq to alter the demographic composition of the population of Kuwait and to destroy the civil records maintained by the legitimate Government of Kuwait;
2. Mandates the Secretary-General to take custody of a copy of the population register of Kuwait, the authenticity of which has been certified by the legitimate government of Kuwait, which covers the population registration up to 1 August 1990;
3. Requests the Secretary-General to establish, in cooperation with the legitimate government of Kuwait, an order of rules and regulations governing access and use of the said copy of the population register.

RESOLUTION 678

Adopted on 29 November 1990 by 12 votes to 2 (Cuba and Yemen), with China abstaining.

The Security Council, . . .
1. Demands that Iraq comply fully with resolution 660 (1990) and all subsequent relevant resolutions and decides, while maintaining all its decisions, to allow Iraq one final opportunity, as a pause of goodwill, to do so;
2. Authorizes member states cooperating with the government of Kuwait, unless Iraq on or before 15 January 1991 fully implements, as set forth in paragraph 1 above, the foregoing resolutions, to use all necessary means to uphold and implement Security Council resolution 660 (1990) and all subsequent relevant resolutions and to restore international peace and security in the area;
3. Requests all states to provide appropriate support for the actions undertaken in pursuance of paragraph 2 of this resolution;
4. Requests the states concerned to keep the Council regularly informed on the progress of actions undertaken pursuant to paragraphs 2 and 3 of this resolution;
5. Decides to remain seized of the matter.

TREATY ON THE FINAL SETTLEMENT WITH RESPECT TO GERMANY

Printed below is the substantive text of the treaty signed in Moscow on 12 September 1990 following the conclusion of the 'two-plus-four' talks between on the one hand the Federal Republic of Germany (FRG) and the German Democratic Republic (GDR), and on the other the World War II allies which exercised post-war responsibility in Germany (the USSR, the USA, the UK and France). Signature of the treaty, by the Soviet, US, UK, French and FRG Foreign Ministers and by the GDR Prime Minister, cleared the path under international law for the formal unification of East with West Germany on 3 October 1990. (Text supplied by German embassy, London.)

Article 1

(1) The united Germany shall comprise the territory of the Federal Republic of Germany, the German Democratic Republic and the whole of Berlin. Its external borders shall be the borders of the Federal Republic of Germany and the German Democratic Republic and shall be definitive from the date on which the present treaty comes into force. The confirmation of the definitive nature of the borders of the united Germany is an essential element of the peaceful order in Europe.

(2) The united Germany and the Republic of Poland shall confirm the existing border between them in a treaty that is binding under international law.

(3) The united Germany has no territorial claims whatsoever against other states and shall not assert any in the future.

(4) The governments of the Federal Republic of Germany and the German Democratic Republic shall ensure that the constitution of the united Germany does not contain any provision incompatible with these principles. This applies accordingly to the provisions laid down in the preamble, the second sentence of article 23, and article 146 of the Basic Law for the Federal Republic of Germany.

(5) The governments of the French Republic, the Union of the Soviet Socialist Republics, the United Kingdom of Great Britain and Northern Ireland and the United States of America take formal note of the corresponding commitments and declarations by the governments of the Federal Republic of Germany and the German Democratic Republic and declare that their implementation will confirm the definitive nature of the united Germany's borders.

Article 2

The governments of the Federal Republic of Germany and the German Democratic Republic reaffirm their declarations that only peace will emanate from German soil. According to the constitution of the united Germany, acts tending to and undertaken with the intent to disturb the peaceful relations between nations, especially to prepare for aggressive war, are unconstitutional and a punishable offense. The governments of the Federal Republic of Germany and the German

Democratic Republic declare that the united Germany will never employ any of its weapons except in accordance with its constitution and the Charter of the United Nations.

Article 3

(1) The governments of the Federal Republic of Germany and the German Democratic Republic reaffirm their renunciation of the manufacture and possession of and control over nuclear, biological and chemical weapons. They declare that the united Germany, too, will abide by these commitments. In particular, rights and obligations arising from the Treaty on the Non-Proliferation of Nuclear Weapons of 1 July 1968 will continue to apply to the united Germany.

(2) The government of the Federal Republic of Germany, acting in full agreement with the government of the German Democratic Republic, made the following statement on 30 August 1990 in Vienna at the negotiations on conventional armed forces in Europe (CFE):

'The government of the Federal Republic of Germany undertakes to reduce the personnel strength of the armed forces of the united Germany to 370,000 (ground, air and naval forces) within three to four years. This reduction will commence on the entry into force of the first CFE agreement. Within the scope of this overall ceiling no more than 345,000 will belong to the ground and air forces which, pursuant to the agreed mandate, alone are the subject of the negotiations on conventional armed forces in Europe. The federal government regards its commitment to reduce ground and air forces as a significant German contribution to the reduction of conventional armed forces in Europe. It assumes that in follow-on negotiations the other participants in the negotiations, too, will render their contribution to enhancing security and stability in Europe, including measures to limit personnel strengths.'

The government of the German Democratic Republic has expressly associated itself with this statement.

(3) The governments of the French Republic, the Union of Soviet Socialist Republics, the United Kingdom of Great Britain and Northern Ireland and the United States of America take note of these statements by the governments of the Federal Republic of Germany and the German Democratic Republic.

Article 4

(1) The governments of the Federal Republic of Germany, the German Democratic Republic and the Union of Soviet Socialist Republics state that the united Germany and the Union of Soviet Socialist Republics will settle by treaty the conditions for and the duration of the presence of Soviet armed forces on the territory of the present German Democratic Republic and of Berlin, as well as the conduct of the withdrawal of these armed forces which will be completed by the end of 1994, in connection with the implementation of the undertaking of the Federal Republic of Germany and the German Democratic Republic referred to in paragraph 2 of article 3 of the present treaty.

(2) The governments of the French Republic, the United Kingdom of Great Britain and Northern Ireland and the United States of America take note of this statement.

Article 5

(1) Until the completion of the withdrawal of the Soviet armed forces from the territory of the present German Democratic Republic and of Berlin in accordance with article 4 of the present treaty, only German territorial defence units which are not integrated into the alliance structures to which German armed forces in the rest of German territory are assigned will be stationed in that territory as armed forces of the united Germany. During that period and subject to the provisions of paragraph 2 of this article, armed forces of other states will not be stationed in that territory or carry out any other military activity there.

(2) For the duration of the presence of Soviet armed forces in the territory of the present German Democratic Republic and of Berlin, armed forces of the French Republic, the United Kingdom of Great Britain and Northern Ireland and the United States of America will, upon German request, remain stationed in Berlin by agreement to this effect between the government of the united Germany and the governments of the states concerned. The number of troops and the amount of equipment of all non-German armed forces stationed in Berlin will not be greater than at the time of signature of the present treaty. New categories of weapons will not be introduced there by non-German armed forces. The government of the united Germany will conclude with the governments of those states which have armed forces stationed in Berlin treaties with conditions which are fair taking account of the relations existing with the states concerned.

(3) Following the completion of the withdrawal of the Soviet armed forces from the territory of the present German Democratic Republic and of Berlin, units of German armed forces assigned to military alliance structures in the same way as those in the rest of German territory may also be stationed in that part of Germany, but without nuclear weapon carriers. This does not apply to conventional weapon systems which may have other capabilities in addition to conventional ones but which in that part of Germany are equipped for a conventional role and designated only for such. Foreign armed forces and nuclear weapons or their carriers will not be stationed in that part of Germany or deployed there. (An agreed minute appended to the treaty stated: 'Any questions with respect to the application of the word "deployed" as used in the last sentence of paragraph 3 of article 5 will be decided by the government of the united Germany in a reasonable and responsible way taking into account the security interests of each contracting party as set forth in the preamble.)

Article 6

The right of the united Germany to belong to alliances, with all the rights and responsibilities arising therefrom, shall not be affected by the present treaty.

Article 7

(1) The French Republic, the Union of Soviet Socialist Republics, the United Kingdom of Great Britain and Northern Ireland and the United States of America hereby terminate their rights and responsibilities relating to Berlin and to Germany as a whole. As a result, the corresponding, related quadripartite agreements, decisions and practices are terminated and all related Four Power institutions are dissolved.

(2) The united Germany shall have accordingly full sovereignty over its internal and external affairs.

Article 8

(1) The present treaty is subject to ratification or acceptance as soon as possible. On the German side it will be ratified by the united Germany. The treaty will therefore apply to the united Germany.

(2) The instruments of ratification or acceptance shall be deposited with the government of the united Germany. That government shall inform the governments of the other contracting parties of the deposit of each instrument of ratification or acceptance.

Article 9

The present treaty shall enter into force for the united Germany, the French Republic, the Union of Soviet Socialist Republics, the United Kingdom of Great Britain and Northern Ireland and the United States of America on the date of deposit of the last instrument of ratification or acceptance by these states.

Article 10

The original of the present treaty, of which the English, French, German and Russian texts are equally authentic, shall be deposited with the government of the Federal Republic of Germany, which shall transmit certified true copies to the governments of the other contracting parties.

ACCOMPANYING GERMAN LETTER

Letter from Foreign Minister Hans-Dietrich Genscher (Federal Republic) and Prime Minister Lothar de Maizière (German Democratic Republic) to the Foreign Ministers of the United States, France, Great Britain and the Soviet Union, concerning the Treaty on the Final Settlement with Respect to Germany.

Mr Foreign Minister,
In connection with the signing today of the Treaty on the Final Settlement with Respect to Germany, we would like to inform you that the governments of the Federal Republic of Germany and the German Democratic Republic declared the following in the negotiations:

1. The Joint Declaration of 15 June 1990, by the governments of the Federal Republic of Germany and the German Democratic Republic on the settlement of outstanding property matters contains, inter alia, the following observations:

'The expropriations effected on the basis of occupation law or sovereignty (between 1945 and 1949) are irreversible. The governments of the Soviet Union and the German Democratic

Republic do not see any means of revising the measures taken then. The government of the Federal Republic of Germany takes note of this in the light of the historical development. It is of the opinion that a final decision on any public compensation must be reserved for a future all-German parliament.'

According to article 41 (1) of the treaty of 31 August 1990 between the Federal Republic of Germany and the German Democratic Republic establishing German unity (Unification Treaty), the aforementioned joint declaration forms an integral part of the treaty. Pursuant to article 41 (3) of the Unification Treaty, the Federal Republic of Germany will not enact any legislation contradicting the part of the joint declaration quoted above.

2. The monuments dedicated to the victims of war and tyranny which have been erected on German soil will be respected and will enjoy the protection of German law. The same applies to the war graves, which will be maintained and looked after.

3. In the united Germany, too, the free democratic basic order will be protected by the constitution. It provides the basis for ensuring that parties which, by reason of their aims or the behavior of their adherents, seek to impair or abolish the free democratic basic order as well as associations which are directed against the constitutional order or the concept of international understanding, can be prohibited. This also applies to parties and associations with national socialist aims.

4. On the treaties of the German Democratic Republic, the following has been agreed in article 12 (1) and (2) of the treaty of 31 August 1990 between the Federal Republic of Germany and the German Democratic Republic establishing German unity:

'The contracting parties agree that, as part of the process of establishing German unity, the international treaties concluded by the German Democratic Republic shall be discussed with the contracting parties in terms of the protection of *bona fide* rights, the interests of the states concerned and the treaty obligations of the Federal Republic of Germany as well as in the light of the principles of a free democratic basic order founded on the rule of law and taking into account the responsibilities of the European Communities in order to regulate or ascertain the continuance, adjustment or termination of such treaties. The united Germany shall lay down its position on the continuance of international treaties of the German Democratic Republic after consultations with the respective contracting parties and with the European Communities insofar as their responsibilities are affected.'

Accept, Mr Foreign Minister, the assurances of our high consideration.

CHARTER OF PARIS FOR A NEW EUROPE

This Charter was signed in Paris on 21 November 1990 by the heads of state or government of the 34 countries of the Conference on Security and Cooperation in Europe (CSCE), i.e. 32 European states (Austria, Belgium, Bulgaria, Cyprus, Czechoslovakia, Denmark, Finland, France, Germany, Hungary, Greece, Holy See, Iceland, Ireland, Italy, Liechtenstein, Luxembourg, Malta, Monaco, Netherlands, Norway, Poland, Portugal, Romania, San Marino, Spain, Sweden, Switzerland, Turkey, USSR, United Kingdom and Yugoslavia) together with the USA and Canada. Its signature, together with a treaty on reduction of conventional armed forces in Europe (see pages 434–8), was officially described as marking the formal end of the Cold War in Europe. (Text supplied by Foreign and Commonwealth Office, London.)

A NEW ERA OF DEMOCRACY, PEACE AND UNITY

We, the heads of state or government of the states participating in the Conference on Security and Cooperation in Europe (CSCE), have assembled in Paris at a time of profound change and historic expectations. The era of confrontation and division of Europe has ended. We declare that henceforth our relations will be founded on respect and cooperation.

Europe is liberating itself from the legacy of the past. The courage of men and women, the strength of the will of the peoples and the power of the ideas of the Helsinki Final Act have opened a new era of democracy, peace and unity in Europe.

Ours is a time for fulfilling the hopes and expectations our peoples have cherished for decades: steadfast commitment to democracy based on human rights and fundamental freedoms; prosperity through economic liberty and social justice; and equal security for all our countries.

The Ten Principles of the Final Act will guide us towards this ambitious future, just as they have lighted our way towards better relations for the past 15 years. Full implementation of all CSCE commitments must form the basis for the initiatives we are now taking to enable our nations to live in accordance with their aspirations.

Human Rights, Democracy and Rule of Law

We undertake to build, consolidate and strengthen democracy as the only system of government of our nations. In this endeavour, we will abide by the following:

Human rights and fundamental freedoms are the birthright of all human beings, are inalienable and are guaranteed by law. Their protection and promotion is the first responsibility of government. Respect for them is an essential safeguard against an over-mighty state. Their observance and full exercise are the foundation of freedom, justice and peace.

Democratic government is based on the will of the people, expressed regularly through free and fair elections. Democracy has as its foundation respect for the human person and the rule of law. Democracy is the best safeguard of freedom of expression, tolerance of all groups of society, and equality of opportunity for each person.

Democracy, with its representative and pluralist character, entails accountability to the electorate, the obligation of public authorities to comply with the law and justice administered impartially. No one will be above the law.

We affirm that, without discrimination, every individual has the right to: freedom of thought, conscience and religion or belief; freedom of expression; freedom of association and peaceful assembly; freedom of movement. No-one will be: subject to arbitrary arrest or detention; subject to torture or other cruel, inhuman or degrading treatment or punishment. Everyone also has the right: to know and act upon his rights; to participate in free and fair elections; to fair and public trial if charged with an offence; to own property alone or in association and to exercise individual enterprise; to enjoy his economic, social and cultural rights.

We affirm that the ethnic, cultural, linguistic and religious identity of national minorities will be protected and that persons belonging to national minorities have the right freely to express, preserve and develop that identity without any discrimination and in full equality before the law. We will ensure that everyone will enjoy recourse to effective remedies, national or international, against any violation of his rights.

Full respect for these precepts is the bedrock on which we will seek to construct the new Europe. Our states will co-operate and support each other with the aim of making democratic gains irreversible.

Economic Liberty and Responsibility

Economic liberty, social justice and environmental responsibility are indispensable for prosperity. The free will of the individual, exercised in democracy and protected by the rule of law, forms the necessary basis for successful economic and social development. We will promote economic activity which respects and upholds human dignity.

Freedom and political pluralism are necessary elements in our common objective of developing market economies towards sustainable economic growth, prosperity, social justice, expanding employment and efficient use of economic resources. The success of the transition to market economy by countries making efforts to this effect is important and in the interest of us all. It will enable us to share a higher level of prosperity which is our common objective. We will co-operate to this end.

Preservation of the environment is a shared responsibility of all our nations. While supporting national and regional efforts in this field, we must also look to the pressing need for joint action on a wider scale.

Friendly Relations among Participating States

Now that a new era is dawning in Europe, we are determined to expand and strengthen friendly relations and cooperation among the states of Europe, the United States of America and Canada, and to promote friendship among our peoples.

To uphold and promote democracy, peace and unity in Europe, we solemnly pledge our full commitment to the Ten Principles of the Helsinki Final Act. We affirm the continuing validity of the Ten Principles and our determination to put them into practice. All the principles apply equally and unreservedly, each of them being interpreted taking into account the others. They form the basis for our relations.

In accordance with our obligations under the Charter of the United Nations and commitments under the Helsinki Final Act, we renew our pledge to refrain from the threat or use of force against the territorial integrity or political independence of any state, or from acting in any other manner inconsistent with the principles or purposes of those documents. We recall that non-compliance with obligations under the Charter of the United Nations constitutes a violation of international law.

We reaffirm our commitment to settle disputes by peaceful means. We decide to develop mechanisms for the prevention and resolution of conflicts among the participating states.

With the ending of the division of Europe, we will strive for a new quality in our security relations while fully respecting each other's freedom of choice in that respect. Security is indivisible and the security of every participating state is inseparably linked to that of all the others. We therefore pledge to cooperate in strengthening confidence and security among us and in promoting arms control and disarmament.

We welcome the Joint Declaration of Twenty-Two States on the improvement of their relations.

Our relations will rest on our common adherence to democratic values and to human rights and fundamental freedoms. We are convinced that in order to strengthen peace and security among our states, the advancement of democracy, and respect for and effective exercise of human rights, are indispensable. We reaffirm the equal rights of peoples and their right to self-determination in conformity with the Charter of the United Nations and with the relevant norms of international law, including those relating to territorial integrity of states.

We are determined to enhance political consultation and to widen cooperation to solve economic, social, environmental, cultural and humanitarian problems. This common resolve and our growing interdependence will help to overcome the mistrust of decades, to increase stability and to build a united Europe.

We want Europe to be a source of peace, open to dialogue and to cooperation with other countries, welcoming exchanges and involved in the search for common responses to the challenges of the future.

Security

Friendly relations among us will benefit from the consolidation of democracy and improved security.

We welcome the signature of the Treaty on Conventional Armed Forces in Europe by 22 participating states which will lead to lower levels of armed forces. We endorse the adoption of a substantial new set of confidence- and security-building measures which will lead to increased transparency and confidence among all participating states. These are important steps towards enhanced stability and security in Europe.

The unprecedented reduction in armed forces resulting from the Treaty on Conventional Armed Forces in Europe, together with new approaches to security and co-operation within the CSCE process, will lead to a new perception of security in Europe and a new dimension in our relations. In this context we fully recognize the freedom of states to choose their own security arrangements.

Unity

Europe whole and free is calling for a new beginning. We invite our peoples to join in this great endeavour.

We note with great satisfaction the Treaty on the Final Settlement with respect to Germany signed in Moscow on 12 September 1990 [see pages xxx–xx] and sincerely welcome the fact that the German people have united to become one state in accordance with the principles of the [Helsinki] Final Act . . . and in full accord with their neighbours. The establishment of the national unity of Germany is an important contribution to a just and lasting order of peace for a united, democratic Europe aware of its responsibility for stability, peace and cooperation.

The participation of both North American and European states is a fundamental characteristic of the CSCE; it underlies its past achievements and is essential to the future of the CSCE process. An abiding adherence to shared values and our common heritage are the ties which bind us together. With all the rich diversity of our nations, we are united in our commitment to expand our cooperation in all fields. The challenges confronting us can only be met by common action, co-operation and solidarity.

The CSCE and the World

The destiny of our nations is linked to that of all other nations. We support fully the United Nations and the enhancement of its role in promoting international peace, security and justice. We reaffirm our commitment to the principles and purposes of the United Nations as enshrined in the Charter and condemn all violations of these principles. We recognize with satisfaction the growing role of the United Nations in world affairs and its increasing effectiveness, fostered by the improvement in relations among our States.

Aware of the dire needs of a great part of the world, we commit ourselves to solidarity with all other countries. Therefore, we issue a call from Paris today to all the nations of the world. We stand ready to join with any and all states in common efforts to protect and advance the community of fundamental human values.

GUIDELINES FOR THE FUTURE

Proceeding from our firm commitment to the full implementation of all CSCE principles and provisions, we now resolve to give a new impetus to a balanced and comprehensive development of our cooperation in order to address the needs and aspirations of our peoples.

Human Dimension

We declare our respect for human rights and fundamental freedoms to be irrevocable. We will fully implement and build upon the provisions relating to the human dimension of the CSCE.

Proceeding from the Document of the Copenhagen Meeting of the Conference on the Human Dimension, we will cooperate to strengthen democratic institutions and to promote the application of the rule of law. To that end, we decide to convene a seminar of experts in Oslo from 4 to 15 November 1991.

Determined to foster the rich contribution of national minorities to the life of our societies, we undertake further to improve their situation. We reaffirm our deep conviction that friendly relations among our peoples, as well as peace, justice, stability and democracy, require that the ethnic, cultural, linguistic and religious identity of national minorities be protected and conditions for the promotion of that identity be created. We declare that questions related to national minorities can only be satisfactorily resolved in a democratic political framework. We further acknowledge that the rights of persons belonging to national minorities must be fully respected as part of universal human rights. Being aware of the urgent need for increased cooperation on, as well as better protection of, national minorities, we decide to convene a meeting of experts on national minorities to be held in Geneva from 1 to 19 July 1991.

We express our determination to combat all forms of racial and ethnic hatred, antisemitism, xenophobia and discrimination against anyone as well as persecution on religious and ideological grounds.

In accordance with our CSCE commitments, we stress that free movement and contacts among our citizens as well as the free flow of information and ideas are crucial for the maintenance and development of free societies and flourishing cultures. We welcome increased tourism and visits among our countries.

The human dimension mechanism has proved its usefulness, and we are consequently determined to expand it to include new procedures involving, inter alia, the services of experts or a roster of eminent persons experienced in human rights issues which could be raised under the mechanism. We shall provide, in the context of the mechanism, for individuals to be involved in the protection of their rights. Therefore, we undertake to develop further our commitments in this respect, in particular at the Moscow Meeting of the Conference on the Human Dimension, without prejudice to obligations under existing international instruments to which our states may be parties.

We recognize the important contribution of the Council of Europe to the promotion of human rights and the principles of democracy and the rule of law as well as to the development of cultural cooperation. We welcome moves by several participating states to join the Council of Europe and adhere to its European Convention on Human Rights. We welcome as well the readiness of the Council of Europe to make its experience available to the CSCE.

Security

The changing political and military environment in Europe opens new possibilities for common efforts in the field of military security. We will build on the important achievements attained in the Treaty on Conventional Armed Forces in Europe and in the negotiations on confidence and security-building measures. We undertake to continue the CSBM negotiations under the same mandate, and to seek to conclude them no later than the Follow-up Meeting of the CSCE to be held in Helsinki in 1992. We also welcome the decision of the participating states concerned to continue the CFE negotiation under the same mandate and to seek to conclude it no later than the Helsinki Follow-up Meeting. Following a period for national preparations, we look forward to a more structured cooperation among all participating states on security matters, and to discussions and consultations among the 34 participating states aimed at establishing by 1992, from the conclusion of the Helsinki Follow-up Meeting, new negotiations on disarmament and confidence- and security-building open to all participating states.

We call for the earliest possible conclusion of the convention on an effectively verifiable, global and comprehensive ban on chemical weapons, and we intend to be original signatories to it. We reaffirm the importance of the 'Open Skies' initiative and call for the successful conclusion of the negotiations as soon as possible.

Although the threat of conflict in Europe has diminished, other dangers threaten the stability of our societies. We are determined to co-operate in defending democratic institutions against activities which violate the independence, sovereign equality or territorial integrity of the participating States. These include illegal activities involving outside pressure, coercion and subversion.

We unreservedly condemn, as criminal, all acts, methods and practices of terrorism and express our determination to work for its eradication both bilaterally and through multilateral co-operation. We will also join together in combating illicit trafficking in drugs.

Being aware that an essential complement to the duty of States to refrain from the threat or use of force is the peaceful settlement of disputes, both being essential factors for the maintenance and consolidation of international peace and security, we will not only seek effective ways of preventing, through political means, conflicts which may yet emerge, but also define, in conformity with international law, appropriate mechanisms for the peaceful resolution of any disputes which may arise. Accordingly, we undertake to seek new forms of co-operation in this area, in particular a range of methods for the peaceful settlement of disputes, including mandatory third-party involvement. We stress that full use should be made in this context of the opportunity of the meeting on the peaceful settlement of disputes which will be convened in Valletta at the beginning of 1991. The Council of Ministers for Foreign Affairs will take into account the Report of the Valletta Meeting.

Economic Co-operation

We stress that economic cooperation based on market economy constitutes an essential element of our relations and will be instrumental in the construction of a prosperous and united Europe. Democratic institutions and economic liberty foster economic and social progress, as recognized in the Document of the Bonn Conference on Economic Cooperation [adopted on 11 April 1990], the results of which we strongly support.

We underline that cooperation in the economic field, science and technology is now an important pillar of the CSCE. The participating states should periodically review progress and give new impulses in these fields.

We are convinced that our overall economic co-operation should be expanded, free enterprise encouraged and trade increased and diversified according to GATT rules. We will promote social justice and progress and further the welfare of our peoples. We recognize in this context the importance of effective policies to address the problem of unemployment.

We reaffirm the need to continue to support democratic countries in transition towards the establishment of market economy and the creation of the basis for self-sustained economic and social growth, as already undertaken by the Group of 24 countries. We further underline the necessity of their increased integration, involving the acceptance of disciplines as well as benefits, into the international economic and financial system.

We consider that increased emphasis on economic cooperation within the CSCE process should take into account the interests of developing participating states.

We recall the link between respect for and promotion of human rights and fundamental freedoms and scientific progress. Cooperation in the field of science and technology will play an essential role in economic and social development. Therefore, it must evolve towards a greater sharing of appropriate scientific and technological information and knowledge with a view to overcoming the technological gap which exists among the participating states. We further encourage the participating states to work together in order to develop human potential and the spirit of free enterprise.

We are determined to give the necessary impetus to cooperation among our states in the fields of energy, transport and tourism for economic and social development. We welcome, in particular, practical steps to create optimal conditions for the economic and rational development of energy resources, with due regard for environmental considerations.

We recognize the important role of the European Community in the political and economic development of Europe. International economic organizations such as the Economic Commission for Europe of the United Nations (ECE/UN), the Bretton Woods Institutions, the Organization for

Economic Cooperation and Development (OECD), the European Free Trade Association (EFTA) and the International Chamber of Commerce (ICC) also have a significant task in promoting economic co-operation, which will be further enhanced by the establishment of the European Bank for Reconstruction and Development (EBRD). In order to pursue our objectives, we stress the necessity for effective coordination of the activities of these organizations and emphasize the need to find methods for all our states to take part in these activities.

Environment

We recognize the urgent need to tackle the problems of the environment and the importance of individual and cooperative efforts in this area. We pledge to intensify our endeavours to protect and improve our environment in order to restore and maintain a sound ecological balance in air, water and soil. Therefore, we are determined to make full use of the CSCE as a framework for the formulation of common environmental commitments and objectives, and thus to pursue the work reflected in the Report of the Sofia Meeting on the Protection of the Environment.

We emphasize the significant role of a well-informed society in enabling the public and individuals to take initiatives to improve the environment. To this end, we commit ourselves to promote public awareness and education on the environment as well as the public reporting of the environmental impact of policies, projects and programmes.

We attach priority to the introduction of clean and low-waste technology, being aware of the need to support countries which do not yet have their own means for appropriate measures.

We underline that environmental policies should be supported by appropriate legislative measures and administrative structures to ensure their effective implementation.

We stress the need for new measures providing for the systematic evaluation of compliance with the existing commitments and, moreover, for the development of more ambitious commitments with regard to notification and exchange of information about the state of the environment and potential environmental hazards. We also welcome the creation of the European Environment Agency (EEA).

We welcome the operational activities, problem-oriented studies and policy reviews in various existing international organizations engaged in the protection of the environment, such as the United Nations Environment Program (UNEP), the Economic Commission for Europe of the United Nations (ECE/UN) and the Organization for Economic Cooperation and Development (OECD). We emphasize the need for strengthening their cooperation and for their efficient co-ordination.

Culture

We recognize the essential contribution of our common European culture and our shared values in overcoming the division of the continent. Therefore, we underline our attachment to creative freedom and to the protection and promotion of our cultural and spiritual heritage, in all its richness and diversity.

In view of the recent changes in Europe, we stress the increased importance of the Cracow Symposium and we look forward to its consideration of guidelines for intensified cooperation in the field of culture. We invite the Council of Europe to contribute to this symposium.

In order to promote greater familiarity amongst our peoples, we favour the establishment of cultural centres in cities of other participating states as well as increased cooperation in the audio-visual field and wider exchange in music, theatre, literature and the arts.

We resolve to make special efforts in our national policies to promote better understanding, in particular among young people, through cultural exchanges, cooperation in all fields of education and, more specifically, through teaching and training in the languages of other participating states. We intend to consider first results of this action at the Helsinki Follow-up Meeting in 1992.

Migrant Workers

We recognize that the issues of migrant workers and their families legally residing in host countries have economic, cultural and social aspects as well as their human dimension. We reaffirm that the protection and promotion of their rights, as well as the implementation of relevant international obligations, is our common concern.

Mediterranean

We consider that the fundamental political changes that have occurred in Europe have a positive relevance to the Mediterranean region. Thus, we will continue efforts to strengthen security and cooperation in the Mediterranean as an important factor for stability in Europe. We welcome the Report of the Palma de Mallorca Meeting on the Mediterranean, the results of which we all support.

We are concerned with the continuing tensions in the region, and renew our determination to intensify efforts towards finding just, viable and lasting solutions, through peaceful means, to outstanding crucial problems, based on respect for the principles of the Final Act.

We wish to promote favourable conditions for a harmonious development and diversification of relations with the non-participating Mediterranean states. Enhanced cooperation with these states will be pursued with the aim of promoting economic and social development and thereby enhancing stability in the region. To this end, we will strive together with these countries towards a substantial narrowing of the prosperity gap between Europe and its Mediterranean neighbours.

Non-governmental Organizations

We recall the major role that non-governmental organizations, religious and other groups and individuals have played in the achievement of the objectives of the CSCE and will further facilitate their activities for the implementation of the CSCE commitments by the participating states. These organizations, groups and individuals must be involved in an appropriate way in the activities and new structures of the CSCE in order to fulfil their important tasks.

NEW STRUCTURES AND INSTITUTIONS OF THE CSCE PROCESS

Our common efforts to consolidate respect for human rights, democracy and the rule of law, to strengthen peace and to promote unity in Europe require a new quality of political dialogue and co-operation and thus development of the structures of the CSCE.

The intensification of our consultations at all levels is of prime importance in shaping our future relations. To this end, we decide on the following:

We, the heads of state or government, shall meet next time in Helsinki on the occasion of the CSCE Follow-up Meeting 1992. Thereafter, we will meet on the occasion of subsequent follow-up meetings.

Our ministers for foreign affairs will meet, as a Council, regularly and at least once a year. These meetings will provide the central forum for political consultations within the CSCE process. The Council will consider issues relevant to the Conference on Security and Cooperation in Europe and take appropriate decisions. The first meeting of the Council will take place in Berlin.

A committee of senior officials will prepare the meetings of the Council and carry out its decisions. The committee will review current issues and may take appropriate decisions, including in the form of recommendations to the Council. Additional meetings of the representatives of the participating states may be agreed upon to discuss questions of urgent concern.

The Council will examine the development of provisions for convening meetings of the committee of senior officials in emergency situations.

Meetings of other ministers may also be agreed by the participating states.

In order to provide administrative support for these consultations we establish a Secretariat in Prague.

Follow-up meetings of the participating states will be held, as a rule, every two years to allow the participating states to take stock of developments, review the implementation of their commitments and consider further steps in the CSCE process.

We decide to create a Conflict Prevention Centre in Vienna to assist the Council in reducing the risk of conflict.

We decide to establish an Office for Free Elections in Warsaw to facilitate contacts and the exchange of information on elections within participating States.

Recognizing the important role parliamentarians can play in the CSCE process, we call for greater parliamentary involvement in the CSCE, in particular through the creation of a CSCE parliamentary assembly, involving members of parliaments from all participating states. To this end, we urge that contacts be pursued at parliamentary level to discuss the field of activities, working methods and rules of procedure of such a CSCE parliamentary structure, drawing on existing experience and work already undertaken in this field.

We ask our ministers for foreign affairs to review this matter on the occasion of their first meeting as a Council.

Procedural and organizational modalities relating to certain provisions contained in the Charter of Paris for a New Europe are set out in the Supplementary Document which is adopted together with the Charter of Paris.

We entrust to the Council the further steps which may be required to ensure the implementation of decisions contained in the present document, as well as in the Supplementary Document, and to consider further efforts for the strengthening of security and cooperation in Europe. The Council may adopt any amendment to the Supplementary Document which it may deem appropriate.

The original of the Charter of Paris for a New Europe, drawn up in English, French, German, Italian, Russian and Spanish, will be transmitted to the government of the French Republic, which will retain it in its archives. Each of the participating states will receive from the government of the French Republic a true copy of the Charter of Paris.

The text of the Charter of Paris will be published in each participating state which will disseminate it and make it known as widely as possible.

The government of the French Republic is requested to transmit to the Secretary-General of the United Nations the text of the Charter of Paris for a New Europe, which is not eligible for registration under article 102 of the Charter of the United Nations, with a view to its circulation to all the members of the Organization as an official document of the United Nations.

The Government of the French Republic is also requested to transmit the text of the Charter of Paris to all the other international organizations mentioned in the text.

Wherefore, we, the undersigned high representatives of the participating states, mindful of the high political significance we attach to the results of the Summit Meeting, and declaring our determination to act in accordance with the provisions we have adopted, have subscribed our signatures below.

UNITED KINGDOM CONSERVATIVE CABINET

(3 January – 1 November 1990)

Prime Minister, First Lord of the Treasury and Minister for the Civil Service	Rt. Hon. Margaret Thatcher, FRS, MP
Lord President of the Council and Leader of the House of Commons	Rt. Hon. Sir Geoffrey Howe, QC, MP[1]
Lord Chancellor	Rt. Hon. The Lord Mackay of Clashfern
Secretary of State for Foreign and Commonwealth Affairs	Rt. Hon. Douglas Hurd, CBE, MP
Chancellor of the Exchequer	Rt. Hon. John Major, MP
Secretary of State for the Home Department	Rt. Hon. David Waddington, QC, MP
Secretary of State for Wales	Rt. Hon. Peter Walker, MBE, MP[2]
	Rt. Hon. David Hunt, MBE, MP[3]
Secretary of State for Employment	Rt. Hon. Michael Howard, QC, MP
Secretary of State for Defence	Rt. Hon. Tom King, MP
Secretary of State for Trade and Industry	Rt. Hon. Nicholas Ridley, MP[4]
	Rt. Hon. Peter Lilley, MP[5]
Chancellor of the Duchy of Lancaster	Rt. Hon. Kenneth Baker, MP
Secretary of State for Health	Rt. Hon. Kenneth Clarke, QC, MP
Secretary of State for Education and Science	Rt. Hon. John MacGregor, OBE, MP
Secretary of State for Scotland	Rt. Hon. Malcolm Rifkind, QC, MP
Secretary of State for Transport	Rt. Hon. Cecil Parkinson, MP
Secretary of State for Energy	Rt. Hon. John Wakeham, MP
Lord Privy Seal and Leader of the House of Lords	Rt. Hon. The Lord Belstead
Secretary of State for Social Security	Rt. Hon. Antony Newton, OBE, MP
Secretary of State for the Environment	Rt. Hon. Christopher Patten, MP
Secretary of State for Northern Ireland	Rt. Hon. Peter Brooke, MP
Minister of Agriculture, Fisheries and Food	Rt. Hon. John Selwyn Gummer, MP
Chief Secretary to the Treasury	Rt. Hon. Norman Lamont, MP

[1] resigned 1 November 1990
[2] resigned 4 May 1990
[3] from 4 May 1990
[4] resigned 14 July 1990
[5] from 14 July 1990

UK CABINET

(2 – 28 November 1990)

Prime Minister, First Lord of the Treasury and Minister for the Civil Service	Rt. Hon. Margaret Thatcher, FRS, MP
Lord President of the Council and Leader of the House of Commons	Rt. Hon. John MacGregor, OBE, MP
Lord Chancellor	Rt. Hon. The Lord Mackay of Clashfern
Secretary of State for Foreign and Commonwealth Affairs	Rt. Hon. Douglas Hurd, CBE, MP
Chancellor of the Exchequer	Rt. Hon. John Major, MP
Secretary of State for the Home Department	Rt. Hon. David Waddington, QC, MP
Secretary of State for Wales	Rt. Hon. David Hunt, MBE, MP
Secretary of State for Employment	Rt. Hon. Michael Howard, QC, MP
Secretary of State for Defence	Rt. Hon. Tom King, MP
Secretary of State for Trade and Industry	Rt. Hon. Peter Lilley, MP
Chancellor of the Duchy of Lancaster	Rt. Hon. Kenneth Baker, MP
Secretary of State for Health	Rt. Hon. William Waldegrave, MP
Secretary of State for Education and Science	Rt. Hon. Kenneth Clarke, QC, MP
Secretary of State for Scotland	Rt. Hon. Malcolm Rifkind, QC, MP
Secretary of State for Transport	Rt. Hon. Cecil Parkinson, MP
Secretary of State for Energy	Rt. Hon. John Wakeham, MP
Lord Privy Seal and Leader of the House of Lords	Rt. Hon. The Lord Belstead
Secretary of State for Social Security	Rt. Hon. Antony Newton, OBE, MP
Secretary of State for the Environment	Rt. Hon. Christopher Patten, MP
Secretary of State for Northern Ireland	Rt. Hon. Peter Brooke, MP
Minister of Agriculture, Fisheries and Food	Rt. Hon. John Selwyn Gummer, MP
Chief Secretary to the Treasury	Rt. Hon. Norman Lamont, MP

(as from 28 November 1990)

Prime Minister, First Lord of the Treasury and Minister for the Civil Service	Rt. Hon. John Major, MP
Lord Chancellor	Rt. Hon. The Lord Mackay of Clashfern
Secretary of State for Foreign and Commonwealth Affairs	Rt. Hon. Douglas Hurd, CBE, MP
Lord Privy Seal and Leader of the House of Lords	Rt. Hon. Lord Waddington of Read, QC
Secretary of State for the Home Department	Rt. Hon. Kenneth Baker, MP
Chancellor of the Exchequer	Rt. Hon. Norman Lamont, MP
Secretary of State for the Environment	Rt. Hon. Michael Heseltine, MP
Secretary of State for Defence	Rt. Hon. Tom King, MP
Secretary of State for Education and Science	Rt. Hon. Kenneth Clarke, QC, MP
Lord President of the Council and Leader of the House of Commons	Rt. Hon. John MacGregor, OBE, MP
Secretary of State for Transport	Rt. Hon. Malcolm Rifkind, QC, MP
Secretary of State for Energy	Rt. Hon. John Wakeham, MP
Secretary of State for Social Security	Rt. Hon. Antony Newton, OBE, MP
Chancellor of the Duchy of Lancaster	Rt. Hon. Christopher Patten, MP
Secretary of State for Northern Ireland	Rt. Hon. Peter Brooke, MP
Minister of Agriculture, Fisheries and Food	Rt. Hon. John Selwyn Gummer, MP
Secretary of State for Employment	Rt. Hon. Michael Howard, QC, MP
Secretary of State for Wales	Rt. Hon. David Hunt, MBE, MP
Secretary of State for Trade and Industry	Rt. Hon. Peter Lilley, MP
Secretary of State for Health	Rt. Hon. William Waldegrave, MP
Secretary of State for Scotland	Rt. Hon. Ian Lang, MP
Chief Secretary to the Treasury	Rt. Hon. David Mellor, QC, MP

UNITED STATES REPUBLICAN CABINET

(as at 31 December 1990)

President	George Bush
Vice-President	J. Danforth Quayle
Secretary of State	James Baker
Secretary of the Treasury	Nicholas Brady
Secretary of Defence	Richard Cheney
Secretary of the Interior	Manuel Lujan
Attorney-General	Richard Thornburgh
Secretary of Commerce	Robert Mosbacher
Secretary of Labour	Lynn Martin*
Secretary of Health & Human Resources	Dr Louis Sullivan
Secretary of Transportation	Samuel Skinner
Secretary of Education	Lamar Alexander*
Secretary of Agriculture	Clayton Yeutter
Secretary of Veteran Affairs	Edward Derwinski
Secretary of Housing and Urban Development	Jack Kemp
Secretary of Energy	James Watkins

CABINET RANK OFFICIALS

Director of the Central Intelligence Agency	William Webster
Director of the Office of Management & Budget	Richard Darman
US Permanent Representative at the United Nations	Thomas Pickering
US Trade Representative	Carla Hills
White House Chief of Staff	John Sununu
Chairman of Council of Economic Advisers	Prof. Michael Boskin
National Security Adviser	General Brent Scowcroft

*Confirmation pending at year's end

OBITUARY

Abdul Rahman, Tunku (b. 1903), Chief Minister of Malaya 1955–57, Prime Minister after independence 1957–63, Prime Minister of Malaysia 1963–70, a barrister by profession, began his political career as president of the United Malays National Organization (UMNO) in 1951. Swept into power in alliance with Chinese and Indian parties, he was one of the architects of independence and of the Malaysian federation. In office he successfully weathered communist terrorism, jungle war with Indonesia, and grave communal disturbance in 1969. Beyond office he became secretary-general of the Islamic Conference, was president of the Malaysian Football Association, and revelled in sport from the racecourse to the bridge table. Died 6 December

Abernathy, Rev Ralph (b. 1926), was Martin Luther King's right-hand man in the non-violent civil-rights campaign in the USA, from the Montgomery bus boycott in 1955 to King's death in 1968. Thereafter he turned sour against King's family, and in his autobiography (1989) exposed his leader's breach of the Seventh Commandment. Died 17 April

Allan, Elizabeth (b. 1910), British actress, had a successful career spanning 50 years on stage, film and television. In the early 1930s she played leading roles with such stars as Clark Gable, Robert Montgomery, Ronald Colman, Katherine Hepburn and Greta Garbo (*q.v.*), then returned to the London stage; a revived film career included *No Highway* (1951) and *Heart of the Matter* (1953), before she concentrated on television. Died 27 July

Althusser, Louis (b. 1918 in French Algeria), French political philosopher, intellectual guru of a generation of middle-class marxist revolutionaries whose day came, and went, in the 1968 'events' in France and elsewhere. His essay collection *Pour Marx* (1965) made his reputation, which later declined, however, after he was committed to a mental hospital (1981) for strangling his wife. Died 20 October

Ames, Leslie (b. 1905), English cricketer, was arguably the best batsman-wicketkeeper the game had ever seen. He played 47 times for England, had a Test average of over 40 runs, scored altogether 102 centuries, and, playing for Kent, held the unbeaten record of 122 batsmen dismissed by a wicketkeeper in an English county season. Died 27 February

Arévalo Bermejo, Juan José (b. 1904), President of Guatemala 1945–50, headed a liberal-reformist regime which inevitably clashed with all-powerful US commercial interests. He spent most of the succeeding counter-revolutionary years in exile. Died 6 October

Averoff, Evangelos (b. 1910), Greek conservative politician, played a leading part in the overthrow of the Colonels' regime in 1974. As Karamanlis' Foreign Minister between 1967 and '73, he had negotiated the Cyprus settlement of 1959. He was Defence Minister 1974–81 and became leader of New Democracy party in opposition, 1981–84. Died 2 January

Bailey, Pearl (b. 1918), black American singer and comedienne, was immensely popular in the 1950s and '60s on Broadway, on the London stage and in Hollywood films, which included *Carmen Jones, Porgy and Bess* and *That Certain Feeling.*

Presidents Ford, Reagan and Bush all appointed her later to special missions to the UN, and she was an ardent Christian evangelist. Died 17 August

Bennett, Joan (b. 1910), American film actress, was, at her best in the 1930s and '40s, one of the brightest stars in the Hollywood firmament. Among her most famous films were *Me and My Girl* (with Spencer Tracy, 1932), *Man Hunt* (with Walter Pidgeon, 1942) and *The Woman in the Window* (with Edward G. Robinson, 1944). Died 7 December

Berger, Erna (b. 1900), German coloratura soprano, began her operatic career in her native Dresden, but sang leading roles with the Berlin State Opera for 20 years from 1934. Her debuts at Covent Garden came in 1935 and at the Metropolitan, New York, in 1949. She played Jenny Lind in a 1940s film. Died 14 June

Bernstein, Leonard (b. 1918), American composer, conductor, pianist and missionary for music, changed the perception of music for millions of people all over the world. For him there was no dividing line between classical and modern music, or between sophisticated and popular music. His most famous creation was *West Side Story* (1957), in form a conventional opera, in content as contemporary as jazz and as catchy as the best of modern stage musicals. In this vein he had already triumphed with music for the Broadway spectacular, *Wonderful Town* (1953), the film *On the Waterfront* (1954) and his own operetta *Candide* (1956). But his compositions ranged beyond the stage and screen to concert pieces and devotional works, mostly Jewish but also Christian. He was a master of the piano, but it was as a conductor that he reached supreme international rank, beginning with a sensational success when aged 25 he stood in for an indisposed Bruno Walter with the New York Philharmonic, of which he became a principal conductor in 1957 and music director in 1958. Thereafter he was in high demand all over the Western world, conducting many forms of orchestral music from Handel to Stravinsky, with a special love for Mahler. His exuberantly energetic style expressed an enthusiasm for music and for life that he passed on to his own and younger generations. The title of his book *The Joy of Music* epitomized the theme of his life. Died 14 October

Bettelheim, Dr Bruno (b. 1903), Austrian psychologist, was the author of important books on the problems of mentally and emotionally disturbed children. His internment, as a Jew, in Dachau and Buchenwald turned his interest to behaviour in extreme situations, the focus of his book *The Informed Heart* (1960), which he wrote while professor of educational psychology and psychiatry at the University of Chicago (1952–73). Died 13 March

Bunshaft, Gordon (b. 1909), American architect, became in 1937 chief designer, New York, of the Chicago firm, Skidmore, Owens & Merrill, whose name concealed his own as architect of many notable buildings. Among the most famous of his works were Lever House (New York, 1952), the Pepsi-Cola building (New York, 1959), the Banque Lambert (Brussels, 1965), a University of Texas complex (1971) and airport buildings at Jeddah. After 42 years with SOM, he retired in 1979. Died 6 August

Caccia, Lord (Harold Caccia, b. 1905), was British ambassador in Vienna 1951–1954 and in Washington 1956–61 and permanent head of the Foreign Office 1962–65. He had been closely involved in Mediterranean policy in World War II and in the post-war unification of the foreign service. Among his subsequent non-diplomatic posts were those of chairman of the Ditchley Foundation, provost of Eton (1965–77), chairman of the MCC and business directorships.

Throughout his career his style was energetic, forthright, hasty and cheerful. Died 31 October

Caradon, Lord (formerly Sir Hugh Foot), PC, GCMG, KCVO, (b. 1907), was among the most distinguished British colonial civil servants in the last phase of a far-flung Empire, conducting one of its most difficult retreats, from ethnically-divided Cyprus. He had served with distinction in the Middle East, Cyprus, Jamaica and Nigeria before becoming governor-in-chief of Jamaica 1951–57 and governor and commander-in-chief of Cyprus 1957–60. After a short period as ambassador to the UN, he was made a peer, a minister of state and permanent representative at the UN under the 1964–70 Labour government, remaining consultant to UNDP 1971–75. Died 5 September

Carruthers, Jimmy (b. 1929), bantamweight boxer, was the first Australian to win a world title in the ring, knocking out the renowned champion Vic Towell in less than three minutes in 1952 and remaining undefeated until he retired two years later. Died 10 August

Chakravarty, Sukhamoy (b. 1934), was the most respected Indian economist of his generation, both academically (in India, England and the USA) and in government service, as chairman of the council of economic advisers to successive prime ministers. Died 22 August

Chastel, André (b. 1912), French art historian, wrote many books, mainly on the Italian renaissance, of which one of the most distinguished was *Myth of the Renaissance* (1969). His highly-valued advice to French governments and museums bore much fruit, including the creation in 1989 of a national art library. Died 18 July

Childs, Marquis (b. 1903), American journalist, exerted much influence on opinion in the USA and abroad through his syndicated column as Washington correspondent of the *St Louis Post-Dispatch*. In 1969 he won the first Pulitzer Prize to be awarded for commentary. Died 30 June

Copland, Aaron (b. 1900), American composer, though of immigrant Lithuanian-Jewish parentage, became the patriot hero of American music. Some of the best and most popular of his many works—which earned him worldwide prestige as one of the great composers of the twentieth century—were inspired by American folktunes and evocations of the prairies and other landscapes of the USA. These included the ballet music for *Rodeo* (1942) and *Appalachian Spring* (his most famous work, 1944), and for the dance-music-drama *Billy the Kid* (1938). Later he composed the scores for a number of films, such as *The Heiress, On the Town* and *Of Mice and Men*. Meanwhile he had composed—as he continued to compose until the late 1960s—equally acclaimed works for the concert platform, like the popular Third Symphony (1946) and his *Twelve Poems of Emily Dickinson* (1950). Like his admirer Leonard Bernstein (see above), he devoted much effort to educating the American public in taste for music, through books and articles, concerts and broadcasts. Died 2 December

Corish, Brendan (b. 1918), Irish politician, was leader of the Labour Party in the Republic 1960–77, and Tánaiste (deputy prime minister) in the Cosgrave administration 1973–77. Died 17 February

Dahl, Roald (b. 1916), British (of Norwegian ancestry) author of morbidly thrilling short stories and imaginative children's books, had a vast readership on both sides of the Atlantic. Among collections of the former were *Someone Like You* (1953) and *Kiss Kiss* (1960), among the latter *James and the Giant Peach* (1961) and *Charlie and the Chocolate Factory* (1964). Died 13 November

Dargaud, Georges (b. 1911), French publisher, gave to the public of all continents two of the world's most famous cartoon characters, Tintin (first created in 1948 by the Belgian artist Hergé) and Asterix (invented by René Gascinn and drawn by Albert Uderzo). Died 18 July

Davis, Sammy, Jr (b. 1925), American entertainer, was bred to the vaudeville stage, on which, with his father, he played from the age of three. In the 1950s, patronised by his lifelong friend Frank Sinatra, and thanks to the exuberance and skill of his performances as dancer, drummer, singer, impersonator, he became a glittering star on stage and screen (*Mr Wonderful* 1956, *Porgy and Bess* 1959), the first black American performer to be accepted on equal terms by white and black audiences alike. He made a triumphant excursion to the legitimate theatre in Odet's *Golden Boy* (1964), but his popularity waned somewhat as his earlier taste for whiskey, marihuana and cocaine took a toll on his health. Died 16 May

Denny, Jacques (b. 1931), French film director, first gained fame with *Lola* (1961), a 'lyrical poem' about Nantes, but was by far best known worldwide for his *Les parapluies de Cherbourg*, starring Catherine Deneuve (1964). Died 27 October

Dexter, John (b. 1925), British stage director, rose from an unlikely early life—a working-class boy, army sergeant, unpromising actor—to become one of the most creative and admired men of the theatre, both legitimate and operatic, classical and contemporary. Associate director at the Royal Court theatre from 1957, in 1963 he took a similar role at the National Theatre. Among the plays and playwrights who owed early fame to him were *The Royal Hunt of the Sun* and *Equus* (Peter Shaffer) and *Roots* (Arnold Wesker). From French classics like *Le Misanthrope* (in English), Dexter progressed to opera, directing successfully for Covent Garden, the English National Opera and the Metropolitan in New York. Among his latest productions were *Heartbreak House* and *Madam Butterfly*. Died 23 March

Doe, Samuel (b. 1950), self-appointed President of Liberia, was a barely literate master-sergeant when in 1980 he led the military coup that overthrew and murdered President Tolbert. In office he had some early successes, but proved himself a corrupt and bloodthirsty ogre, not above cannibalism. Rebellion, largely tribal, brought him the same fate as his predecessor. Died 10 September

Duarte, José Napoléon (b. 1925), co-founder of El Salvador's Christian Democrats in 1960 and President of his country in 1980–82 and 1984–89, was associated with US attempts to resolve internal conflict through an alliance of army moderates and centrist reformers, but his influence waned during his second term, especially after he was diagnosed as suffering from terminal cancer. Died 23 February

Dunne, Irene (b. 1901), American actress and singer, was a star of stage musicals like *Show Boat* (1929) before she went to Hollywood in the 1930s to play in both musical and dramatic films, in the latter opposite such co-stars as Robert Taylor (*Magnificent Obsession*), Cary Grant (*My Favourite Wife* and *Penny Serenade*) and Charles Boyer (*Love Affair* and *When Tomorrow Comes*). She will also be remembered for her more mature parts in *Anna and the King of Siam* (1946), *I Remember Mama* (1947) and *Life With Father* (1948). Died 4 September

Durrell, Lawrence (b. 1912), British author, gained instant fame with his four-volume novel *The Alexandria Quartet* (1957–60), but he was also a fine poet (*Collected Poems,* 1980) and an entertaining writer of plays, essays and short pieces for the press. Died 7 November

Dürrenmatt, Friedrich (b. 1921), Swiss playwright and author, was best known among English-speakers for his black comedy *The Visit* (*Besuch der alten Dame*, 1956), which was later made into an opera. Other plays of international renown included *The Physicists* and *Meteor*. He also wrote successful detective novels (among them *The Judge and the Hangman*, 1954), short stories and television scripts. Died 14 December

Emmett, Rowland (b. 1906), British cartoonist, won worldwide fame for his drawings and models of fantastic machines and crazy trains. Died 13 November

Erté, *see* Tirtoff, Romain de

Esmond, Jill (b. 1908), British actress, was remembered as Laurence Olivier's first wife (1930–40), but in those days she actually outshone him as a star of stage and screen in England and America. She returned successfully to Broadway and Hollywood 1942–46, but retired in the 1950s. Died 28 July

Fabrizi, Aldo (b. 1905), Italian actor and film director, played the lead part in *Roma, città aperta* (1945), which first gained him wide fame; other films that his acting adorned included *Vivere in pace* (1946), *Prima communione* (1950) and *Guardie e ladri* (1951). As a director he was less successful than he was as actor and cookery expert. Died 2 April

Fahd al-Ahmad as-Sabah, Sheikh (b. 1945), a scion of Kuwait's ruling house, was a member of the International Olympic Committee, president of the Olympic Council of Asia and a vice-president of FIFA, the global governing body of association football. Besides his interests in sport, he had fought on the Palestinian side in the Arab-Israeli war of 1967, but his influence in Arab society, as in sport, was diplomatic and liberal. Killed in action against the Iraqi invasion, 2 August

Figgures, Sir Frank, KCB (b. 1910), was the first secretary-general of the European Free Trade Association (EFTA) 1960–65. Died 27 November

Figueres Ferrer, José (b. 1906), was President of Costa Rica 1948–49, 1953–58 and 1970–74. A social democrat wafted to power by popular hatred of the oppressive regime of Rafael Calderón, he applied a number of radical reforms, and despite serious setbacks earned respect as a major statesman of Central America. Died 8 June

Fleming, Rt Rev Launcelot, KCVO (b. 1906), British scientist, explorer and ecclesiastic, was a member of the Grahamland expedition to the Antarctic 1934 and director of the Scott Polar Research Institute 1947–49; chaplain, fellow and later dean of Trinity Hall, Cambridge 1933–49; bishop of Portsmouth 1949–59, of Norwich 1959–71; thereafter dean of Windsor and domestic chaplain to the Queen. Always deeply concerned for young people, he was one of the founders of Voluntary Service Overseas. Died 30 July

Foot, Sir Hugh, *see* Caradon, Lord.

Forbes, Malcolm (b. 1919), American business journal publisher and multi-millionaire, became in 1954 sole proprietor and editor-in-chief of *Forbes Magazine,* founded by his father, whose circulation he multiplied sevenfold. Died 24 February

Fricker, Peter Racine (b. in England 1920), musical composer and teacher, after war service in the RAF succeeded his early mentor Michael Tippett as director of music at Morley College 1952–64. Drawn to UCLA at Santa Barbara in 1964 by a visiting professorship, he held its chair of music for the rest of his life, though often revisiting and composing for his native land. His compositions, ranging from violin concertos to songs and short pieces for many instruments, were numerous, eclectic and latterly avant-garde. Died 1 February

Garbo, Greta (b. Greta L. Gustafsson in Sweden 1905), the greatest of all film stars, was a magnificent actress as well as a supreme beauty. In 1925 the Swedish film director Mauritz Stiller took her to Hollywood, where she entered a career-long association with Metro-Goldwyn-Mayer. Critics soon noted her talent, but for her first really successful film, *Flesh and the Devil* (with John Gilbert), she had to wait until 1927. Thenceforward she was a cinema idol. The coming of sound films only enhanced her appeal—her husky, resonant voice was unique and unforgettable—and the list of her 'talkies' included many of the most triumphant films of the 1930s: *Anna Christie* (1930), *Mata Hari* (1932), *Grand Hotel* (1932), *Queen Christina* (1933), *The Painted Veil* (1934), *Anna Karenina* (1935), *Camille* (1936), *Ninotchka* (1939). In 1941 she resigned from the cinema, to lead a solitary and reclusive life for nearly half a century. Died 16 April

Gardiner, Lord, PC, CH (b. 1900), as Lord Chancellor in the Labour governments of 1964–70, was a notable reformer of English law. He was responsible for the abolition of the death penalty, the liberalization of the laws on homosexual conduct and abortion, three major statutory reforms of the criminal law, creation of the Family Division of the High Court, and of the permanent Law Commission to study existing law and recommend changes in the interest of justice. Before becoming a life peer in 1963, as Gerald Gardiner, QC, he had been a highly-rewarded barrister, best known to the general public for his successful defence of the publishers of *Lady Chatterley's Lover* against a charge of obscenity. Died 7 January

Gardner, Ava (b. 1922), American film actress, was admired more for her exquisite beauty than for her acting, but she effectively played leading roles in many good films, from *The Killers* (1946) to Huston's *Night of the Iguana* (1964). The last two decades of her life were spent in quiet semi-retirement in England. Of her three husbands the last was Frank Sinatra. Died 25 January

Gavin, Lieut. Gen. James (b. 1907), commanded the famous 82nd US airborne division in the last months of World War II in Europe, where his personal valour matched his tactical brilliance. Though US ambassador to France 1961–62, he was no establishment figure, but a fierce critic of American involvement in Vietnam. Died 23 February

Genière, Renaud de la (b. 1925), was governor of the Bank of France 1979–84 and chairman of the Compagnie Financière de Suez 1986–90. Died 16 October

Girodias, Maurice (b. 1919), French publisher, defied convention and censorship, most spectacularly with publication by his Olympia Press of Nabokov's *Lolita* (1955). He also published the disputed homosexual 'Black Diaries' of Sir Roger Casement, executed for high treason in 1916. Later he moved to the USA and became an American citizen. Died 3 July

Goddard, Paulette (b. Marion Levy 1911), American film actress, was discovered playing small parts by Charlie Chaplin, with whom she starred in *Modern Times* and *The Great Dictator,* and to whom she was married 1935–42. She acted in a number of successful films in the 1940s but her star career was ended and she retired to Switzerland. (Her fourth husband, from 1958 until his death in 1970, was the author Erich Maria Remarque.) Died 23 April

Goldberg, Arthur J. (b. 1908), American lawyer and politician, was US ambassador to the UN 1965–68. As counsel to the Council of Industrial

Organizations he had been a prime mover in the AFL/CIO merger of 1955 which united the two branches of American trade unionism. He became Secretary of Labor in President Kennedy's 1961 administration but was moved to the US Supreme Court bench the following year. Died 19 January

Graziano, Rocky (b. Rocco Barbella 1922), American boxer, was world middleweight champion for only a short time (1947–48), but despite his youthful criminal record became a folk hero by virtue of his warm personality and his ability to give and take the heaviest punishment; his life was presented in the highly successful film *Somebody Up There Likes Me* (1956, with Paul Newman). Died 22 May

Gucci, Aldo, (b. 1905), Italian businessman, turned a family saddlery firm into a worldwide empire famous for expensive and elegant leather goods. In 1986 he served a short gaol sentence in the US for multi-million tax evasion, for which he blamed an accountant and which he redeemed in full. Died 20 January

Hammer, Dr Armand (b. 1898), American businessman and philanthropist, won world renown as a middleman between the USSR and US administrations, having established personal friendships with successive Soviet leaders, starting with Lenin in the 1920s. An incessant worker, he made fortunes from pharmaceuticals and oil, in the latter trade raising Occidental from a poor little company to a major global force. Much of his multimillion profits he spent on a magnificent art collection and on medical and other charities. Died 10 December

Harrison, Sir Rex (b. 1908), British actor, after early experience in repertory and touring companies, rose to national stardom in Rattigan's *French Without Tears* (1936), in a role displaying his unique stage personality—urbane, humorous and commanding. On stage and screen in the 1930s, '40s and '50s (with a wartime interval in the RAFVR), he acted to the acclaim of critics and public in the plays of Shaw, Coward, Behrman, Eliot, Fry, among other modern classics; but his most enduring triumph came in 1956, when he played Professor Higgins in Lerner and Loewe's musical *My Fair Lady* (based on Shaw's *Pygmalion*), a part for which, when it was translated from the theatre to the cinema, he won an Oscar for best actor—this despite his total inability to sing. He continued acting to the end, and was appearing on Broadway in Somerset Maugham's *The Circle* when he died, 2 June

Henson, Jim (b. 1936), American puppeteer, created the Muppets (among them Kermit the Frog, speaking with Henson's own voice), who first appeared in a highly successful children's educational programme in the US, *Sesame Street,* and from 1976 in the British-based *Muppet Show,* one of the most popular television series in the world, shown in 100 countries. Died 16 May

Hofstadter, Dr Robert (b. 1915), shared with Rudolf Mossbauer the 1961 Nobel prize for physics for their work on the structure of the atomic nucleus. Stanford University, California, was the scene of his teaching and research 1950–85. Died 17 November

Hopkinson, Sir Tom (b. 1905), British journalist, made a great name for himself as editor 1940–53 of *Picture Post*, the British counterpart of *Paris Match*. In 1957–61 he edited *Drum*, the South African picture magazine for Africans. Next, he was founder-director of the International Press Institute's Nairobi centre for training Africans in journalism. From 1967, he taught journalism studies at university level in England, the USA and Wales. Died 20 June

Hussein Onn, Tun (b. 1922), was

Prime Minister of Malaysia 1976–81. After serving as an officer in the Indian Army he supported his father, Chief Minister of Johore, in founding the United Malays National Organization (UMNO), and held ministerial office from 1970 in the ruling coalition, which he led to electoral victory in 1978. Died 30 May

Hutton, Sir Leonard (b. 1916), English cricketer, made batting scores which stood as records for many years, some still unsurpassed: 364 in a Test match against Australia (1938), a first-wicket stand of 359 with Washbrook against South Africa (1948), the highest total of runs in one month of the English season (1,294 in June 1949). In Test and county cricket he scored in all 40,140 runs, took 173 wickets as a bowler and held 369 catches; his average score in Test matches was 56.67. He was the first professional player to captain England (1952). A calm and modest man, he was widely respected throughout the sporting world. Died 6 September

Kagan, Oleg (b. 1946), Russian violinist, was profoundly admired in the USA and Germany as well as the USSR for his playing of both classical and contemporary music. Died 15 July

Karjalainen, Dr Ahti (b. 1923), Finnish Centre (Agrarian) Party politician, was Prime Minister 1962–64 and 1970–71: he was Foreign Minister 1961–62, '64–70 and '72–75, governor of the Bank of Finland 1982–83 and chairman of the Finnish-Soviet economic commission 1967–83. Died 7 September

Kendall-Carpenter, John (b. 1925), played rugby football for England 1948–54, latterly as captain. Later he became president of the RFU and chairman of the Rugby World Cup organizing committee. Off the field he was a highly-respected school headmaster. Died 23 May

Keswick, Sir William ('Tony') (b. 1903), as director of Matheson & Co. 1943–75 (chairman 1949–66), was the leading British figure in Far East trade for a generation. He was a director of the Bank of England 1955–73, of Hudson's Bay Co. 1943–72 (governor 1952–65) and of British Petroleum 1950–73. He was also a patron of the arts, notably of Henry Moore, several of whose famous sculptures stand in the open on Keswick's Scottish estate, and was a trustee of the National Gallery and the National Theatre. Died 16 February

Kreisky, Dr Bruno (b. 1911), was Federal Chancellor of Austria 1970–83. Though from an affluent background he was from his youth an ardent socialist, who suffered imprisonment after the Anschluss before escaping to Sweden, where he spent the next dozen years. Elected to Parliament in 1956, he became chairman of the Socialist Party in 1967, a post he retained after election to the chancellorship in 1970, and again in 1971, 1975 and 1979. His regime was marked by economic and financial stability and social reform. A Jew by birth but not by observance, he pursued an even policy towards Jewish and Arab causes in the Middle East; his grant of diplomatic recognition to the PLO called down the bitter enmity of Zionists. Died 29 July

Kuznetsov, Vasiliy (b. 1901), was Brezhnev's deputy chairman of the Presidium of the Supreme Soviet 1977–85. An orthodox communist, he had served in high offices, including those of Deputy Foreign Minister and ambassador to China, under all general secretaries from Stalin onwards. Died 5 June

Larsen, Leif (b. 1906), hero of Norwegian resistance in World War II, constantly risked his life in small ships bringing agents and supplies across the North Sea, for which service he was five times decorated by Britain. Died 12 October

OBITUARY

Le Duc Tho, (b. 1911), Vietnamese Communist official, led for North Vietnam in the negotiations which ended the Vietnam war. He and his US counterpart, Henry Kissinger, were jointly awarded the Nobel peace prize, which Le Duc Tho refused to accept, believing that no more than an armistice had been achieved. Died 13 October

Lehmann, Rosamond (b. 1901), British author, won instant acclaim from critics and the public with her first novel, *Dusty Answer* (1921), and thereafter held her place among the best novelists of her time. Among her later books were *Invitation to the Waltz* (1932), *The Ballad and the Source* (1944), *The Echoing Grove* (1953) and a collection of short stories, *The Gypsy's Baby* (1946). She also translated Cocteau and Lemarchand from the French, and her play *No More Music* was produced in 1939. She was for many years president of the English centre of the PEN Club. Died 12 March

Liaquat Ali Khan, Begum Raana (b. 1905), widow of Pakistan's first Prime Minister, worked alongside her husband, under M. A. Jinnah's leadership, for the birth of a new nation for India's Muslim people. After its traumatic delivery, she founded the influential All Pakistan Women's Association and held important public posts, as ambassador and as governor of Sind (1973–76). In 1979 she received the UN's Human Rights Award. Died 13 June

Lleras Camargo, Dr Alberto (b. 1906), was President of Colombia 1945–46 and 1958–62. He had been ambassador to the USA in 1943 and the first secretary-general of the OAS 1947–54. A liberal in Colombian terms, he was at the same time vehemently anti-communist, both in political office and as a newspaper editor. Died 4 January

Lo-Johannson, Ivar (b. 1901), Swedish author and poet, wrote many novels, mostly about life among the poor—share-croppers and others—of which *Godnatt Jord* (*Good Night Earth,* 1933) was reckoned one of the finest, ranking with Steinbeck's *The Grapes of Wrath,* Died 11 April

Lockwood, Margaret (b. 1916), British actress, had her era of global stardom playing, in such films as *The Lady Vanishes* (1938), *Night Train to Munich* (1942), *The Man in Grey* (1943), *The Wicked Lady* (1945), the parts of chiselled beauties whom you would rather see on the screen than in your home. Demodée as a film star, she turned successfully to the stage, adding high merit as a comedy actress to her natural beauty and presence. Died 15 July

Logoreci, Anton (b. in Albania 1910), British author and broadcaster, was from 1961 until 1989 the *Annual Register*'s contributor on his native land. A mature student in London when Mussolini seized Albania, and strongly hostile to the succeeding Hoxha regime, he spent the rest of his life in exile, a balanced, unembittered exponent of Albania's affairs and culture in print and for the BBC. Died 23 September

Loss, Joe (b. 1909), British dance band leader, became a household name in the 1930s, during World War II (with *Music While You Work*) and in the subsequent television era. Patronized by the Queen and other members of the Royal Family, he won the top honour of the dance world, the Carl Alan Award, 14 times. Died 6 June

Macé, Gabriel (b. 1919), French journalist, was editor-in-chief of the Paris satirical journal *Le Canard Enchainé* for 21 years from 1969. Died 23 June

Maclean, Lord, KT, PC, GCVO, KBE (b. Charles Maclean 1916), as Chief Scout of the UK 1959–71 and of the Commonwealth 1959–75, modernized the worldwide Scout movement, and as Lord Chamberlain of Her Majesty's Household 1971–85 planned the ceremonial for the Queen's silver wedding and silver jubilee, and other royal celebrations. He had served with distinction in the Scots Guards in World War II. Died 8 February

Marble, Alice (b. 1913), American tennis player, won the women's US national singles title in 1936, '38, '39 and '40 and the Wimbledon singles title in 1939; in doubles she shared the US title four times and the Wimbledon title five times. She was credited with bringing masculine style and tactics to the feminine game. Died 13 December

Margerie, Roland de (b. 1899), as France's ambassador to Bonn from 1962 (after embassies to the Vatican and Madrid), was a prime instrument of the Franco-German reconciliation achieved by President de Gaulle and Chancellor Adenauer in 1963. Died 13 July

Menninger, Dr Karl (b. 1893), American psychiatrist, founded, with his doctor father, the Menninger Clinic in Topeka, Kansas, in 1925, and with his brother William the far-famed Menninger Foundation in 1941. He was specially concerned with crime and punishment, and was an ardent opponent not only of the death penalty but also of most imprisonment, which he deemed to enlarge the evil that it aimed to check. Died 22 July

Middleton, Drew (b. 1913), American journalist, correspondent of the *New York Times* in London and on war fronts 1942–44, in West Germany 1947–53 and again in London 1953–63, was a highly-respected interpreter of British, Allied and European affairs for a generation. After further foreign service he was military correspondent of the *New York Times* 1970–84. Died 10 January

Minotis, Alexis (b. 1900), Greek tragedian and theatrical director, was famed throughout the civilized world for his acting of the great roles in classical Greek drama, especially at the ancient theatre at Epidaurus, but he was also a fine interpreter of Shakespeare's tragic characters, and took both Sophocles and Shakespeare to London, New York and other countries. He was closely associated with the Greek National Theatre from its birth (artistic director 1964–67, director-general 1974–80, president of the board 1980–81, 1985–86). Died 11 November

Moravia, Alberto (b. 1907), Italian author, dramatist and political figure, was reckoned to be one of the great European novelists of the century. His most famous work was *La Romana* (1947), translated as *The Woman of Rome,* but he had made his mark much earlier with *Gli indifferenti* (1929) (*Time of Indifference*); other world-renowned novels included *La Ciociara* (1945) (*Two Women*), later filmed with Sophia Loren, and *La Noia* (1960) (*The Empty Canvas*). He was also a prolific journalist, film critic and travel writer. Far to the left but not a communist, he was elected to the European Parliament in 1983. Died 26 September

More O'Ferrall, Roderick (b. 1903), was in his day Ireland's greatest breeder and trainer of racehorses, and a winning owner besides. He trained the winners of five Irish classics, and bred twelve classic winners. Died 29 October

Mothopeng, Zephania (b. 1913), South African black activist, was one of the founders of the Pan Africanist Congress in 1959 and became its president in 1986, holding unswervingly to the PAC's policy of no compromise or negotiation with whites in the struggle for black rule. Died 23 October

Moynihan, Rodrigo, RA (b. 1910), British artist, was famed in mid-career for his portraits, but from 1957 onward he developed the abstract impressionism that had inspired his early work, an abstraction less austere in later paintings. From 1948 to 1957 he was professor of painting at the Royal College of Art. Died 6 November

Muggeridge, Malcolm (b. 1903), British journalist, author and broadcaster, editor of *Punch* 1952–57 and witty scourge of establishment attitudes of both left and right throughout most of his career, which made him one of the early stars of the television age. More admired among media professionals than by the wider public, he combined a trenchant writing style with a gift for controversy, notably over his 1957 critique of the British monarchy. Once a devotee of earthly pleasures, he became in later life an ascetic and in old age was received into the Roman Catholic Church. Died 13 November

Müller, Dr Gebhard (b. 1900), was president of the constitutional court of West Germany 1959–71, playing a vital role in the interpretation and elaboration of the Federal Republic's Basic Law. He had been prime minister of Baden-Württemberg 1953–59 and one of the founders of the Christian Democratic Union. Died 7 August

Mumford, Lewis (b. 1895), American author and lecturer, became a venerated prophet and seer of the world of architecture and town planning, especially through two of his many books, *Technics and Civilization* (1934) and *The Culture of Cities* (1938). His thought was, in essence, to keep the ideals of humanism in a technical age. Died 26 January

Nono, Luigi (b. 1924), Italian composer, applied to his work the belief that music should express political ideology, his own being far to the left. His international fame rested largely on *Il canto sospeso* (1956), a choral composition celebrating resistance fighters. Not surprisingly, most of his later music employed electronic sound. Died in May

Noyce, Robert (b. 1927), American electronic engineer, invented in 1957 (simultaneously with Jack Kelly) the microchip, the key element in most subsequent development of computer and other high technology. He was then working at the Fairchild Instruments Corporation, but in 1968 he and a colleague set up Intel Corp., a successful computer business. Died 3 June

Ó Fiaich, HE Cardinal Tomás, Archbishop of Armagh (b. 1923), was both a profound scholar of the history and language of his country and a devoted, humane pastoral priest, but these were not the most apt qualities for the headship of the Roman Catholic Church in an Ireland bitterly divided by nationalism allied to religion; despite his own sincere ecumenical hopes and denunciation of violence he appeared to many Northern Protestants and even some of his own faith to give undue sympathy to republican terrorists. Born in Crossmaglen, the scene of much intercommunal murder and destruction, after a brilliant scholastic career he became professor (1959) of modern history at Maynooth College, and its president in 1974. Never previously a bishop, he was made Archbishop of Armagh, Ireland's primal see, in 1977 and a cardinal in 1979. He had also been chairman of the government commission on the restoration of the Irish language. Died 8 May

Oakeshott, Professor Michael (b. 1901), British philosopher, was professor of political science at the London School of Economics 1951–69. His anti-corporatist and sceptical political philosophy, founded on the classical ideal of civil association, had a profound effect on a generation which matured in the 1980s. His influential books included *Experience and its Modes* (1933), *On Human Conduct*

(1975) and *On History* (1983). Died 19 December

O'Neill of the Maine, Lord (b. 1914), was, as Capt. Terence O'Neill, Prime Minister of Northern Ireland 1963–69. A descendant of the aristocratic Irish Protestant 'Ascendancy', he strove to moderate communal passion in the province, but was obliged to resign office by the more extreme temper of his Unionist party. Died 12 June

Paley, William S. (b. 1901), was chairman of the Columbia Broadcasting System 1928–46, and its board chairman 1946–83 and again 1986–90, raising it from a small radio network to a multibillion conglomerate and one of the most powerful media businesses in the world. A champion of news and public affairs programmes, he enlisted such famous news broadcasters as Ed Murrow, William Shirer, H. V. Kaltenborn and Walter Cronkite, but he had an equal flair for popular music and among his early recruits were Frank Sinatra and Bing Crosby. He used much of his great wealth as a patron of music and founder of the Museum of Broadcasting in New York. Died 26 October

Pandit, Mrs Vijaya Lakshmi (b. 1900), sister of Prime Minister Jawaharlal Nehru, was the first woman to hold ministerial office in India, in the United Provinces government 1937–39. Among her subsequent posts were ambassador to Moscow 1947–49, to Washington 1949–51, president of the UN Assembly 1953, high commissioner to the UK 1954–61, and governor of Maharashtra 1962–64. Died 1 December

Paradjanov, Sergei (b. 1924), Soviet (Armenian) film director, responsible for two of the finest films to come from the USSR, *Shadows of Our Forgotten Ancestors* (1965) and *The Colour of Pomegranates* (1968), was nevertheless (or therefore) persecuted intermittently by the Soviet authorities. Died 20 July

Penston, Dr Michael (b. 1943), British astronomer, earned worldwide fame as the first to identify and quantify a 'black hole' of huge concentrated mass, whose existence as a feature of the universe had been predicted by Penrose and Hawking: this he did in 1983. From 1965 he worked at the Royal Greenwich Observatory, but he also had spells at the Hale observatory in California, at the Anglo-Austrian observatory and at the European Space Agency station in Madrid, where he was highly successful as international ultraviolet explorer. Died 23 December

Pertini, Sandro (b. 1896), Italian socialist politician, was President of Italy 1978–85. After distinguished military service in World War I he had joined the Socialist Party, and under Mussolini's rule he was tried and imprisoned for subversive activity, escaped to France from subsequent internal exile, and on his clandestine return in 1929 was identified and condemned to 11 years in gaol, five years of which he served before again suffering internal exile. Brave service in the wartime resistance earned him the Gold Medal of Valour. Elected to the constituent assembly in 1946, a life senator from 1948, and a member of the Chamber of Deputies from 1963, he was its Deputy Speaker 1963–68 and Speaker 1968–78. Died 24 February

Petersen, Jack (b. 1911), was British and Empire heavyweight boxing champion 1934–36. Died 22 November

Pimen, HH Patriarch (b. 1910), was head of the Russian Orthodox Church as Patriarch of Moscow and all Russia from 1971. As priest and bishop he had suffered imprisonment and forced army service under Stalin. As Patriarch he kept his head well below the parapet (or pulpit), passively submitting to state fetters on religion until the eve of *glasnost* in 1987. Died 3 May

Piper, Sir David (b. 1918), was director of the Ashmolean Museum,

Oxford, 1973–85, after similar service to the National Portrait Gallery and Fitzwilliam Museum, Cambridge. To his scholarship and skill as a museum director he added sensitive art as author: his books included *Trial by Battle* (a novel), *The English Face* and *The Companion Guide to London*. Died 29 December

Pochin, Sir Edward, KBE (b. 1909), British physician, who became a worldwide authority on risks from radiation, was chairman of the International Commission on Radiological Protection 1962–69, author of a seminal report (1957) on radiological health and safety at Britain's Atomic Weapons Research Establishment, and UK delegate to the UN Committee on the Effects of Atomic Radiation 1956–82. Died 29 January

Powell, Michael (b. 1905), British film-maker, enjoyed his most successful period in partnership with Emeric Pressburger, whose key role was that of script-writer. Together they made such films as *49th Parallel, The Life and Death of Colonel Blimp, A Matter of Life and Death, Black Narcissus, The Red Shoes, The Small Back Room, The Tales of Hoffmann* and *Ill Met by Moonlight*. After parting from Pressburger in the late 1950s, he made, among other films, *They're a Weird Mob* and *Peeping Tom*. Died 19 February

Puig, Manuel (b. 1932), Argentinian popular novelist, was best known elsewhere for his *Kiss of the Spiderwoman* (1976), which was made into a brilliant film (1985). Died in Mexico 22 July

Rajneesh, Bhagwan Sri (b. 1931), fraudulent Indian guru, promoted from a US base a new 'religion', embracing free love and pseudo-psychology, which in its heyday claimed hundreds of thousands of devotees and made him a multi-millionaire. Deported on criminal charges, he returned to India but still drew thousands of gullible disciples. Died 19 January

Rashid bin Saeed al Maktoum, Sheikh (b. 1914), was Emir of Dubai from 1958. At home a progressive monarch, he was chief architect of the United Arab Emirates in 1971. Died 7 October

Rasmussen, Steen Eiler (b. 1898), Danish architect, had a powerful influence on architectural thought in Scandinavia, Britain and the USA, through his books (above all *London, the Unique City*, 1937) and his teaching in all those countries. Died 20 June

Reid, Major Pat (b. 1910), was escape officer at Colditz prison camp in Germany 1940–42, and himself escaped to Switzerland. His book *The Colditz Story* (1953) became a best-seller, was made into a film, and was the basis of a popular semi-fictional television series (1973). Died 22 May

Ritsos, Yannis (b. 1909), Greek poet and left-wing activist, became a popular patriotic hero with his poem *O Epitafios* (1936), which was later set to music; but the literary world admired more his shorter lyrical poems, of which a selection was published in English translation (*Gestures*, 1971), Died 11 November

Robles, Marcos (b. 1905), was President of Panama 1964–68. The main achievement of his term of office was negotiation of a draft Canal Treaty with the USA, but it was frustrated by his own electoral defeat, shortly followed by a military coup. Died in exile 14 April

Rothschild, Lord, GBE, GM, FRS (Victor Rothschild) (b. 1910), British polymath and public servant, inherited the leadership of the English Rothschild clan, and for a time in the 1970s became executive chairman of the family bank, but his main interests lay elsewhere. In World War II he earned the George Medal as an anti-sabotage officer. A brilliant biologist, he was chairman of the Agricultural Research Council 1948–58, while continuing his zoological research at Cambridge University, then became research coordinator of the Royal Dutch Shell group 1965–70. When, in 1971, Prime Minister Heath set up a Cabinet Office 'think tank', the Central Policy Review Staff, he invited Rothschild to be its first director-general, but Rothschild's far-sighted radicalism pleased neither the Conservative nor the succeeding Labour Prime Minister, and he resigned in 1974, not before imprinting a lasting mark upon Whitehall and political thinking. Died 20 March

Rubin, HE Cardinal Wladyslaw (b. 1917), Polish priest, was ordained in Lebanon after serving in the free Polish army. Called to Rome in 1949, he became chaplain to the Polish refugees, and in 1964, now a bishop, pastor of emigré Poles worldwide. Ten years as general secretary of the Synod of Bishops were followed by his appointment in 1980 (cardinal 1979) as prefect of the Congregation for the Eastern Churches. Died 29 November

Rumor, Mariano (b. 1915), was Prime Minister of Italy for five short periods between 1968 and 1974. A Christian Democrat, he had previously been Minister of Agriculture and of the Interior, and was later Minister of the Interior again and of Foreign Affairs 1974–76. He was president of the European Union of Christian Democrats from 1965 and a member of the European Parliament from 1969. Died 22 January

Selznick, Irene (b. 1907), daughter of Louis B. Mayer, the tycoon of MGM, and wife (1930–48) of David O. Selznick, the Hollywood film director, carved a glittering personal career as producer for the New York stage: *Streetcar* and *The Chalk Garden* were among her famous 'firsts'. Died 10 October

Shepherd, General Lemnel C. (b. 1896), attained command of the US Marine Corps in 1952 and was the first marine to serve on the US joint chiefs of staff committee; the summit of his fighting career was the battle for Okinawa in 1945, when he commanded the 6th Marine division in a decisive, bloody action. Died 6 August

Smith, Dodie (b. 1896), British playwright and novelist, won her greatest successes with the comedy *Autumn Crocus* (1931), the novel *I Capture the Castle* (1948) and the children's story *The Hundred and One Dalmatians* (1956), which was translated into a money-spinning film by Walt Disney. Died 24 November

Soupault, Philippe (b. 1897), French poet and novelist, shared with André Breton the claim to have launched the surrealist movement with their poem *Les champs magnétiques,* published in 1921, though his friends Louis Aragon and Guillaume Apollinaire were also among its founders. In 1974, after a varied career as writer, teacher and propagandist, he was awarded the Grand Prix de Poésie by the Académie Française. Died 11 March

Soustelle, Jacques (b. 1912), French politician, as governor-general of Algeria 1955–56 broke with General de Gaulle, whom he otherwise admired and followed, over his own ardent aim of keeping Algeria part of France. Died 6 August

Spear, Ruskin, RA (b. 1911), British artist, was greatly admired both by the public and by the art-critical world for the vigour and insight of his portraits, whether of the famous or of the obscure, and the poetry of his rarer landscapes. At first regarded by the orthodox as a rebellious modernist, he was a caustic critic of much contemporary abstract art, but as an Academician and as a teacher (tutor at the Royal College of Art 1948–75) he encouraged the new and venturesome in painting, while retaining his own direct and forthright style. Died 17 January

Stanwyck, Barbara (b. Ruby Stevens 1907), American actress, played leading roles in Hollywood films for 30 years, retiring from the cinema in 1965 to make another glittering career in television and winning three Emmy awards for her acting in her own show and in *The Big Valley* and *The Thorn Birds*. Most of her best film performances were as tough, worldly but essentially feminine characters, as in *Union Pacific, The Lady Eve,* and *The File on Thelma Gordon*. At one time she was reckoned to be the most highly-paid woman in the USA. Died 20 January

Stewart, Very Rev James (b. 1896), was moderator of the General Assembly of the Church of Scotland 1963–64 and chaplain to the Queen. A great preacher, he published two books of sermons and two of lecture series on the ethos of preaching the faith. In public affairs he held firmly to the doctrine that 'Jesus must either be King everywhere or else King nowhere at all'. Died 1 July

Takayanagi, Kenjiro (b. 1899), Japanese scientist and businessman, rivalled Baird and Zworykin as inventor of electronic television, with the 40-line picture he produced in December 1926. Later, as vice-president of the Victor Co. of Japan, he helped to make that firm the world leader in video-recorders. Died 23 July

Taylor, A.J.P. (b. 1906), British historian, fellow of Magdalen College, Oxford, 1938–76, was the most widely read, heard and seen exponent of history in the English-speaking world. A brilliant tutor and lecturer, soaked in historical knowledge and gifted with a phenomenal memory as well as a love of paradox, he had an immense audience both for his studies of history—which most of his academic peers thought eccentric, and some thought mischievous—and for his excursions into politics, as a socialist and a nuclear disarmer. His most important books were *The Struggle for Mastery in Europe 1848–1918* (1954) and *English History 1914–45* (1965); his most controversial was *The Origins of the Second World War* (1961), which held the field for nearly 30 years. Other works included a life of his patron, *Beaverbrook* (1972), and an autobiography, *A Personal History* (1983). Died 7 September

Tinling, Ted (b. 1910), British dress designer and lawn tennis official, became famous in the 1940s for the innovative clothes he designed for leading women tennis players, but he was also a much-respected mediator in the international game. Died 22 May

Tirtoff, Romain de, (professionally known as Erté) (b. 1892), Russian-born French designer, was called the father of Art Deco; his sculptures and pictures were highly prized, but to a wider public he was most famous for his gorgeous stage designs and costumes, especially those for the revue theatres of Paris. He arrived in Paris in 1912, and in 1915 he began designing for such stars as Yvonne Printemps, Mistinguett, Maurice Chevalier and Gaby Deslys and producing many lavish shows for the Folies-Bergère and Broadway impresarios. After the 1929 stock market crash he switched to designing for the smaller stage (Bal Tabarin, London theatres) and the cinema, and after World War II for opera and ballet, continuing into his 80s and 90s with productions of *Der Rosenkavalier* at Glyndebourne (1980) and *Anatol* in Los Angeles (1985). Meanwhile his work had been celebrated by international exhibitions and by a number of books, including his own memoirs. Died 21 April

Tortelier, Paul (b. 1914), French cellist, made his London debut under Beecham in 1947 and his American solo debut in 1955, after leading the cello section of the Boston Symphony Orchestra. His romantic sensitivity and purity of tone made him one of the great cellists of his time. Died 18 December

Turner, Dame Eva (b. 1892), British opera singer, was deemed among the greatest sopranos of the century, which her life nearly spanned. Her Turandot, in particular, was held supreme above all rivals. The *Times* obituarist wrote: 'Once she began to sing, a steady, well-integrated body of tone emerged from her frame . . . . She produced a seamless legato and an inexhaustible reserve of voice, supplemented by excellent diction.' A student of the Royal Academy of Music, she first sang at Covent Garden in a Carl Rosa season in 1920, before taking major parts there in the grand opera season of 1928, having meanwhile sung at La Scala under Toscanini and elsewhere in Europe and South America. Her American debut came later in the same year. World War II interrupted her career, to which she briefly returned at Covent Garden in 1947–48, retiring then to teach, first at the University of Oklahoma and then at the RAM. Died 16 June

van Praagh, Dame Peggy, DBE (b. in England 1910), Australian ballet dancer and director, founded Australian Ballet in 1959 and directed it from 1962 to 1974. In London she had danced, starting in 1929, in companies led by Anton Dolin, Marie Rambert, Antony Tudor and Ninette de Valois, until in 1946 she became ballet mistress and later assistant director of Sadlers Wells Theatre Ballet, which she left in 1955 to produce, direct and teach ballet as a freelance, a role that took her to Australia in 1959. Died 15 January

Vaughan, Sarah (b. 1924), black American jazz singer, won *Down Beat* magazine's poll as the best female jazz vocalist for six years 1947–52, and a Grammy award in the dame class in 1982 for her album *Gershwin Lives.* Died 3 April

Wall, Max, (b. Maxwell Lorimer 1908), British comedian and dancer, had an up-and-down career on the variety, musical and legitimate stage and on radio and television. Its peaks were in revue in the 1930s, on radio after World War II, in the American musical *The Pajama Game* (1955–56) and in contemporary theatre (Wesker, Osborne, Beckett, Pinter) in the 1970s, when he became a cult figure. Died 22 May

White, Patrick (b. 1912), Australian novelist, won the Nobel prize for literature in 1973. His most famous novel was *Voss* (1957); others included *The Solid Mandala* (1966) and *The Eye of the Storm* (1973). Born and largely educated in England, White was quintessentially Australian in ancestry and in the themes and background of his books. His politics were left-wing, his personality abrasive. Died 30 September

Williams, Rt Rev Gwylim (b. 1913), Archbishop of Wales 1971–82, champion of ecumenical causes and of a bilingual Welsh Church of the Anglican communion, died 23 December

Wynne, Greville (b. 1918), a British spy in the Cold War era, using semi-genuine cover as an engineering exporter, claimed to have been the channel though which Lieut.-Col. Oleg Penkovsky leaked crucially important Soviet information. Arrested in Hungary in 1962, he was tortured and sentenced to eight years in prison, but in 1964 was swapped for Gordon Lonsdale, a Soviet spy convicted in England. Died 27 February

Yun Po-sun (b. 1899), was President of South Korea 1960–62, resigning in protest against the arbitrary antidemocratic actions of Park Chunghee's military junta, and thereafter striving against personal harassment and nationwide oppression. Died 18 July

CHRONICLE OF PRINCIPAL EVENTS IN 1990

A detailed chronology of the Gulf crisis appears in this volume on pages 7–9.

JANUARY

3   In UK, Norman Fowler resigned as Secretary of State for Employment and was succeeded by Michael Howard.
    300 died in Pakistan's worst rail disaster.
4   Former Panamanian leader Gen. Noriega surrendered to US authorities, having sought refuge in papal nunciature in Panama City in Dec. 1989; he was taken to Florida to face drug-trafficking charges.
    President Gorbachev cancelled engagements with foreign politicians because of growing domestic troubles.
6   Muslims in southern Azerbaijan tore down border installations, demanding easier access to Iran.
9   A two-day ministerial meeting of Comecon opened in Sofia: moves towards a free-market trading system were agreed.
10 China lifted martial law, imposed in May 1989 because of pro-democracy demonstrations; 18 Jan. release of 573 detainees announced.
11 President Gorbachev visited Lithuania: he offered new legislation to allow for self-determination (see 24 Feb., 11 Mar.)
12 Interim government of Romania, bowing to protests, outlawed Communist Party but subsequently announced referendum on issue (see 18 Feb., 20 May, 18 Nov.).
13 Thirty dead in inter-communal fighting in Baku, Azerbaijan (see 18 Jan.)
14 In Spain, 43 died in discotheque fire in Zaragoza.
    One hundred and seventy dead in ferry disaster in Bangladesh.
15 President Gorbachev declared state of emergency in Nagorno-Karabakh and sent in troops because of continuing ethnic violence.
    Bulgarian National Assembly, in response to demonstrations, voted to end communist monopoly (see 17 June).
17 Indian government ordered mass resignation of state governors, alleging that Congress (I) party had broken tradition of non-political appointments.
18 Azerbaijan declared war on neighbouring republic of Armenia; 19 Jan. more than 80 died when Soviet troops fired on demonstrators in Baku; 22 Jan. 750,000 gathered in Baku for funerals (see 23 Jan.)
    Czechoslovak PM Marian Čalfa resigned from Communist Party.
20 President Prosper Avril of Haiti declared state of siege because of escalating violence (see 10 Mar., 16 Dec.).
21 100,000 Ukrainians formed a 300-mile human chain to commemorate period of independence in 1919.
    In Mongolia, thousands demonstrated in Ulan Bator, demanding political change (see 29 July).
22 League of Communists of Yugoslavia voted to end party monopoly on power.
23 Soviet troops ended a five-day Azerbaijani naval blockade of Baku harbour; general strike had halted city.
24 Commonwealth Games opened in Auckland, New Zealand, ending 3 Feb.; several competitors disqualified for drug-taking.
25 In UK, 47 died in storms; widespread damage caused by winds up to 110 mph.
    In USA, 66 dead in plane crash on Long Island.
    Pope John Paul II began five-nation tour of W. Africa.
26 Indian troops moved into Kashmir to enforce curfew; many had died in separatist

violence following resignation of state government and imposition of direct rule (see 21 May, 8 July).
29 In Poland, Aleksander Kwasmiewski elected chairman of General Council of Social Democracy (new left-wing party formed after demise of Communist Party).
In USA, President Bush presented $1,230,000 million budget to Congress: it envisaged halved 1991 budget deficit and unveiled plans to wind down 69 military bases (see 4 Oct.).
30 In UK, Public Expenditure White Paper proposed rise of £5,500 million in spending, including more for health, roads, arts and higher education.
31 In State of Union address, President Bush proposed massive reduction of US and Soviet troops in Europe.

FEBRUARY

1 Bulgarian government resigned; a new all-communist government, led by Andrei Lukanov, was formed on 8 Feb. (see 17 June, 29 Nov.).
2 In S. Africa, President de Klerk ended 30-year ban on ANC (see 11 Feb.).
4 In USSR, 300,000 took part in largest anti-government demonstration in Moscow since 1917 revolution.
In Egypt, 10 died in attack on tourist bus travelling to Israeli-occupied Gaza Strip.
In Costa Rica, Rafael Angel Calderón (Social Christian) defeated Carlos Manuel Castillo in presidential election.
Slovene communists seceded from League of Communists of Yugoslavia.
Thirty dead in violent storms in northern France and Germany.
6 In UK, White Paper, *Crime, Justice and Protecting the Public* (Cmnd. 965), proposed more severe punishment for serious offenders.
7 In USSR, central committee of CPSU voted to end party monopoly on power; politburo to be replaced by a larger party presidium (see 15 Mar.).
8 In UK, Scout Association decided to admit girls.
10 Chancellor Kohl of W. Germany said in Moscow that Gorbachev saw no obstacles to reunification of Germany.
11 In S. Africa, ANC leader Nelson Mandela released after 27 years in gaol; 50 died in violence between rival black factions in Natal celebrating his release.
13 S. African Cricket Union abandoned remaining matches of controversial tour by rebel English side.
Thirty-seven reported dead in ethnic unrest in Soviet republic of Tajikistan; violence also reported in Khirgizia.
15 President Bush held talks on anti-drugs programme with Presidents of Peru, Bolivia and Colombia in Cartagena, Colombia.
Britain and Argentina agreed to resume diplomatic relations, broken in 1982 over Falklands war.
16 UK Foreign Secretary confirmed that government had accepted strict Chinese limits on number of democratically-elected seats in Hong Kong Legislative Assembly after Chinese takeover in 1997; protesters demonstrated in colony on 18 Feb.
SWAPO leader Sam Nujoma elected Namibia's first President after independence (see 21 March).
Kenyan Foreign Minister Robert Ouko found murdered.
18 In Japanese general election, ruling LDP, led by Toshiki Kaifu, returned with slightly reduced majority.
In Romania, demonstrators stormed government offices, protesting at presence of known Ceauşescu supporters.
21 In Yugoslav province of Kosovo a curfew was imposed, 30 having died in month of unrest.

CHRONICLE OF EVENTS 597

President Havel of Czechoslovakia, addressing US Congress, called for peace conference to end post-war divisions of Europe.
23 Prince Sihanouk returned to Kampuchea after 11 years' exile.
In UK, six-month ambulance dispute settled.
24 Nationalists overwhelmingly defeated communist candidates at elections in Lithuania (see 11 Mar.); 200,000 took part in pro-democracy rally in Moscow on 25 Feb.
25 In talks at Camp David, President Bush and Chancellor Kohl reaffirmed that a united Germany should remain a full member of NATO.
At elections in Nicaragua, US-backed coalition led by Violeta Chamorro defeated President Ortega's Sandinista government; she was sworn in as President on 25 April (see 19 April).
26 Following talks in Moscow, President Havel announced that USSR had agreed to withdrawal of its 73,500 troops from Czechoslovakia by July 1991.
27 Eighteen dead in two days of violent storms across Britain and northern Europe where many more died.

MARCH

4 In S. Africa, President Lennox Sebe ousted in military coup in Ciskei homeland; S. African forces sent in on 5 Mar. to restore order.
At elections in Russian Federation, Ukraine and Byelorussia, reformists made substantial gains (see 18 Mar.).
5 President Mengistu of Ethiopia outlined proposals for political and economic reform.
In UK, five arrested in anti-poll-tax demonstration in Nottingham; further violent protests occurred around the country in subsequent days.
6 In Afghanistan, an attempted coup against government of President Najibullah was quashed.
7 In UK, DTI report claimed that Fayed brothers had lied persistently to gain approval for takeover of House of Fraser group, including Harrods store, in 1985.
10 Gen. Avril resigned as President of Haiti; he was succeeded by Ertha Pascal-Trouillot on 12 Mar. (see 16 Dec.).
11 Patricio Aylwin Azócar (elected Dec. 1989) sworn in as Chile's first democratically-elected President since 1973 coup.
Lithuania declared unilateral independence from USSR, by whom it had been annexed in 1940; Dr Vitautis Landsbergis elected Lithuanian President on 12 Mar.; Soviet Congress declared move illegal; 25 Mar. Soviet tanks sent to Vilnius as Moscow called for backdown on secession move (see 15, 18 April, 9, 17 May, 29 June).
12 Said Mohammed Djohar elected President of Comoros.
13 Israel's national unity coalition government collapsed following dismissal of Labour leader Shimon Peres (see 12 June).
15 Iraq executed a British journalist, Farzad Bazoft, for alleged espionage; a British nurse convicted with him was released on 16 July after intervention of President Kaunda of Zambia.
In USSR, Gorbachev sworn in to new office of executive President approved earlier by Supreme Soviet which had also voted overwhelmingly to renounce communist monopoly.
Fernando Collor de Mello sworn in as President of Brazil.
17 Works of art valued at $130 million stolen from Garner Museum, Boston, USA.
18 E. Germany held first free elections since 1933; conservative alliance gained 49 per cent of vote; Lothar de Maizière sworn in at head of coalition government on 12 April (see 5 April, 19 Aug., 3 Oct., 17 Dec.).

20 In UK, budget day: Chancellor announced new tax incentives for savers (TESSAS) and raised tax allowances in line with inflation; separate taxation of married women would begin on 6 April.
21 President Havel of Czechoslovakia on three-day visit to UK.
  Delegates from 150 nations attended Namibian independence celebrations; Soviet Foreign Minister Shevardnadze held talks with S. African President de Klerk in Windhoek.
  In Romania, three dead, 200 injured in Tirgu Mures, where troops had been sent in to counter intimidation of ethnic Hungarians.
22 In UK, Labour won previously safe Tory Mid-Staffordshire seat, its biggest by-election success for 50 years.
24 In Australian general election, ruling Labour Party, led by PM Bob Hawke, returned with narrow majority (see 3 April).
28 In UK, customs officers foiled an attempt to smuggle nuclear bomb trigger devices onto an Iraqi airliner at Heathrow airport.
30 Parliament of Estonia overwhelmingly rejected Soviet authority over its territory, declaring itself an occupied state.
31 In UK, some 330 police and 80 others injured in violent anti-poll-tax rioting around Trafalgar Square in London.
  In UK, Oxford won university Boat Race by 2¼ lengths.

APRIL

1 At general election in Zimbabwe, ruling ZANU-PF won 117 out of 120 seats; Robert Mugabe overwhelmingly defeated opposition leader Edgar Tekere in presidential contest.
2 In UK, Defence White Paper (Cmnd. 1022) emphasized government's intention to maintain a cautious approach to defence strategy in spite of 'tremendous events' in E. Europe.
  N. Wales hit by second largest earthquake to affect Britain in 100 years.
3 Dr John Hewson succeeded Andrew Peacock as leader of Australian Liberal Party; Tim Fischer succeeded Charles Blunt as leader of National Party on 10 April.
4 Chinese People's Congress approved the Basic Law, mini-constitution for Hong Kong after 1997 Chinese takeover.
5 E. Germany's first freely-elected parliament (Volkskammer) since Nazi takeover in 1933 met for first session.
6 In Nepal, many died when army fired on pro-democracy demonstrators in Kathmandu; 8 April, King Birendra ended 30-year ban on political parties (see 19 April).
7 At least 159 died in fire on ferry *Scandinavian Star* off Swedish coast.
  In UK, Grand National won by Mister Frisk at 16–1.
8 In Greek general election, New Democracy party gained narrow majority; Constantine Mitsotakis took office as PM on 11 April.
  In Hungarian general election, centre-right Democratic Forum and its allies, led by József Antall, gained landslide victory.
9 World ministerial drug summit opened in London, ending 11 April; declaration called for national strategies to combat drug abuse and trafficking.
10 Three European hostages released in Beirut following secret deal with France for delivery of Mirage jets to Libya.
11 In UK, customs officers on Teeside detained consignment of steel tubes destined for Iraq; they were believed to be components for a 140-ton gun capable of firing nuclear or chemical shells.
12 Polish President Jaruzelski on three-day visit to USSR during which Soviets finally admitted responsibility for massacre of 15,000 Polish officers at Katyn in 1940.

13 President Bush and Mrs Thatcher held summit talks in Bermuda.
15 President Landsbergis of Lithuania appealed to West for support in face of threatened Soviet sanctions.
    ANC leader Nelson Mandela on two-day visit to UK: a Wembley pop concert in his honour was attended by 72,000 people.
18 USSR cut off supply of oil to secessionist Lithuania (see 9, 17 May, 19 June).
19 British Nationality Bill (Hong Kong) obtained second reading in House of Commons: British passports would be granted to 50,000 Hong Kong residents.
    K. P. Bhattarai sworn in as PM of Nepal, ending 30 years of direct royal rule.
    Sandinista army and US-backed Contra rebels signed ceasefire ending nine-year war in Nicaragua.
20 Eastern Australia affected by worst floods for 30 years; thousands homeless.
21 Pope John Paul II on first visit to Czechoslovakia.
    In Poland, Lech Walesa overwhelmingly re-elected chairman of Solidarity (see 9 Dec.).
22 Presidential election in Turkish sector of Cyprus returned Rauf Denktash for further term.
    US hostage Robert Polhill released after 30 months captivity in Beirut; another American, Frank Reed, was released after four years on 30 April.
    Troops loyal to President Babangida foiled attempted coup in Nigeria; 42 coup plotters were executed on 27 July.
    In UK, tenth London Marathon won by Allister Hutton in 2 hrs 10 min 10 sec.
23 Chinese PM Li Peng on official visit to Moscow.
    In UK, MPs in a free vote rejected amendment to ban all human embryo research; they voted on 24 April to reduce time-limit for abortion from 28 to 24 weeks.
24 Chancellor Kohl of W. Germany and E. German PM de Maizière agreed currency union of two countries (see 2 July).
25 In UK, prison officers stormed Strangeways gaol, Manchester, ending 25-day siege by inmates causing estimated £50 million damage.
    Mrs Thatcher attended ceremonies in Turkey to mark 75th anniversary of Gallipoli campaign.
26 Chancellor Kohl and President Mitterrand held 55th Franco-German summit in Paris: they declared intention to press for swift progress towards European political union.
28 EC heads of government held informal summit in Dublin: they welcomed prospect of German reunification.

MAY

1 In USSR, 40,000 demonstrators disrupted May Day parades in Moscow.
2 Three days of talks between ANC and S. African government opened in Cape Town; a communique pledged commitment towards ending violence and work towards political settlement.
   President Mubarak of Egypt began first official visit to Syria since severance of relations in 1977.
3 In local elections in UK, Labour made net gain of 300 seats.
4 Latvia declared itself an independent sovereign republic, deputies voting to restore parts of pre-war constitution; Estonia took similar decision on 8 May.
   President Ochirbat of Mongolia in Beijing for bilateral talks, the first high-level contact since 1962.
   Constantine Karamanlis elected President of Greece for second term.
   In UK, Mrs Thatcher and President Mitterrand held talks on security and defence.
5 Four World War II Allied powers, meeting in Bonn, agreed that German reunification should go ahead without delay.

- 6 Pope John Paul II began nine-day visit to Mexico and Curaçao.
  Eleven died in bomb explosion on Pakistani train near Indian border.
- 8 President de Klerk began 18-day tour of Europe; he held talks with Mrs Thatcher on 19 May.
- 9 Lithuanian PM Kazimiera Prunskiene in London for talks with Mrs Thatcher.
- 12 At least 26 dead in three bomb explosions in Colombia, believed to be work of drug-traffickers.
- 13 Government forces put down attempted coup in Madagascar.
- 15 Report of US presidential commission into Lockerbie disaster (see AR 1988, p. 38) criticized Pan Am and FAA for security lapses (see 1 Oct.).
  In UK, public concern over so-called 'mad cow disease' (BSE) led to banning of home-produced beef in schools and hospitals.
  Van Gogh's *Portrait of Dr Gachet* sold for $82.5 million, a new record, at Christie's, New York.
- 16 Presidential election in Dominican Republic; on 12 June President Balaguer declared himself winner despite accusations of fraud.
- 17 Lithuanian PM in Moscow to discuss proposals for independence (see 29 June).
- 18 E. and W. Germany signed treaty on economic, currency and social union (see 2 July).
- 20 Romania held first free elections for 53 years; Ion Iliescu won landslide victory in presidential contest; National Salvation Front (NSF) took two-thirds of seats in new parliament (see 14, 20 June).
  Lone Israeli gunman massacred seven Arab workers near Tel Aviv; other Arabs died when Israeli troops dispersed protest riots in Gaza.
- 21 Forty dead in violence in Kashmir following assassination of Mirwaiz Maulvi Farooq, a leading political and religious figure.
- 22 North and South Yemen formally merged to become new Yemen Republic.
  In India, 1,000 dead in cyclone in Andhra Pradesh.
- 24 France sent troop reinforcements to Gabon; rioters were demanding end to Bongo regime.
  Princess Royal on 13-day tour of USSR, first official British royal visit since before 1917 revolution.
- 25 President Mitterrand in Moscow for talks on German unity and European confederation.
  Mrs Thatcher called for a 'giant international effort' to save Earth from consequences of global warming.
- 26 Panic buying in Moscow followed announcement of steep price rises for basic foods.
- 27 Presidential election in Colombia won by César Gaviria Trujillo of ruling Liberals.
  Burma (Myanmar) held first multi-party elections for 30 years: National League for Democracy claimed victory but was banned on 20 Dec. by military who refused to hand over power.
  In Poland, local elections (country's first free vote for 50 years) were held in 48,000 constituencies.
  Veterans gathered in Dunkirk to mark 50th anniversary of World War II evacuation.
  Two Australian tourists shot dead by IRA gunmen in Netherlands.
- 28 Twenty-two reported dead in clashes between Armenians and Soviet troops.
- 29 Boris Yeltsin elected President of Russian Federation.
  President Gorbachev on two-day visit to Canada.
  Hau Po-tsun appointed PM of Taiwan amid violent protests.
- 30 Seventy dead in earthquake in E. Europe; 100 dead in earthquake in Peru.
  Eight Hong Kong people hanged in Malaysia for drug-trafficking.
- 31 Presidents Bush and Gorbachev began three-day summit in Washington; a trade

CHRONICLE OF EVENTS 601

agreement was concluded and outline agreement on reduction of strategic arms reached.
In Pakistan, 40 dead in ethnic clashes around Karachi.

JUNE

1 In UK, Social Democratic Party wound up after nine years.
4 President Gorbachev and President Roh Tae Woo of S. Korea held first-ever talks in Washington.
5 Communist hardliner Vladimir Ivashko elected president of Ukraine.
  In UK, government defeated in House of Lords on War Crimes Bill: it would have permitted trials of alleged Nazi war criminals.
6 In UK, Derby won by Quest for Fame at 7–1.
7 A one-day meeting of Warsaw Pact in Moscow proposed radical reforms to Pact and formation of joint bodies with NATO to set seal on end of Cold War; NATO foreign ministers, meeting in Scotland, heard Mrs Thatcher call for alliance to move towards new role of peace-building in Europe.
  Mrs Thatcher began visit to Moscow, Ukraine and Armenia.
  President de Klerk ended four-year state of emergency in most of S. Africa; remaining security controls in Natal were lifted on 18 Oct.
8 At first free elections in Czechoslovakia since 1946, Civic Forum won outright majority in federal parliament.
  Congress of Russian Federation approved declaration of sovereignty.
  World Cup Football opened in Italy: W. Germany defeated Argentina 1–0 in final in Rome on 8 July.
10 Alberto Fujimori, of Japanese ancestry, defeated Mario Vargas Llosa in presidential election in Peru; he was sworn in on 28 July.
11 Former US National Security Adviser John Poindexter gaoled for his role in the Iran-Contra affair.
12 Yitzhak Shamir formed new right-wing coalition government in Israel; David Levy appointed Foreign Minister.
   In Algeria's first multi-party elections for local councils, fundamentalist Islamic Salvation Front gained 55 per cent of poll.
14 In Romania, 10,000 coalminers patrolled Bucharest in mobs, attacking demonstrators who claimed that NSF (see 20 May) was composed of neo-communists.
   In UK, Transport Secretary shelved high-speed rail link to Channel Tunnel.
17 At elections in Bulgaria, Socialist Party (former communists) gained more than half of seats in Grand National Assembly (see 6 July).
19 President Gorbachev warned Russian (RSFSR) Communist Party that radical actions could threaten downfall of USSR as a whole.
20 Sixteenth Franco-African summit opened in La Baule, France.
   Ion Iliescu sworn in as President of Romania.
   Soviet republic of Uzbekistan approved declaration of sovereignty.
21 70,000 died in earthquake in north-western Iran.
22 In Canada, Manitoba and Newfoundland refused to ratify Meech Lake Accord recognizing Quebec as a 'distinct society'.
25 Two-day summit conference of EC heads of government opened in Dublin; an aid package to assist collapsing Soviet economy was agreed.
   In UK, four injured in IRA bomb explosion at Carlton Club, London.
26 Hungarian parliament voted for withdrawal from Warsaw Pact.
28 A 35-nation CSCE conference on human rights, meeting in Copenhagen, agreed a declaration guaranteeing rights of citizens and committing governments to multi-party democracy.

29 Lithuania agreed to suspend its declaration of independence, pending negotiations with Soviet government.
30 HM Queen Elizabeth II on five-day visit to Canada.

JULY

1 Deutschmark became official currency of E. Germany, marking official economic union with W. Germany (see 3 Oct.).
2 Twenty-eighth congress of CPSU opened in Moscow; Gorbachev warned of 'dark times' ahead if perestroika reforms were not pursued.
   In Saudi Arabia, 1,400 pilgrims died in stampede near Mecca.
   In New York, Imelda Marcos, widow of former Philippines dictator, acquitted of plotting with him to steal £114 million from her country for personal use.
4 Nelson Mandela in London for talks with Mrs Thatcher at end of 13-nation tour which included talks in Washington with President Bush.
5 Two-day NATO summit conference opened in London; final communique included invitation to Warsaw Pact allies to sign joint declaration on non-aggression; invitation to Gorbachev to address N. Atlantic Council; intensified negotiations on conventional forces; nuclear arms to be 'weapons of last resort'; and a stronger role for CSCE (see 14 July).
6 Petar Mladenov resigned as President of Bulgaria; he was succeeded by Zhelyn Zhelev on 1 Aug.
8 Indian army took direct control of Kashmir under emergency regulations imposed because of separatist violence.
   In Albania, 6,000 refugees sheltered in Western embassies amid mounting anti-government protests; 9 July, President Alia reshuffled cabinet as first refugees were evacuated to Prague; 4,000 others later sailed to Brindisi (see 11 Dec.).
   In UK, Stefan Edberg defeated Boris Becker in men's tennis final at Wimbledon.
9 Western economic summit opened in Houston (USA); an agreed document, *Securing Democracy*, encouraged economic and financial assistance to USSR.
11 Nine reported dead in Kenya in demonstrations against one-party rule.
12 In USSR, Boris Yeltsin and other reformists resigned from Communist Party.
13 In USSR, CPSU congress elected new central committee, dropping several leading conservatives.
14 In UK, Nicholas Ridley resigned as Trade and Industry Secretary over anti-German remarks in a *Spectator* interview; he was replaced by Peter Lilley.
   NATO Secretary-General Manfred Wörner held first-ever such talks with Gorbachev in Moscow; Gorbachev accepted invitation to visit NATO HQ in Brussels.
16 Ukrainian parliament voted for sovereignty, declaring its intention to become a neutral state.
   After talks in Moscow with Chancellor Kohl, Gorbachev said USSR was willing to accept united Germany as member of NATO (see 31 Aug., 3 Oct.).
   An earthquake in northern Philippines killed 1,500.
19 In UK, Environment Secretary announced £3,000 million package for local government to ease 1991 poll tax bills.
23 Indian PM V. P. Singh in Moscow for talks with Gorbachev.
24 30,000 Iraqi troops reported massed on Kuwait border amid dispute over oil-production and territorial claims.
   In Ireland, three policemen and a nun died in IRA bomb explosion near Armagh.
25 In UK, Rt Rev George Carey, Bishop of Bath and Wells, named to succeed Dr Runcie as Archbishop of Canterbury in 1991.
   In UK, defence review proposed 18 per cent cut in armed forces and halving of Rhine army within five years.
27 In UK, at a Lord's Test match v. India, Graham Gooch scored 333, only 11th man to score triple Test century.

CHRONICLE OF EVENTS 603

In Trinidad & Tobago, black Muslim rebels attempted to stage coup, taking PM and others hostage in parliament building; 1 Aug. rebels surrendered; 30 dead.

29 Mongolia held first free elections for 69 years; ruling CP took majority of seats in upper house; other parties gained nearly half seats in legislature (see 3 Sept.).
In Liberia, 600 refugees massacred in Monrovia where rebels were seeking overthrow of Doe regime (se 7 Aug., 10 Sept.).
USSR and Albania agreed to resume diplomatic relations broken in 1961.

31 Two-day 'Pentagonale' summit opened in Venice, attended by Austria, Hungary, Italy, Yugoslavia and Czechoslovakia; final declaration pledged regional cooperation and safeguarding of human rights.
President Chissano of Mozambique announced adoption of multi-party system for 1991 elections (see 3 Nov.).

AUGUST

2 Iraqi forces invaded Gulf state of Kuwait; deposed Emir fled to Saudi Arabia; US, UK and France immediately froze Iraqi and Kuwait assets; UN Security Council adopted resolution 660 calling for unconditional withdrawal.
Mrs Thatcher held talks in Colorado with President Bush; in speech to Aspen Institute on 5 Aug. she called for 'a world in which true democracy and the rule of law are extended far and wide', for a European Magna Carta and a rejuvenated UN.

3 Arpad Göncz sworn in as President of new Democratic Republic of Hungary.
Britain experienced its hottest day on record: 98.8°F (37.1°C) recorded at Cheltenham.

4 In UK, Queen Elizabeth the Queen Mother celebrated her 90th birthday.

5 Iraq named a 'free provisional government' of Kuwait, formed entirely of Iraqi nationals.

6 UN Security Council resolution 661 imposed mandatory sanctions against Iraq, including oil embargo.
President Ghulam Ishaq Khan of Pakistan dismissed government of Benazir Bhutto, alleging corruption and ineptitude (see 10 Sept., 24 Oct.).

7 President Bush ordered US planes and troops to Saudi Arabia amid fears of imminent Iraqi invasion; Turkey closed pipeline carrying Iraqi oil.
West African leaders, meeting in Gambia, agreed to send forces to Liberia to intervene in civil war (see 2, 10 Sept.)

9 Iraq announced it had annexed Kuwait; UK announced it would join US forces massing in Gulf.

10 At emergency Arab League summit in Cairo, 12 nations voted to condemn Iraqi invasion of Kuwait and join international sanctions against Iraq.

14 In USSR, Gorbachev issued decree rehabilitating those repressed by Stalin; another decree restored citizenship to Alexander Solzhenitsyn and 22 exiled dissidents.

15 President Saddam Husain of Iraq made peace with Iran, accepting all Iranian demands including release of POWs and reinstatement of 1975 Algiers Treaty dividing Shatt al-Arab waterway, dispute over which had led to 1980–88 Gulf war.

19 Iraq began rounding up Western nationals in Kuwait for internment: they were to be used as a 'human shield' to deter air attacks on military installations in Iraq.
East Germany's coalition government, led by Lothar de Maizière, collapsed.

21 In S. Africa, 400 reported dead in eight days of clashes in Transvaal townships between supporters of ANC and Inkatha Zulu organization led by Chief Buthelezi (see 24 Aug.)

22 President Bush announced call-up of 40,000 US reservists for service in Gulf.
Jordan temporarily closed border with Iraq because of influx of refugees fleeing Gulf crisis.

23 President Saddam Husain of Iraq appeared on television with British hostages.
24 S. African government declared 27 townships around Johannesburg 'unrest areas' under Public Safety Act; 500 had died in two weeks of violence.
An Irishman, Brian Keenan, released after four years as a hostage of Muslim extremists in Lebanon.
25 UN Security Council resolution 665 authorized use of 'measures commensurate' to stop violation of trade embargo against Iraq.
26 King Husain of Jordan began peace mission among Arab leaders.
Romanian riot police on streets of Bucharest to deal with continuing anti-government protests.
28 President Saddam Husain announced that all foreign women and children could leave Kuwait; Iraq said Kuwait had become its 19th governorate.
In UK, former Guinness chairman Ernest Saunders and others gaoled for illegal share support operation during takeover of Distillers in 1986; the 112-day trial, with £25 million costs, was the most expensive in British legal history.
30 UN Secretary-General Pérez de Cuellar in Amman for talks with Iraqi Foreign Minister on Gulf crisis.
31 In S. Africa, President de Klerk announced that membership of National Party would be open to all races for first time since its foundation in 1915.
E. and W. Germany signed treaty sealing unification of their political and legal systems on 3 Oct.

SEPTEMBER

1 Pope John Paul II began five-nation African tour; on 10 Sept. he consecrated £100 million basilica at Yamoussokro (Côte d'Ivoire), world's largest church.
Seven southern African front-line states held summit talks in Lusaka; they expressed concern over black-against-black violence in S. Africa (see 21, 24 Aug.)
2 W. African peacekeeping force reported in control of Monrovia, Liberia (see 7 Aug., 10 Sept.).
3 Ethnic Albanians staged 24-hour strike in Kosovo where repression had increased following imposition of direct Serbian rule (see 28 Sept.).
New Mongolian parliament (see 29 July) elected communist leader Punsalmaagiyn Ochirbat as President.
4 Geoffrey Palmer resigned as Labour PM of New Zealand and was succeeded by Michael Moore (see 27 Oct.).
5 PMs of N. and S. Korea held talks on reunification in Seoul.
6 In UK, parliament recalled to debate Gulf crisis; government had majority of 402 at end of two-day debate; Mrs Thatcher announced that more British troops would go to Gulf.
9 Presidents Bush and Gorbachev held summit talks in Helsinki: they demanded unconditional withdrawal from Kuwait by Iraq.
10 In Liberia, President Doe died after being captured by rebel faction; Prince Johnson, a rebel leader, said he would run country pending formation of transitional government.
In Pakistan, former PM Benazir Bhutto charged with misuse of power.
11 Parliament of Russian republic (P.SFSR) adopted programme aiming to introduce market economy within 500 days.
In UK, Church of England report, *Faith in the Countryside*, called for government action to provide better homes, transport, health care and job prospects for rural communities.
12 Foreign ministers of four victorious wartime Allied powers and of E. and W. Germany signed agreement (see DOCUMENTS) in Moscow enabling reunification of two German states (see 3 Oct.).

CHRONICLE OF EVENTS 605

In USSR, Gorbachev outlined compromise programme of economic reform based on ideas of Stanislav Shatalin but containing elements of PM Ryzhkov's plan.
13 W. German and Soviet Foreign Ministers initialled 20-year Treaty on Good Neighbourliness, Partnership and Cooperation.
UK Defence Secretary announced deployment of 7th Armoured Brigade in Gulf.
In S. Africa, 26 black commuters died in shooting on train in Johannesburg.
14 US Secretary of State Baker held crisis talks in Damascus with President Asad.
17 Mrs Thatcher on two-day visit to Czechoslovakia, first by a British PM for 50 years; she later visited Switzerland and Hungary.
18 In UK, former governor of Gibraltar, Sir Peter Terry, injured in IRA gun attack.
In S. Africa, Winnie Mandelá charged with kidnapping and assault.
In Romania, Nicu Ceauşescu, son of executed dictator, gaoled for 20 years for his role in deaths of 91 civilians in Dec. 1989 revolution.
22 Asian Games opened in Beijing; Iraq banned because of Kuwait invasion.
23 Iraq threatened to attack Israel and Middle East oilfields if it was strangled by economic sanctions.
24 President de Klerk became first S. African head of state to be received at White House since 1948 imposition of apartheid.
President Weizsäcker of W. Germany signed treaty for reunification of Germany; E. Germany formally withdrew from Warsaw Pact.
In USSR, Supreme Soviet voted to give Gorbachev sweeping powers to implement economic reforms and steer country towards market economy within 18 months.
25 In UK, White Paper, *The Common Inheritance: Britain's Environmental Strategy* (Cmnd. 1200), outlined proposals to counter global warming, combat pollution and protect countryside and national heritage.
UN Security Council resolution 670 called for air blockade to reinforce economic sanctions against Iraq.
26 US Defence Secretary announced plans for withdrawal of 40,000 troops from Europe.
27 Britain and Iran agreed to resume diplomatic relations broken in 1989 over *Satanic Verses* affair.
In UK, Labour retained seat in by-election at Knowsley S. with reduced majority.
28 Serbian parliament adopted new constitution, stripping Albanian enclave of Kosovo of its autonomy.
Soviet republic of Kazakhstan declared eastern region a disaster area; an accident on 12 Sept. at nuclear fuel plant near border with Mongolia and China had released toxic gas.
29 In New York, world leaders attended largest summit in history, the World Summit for Children.

OCTOBER

1 Labour Party conference opened in Blackpool, ending 5 Oct.; delegates voted to study electoral reform.
In Scotland, inquiry opened at Dumfries into bombing of Pan Am jet in Dec. 1988 at Lockerbie in which 270 died.
2 In China, 132 died when hijacked Boeing 737 crashed at Canton airport.
3 E. and W. Germany reunified as one nation after 45 years of division; newly-constituted Bundestag held first meeting in Berlin on 4 Oct.
4 In USA, House of Representatives voted against President's budget proposals; 8 Oct. Democratic leaders forced through a compromise package diluting Bush proposals; 9 Oct. Bush signed bill to provide emergency funding as disagreement continued.
France and Belgium agreed to send troops to Rwanda where rebel invasion from Uganda threatened safety of their nationals.

CHRONICLE OF EVENTS

7   In Austrian parliamentary elections Socialists, led by Franz Vranitzky, remained dominant; new coalition with People's Party formed on 17 Dec.
8   Britain became a full member of the European exchange rate mechanism (ERM).
    At least 17 Palestinians died when Israeli police fired on demonstrators at the Temple Mount, Jerusalem.
9   Soviet parliament approved draft legislation to reform banking system.
    President Saddam Husain of Iraq threatened missile strike against Israel in retaliation for Temple Mount deaths; Arab League condemned Israeli action.
    In India, eight students committed suicide over government plans to reserve more jobs for low-caste masses.
12 Lebanese Christian militia leader, Gen. Michel Aoun, took refuge in French embassy in Beirut after his HQ was bombarded by Syrian and Lebanese forces (see 25 Nov., 3 Dec.).
    Egyptian parliamentary Speaker Rifa'at Mahjub assassinated in Cairo.
14 Mrs Thatcher and President de Klerk of S. Africa held talks at Chequers.
15 Nobel Peace Prize awarded to Soviet President Mikhail Gorbachev; 28 Nov. Gorbachev said he was unable to go to Oslo for award ceremony because of deteriorating situation at home.
    In S. Africa, Separate Amenities Act erased from statute book.
    British Foreign Secretary Hurd began controversial visit to Israel which accused him of anti-Israel remarks following Temple Mount shootings; Palestinian delegation cancelled meeting, alleging he was opposed to Palestinian state.
18 In UK, Liberal Democrats overturned 17,000 Tory majority in Eastbourne by-election.
    Romanian PM announced currency devaluation and radical economic reforms.
    UN Secretary-General abandoned mission to investigate Temple Mount shootings because of Israeli refusal to cooperate.
    In UK, charges against employees of P&O, arising from Zeebrugge ferry disaster in 1987, dropped for lack of evidence.
21 In Lebanon, Dany Chamoun, leader of National Liberal Party, assassinated with his family.
    In Malaysia, ruling National Front coalition led by Mahathir Mohamed gained two-thirds majority in parliamentary elections.
23 Thirty-three hostages released by Iraq returned to UK with former UK PM Edward Heath who had made a humanitarian mission to Baghdad; Iraqi parliament voted to release all 330 French hostages.
    President Cossiga of Italy on four-day state visit to UK.
24 Benazir Bhutto's Pakistan People's Party suffered crushing defeat by Islamic Democratic Alliance in general election; Nawaz Sharif sworn in as PM on 6 Nov.
    Six solders and a civilian died in IRA bombings at army checkpoints in N. Ireland.
    Soviet envoy, Yevgeny Primakov, in Cairo at start of Gulf peace mission; he held fruitless talks with Saddam in Baghdad on 29 Oct.
25 Israel rejected UN Security Council resolution calling for its acceptance of UN mission to investigate Temple Mount killings.
26 President Gorbachev on visit to Spain.
27 Two-day summit conference of EC heads of government opened in Rome; with exception of UK, they voted to begin second stage of economic and monetary union in 1994 and to aim for single European currency by 2000; declaration said that EC members would not negotiate with Saddam Husain.
    In elections in New Zealand, National Party, led by James Bolger, defeated incumbent Labour Party.
28 In USSR, elections in Georgia were won by non-communist parties calling for independence and adoption of market economy.
    Soviet troops sent to Moldavia to prevent ethnic clashes.

CHRONICLE OF EVENTS

In first contested presidential election in Côte d'Ivoire, Félix Houphouët-Boigny re-elected for seventh term amid fraud allegations.

29 UN Security Council passed composite resolution (674) condemning Iraq's hostage-taking and pillage of Kuwait.
In Norway, coalition government of Jan Syse resigned in dispute over EC links; on 30 Oct. Gro Harlem Brundtland agreed to form minority Labour government.

30 In India, five died when police fired on Hindu militants who stormed a Muslim mosque in Ayodhya, Uttar Pradesh; further deaths occurred in continuing violence on subsequent days.

31 Irish PM Haughey sacked deputy PM Brian Lenihan following no-confidence vote in Dáil over so-called 'Dublingate' affair (scc 7 Nov.).

NOVEMBER

1 In UK, Sir Geoffrey Howe (Leader of House of Commons) resigned from government over differences with Mrs Thatcher on approach to EC; his resignation speech on 13 Nov. accused her of risking Britain's future by her attitude; Mrs Thatcher reshuffled cabinet on 2 Nov.

2 In UK, Sky Television and British Satellite Broadcasting (BSB) announced merger.

3 People's Assembly of Mozambique voted to adopt new constitution, ending 15-year marxist experiment.

5 Rabbi Meir Kahane, founder of Jewish Defence League, assassinated in New York.

6 In mid-term elections in USA, Democrats strengthened their hold on Congress and increased Senate majority by one.
Bishop Cahal Daly named as new Archbishop of Armagh and Primate of Ireland.

7 In Ireland, Mary Robinson (independent) defeated Brian Lenihan to become Republic's first woman President; she was sworn on on 3 Dec.
In India, government of V. P. Singh resigned; a minority government led by Chandra Shekhar was sworn in on 10 Nov.
In UK, state opening of parliament: Queen's speech foreshadowed 15 bills dealing mainly with transport and fight against crime.
Delegates attending World Climate Conference in Geneva agreed to drawing-up of treaty to protect atmosphere by 1992.

8 In UK, Labour retained seats in by-elections at Bootle and Bradford N.

9 President Gorbachev on two-day visit to Bonn.

11 Ruling Christian Democrat Party routed in first round of presidental election in Guatemala; run-off to take place on 6 Jan. 1991.

12 Emperor Akihito enthroned as Japan's 125th monarch.

14 A treaty confirming Oder-Neisse line as frontier between Germany and Poland was signed in Warsaw.
Soviet government announced freeing of prices of 'luxury' goods.

17 Soviet parliament approved in principle Gorbachev's proposals for new political structure but rejected increase in presidential powers.
President Bush addressed crowds during 24-hour visit to Prague.

18 President Gorbachev had audience at Vatican; he renewed invitation to Pope to visit USSR.
President Bush and Chancellor Kohl held talks at Oggersheim, Germany: they pleased for peaceful solution of Gulf crisis.
A recreated Communist Party, Socialist Party of Labour, founded in Romania.

19 Three-day CSCE summit opened in Paris attended by representatives of 34 nations; historic arms (CFE) treaty eliminating more than 60,000 tanks, artillery and other weapons was signed by NATO and Warsaw Pact leaders; delegates also signed

Charter of Paris for a new Europe marking end of Cold War and affirming supremacy of democratic process (see DOCUMENTS).

A three-week meeting of parties to 1961 Antarctica treaty opened in Chile.

20 In UK, Conservative Party held ballot for leadership; Michael Heseltine obtained 152 votes; with 204 votes, Mrs Thatcher was four short of number required for outright win; on 22 Nov. she announced her intention to resign as PM (see 27 Nov.).

Hungarian PM announced at CSCE conference that Warsaw Pact organization would be scrapped by 1992.

22 President Bush visited US troops in Saudi Arabia; on 23 Nov. he held talks with President Asad of Syria in Geneva.

23 Soviet parliament granted President Gorbachev additional powers permitting him to take emergency measures to maintain order in USSR.

25 In Lebanon, Christian militias withdrew from E. Beirut under a peace agreement intended to reunify city which would be policed by government troops and Syrian soldiers (see 3 Dec.).

26 Lee Kuan Yew resigned as PM after 31 years as Singapore's leader; his successor, Goh Chok Tong, was sworn in on 28 Nov.

27 In UK, Conservative Party held second round of leadership ballot; John Major was within two votes of outright victory and his opponents Michael Heseltine and Douglas Hurd conceded defeat.

Government of Bangladesh imposed state of emergency in face of violent campaign by opposition parties (see 4 Dec.).

Soviet Defence Minister Marshal Yazov announced sweeping new powers to combat attacks on army and maintain law and order.

28 In UK, Mrs Thatcher tendered her resignation to the Queen; Mr Major took office as PM and undertook extensive cabinet reshuffle; Norman Lamont appointed Chancellor of Exchequer.

29 UN Security Council by 12–2 vote adopted resolution 678, authorizing use of force against Iraq after 15 Jan. 1991; China abstained.

Germany began airlift of food supplies to USSR which was suffering worst shortages since World War II.

In Bulgaria, government of Andrei Lukanov (formed on 8 Feb.) resigned.

30 President Bush offered to send Secretary of State Baker to Baghdad for talks on Gulf crisis with President Saddam Husain between 15 Dec. and 15 Jan. 1991; no date had been agreed by year end.

DECEMBER

1 British and French construction workers marked historic breakthrough in Channel Tunnel project: for first time it was possible to walk from Britain to France.

2 Voters in united Germany went to polls for first time since 1932; Helmut Kohl was returned as Chancellor; CDU, CSU and FDP would form coalition, SDP vote having fallen.

In USSR, Interior Minister Vadim Bakatin replaced by Boris Pugo.

In Chad, rebel forces led by Idriss Deby overthrew regime of Hissène Habré; on 4 Dec. Deby declared himself President and appointed Council of State.

Ruling National Democratic Party gained overwhelming majority in parliamentary elections in Egypt.

3 In Lebanon, withdrawal of Christian Lebanese Forces left Beirut free of all private militias for first time since 1976.

In Brussels, riot police dispersed 30,000 farmers demanding protection of their subsidies as delegates from 107 countries met for Uruguay round of GATT talks aimed at freeing world trade; talks collapsed on 7 Dec.

President Bush in Brazil at start of five-nation tour of Latin America.

CHRONICLE OF EVENTS

4 EC foreign ministers agreed to start food convoys to USSR.
5 In UK, twelve regional electricity companies offered for sale in government's biggest-ever privatization issue which was massively oversubscribed.
6 President Saddam Husain announced that all Western hostages in Kuwait and Iraq would be freed; evacuation began on 9 Dec. and was complete by Christmas.
  Gen. Ershad resigned as President of Bangladesh; he was placed under house arrest on 12 Dec.; Chief Justice Shahabbudin Ahmed appointed to head caretaker government pending elections.
9 Former Solidarity leader Lech Walesa won landslide victory in Polish presidential election (see 14 Dec.).
  Slobodan Milosevic (Serbian Socialist Party) gained overwhelming victory in Serbia's first free elections for 50 years for presidency of republic.
11 KGB chairman Vladimir Kryuchkov announced that KGB would use its authority throughout USSR to prevent national collapse.
  Amid mounting unrest in Albania, ruling Communist Party dismissed five members of politburo and said opposition parties should be allowed.
  Israeli PM Shamir in Washington for talks with President Bush.
12 Following talks in Washington with Soviet Foreign Minister Shevardnadze, President Bush announced lifting of trade restrictions and promised credit guarantees worth $1,000 million to enable USSR to buy grain and other agricultural commodities on favourable terms.
  Opposition Social Democrats made substantial gains in Danish general election; PM Schlüter would continue to lead minority coalition.
13 ANC president Oliver Tambo returned to S. Africa after 30 years in exile.
14 Two-day summit conference of EC heads of government opened in Rome; leaders agreed to begin a £200 million food-aid package to USSR; two inter-governmental conferences (IGCs) on political union and on economic and currency union opened immediately after summit.
  In Poland, government of Tadeusz Mazowiecki resigned; President Walesa nominated Jan Krzysztof Bielicki as PM on 29 Dec.
16 In Haiti, Fr Jean-Bertrand Aristide won presidential election.
17 In UK, House of Commons rejected motion to reintroduce death penalty.
  Lothar de Maizière, deputy leader of CDU and last PM of GDR, resigned from German government following allegations that he had worked for 'Stasi' secret police.
19 Salim al-Hoss resigned as PM of Lebanon; President Hrawi invited Omar Karami to form new government.
20 Eduard Shevardnadze resigned as Soviet Foreign Minister, declaring that USSR was heading for dictatorship.
21 British PM John Major in Washington for talks with President Bush.
22 Prince of Wales visited British forces in Gulf.
23 Slovenia voted in plebiscite for independence.
27 Gennadi Yanayev elected Soviet Vice-President at Congress of People's Deputies; Russian Federation said it would withhold much of its contribution to central budget in 1991.
28 In UK, Defence Secretary announced biggest call-up of reservists since 1956 Suez crisis for service in Gulf.

INDEX

Page references in bold indicate location of main coverage.

ABACHA, Sanni, 259
ABALKIN, Leonid, 86, 112
ABDALLAH, Ahmed, 330–1
ABDELAZIZ, Mohamed, 244
ABDUL WAKIL, Idris, 253
ABDUL RAHMAN, Tunku, death, 338; obit., 579
ABDULLAH, Ahmed Sulayman, 249
ABE, Shintaro, 361
ABERNATHY, Rev Ralph, obit., 579
ABRAHAM, Gen. Hérard, 86
ABU DHABI, 223, 228
ABULHASAN, Mohammad A., 387
ACHESON, Donald, 296
ACKFORD, Paul, 527
ACKROYD, Peter, 517, 521
ADAM, Marcus, 528
ADAMI, Dr Eddie Fenech, Prime Minister of Malta, 187
ADAMS, Richard, 518, 522
ADAMSON, J. B., 449
ADRIEN, Fr Antoine, 86
ADVANI, L. K., 313
AFGHANISTAN, 67, 307, **309–11**, 597
AFRICAN CONFERENCES & ORGANIZATIONS, 244, 257, 258, 261, 264, 281, 394, **419–21**
AGANBEGYAN, Abel, 112
AGASSI, Andre, 533
AGONDJO-OKAWE, Maître, 275
AGUILAR MAWDSLEY, Andrés, 469
AHMED, Shahabuddin, Acting President of Bangladesh, 320, 609
AHMED ALI, Gen. Fathi, 228
AHO, Esko, 175
AHOMADEGBE, Justin, 272
AIDS (Acquired Immune Deficiency Syndrome), 42, 252, 254, 257, 294, 336, 425, **455–7**
AIME, Jean-Claude, 391
AISHWARYA, HM Queen, of Nepal, 324
AITKEN-WALKER, Louise, 534
AJMAN, 223
AKABUSI, Kriss, 529
AKBULUT, Yildirim, Prime Minister of Turkey, 193
AKHMATOVA, Anna, 520
AKIHITO, HM Emperor, of Japan, 363–4, 449, 607
AKSOY, Muammer, death, 195
ALAOUI, Moulay Ahmed, 243
ALATAS, Ali, 343, 356
ALBANIA, **137–9**, 190, 365, 414, 445, 587, 602, 603, 609
ALDISS, Brian, 522
ALEXANDER, John, death, 484
ALEXANDER, Lamar, 578
ALFONSÍN FOULKES, Raúl, 578
ALGERIA, 145, 221, 235, **237–41**, 244, 245, 268, 284, 412, 449, 601
ALHAJI, Alhaji Abubakar, 261

ALI, Brig.-Gen. Moses, 255
ALI, Muhammad, 217
ALI, Tariq, 494
ALIA, Ramiz, Head of State of Albania, 137–9, 602
ALINGUÉ, Jean B., 274
ALLAN, Elizabeth, obit., 579
ALLEN, Woody, 496
ALLENDE GOSSENS, Salvador, 79
ALMODOVAR, Pedro, 499
ALPTEMOÇIN, Ahmet Kurtçebe, 194
ALSTON, Richard, 489
ALTHUSSER, Louis, obit., 579
AMERICAN SAMOA, **383, 384**
AMES, Leslie, obit., 579
AMIN, Idi, 255, 257
AMIS, Sir Kingsley, 516, 520
AMNESTY INTERNATIONAL, 78, 219, 223, 229, 242–3, 266, 269, 277, 322, 323
AMOUR, Dr Salmin, 253
ANANIASHVILI, Nina, 488
ANDEAN PACT, **426**
ANDERSON, Frank, 491
ANDERSON, Chris, 292
ANDORRA, 472
ANDREOTTI, Giulio, Prime Minister of Italy, 155, 157–9
ANDREW, Christopher, 515, 523
ANDRIESSEN, Louis, 488
ANGIER, Carole, 518, 521
ANGOLA, 279, **286–8**
ANGUILLA, **103**
ANNAN, Noel, 523
ANTALL, József, Prime Minister of Hungary, 124–6, 401, 439, 598
ANTARCTICA, 381, 396
ANTIGUA & BARBUDA, **100, 101,** 428
ANTONIO, Manuel, 285
ANWAR IBRAHIM, Datuk Seri, 337–8
ANYAOKU, Chief Emeka, 398–9
AOUN, Gen. Michel, 211–14, 606
APPADORAI, Prof. A., 315
APPIAH, Joe, 258
APPIAH, Peggy, 258
AQUINO, Benigno, 344
AQUINO, Corazon, President of the Philippines, 343–5
ARAB COOPERATION COUNCIL (ACC), 207, 222
ARAB LEAGUE, 7, 202–3, 205, 207, 210, 216, 220, 223, 229, 236, 243, 249, 268, 387, 389, 603
ARAB MAGHREB UNION (AMU), 232, 236, 421
ARAB STATES OF THE GULF, **223–8,** 230
ARAB WORLD, **200–3**
ARAFAT, Yassir, 202, 205, 210–11, 302, 391
ARCAND, Denys, 499
ARCHITECTURE, **509–11**
ARÉVALO BERMEJO, Juan José, obit., 579

INDEX

ARGAÑA, Luis Maria, 82
ARGENTINA, **74–6**, 78, 82, 83, 389, 394, 412, 525, 526, 527, 533, 591, 596
ARGENTO, Dominick, 483
ARIAS SÁNCHEZ, Oscar, 88
ARIDOR, Yoram, 392
ARISTIDE, Fr Jean Bertrand, President of Haiti, 87, 609
ARLOTT, John, 522
ARMS CONTROL (*see also* Conference on Security and Cooperation in Europe, North Atlantic Treaty Organization, Warsaw Pact), **430–43**; CFE Treaty, 40, 53–4, 66, 67, 145, 177, 430, **432–4, 435** (*diagrams*), **436** (*map*), **437–40**; chemical weapons, 65, 113, 425; CSBM, 434, **438**; Germany, 151, **430–2**; START, 65, 113, **440–1**; UN, 394–5
ARMYTAGE, Marcus, 534
ARONSON, Theo, 522
ART, **504–8**, 597, 600
ARUBA, **104**
ASAD, Hafiz al-, President of Syria, 9, 210–12, 307, 605, 608
ASHDOWN, Paddy, MP, 26, 28
ASHFORD, John, 490
ASIA-PACIFIC DEVELOPMENT COUNCIL (APDC), **424**
ASPE ARMELLA, Pedro, 91
ASSOCIATION OF SOUTH-EAST ASIAN NATIONS (ASEAN), 346, 347, **423–4**
ASYLMURATOVA, Altynai, 488
ATANASOV, Georgi, 131
ATHERTON, Michael, 529–30
ATKINSON, Rick, 522
ATTALI, Jacques, 539
ATTALLAH, Naim, 523
AUSTRALIA, 219, 347, 358, **372–6**, 377, 398, 424, 425, 452, 455, 464, 487, 527, 531, 532, 534, 540, 581, 594, 598, 599, 600
AUSTRIA, 8, 122, 126, **175–8**, 187, 217, 387, 409, 416, 569, 580, 586, 603, 606
AVENSON, Don, 58, 60
AVEROFF, Evangelos, obit., 579
AVRIL, Gen. Prosper, 86, 595, 597
AYA, Prince, of Japan, 363
AYAH, Wilson Ndolo, 251
AYCKBOURN, Alan, 492, 495
AYLWIN AZÓCAR, Patricio, President of Chile, 78, 597
AZAHARUDDIN, Mohammad, 529
AZIZ, Tariq, Foreign Minister of Iraq, 8, 69, 215–16
AZNAR, José Maria, 181

BABA, Ghafar, 337
BABANGIDA, Gen. Ibrahim, Head of State of Nigeria, 259–60, 262, 277, 599
BACKLEY, Steve, 528
BADR, Gen. Zaki, 205
BADRAN, Mudar, Prime Minister of Jordan, 209
BADRI, Abdullah al-, 231
BAGGIO, Roberto, 526

BAHAMAS, **99**
BAHRAIN, **224**, 226, 227, 228, 391, 442
BAILEY, Paul, 522
BAILEY, Pearl, obit., 579–80
BAINBRIDGE, Beryl, 516
BAIR, Deidre, 517, 521
BAKATIN, Vadim, 608
BAKER, James, US Secretary of State, 7, 9, 65–7, 69, 193–4, 200, 202, 210, 340, 346–7, 353, 370, 434, 440, 578, 605, 608
BAKER, Kenneth, MP, 12, 29, 33, 42, 520, 576–7
BAKER, Nicholson, 517, 520
BALAGUER, Joaquín, President of Dominican Republic, 87, 600
BALCEROWICZ, Leszek, 115
BALLARD, J. G., 520
BALLESTEROS, Seve, 531
BALLET, *see* Dance/Ballet
BANDA, Hastings Kamuzu, President of Malawi, 290–1
BANDAR BIN SULTAN, Prince, 220
BANGLADESH, **318–21**, 412, 422, 464, 595, 608, 609
BARBADOS, **96–7**, 399, 428
BARCO VARGAS, Virgilio, 80
BARKWORTH, Peter, 495
BARLOW, Frank, 500
BARRE, Abdurahman Jama, 248
BARRETT, Anthony A., 522
BARRIE, Dennis, 508
BARROW, Dame Nita, 97
BARRY, Gerald, 483
BARRY, Marion, 61, 63–4
BARYSHNIKOV, Mikhail, 490
BASHIR, Lt.-Gen. Omar Hasan Ahmed al-, Prime Minister of Sudan, 205, 229, 232
BATBAYAR, Bat-Erdeniyn, 369
BATMÖNH, Jambyn, 369
BAT-ÜÜL, Erdeniyn, 368
BAUCKHAM, R., 449
BAYKAL, Deniz, 195
BAZIN, Marc, 87
BAZOFT, Farzad, 25, 215, 597
BEATTY, Warren, 497
BECKER, Boris, 533, 602
BEDFORD, Sybille, 522
BEEVOR, Antony, 523
BELAU, **383, 384–5**
BELEZA, Miguel, 184
BELGIUM, **159–61**, 163, 229, 279, 281, 361, 387, 403, 442, 474, 569, 605
BELHADJ, Ali, 238, 240
BELICHENKO, Albert, 411
BELIZE, **97**
BELLO, Usman, 259
BELLOTTI, David, MP, 35
BELLOTTI, Francis X., 59
BELSTEAD, Lord, 576–7
BEN ALI, Gen. Zayn al-Adin, President of Tunisia, 233–6
BEN BELLA, Ahmed, 240
BEN-PORATH, Miriam, 199
BENIN, **271–2**, 445

BENN, Nigel, 528
BENN, Tony, MP, 9, 26, 217
BENNETT, Alan, 493
BENNETT, Joan, obit., 580
BENNETT, Nicholas, MP, 47
BENSON, Peter, 515
BERBEROVA, Nina, 520
BÉRÉGOVOY, Pierre, 405
BÉRENGER, Paul, 328
BERESFORD, Bruce, 496
BERGER, Erna, 484; obit., 580
BERGHOFER, Wolfgang, 147
BERGREEN, Laurence, 521
BERLIN, Isaiah, 522
BERNSTEIN, Leonard, death, 484, 487–8; obit., 580
BERON, Petar, 132
BERRADA, Mohamed, 241
BERRYMAN, John, 520
BETTELHEIM, Dr Bruno, 522; obit., 580
BHATTARAI, K. P., Prime Minister of Nepal, 324–5, 599
BHUTAN, **325–6**, 422
BHUTTO, Benazir, 316–17, 603–4, 606
BIBALO, Antonio, 484
BID, Ali Salim al-, 222
BIELICKI, Jan Krzysztof, Prime Minister of Poland, 118, 609
BILDT, Carl, 418
BINTLEY, David, 488
BIRD, Lester, 101
BIRD, Vere, Prime Minister of Antigua & Barbuda, 101
BIRD, Vere, Jr., 101
BIRENDRA, HM King, of Nepal, 324–5, 598
BIRLA, M. P., 315
BISHOP, Maurice, 98
BITAT, Rabah, 239–40
BIYA, Paul, President of Cameroon, 273
BLACK, Roger, 528
BLACK, Yondo, 273
BLAIZE, Herbert, 98
BLAKE, George, 522
BLAKE, Lord, 521
BLAKEMORE, Michael, 494
BLOCH, Michael, 521
BLOM-COOPER, Louis, QC, 101
BLUNDY, David, 519
BLUNT, Charles, 373
BLYTON, Enid, 519
BOLGER, Jim, Prime Minister of New Zealand, 378–81, 606
BOLIVIA, **76–7**, 80, 82, 83, 358, 426, 427, 596
BOLKIAH, Sir Hassanal, Sultan of Brunei, 338
BOMANI, Paul, 253
BOND, Alan, 374
BONGO, Omar, President of Gabon, 144, 275, 600
BOOTH, Laurie, 490
BORJA CEVALLOS, Rodrigo, President of Ecuador, 81
BORK, Robert, 61
BORLAND, Maureen, 521

BOSCH, Juan, 87
BOSE, Hans-Jürgen von, 485
BOSKIN, Michael, 578
BOSSANO, Joe, Chief Minister of Gibraltar, 186–7
BOTHA, P. W., 303
BOTHA, R. F. (Pik), 253
BOTSWANA, **296–7**
BOUCHARD, Lucien, 71, 73
BOULARES, Habib, 236–7
BOURASSA, Robert, 70–2
BOURDEAUX, M., 450
BOURGUIBA, Habib, 234
BOUTERSE, Lt.-Col. Desi, 102
BOWEN, Gen. Hezekiah, 264
BOYD, Brian, 521
BOYD, William, 516
BOZER, Ali, 194
BRADLEY, Senator Bill, 60
BRADY, Nicholas, 578
BRAGA, Enrique, 84
BRAHIMI, Abdelhamid, 238, 240
BRAITHWAITE, Nicholas, 98
BRANAGH, Kenneth, 491–2, 498
BRANDSTRUP, Kim, 490
BRANDT, Willy, 9, 217
BRANSTAD, Terry E., 58, 60
BRAUDEL, Fernand, 523
BRAUN, Helena, death, 484
BRAYBROOKE, M., 450
BRAZIL, 76, **77–8**, 82, 389, 412, 446, 531, 532, 538, 597, 608
BREDIN, Jean-Denis, 470
BREHME, Andreas, 525
BRELAND, Mark, 528
BRENDEL, Alfred, 522
BRENNAN, Joseph, 60
BRENNAN, William J., 61
BRENTON, Howard, 494–5
BREYTENBACH, Col. Jan, 287
BREZHNEV, Leonid, 1, 3
BRIERS, Richard, 492
BRISTOW, Eric, 534
BRITISH VIRGIN ISLANDS, 428
BRITTAN, Sir Leon, 33
BROADCASTING, see Television and Radio
BROOKE, Peter, MP, 48–9, 165, 576–7
BROOKNER, Anita, 520
BROOME, John, 509
BROWN, Christy, 167
BROWN, Simon, 476
BROWNE-WILKINSON, Sir Nicholas, 475
BRUCAN, Silviu, 127
BRUCCOLI, Matthew J., 522
BRUNDTLAND, Gro Harlem, Prime Minister of Norway, 172, 418, 607
BRUNEI, **338–9**, 423
BRUNSWIJK, Ronnie, 102
BRUTON, John, 166
BRYSON, Bill, 521
BRZEZINSKI, Zbigniew, 515, 523
BUCARAM ORTIZ, Averroes, 82
BUCHAN, William, 522
BULGARIA, **130–3**, 176, 194, 401, 410, 414, 431, 444–5, 569, 595, 596, 601, 602, 608

INDEX

BULL, Deborah, 488
BUNSHAFT, Gordon, obit., 580
BURGESS, Anthony, 495, 518, 522
BURKE, Ray, 167
BURKINA FASO, 265, **270**, 465, 499
BURMA, see Myanmar
BURT, Richard, 441
BURUNDI, **280**
BUSH, George, President of USA, 578; arms control and defence, 54, 425, 433–4, 596–7; drugs, 54, 80, 596; environment, 465; foreign affairs, 22, 52, 65–7, 76, 80, 92, 79, 113, 122, 193, 213, 233, 251, 279, 302, 353, 362, 426–7, 440–1, 599–600, 602–3, 607–9; Gulf crisis, 7, 8, 9, 44, 52–3, 67–9, 208, 210, 218, 221, 388, 500, 603–4, 607–8; home affairs, 52–7, 61–3, 542, 596, 605
BUSH, Neil, 62
BUSKE, Norman, 384
BUSSELL, Darcey, 488
BUTCHER, Rosemary, 490
BUTHELEZI, Chief Mangosuthu, 300, 303
BUTRIMENKO, Aleksandr, 410
BUYOYA, Pierre, President of Burundi, 280
BYAMBASÜREN, Dashiyn, Prime Minister of Mongolia, 368, 370–1
BYATT, A. S., 516, 520

CABRAL, Bernando, 78
CABRERA, Alfonso, 90
CACCIA, Lord, obit., 580–1
CÁCERES, Gen. Isidro, 75
CAFIERO, Antonio, 75
CAGE, John, 486
CAIN, John, 374
CAIRD, John, 495
CALATRAVA, Santiago, 511
CALDERÓN FOURNIER, Rafael Angel, President of Costa Rica, 90, 596
ČALFA, Marian, Prime Minister of Czechoslovakia, 595
CALLEJAS, Rafael Leonardo, President of Honduras, 90
CAMARA, Col. Iafai, 282
CAMBODIA, see Kampuchea
CAMEROON, 261–2, **273,** 274, 277, 525–6
CAMPBELL, Carroll, 58, 60
CAMPBELL, Kim, 73
CÁMPORA, Mario, 76
CAMPS, Gen. Ramón, 75
CANADA, 66, **69–74,** 113, 252, 323, 358, 387, 390, 398, 399, 425–6, 446, 464, 499, 539, 540, 561, 600, 601, 602
CANETTI, Elias, 522
CANNADINE, David, 519, 522
CAPE VERDE, **282**
CAPRIATI, Jennifer, 533
CAPUCINE, death, 499
CARADON, Lord, obit., 581
CARDOSO DE MELLO, Zélia, 77
CAREY, Rt Rev Dr George, Archbishop-designate of Canterbury, 23, 602
CARIBBEAN ORGANIZATIONS, 94, **427–8**
CARLING, Will, 527

CARLSON, Frank, 60
CARLSSON, Ingvar, Prime Minister of Sweden, 172–3
CARPIO, Jorge, 90
CARR, Edwin, 487
CARRINGTON, Lord, 504
CARRON, Owen J., 51
CARRUTHERS, Jimmy, obit., 581
CARSON, Willie, 533
CARTER, Ian, 521
CARTER, Jimmy, 52, 68
CARTER-RUCK, Peter, 522
CARTLAND, Dame Barbara, 513
CARTWRIGHT, Justin, 520
CARVALHAS, Carlos, 184
CASSIDY, Stuart, 488
CASTILLO, Carlos Manuel, 90, 596
CASTRO RUZ, Fidel, President of Cuba, 85
CATÁ, Alfonso, 491
CATON JONES, Michael, 498
CAVACO SILVA, Anibal, Prime Minister of Portugal, 183–5
CAYGILL, David, 379
CEAUŞESCU, Nicolae, 127, 129, 291, 444, 596
CEAUŞESCU, Nicu, 129, 605
CECIL, Hugh and Mirabel, 521
CENTRAL AFRICAN REPUBLIC, **275–6**
CENTRAL AMERICA, **87–91**
CEREZO ARÉVALO, Vinicio, President of Guatemala, 90
ÇETIN, Hikmet, 195
CHAD, 144, 230, 232–3, **274–5,** 420, 468, 608
CHADLI, Bendjedid, President of Algeria, 221, 239, 244
CHAKRAVARTY, Sukhamoy, obit., 581
CHALERM YUBAMRUNG, Captain, 335–6
CHAMLONG SRIMUANG, 336
CHAMORRO, Pedro Joaquín, 88
CHAMORRO, Violeta Barrios de, President of Nicaragua, 88, 597
CHAMOUN, Dany, death, 213, 606
CHANG, Michael, 533
CHANNING, Stockard, 496
CHAOVALIT YONGCHAIYUT, Gen., 335–6
CHAPMAN, Robert L., 523
CHARFI, Mohammed, 234
CHARLES, Eugenia, Prime Minister of Dominica, 101
CHARLTON, Jack, 167, 526
CHARLTON, Roger, 534
CHASTEL, André, obit., 581
CHATICHAI CHOONHAVAN, Maj.-Gen., Prime Minister of Thailand, 335–6
CHEA SIM, 348
CHEN LI-AN, 357
CHENEY, Richard, 9, 68, 220, 578
CHENG, Vincent, 339
CHEVÈNEMENT, Jean-Pierre, 145
CHIANG CHING-KUO, 357
CHIDZERO, Dr Bernard, 294
CHIEN, Frederic, 357
CHILDS, Marquis, obit., 581
CHILE, 76, **78–9,** 83, 381, 424, 597, 608
CHILES, Senator Lawton, 59–60

CHINA, PEOPLE'S REPUBLIC OF, **349–56;**
arts, 499; economy, 349–53, 538;
external relations, 66, 67, 139, 144,
220, 254–5, 334, 340, 341, 342, 346,
347, **353–6,** 357, 358, 359–60, 363, 366,
367–8, 370–1, 376, 386, 390, 396, 424,
561, 566; Gulf crisis, 9, 353–4, 356,
386, 561, 566; religion, 445; science,
455
CHIPPINDALE, Peter, 519, 523
CHIRAC, Jacques, 141
CHISSANO, Joaquim Alberto, President of
Mozambique, 283–4, 603
CHOI HO JOONG, 367
CHOUDHURY, Abdul Hussain, 448
CHRÉTIEN, Jean, 71
CHRISTIE, Linford, 528
CHRONICLE OF 1990, **595–609**
CINEMA, 167, **496–500**
CLAIBORNE, Robert, 521
CLARK, Petula, 495
CLARKE, J. P., 51
CLARKE, Kenneth, MP, 17, 37, 576–7
CLIBERTO, José Angel, 85
COCK, Anna Somers, 508
COCKETT, Richard, 522
COCTEAU, Jean, 522
COETZEE, J. M., 516, 520
COHEN, Herman, 247
COLEMAN, Peter, 384
COLLINS, Gerard, 134, 164–5
COLLINS, Joan, 492
COLLOR DE MELLO, Fernando, President
of Brazil, 76–7, 538, 597
COLOMBIA, **80–1,** 83, 101, 163, 387, 390,
392, 412, 426, 427, 526, 561, 587, 596,
600
COMECON (Council for Mutual Economic
Assistance), 115, 122, 123, **408–11,** 595
COMMONWEALTH, THE, 94, 98, 383, **397–9,**
528, 595
COMOROS, 327, **329–31,** 597
COMPAORÉ, Capt. Blaise, Head of State
of Burkina Faso, 270
COMPTON, John, Prime Minister of St
Lucia, 101
CONABLE, Barber, 420
CONFERENCE ON SECURITY AND
COOPERATION IN EUROPE (CSCE), 1, 2,
40, 113, 123, 138, 145, 159, 177, 182,
411, 413, 415, 430, **432–40,** 443, 569–76
(*text*), 607–8
CONGO, **276**
CONJUANGCO, Eduardo, 344
CONNELL, Laurie, 375
CONNOLLY, Cyril, 517, 520
CONQUEST, Robert, 515, 523
CONRAD, Peter, 522
COONEY, Ray, 495
COOPER, Roger, 307
COOPER, William, 522
COPLAND, Aaron, 483; death, 488; obit.,
581
COREY, Elias James, 458
CORISH, Brendan, obit., 581
CORNEA, Doina, 127

CORREA, Charles, 511
COSSEY, Caroline, 415
COSSIGA, Francesco, President of Italy,
156–7, 159, 606
COSTA RICA, **88,** 89, **90,** 583, 596
CÔTE D'IVOIRE, 156, 265, 266, **269–70,**
446–7, 561, 604, 607
COTRET, Robert de, 73
COTTI, Flavio, 180
COUNCIL OF EUROPE, 123, 126, **414–5**
COVELL, Roger, 487
COX, Brian, 492
CRAM, Steve, 529
CRASKE, Margaret, death, 491
CRAXI, Bettino, 155
CRISTIANI BURKARD, Alfredo, President
of El Salvador, 89
CRUISE, Tom, 497
CUBA, 4, 9, **85–6,** 286, 287, 387, 389, 390,
392, 396, 408, 409, 412, 426, 561–6
CULCSI, Pastor, 444
CUNHAL, Alvaro, 184
CUNNINGHAM, Merce, 489, 491
CUOMO, Mario, 60
CURRIE, Austin, 166
CYPRUS, 187, **191–2,** 193, 386, 389, 394,
472, 569, 599
CZECHOSLOVAKIA, 23, **119–24,** 126, 158,
176, 226, 366, 401, 408, 410, 414, 415,
417, 431, 438, 439, 445, 447, 471, 532,
536, 569, 595, 596, 597, 598, 605

DA COSTA, Manuel Pinto, President of
São Tomé and Príncipe, 283
DAHL, Roald, death, 519; obit., 581
DALY, Cahal, Primate of Ireland, 447,
607
DANCE/BALLET, **488–91**
DANIELS, Anthony, 523
DARGAUD, Georges, obit., 581
DARLEY, Gillian, 521
DARMAN, Richard, 578
DAVIDSON, Max, 520
DAVIES, Dido, 521
DAVIES, Jonathan, 527
DAVIES, Russell, 521
DAVIS, Paul, 523
DAVIS, Sammy, Jr., death, 499; obit., 581
DAVIS, Steve, 534
DAVIS-GOFF, Annabel, 522
DAY-LEWIS, Daniel, 167, 498
DE GRUNWALD, Dimitri, death, 500
DE KLERK, F. W., President of South
Africa, 295, 299–305, 394, 596, 598,
600–1, 604–6
DE MAIZIÈRE, Lothar, 148–9, 153, 568,
597, 599, 603, 609
DE MARCO, Guido, 187, 386
DE MELO, Eurico, 183
DE MICHELIS, Gianni, 157–8
DE OLIVEIRA, Veiga, 184
DE VALOIS, Dame Ninette, 489
DE ZOYSA, Richard, 323
DEBT PROBLEMS, (*see also* International
Monetary Fund, World Bank), Africa,

252, 258, 260–1, 285, 290; Americas, 76, 91, 93, 94, 99; Arab world, 206, 208–9, 211, 215, 216, 238, 240, 241; Asia, 318, 319, 329, 332, 352, 371; E. Europe, 115, 122, 131
DEBY, Idriss, President of Chad, 274, 608
DELANEY, J. P. G., 521
DELORS, Jacques, President of the EC Commission, 31, 43, 402
DEMIREL, Süleyman, 194
DEMPSTER, Dallas, 375
DENG XIAOPING, 355
DENKTASH, Rauf, President of Turkish Republic of N. Cyprus, 191, 193, 599
DENMARK, **167–9**, 183, 186, 408, 417, 491, 569, 591, 609
DENNING, Lord, 31
DENNY, Jacques, obit., 582
DEPARDIEU, Gérard, 498–9
DER'I, Arie, 196, 199
DERWINSKI, Edward, 578
DEV, Kapil, 529
DEVINE, Michael, 90
DeVITO, Danny, 497
DEWAR, Donald, MP, 44
DEXTER, John, obit., 582
DEZOTTI, Gustavo, 525
DICKINSON, Peter, 516, 520
DIENG, Amadou, 266
DIENSTBIER, Jiři, 122–3
DIMITROV, Filip, 132
DINKA, Tesfaye, 247
DINKINS, David, 53, 64
DiPRETE, Edward, 60
DIRIA, Ahmed Hassan, 253
DIRO, Ted, 378
DISARMAMENT, see Arms Control, Conference on Security and Cooperation in Europe
DISASTERS AND ACCIDENTS, Australia, 599; Bangladesh, 595; Dominica, 101; Germany, 596; Grenada, 98; India, 600; Iran, 308, 601; Morocco, 467; Pakistan, 595; Peru, 600; Philippines, 343, 602; Saudi Arabia, 220, 221, 448, 602; S. Pacific, 385; Spain, 595; Sweden, 598; Tanzania, 255; UK, 15–16, 46, 47, 595, 597, 598; USA, 53, 467, 595; USSR, 467, 605
DISSANAYAKE, Gamini, 323
DIXON, Sharon Pratt, 61
DJIBOUTI, **250**
DJOHAR, Said Mohammed, President of Comoros, 330, 597
DLAMINI, Obed Mfanyana, Prime Minister of Swaziland, 298
DO MUOI, Prime Minister of Vietnam, 346
DOAN KHUE, Gen., 336
DOE, Gen. Samuel, 264; death, 264, 421, 604; obit., 582
DOGAN, Hüsnü, 194
DOI, Takako, 361
DOMINICA, **100, 101**, 428
DOMINICAN REPUBLIC, **86–7**, 428, 600
DONALD, Mike, 531
DONALDSON, Frances, 518, 522

DONNELLY, Martin, 532
DORLIGJAV, Dambiyn, 370
DOS SANTOS, José Eduardo, President of Angola, 286
DOTAN, Brig.-Gen. Rami, 199
DOUGLAS, Dick, MP, 13, 45
DOUGLAS, James 'Buster', 528
DOUGLAS, Roger, 379
DOUGLAS, Roy, 522
DOURDA, Abu Zaid Omar, 231
DOWD, Ronald, 484
DOWELL, Anthony, 488
DRASKOVIC, Vuk, 134
DRUG-TRAFFICKING, Africa, 288, 338; Americas, 63–4, 76, 77, 80–1, 82, 97, 101, 103, 104, 426, 598; Asia, 338, 600; Europe, 157, 163, 180; UN, 395, 470
DU PLESSIX GRAY, Francine, 515, 523
DUARTE, José Napoléon, obit., 582
DUBAI, 223, 228, 591
DUBČEK, Alexander, 122
DUFF, Robin, death, 491
DUGAN, Gen. Michael, 68
DUKAKIS, Michael, 59
DUKES, Alan, 166
DUMAS, Roland, 244
DUMBUTSHENA, Justice Enoch, 293
DUNNE, Irene, obit., 582
DUPOND, Patrick, 491
DURANTE, Viviana, 488
DURENBERGER, Senator David, 62
DURRELL, Lawrence, 523; death, 519; obit., 582
DÜRRENMATT, Friedrich, obit., 582
DURSCHMIED, Erik, 522
DUTFIELD, Michael, 523
DZARDYHAN, Kinayatyn, 370
DZORIG, Sanjaasürengiyn, 368, 370

EASLEY, Mike, 58
ECONOMIC AND SOCIAL AFFAIRS, **536–60**; international economy, 407–8, **538–40**; Poland and E. Europe, **536–8**; statistical data, **546–60**
ECONOMIC AND SOCIAL COMMISSION FOR ASIA AND THE PACIFIC, **424–5**
ECONOMIC COMMUNITY OF CENTRAL AFRICAN STATES (CEEAC), 421
ECONOMIC COMMUNITY OF WEST AFRICAN STATES (ECOWAS), 258, 261, 263, 264, 265, 267, 421
ECUADOR, **81–2**, 387, 424, 427, 533
EDBERG, Stefan, 533, 602
EDDERY, Pat, 534
EDELSTEIN, Victor, 489
EDGAR, David, 493
EDWARDS, Tracy, 534
EGYPT, 4, 7, 8, 9, 197, 198, 200, 202–3, **204–6,** 207, 209, 210, 216, 217, 220, 222, 226, 230, 231, 232, 233, 236, 243, 364, 389, 397, 403, 412, 420, 596, 599, 606, 608
EL SALVADOR, **87–9**, 469, 582
ELIZABETH II, HM Queen, 328, 381, 602, 608
ELIZABETH, HM The Queen Mother, 603

ELLIOTT, Peter, 528–9
ELLIS, Bret Easton, 517
EMMETT, Rowland, obit., 582
ENDARA GALLIMANY, Guillermo, President of Panama, 88, 426
ENGHOLM, Björn, 153
ENRIGHT, D. J., 520
ENRILE, Juan Ponce, 344
ENVIRONMENT, 24, 54, 156–7, 162, 179, 320–1, 332, 381, 384, 399, 423, 425, **464–7**, 600, 605, 607
EQUATORIAL GUINEA, **276–7**
ERMLER, Mark, 489
ERSHAD, Hussain Mohammad, 318–20, 422, 609
ERTÉ, *see under* Tirtoff, Romain de
ESCHEIKH, Abdelhamid, 234
ESCOBAR GAVIRIA, Pablo, 80
ESMOND, Jill, 583
ESTÈVE-COLL, Elizabeth, 507
ESTONIA, 487, 598, 599
ETHIOPIA, 230, **246–8**, 291, 387, 465, 561, 597
EUBANK, Chris, 528
EUROPEAN BANK FOR RECONSTRUCTION AND DEVELOPMENT (EBRD), 134, 411, 539
EUROPEAN COMMUNITY (*see also* European Community Law), **399–406**; EFTA, 168, 170, 171–2, 174, 175, 176, 178, 415–7, 418, 472; EMU, 33, 36, 157, 159, 168, 404–5, 472; environment, 464, 465, 466; external relations, 66, 91, 96, 123, 130, 134, 144, 168, 170, 173–4, 176, 178, 179, 187, 188, 192, 193, 208, 210, 232, 233, 236, 304, 307, 323, 327, 334, 380, 401–2, 423–4, 426, 427; GATT, 405–6, 407; Gulf crisis, 7, 8, 158, 160, 208, 400, 402–4; research & development, 462; Schengen agreement, 472; UK, 14–5, 20, 21, 28, 31–2, 33–4, 36–9, 43–4, 46, 50, 404, 539–41, 545; WEU, 443
EUROPEAN COMMUNITY LAW, 401, **471–4**, 474–5, 477–8
EUROPEAN COURT OF HUMAN RIGHTS, 415, 470–1, 476
EUROPEAN COURT OF JUSTICE, **473–4**, 474–5
EUROPEAN FREE TRADE ASSOCIATION (EFTA), 168, 170, 171–2, 174, 175, 176, 178, **415–7**, 418, 472, 583
EVANS, C. F., 449
EVDOKIMOVA, Eva, 489
EWING, Margaret, 45
EYADEMA, Gen. Gnassingbe, President of Togo, 272
EYRE, Richard, 493
EYSENCK, H. J., 522

FABRIZI, Aldo, death, 499; obit., 583
FADEYECHEV, Alexei, 488
FAHD AL-AHMAD AL-SABAH, Sheikh, obit., 583
FAHD IBN ABDUL AZIZ, HM King, of Saudi Arabia, 8, 221, 448–9
FALDO, Nick, 530–1
FALKLAND ISLANDS/MALVINAS, 394, 596
FAMA, Joseph, 64
FANE, Julian, 521
FANG LIZHI, 350
FARIAS, Paulo César, 78
FAROOQ, Mirwaiz Maulvi, 600
FARRELL, Terry, 510
FASHION, **511–3**
FAYED, Mohammed and Ali, 338, 597
FEBRES CORDERO RIVADENEIRA, León, 81
FEINSTEIN, Dianne, 58, 60
FELDT, Kjell-Olof, 172
FETTAH, Mohamed, 242
FIELDING, Xan, 521
FIGGURES, Sir Frank, death, 416; obit., 583
FIGUERES FERRER, José, obit., 583
FIJI, 381, **382–3**
FILMON, Gary, 73
FINLAND, 168, **174–5**, 387, 409, 416, 417, 499, 540, 561, 569, 586
FINN, William, 496
FINNEY, Joan, 60
FINUCANE, D., 51
FIRMENICH, Mario Eduardo, 76
FISCHER, Tim, 373, 598
FISK, Robert, 514, 523
FITERMAN, Charles, 141
FITZGERALD, Penelope, 516, 520
FLEMING, Rt Rev Launcelot, obit., 583
FLEUTIAUX, Perrette, 515, 520
FLOYD, Ray, 530
FONCHA, John Ngu, 273
FORBES, Malcolm, obit., 583
FORBES, Ralph, 58
FORD, Richard, 517, 520
FOREMAN, George, 528
FORMAN, Sir Denis, 518, 522
FORSTER, Margaret, 516, 520
FORSYTH, Michael, 45
FOSTER, Norman, 511
FOURAS, Dana, 488
FOWLER, Sir Norman, MP, 11, 595
FRANCE, **140–5**; arts, 483, 491, 498, 507, 515; broadcasting, 503; Corsica, 142–3; defence, 145; DOM & TOM, 143–4, 382–4, 425, 428; economy, 142, 143, 408, 539, 544; environment, 465; external relations, 23, 29, 33, 66, 113–4, 122, 138, **144–5**, 151, 176, 181, 183, 208, 213–4, 226, 232, 239, 243–4, 250, 261, 274, 277, 281, 296, 319, 330, 331, 332, 342, 353, 361, 386, 390, 395, 400, 403, 404–5, 406, 422, 425, 430, 431, 442–3, 469–70, 566, 569–76; Gulf crisis, 8, 143, 144, 145, 208, 226, 386, 390, 403, 430, 442–3, 561; immigration, 141, 142; politics, 140–1; sport, 527, 529, 531, 534
FRANCOPHONIE, 70–1, 144, 267, 271, 276, 330, 422, 601
FRANK, Barney, 62
FRANK, Katherine, 521
FRANKS, Gary, 61
FRASER, Angus, 529

FREEDMAN, Lawrence, 522
FRENCH POLYNESIA, 144, **383, 384**
FRICKER, Brenda, 167
FRICKER, Peter Racine, obit., 583–4
FRIDERICIA, Allan, 491
FRIEDMAN, Jerome, 458–9
FRIEDRICH, Götz, 482, 484
FRIEL, Brian, 493
FRIEND, Richard, 454
FUENTES, Carlos, 520
FUGARD, Athol, 493
FUJAIRAH, 223
FUJIMORI, Alberto Keinya, President of Peru, 83–4, 426, 601
FULLER, Peter, death, 508

GABO, Naum, 508
GABON, 144, 232, **275–6,** 277, 600
GAGE, Nicholas, 522
GAIREY, Sir Eric, 98
GALE, Iain, 521
GALLIANO, John, 489
GAMBA-STONEHOUSE, Virginia, 522
GAMBIA, THE, **263,** 264, 265, 266, 603
GAMEZ, Robert, 531
GAMSAKHURDIA, Zviad, 111
GANBOLD, Davaadorjiyn, 369–70
GANDHI, Indira, 314
GANDHI, Maneka, 313
GANDHI, Rajiv, 313
GANTT, Harvey, 58, 61
GARBA, Gen. Joseph N., 187
GARBO, Greta, death, 499; obit., 584
GARCÍA PÉREZ, Alan, 76, 426
GARDINER, Lord, obit., 584
GARDNER, Ava, death, 499; obit., 584
GAREL-JONES, Tristan, MP, 186
GARLAND, Nicholas, 519, 522
GARRISON, Zena, 533
GARTON ASH, Timothy, 515, 523
GASCOIGNE, Paul ('Gazza'), 526
GATTING, Mike, 530
GAVIN, Lt.-Gen. James, obit., 584
GAVIRIA RIVERO, Gustavo de Jesús, 80
GAVIRIA TRUJILLO, César, President of Colombia, 81, 600
GAYOOM, Maumoun Abdul, President of Maldives, 331, 422
GBAGBO, Laurent, 269–70
GEAGEA, Samir, 212–13
GEBLER, Carlo, 520
GEHRING, Walter, 454–5
GEINGOB, Hage, 295
GELLI, Licio, 157
GENERAL AGREEMENT ON TARIFFS AND TRADE (GATT), 44, 50, 66, 85, 164, 179, 312, 380, 395, 400, 407, 413, 423, 424, 425, 540, 608
GENIÈRE, Renaud de la, obit., 584
GENSCHER, Hans-Dietrich, 151, 568
GERMANY, **146–55;** arts, 484, 485, 498, 505; East Germany, **146–9;** economy, 146–7, 148–9, 152, 154, 408, 536, 538, 539, 540; elections, 147–8, 153–4; external relations, 22, 23, 24, 29, 31, 32, 33, 66, 74, 114, 118, 122, 123, 138, 144, 151, 158, 168, 175, 176–7, 354, 361, 400, 404–5, 406, 409, 430–2, 433, 434, 442–3, 569; Gulf crisis, 8, 217, 403; immigration, 151, 154–5; sport, 155, 528, 532; unification, 1, 23, 31, 114, 118, 122, 123, 144, **146–55,** 158, 164, 168, 176, 354, 400, 402, 409, 430–2, 433, 434, 471–2, 566–9 (*text*); West Germany, 151–5
GHANA, **257–8,** 264, 272
GHANOUCHI, Mohammed, 234
GHANOUCHI, Rachid, 235
GHOZALI, Sid Ahmed, 241
GIACOMELLI, Giorgio, 392
GIBRALTAR, 182, **185–7,** 605
GIEDEON, Torsten, 531
GILBERT, Brad, 533
GILLEY, Sheridan, 521
GINGRICH, Newt, 56
GINSBERG, Allen, 485
GIRAY, Safa, 194
GIRODIAS, Maurice, obit., 584
GIROUARD, Mark, 523
GISCARD D'ESTAING, Valéry, 141
GLASS, Charles, 514, 523
GLASS, Philip, 485
GLEMP, HE Cardinal Jozef, 447
GLENNY, Michael, 515, 523
GLISTRUP, Mogens, 168
GODDARD, Paulette, death, 499; obit., 584
GODFREY, Paul, 494
GODOY, Virgilio, 89
GOH CHOK TONG, Prime Minister of Singapore, 339–40, 608
GOHLKE, Reiner, 149
GOLDBERG, Arthur J., obit., 584–5
GOLDSTONE, Mr Justice, 301
GOMBOJAV, Jambyn, 370
GOMEZ, Andres, 533
GONCHIGDORJ, Radnaasümbereliyn, 368–70
GÖNCZ, Árpád, President of Hungary, 125, 603
GONZÁLEZ, Antonio Ermán, 74
GONZÁLEZ, Felipe, Prime Minister of Spain, 180–2
GOOCH, Graham, 529–30, 602
GOODALL, Jane, 522
GOPALAKRISHNAN, Adoor, 499
GORANI, Hajrullah, 136
GORBACHEV, Mikhail, President of USSR, 130, 402, 471, 515, 606; defence and arms control, 33, 431–2, 434, 439, 441, 602; environment, 466; foreign affairs, 33, 65–6, 113–4, 144, 151, 354, 361, 366, 440, 595–6, 600–3, 606–7; Gulf crisis, 8, 68, 604; home affairs, 23, 105–12, 307, 444, 595–6, 601–2, 605, 607–8
GORDIEVSKY, Oleg, 515, 523
GORDIMER, Nadine, 517, 520
GORDON, Mary, 520
GORE, Senator Al, 61
GOULD, Bryan, MP, 42
GOW, Ian, MP, death, 23, 35

GOWER, David, 529–30
GRADY, Wayne, 531
GRAF, Steffi, 532–3
GRAHAM, A. C., 450
GRAHAM, Martha, 490
GRAY, Robert, 522
GRAY, Simon, 495
GRAZIANO, Rocky, obit., 585
GREECE, 139, **188–91**, 192, 193, 471, 540, 569, 579, 588, 591, 598, 599
GREEN, Ben, 487
GREEN, Michael, 519, 522
GREENAWAY, Peter, 498
GREENE, Graham, 520, 522
GREENE, Harold, 63
GREENLAND, 418
GRENADA, **98**, 428
GRIMSHAW, Nicholas, 510
GRIMSSON, Olafur Ragnar, 169–70
GRIST, Ian, MP, 47
GUADELOUPE, 143, 428
GUARE, John, 496
GUATEMALA, **87**, **89–90**, 579, 607
GUBBAY, Chief Justice Tony, 293
GUBENKO, Nikolai, 485
GUCCI, Aldo, obit., 585
GUERRA, Alfonso, 180
GUERRA, Juan, 180–1
GUILLAUME, Gilbert, 469
GUILLEM, Sylvie, 488
GUINEA, 264, **267**
GUINEA-BISSAU, 265, 266, **282**, 445, 468
GULF COOPERATION COUNCIL (GCC), 226, 227, 228, 250
GULF CRISIS (*see also* Iraq, Kuwait), Algeria, 241; AMU, 421; Argentina, 76; Australia, 376; Austria, 176; Belgium, 160; Belize, 97; Bulgaria, 132; Cameroon, 273; Canada, 73–4; Caribbean, 428; China, 9, 350, 353–4, 356, 386, 561, 566; chronology, 7–9; Denmark, 168; editorial, 1–6; EC, 400, 402–4, 405; Egypt, 204–6; ESCAP, 425; Ethiopia, 247; France, 8, 143, 144, 145, 208, 226, 386, 390, 403, 430, 442–3, 561; Gabon, 275; Greece, 192; Gulf states, 224–8; Hungary, 126; Indonesia, 343; Iran, 306–7, 308; Ireland, 165; Israel, 197, 198; Italy, 157–9; Japan, 364–5; Jordan, 207–9; Lebanon, 212; Libya, 233; Malaysia, 338; Malta, 187; Mauritania, 268; Mexico, 91; Morocco, 243; Netherlands, 162; Niger, 271; Nigeria, 260, 262; Non-Aligned, 411–2; Pakistan, 318; Philippines, 343; Poland, 115; Portugal, 185; Romania, 129; SAARC, 423; Saudi Arabia, 219–21; Senegal, 266; Singapore, 340; Somalia, 249; Sri Lanka, 323; Sudan, 229–30; Trinidad & Tobago, 96; Tunisia, 236–7; Turkey, 192–5; UK, 4, 7, 8, 9, 24–7, 29, 38, 43–4, 158, 208, 210, 215, 216, 217, 223, 226, 386, 388, 390, 403, 430, 442–3, 446, 561; UN, 1, 4–6, 7, 8, 9, 25–7, 29, 68–9, 73, 129, 132, 145, 158, 160, 165, 168, 176, 193, 198, 208, 215–8, 223, 224, 226, 236, 243, 247, 306, 338, 376, 386–90, 395, 397, 412, 419, 430, 561–6 (*texts*); USA, 4–6, 7, 8, 9, 52, 53, 59, 67–9, 158, 176, 192, 198, 203, 205–6, 207–8, 210, 215–8, 219–21, 223, 224, 225, 226, 233, 236, 241, 243, 247, 271, 318, 338, 350, 353–4, 356, 386, 387–90, 403, 430, 441, 442–3, 446–7, 561; USSR, 114, 386, 388–9, 390, 561; WEU, 442–3; Yemen, 221–3
GULF STATES, *see* Arab States of the Gulf
GUMMER, John Selwyn, MP, 576
GUNGAADORG, Sharavyn, 369
GÜRES, Gen. Dogan, 194
GURNEY, A. R., 495
GUTMAN, Yisrael, 450
GUYANA, 85, **93–5**, 399
GWYN, Peter, 518, 522
GYSI, Gregor, 154

HAAS, Bishop Wolfgang, 446
HABBASH, George, 203, 208
HABRÉ, Hissène, 232, 274, 608
HABYARIMANA, Maj.-Gen. Juvénal, President of Rwanda, 256, 281
HADDAOUI, Rafiq, 242
HADLEE, Sir Richard, 529
HAFIZ, Amin al-, 211
HAGER, Bengt, 491
HAIDER, Jörg, 177
HAINES, Janine, 373
HAITI, **86–7**, 94, 428, 595, 597, 609
HAITINK, Bernard, 489
HALL, Sir Peter, 495
HALPERIN, John, 521
HAMILTON, Ian, 523
HAMMER, Armand, obit., 585
HAMROUCHE, Mouloud, Prime Minister of Algeria, 239–40
HANDS, John, 515, 520
HANDS, Terry, 494–5
HANLEY, Ellery, 527
HANNIBALSSON, Jón Baldvin, 169
HANSON, Johnny, 258
HAQ, Wahidul, 319
HARBISON, John, 486
HARE, David, 493
HARMS, Mr Justice, 303–4
HARRIES, Rt Rev Richard, 446
HARRIS, Kenneth, 58
HARRIS, Robert, 521
HARRISON, Carey, 520
HARRISON, Sir Rex, death, 499; obit., 585
HARRISON, Tony, 494
HART-DAVIS, Duff, 519, 523
HARTNELL, Tony, 375
HARWOOD, Elizabeth, 484
HASHIMOTO, Ryutaro, 362
HASSAN II, HM King, of Morocco, 9, 145, 241–5, 420
HASSELL, Fey von, 522
HASTINGS, Gavin, 527
HATCH, N. O., 450
HAU PO-TSUN, Prime Minister of Taiwan, 357, 600

INDEX

HAUGHEY, Charles, Prime Minister of Irish Republic, 164, 166
HAVEL, Václav, President of Czechoslovakia, 120–3, 415, 445, 597–8
HAWATMEH, Naif, 203, 208, 214
HAWKE, Bob, Prime Minister of Australia, 372, 598
HAWKINS, Yusuf, 64
HAWLEY, Steve, 451
HAYMAN, Ronald, 521
HAYNE, Desmond, 529
HEAL, Sylvia, MP, 15
HEALEY, Denis, MP, 38
HEATH, Edward, MP, 8, 26, 41, 217, 606
HEATH-STUBBS, John, 520
HEKMATYAR, Gulbuddin, 309–10
HELLSTRÖM, Mats, 418
HELMS, Jesse, 58, 61
HEMMINGS, Eddie, 529
HENDRY, Stephen, 534
HENSON, Jim, death, 500; obit., 585
HENZE, Hans Werner, 484–5
HERATH, Harold, 323
HERBERT, David, 522
HERMANSSON, Steingrimur, Prime Minister of Iceland, 170
HERRERA HASSAN, Eduardo, 91
HERRIGEL, Otto, 295
HERSCU, George, 374
HEWSON, John, 373, 598
HESELTINE, Michael, MP, 12, 15, 39–42, 47, 511, 577, 608
HEYM, Stephen, 148
HIBBERT, Christopher, 522
HICKEL, Walter, 60
HIDOUCI, Ghazi, 240
HIJUELOS, Oscar, 517, 520
HILAIRE, Laurent, 488
HILLS, Carla, 578
HINSLEY, F. H., 522
HINZE, Russell, 375
HITCHENS, Christopher, 523
HO CHI MINH, 346
HOARE, Philip, 521
HOFSTADTER, Dr Robert, obit., 585
HOGGART, Richard, 522
HOLDEN, Anthony, 523
HOLKERI, Harri, Prime Minister of Finland, 175
HOLLINGWORTH, Clare, 519, 522
HOLLOWAY, Robin, 483, 487
HOLLWEG, Ilse, death, 484
HOLLYFIELD, Evander, 528
HOLMES À COURT, Robert, 374
HOLOMAN, D. Kern, 488
HOLOMISA, Gen. Bantu, 300
HONDURAS, **87, 90,** 468, 469
HONECKER, Erich, 146
HONEYGHAN, Lloyd, 528
HONG KONG, 334, 336, 338, 354, 355, 356, 358, **359–60,** 369, 596, 598, 599, 600
HOPE, Christopher, 515, 523
HOPKINSON, Sir Tom, obit., 585
HOPKIRK, Peter, 523
HORNE, Marilyn, 482
HORRIE, Chris, 519, 523

HOSS, Salim al-, 609
HOUPHOUËT-BOIGNY, Félix, President of Côte d'Ivoire, 269–70, 447, 607
HOWARD, Anthony, 518, 521
HOWARD, John, 373
HOWARD, Michael, MP, 11, 576–7, 595
HOWE, Sir Geoffrey, MP, 19, 32, 35–8, 79, 576, 607
HOXHA, Enver, 138
HOYTE, Desmond, President of Guyana, 95
HRAWI, Elias, President of Lebanon, 211–14, 609
HUGHES, Gwyn and Maureen, 495
HUGHES, Robert, 523
HUGHES, Simon, MP, 18
HUMBLE, Keith, 487
HUME, HE Cardinal Basil, 447
HUME, John, MP, 49
HUN SEN, Prime Minister of Kampuchea, 347–8
HUNGARY, 23, 32, 122, 123, **124–6,** 130, 158, 176, 361, 366, 401, 408, 410, 411, 414, 417, 431, 433, 434, 439, 444, 447, 471, 536, 569, 598, 601, 603, 605, 608
HUNT, David, MP, 11, 46–7, 576–7
HURD, Douglas, MP, 23, 26–7, 31–2, 37, 40–1, 43, 307, 359, 388, 420, 576–7, 606, 608
HURTADO MILLER, Juan Carlos, 83
HUSAIN, HM King, of Jordan, 7, 8, 9, 202–3, 207–9, 217, 220, 229, 389, 467, 604
HUSAIN, Saddam, *see under* Saddam Husain
HUSAINI, Faisal al, 200, 202
HUSSEIN ONN, Tun, obit., 585–6
HUTCHINSON, Max, 509, 511
HUTTON, Alister, 599
HUTTON, Sir Leonard, 530; obit., 586

IBRAHIM, Ilyas, 331
ICELAND, **169–70,** 416, 417, 569
IKIMI, Chief Tom, 260
ILIESCU, Ion, President of Romania, 128–30, 600–1
INAMURA, Toshiyuki, 365
INDIA, 2, **311–5,** 317–8, 319, 320, 321, 322, 325, 326, 331, 383, 387, 412, 422, 449, 499, 511, 529, 530, 581, 590, 591, 595, 600, 602, 606, 607
INDONESIA, 220, 340, **341–3,** 346, 347, 350, 356, 412, 423, 424, 538
INGRAO, Pietro, 155
INÖNÜ, Erdal, 194–5
INTERNATIONAL COURT OF JUSTICE (ICJ), 233, 275, **468–9**
INTERNATIONAL MONETARY FUND (IMF) (*see also* Debt Problems, World Bank), Africa, 254, 258, 262, 263, 269, 285, 289, 291, 332; Americas, 74, 78, 84, 93, 94, 95, 427; Arab world, 206, 209, 211, 230, 242; Asia, 318, 346; Europe, 122, 132, 134, 189, 401
IRAN, 8, 25, 63, 144, 165, 200, 210, 211, 212, 213, 214, 215, 216, 217, 220,

226–7, 230, **306–9**, 380, 389, 396, 397, 448, 513–4, 595, 603, 605
IRAQ, 1, 3–4, 6, 7, 8, 9, 24–7, 43, 52, 67–9, 73, 114, 122, 129, 145, 158, 162, 165, 176, 192, 193, 197, 198, 200, 201 (*map*), 202–3, 204, 205, 206, 207, 208, 210, 211, 212, **215–8,** 219–21, 222, 223, 224–8, 229–30, 236–7, 241, 243, 247, 249, 250, 260, 262, 266, 268, 306–7, 308, 318, 338, 340, 343, 356, 364, 370, 376, 386–90, 396, 402, 403, 411, 412, 419, 423, 430, 442, 449, 514, 538, 561–6, 597, 598, 602, 603–9
IRELAND, Jill, death, 499
IRELAND, NORTHERN, *see* Northern Ireland
IRELAND, REPUBLIC OF, 48–9, 51, 134, **164–7**, 183, 213, 296, 400, 408, 447, 516, 526, 527, 531, 534, 569, 581, 588, 589, 607
IRWIN, Hale, 531
ISAKSON, Johnny, 59
ISLAMIC CONFERENCE ORGANIZATION (ICO), 266
ISLAMIC FUNDAMENTALISM, 95, 145, 195, 203, 205, 207, 209, 212–4, 222, 229, 234–5, 237–40, 242, 307–8, 309–11, 317, 342, 448, 449, 513–4
ISRAEL, 4, 5, 7, 8, 9, 101, 122, 190, **196–200**, 202, 203, 204, 207, 209, 210, 212, 213, 214, 215, 216, 217, 223, 232, 243, 247, 390–3, 396, 402, 404, 447–8, 514, 597, 600, 601, 606, 609
ITALY, 66, 122, 134, 138, **155–9,** 176, 183, 361, 389, 404, 408, 442, 443, 447, 472, 498, 504, 511, 525, 526, 532, 535, 539, 544, 569, 583, 585, 588, 589, 590, 592, 603, 606
ITURRALDE BALLIVIÁN, Carlos, 77
IVANOVA, Veronika, 490
IVASHKO, Vladimir, 601
IVORY COAST, *see* Côte d'Ivoire

JABIR AL-AHMAD AL-JABIR AS-SABAH, Emir of Kuwait, 7, 225, 389, 603
JACKSON, Colin, 528–9
JACKSON, Rev Jesse, 61, 217
JACOBI, Lotte, death, 508
JACOBS, Eric, 10
JAFFÉ, Nigel A., 491
JAGAN, Cheddi, 95
JAMAICA, **92–3**, 398, 412, 427, 428
JAMES, P. D., 513
JANKOWITSCH, Dr Peter, 178
JAPAN, **360–5;** arts, 499; broadcasting, 504; economy, 362, 408, 538, 539, 540; enthronement, 363–4, 449; environment, 464, 465; external relations, 8, 66, 177, 186, 208, 230, 312, 334, 340, 346, 347, 349, 350, 353, 366, 368, 371, 381, 384, 389, 397, 407, 424, 427; politics, 361, 364–5; scandals, 365; space, 453
JARAMILLO OSSA, Bernardo, 80
JARRETT, Tony, 529
JARUZELSKI, Gen. Wojciech, 117, 598
JATOI, Ghulam Mustapha, 316–17
JAWARA, Sir Dawda Kairaba, President of the Gambia, 263
JENKINS, Alan, 520
JENNINGS, Alex, 495
JENNINGS, Robert, 469
JI PENGFEI, 359
JIANG ZEMIN, General Secretary of Chinese Communist Party, 367
JIMÉNEZ DE ARÉCHAGA, Eduardo, 470
JINGME SINGYE WANGCHUK, HM King, of Bhutan, 325–6, 422
JOHN PAUL II, HH Pope, 122, 159, 187, 280–2, 445–6, 595, 599–600, 604, 607
JOHNSON, Prince Yormie, 264, 604
JOHNSTON, John, 523
JOLLY, Rob, 374
JONES, Ben, 98
JONES, Dame Gwynneth, 482
JONES, P. F., 450
JORDAN, 7, 8, 9, 202, 203, **207–9,** 217, 220, 229, 364, 389, 392, 393, 397, 403, 449, 467, 603, 604
JORDAN, Louis, 495
JOSEPH, Wilfred, 483
JOSPIN, Lionel, 141
JOVIC, Borisav, 135
JUDD, Alan, 517, 521
JUGNAUTH, Sir Aneerood, Prime Minister of Mauritius, 327–8

KACZYNSKI, Jaroslaw, 117
KADARE, Ismail, 138
KADRI, Abdullah, 242
KADZAMIRA, Cecilia, 291
KAGAN, Oleg, obit., 586
KAHANE, Rabbi Meir, death, 198, 203, 448, 607
KAHVECI, Adnan, 194
KAIFU, Toshiki, Prime Minister of Japan, 312, 360–5, 371, 596
KAMBA, Walter, 293
KAMIL JAFFAR, Datuk Nik, 397
KAMPUCHEA, 66, 67, 343, 346, **347–8,** 356, 363, 387, 393, 423, 597
KANEMARU, Shin, 368
KANG YUNG-HOON, 366–7
KANTOR, Tadeusz, death, 508
KAPOLKAS, Donald, 384
KAPOOR, Anish, 506
KAPUSCINSKI, Ryszard, 519, 523
KARAMANLIS, Konstantinos, President of Greece, 189, 599
KARAMI, Omar, 214, 609
KARJALAINEN, Dr Ahti, obit., 586
KASHOGGI, Adnan, 220
KASSEBAUM, Senator Nancy, 61
KAUFMAN, Gerald, MP, 27, 29
KAUNDA, Kenneth, President of Zambia, 288, 290, 597
KAURISMAKI, Aki, 499
KAVANAGH, P. J., 522
KAWASHIMA, Kiko, 363
KAWAWA, Rashidi, 254
KAYE, M. M., 518, 522

KEITH, Kenneth, 470
KEMP, Jack, 578
KENDALL, Henry, 459
KENDALL-CARPENTER, John, obit., 586
KENILOREA, Sir Peter, 384
KENNARD, George, 522
KENNEDY, Arthur, death, 499
KENNEDY, Senator Edward, 61, 69
KENNEDY, Ian, 455
KENNEDY, Ludovic, 523
KENYA, 229, **250–3**, 255, 284, 447, 596, 602
KENYON, Ian R., 394
KERR, Philip, 523
KEREKOU, Brig.-Gen. Mathieu, President of Benin, 272
KESWICK, Sir William ('Tony'), obit., 586
KHAMENEI, Ayatollah Ali, 307, 448
KHAN, Maj.-Gen. Nuruddin, 319
KHAN, Ghulam Ishaq, President of Pakistan, 316, 603
KHAN, Sahibzada Yaqub, 317
KHELIL, Ismail, 234, 236
KHOMEINI, Ayatollah Sayyed Ruhollah, 513
KIBONA, Stephen, 253
KIDD, Charles, 523
KIM IL SUNG, President of N. Korea, 291, 366
KIMARIO, Maj.-Gen. Muhiddin, 253
KING, Don, 527–8
KING, Francis, 520
KING, Tom, MP, 9, 24, 576–7
KINGIBE, Alhaji Babagan, 260
KINGSMAN, Alan, 456
KINGSMAN, Sue, 456
KINNOCK, Neil, MP, 13–14, 21–2, 26, 28–30, 34, 42, 49
KIRIBATI, **382, 384**
KIRNER, Joan, 374
KIS, János, 125
KISZCZAK, Gen. Czeslaw, 116
KITE, Tom, 531
KITINGAN, Datuk Joseph Pairan, 337
KIYONGA, Crispus, 256
KLAUS, Václav, 121
KLIBI, Chedli, 202, 236
KLIMA, Ivan, 517, 520
KNAPMAN, Roger, MP, 31
KOCHNO, Boris, death, 491
KOHL, Helmut, Chancellor of Federal Republic of Germany, 9, 33, 114, 118, 122, 148, 151–3, 354, 400, 404, 432, 434, 596–7, 599, 602, 607–8
KOIVISTO, Mauno, President of Finland, 174
KOLODZIEJCZYK, Piotr, 116
KAYSONE PHOMIVANE, Prime Minister of Laos, 349
KEATING, Paul, 375
KEENAN, Brian, 48, 51, 165, 604
KOLINGBA, Gen. André, 275
KOLTAI, Ralph, 489
KOMOÉ, Moïse Koffi, 269
KONAN-BÉDIE, Henri, 270
KOPP, Elisabeth and Hans, 178

KOREA, DEMOCRATIC PEOPLE'S REPUBLIC OF (North Korea), 291, 366, **367–8**, 604
KOREA, REPUBLIC OF (South Korea), 123, 334, 355, 362–3, **365–7**, 368, 369, 538, 594, 601, 604
KOZLOWSKI, Krzysztof, 116
KREAMER, Peter, 509
KREISKY, Dr Bruno, death, 176; obit., 586
KRIER, Leon, 509
KRYUCHKOV, Vladimir, 609
KUCZYNSKI, Waldemar, 115
KUPFER, Harry, 484
KUO, Shirley, 357
KURDISH QUESTION, 195
KUREISHI, Hanif, 516, 520
KUROSAWA, Akira, 499
KUWAIT, 1, 3–4, 5, 6, 7, 8, 9, 24–7, 38, 43, 52, 67–9, 73, 114, 145, 158, 162, 165, 176, 192, 193, 197, 200, 201 (*map*), 202–3, 204, 205, 206, 207, 208, 209, 210, 211, 215–8, 219–21, 222, **224–8**, 229–30, 236–7, 241, 243, 247, 249, 260, 266, 268, 306–7, 308, 318, 340, 343, 356, 364, 370, 386–90, 402, 403, 411, 412, 419, 430, 467, 514, 538, 561–6, 583, 602, 603–9

LACALLE HERRERA, Luis Alberto, President of Uruguay, 82, 84
LACAYO, Raúl, 89
LACOUTURE, Jean, 518, 521
LAFONTAINE, Oskar, 153
LAGERFELD, Karl, 512
LAHUD, Gen., 213
LAL, Devi, 313–14
LALONDE, Brice, 465
LAMBERT, Gavin, 521
LAMONT, Norman, MP, 42–3, 545, 576–7, 608
LANCASTER, Mark, 489
LANDSBERGIS, Vitantis, 597, 599
LANG, David, 485
LANG, Ian, MP, 42, 45, 577
LANGE, David, 380
LANGER, Bernhard, 531
LAOS, **348–9**
LAPINE, James, 495–6
LAQUEUR, Walter, 521
LARIDH, Ali, 234–5
LARKIN, Philip, 519
LARSEN, Leif, obit., 586
LARSSON, Allan, 173
LATIN AMERICAN ORGANIZATIONS, 96, **425–7**
LATVIA, 599
LAURENSON, James, 494
LAW AND LEGAL MATTERS, European Community law, 31, 401, 406, **471–4**; international law, 233, 275, 415, **468–71**; UK law, 415, **474–7**; US law, 61–2, **479–81**
LAWRENCE, Ashley, death, 491
LAWRENCE, Carmen, 374
LAWSON, Nigel, MP, 14, 34, 38
LE DUC THO, death, 346; obit., 587

LE PEN, Jean-Marie, 141, 239
LEADBETTER, David, 530
LEBANON, 65, 144, 145, 210, 211, **212–4**, 216, 307, 386, 396, 514, 604, 606, 608, 609
LEE HSIEN LOONG, Brig.-Gen., 339–40
LEE KUAN YEW, 339–40, 356, 608
LEE TENG-HUI, President of Taiwan, 357
LEHMANN, Rosamond, death, 519; obit., 587
LEIGH GUZMÁN, Gen. Gustavo, 79
LEKHANYA, Maj.-Gen. Justin, Head of Government of Lesotho, 297–8
LEMOND, Greg, 534
LENDL, Ivan, 532–3
LENIHAN, Brian, 166, 607
LEÓN GÓMEZ, Carlos Pizarro, 80
LÉOTARD, François, 140
LESOTHO, **297–8**
LETELIER, Orlando, 79
LETSIE, Col. Sekhobe, 297
LETSIE, Col. Thaabe, 297
LEVI, Peter, 517, 520, 521
LEVI, Primo, 520
LEVI, Wayne, 531
LEVY, David, 601
LEWIS, Richard, death, 484
LEZHNINA, Larissa, 490
LI PENG, Prime Minister of China, 340, 350–1, 354, 356, 359, 367, 599
LI SHUXIAN, 350
LIAQUAT ALI KHAN, Begum Raana, obit., 587
LIBERIA, 258, 261, 262, 263, **264–5**, 267, 270, 421, 456, 582, 603, 604
LIBERIA PETERS, Maria, Prime Minister of Netherlands Antilles, 104
LIBYA, 144, 187, 202, 204, **231–3**, 247, 249, 270, 274, 302, 420, 468, 598
LIECHTENSTEIN, 387, 416, 569
LIEN CHAN, 357
LILBURN, Douglas, 487
LILLEY, Peter, MP, 22, 576–7, 602
LILOV, Aleksandar, 131–2
LIM, Paul, 534
LINEKER, Gary, 526
LINI, Walter, Prime Minister of Vanuatu, 384
LITERATURE, **513–24**
LITHUANIA, 66, 595, 597, 599, 600, 602
LLERAS CAMARGO, Dr Alberto, obit., 587
LLOREDA, Rodrigo, 81
LLOYD WEBBER, Andrew, 495
LO-JOHANNSON, Ivar, obit., 587
LOADES, David, 523
LOCKWOOD, Margaret, obit., 587
LOCKWOOD, Stuart, 500
LOGORECI, Anton, obit., 587
LONCAR, Budimir, 412
LONG, Richard A., 491
LÓPEZ ALBÚJAR, Gen. Enrique, 83
LÓPEZ PORTILLO, Gustavo, 91
LOSS, Joe, obit., 587
LOY, Rosetta, 517, 520
LUBOWSKI, Anton, 295
LÜDER, Italo, 75

LUJAN, Manuel, 578
LUKANOV, Andrei, 131–3, 596, 608
LUNYOV, Alexander, 490
LUTCHMEENARAIDOO, Seetanah, 327
LUXEMBOURG, **163**, 442, 569
LYNCH, David, 497
LYNN, Jonathan, 498

McADAM, Keith, 456
McBEAN, Angus, death, 491
MacCAIG, Norman, 520
McCARTNEY, Paul, 487
McCARTHY, John, 165
MacCORMAC, Richard, 509–10
McCRAY, Antron, 65
McCULLIN, Don, 519, 522
McCUSKER, Harold, MP, 49
MacDONALD, Flora, 399
MacDONALD, Malcolm, 488
MacDONALD, George, 520
MacDONOGH, Giles, 521
MACÉ, Gabriel, obit., 587
McEWAN, Ian, 520
MacFARLANE, John, 489
McGAHERN, John, 516, 520
McGEECHAN, Ian, 527
MacGREGOR, John, MP, 37, 576–7
MACK, Mirna, 90
MACKAY OF CLASHFERN, Lord, 576–7
McKEAN, Tom, 529
McKELLEN, Sir Ian, 493
McKIBBEN, Bill, 523
McKINNON, Don, 381
MACLEAN, Lord, obit., 587–8
MACLEOD, Iseabail, 523
MacMILLAN, Sir Kenneth, 488, 491
McMURTRY, Roy, 398
McNULTY, Mark, 530
MACQUARRIE, J., 449
MacSHARRY, Ray, 164, 406
MADAGASCAR, 327, **332**, 469, 600
MADANI, Abassi, 240
MADAR, Mohamed Hawatie, Prime Minister of Somalia, 248
MADONNA, 487
MAGA, Hubert, 272
MAGAE, Festus, 296
MAGHREB, *see* Arab Maghreb Union
MAGOCHE, Emmanuel, 292
MAHATHIR MOHAMAD, Dr, Prime Minister of Malaysia, 337–8, 340, 398, 606
MAHDI, Mubarak al-, 229
MAHDI, Sayyid Sadiq al-, 229
MAHJUB, Rifa'at, death, 205, 606
MAJOR, John, MP, Prime Minister of UK, 11, 14, 31, 33–37, 40–2, 42–4, 47, 49, 210, 404, 544, 545, 576–7, 608–9
MAKAROVA, Natalia, 488
MAKHALINA, Yulia, 490
MAKOTO, Tanabe, 368
MALAMUD, Bernard, 520
MALAN, Gen. Magnus, 304
MALAN, Rian, 515, 522
MALAWI, 285, **290–1**
MALAYSIA, **337–8**, 340, 387, 390, 392,

397, 398, 412, 413, 424, 538, 561, 579, 585–6, 600, 606
MALCOLM, Devon, 529
MALDIVES, **331**, 422–3
MALECELA, John, Prime Minister of Tanzania, 253
MALI, 264, **267–8**, 465
MALLON, Seamus, 49
MALTA, **187–8**, 386, 399, 472, 569
MAMALONI, Solomon, Prime Minister of Solomon Islands, 384
MANDAL, B. P., 312
MANDELA, Nelson, 24–5, 288, 292, 299–305, 394, 398, 420, 515, 596, 599, 602
MANDELA, Winnie, 605
MANGANO, Silvano, death, 499
MANLEY, Michael, Prime Minister of Jamaica, 93
MANN, Simranjit Singh, 314–15
MANSELL, Nigel, 532
MANZ, Johannes, 244
MAPPLETHORPE, Robert, 508
MARA, Ratu Sir Kamisese, Prime Minister of Fiji, 381
MARADONA, Diego, 525
MARBLE, Alice, obit., 588
MARCHAIS, Georges, 141
MARCOS, Ferdinand, 344
MARCOS, Imelda, 602
MARGERIE, Roland de, obit., 588
MARGRETHE, HM Queen, of Denmark, 491
MARKOVIC, Ante, Prime Minister of Yugoslavia, 133–5
MARKOWITZ, Harry, 540
MARKWELL, James, 54
MARSHALL ISLANDS, 383, 385
MARTIN, Lee, 526
MARTIN, Lynn, 578
MARTINEZ, Bob, 59–60
MARTINIQUE, 428
MARTYN, Barrie, 488
MASIRE, Quett, President of Botswana, 296–7
MASLEN, John, 411
MASSERA, Admiral Emilio, 75
MASSIE, Allan, 517, 520
MASSUD, Ahmed Shah, 310
MATAR, Faoud, 521
MATIBA, Kenneth, 251
MATTERS, Arnold, death, 484
MATTHAUS, Lothar, 526
MATTHEWS, John, 523
MATTHUS, Siegfried, 483
MATTOX, Jim, 58
MAUDE, Francis, MP, 186, 354
MAURITANIA, 265, 266, **268–9**, 420, 465
MAURITIUS, **327–8**
MAW, Nicholas, 484, 487
MAYOR, Federico, 396
MAZILU, Dumitru, 127
MAZOWIECKI, Tadeusz, Prime Minister of Poland, 115–8, 415, 609
MBA-ABESSOLE, Fr, 275
M'DAGHRI, Moulay Driss Alaoui, 242

MÉDECIN, Jacques, 141
MEDICINE AND MEDICAL RESEARCH (*see also* AIDS), **454–8**
MEDITERRANEAN, 183, 187, 413
MELLOR, David, MP, 502, 577
MELNIKOV, Kirill, 490
MENDES, Frederico, 527
MENEM, Carlos Sául, President of Argentina, 75–6, 525
MENEM, Eduardo, 75
MENEM, Zulema Yoma de, 75
MENGISTU HAILE-MARYAM, Lt. Col., President of Ethiopia, 246–7, 597
MENINGA, Mal, 527
MENNINGER, Dr Karl, obit., 588
MERBAH, Kasdi, 240
MERCER, Derrik, 523
MERINO, Dan, 534
MESIC, Stjepan, 135
METCALF, John, 483
MEXICO, 89, **91–2**, 358, 412, 424, 428, 515, 600
MEYER, Sir Anthony, MP, 39, 47
MEYERS, Jeffrey, 521
MFANASIBLI, Prince, 298
MHANGO, Mkwaptira, 291
MICHAEL, ex-King of Romania, 129
MICHAELS, Leonard, 521
MICHEL, James, 329
MICHIKO, HM Empress, of Japan, 364
MIDDLETON, Drew, obit., 588
MIKHAILOVICH ALEKSI, Patriarch, 444
MILES, Barry, 521
MILITARU, Gen. Nicolae, 127
MILKEN, Michael, 541
MILLER, Arthur, 492, 494
MILLER, Jonathan, 492
MILLER, Judith, 514, 523
MILLER, Merton, 540
MILLER, Zell, 59–60
MILOSEVIC, Slobodan, 135, 609
MINOTIS, Alexis, obit., 588
MIRGHANI, Sayydi Muhammed Otham al-, 229
MITCHELL, James, Prime Minister of St Vincent, 101
MITCHELL, Theo, 58, 60
MITRA, Ramon, 344
MITSOTAKIS, Konstantinos, 188–90, 598
MITTERRAND, Danielle, 244
MITTERRAND, François, President of France, 122, 140–1, 144–5, 319, 330, 332, 384, 400, 404, 422, 599–600
MKAPA, Benjamin, 253
MLADENOV, Petar, 131–2, 602
MOBUTU SESE SEKO, President of Zaïre, 278–9, 286
MOCK, Dr Alois, 178
MODROW, Hans, 146–7
MOHAMMAD, Shaoib, 530
MOI, Daniel Arap, President of Kenya, 250–1
MOKHANTSO, Col. Monyane, 297
MOLTKE, Helmuth James von, 519, 522
MOLYNEAUX, James, 48

MOMOH, Joseph Saidu, President of Sierra Leone, 262
MONACO, 569
MONDELLO, Keith, 64–5
MONGOLIA, **368–71,** 409, 410, 424, 445, 595, 599, 603, 604, 605
MONK, Ray, 517–8, 521
MONTANA, Claude, 512
MONTEGRIFFO, Peter, 186
MONTSERRAT, **103,** 428
MONZON, Pierre, 525
MOORE, Brian, 516, 520
MOORE, Michael, 378–9, 604
MOORHOUSE, Adrian, 528
MORAVIA, Alberto, 517, 520; obit., 588
MORE O'FERRALL, Roderick, obit., 588
MOREIRA, Tavares, 184
MOREIRA, Vital, 184
MORGAN, Edwin, 520
MORGAN, Kenneth O., 523
MORGAN, Peter, 21
MORGAN, Gen. Said Hirsi, 249
MORGAN, Ted, 523
MORHANGE-BÉGUÉ, Claude, 519, 522
MOROCCO, 9, 145, 203, 232, **241–4,** 245, 268, 394, 420–1, 467
MORPURGO, J. E., 522
MORRIS, Mark, 490
MOSBACHER, Robert, 578
MOSER, Charles A., 521
MOSHOESHOE II, HM King, formerly of Lesotho, 297–8
MOSLEY, Nicholas, 516, 520
MOSOEUNYANE, Col. Khetang, 297
MOTHOPENG, Zephania, obit., 588
MOYNIHAN, Senator Daniel, 54
MOYNIHAN, Rodrigo, death, 508; obit., 588–9
MOZAMBIQUE, 253, **283–5,** 445–6, 603, 607
MSWATI III, HM King, of Swaziland, 298
MUBARAK, Husni, President of Egypt, 7, 8, 204–5, 210, 216, 222, 232, 420, 599
MUGABE, Robert, President of Zimbabwe, 292–3, 598
MUGE, Bishop Alexander, death, 251, 447
MUGGERIDGE, Malcolm, obit., 589
MUIR, Frank, 524
MUKAHAMEDOV, Irek, 488
MULDOON, Sir Robert, 379
MULLEN, Richard, 518, 521
MÜLLER, Dr Gebhard, obit., 589
MULRONEY, Brian, Prime Minister of Canada, 70–2
MUMFORD, Lewis, obit., 589
MUNRO, Alice, 516, 520
MUNTASSIR, Omar Mustafa al-, 231
MURDOCH, Rupert, 500–1
MURRAY, Joseph, 458
MURRAY, Yvonne, 528
MUSAVI, Husain, 213
MUSEVENI, Yoweri, President of Uganda, 255, 257, 281, 420
MUSIC, 167, **484–8**
MUTI, Riccardo, 483
MUWANGA, Paulo, 257
MUZENDA, Simon, 292–3

MWINYI, Ali Hassan, President of Tanzania, 253–4
MYANMAR (BURMA), **333–5,** 449, 600
MYLROIE, Laurie, 514, 523

NABOKOV, Dmitri, 522
NACCACHE, Anis, 144
NADIR, Asil, 192
NAGY, Gyula, 444
NAGY, Ivan, 489
NAIFEH, Steven, 518, 521
NAIPAUL, V. S., 524
NAJIBULLAH, Mohammed, President of Afghanistan, 309–11, 597
NAKAYAMA, Taro, 349, 362, 389
NAMALIU, Rabbie, Prime Minister of Papua New Guinea, 378
NAMIBIA, **295–6,** 297, 319, 387, 393, 398, 413, 420, 421, 596, 598
NAMUTH, Hans, 508
NANNINI, Alessandro, 532
NAPIER, Priscilla, 523
NARAYAN, R. K., 520
NASSER, Khalid, 205
NASSER AL-KIDWAR, 392
NAURU, 425
NAVARRO WOLFF, Antonio, 81
NAVRATILOVA, Martina, 533
NEAOUTYINE, Paul, 383
NÉMETH, Miklós, 414
NEPAL, **324–5,** 422, 598, 599
NETANYAHU, Benjamin, 391
NETHERLANDS, THE, 102, 103, 104, **161–2,** 403, 442, 464, 505–6, 511, 526, 530, 569, 600
NETHERLANDS ANTILLES, **104**
NEUMEIER, John, 490
NEW CALEDONIA, **382–4,** 425
NEW ZEALAND, 144, 219, **378–82,** 469–70, 487, 489, 504, 527, 528, 529, 530, 540, 604, 606
NEWSOM, Lloyd, 490
NEWTON, Anthony, MP, 576–7
NEZZAR, Maj.-Gen. Khaled, 239
NGEI, Paul Joseph, 252
NGUEMA MBASOGO, Col. Teodoro Obiang, President of Equatorial Guinea, 277
NGUYEN CO THACH, 336, 346
NGUYEN VAN LINH, 346
NICARAGUA, 63, 86, **87–9,** 358, 447, 468–9, 597, 599
NICHOLAS, Sir David, 500
NICHOLLS, C. S., 521
NICKLAUS, Jack, 530
NIE, Yanfu, 455
NIGER, 268, **271**
NIGERIA, 258, **259–62,** 264, 265, 272, 274, 277, 398, 412, 420, 599
NIKITIN, Vladilen, 371
NIMLEY, Gen. David, 264
NKOMO, Joshua, 293
NKRUMAH, Kwame, 258
NO CHE BONG, 367
NOBEL PRIZES,
economics, 540

INDEX

literature, 515
peace, 114, 606
sciences and medicine, 458–9
NOBLE, Adrian, 494
NOIR, Michel, 140–1
NON-ALIGNED MOVEMENT, 3, **411–3**
NONO, Luigi, death, 484, 488; obit., 589
NORDIC COUNCIL, **417–8**
NORIEGA MORENO, Gen. Manuel, 52, 90–1, 595
NORMAN, Denis, 292
NORMAN, Geraldine, 504
NORMAN, Greg, 531
NORMAN, Jessye, 483
NORTH, Lt.-Col. Oliver, 62–3
NORTH ATLANTIC TREATY ORGANIZATON (NATO) (*see also* Arms Control, Western European Union), 3, 23–24, 31–2, 53–4, 67, 114, 123, 151, 158, 164, 168, 182, 183, 192, 193, 194, 405, 415, **430–40**, 442–3, 597, 601, 602
NORTHERN IRELAND, **48–51**, 165–6, 606
NORWAY, **171–2**, 252, 389, 397, 416, 417, 418, 464, 540, 569, 586, 607
NOVAK, C., 450
NOYCE, Robert, obit., 589
NUCCI, Christian, 141
NUJOMA, Sam, President of Namibia, 295, 420, 596
NUREYEV, Rudolf, 491
NYERERE, Dr Julius, 254, 412, 420

Ó FIAICH, HE Cardinal, death, 48, 447; obit., 589
OAKESHOTT, Prof. Michael, obit., 589–90
OBANDO Y BRAVO, HE Cardinal Miguel, 89
OBITUARIES, **579–94**
OBOTE, Milton, 257
O'BRIEN, Edna, 520
O'BRIEN, Timothy, 495
O'BRIEN, Vincent, 533
O'NEILL OF THE MAINE, Lord, obit., 590
OCCHETTO, Achille, 155–6
OCHIRBAT, Gombojavyn, 369, 371
OCHIRBAT, Punsalmaagiyn, President of Mongolia, 369–71, 599, 604
ODINGA, Oginga, 251
OFFIAH, Martin, 527
OGATA, Sadako, 397
OIL (*see also* Organization of Petroleum Exporting Countries), 86, 96, 97, 115, 129, 132, 159, 174–5, 193, 202, 206, 208, 211, 215, 216, 219, 220, 224–8, 231–2, 240, 260–1, 275, 308, 342, 346, 539
OKULLU, Bishop John, 447
OLAZABAL, José-Maria, 531
OMAN, **224, 226–8**, 307
ONASSIS, Jacqueline Kennedy, 512
ONG TENG CHEONG, 339
OPERA, **482–4**, 485, 487
OQUELÍ COLINDRES, Héctor, 89
ORGANIZATION FOR ECONOMIC COOPERATION AND DEVELOPMENT (OECD), 189, **407–8**, 538, 539, 540

ORGANIZATION OF AFRICAN UNITY (OAU), 244, 257, 266, 281, 394, **419–21**
ORGANIZATION OF AMERICAN STATES (OAS), **425–6**
ORGANIZATION OF PETROLEUM EXPORTING COUNTRIES (OPEC) (*see also* Oil), 8, 216, 224, 230, 540
ORKAR, Maj. Gideon N., 259
ORTEGA SAAVEDRA, Daniel, 89, 597
OSBORNE, John, 103
OUATTARA, Alassane, Prime Minister of Côte d'Ivoire, 269–70
OUEDDEYE, Goukouni, 274
OUEDRAOGO, Idrissa, 499
OUKO, Dr Robert, death, 250–1, 596
OUMAR, Acheikh Ibn, 233
OWEN, Dr David, MP, 19
OZ, Amos, 514, 523
ÖZAL, Turgut, President of Turkey, 193–4
OZBEK, Rifat, 512

PACIFIC REGION, 381, **382–5, 425,** 538
PACKER, Kerry, 374
PADFIELD, Peter, 523
PAEINIU, Bikenibeu, Prime Minister of Tuvalu, 384
PAGE, Ashley, 488–9
PAISLEY, Rev Ian, 48
PAKDEMIRLI, Ekrem, 194
PAKISTAN, 2, 307, 309, 310, 312, **315–8,** 422, 448, 449, 529, 530, 587, 595, 600, 601, 603, 604, 606
PALAU, *see* Belau
PALESTINE LIBERATION ORGANIZATION (PLO), 197, 202, 203, 211, 214, 226, 302, 391
PALESTINIAN PEOPLE, 8, 26, 27, 145, 197–200, 202, 203, 204, 205, 207, 210, 211, 214, 216, 218, 225, 226, 338, 386, 388, 390–3, 412, 448, 606
PALEY, William S., obit., 590
PALMER, Geoffrey, 379, 604
PALUMBO, Peter, 510
PALUTNIK, Jean, 465
PANAMA, 52, 54, **88, 90–1,** 97, 396, 426, 491, 595
PANCRAZI, Jean-Noel, 515, 520
PANDIT, Mrs Vijaya Lakshmi, death, 315; obit., 590
PANKOVA, Yelena, 490
PANUFNIK, Andrzej, 486
PAPANDREOU, Andreas, 188–9
PAPP, Bishop Laszlo, 444
PAPUA NEW GUINEA, **377–8,** 424
PARADJANOV, Sergei, obit., 590
PARAGUAY, **82,**
PARIS, Barry, 521
PARISH, Daphne, 25
PARKER, Tony, 524
PARKINSON, Cecil, MP, 22, 42, 576–7
PARKINSON, Norman, death, 508, 513
PARKS, Mama Lu, 491
PARRETTI, Giancarlo, 497
PÄRT, Arvo, 487
PARTRIDGE, Frances, 522
PASCAL-TROUILLOT, Ertha, 86, 597

PASHKO, Gramos, 139
PASQUA, Charles, 141
PASSARINHO, Jarbas, 78
PASTERNAK, Evgeny, 521
PATTEN, Christopher, MP, 12, 16, 35, 42, 510–11, 576–7
PATTERSON, Percival, 93
PAVAROTTI, Luciano, 482
PAZ, Octavio, 515
PAZ ZAMORA, Jaime, President of Bolivia, 77, 426
PEACOCK, Andrew, 598
PEASE, Henry, 83
PELLI, Cesar, 510
PENDERECKI, Krzysztof, 483
PENSTON, Dr Michael, obit., 590
PENTAGONALE, 122, 126, 158, 603
PEREIRA, Aristides, President of Cape Verde, 282
PERES, Shimon, 196–7, 200, 204, 597
PÉREZ, Carlos Andrés, President of Venezuela, 85, 426
PÉREZ DE CUELLAR, Javier, UN Secretary- General, 8, 9, 139, 244–5, 386–96, 470, 604
PERRAULT, Gilles, 243
PERTINI, Sandro, death, 159; obit., 590
PERU, 80, **83–4,** 358, 412, 424, 426, 427, 596, 600, 601
PERUMAL, Varadaraja, 321
PETERS, Clarke, 495
PETERS, Winston, 379, 381
PETERSEN, Jack, obit., 590
PETERSON, David, 73
PETHERBRIDGE, Deanna, 489
PHILIPPINES, 209, **343–5,** 358, 424, 538, 602
PICASSO, Jacqueline, 507
PICKERING, Thomas R., 387, 578
PICKFORD, Errol, 488
PIGGOTT, Lester, 533
PIMEN, HH Patriarch, death, 444; obit., 590
PINDLING, Sir Lynden, Prime Minister of the Bahamas, 99
PINOCHET UGARTE, Gen. Augusto, 79
PINTER, Harold, 448, 495
PIPE, Martin, 534
PIPER, Sir David, obit., 590–1
PIQUET, Nelson, 532
PLAKA, Sokrat, 190
PLATT, David, 526
PLOWRIGHT, Joan, 492
POCHIN, Sir Edward, obit., 591
POCOCK, Tom, 519, 521
POHIVA, Akilisi, 384
PÖHL, Karl-Otto, 38
POINDEXTER, John M., 62–3, 601
POLAND, **114–8,** 123, 126, 144, 151–2, 158, 176, 361, 401, 408, 410, 411, 414, 415, 417, 431, 439, 447, 471, 486, **536–8,** 566, 569, 592, 596, 598, 599, 600, 607, 609
POLHILL, Robert, 65, 213, 599
POLOZKOV, Ivan, 111
POPOV, Dimitar, 133

PORCA, Francesca, 157
PORTA, Hugo, 527
PORTUGAL, 182, **183–5,** 287, 569
POWELL, Anthony, 518, 521
POWELL, Enoch, 520
POWELL, Janet, 373
POWELL, Michael, death, 500; obit., 591
PRABHAKARAN, Vellupillai, 321
PRAMUAL SABHAVASU, 335
PREBBLE, Richard, 380
PREFERENTIAL TRADE AREA (PTA), 421
PREMADASA, Ranasinghe, President of Sri Lanka, 323
PRIBYL, Vilem, death, 484
PRICE, George, Prime Minister of Belize, 97
PRIMAKOV, Yevgeny, 8, 218, 606
PRITCHETT, V. S., 516, 520, 522
PROST, Alain, 531–2
PRUNSKIENE, Kazimiera, 600
PRUSINER, Stanley, 457
PUCCI, Emilio, 512
PUGO, Boris, 608
PUIG, Manuel, obit., 591
PŪREV, Jambyn, 371
PŪREVDORJ, Choyjilsürengiyn, 370
PUTTNAM, David, 498
PYNCHON, Thomas, 517, 520

QABOOS BIN SAID, Sultan, 227
QADAFI, Col. Muammar, Libyan leader, 144, 204, 231–3, 302
QARWI, Dr Hamid, Prime Minister of Tunisia, 236
QATAR, **224,** 226, 227
QIAN QICHEN, 220, 353–4
QUARSHIGAH, Maj. Courage, 258
QUAYLE, Anthony, 518, 522
QUAYLE, J. Danforth, Vice-President of USA, 221, 340, 578

RABAN, Jonathan, 524
RABIN, Yitzhak, 197
RACIAL AND ETHNIC CONFLICT, Austria, 176, 177; Belgium, 160; Bhutan, 326; Bolivia, 77; Burundi, 280; Cameroon, 273; Canada, 70–1, 72; Cyprus, 191, 193; Czechoslovakia, 119, 121; E. Europe, 119, 121, 126, 128, 130, 132, 134–7, 139, 152, 154–5, 447; Ethiopia, 246–8; Fiji, 383; France, 141–2, 447; Germany, 447; Greece, 188, 190; Guinea-Bissau, 282; India, 311–5; Israel, 198, 200, 448; Italy, 156, 447; Kenya, 251; Lebanon, 212–4; Malaysia, 337–8; Mali, 268; Mauritania, 269; Mauritius, 328; Myanmar, 334; Netherlands, 162; New Caledonia, 383–4; New Zealand, 381; Niger, 271; Rwanda, 281; Senegal, 266; South Africa, 299–305; Sri Lanka, 321–3; Sweden, 447; Switzerland, 179–80; Turkey, 195; UK, 26, 447; USA, 58–9, 61, 63–5; USSR, 1, 2, 106, 109–11; Yugoslavia, 134–7
RADU, Nicolae, 128

INDEX

RAE, Bob, 73
RAFSANJANI, Hojatolislam Hashemi, President of Iran, 210, 217, 306–7
RAHMAN, Lt.-Gen. Atiqur, 319
RAHMAN, Sheikh Mujibur, 320
RAINE, Craig, 521
RAJNEESH, Bhagwan Sri, obit., 591
RAMADAN, Taha Yasin, 243
RAMOS, Gen. Fidel, 344
RAMPHAL, Sir Shridath, 397–8
RAMUSHWANA, Col., 300
RANJEVA, Raymond, 469
RANSMAYR, Christoph, 520
RAPHAEL, Adam, 524
RAPPENEAU, Jean Paul, 498
RAS AL-KHAIMAH, 223
RASHID BIN SAEED AL-MAKTOUM, Sheikh, death, 227; obit., 591
RASMUSSEN, Steen Eiler, obit., 591
RAŢIU, Ion, 128
RATSIRAKA, Didier, President of Madagascar, 332
RATUSHINSKAYA, Irina, 523
RATZINGER, HE Cardinal Joseph, 446
RAY, Satyajit, 499
RAZALEIGH HAMZAH, Tengku, 337–8
REAGAN, Ronald, 22, 53, 62–3, 479, 542
REED, Frank, 65, 213, 599
REGIS, John, 528
REICH, Steve, 486
REID, Maj. Pat, obit., 591
RELIGION (*see also* Islamic Fundamentalism, Vatican), **444–50**; Africa, 270, 330, 446–7, 449; anti–semitism, 447–8; Asia-Pacific, 313, 314, 382, 445, 449; debates, 446–7; E. Europe, 128, 139, 444–5; Islamic tensions, 448–9; religious freedom, 444–5; UK, 23, 446, 447, 448
RENDELL, Ruth, 520
RENÉ, France-Albert, President of Seychelles, 329–30
REVKIN, Andrew, 515, 523
REX, Robert, Prime Minister of Niue, 384
REZZORI, Gregor von, 518, 522
RICHARDS, Ann, 58, 60
RICHARDS, Susan, 515, 523
RICHARDSON, Ruth, 379
RICHLER, Mordecai, 516, 520
RICKS, Christopher, 521
RIDLEY, Nicholas, MP, 22, 32–3, 36, 510, 576, 602
RIEGLER, Josef, 177
RIFKIND, Malcolm, MP, 22, 42, 44–5, 576–7
RIPERT, Jean 143
RITHAUDDEEN, Tengku Ahmad, 337
RITT, Martin, death, 500
RITSOS, Yannis, obit., 591
ROBERTS, Barbara, 60
ROBERTS, Sir Wyn, MP, 47
ROBINSON, Arthur N., Prime Minister of Trinidad & Tobago, 95
ROBINSON, Mary, President of Republic of Ireland, 166, 607
ROBINSON, N., 450

ROBLES, Marcos, obit., 591
ROBSON, Christopher, 485
ROCARD, Michel, Prime Minister of France, 141–2
RODRIGUES, Ferro, 184
RODRÍGUEZ, Gen. Andrés, President of Paraguay, 82
RODRÍGUEZ, Miguel, 85
RODRÍGUEZ CAMPOS, Orestes, 84
ROGERS, Richard, 509
ROH TAE WOO, President of S. Korea, 362, 366–7, 601
ROKORO, Vekuli, 295
ROMAN, Petre, Prime Minister of Romania, 129
ROMANIA, 126, **127–30**, 176, 194, 291, 366, 390, 401, 410, 414, 431, 444, 447, 526, 561, 569, 595, 596, 598, 600, 601, 604, 605, 606, 607
ROMERO, Humberto, 75
RONAY, Gabriel, 523
ROSE, Barbara, 508
ROSE, Michael, 454
ROSEN, Chief Rabbi Moses, 444
ROSEN, Elsa Marianne von, 491
ROSS, Steven, 504
ROSSI, Aldo, 511
ROSTENKOWSKI, Dan, 56
ROTHSCHILD, Lord, obit., 591–2
ROUAUD, Jean, 515, 520
ROUSE, Edmund, 375
ROYAL, HRH The Princess, 23, 600
RUBIA, Charles, 251
RUBIN, HE Cardinal Wladyslaw, obit., 592
RUBINSTEIN, Helge, 524
RUDOLPH, Piet 'Skiet', 302
RUFFILLI, Roberto, 157
RUMOR, Mariano, obit., 592
RUNCIE, Most Rev Dr Robert, Archbishop of Canterbury, 23, 446
RUSHDIE, Salman, 25, 307, 448, 477, 513–14, 520
RUTHVEN, Malise, 514, 523
RUZIMATOV, Farouk, 490
RWANDA, 144, 256, **280–1**, 605
RWIGYEMA, Maj.-Gen. Fred, 256; death, 281
RYZHKOV, Nikolai, Prime Minister of USSR, 112, 340, 605

SAADI, Moussa, 242
SABAT TALAT KADRAT, 387, 389
SABATINI, Gabriela, 533
SACHS, Jeffrey, 537
SADDAM HUSAIN, President of Iraq, 1, 7, 8, 9, 26, 38, 43, 67–8, 114, 129, 197, 200, 202–7, 210, 215–18, 221–2, 229–30, 241, 243, 247, 268, 402, 412, 449, 500, 603–4, 606, 608–9
SAHAY, Subodh Kant, 314
SAIBOU, Brig. Ali, President of Niger, 271
SAID AWANG, Mohamed, 338

SAINSBURY, Timothy, MP, 396
ST JOHN OF FAWSLEY, Lord, 510
ST KITTS-NEVIS, **100–1,** 428
ST LUCIA, **100, 101,** 428
ST VINCENT AND THE GRENADINES, **100, 101–2,** 428
SAITO, Ryoei, 505
SAITOTI, Prof. George, 252
SAKHAROV, Andrei, 515, 523
SALAAM, Yusuf, 65
SALEH, Gen. Ali Abdullah, President of Yemen, 222
SALINAS DE GORTARI, Carlos, President of Mexico, 91
SALMOND, Alex, 45
SALONGA, Jovito, 344
SAMATER, Mohammed Ali, 248
SAMPAIO, Dr Jorge, 184
SAMPRAS, Peter, 533
SAN MARINO, 569
SANDERS, Bernie, 61
SANDERS, E. P., 450
SANDERSON, Lord, 45
SANDERSON, Tessa, 528
SANDIFORD, Erskine, Prime Minister of Barbados, 96–7
SANGUINETTI CAIROLO, Julio Maria, 84
SANSOM, Bruce, 488
SANTANA, Raymond, 65
SÃO TOMÉ & PRÍNCIPE, **283**
SARID, Yossi, 198
SARO-WIWA, Ken, 523
SARTZETAKIS, Khristos, 188
SASSOU-NGUESSO, Col. Denis, President of Congo, 276
SAUD AL-FAISAL, HRH Prince, 220, 389
SAUDI ARABIA, 7, 8, 9, 25, 26, 52, 67, 145, 194, 202, 203, 204, 205, 207, 208, 210, 216, 217, **219–21,** 222, 223, 225, 226, 230, 241, 243, 266, 271, 307, 318, 389, 430, 448, 464, 602, 603, 608
SAUNDERS, Ernest, 477, 604
SAVIMBI, Jonas, 286–7
SAW MAUNG, Gen., 335
SAWYER, Dr Amos, 265, 421
SAYED, Bachir Mustafa, 245
SCHAUFUSS, Peter, 489
SCHIFANO, Laurence, 521
SCHIFTER, Richard, 354
SCHILLACI, Salvatore, 526
SCHLÜTER, Poul, Prime Minister of Denmark, 168–9, 609
SCHNITTKE, Alfred, 486
SCHØNBERG, Bent, 491
SCHONBERGER, Elmer, 488
SCHWARTZ, Stephen, 495
SCHWARZENEGGER, Arnold, 497
SCIENCES (*see also* Environment, Medicine and Medical Research, Technology), astronomy & space research, 55, **451–3;** Nobel prizes, **458–9;** physics, **453–4**
SCOTLAND, 13, 19, 28, **44–6,** 159, 526, 527, 534, 593, 605
SCORSESE, Martin, 497
SCOWCROFT, Gen. Brent, 578

SCUDAMORE, Peter, 534
SCULTHORPE, Peter, 487
SEABRA, Zita, 184
SEAGA, Edward, 93
SEBE, Lennox, 300, 597
SECORD, Richard, 62
SÉGUIN, Philippe, 141
SELBOURNE, David, 515, 523
SELES, Monica, 532–3
SELLARS, Peter, 482
SELZNICK, Irene, obit., 592
SEN, A. K., 313
SENEGAL, 156, 263, **265–6,** 268, 269, 274, 282, 412, 413, 420, 468
SENEILDÍN, Mohammed Ali, 75
SENNA, Ayrton, 531–2
SEROTA, Nicholas, 506
SERRA, Narcís, 182
SEVILLANO, Trinidad, 489
SEYCHELLES, **329–30**
SHAFFER, Peter, 496
SHAKSHUKI, Fawzi al-, 231
SHAMIR, Shimon, 197
SHAMIR, Yitzhak, Prime Minister of Israel, 196–7, 200, 201–4, 601, 609
SHANKAR, Ramsewak, 102
SHANSHAL, Gen. Abdel-Jaber Khalil, 9
SHANTARAM, V., death, 500
SHARIF, Nawaz, Prime Minister of Pakistan, 316–17, 606
SHARJAH, 223
SHARON, Ariel, 196
SHARPE, William, 540
SHARPTON, Rev Al, 64–5
SHATALIN, Stanislav, 112, 605
SHEKHAR, Chandra, Prime Minister of India, 313–15, 607
SHEPHERD, Gen. Lemnel C., obit., 592
SHEPPARD, John, 454–5
SHEVARDNADZE, Eduard, 65, 67, 114, 287, 388–9, 434, 439, 598, 609
SHORT, Michael, 488
SHOSTAKOVICH, Maxim, 484
SHUKLA, V. C., 313
SIDDHI SAVETSILA, 335
SIDDIQUI, Abdul Kader ('Tiger'), 320
SIERRA LEONE, **262–3,** 264
SIEW, Vincent, 357
SIHANOUK, Prince Norodom, 347, 597
SIKORSKI, Radek, 524
SILBER, John, 59
SIMKINS, C. A. G., 522
SIMON, Josette, 494
SIMON, Senator Paul, 61
SIMPSON, Helen, 520
SINCLAIR-STEVENSON, Christopher, 517
SINDEN, Donald, 495
SINGAPORE, **339–40,** 350, 356, 369, 424, 538, 608
SINGH, Rao Birendra, 313
SINGH, Sanjay, 313
SINGH, Vishwanath Pratap (V. P.), 311–14, 602, 607
SINGHER, Martial, death, 484
SITHOLE, Ndabaningi, 292
SIWICKI, Florian, 116

INDEX

SIYAD BARRE, Brig. Maslah Mohammed, 249
SIYAD BARRE, Maj.-Gen. Mohammed, President of Somalia, 248–9
SKINNER, Samuel, 578
SKUBISZEWSKI, Krzysztof, 118
SMITH, Dodie, death, 519; obit., 592
SMITH, John, MP (Labour Shadow Chancellor), 14, 29, 37
SMITH, Dame Maggie, 496
SMITH, Michael, 487
SOARES, Mário, President of Portugal, 184
SODNOM, Dumaagiyn, 369
SOGLO, Nicéphore, Prime Minister of Benin, 272
SOLCHAGA, Carlos, 181–2
SOLE, David, 527
SOLOMON, Gershon, 448
SOLOMON ISLANDS, **382, 384**
SOLZHENITSYN, Alexander, 603
SOMALIA, **248–9**, 250
SOMOZA, Anastasio, 88
SONDHEIM, Stephen, 487, 495
SOUPAULT, Philippe, obit., 592
SOUSTELLE, Jacques, obit., 592
SOUTER, David H., 61–2
SOUTH AFRICA, 24–5, 44, 162, 253, 279, 285, 287, 288, 292, 295, 296, 297, 298, **299–305**, 394, 397–8, 419, 420, 447, 516, 530, 588, 596, 597, 598, 599, 600, 601, 602, 603, 604, 605, 606, 609
SOUTH ASIAN ASSOCIATION FOR REGIONAL COOPERATION (SAARC), 313, 319, 325–6, **422–3**
SOUTH-EAST ASIAN ORGANIZATIONS, **423–4**
SOUTHERN AFRICAN DEVELOPMENT COORDINATION CONFERENCE (SADCC), 296, 421
SPACE EXPLORATION, 55, **451–3**
SPAIN, 79, 113, **180–3**, 186, 277, 408, 499, 504, 531, 532, 569, 595, 606
SPALDING, Julian, 505
SPARK, Muriel, 520
SPARKS, Allister, 514, 523
SPEAR, Ruskin, obit., 592–3
SPENCER, Stanley, 506
SPILLANE, Mickey, 517, 520
SPORT, 155, 159, 167, 190–1, 397–8, **525–35**
SPURLING, Hilary, 517, 521
SRI LANKA, **321–3**, 422, 469
STAMPS, Dr Timothy, 292
STANGERUP, Henrik, 517, 520
STANWYCK, Barbara, death, 499; obit., 593
STEBER, Eleanor, 484
STEWART, Very Rev James, obit., 593
STEWART, Payne, 530
STILLMAN, Whit, 497
STIRLING, James, 510
STOCKHAUSEN, Karlheinz, 485
STOLTENBERG, Thorvald, 397
STONE, John, 373
STONE, Norman, 515, 523
STONE, Oliver, 497
STROESSNER, Gen. Alfredo, 82
STRONG, Patience, death, 519
STROOCK, Thomas, 89
STRUGNELL, John, 200
SUÁREZ MASON, Gen. Guillermo, 75
SUÁREZ Y ESQUIVEL, José, 79
SUBEV, Fr Hristofor, 445
SUCHINDA KRAPAYOON, Gen., 335–6
SUDAN, 202, 205, 218, **228–30**, 231, 232, 248, 257, 274, 449, 465
SUDHARMONO, Lt.-Gen., 341
SUHARTO, Gen. T. N. J., President of Indonesia, 341–2, 346, 356
SULLIVAN, Louis, 578
SULTAN, Prince, 220
SUMPTION, Jonathan, 518–9, 523
SUNDLUN, Bruce, 60
SUNESSON, Fanny, 530
SUNUNU, John, 578
SURINAME, **102–3**
SUTHERLAND, Dame Joan, 482
SUTHERLAND, John, 521
SUVAR, Stipe, 135
SWAZILAND, **298–9**
SWEDEN, 168, **172–4**, 389, 416, 417, 418, 447, 472, 533, 569, 584, 587, 598
SWITZERLAND, **178–80**, 416, 446, 455, 540, 569, 583, 605
SYRIA, 4, 9, 25, 65, 193, 202, 204, **209–11**, 212, 213, 214, 216, 220, 232, 243, 307, 599, 605, 606
SYSE, Jan Peder, 171–2, 607
SZYMANOWSKI, Karel, 486

TAIWAN, 144, 340, 346, 355, 356, **357–8**, 369, 538, 600
TAKAYANAGI, Kenjiro, obit., 593
TAKI, Mohammed, 330
TALHI, Jadallah Azouz al-, 187
TAMBO, Oliver, 304, 609
TANAY, Lt.-Gen., 309
TANZANIA, **253–5**, 280, 281, 420
TAUBERT, K. H., death, 491
TAYLOR, A. J. P., death, 519; obit., 593
TAYLOR, Charles, 264–5, 270
TAYLOR, David, 103
TAYLOR, Elizabeth, 512
TAYLOR, Gary, 518, 521
TAYLOR, Phil, 534
TAYLOR, Richard, 459
TAYLOR-MORGAN, Tommy, 262
TEBBIT, Norman, MP, 514
TECHNOLOGY, **459–63**
TEKERE, Edgar, 292, 598
TELEVISION AND RADIO, 157, 167, **500–4**
TEMBO, Lt.-Gen. Christon, 289
TEMBO, John, 291
TENDULKAR, Sachin, 529
TEO SOH LUNG, 339
TERRY, Sir Peter, 605
TERRY-THOMAS, death, 499
THAILAND, **335–6**, 346, 538
THAMBIMUTTU, Sam, 322
THATCHER, Margaret, MP, Prime Minister of United Kingdom, 28, 47, 576–7; defence, 23–4, 40, 599, 601; drugs, 395; environment, 24, 600;

European Community, 14–15, 31, 33–4, 36, 38, 404; foreign affairs, 23–5, 32, 122, 302, 304, 485, 599–600, 602–3, 605–6; Gulf crisis, 8, 25–6, 29, 38, 604; home affairs, 12, 17, 20–21, 35, 49, 498, 506; Tory leadership election and resignation, 10, 12, 15, 36–41, 46, 210, 262, 404, 607–8
THEATRE, **491–6**
THEOCTIST, Patriarch, 444
THOMAS, Donald, 518, 521
THOMAS, Donnall, 458
THOMAS, R. S., 520
THOMPSON, Dudley, 398
THOMPSON, Laird, 452
THOMPSON, Mark, 493
THOMSON OF MONIFIETH, Lord, 502
THORNBURGH, Richard, 578
THWAITE, Ann, 517, 521
TIAN ZENGPEI, 354
TIBET, 445
TIMEON, Peter, 384
TINDALL, Gillian, 520
TINLING, Ted, obit., 593
TIPPETT, Sir Michael, 482
TIRTOFF, Romain de (Erté), death, 513; obit., 593
TITO, Josip Broz, 137
TIZARD, Dame Catherine, Governor-Gen. of New Zealand, 382
TOGO, 264, **271–2**
TOHIAN, Paul, 377
TOIBIN, Colm, 516, 520
TÖKÉS, László, 444
TOLBA, Mostafa, 396
TOMALIN, Claire, 517, 521
TONGA, **383, 384**
TORNATORE, Giuseppe, 498
TORTELIER, Paul, death, 488; obit., 593–4
TOURÉ, Sekou, 267
TOV, Emmanuel, 200
TOWER, Joan, 486
TOWER, John,
TRAN XUAN BACH, 345
TRAORÉ, Gen. Moussa, President of Mali, 267
TREURNICHT, Dr. A. P., 302
TREVOR, William, 516, 520
TRIMBLE, David, 49
TRINIDAD & TOBAGO, **95–6,** 427, 428, 603
TRUDEAU, Pierre, 71
TSEDENBAL, Yumjaagiyn, 369
TUBIN, Eduard, 487
TUDJMAN, Franjo, 135
TUNISIA, 202, **233–7,** 307, 412
TUMA, Romeu, 77
TURKEY, 7, 162, 176, 179, 187, 190, **192–5,** 210, 216, 220, 307, 364, 376, 397, 403, 408, 471, 569, 599, 603
TURKS & CAICOS ISLANDS, 428
TURNER, Dame Eva, death, 482, 468; obit., 594
TURNER, John,
TURNER, Ted, 500
TUTU, Most Rev Desmond, Archbishop of Cape Town, 303
TUVALU, **382, 384,** 385
TYMINSKI, Stanislaw, 117–8
TYSON, Mike, 527-8

ÜCOK, Bahriye, death, 195
UGANDA, 229, 230, 252, **255–7,** 281, 422, 605
UMM AL-QAIWAN, 223
UNDERWOOD, Rory, 527
UNION OF SOVIET SOCIALIST REPUBLICS (USSR), **105–14;** arts, 484, 490, 499; Baltic Republics, 106, 110, 111; constitution, 105, 106, 108–9; CPSU, 105, 106–8; economy, 2, 105, 106, 111–3, 408–11, 536; environment, 464–7; external relations, 1, 2–3, 23, 24, 31, 40, 44, 53, 65–8, 76, 86, 105, 113, 114, 118, 122, 123, 130, 132, 134, 139, 144–51, 147, 159, 164, 174–5, 176, 183, 194, 198–9, 200, 202, 204, 207, 209–10, 218, 220, 222, 226, 247, 286–7, 307, 309–10, 312, 340, 345–6, 347–8, 354, 361, 363, 366, 367, 369, 371, 380, 386, 388–9, 390, 400, 401–2, 405, 409–10, 412, 414, 424, 569; German unification, 114, 151, 409, 430–2, 566–9; Gulf crisis, 114, 386, 388–9, 390, 561; national unrest, 1, 2, 106, 109–11; religion, 444; Shevardnadze resignation, 114; space, 453
UNITED ARAB EMIRATES (UAE), 7, 202, 215, 216, **223–4, 226–8**
UNITED KINGDOM, **10–51**
EXTERNAL RELATIONS (*see also* Arms Control, Conference on Security and Cooperation in Europe, Gulf Crisis, North Atlantic Treaty Organization, Western European Union), **23–7, 30–4;** Africa, 24–5, 44, 262, 263, 297, 302, 304; aid, 420; Americas, 22, 25, 31, 44, 66, 76, 79, 91; Antarctica, 381; Arab world, 4, 7, 8, 9, 24–7, 29, 38, 43–4, 158, 208, 210, 213, 215, 216, 217, 223, 226, 386, 388, 390, 403, 430, 442–3, 446, 561; Asia, 336, 338, 340, 354, 359–60, 361; dependencies, 103, 182, 186, 428, 359–60; diplomatic relations, 25, 76, 210, 307, 394; Europe, 14–5, 22, 23–4, 28, 30–4, 36, 37, 38–9, 40, 43–4, 122, 139, 151, 157, 159, 176, 402, 403, 404–5, 442–3, 569; Ireland, 48–9; 165–6
HOME AFFAIRS (*see also* Northern Ireland, Scotland, Wales), architecture, **509–11;** arts, **482–524;** by-elections, 15, 19, 29, 35, 38, 45–6, 49; broadcasting, 19–20, **500–3;** Channel tunnel, 30–1; defence, 23, 24, 29, 40; disasters, 15, 46, 47; economy, 11, 13, 14, 29, 33–4, 35, 37, 43, 46, 47, 50–1, 539, **542–5;** ERM, 14–5, 33–4, 38, 43, 404, 539, 540, 541, 545; environment, 24, 28, 35–6, 465, 466; government changes, 11, 22, 37, 46, 47, 576–7 (*lists*); law, 415, **474–7;** local elections, 18–9, 45; parties, 10, 11, 12, 13, 16, 19, 20, 22, 27, 28–30,

34–5, 36, 40–2, 44–5, 47, 49; poll tax, 10, 12–3, 15, 16–8, 39–40, 42–3, 44, 475; religion, 23, 446, 448; riots, 16, 18; scandals, 21–2, 192, 338–9, 474, 477; science & medicine, 453–4, 456–7; terrorism, 22–3, 35, 48, 50, 51; Thatcher's fall, 1, 10, **36–40,** 41–2, 47; TUC, 28; War Crimes Bill, 19
UNITED NATIONS (*see also* General Agreement on Tariffs and Trade, International Court of Justice), **386–97;** Afghanistan, 309–11; Angola, 287; Antarctica, 396; Arab-Israeli dispute, 198, 202, 203, 386, 390–3, 412; children, 396–7, 470; Cyprus, 191–2, 386, 394; disarmament, 394–5; drugs, 395, 470; economy & trade, 395; E. Europe, 139; environment, 320, 396, 423, 425, 464–5, 466; Eritrea, 247; Falklands, 394; famine & refugees, 397; Gulf crisis, 1, 4–6, 7, 8, 9, 25–7, 29, 68–9, 73, 129, 132, 145, 158, 160, 165, 168, 176, 193, 198, 208, 215–8, 223, 224, 226, 236, 243, 247, 306, 338, 376, 386–90, 395, 397, 412, 419, 430, 561–6 (*texts*); human rights, 396; Kampuchea, 66–7, 347, 387, 393; Latin America, 85; Namibia, 295, 296, 387, 393; population, 328, 396; *Rainbow Warrior*, 144, 470; South Africa, 162, 394; South Pacific, 384; UNESCO, 396; Western Sahara, 244–5, 387, 393–4, 421
UNITED STATES OF AMERICA (USA), **52–69** EXTERNAL RELATIONS (*see also* Arms Control, Conference on Security and Cooperation in Europe, North Atlantic Treaty Organization, Organization of American States), **65–9;** Africa, 247, 249, 251, 265, 274, 275, 279, 286, 287, 291, 302, 332; Arab-Israeli dispute, 197, 198, 200, 202, 203, 204, 210, 213, 218, 391, 412; Arab world, 212, 213, 222, 229, 230, 233; Asia, 66, 67, 318, 334, 339, 340, 343–4, 346, 347, 349, 350, 353–4, 356, 361, 362, 370, 423, 424; China, 66, 67, 350, 353–4, 356; Caribbean, 96, 426–7; Europe, 53, 66, 122, 130, 139, 151, 168, 176, 190, 192–4, 403, 406, 415, 442–3, 566–9; GATT, 66, 164, 312, 406, 407; Gulf crisis, 4–6, 7, 8, 9, 52, 53, 59, 67–9, 158, 176, 192, 198, 203, 205–6, 207–8, 210, 215–8, 219–21, 223, 224, 225, 226, 233, 236, 241, 243, 247, 271, 318, 338, 350, 353–4, 356, 386, 387–90, 403, 430, 441, 442–3, 446–7, 561; Japan, 361, 362; Latin America, 76, 77, 78, 79, 84, 85, 86, 88–91, 426–7; Pacific, 380, 381, 384, 385, 424–5; Panama, 52, 54, 90–1; USSR, 53, 65–6, 67, 68, 113, 430–43 HOME AFFAIRS, **53–65;** appointments, 61–2, 578 (*list*); arts, 483, 485–7, 490–1, 495–6, 504–6, 507–8; broadcasting, 500, 503, 504; defence, 53–4, 55; drugs & crime, 53, 63–5; disasters,

53; economy, 52, 53–8, 408, 538, 539, **540–2,** 544; elections, 53, 57, 58–61, 64; environment, 54, 464, 465, 467; Iran-Contra affair, 62–3; law, 61–2, **479–81;** racial issues, 58–9, 61, 63–5; Savings & Loan scandal, 62; science & medicine, **451–9;** space, 55, 451–3; sport, 526–7, 530, 532–3, 534–5; State of the Union, 53–5
UPDIKE, John, 517, 520
URUGUAY, 78, 82, **84**
UTLEY, Roger, 527

VALLELY, P., 450
VAN DER KAMP, John, 58
VAN EYCK, Aldo, 511
VAN PRAAGH, Dame Peggy, death, 491; obit., 594
VANSITTART, Peter, 517, 520
VANUATU, **382, 384,** 425
VARGAS LLOSA, Mario, 83, 520, 601
VASSILIOU, Georgios, President of Cyprus, 191
VATICAN, 122, 123, 128, 159, 280, 282, 361, 445, 446, 569, 595, 599, 600, 604, 607
VAUGHAN, Sarah, obit., 594
VÄYRYNEN, Paavo, 175
VELAYATI, Ali Akbar, 306–7
VENEZUELA, 83, **85,** 412, 413, 426, 427, 428, 469
VENKATARAMAN, Ramaswamy, President of India, 313
VENTO, John, 64
VERHOEVEN, Paul, 497
VERMA, Jatinder, 492
VERSACE, Gianni, 512
VEZIROV, Abdul Rakhman, 110
VIDELA, Gen. Jorge, 75–6
VIETNAM, 66, 67, 335, 336, **345–6,** 347, 356, 408, 409, 423, 424, 445, 587
VINE, Carl, 487
VIOLA, Gen. Robert, 75
VISHNIAC, Roman, death, 508
VITALIEV, Vitali, 515, 523
VLASI, Azem, 136
VRANITZKY, Dr Fred, Chancellor of Austria, 177, 606

WADDINGTON OF READ, Lord (David Waddington), 16, 42, 576–7
WAGONER, Dan, 490
WAITE, Terry, 213
WAJED, Sheikh Hasina, 320
WAKEHAM, John, MP, 576–7
WALLOTT, Derek, 518, 520
WALDEGRAVE, William, MP, 37, 577
WALDHEIM, Dr Kurt, President of Austria, 8, 176, 217
WALES, 28, **46–8,** 527, 531, 594, 598
WALES, HRH Prince of, 364, 509, 609
WALES, HRH Princess of, 364
WALESA, Lech, President of Poland, 114, 116–8, 447, 537, 599, 609
WALKER, Peter, MP, 11, 46, 576
WALL, Max, death, 499; obit., 594

INDEX

WALLACE, Irving, death, 519
WAMWERE, Koigi wa, 252
WANG BINGQIAN, 351
WANG CHIEN-HSUAN, 357
WARIOBA, Joseph, 253
WARNER, Deborah, 492
WARSAW PACT (*see also* Arms Control), 1, 3, 23, 67, 116, 123, 129, 151, 410–11, **431–40,** 601, 602, 608
WARWICK, Derek, 532
WATANJAR, Mohammed Aslam, 310
WATKINS, Alan, 524
WATKINS, Glenn, 488
WATKINS, James, 578
WATKINS, Paul, 515
WATSON, Tom, 531
WAUGH, Auberon, 518, 521
WEATHERBY, W. J., 521
WEBSTER, Paul, 523
WEBSTER, William, 68, 578
WEERAMANTRY, Christopher, 469
WEICKER, Lowell, Jr, 60
WEIR, Judith, 483
WEIZSÄCKER, Richard von, President of Germany, 354, 605
WELD, William, 59
WESLEY, Mary, 516, 520
WESLEY-SMITH, Martin, 487
WESSELS, Anton, 450
WESTERN EUROPEAN UNION (WEU), 8, 164, 183, 220, **442–3**
WESTERN SAHARA, 232, 242, 243, **244–5,** 268, 387, 393–4, 420–1
WESTERN SAMOA, **383, 384,** 385, 425
WESTWOOD, Vivienne, 513
WHEATON, David, 533
WHEEN, Francis, 518, 521
WHITCOMB, Noel, 522
WHITE, Patrick, death, 376, 519; obit., 594
WHITE SMITH, Gregory, 518, 521
WICKE, Peter, 488
WIGGINS, Marianne, 514
WIJERATNE, Ranjan, 323
WILDER, Douglas, 63
WILEY, Roland J., 491
WILLIAMS, Alan, MP, 48
WILLIAMS, Aubrey, death, 508
WILLIAMS, Clayton, 58, 60
WILLIAMS, Rt Rev Gwylim, obit., 594
WILLIAMS, Hugo, 521
WILLIAMS, Joy, 520
WILLIAMS, Michael, 495
WILLIAMSON, David, 523
WILLIS, Norman, 28
WILSON, A. N., 517, 521
WILSON, August, 496
WILSON, Sir David, Governor of Hong Kong, 359
WILSON, Gordon, 45
WILSON, Michael, 73
WILSON, Senator Pete, 58, 60
WINSTONE, H. V. F., 521
WISMOYO ARISMUNANDAR, Maj.-Gen., 341
WOOD, John, 491
WOOSNAM, Ian, 530–1
WORLD BANK (IBRD), 87, 94, 115, 206, 254, 261, 269, 277, 285, 350, 395, 420, 427, 429
WORLD HEALTH ORGANIZATION (WHO), 455, 456
WÖRNER, Gen. Manfred, NATO Secretary-General, 602
WORSNIP, Glyn, 522
WRIGHT, Peter, 489
WYATT, Lord, 502
WYNNE, Greville, obit., 594

XENAKIS, Iannis, 486
XU DUNXIN, 346

YANAEV, Gennadi, 609
YANG SHANGKUN, President of China, 355, 367
YAZOV, Marshal, 608
YELTSIN, Boris, 111, 366, 515, 523, 600, 602
YEMEN, REPUBLIC OF, 4, 9, 202, 217, 218, 220, **221–3,** 247, 387, 388, 389, 390, 392, 412, 413, 449, 561–6, 600
YEO, Brig.-Gen. George, 339
YEUTTER, Clayton, 578
YILMAZ, Mesut, 194
YON HYONG MUK, Prime Minister of North Korea, 367
YONG, Datuk Amar Stephen, 337
YOUNG, Andrew, 59
YOUNG, Douglas, 45
YOUNIS, Waqar, 529–30
YUGOSLAVIA, 122, 126, **133–7,** 158, 176, 190, 205, 366, 401, 409, 411, 412, 413, 414, 417, 525, 528, 532, 569, 595, 596, 603, 609
YUN PO-SUN, 594
YUNIS, Col. Abu Bakr, 232

ZAÏRE, 230, 274, **278–80,** 281, 286, 561
ZAKLINSKY, Konstantin, 488
ZAMBIA, 255, 257, **288–90,** 412, 597
ZANZIBAR, 253, **254–5**
ZARDARI, Asif, 316
ZAWODINSKI, Stefan, 411
ZAYYAD, Dr Hamza, 261
ZEHJNULAHU, Jusuf, 136–7
ŻELAZNY, Jan, 528
ZELENSKY, Igor, 490
ZHAO ZIYANG, 350
ZHELEV, Zhelyu, President of Bulgaria, 132, 602
ZHIVKOV, Todor, 131
ZHOU ENLAI, 354
ZHOU NAN, 359
ZIA, Begum Khaleda, 320
ZIA-UI-HAQ, Gen. Mohammad, 317
ZIEGLER, Philip, 518, 521
ZILITNI, Said al-, 231
ZIMBABWE, 284, 285, **291–4,** 387, 412, 530, 598
ZIMMERMANN, Bernd Alois, 484
ZINSOU, Emile, 272
ZOLOTAS, Xenophon, 188
ZWANE, Dr Ambrose, 298

REF D 2 .A7 1990